A Great Gay Book

Editor: Zack Knoll
Designer: Diane Shaw
Managing Editor: Annalea Manalili
Production Manager: Denise LaCongo

Library of Congress Control Number: 2023946461

ISBN: 978-1-4197-6678-7
eISBN: 978-1-64700-938-0

For additional credits, see page 428

Printed and bound in China
10 9 8 7 6 5 4 3 2 1

ABRAMS The Art of Books
195 Broadway, New York, NY 10007
abramsbooks.com

A Great Gay Book

Stories of Growth, Belonging & Other Queer Possibilities

Edited by **RYAN FITZGIBBON**
Founder of *Hello Mr.* magazine

ABRAMS, NEW YORK

9
HELLO AGAIN
Ryan Fitzgibbon

16
On Writing a Great, Gay Book
Hanya Yanagihara, Garth Greenwell

28
SLUTBOYS
Ben French

31
Snob Queer
Jeremy Atherton Lin

41
Navot and His Kind: Portraits, Penises, and Peyes
Michele Fossi

53
Star Beings
Alexander Chee

58
On the Move: A Life: Brian Anderson
Samuel Bradley

66
Who Conquers Who, or Surprisingly Good Airplane Food
Tommy Pico

69
Shut Up After You're Thirty: Charles Rogers in Search of John Waters's Approval
Charles Rogers

81
Sanctuary
Jen Silverman

95
Blurry Soles
Mathew Rodriguez

103
Anal Fisting: A Case Study of the Mental and Rectal Elasticity of the Human Male
Sam Finkelstein

114
Forgiveness
Christopher Soto

117
The Recording
Khalid El Khatib

127
Back to Start: The "Lady" Bunny
Martin Belk

135
FAG SCHOOL #6½
Brontez Purnell

147
All These Cats Have AIDS
Jason Villemez

162
Fire Island
Robert Andy Coombs

175
Kehinde Wiley in 3D: An Artist's Quest to Unflatten Black America
Antwaun Sargent

183
The House of the Sleeping Beaus
John Better Armella

190
Good Dick Is a Myth
Mack Rogers

216
History of My Blood
Mason Pippenger

221
Notebook Fragments
Ocean Vuong

226
Camp
Michael Huey

193
We Meet Again: Familiar Faces of *Hello Mr.*
Ernesto Macias

194
Nic Dorward

197
Ed Droste

198
Dan Donigan

201
Saeed Jones

202
Mike Hadreas

205
Parson James

206
Stephen Galloway

209
Brian Anderson

210
John Early

213
Tunde Olaniran

214
Olly Alexander

230
He Opened Up Somewhere Along the Eastern Shore
Jason Hanasik

238
A Compendium of Loss
Thom James Carter

247
Javier Muñoz: *Hamilton*'s New Hamilton
Scott Bixby

256
Close Encounter
Noah Michelson

258
Clear Constellations: Mapping the Cultural Pinpoints of Critic Wesley Morris
J Wortham

267
Falling Prey
Fran Tirado

277
Jello Boy
Calvin Gimpelevich

281
What's Left of Marcus Leatherdale?
Martin Belk

290
On Watching MormonBoyz Porn as a Gay Ex-Mormon
Craig Mangum

301
Queering Space
Davy Pittoors

318
1st Samuel, 1st Love
Kitsch Harris

320
How to Unerase Yourself with Garrard Conley
Scott Bixby

326
Learning I'm Susceptible to Cults
Andrew Ketcham

328
Maggie and Olivia, or: Flickering In and Out of Many Things
Erin Riley

339
Cryin' These Cocksucking Tears: Remembering My Friend, Patrick Haggerty
Andrew Sa

344
Nature Poem
Tommy Pico

349
Chani Nicholas Is in Your House
Alexander Chee

357
Violets
Steve Orlando, Derek Charm

362
Just Be Cool
Matthew Harris

367
Selected Poems from *The Walt Whitman Reader*: An English-to-English Translation
Paul Legault

370
The Mother, the Son, and the Holy Spirit
Dany Salvatierra

381
Screen Test
Daniel Shea

388
Saying Hello to New Queer Voices
Colby Anderson, Yezmin Villarreal

396
How to Talk to Strangers
Bryan Washington

401
The Perfect Imbalance of Raul Lopez
Ernesto Macias

409
The Wound
Riley Yaxley

416
we know the weight is human
Tate Justus

424
Contributors

428
Credits

430
Acknowledgments

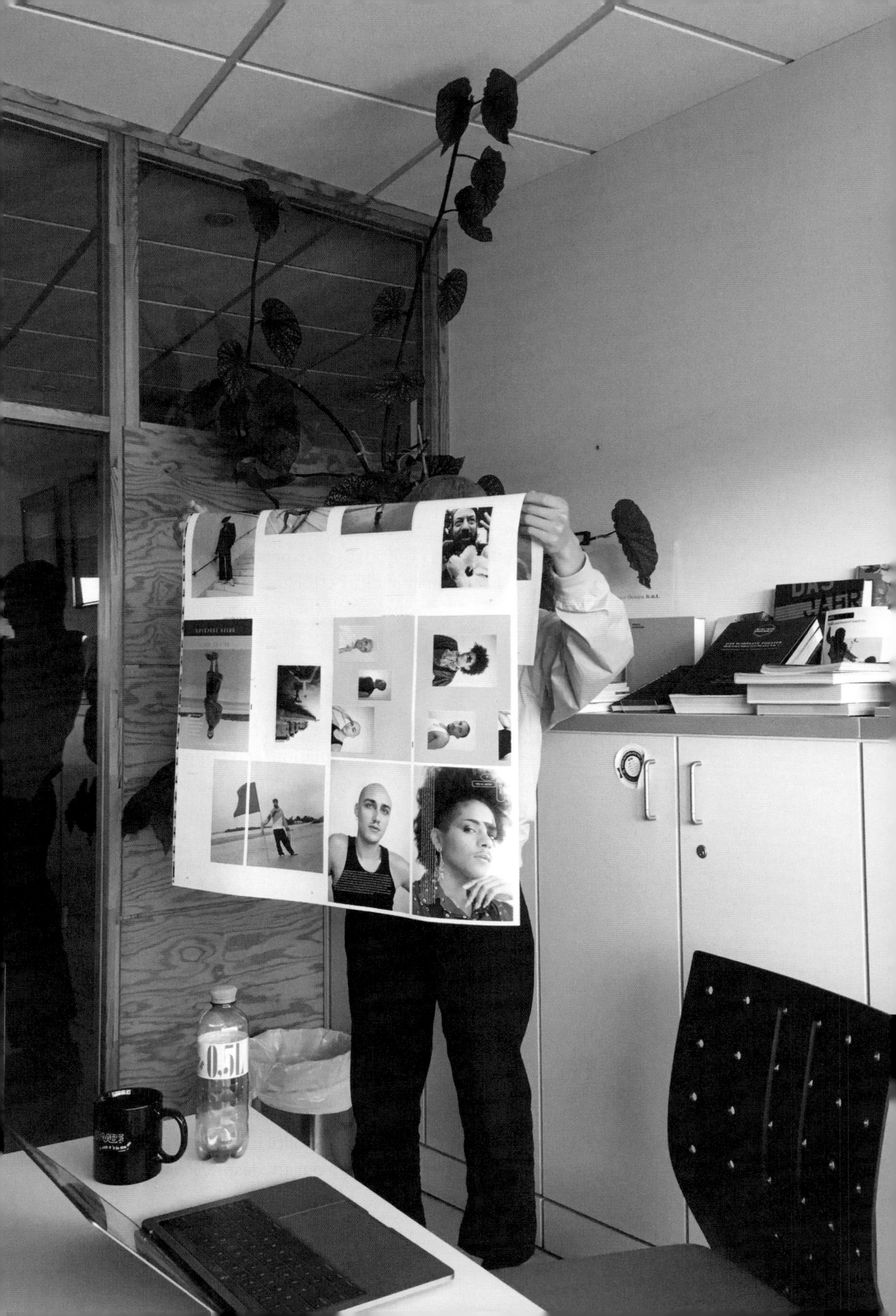

Hello Again

Ryan Fitzgibbon

Aligning with the truth comes naturally when we're young. Over time, as our instincts are challenged, trusting our sense of what's possible becomes a practice. Ridding ourselves of expectations, of shame, to do things *our* way. Not just imagining a better (more honest) future, but playing a role in creating one. This book is the product of that knowing; the pursuit of something true.

A Great Gay Book is a collection of essays, poems, interviews, profiles, short fiction, art, zines, and photographs by many of the great gay and queer voices of the last decade. The stories that fill these pages form a capsule of joy, grief, pleasure, contemplation, and hope. One piece alone can not capture the multitudes contained by our community. Collectively, even, the temptation to claim something "universal" would be dishonest, and counter to progress. So, the intention of this compendium is to encourage reflection—considering your proximity to each story—as a mirror to conceive new possibilities.

This vision was charted by *Hello Mr.* when I released the first of ten issues of the magazine "about men who date men" in 2013. It was an invitation to start a conversation about a future where the gay experience is not assumed, does not fit a mold, and will not be erased. Over the years, as my team and the audience it reached expanded, encapsulating "queerness" more broadly, so did the mission. The long-held practice of banning LGBTQ+ books, and decades of queerphobic censorship, have been desperate attempts by those in power to deny our existence and retain their sense of control. Defying this politicization by telling our stories and expressing ourselves through our art, despite it, is inherent to our survival.

The author Garth Greenwell once suggested that "being an artist means trying to tell the truth as much as you can." This was proposed in conversation with the author Hanya Yanagihara in 2016, for our eighth issue; Yanagihara responded that the work of artists is "tough work . . . that it is uncompromising, not just in its subject matter necessarily, but because you have the sense that the artist is really forgetting their audience."

The privileges afforded to me and my unique perspective as the creator of *Hello Mr.* is one I've approached and analyzed with great intention in the years at its helm. At the outset, it was an ambitious venture with something to prove. Now, a record of resilience that speaks for itself.

The first time my heart broke, I fled Michigan for San Francisco. Twenty-one and newly out, I fought big emotions with big actions. I found an open room on Craigslist in an apartment shared by two women in the centrally located SoMa (South of Market) district. We lived on the top floor of the last house at the end of Dore Street, the home to Up Your Alley, a smaller version of Folsom Street Fair, the annual leather, BDSM, and kink fest. "Up Your Alley is not for the faint of heart—where," according to the Folsom Street official website, "leather daddies rule the streets."

The weekend after I arrived, my roommates took off on a road trip and left me, but a twink, without warning, for this reveal of a lifetime. It was a rare scorcher of a day for the typically overcast Bay Area. Walking down Folsom, stimulated by acts of the abominable, a gleeful voyeur strolling behind said exactly what I was thinking: "This is what hell is going to be like, isn't it?"

A year later, I traded alley afterlife for an alternate reality in the historic Castro district. I replied to a listing titled "Two Gays Looking for a Third" and sealed the deal with a six-pack of beer. Grindr had only just debuted, so Craigslist is still where we found most connections.

My new roommates, Gay One and Gay Two—not a couple—were shuffling rooms to make space for the wardrobe and growing wig collection of Lychee Minelli, the newest member of the Rice Rockettes. My bedroom window doubled as a backboard for the basketball hoop at Harvey Milk Civil Rights Elementary. In our shared backyard, fig trees grew and faeires gathered. On Mondays, the Rockettes crammed into our living room to watch the second season of *RuPaul's Drag Race* while getting tips from mutha, Estee Longah, on painting for the back row. If what I'd witnessed before was hell, then surely, this was heaven.

By the end of my two years on Collingwood Ave., Lychee had been crowned Miss GAPA (Gay Asian Pacific Alliance), Proposition 8 was auditioning "Love is Love" for national deployment, and I had the beginnings of a magazine that would ultimately lead me here.

Of the many unexplainable moments in life when a path reveals itself, founding *Hello Mr.* is undoubtedly top. The early days—scattered, like seeds, in the moonlit hours of 2012—had a current to them. As its conduit, I started to recognize a distancing when observing, rather than participating in life around me. Contemplating instead of allowing. I understand, now, how easy it is to be fooled by thoughts; feeling your way to knowing takes nerve.

I had a dream job for a think tank in Palo Alto, known for their human-centered approach to design. The commute took up to ninety minutes each way, so my days were long, leaving only nights and weekends to develop the foundation of *Hello Mr.* I didn't go out as often as I suspected other twenty-four year old gays living in the Castro did, but occasionally I could be coerced. One of those rare nights, instigated by my roommate (Lychee), led me down the street and around the corner to The Mix where I met Max, the student from Australia, which led me to Melbourne later that year after his visa expired.

Two weeks after arriving in the land Down Under, I failed to hold back tears on the dance floor at Poof Doof when the chorus reached "with somebody who loves me!" I walked back to the flat I was subletting, knowing that a gesture as grand as an intercontinental move wouldn't change the fact that our relationship had run its course. I'd end up staying a year, never again seeing Max, and dedicated myself full-time to *Hello Mr.* (Like I said, big emotions were met with big actions.) After launching the first issue at Sydney Mardi Gras, I took off for New York, where I spent the next six years publishing under this moniker.

It was refreshing to have a gay magazine on newsstands that promised depth. "More than what meets the eye," as the mission stated. Void of a comment section, print prompted introspection for readers. And with the advent of Instagram, community formed around the content, prompting meet-ups, salons, and large-scale events, like our annual "Hello Love" party, which drew hundreds of lonely, horny, or otherwise preoccupied hearts to the dance floor each Valentine's Day. As awareness of what *Hello Mr.* was about grew, the team that made it all happen did too. Writer Fran Tirado was one of the magazine's first accomplices. We met shortly after I landed in Brooklyn, as issue 02 was going to print. I was renting a desk in the Pencil Factory on Greenpoint Avenue, where I was befriended by art director Zhang Qingyun. Issue-over-issue, these two great minds elevated the written and visual stature of our content, respectively, and led a cast of supporting characters alongside me until the publication's bittersweet end.

Over its lifespan, nearly 65,000 magazines traveled around the world, amplifying the voices of over five hundred LGBTQ+ artists and writers. It's difficult to capture the impression made through numbers, but within them were several firsts. For many, *Hello Mr.* was the first gay magazine they purchased. For others, a publishing debut. The personal expansion it facilitated was its magic. A promise kept.

By 2018, I arrived at the conclusion that it was time to focus on my own growth. I was proud of the role *Hello Mr.* played, and trusted that the impact of the ten issues published would continue to be felt. But keeping my head above water and sustaining a team of queer creatives in New York City—particularly through the Trump years—wore on me. I knew I needed to let go and start experiencing life for myself.

I spent the following year back in Michigan searching for my next new. Watching TV one morning, I learned about an initiative that paid people to move to Tulsa, Oklahoma. Desperate to start 2020 anywhere but under my parent's roof (love you), I applied while the segment was still airing. Come January, I was settling into my new home as a registered voter of Oklahoma.

A friend I'd made in my first weeks invited me to a drag brunch on March 15. Reports of a new coronavirus hitting coastal cities dominated headlines, but fear of it reaching the Plains was just an apt punchline for the queens hosting at the Dust Bowl. I don't remember the song, but the bit involved an economy-size jug of sanitizer waltzed around the bowling alley, haphazardly pumped into the hands of patrons like me in line for the breakfast buffet. Sometimes, in trade for a tattered dollar

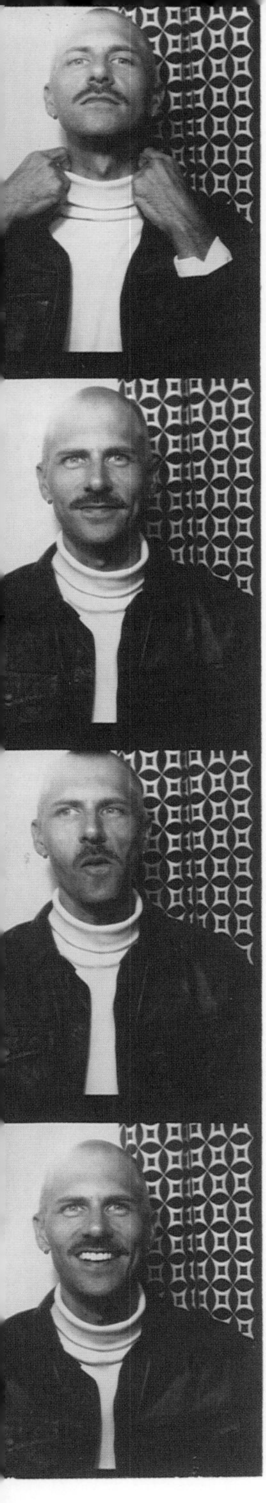

bill. Lockdown was ordered the next day, and when I woke up covered in sweat, I knew the jig was up. I sheltered in place as my symptoms escalated over the next ten days. Two months later, when it felt relatively safe to mask up and see a doctor—expecting Covid antibodies—I learned that my body had seroconverted to HIV positive.

While waiting to begin treatment, my hometown experienced its worst flood in decades, Larry Kramer was laid to rest, footage of George Floyd's murder ignited an uprising, and Trump announced a rally in Tulsa on Juneteenth, three blocks from where I had just become immunocompromised. During my intake appointment, I couldn't help but think of loss. Before a physician would look me in the eye and confirm my status, a scale greeted my disbelief. Everything felt heavy, while a familiar version of me stood facing an unfamiliar wall. Our bodies are always speaking to us, and I had no reason not to trust what it was telling me now.

As I'm writing this, three years after reaching undetectable, my body feels content and grateful for slowing down and listening. For showing up and being intentional about healing, and for translating these feelings into words; something others could grab on to. That was how this all began, the book you're holding. *A Great Gay Book*, and the *Stories of Growth, Belonging, and Other Queer Possibilities* within is a tome of truths. It's a gift to have had this opportunity to reflect on the meaning of it all, and has been an absolute pleasure to create.

Nurture your feelings. Listen for the truth. Act accordingly.

Always with love,

Ryan

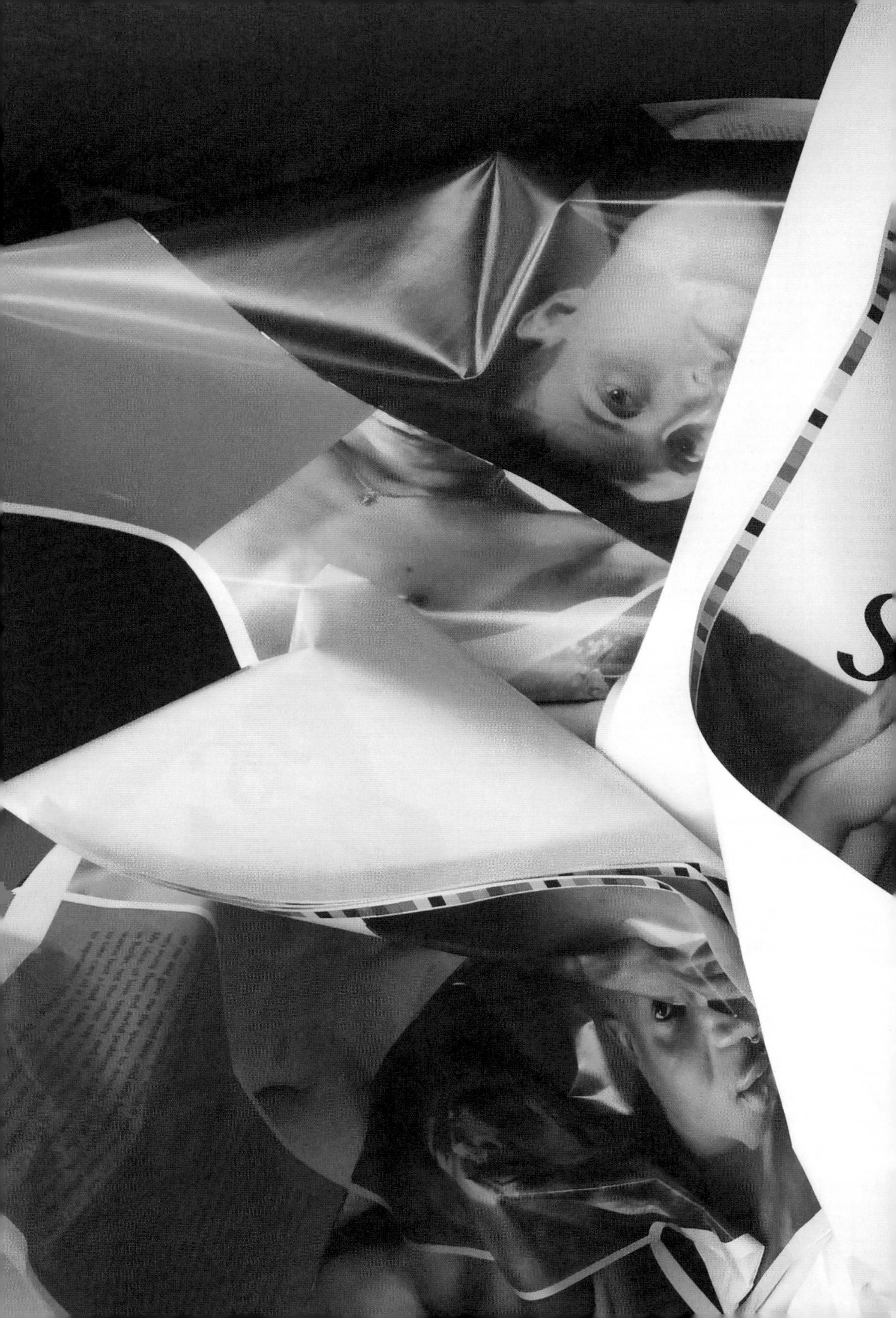

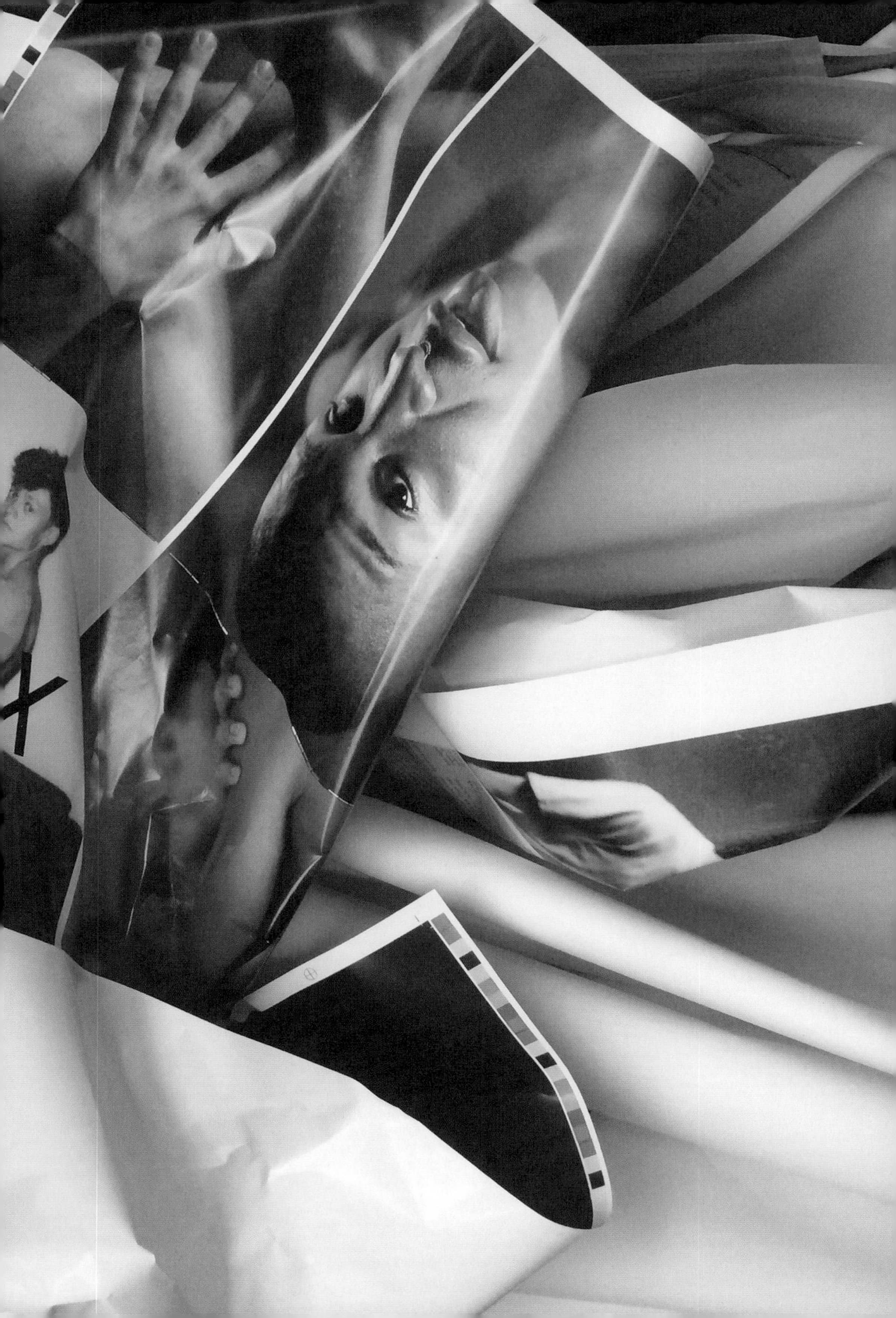

ON WRITING A GREAT, GAY BOOK

Hanya Yanagihara
in Conversation with
Garth Greenwell

HANYA YANAGIHARA: I'm going to go for the big question. What does it mean to write a gay book? Is it the fact that the writer is gay that makes a book gay? What does making gay literature mean at this particular moment?

GARTH GREENWELL: I don't really have an answer for that. I think anyone who cares about the question is going to have a different answer.

HY: But do you think there's such a thing as a queer aesthetic? I know that you've argued persuasively that there is this idea of an extravagance of emotion, a bigness of mood, a sort of tonality. I think especially when gay art—in film or music or books—had to disguise this idea of gayness, there was this twinning of shame and eroticism that they had to express in a different language. Is that still true?

GG: I don't think that there's a queer aesthetic, I think there are many queer aesthetics. And I actually don't think it has anything to do with—well I don't think it's determined by an artist's identity. Because I don't think you're born into a queer aesthetic, I think you have to work for it, learn it. I think there are styles that queer artists have chosen, and I certainly feel that when I think about the kind of sentences I'm drawn to. Whether you're thinking of Proust or James or Woolf, that comes out of a queer tradition. And yeah I do think there are modalities that have been coded queer both adversarially and in a sort of identificatory way. So it does feel meaningful to me to think about queer art. Maybe more intensely because queer life and queer culture have been so mainstreamed.

HY: A very limited sense.

GG: That's exactly right. In a way that excludes, that can feel constraining, or that can feel like it sacrifices too much. There is this kind of desire, among a lot of queer writers and artists I know, to push back and to assert a kind of queerness that has fallen out of the marriage—equality—picture of gay life.

HY: When you were writing [*What Belongs to You*], were you conscious of following in a certain tradition of a "queer aesthetic?" Whatever you write, now and in the future, even if your writing, subject-wise, seems to have nothing to do with gay life or gay history or gay experience, is it still, by your experience, a gay book?

GG: Beyond my current projects I have no idea. The current projects are queer in both of those senses. I don't think queerness in art is necessarily or primarily about subject matter. In David Halperin's book *How to Be Gay*, he makes this argument that things like opera and Broadway musicals are more expressive of queerness than something like *Brokeback Mountain*. In that, objectively queer content puts more pressure on the queerness of the style. That's an interesting argument to me, but I don't know if it's exactly true. I think Genet's novels are as queer as anything could ever get, both stylistically and in terms of subject matter. But Alexander Chee's *The Queen of the Night*—there's not a lot of objective queerness in that, but it's a super gay novel.

HY: It is super gay. I do agree with you that it's like that famous line about pornography—you can't define it until you see it. But I also think there is a queer aesthetic in a way that there is perhaps not an Asian-American aesthetic.

I don't think that there's a queer aesthetic, I think there are many queer aesthetics.

GG: Oh, that's interesting.

HY: I thought lots about what makes a gay book or not. Is it the content, is it who's writing it, is it the themes, or is it the tone? What is it? Because one of the questions I thought I'd get asked a lot, and didn't, is: *Why are there no Asian-American characters in my book? And are you an Asian-American writer?* In the end, I was asked it only twice, both by Asian-American writers, and the answer to both is: "Yes." I think that much of Asian-American history in America has been, largely for cultural reasons, accepting what's handed to us. It comes down to a philosophical difference of thinking that life can't be changed, versus thinking that if you push hard enough against circumstances they will change, which is a very Western way of thinking. There's a Japanese phrase *shikata ga nai*, "it can't be helped," and the Eastern way of thinking is simply that. Which is why, for example, people find it perplexing that Japanese-Americans never uprose in large numbers when they were put in internment camps. It simply wasn't part of their philosophy. And in that way, I thought my first book [*The People in the Trees*] was an indictment of how Asian-Americans have allowed themselves to be treated in this country. I did think that was a very Asian-American book. But no one has called it that, even though I do. So I'm not sure there's a certain Asian-American aesthetic the way there is definitely a queer aesthetic.

GG: Well part of that may be that Asian-American identity—

HY: You can't hide it.

GG: You can't hide it, and also you're born into it, you can't deny it.

HY: It's not associated with shame and hiding and a process of discovery.

GG: And education, or initiation. Because I think with gay identity, there's a kind of initiation to it.

HY: It's something you have to act upon.

GG: And it's something you have to seek out. I remember, because I grew up in a very un-gay environment, there were no gay people around me for a long time, and I had to seek out gayness and try to find images of myself that made me not want to die. And that in itself was a kind of training. When I was thirteen, I went to this bookstore in Louisville that had a lesbian and gay section. I didn't know anything about literature, I was in Kentucky public schools, and I would just pull books at random.

HY: Do you remember a book you read that you saw yourself in?

GG: I remember *Giovanni's Room*, *Our Lady of the Flowers*, and *Confessions of a Mask*.

HY: Wow, you really went for the trio.

GG: There's a way in which, because of that section, I knew that any book I pulled out would speak to me in a way.

HY: There is this idea of the [queer] tribe—the emotions are the same, the process is the same. If you are gay, the process of becoming a gay adult is much more similar than not. The circumstances might be different, but the emotions are all the same. And it does cut across nationality and race and so on and so forth.

GG: In that way I could read Mishima and feel that his books were about me. Even though they were books about a world very separate from Kentucky in the early nineties, I could say, "This is a book about me."

HY: What does it mean to write a post-gay novel? If you believe such a thing exists?

GG: I want to hear your answer to that.

HY: I don't believe it exists. I understand what it means insofar that gay desire isn't something that has to be written about in code. You don't have to sort of ferret it out in a book. It's not subtext, it's text. I suppose that that could be a definition of a post-gay literary age. But I think "post-gay" assumes that everyone understands and accepts what gayness is. "Post-gay" suggests that gayness is something that isn't expansive in of and itself, that it's something that isn't universal in of itself, that it's something that has to be moved beyond, and I just don't think that's true. What do you think?

GG: The idea of post-gay is bound up in a narrative of gayness and gay community as a response to shame.

HY: Or sex.

GG: Or sex. But if we can get beyond shame then the bonds that might make the identity and the community intelligible will be gone. It's a kind of wishful thinking that we've cleared away all the prejudice and now we can live more expansively, and it's an understanding of gayness that is far too narrow—it buys into this bogus idea of "the universal." The idea of "the universal" is something that's scrubbed clean of particularities—all that does is let it be white. All that does is let it be straight.

HY: What is a gay book without sex?

GG: That seems like a really easy question to answer. A book doesn't have to have sex in it. In your book [*A Little Life*] Willem feels a great deal of desire for Jude. Some people would say "obviously it's not a gay novel, Willem says he's not gay but he just loves Jude." And I'm like, that's the gayest thing anyone could ever say.

HY: I know [laughs].

GG: Of course you can have central, primary, nourishing, important gay relationships without sex, just like you can have heterosexual relationships that have all of those qualities that don't have sex at the heart.

HY: Yes, it's a very limited way of thinking. I think all of us, gay people and not-gay people, are guilty to a certain extent of assuming that a central part of a gay relationship is sex. One of the things that I wanted to discuss in the book is how limited the idea of sexuality is for men. Women don't have as much power as men and so we are therefore left more to ourselves to glide up and down the spectrum of sexuality. If you're a woman who identifies as straight and you end up sleeping with another woman and you still want to claim yourself as straight, no one really cares. If you're a man, it doesn't work that way. Being gay as a man threatens the idea of masculinity in a way that being gay as a woman does not threaten the idea of, if not femininity, then womanhood. Love between men, in its most beautiful and fluent expression, has traditionally been between gay men because it is assumed to be part of the expression of what a gay man is. Not that straight men aren't capable of that, but they're certainly not allowed to access it. So it was, in its truest sense, a book about the depth and the complexity of love between men. I remember when I was first thinking of this book I was at a dinner party with the great publisher Ann Godoff, and she was saying that what you saw during the worst years of New York's AIDS crisis was a flowering of friendship and a testament to the elasticity of friendship that modern times have never seen before. And it was because of gay men. It was gay men who created that and showed how durable and how expansive the relationship could be. In that way the book was inspired by a part of gay history. But I wasn't consciously writing a book about gay life. I will say that when I turned it into Anna, our agent, the first thing she said was, "There are too many gay people in this book."

GG: [Laughs] Bad Anna.

The idea of 'the universal' is something that's scrubbed clean of particularities—all that does is let it be white. All that does is let it be straight.

HY: And that it wasn't realistic because of that. But it is realistic! If you're in a certain city, if you're in a certain class, if you're in a certain circle, if you're in a certain industry, that is what you see. And you see these mini-utopias of people who have found, in perhaps very small universes but complete ones, places where love and affection and physical intimacy and romance and sex and friendship and jealousies, and all of the things that love can be between men, are profoundly and imperfectly and wonderfully expressed.

GG: Some people responded very strongly against the idea that *A Little Life* is a gay novel, or that it could be claimed as a gay novel. There were categories those responses fell into, and I sort of ranked them from stupid to non-stupid. The most stupid was "This can't be a gay novel because it is written by a woman."

HY: Well, listen, if you came to me and said, "Garth Greenwell wrote the great Asian-American novel," I would think, *No, he didn't.*

GG: Right. Like Darryl Pinckney said, "But it has been such a battle for these stories to be told." Not just queer stories; he was talking about Black stories and about the Black experience and for these stories to be told in their own voices. That has important value, too. And he said this beautiful thing about how we have to be able to hold contradictions and hold contradictory things to be true. Writers have to write what they have to write, and they have to be free to write that and it is also important that stories be told in their own voices. It's not a contradiction to assert that however perilous and difficult, it is possible and also valuable to write across difference. We all have to be invested in creating more spaces for voices that have not been heard, for voices that are structurally de-privileged to be heard.

HY: I feel like if you're really concerned that you can't write across difference, there is a bigger problem with you, yourself, as an artist and a person. But I also think that in the conversation, of writing across race or sexuality or gender or religion, we forget that there's another way to write across difference. The way that the characters think and move in my book—and certainly many authors would say the same about the characters in their books—are not necessarily how I think or how I've been trained to think. The sense of privilege these characters have, their sense of ease, are not things that I am privy to necessarily, and that, too, is a writing across difference.

GG: No question. And to think about what it takes to write across difference? It seems to me it takes a kind of emotional investment that puts the writer at risk. It takes work.

HY: Let me ask you something else. What are you tired of seeing in queer books [laughs]?

GG: There's nothing I'm tired of. I'm not tired of coming-out narratives—that's an incredibly rich experience that's inflected by all sorts of different categories. I don't think that sex work is a story that we wear out, because it's this humanly rich, infinitely varied experience. Just like, I don't think we're going to wear out boy meets girl or girl meets boy, I don't think we're going to wear out these sort of fundamental human stories that we're going to tell. And the sort of lie at the heart of that complaint of "Ugh, are we going to see another coming-out narrative, or another narrative about sex in bathrooms," is this assumption that these experiences are less valuable because they're gay. I think it is just homophobic.

HY: Also this idea that there's a sameness to the coming-out narrative.

GG: There's a sameness to any growing-up narrative. There's a sameness to growing up in a household and then leaving it. These are just fundamental experiences. Really there aren't new stories. Human life follows a limited number of patterns.

HY: Let me ask you about this. Is it the artist's obligation to be political, and what does that mean in this day and age? Does a gay writer, a self-proclaimed gay writer, writing these days have any sort of responsibility?

GG: No. I think there's a lot at stake for everybody in protecting writers, in protecting artists from those kinds of demands. I do see a conflict between my work and my identity as an activist, as someone who is interested in politics and political change. My work and my identity as an artist is all about ambivalence and ambiguity, but work in the political sphere, it cannot entertain that kind of ambivalence and ambiguity. I think there is a flattening out of vision when you are engaged in the important work of political change that is damaging to the artist. Fighting for political change for queer people has meant presenting a kind of narrative that is true and false, and I think being an artist means trying to tell the truth as much as you can. In that way I do feel a conflict between my art and my politics. It does feel like a split allegiance, because both of those endeavors feel really important to me.

I do see a conflict between my work and my identity as an activist.

HY: I will say that we're in a period of gay literature in which you can have unhappy gay characters, loathsome gay characters. Our understanding, perhaps in limited spheres of what it means to be gay and to have a gay life, has advanced far enough that I don't think writers worry as much about positive representation. Whereas I don't know if trans writers feel that they have to reassure, that they have to make an ending that feels unambiguous somehow. I suppose that is cultural and artistic progress when you have a broader diversity of gay life and gay outcomes and gay endings in literature, when you don't feel the burden perhaps of speaking for an entire community.

GG: Not just the burden of speaking for but the burden of speaking to.

HY: And of knowing your book is going to be the one in which some kid finds salvation, which is crippling for art.

GG: What political change for minority groups means in a democracy is making a case to the majority. It means translating the values of particular lives and packaging that value in a way that will be legible to the majority, packaging them in a way that they're palatable to the people who are disgusted by the idea of queer life.

You go back and you read some of the Congressional debates around the AIDS crisis, and the ways in which queer bodies are just demonized and vilified and spoken of in animalistic terms. Just this disgust, which was unashamed then. And that's what the political fight had to counter.

HY: It meant everyone had to be on their best behavior. And now you don't have to be as much.

GG: I think that that's just part of what fighting for minority rights entails. For queer people it meant getting them thinking about everything except anal sex, because straight people are disgusted by two men fucking. And so getting them thinking about everything else. So maybe that was necessary, but it's also necessary now to push back against that and try to recover, to try to restore the reality of queer experience.

HY: Well, I mean, that's one of the things I love so much about Edmund White's books. They're unabashedly, often very funnily, but unflinchingly, delightedly about sex, especially *City Boy*.

GG: I think that's a great subversion.

HY: Did you—this is going to be a really terrible word in this context—did you really enjoy larding it up in your book [laughs]? Because the sex scenes are very sexy and they're very much about sex. You can't pretend they're just sort of having frottage in the Equinox.

GG: Or in *Giovanni's Room*, where the bodies just disappear when they have sex.

HY: They sort of conveniently fade.

GG: I don't think there's nearly enough sex in *What Belongs to You*. I don't think there's enough of it. For the last twenty years, there has not been a lot of visible gay fiction that has gotten attention that has explicit sex in it.

HY: Hollinghurst has.

GG: I think *The Swimming-Pool Library* has it. That is the book that managed to get prestige and attention even though it had a lot of gay sex in it. Samuel Delany is one of the writers doing the most remarkable sex writing, but those books aren't being widely read. Edmund White has never been recognized as the genius he is by the broader literary sphere. His fiction has never won the huge prizes he should have. Even if you look at a writer I adore, Andrew Holleran, who I think is a great American writer who has never been recognized.

HY: Not that we should say winning is—

GG: Right, but—

HY: But it is a recognition from some sort of academy that what you're writing is relevant to culture.

GG: Oh! David Leavitt, too. *The Lost Language of Cranes*.

HY: I've always loved it. My father got it for me when I was twelve.

GG: [Laughs]

HY: Yeah, I don't think he knew what it was about.

GG: That's a wonderful book to read when you're twelve.

HY: When I think about it, who really does write gay sex ecstatically?

GG: In the stuff that I'm working on now, there's a lot more sex. It's much more explicit. I am interested in pushing that further. I do think it is this almost unique tool for a writer, it puts so much stuff under pressure.

HY: That's an interesting way to think about sex—both as an announcement and a pressure applier for the rest of the book.

GG: I think of sex as this experience that captures a whole series of interlocked contradictions. It's when we're at our most vulnerable and our most performative. It's when we're most thrust into our own sensations. And, if it's interesting sex or if it's good sex, most attentive to the sensations of another. I think it's when we're most bodily animal beings, and when we have our greatest intimations of the metaphysical.

HY: I suppose if *A Little Life* suggests anything about sex, it's that it's not fundamentally necessary to the human condition. That sex might be something that is not afforded to everyone and is not central to everyone.

I think of sex as this experience that captures a whole series of interlocked contradictions.

GG: The much better arguments about the book are in thinking about it as the first great asexual novel.

HY: Yes! And hearing from readers who have taken the time to write very thoughtful and interesting notes, I wonder, are we at a moment in a particular slice of gay America, the slice of gay America that you inhabit and that many people in this city inhabit, in which there is a terrific amount of pressure as a gay man to have sex, to be talking about sex, to be fluent in sex? One of the interesting through-lines of these letters has been these sorts of confessions of, "I don't really like it that much," "I don't have it enough," "I feel like I'm failing as a gay man because I'm not doing it enough," "I'm not enjoying it enough," "I'm not experimental enough." Certainly, I don't think any other group has that sort of pressure.

GG: You can't question it. I think there was a moment where straight women had to prove it, too.

HY: I agree, but that moment has sort of passed.

GG: Sexual liberation does not mean your whole life is centered on sex. I do think that's something that's been recognized in gay literature. I think you see this in Edmund White, you see this in Andrew Holleran quite explicitly. Part of recognizing the richness of sex and sexuality is recognizing that it accommodates tedium as well. Part of the richness of sex and sexuality is the fact that it is possible for it to be not very meaningful.

HY: What do you think about this idea that for many years, and certainly still in many places, gay life was inextricable from danger? This idea of a fearfulness of potential new encounters, very broadly defined. That part of the thrill of going to the park at three A.M. was that you might get arrested, but it was also a necessity.

> You should be making mistakes on the page, you should be reaching for something uncomfortable, you should be less worried about prettiness.

GG: I do think one of the most dangerous things in American culture is that timidity, that fear of Otherness, that fear of crossing these boundaries we inscribe our lives with. It is true that much of what seems the radicality of queer life, or the potential radicality, is that it did all of those things. When you went to the cruising park you would meet all kinds of people. There could be a heightened danger but also a heightened possibility. And I think we are so obsessed with safety. We are so obsessed with safety and that is totally stifling. I do think risk is really important.

HY: Hmm. The closing of the American mind to risk. And the defanging of gay life for acceptance and visibility. And the seizing of a certain type of gay life or representation of gay life as entertainment, is dangerous. Not all representation is helpful representation, especially when the representation is as a sort of clown.

GG: Then the question becomes, certainly as a writer, how do you put the fangs back? Or how do you reclaim some of what's been lost in exchange for a kind of acceptance. This is a thing that unites all responses to *A Little Life*, people who love it and people who hate it, is the intensity. I think it's owed to the intensity of the experience that is reading that book. I think everyone should read the book. I tell them, I'm not sure if you will love this book or if you will hate it, but it will be a landmark. After you finish this book you will be in a different place. It is a book that feels like it assaults you. How intentional was that when you made it? How much is that a quality of the art that you love, the adversarial quality?

HY: I suppose the easy answer is that I wasn't trained as a writer. I didn't know what kind of mistakes I should be avoiding. But if there's something I don't like in literature right now it's the safety of it. I think artists of all sorts should be encouraged to make big mistakes. You should be making mistakes on the page, you should be reaching for something uncomfortable, you should be less worried about prettiness. And I think we're at a moment in American literature where a lot of the work is polished, it's contained, it's buffed, it's perfectly fine. It's often technically perfect. But that's not what a book should be doing—a book should be trying to make something new, and by making something new it should have bolts and nails showing. It should be something that makes you a little uncomfortable to do, or a lot uncomfortable to do. It should be something that makes you sometimes queasy, something that makes you actively challenge yourself to do something ugly. I do think that every writer has an obligation to reach for something big and to be unafraid of being unliked. When you look at photography, which I've been collecting for a while, the word that photo editors will often use to distinguish a work they don't like from one they do is—this is a very damning word—"easy." A photo director will often say, "Have you seen so and so's work?" And they'll say, "Oh yeah, it's tough work." And what they mean by that, obviously, is that it is work that is uncompromising, not just in its subject matter necessarily, but because you have the sense that the artist is really forgetting audience. It's really hard to forget your audience when you're creating a visual work, and someone's walking by or a gallery owner is flipping through your portfolio, and you have a second or a micro-second to catch their attention. You don't want to put in the tough work. But the tough work is the work that announces you have something to say, that you are seeing something and that something is seeing you back. And if you can't do the tough work, if you can't forget about the audience enough, then you shouldn't do the work at all. Do commercial work, that's fine. I look at my collection here in my apartment and a lot of these pieces are not pieces that are going to endure. They're tough pieces, they're unlikable pieces. But I always admire the artist who has something to say and is going to say it without thinking about who's actually going to see it.

It's the privilege of marginality—that is the privilege of queerness. That exclusion.

GG: The thing that is scariest to me about the process of the publishing and the reception of the book is that when you're promoting a book, you are in this very artificial environment that has this incredibly strong gravity that distorts values. I was an opera singer and then I was a poet, those were my trainings in art.

HY: So you left the money-making world behind [laughs].

GG: I've always admired writers who seemed utterly unconcerned with any conventional measures of success. For the first time in my life, I'm aware of sales figures, and I hate that. There's such intense pressure put on writers now. If you're going to publish with a publisher like Doubleday or FSG then people are going to care about sales figures and you're going to be put into this machine. And the question I have now is how do you get back to that place where you're not thinking about an audience? Where you can have the fangs?

HY: Yeah, and there's nothing sweeter than, in retrospect, when you're writing your first. No one knows, no one's read it, the book could be anything. It's as close as you can get to a pure state of writing. There's something very sweet about that. In order to be an artist, it's useful if you're in some sort of state of constant humility. Whether it's living in another country, or surrounding yourself with another form of art you can't quite understand or won't or don't have any pure, true access to. Or you're surrounded by others who don't understand you, or are in a job where you are diminished somehow. It's necessary.

GG: It's the privilege of marginality—that is the privilege of queerness. That exclusion.

HY: Right. If you're lucky enough to exercise it.

GG: I do think that writing across difference, if it's done in a way that feels authoritative and not objectionable, has to be earned.

HY: I think people get into trouble because of two things: you create a character and you try to make this character, their Otherness, be incidental to who they are; or you try to make their Otherness all of who they are.

GG: Absolutely.

HY: They're the same problem. It's the same way that people will say "My Black friend so-and-so," or "I don't see race." As offensive as that is, and as problematic as that is, and as willfully blind as that is, in life so too is it in art.

GG: I think especially in this country it's just agonizing to wrestle with those things. Especially around race, more around race than around sexual identity, even though both of those minorities have been subjected to such violence. It is a kind of agony. To me, the authenticity, or sort of the legitimacy of writing across difference, is the extent to which you are willing to confront and take on and feel that agony.

HY: Yes, and I certainly don't think you can announce, "I'm going to write a gay book." That's where you really run into problems.

GG: You have to do the work of trying to understand not just your ideas or the myths you've been told about another group's experiences, but about that experience itself. Writing across difference becomes objectionable when it is cartoonish in the sense that it is just inhabiting myth.

HY: And it can't be your sort of challenge for that particular month, or that particular book. It's not Kilimanjaro and you're not going to climb it and it's not going to be something you dust off your hands at the end. It should leave you with more questions and toward a greater sort of searching. And if it doesn't, you're not doing it right.

GG: Absolutely.

In order to be an artist, it's useful if you're in some sort of state of constant humility.

HY: Yet how extraordinary it remains, and how meaningful it might be, to have the sense that you are being recognized by someone not of your tribe, as being a full human, a full member of what humanity is. I suppose that's what I find the most moving. When we talk about a work of art as "universal," what we're really talking about is its particularities. We're not talking about a generic person in a generic landscape dealing with generic problems, however you might define that. What makes a book universal is the problems of the particular. By saying that this is territory that can only be told or trod by a gay writer means that you are taking away your right to be recognized as the universal. I hope that other writers would think that a gay life is just as meaningful, just as universal, as a life that conforms to the contours of heteronormative society. But someone else talking about a queer life who's not queer does not mean that other people won't have their chance, nor does it mean the narrative that comes from experience is less meaningful.

ORIGINALLY PUBLISHED IN *HELLO MR.* ISSUE 08 IN 2016.

Slutboys

Ben French

Let's hear it for the slutboys. For all the hipster beardies slurping Peebers on tattered basement couches. All the twinks hurling themselves at boys like walls, sloshing rosé. All the sober otters and road-worn chubs found chain-smoking, legs dangling from rooftops downtown like matchsticks. Music: Sylvester. Club queens ballistic. Snatched little angels puking in gold-leaf toilets, shitshow frescos. Turn up for the holy glory only found in dive bar glory holes. Cyan karaoke slingers. Backseat truckstop fuckers. Dartboard pin-up boys. Let's hear it for the harnessed pigs swimming in seas of sweat and slop, hot pink thongs and wet mesh barbacks. For cotton candy lace fronts, secondhand nylons: Sissy's first time in drag, stumbling stilettos. Body electric. Lip sync fantastic. Mic drop, death drop, act up, listen up. This is for the gaymers and geeks in dark bar corners toggling cocks like Xbox controllers, deftly fingering schoolboy come-ups. All the boys on knees tonguing black clone boots, concrete on cheek, a newfound sin. All the clubs, churches. All the strobe lights, penance heaven sent. Drinks like Sunday wine, drunken gear night chainlink church choir. Sing "Come On." Sing "Mighty Real." Sing "Somewhere Over the Rainbow." There's sweat, there's blood, there's cum, there's dirt. Above all, there's slutboys: fairies and faggots reconfiguring sadness, susurrating leather. Every form of worship, the body. Scruff on scruff, tongue in cheek, hand in the bush, blood of my blood. Our histories live in our bodies the only way they know how: moving. Constant. In my slutboy mouth, a thousand homos' clenched fists. In my scrawny slutboy arms, the strength of Stonewall bricks cracking glass like shame. In my slutboy hips, a thousand Castro queens, late night wine-drunk on tattered yellow mattresses organizing action. When you slice my slutboy wrists, red satin sheets unfurl like sunsets. When you grab my slutboy cock, a whole history stands at attention. When you call me a slut, I slay you with silence, make my own magic, dig graves with my laugh.

ORIGINALLY PUBLISHED IN *HELLO MR.* ISSUE 09 IN 2017.

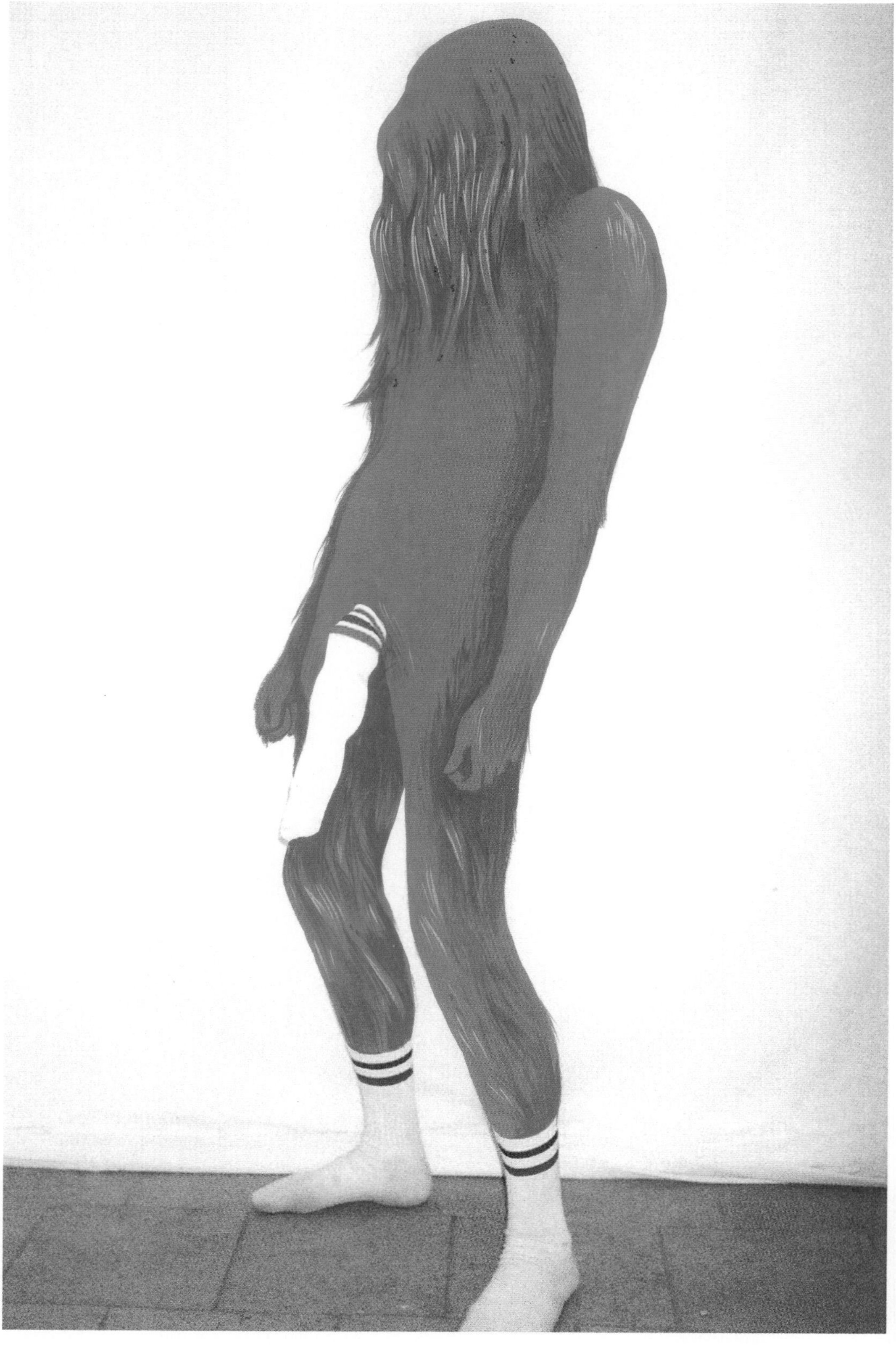

Snob Queer

Jeremy Atherton Lin

Art by Gorsad & Vito Montolio

Nearing late September, I received a text: *Hi boys! I don't suppose you're going to this . . .* The link was to Queer Bloomsbury, an event at Charleston, the farmhouse and garden not far from the coastal town where FBR and I live in East Sussex, England.

Oh, no, queer!, I thought, without exactly knowing why.

In 1916, the artist Vanessa Bell moved to Charleston with her lover Duncan Grant plus his other lover David Garnett, also known as Bunny. They were members of the Bloomsbury Group, those dazzling talents, generally from upper-middle-class backgrounds, including Bell's husband Clive and sister Virginia Woolf, as well as Grant's cousin—and briefly paramour—Lytton Strachey. As the staff at Charleston puts it, "The Bloomsbury group were at the vanguard of imagining new ways of living and loving." A century later, Queer Bloomsbury was a forum for contemporary reimaginings by a new generation. Why, then, did it sound so stuffy?

When people say *queer*, what I hear is *quaint*. Especially after the 2017 exhibition *Queer British Art 1861–1967* at Tate Britain. In the gallery's custom typeface, QUEER became institutionalized, or rather a selection of non-heteronormative art was deemed worthy of designating national heritage. Since then, I've thought of *queer* as akin to *eccentric*, which is what posh people get to be when they diddle their own cousin.

As such, despite queer's radical detours—very nineties—the word now presents as legitimate. I'm likely to find myself self-defining as queer when I am, say, submitting a proposal to a panel. If I call myself queer, the judges are unlikely to imagine me rimming bussy or chewing my own sock while gooning on Berlin XXX. They're conjuring me, like, wearing a cravat.

On the Sunday morning of Queer Bloomsbury, I remained undecided over whether to attend. It promised a panel of fierce nonbinary writers and durational performance art. It was also a chance to catch *Very Private?*, an exhibit featuring a few of the hundreds of erotic drawings by Duncan Grant, which had passed between lovers and friends through six furtive decades.

Are you buying the £35 ticket?, I texted indignantly to the pal who invited me.

I am, he replied. *Homophobic price.*

The first recorded use of the word *queer*, in the sense of a homosexual man, conflates perversion with elitism. A letter was read aloud at Oscar Wilde's 1895 trial, written the previous year by John Douglas, 9th Marquess of Queensberry, father of Wilde's young lover Lord Alfred Douglas, also known as Bosie. Writing spitefully to his father-in-law, Queensberry furiously attempted to hold someone to account for the death of his eldest son, Francis Archibald Douglas, Viscount Drumlanrig, "who was killed," according to his gravestone, "by the accidental discharge of his gun" at the age of twenty-seven.

"I write to tell you that it is a *judgment* on the whole *lot of you*," Queensberry raged, believing both sons had been corrupted by older men including "The Snob Queers like Rosebery." That would be Archibald Primrose, 5th Earl of Rosebery, also prime minister. A proponent of imperialism, Rosebery was also believed to be a homosexual who bedded Queensberry's late son. It's been speculated that Queensberry threatened to expose the prime minister if he did not ensure the vigorous prosecution of Wilde for acts of gross indecency with his younger son, Bosie. Through this obsessive campaign to depict his progeny as defiled victims, Queensberry rendered an indelible image of homosexual men as not only predatory but highfalutin.

I like to refer to myself as an old-school homosexual, not a queer. But that's just me.

In the end, we were too hungover to get to Queer Bloomsbury. All I wanted was to stay close to our apartment, maybe scarf down spring rolls from You's Chinese. Waiting for the order, FBR and I bought some half-price Hay stacking crates from TK Maxx across the street. We took our greasy snack down to the beach, where we tried to figure out why exactly we were put off by the word *queer*. For one thing, as a writer often classified as such, a Queer Event always strikes me a little like work.

One writer who does not want to be classified as such, David Sedaris, happens to live in an adjacent county, West Sussex. And coincidentally, in October, around a month after Queer Bloomsbury, Sedaris delivered a satirical commentary on *CBS Sunday Morning*, in which he announced he was "simply done fighting the term 'queer.'"

I find myself somewhat aligned with Sedaris where his view is that the term, intended to be inclusive, may instead be an ill-fated attempt at all-encompassing. "I read an interview with a woman who identifies as queer because she's tall," Sedaris quipped. Similar things have been said before, by people younger and more punk. Brontez Purnell in *Bookforum* in 2016: ". . . it's like everyone's queer now. I'll be sitting there talking to a guy who vaguely thought about sucking a dick in college, sort of. And he's like, 'Our struggle is queer freedom.' I like to refer to myself as an old-school homosexual, not a queer. But that's just me."

Sedaris invents an absurdist twist, claiming he's decided to self-identify as straight. But his satire defaults to essentialism: "I'm going with heterosexual because, like the words *Jewish* or *female*, it rarely if ever changes." This apparent defense of fixed identity categories wound up coming across as out-of-touch. The bigger problem may be context. One brilliant writer pointed out to me that Sedaris should know better than to risk amplifying divisiveness on a platform as massive as CBS. Nuance is hard to achieve in ninety seconds. (And that's before the paraphrasing. I first caught wind of the whole thing from a friend: *David Sedaris defines* queer *as tall women and short men.*)

In her concurring *New York Times* op-ed "Let's Say Gay," Pamela Paul attempted to expose *queer* as a shibboleth, with its self-consciously

Not gay as in happy, but queer as in fuck you.

marginal connotations. "Many gay people simply prefer the word 'gay.' 'Gay' has long been a generally positive term," she proclaimed, breezily erasing its ubiquity as a playground taunt. Paul's glib take relied on anecdotal evidence. "What I hear most often from gay and lesbian friends regarding the word 'queer' is something along the lines of what Sedaris pointed out: 'Nobody consulted me!' This wasn't their choice." By contrast, in a takedown of Sedaris in *Jezebel*, Rich Juzwiak brought up the long history of the word as self-identification, citing George Chauncey's assertion in the book *Gay New York* that, prior to World War II, some men self-defined as queer because they "saw themselves as 'special'—more sophisticated, more knowing—and took pleasure in being different from the mass."

But Chauncey's research involves a complicated, class-based timeline of the implied meanings of *queer*. In the early decades of the twentieth century, the term could be used within working class culture to connote womanlike behavior, or alternatively as a self-definition by middle-class homosexuals who considered *faggot* and *fairy* derogatory whereas "*queer* did not presume that the men it denoted were effeminate, for many queers were repelled by the style of the fairy and his loss of manly status." *Fairy* brought to mind a mincing streetwalker. *Faggot* was used more commonly on the Harlem scene. By contrast, "the cultural stance of the queer embodied the general middle-class preference for privacy, self-restraint, and lack of self-disclosure, and for many men this constituted part of its appeal."

According to Chauncey's research, these bougie types "created a place for themselves in middle-class culture by constructing a persona of highly mannered—and ambiguous—sophistication." This often entailed Anglophilia, specifically admiration of the English gentry. "While the fairy intended his style to mark him as a sexual invert," Chauncey writes, "the queer intended his style to deflect such suspicions." This "did not entirely protect queers from ridicule for gender nonconformity, but it did allow them to recast, denigrate, and dismiss such ridicule as a sign of lower-class brutishness." In fact, Chauncey provides a range of evidence that straight working-class men were more tolerant to homos in their midst (and more open to their advances). Queer, in the sense of discreet homosexuality, was a response to middle-class hostility. And middle-class queers were just as capable of camping it up and tossing feminine pronouns around, they just did not do so in public. Chauncey describes the queers' disparaging of fairies as class-based antagonism.

"Many middle-class queers blamed anti-gay hostility on the failure of fairies to abide by straight middle-class conventions of decorum in their dress and style."

In the Sedaris debate, much more than class, a generational divide was obvious. Among the letters to the editor published by the *Times*, a teenager contended that "silencing the word 'queer' mutes the politically charged history of the community," which defers to queer activist jargon of the past few decades. *(Not gay as in happy, but queer as in fuck you.)* To one gay man in his sixties, though, "it feels as if the pioneers of gay liberation . . . are disregarded as irrelevant because the new generation sees itself as the true liberators." Every pundit seemed concerned with respecting history, yet chose a different Queer Common Era.

The comments below the *Jezebel* hatchet job tended to be of the "OK, boomer" variety. But they don't quite agree on what *queer* represents: weapon of agitation, or Dumbo's feather? One comment went: "I also can't say I have much patients [*sic*] for a middle aged white man telling people the labels that give them comfort are pointless." Is satire ever meant to provide comfort? Is queerness?

The etymological roots of *queer* are entwined with the oblique and off-center, as in German *quer*, meaning diagonal. It makes sense that *queer* works as a synonym for *kooky*. This is one reason I bristle at the portmanteau *queerdo*—as with *ginormous*, it's redundant.

East Sussex, where we live, is a pretty queer—as in weird—county. There are softly undulating hills, called *downs*, and little residential passageways, called *twittens*. Then suddenly, the turbulent sea. One evening, FBR and I watched the arrival of a dinghy crammed with some thirty asylum seekers. Local supporters, mobilized via WhatsApp, arrived in sedans with provisions in the trunk. A woman handed a shivering man the coat off her back. A red-faced local marched toward the migrants, shouting and expanding his arms into a one-man wall, but he found himself outnumbered by compassionate teens. A remarkable number of youth in the region identify as catgender. They eat on the floor, nuzzle human companions, and expect teachers to use their correct pronouns, nya/nyan. There is also evidence of a thriving local community of Satanists. One of our newer shops sells homoerotic skate gear. Last time I passed, a t-shirt displayed in the window was printed with a photo of hairy calves and the dirty soles of white socks. £75. The titillation brought on by encountering the image openly displayed: free.

On the seafront, a snazzy bar prides itself on providing an LGBTQIA+ safe space. FBR and I went on the Saturday before Halloween dressed as Bill and Ted. A reasonably attractive shortie demanded I stop looking at him. (I thought he was looking at me!) He'd been dancing close, then seemed to switch, aggressively proclaiming that he, a *straight*, normally felt *very comfortable* at this bar and chose to go there *frequently*. But my stare he found unnerving.

"It's *creepy*," he said.

I told myself I only looked creepy because I was several gins deep and wearing a wig that no longer gave the slightest hint of Keanu Reeves. I told myself that he just couldn't cope with the palpable mutual desire. (*I felt it, too!*, FBR assured me.) This guy had every right to scorn my glance, tell it to me straight, move away. I had every obligation not to pursue (which, having not yet received the monkeypox jab, I wouldn't have anyway). But his tactic was to proclaim his sense of belonging over mine. I fiercely told him it was a fucking gay bar. Jesus, I thought, I literally wrote the book. His girlfriend kept apologizing to me. Others tried to get involved—"Everything OK?"—but I was done.

We exited, then plopped onto a bench by the sea.

"What makes me mad is that it's us who left," FBR said.

"It's OK," I said. "I was ready to go."

"I should have known by his shoes," FBR huffed.

That guy is nothing new—the conditional ally, for whom tolerance requires desexualizing. In Angus Wilson's 1952 novel *Hemlock and After*, a character says, "I'm not medieval or something. I quite like queers if it comes to it, so long as they're not on the make."

Our working definitions of *queer*—very academia in the nineties—tend to describe a quality independent of sexual orientation. Eve Kosofsky Sedgwick gave us: "the open mesh of possibilities, gaps, overlaps, dissonances and resonances, lapses and excesses of meaning when the constituent elements of anyone's gender, of anyone's sexuality aren't made (or *can't be* made) to signify monolithically." In this vein, bell hooks once identified as "queer-pas-gay," the *pas* enacting, as in dance vocabulary, a stepping past homosexuality to queer positionality, or being "at odds with." David Halperin chimed, "Queer is by definition *whatever* is at odds with the normal, the legitimate, the dominant. *There is nothing in particular to which it necessarily refers.*"

FBR and I finally ventured to Charleston on an ordinary Friday in November. The *Very Private?* show of Duncan Grant's erotic drawings was still on; as soon as FBR entered the lobby to ask where we could park our bikes, he encountered several depictions of penis. Meanwhile, I spotted a cravat, worn with a blue chore jacket by a bespectacled boy who sat making paper chains in preparation for Christmas. I overheard a man who looked like Bob from *Twin Peaks* donning Junya Watanabe remark on the house's interior design: "What they were *not* looking for was Instagram likes." Visitors seemed largely divided into two categories: high art and country living. In the former group: avant-garde Bob, a middle-aged woman who wore her hair in a long plait like the author Renata Adler, a twink with a single drop pearl earring. The rural set sported Barbour jackets. In the café, one of these old white guys was apoplectic at being kept waiting for his gnocchi.

That guy is nothing new—the conditional ally, for whom tolerance requires desexualizing

He and his wife and their mirror-couple friends were also booked into the 2:40 P.M. tour of the house, along with a gaggle of student types, including the boy with the pearl earring. The tour guide, plausibly a reincarnation of Virginia Woolf, was flummoxed that we were all in the same time slot. One of the Barbour wives confirmed, "We are a very mixed group."

At Charleston, the mantelpieces are painted like geometric cosmos, it's said because Vanessa Bell worked there to keep warm by the fire. The lampshades are upside-down colanders. The color scheme is salmon and asparagus, butter and duck egg blue.

The tour guide closed a slanted door, revealing a mural on the back. "There's nothing straight in Charleston," she said, and everyone ha-ha-ha'ed like you do watching Shakespeare. The dining table, she pointed out, was round, making gatherings non-hierarchical. "Although I'd argue," she said, "that whoever served the food—Vanessa Bell—was the true head of the table."

Mr. No Gnocchi, standing in front of a small painting, announced that the original that Duncan Grant had copied was by Piero della Francesca.

"I know this because we saw it at the Uffizi!" It goes without saying, the mansplaining seal had been broken.

The other Barbour husband stood in front of a fantastical wardrobe and muttered something about not being able to fathom the time and inclination to decorate so intensely. His (or was it the other) Barbour wife added: "While thinking Greek Thoughts!"

The queerness of Charleston was somehow not aligned with *my* queerness—lovely, but telegraphing privilege, in that rundown, damp, very English way. Yet I couldn't help feeling the place belonged more to *us* than *them*. In still other moments, I saw how the Barbour team connected to the English sensibility, respected the poshness. Until the eclecticism of the objects began to grate.

"It's so . . . random!" one of the men remarked.

"It's the accumulation of life over time," the tour guide explained.

The last room on the tour is the glorious custom-built studio; in the middle, a tasteful male nude by Grant is proudly displayed on an easel. A Barbour enquired about his identity. Turns out he was the local electrician. We tittered. The Barbours turned their attention to a landscape instead. "Where exactly in France is that?" they demanded.

We speculated the Barbours wouldn't have purchased the combination ticket to see *Very Private?*. Yet there they were, wandering into the gallery after touring the garden, giving off a slight air of obligation with that edge of oh, yeah, so what?

A viewer might first notice work by Ajamu X, monochrome photographs of Black bodies in close-up. He is one of a small group of contemporary artists whose work had been hung in conversation with Grant's drawings. But Grant's decades-old sketches were probably the most explicit on display. There are not only erections, there is handstand rimming. There are balls, sailor caps, armpits, feet. The images are very oral, with a tender, if not worshipful, feeling for penis. Some of the boys are in mesh undergear. They look comfortable in transgression, masculine the way that fey dancers can be, standing still, stinking. I felt a surge of vindication as the Barbours swiftly left. The private Duncan Grant was not just queer, he was all horned up.

The private Duncan Grant was not just queer, he was all horned up.

In the gift shop, I ran into an amiable straight guy I know, a graphic designer down from London with his pretty wife. We spoke about what we were up to. Nothing much. We spoke about unproductivity-as-process. His wife was very encouraging about unproductivity. I told her she should record a do-nothing meditation for the Calm app.

It was nice to see that dude. I sometimes think about the time he told me that he nicknamed his young daughter Creep. For a second there, I was slightly aghast.

"It just stuck," he'd shrugged.

And I could sense how the word must sound snuggly and familiar in their household. It didn't need to mean anything in particular. It was funny. It stuck. A pretty good nickname, I realized. I also imagine that one day the daughter will insist her daddy stop calling her that.

WORKS CITED

Chauncey, George. *Gay New York: Gender, Urban Culture, and the Making of the Gay Male World, 1890-1940* (New York: Basic Books, 1994).

Halperin, David. *Saint Foucault: Towards a Gay Hagiography* (New York: Oxford University Press, 1997).

Sedgwick, Eve Kosofsky. *Tendencies* (Durham, NC: Duke University Press 1994).

Wilson, Angus. *Hemlock and After* (New York: Viking Press, 1952).

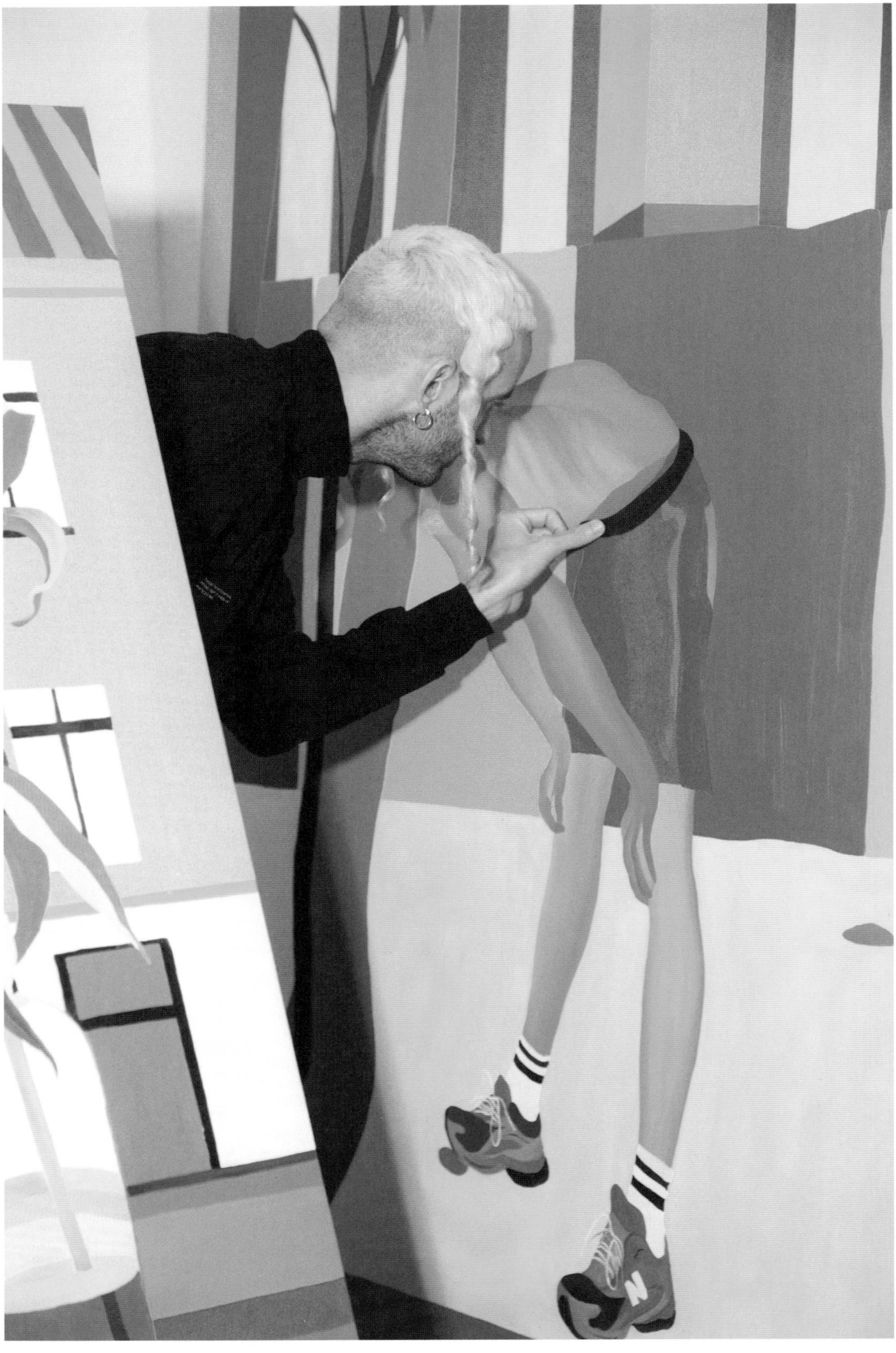

Navot and His Kind: Portraits, Penises, and Peyes

Michele Fossi | Photos by Luke Abby

On a gloomy Berlin day, among the grayness of the surrounding buildings, Navot Miller's atelier in Berlin-Tempelhof is a sudden epiphany of color, making it impossible to miss. After welcoming me inside, the Israeli-American painter, since nearly a decade an adoptive Berliner, shows me several unfinished oil paintings he is currently working on, all painted with his contradistinctive vivid, comic-like colors and invariably showing his equally contradistinctive mix of Jewish and gay imagery.

"Art was in fact my backup plan: My original idea was to study architecture in Berlin," he confessed. "But three times I applied to different architecture schools and three times I was rejected. Eventually, I was accepted at the art school Kunsthochschule Berlin Weissensee. I didn't immediately give up my dream of becoming an architect, though. My early drawings were dominated by geometric patterns and simple architectural structures, such as house shapes, trees, and lamp posts."

Navot Miller was born in the rural small town of Shadmot Mehola, a national-religious Israeli settlement in the West Bank, in 1991, to an American mother and an Algerian-French father. "As a child, I grew up in a conservative Orthodox community that followed strict religious rules, and I never felt I could be accepted there as a homosexual. Although I received care and support from my family, from a very young age I told myself that if I ever had the possibility of trying to live someplace else, I'd do it." In a colorful zine containing a few short autobiographical texts interspersed with a selection of his early painted works, published on the occasion of his group show *Posts Paris Ass* at Palais de Tokyo in 2018, he dedicated a few lines to his hometown. Intentionally opting for an infantile, ungrammatical language, suggesting it's his inner child speaking, he writes: "In shadmot mehola the light is too bright, too white. In shadmot mehola everyone is heterosexuals. In shadmot mehola who isn't heterosexual doesn't live in shadmot mehola they live somewhere else."

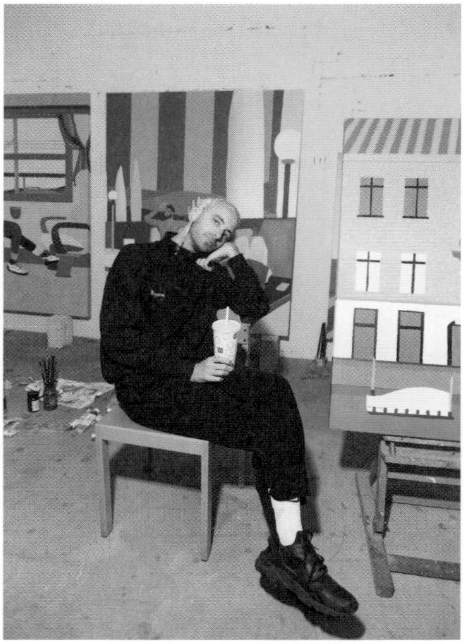

The painter ascribes his unrelenting creative artistic drive in the past years to the existential need to bring together the schizophrenic ends of his biography—the orthodox past, full of no-goes and taboos, and the secular, liberated gay present. "With its tolerant atmosphere and vibrant gay scene, Berlin was the theater of a gay Renaissance for me—a real tsunami. Like Patti Smith says of New York, Berlin was for me the city that 'de- and reformed me,'" he reveals. "My fascination with symmetry and geometry soon gave way to an intense artistic drive to explore the subject of sexuality. I found myself creating oddly arranged collages of newspaper and magazine clippings, mixing images from both Orthodox Judaism lifestyle and gay porn; in another drawing, the windows of a synagogue took the shape of penises."

Opposite: Fig. 1

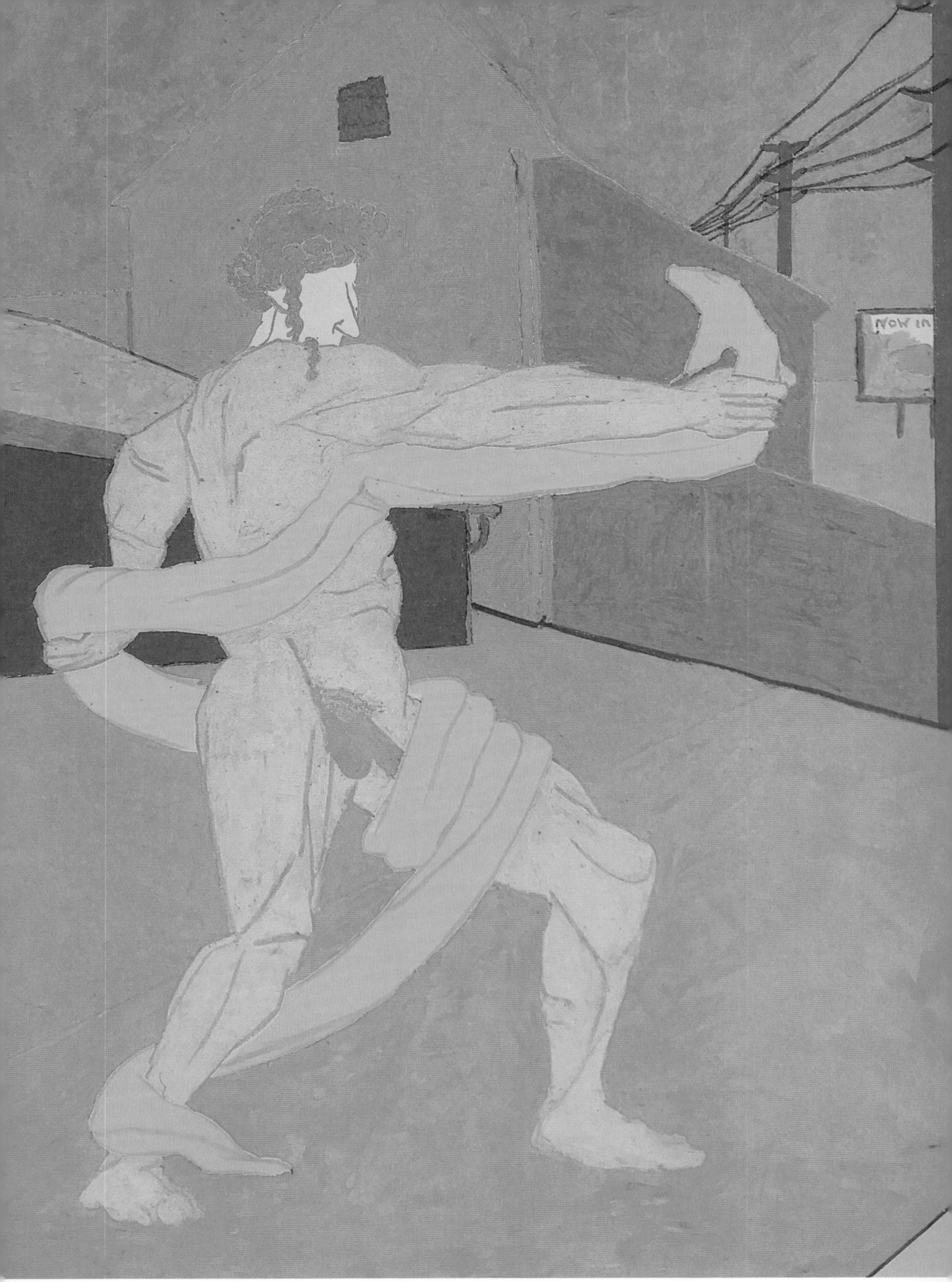
NOW IN

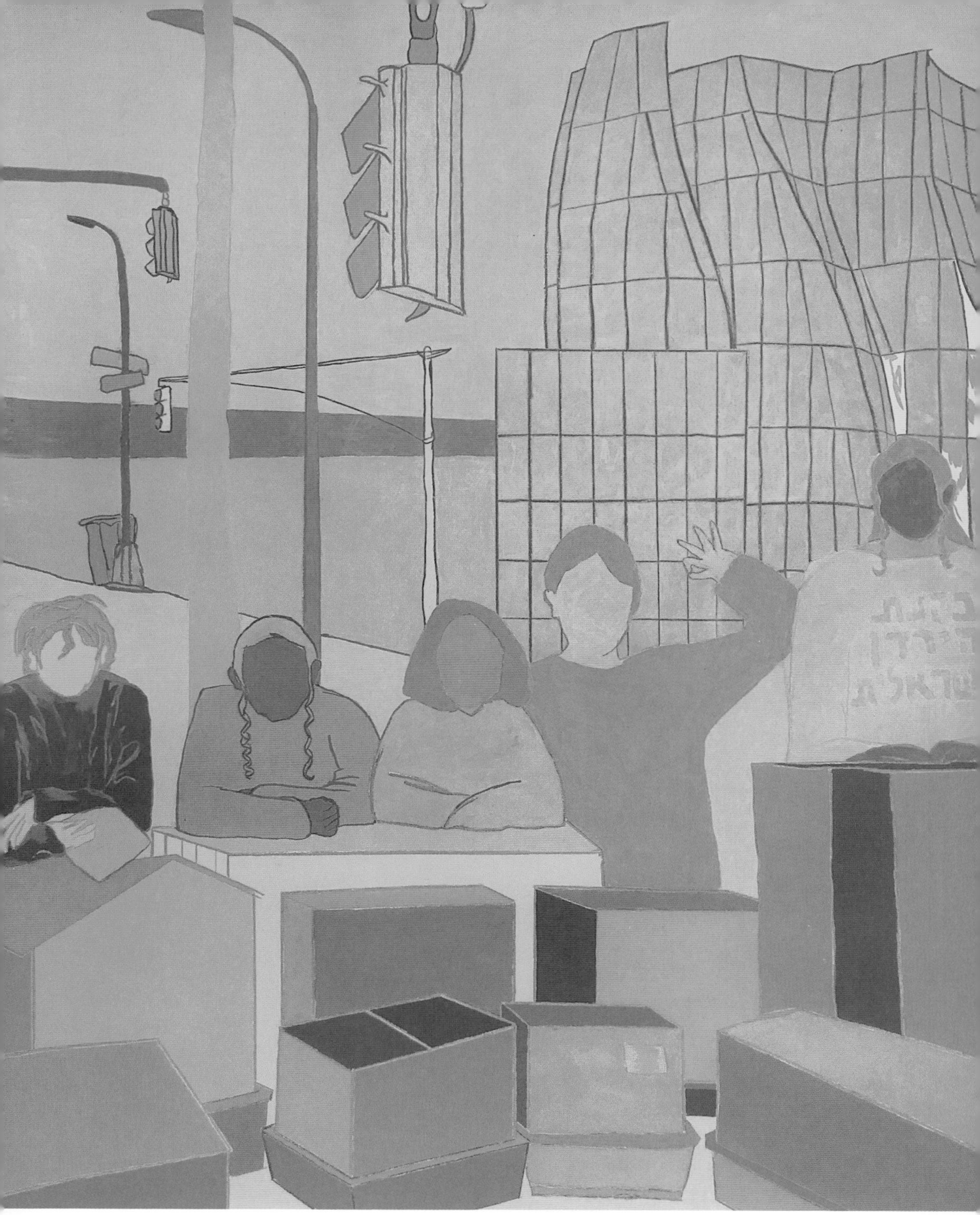

Above: Fig. 3, Opposite: Fig. 2

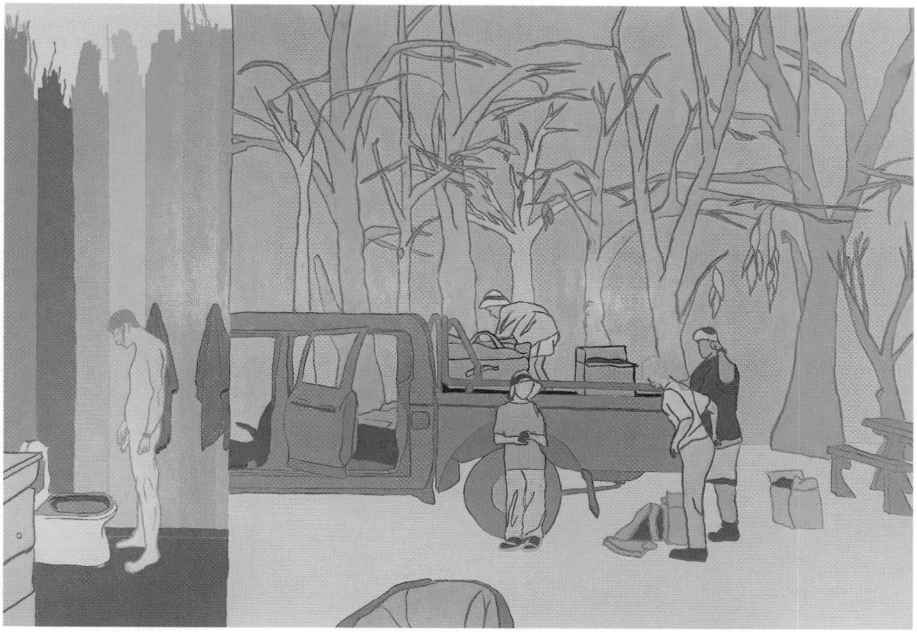

He goes on to describe a visit to the Abguss-Sammlung Antiker Plastik in Charlottenburg, in 2018, as "the Road to Damascus moment" that marked a point of non-return in his artistic journey. "Appealing to my homoerotic taste, the muscular sculptures of Greek deities and heroes in the museum's collection made a great impression on me. In the following days, I began drawing relentlessly those mythological athletic figures, often characterizing them as Orthodox Jews." This is best epitomized by *Apollo as a Jew* (Fig. 1), a wax pastel drawing that depicts the god engaged in a battle against the mythical snake monster Python, embellished with sidelocks (in Yiddish: *Peyes*) dangling down his head. "This work is particularly dear to me: It represents my first conscious attempt to blend in my practice my Jewish religious background with my contemporary, sexually liberated lifestyle in Berlin. Around the same time," he continues, "I started combining childhood images with scenes from my everyday life today, attempting a cathartic conciliation between otherwise far-away, irreconcilable sides of my identity. Although no glue is involved, I like to refer to such works as *collages*—juxtapositions of images that otherwise would be unconnected in time and space." In *The Millers and Zach* (Fig. 2), his former partner, portrayed while pissing, makes his unexpected appearance in the middle of a family trip in a natural park in Israel dating at least twenty years before. In *Hamster club* (Fig. 3), he portrays a group of young kids from Shadmot Mehola in front of hamster cages, including himself, with Frank Gehry's IAC building in New York and the Hudson River as a background.

"Around the same time, I started dealing with the documentation—or better, the 'Navotization,' as I had done with Apollo—of my casual lovers' bodies, usually starting with a snapshot taken on my phone after sex, which I subsequently transform into a drawing in my studio." A good example is the homoerotically charged *Willi in Wedding before bed* (Fig. 4), where the naked lover's reflection in the mirror portrays him as an Orthodox Jew. In *Boy on balcony* (Fig. 5), a lover in underwear is smoking an after-sex cigarette on the balcony of a lakeside hotel; at a second glance, the balcony's metallic bars appear strangely bent, forming a menorah. Recently, Miller has focused on some more sexually explicit works—a shift he attributes to a visit to the Tom of Finland Foundation show in Venice in 2022. "I felt like my practice was not nearly as gay as some of the works I saw in this show." As soon as he returned to Berlin, he began painting scenes associated with Berlin's liberated and sex-positive gay lifestyles. In *Water-Break* (Fig. 6), he portrays a group of men engaging with each other in what seems to be an outdoor dark room during a festival. In *Wedding* (Fig. 7), we see a group of half-naked bodies gathered indoors as part of an after-hours orgy.

The use of vibrant, pastel-like, neon colors, which since *Apollo as a Jew* became his painting style's most distinctive feature, fulfills a similar conciliatory function, he explains. "I see bright, positive colors as a way to add a queer touch to my religious past," he says while touching one of the two blond-dyed Peyes running down his head. "Yes, my Peyes underwent a similar queering process," he adds, smiling. "A Jewish Orthodox embracing a secular gay lifestyle would normally cut

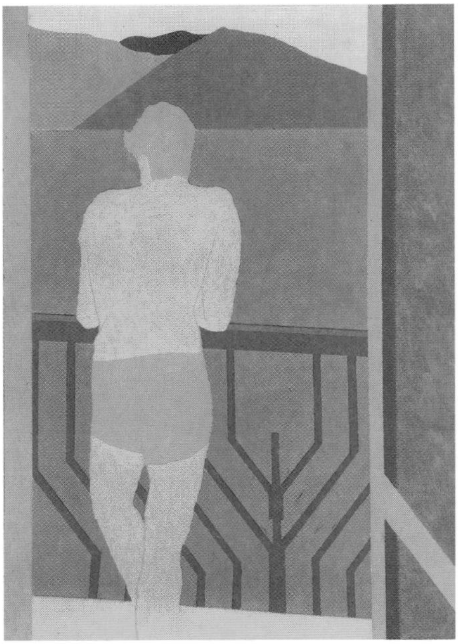

them. I made them blond instead, in the attempt to integrate this religious symbol into my gay identity." He goes on to share his vision for a future show in Berlin, that will not fail to stir controversy. "I am planning to transform a gallery into a synagogue painted entirely in pink," he reveals. "My intention is not merely to provoke, let alone offend anyone. I want to create an inclusive place of worship open to everyone, regardless of religious faith, skin color, gender, and sexual orientation, where my religious upbringing and gay identity can intersect and coexist. I am also excited at the idea of bringing my practice from 2D to 3D, combining my stark interests in architecture as well as in painting."

It would be reductive, however, to consider his peculiar, flamboyant use of color as a mere queer signifier. Deliberately unrealistic (a human skin can be blue, a tree can be red, or a windmill purple),

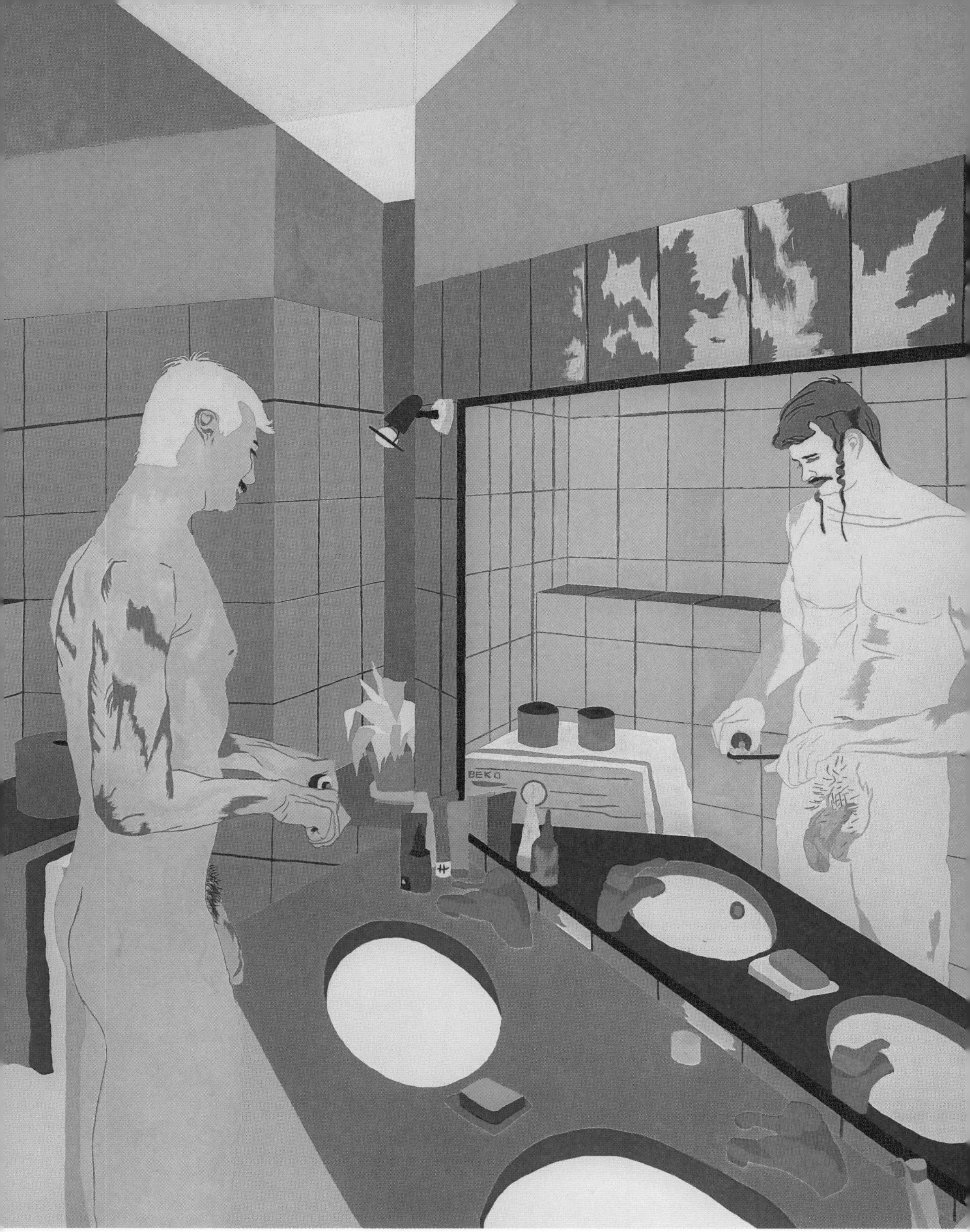

Opposite: Fig. 5, Above: Fig. 4

yet carefully chosen so as to create a harmonious color palette, vibrant colors in Miller's practice are there to signify to the viewer that what they see is a highly subjective re-examination of reality, seen through a lens of memories and feelings. Re-elaborations of the subconscious in the form of free, often paradoxical associations of people, places, buildings, and objects that would not be possible in real life, his works are mesmerizing lucid dreams. At times, their suspended, hallucinated atmospheres leave the viewer puzzled, prompting them to revisit each image multiple times.

Particularly intriguing are the paintings set in carefully designed interiors, where the artist's eye for architecture is explicitly evident (Fig. 8). In these works, much like David Hockney (whom, not surprisingly, he acknowledges as his greatest reference), Miller gives us a vantage point from which to witness and participate in queer life—making us, whether we like it or not, voyeurs.

The representation of queer life he offers us, however, is neither documentary nor pornographic but one always filtered through the prism of his emotions: In his multi-colored, non-realistic portrayal of friends and lovers, the interplay between people and the spaces they inhabit always suggests revelations of the soul. "With few models to draw upon in the tradition, the notion of 'queer space' is all but a given—it is something many gay people taking their first steps in the gay world have to create by themselves, an exciting and frightening task at the same time. For this very reason, queer space is often an emotionally charged space." From Miller's perspective as an artist, a very colorful one.

Opposite: Fig. 8

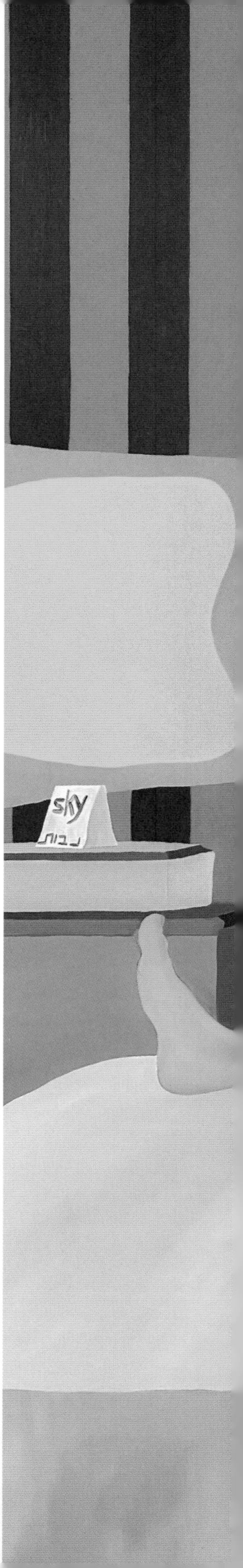

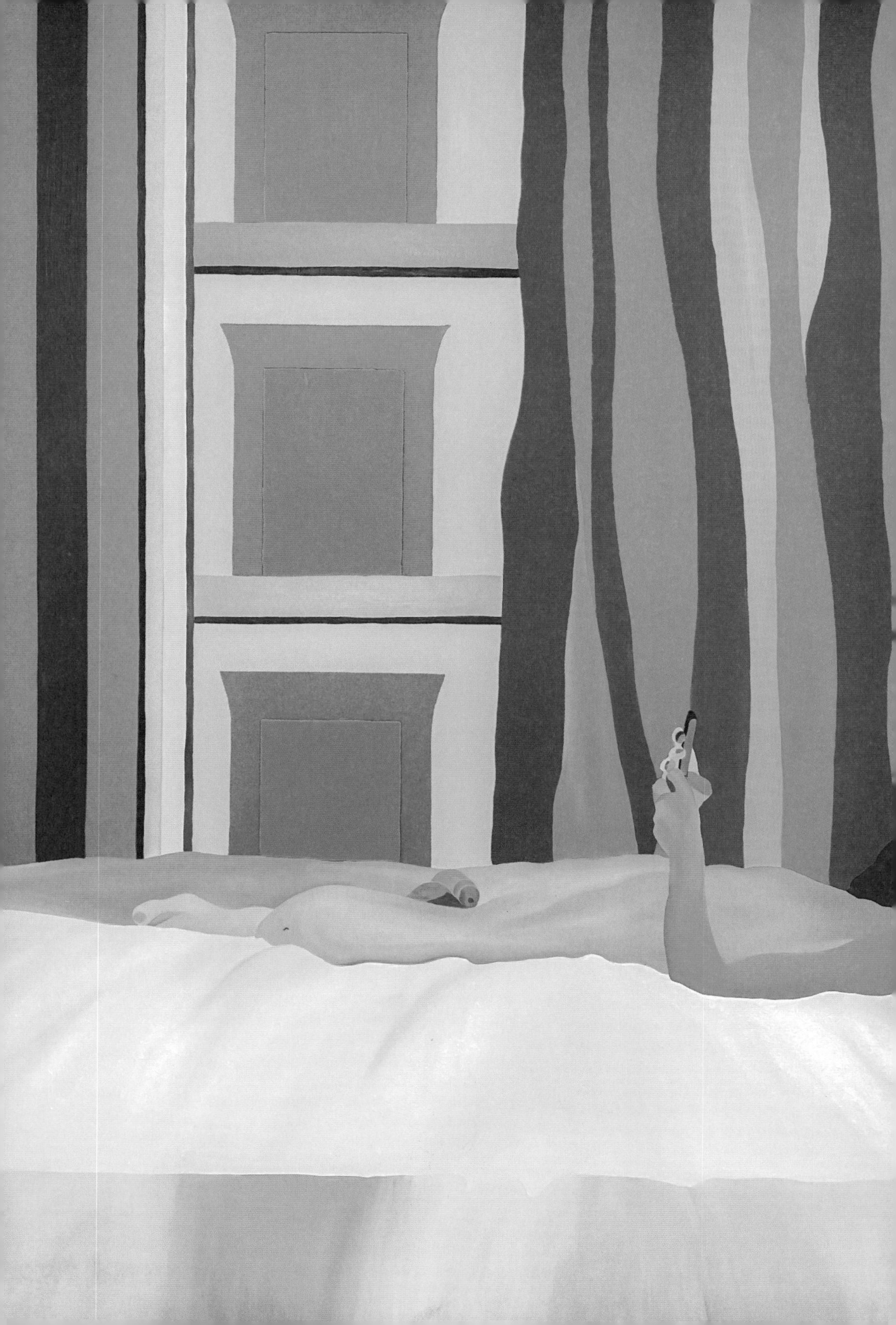

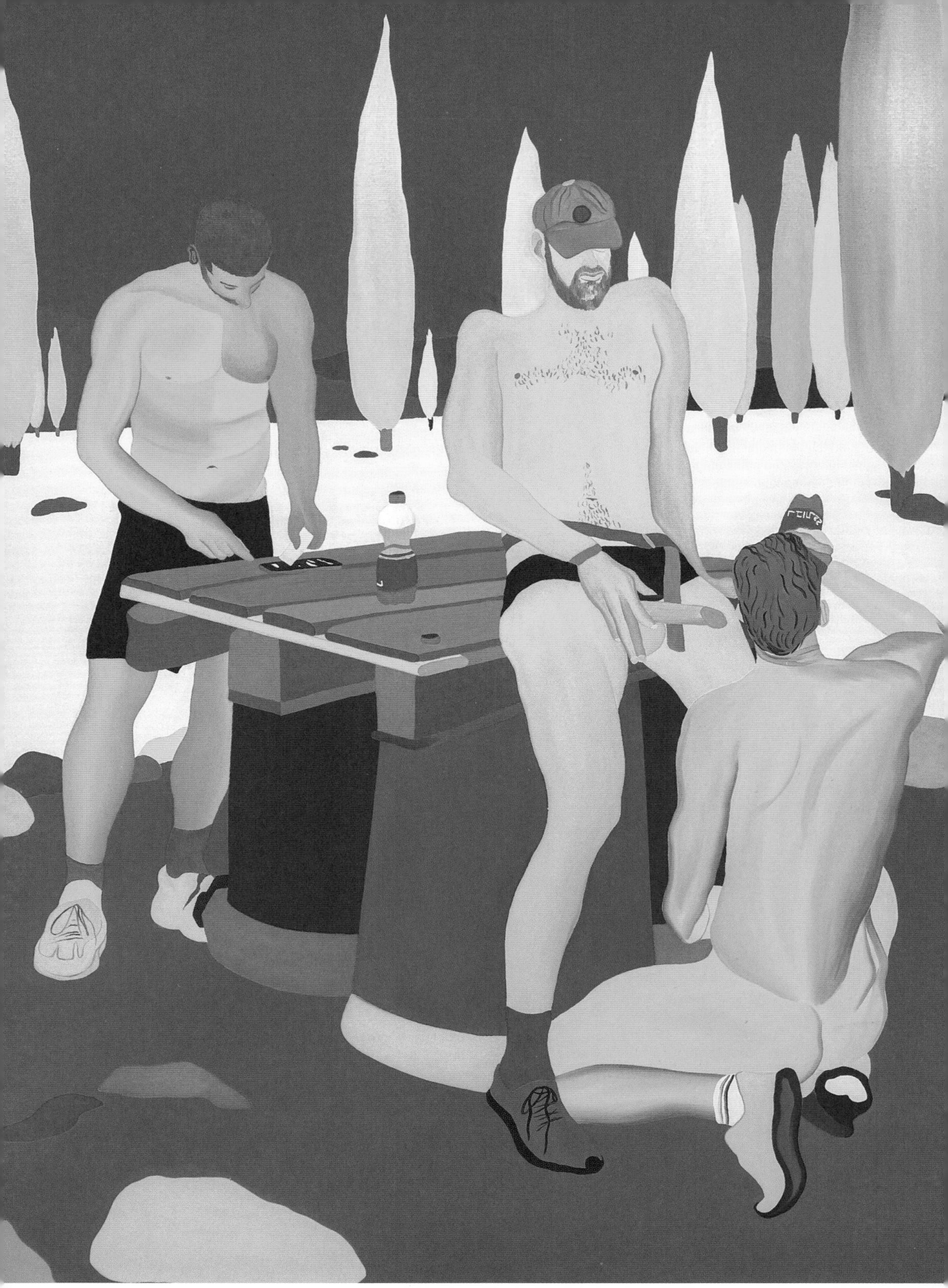

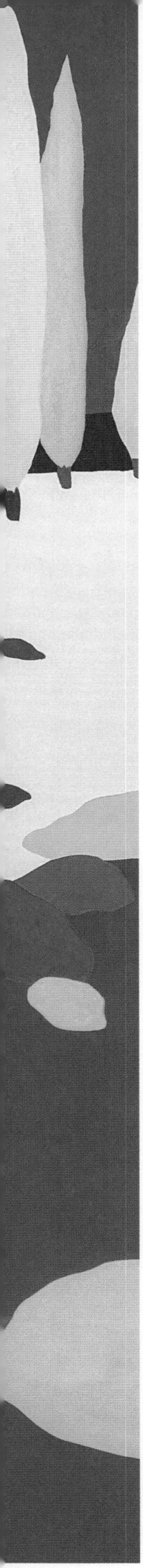

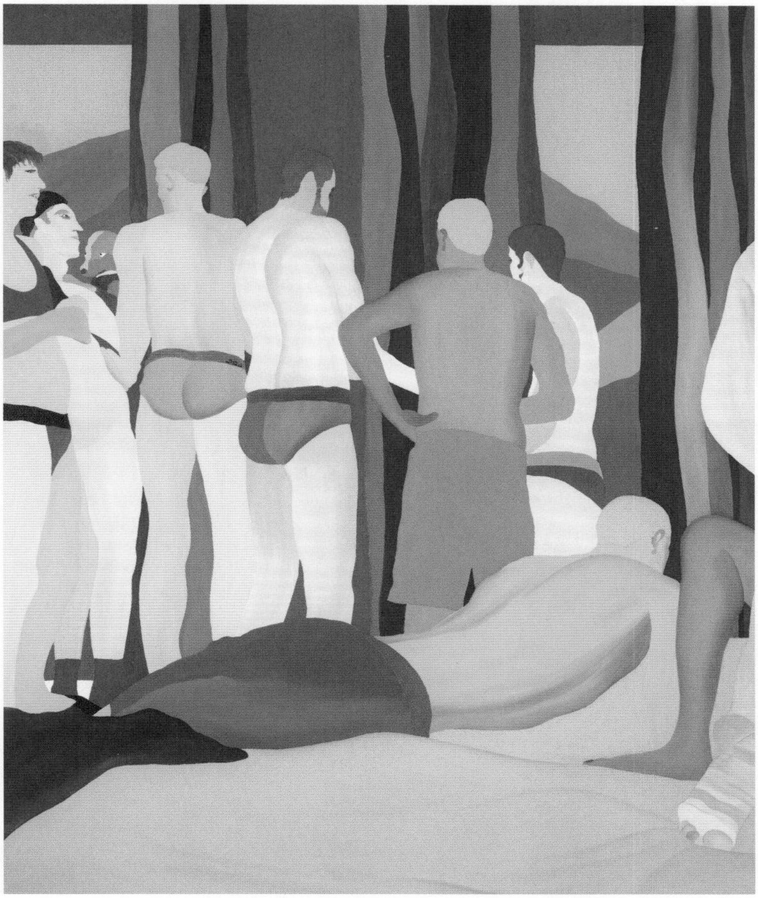

Opposite: Fig 6, Above: Fig. 7

Fig. 1 *Apollo as a Jew*, 2018, water-soluble wax pastel on paper, 100 × 150 cm, courtesy of the artist (p. 43)

Fig. 2 *The Millers and Zach*, 2020, water-soluble wax pastel on paper, 150 × 190 cm, courtesy of the artist (p. 45)

Fig. 3 *Hamster club*, 2019, water-soluble wax pastel on paper, 150 × 190 cm, courtesy of the artist (p. 44)

Fig. 4 *Willi in Wedding before bed*, 2020, water-soluble wax pastel on paper, 150 × 190 cm, courtesy of the artist (p. 47)

Fig. 5 *Boy on balcony*, 2019, water-soluble wax pastel on paper, 72 × 102 cm, courtesy of private collection Helsinki (p. 46)

Fig. 6 *Water-Break*, 2022, oil on canvas, courtesy of the artist (p. 50)

Fig. 7 *Wedding*, 2022, oil on canvas, courtesy of the artist (p. 51)

Fig. 8 *Riccardo on bed*, 2022, oil on canvas, courtesy of the artist (p. 49)

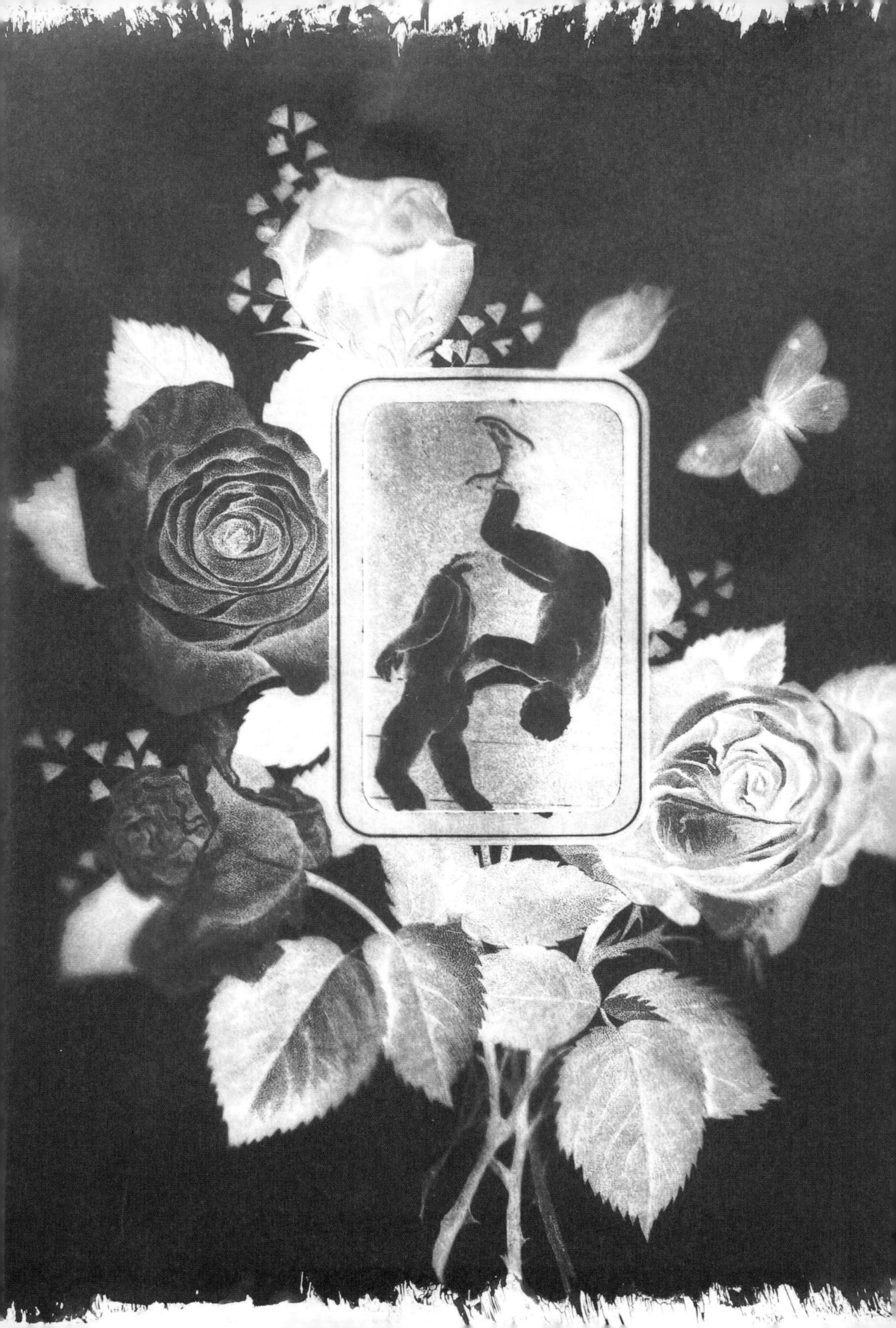

STAR BEINGS

Alexander Chee | Art by Jason Edward Tucker

I met Bobby at the party of a yoga teacher we had in common. It was summer of 1999 and the party was in the garden behind his beautiful apartment in Chelsea. Margaritas were being served. The yoga teacher lifted his and said, "We do yoga so we can do this," and we toasted him and everyone laughed and drank.

We did whatever he did, as it had rewarded him richly. He was a supernaturally good looking, supernaturally young looking man of fifty, like a movie star, handsome in the old "dark handsome stranger" way of movies from the earlier part of the twentieth century, as if he'd escaped from them with his good looks intact. We loved him and it was his birthday, and the love moved around the room, doing things.

Bobby was, for example, chatting up another man, who was also pretty cute, and they would each look over at me periodically, so I walked over. For a while after that, the three of us were chatting each other up, flirting, and then at some point, Bobby seemed to decide on the other guy. I was feeling a little drunk and daring, though, so I still gave Bobby my number. My way of saying *It isn't going to work out with him. So here is this for when it doesn't work out with him and you come around.*

I was very involved with the New Age, it should be said. I was taking a lot of yoga classes, sometimes twice a day. My body was changing. My whole life I'd lifted weights, but once I began doing yoga, I started to look like I really lifted weights, strong and masculine. My shoulders filled out, my thighs became powerful. "Are you lifting," people would ask, and I would say, "I'm lifting me." The kind of yoga I did was intensely athletic, circus tricks I called it sometimes. I perfected the art of putting a beer glass on my head and balancing it there, and then going down to my knees without spilling a drop. And then, once people thought the trick was over, I'd slide across the floor to the other person, on my knees.

But we were drinking margaritas that night, and so Bobby had no way of knowing this about me.

I left, and somehow knew he would call me, and so when he did, I tried to act surprised, and I even was. A little.

"It didn't work out with that guy," he said.

"I'm sorry," I said, in a mock-sorrowful tone.

He lived in Hoboken, so we went there, walked the stairs to his railroad apartment and sat down on his bed. He told me he had a spirit animal, also an inner child. He had guides, he said. He went over to a statue of a rabbit on his television and picked it up. It was hollow and there were all these things inside that he took out. "The rule," he said, "with the rabbit, is that if you pick it up, you have to open it up and take everything out."

"Sort of like you," I said.

I have this thing with my mouth that I call "mouth of evil," where it just says things like that. It's sort of like I'm following this nasty kid around who sits on my face and seems to have some kind of death wish. I could feel the joke unspoken in the air, and the way it filled my mouth, hoping to be born, and how I could almost have stopped it. But did not.

What happened is, his eyes went wide and he laughed as he jumped on the bed with a sort of smiling grimace. I laughed up at him, or, the mouth of evil did, and he pushed me down.

"It's okay," I said. "I get it. You're not a person," I said, looking up at him. He was holding back a laugh. "You're a team."

That first night I called him Team Bobby and it stuck. *Team Alex wants to know if Team Bobby wants a drink*, I'd write, in emails to him. *Team Alex wants to get Thai afterward.*

Because he worked all day with essential oils, he smelled great and the room around him always smelled great, like vetiver or lemongrass.

"I feel like you're here to teach me a lesson," he'd say, as our New Age heroic bodies lay at rest side by side after fairly conventional but satisfying sex.

Whenever people said this to me, in the New Age, I always felt anxious. It was like they were saying, *Someday you will cause me so much pain I will remember you forever*, and that just didn't seem to bode well. But I said nothing, as he stroked my shoulder in the dark with his beautifully scented hands.

I knew, someday, I'd probably hate him. But for now, it was fine.

It had just become common to talk about what you were working on then. Yoga was a practice and we were all just practicing, all the time, a long rehearsal that eventually revealed itself as also being the show. I didn't like talking about what I was working on, and I was sometimes embarrassed enough that I considered just never saying anything. But I had found a way to participate. I had always thought I wasn't a physical person before yoga, for example, but this turned out to be wrong—I was just bored of other ways of using the body. I was working on thinking of myself as a physical person. I told him this.

"I'm working on my relationship to money," he said, by way of a reply. "I'm learning lessons about money."

I nodded, making us breakfast. We were in his apartment in Hoboken.

"I listen to these tapes," he said.

I raised my eyebrows, to silently say, *Yeah?*

"They're by this woman who channels these star beings," he said.

In the mornings, without knowing it, I try to say nothing. I don't like to speak until around ten A.M. The mouth of evil needs rest, I guess. But he wanted me to speak. He wanted to talk.

"Star beings?" I asked.

"The Pleiadeans," he said. "The Pleiades aren't stars. They're enormous spiritual beings and they have messages for humanity. She can hear them; she channels them."

"Who is she," I asked.

"This woman out in California," he said.

It seemed to me that if a being larger than our planet had a message for our planet, it would talk to the planet, or it would find someone really important, like Henry Kissinger or Vaclav Havel to speak with, and not an otherwise unknown woman in California, but it may be that stature and status are hard to see from that far away. It may be that when you look at Earth from that far away, our most important people seem unimportant, and so the messages go to other people. Who may in fact be secretly important. But all of this seemed so unlikely, that this being would want to instruct us on how to save more money. Or on how to be happy.

If you were the size of a star, how could these matters even register?

All of that was approximately what the mouth of evil rejected as I thought about what to say. It wasn't fast and funny, it was too thoughtful a critique.

So instead, I said the thing the mouth and I had agreed on years ago as middle ground.

"Interesting," I said.

While he listened to his tapes, I would lie in bed and try to pretend to read a book, but instead I was watching him.

When I said back then that I was working on thinking of myself as a physical person, what I mean is that I was using it to figure myself out. It was a way of talking to myself that resembled nothing else, except, of course, the mouth of evil, which I knew was really just truth—truth of the kind that no one wanted to hear but everyone needed to know. My mother likes to tell the story of me as a child asking a model at a swimsuit shoot why she wore a bathing suit that was too small for her. I grew up to be the person who says "You're not more important than me" when someone tries to cut in front of me. And if the house is on fire, I shout "Fire!"

But somewhere along the line something had gone wrong. In my first yoga classes with the handsome teacher who introduced me to Bobby, I would lie on my back in corpse pose and hear someone screaming "Help me," as if they had fallen down a canyon, except it was me and the canyon was me also. Some people treated yoga like a workout, and if that's what they needed then fine, but I had come to think of it as a kind of sign language to talk to the universe, spelling out my life with my whole body. Each yoga pose was me hanging off the cliff of myself, reaching for the part of me at the bottom of that canyon. Each one was me diving down to the bottom of the wreck of me, hoping for survivors. I could say I was going to class twice a day or I could say that time felt like it was running out for the search party, though I had not worked out what I would do with what I would find.

When we had been together long enough, about two months, people who knew us started to say, "You guys make a great team," and we would say, simultaneously, "Yes," as our eyes met, and then we would laugh a little inside at the memory of my Team Bobby joke that had in fact become something different. His sense of humor was still one of the signs to me that it would work out with us.

I was trying to extend myself into his belief system as a way to tell him I loved him, even a little further than I had. Until now I had left the difference between us at "If you believe it, I believe you." But that was how I treated everyone and I wanted to be different for him. Back then I had a problem almost as old as me, which was that there was a man I would have sex with and a man I loved, and they were never the same man. I would never try to love the man I had sex with, and I would only try to have sex with the man I loved for a little while, in the way of someone who is certain something should work without having checked first. Bobby was, I thought, a good candidate for bringing this all together in one man. I both lusted after him and found him sweet and liked to lie there with him, smelling of lemongrass. The only problem was that he was at least as bad off as I was, because so much had happened to him he needed a team to help.

And maybe I did, too.

I tried on this idea of the two of us, a team. I began by thinking of what my spirit animal could possibly be. Before I filled with contempt for myself at the idea of even doing it, I came up with the corniest one ever: the dolphin. But I felt it had to be true. As a child I had taught myself to swim like one, my arms at my side like Patrick Duffy in *Man from Atlantis*, and held my breath in contests with my brother and father. I had been asthmatic as a kid but this had succeeded in expanding my lungs, as I thought yoga had also. With some distance I think Patrick was my spirit animal, but I was, am, literal-minded.

I tried this theory out on Bobby. That maybe the dolphin had taught me this.

He nodded, a little unsure, I think, if I was making fun of him. And I felt so alone as I watched this, even a little angry at myself for even trying to have a spirit animal.

I want you to know that I did love him, even though we didn't make it out together. I just wasn't able to defeat my pattern. I probably needed both him and the other guy at the party. I just didn't know how to say it. I did need a team, just . . . a different one.

What I remember now is that when Team Bobby would put on headphones and lie down and listen intently to the tapes, he had the most incredible expression on his face, a sweet faith that made me like him even more, though it also terrified me when he did this. I had come to an understanding of him that I somehow didn't have earlier.

We were more alike than not, though I liked to think of us as opposites. We were about the same height, we both had brown hair. His was longer and curly, mine was cropped off. He was like a piece of the sweet intense universe that had never quite found a home, in the shape of a good-looking Jewish man in his late twenties. I was, at the same age, dressed up as a piece of what I smilingly thought of as the sweet evil, a so-called "exotic" multiracial, literally hard to pin down. But we had met because we *were* so alike, both so at the end of our ropes, maybe even at the end of the same rope. Yoga, as another yoga teacher friend of mine would say, was a good place for broken people. It said a lot to me that he was as far out as he was, because there wasn't much further to go—everything else had failed him. If the answers weren't out there at the edge of the known universe and whispering themselves into his ears through his headphones, I worried that he wasn't likely to live very long. And he smelled sweet and was good in bed, and so kind, so that would have been bad. There were other, better candidates for traveling out past the edge of the universe, people who deserved this world even less than he did, or at least, that was what the mouth of evil told me. Because the secret to the mouth of evil was that it wanted only the good. For everyone. It just could only talk about the bad.

The big difference between us was this: Unlike me, he trusted things without putting them through tests—the trust *was* the test. And so as I watched him, I felt like I was waiting for him to figure out that it was all bullshit. I hated the star beings for even putting him on the line.

Tell him, I would silently shout across the light-years, at those stars he was listening to so intently. *Tell him what he needs to live.*

ORIGINALLY PUBLISHED IN *HELLO MR.* ISSUE 09 IN 2017.

On the Move: A Life: Brian Anderson

Photos by Samuel Bradley

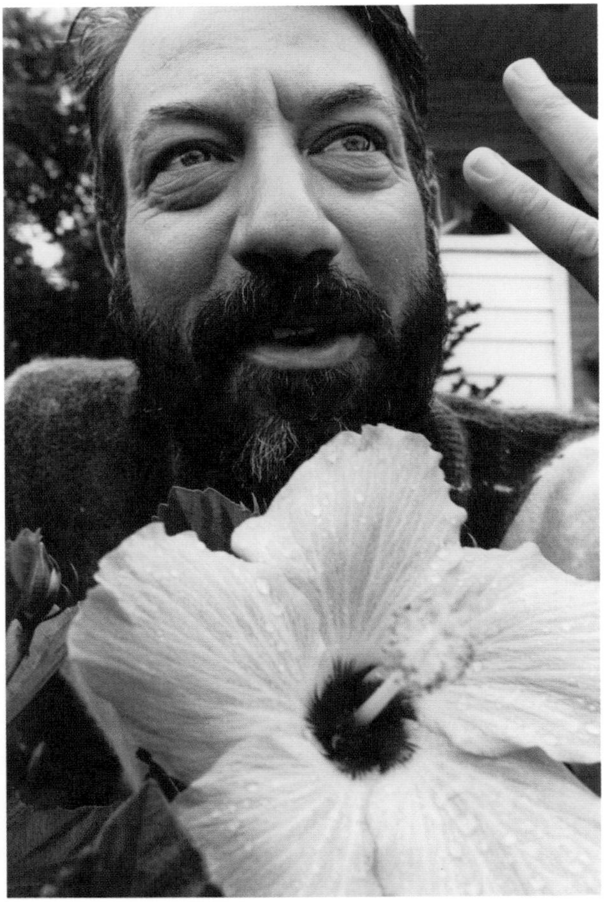

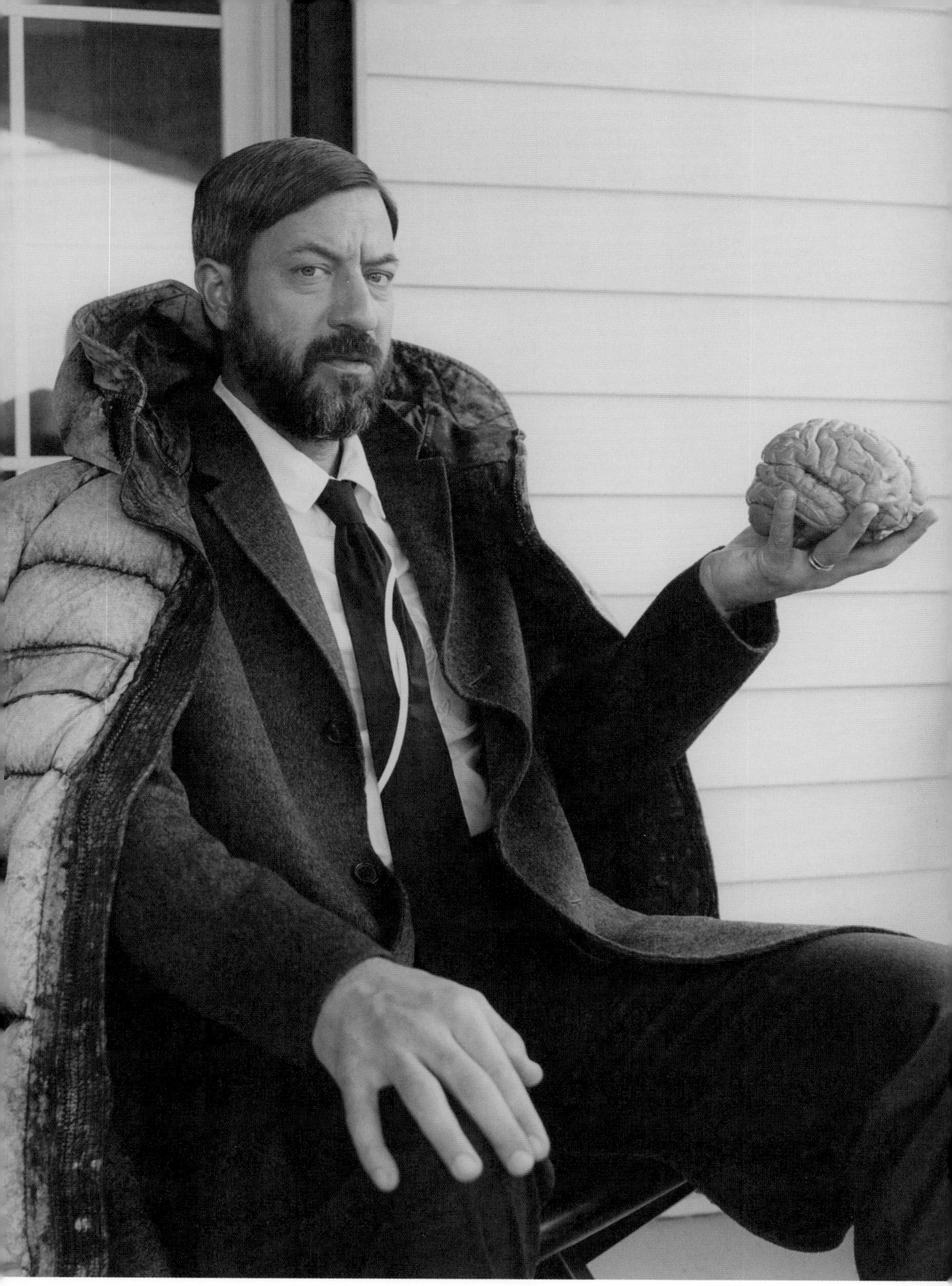

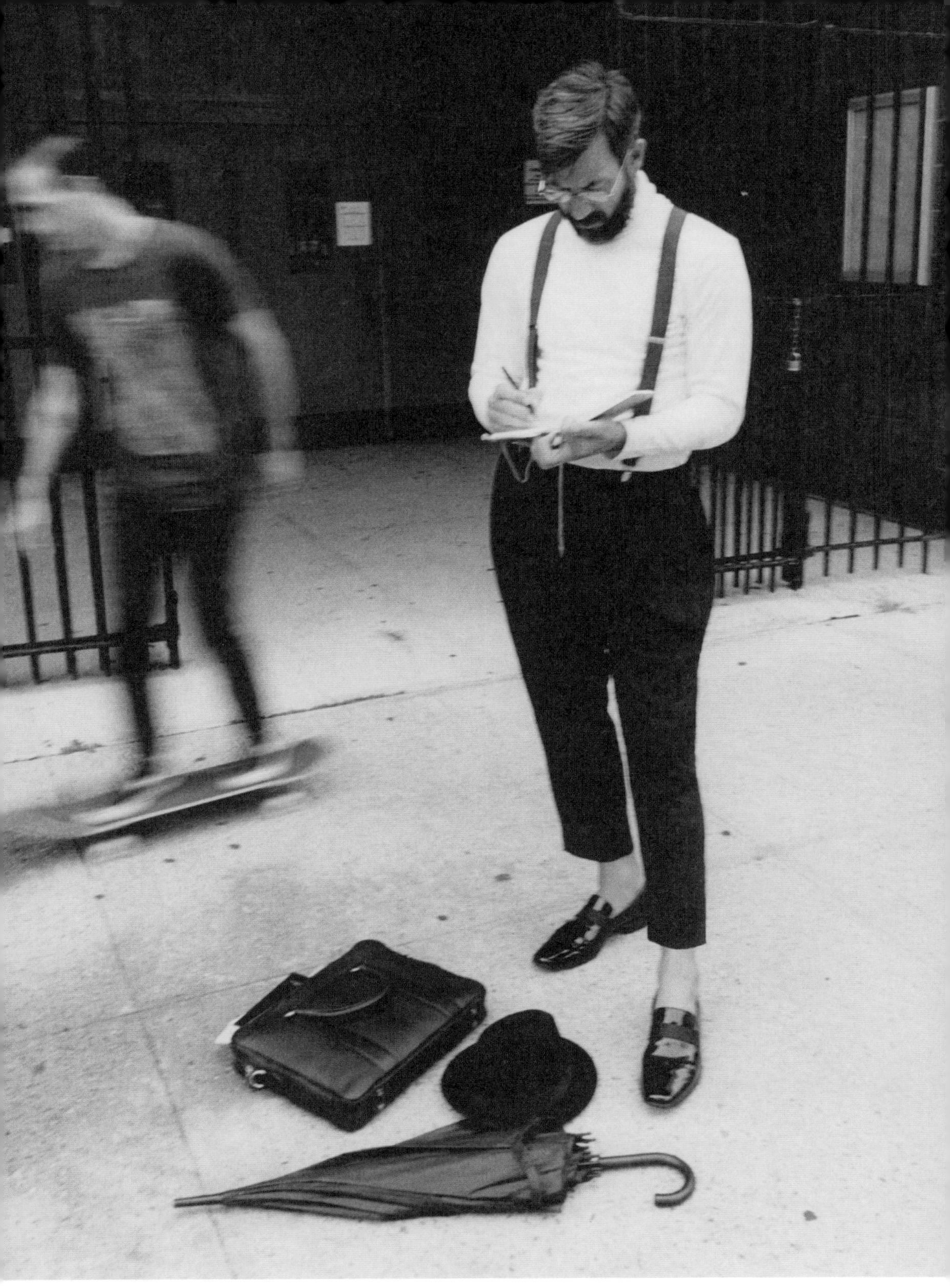

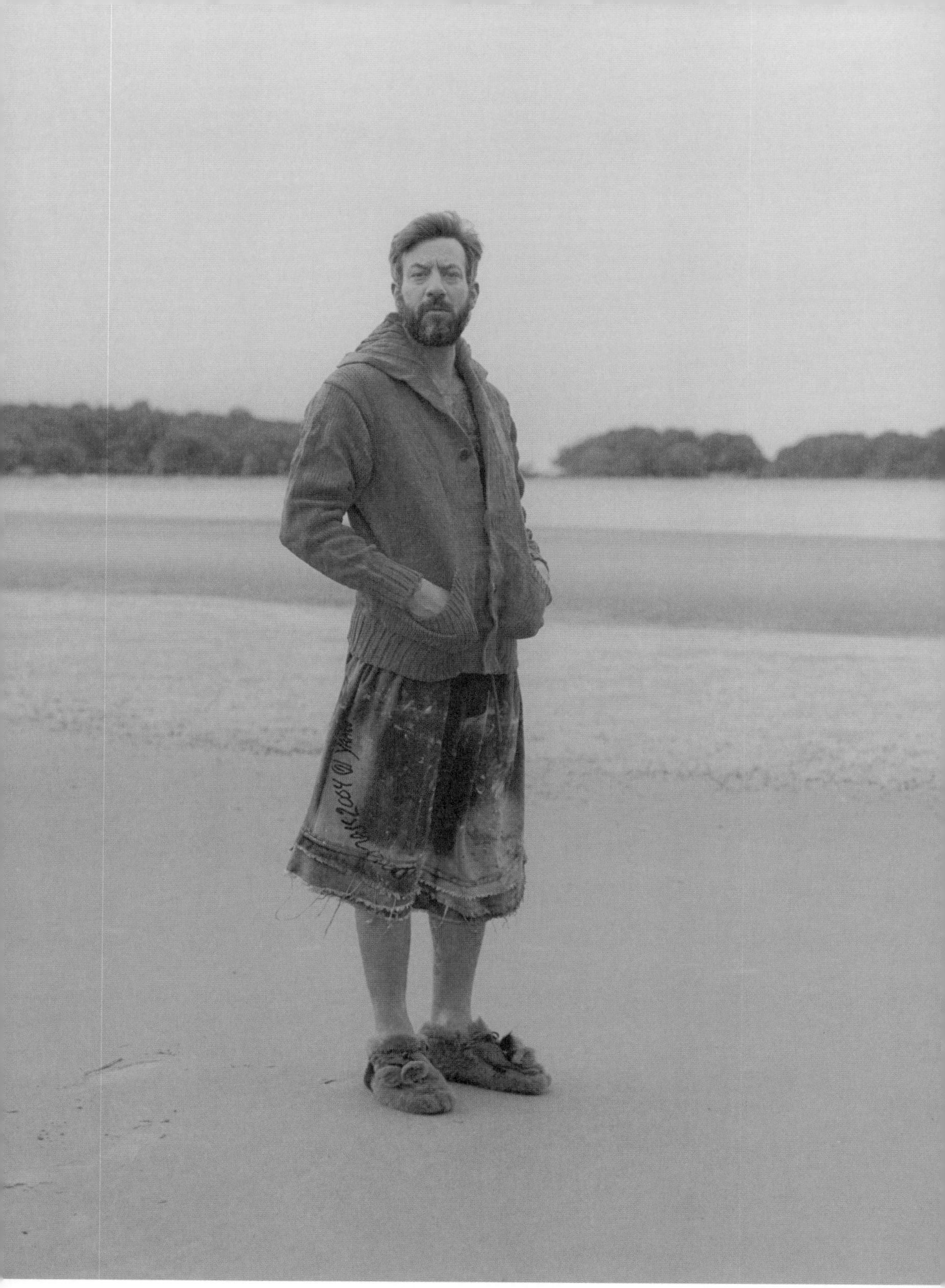

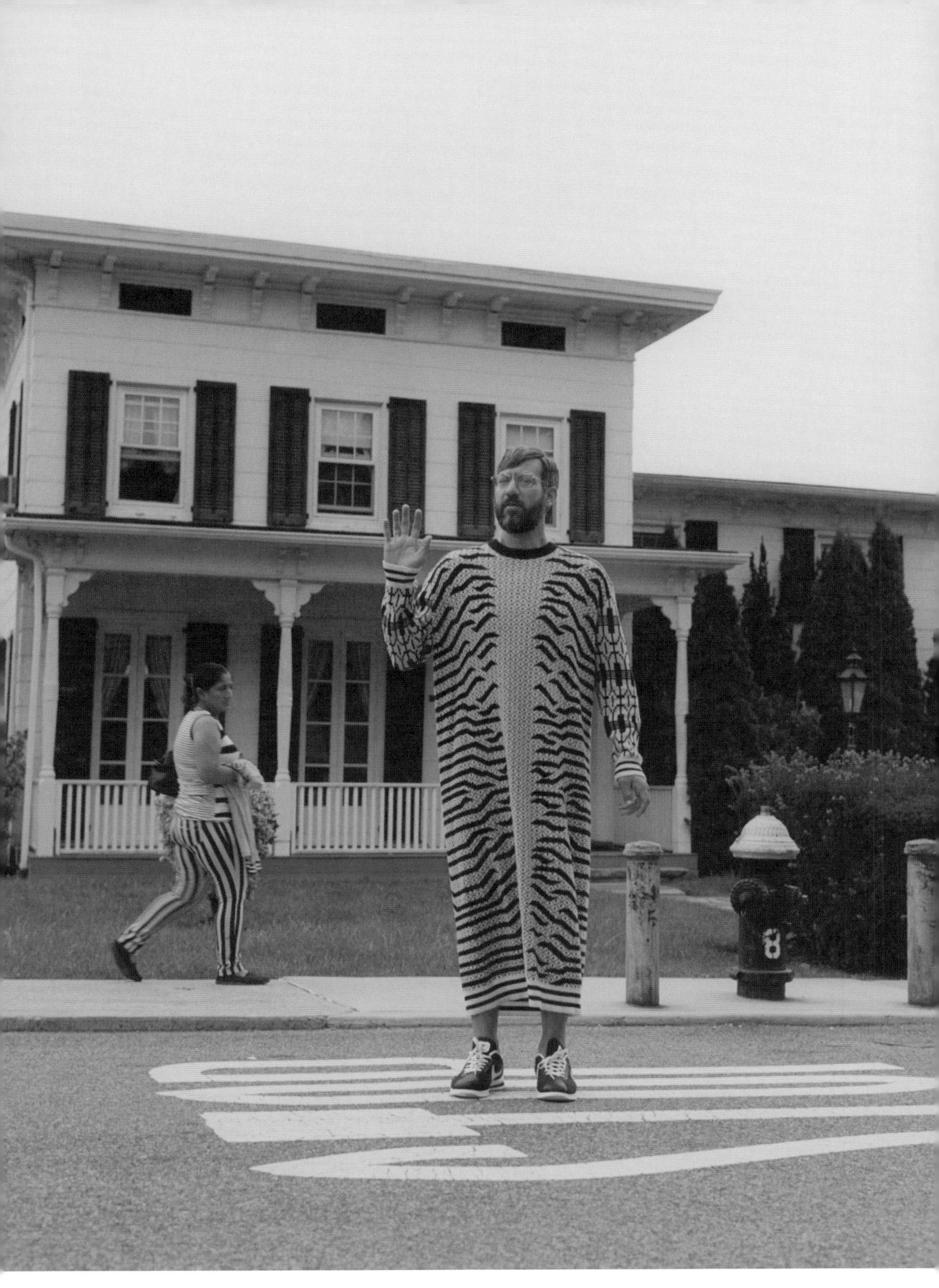

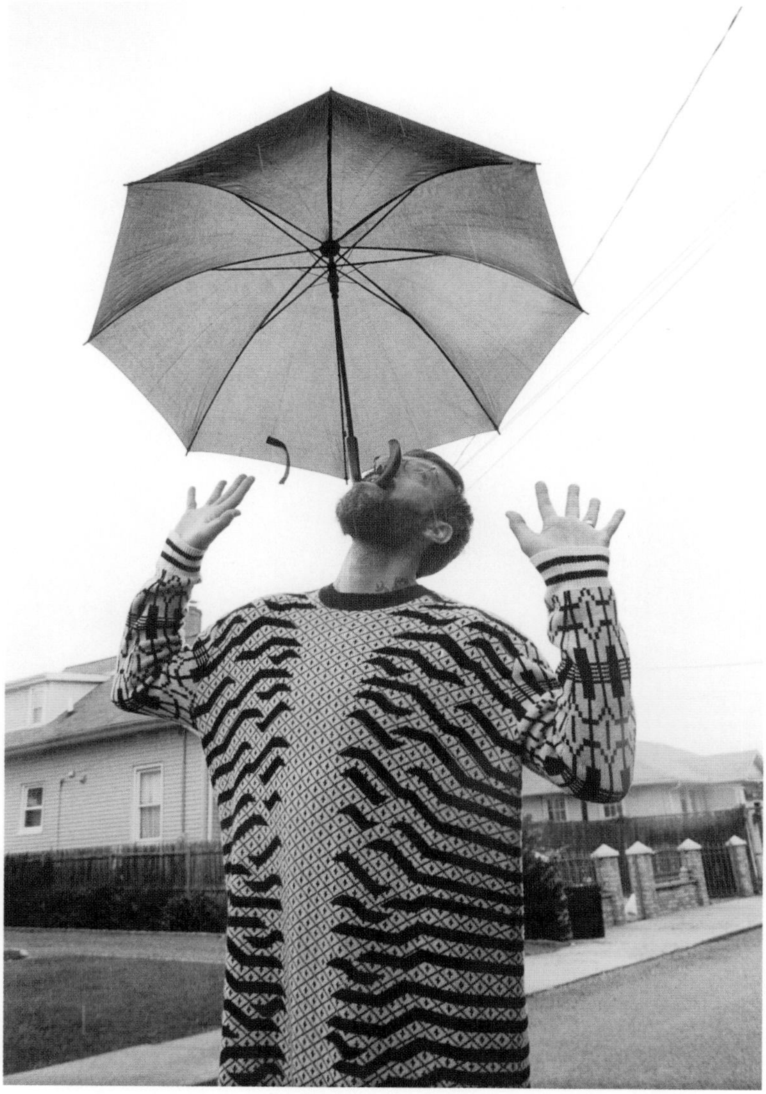

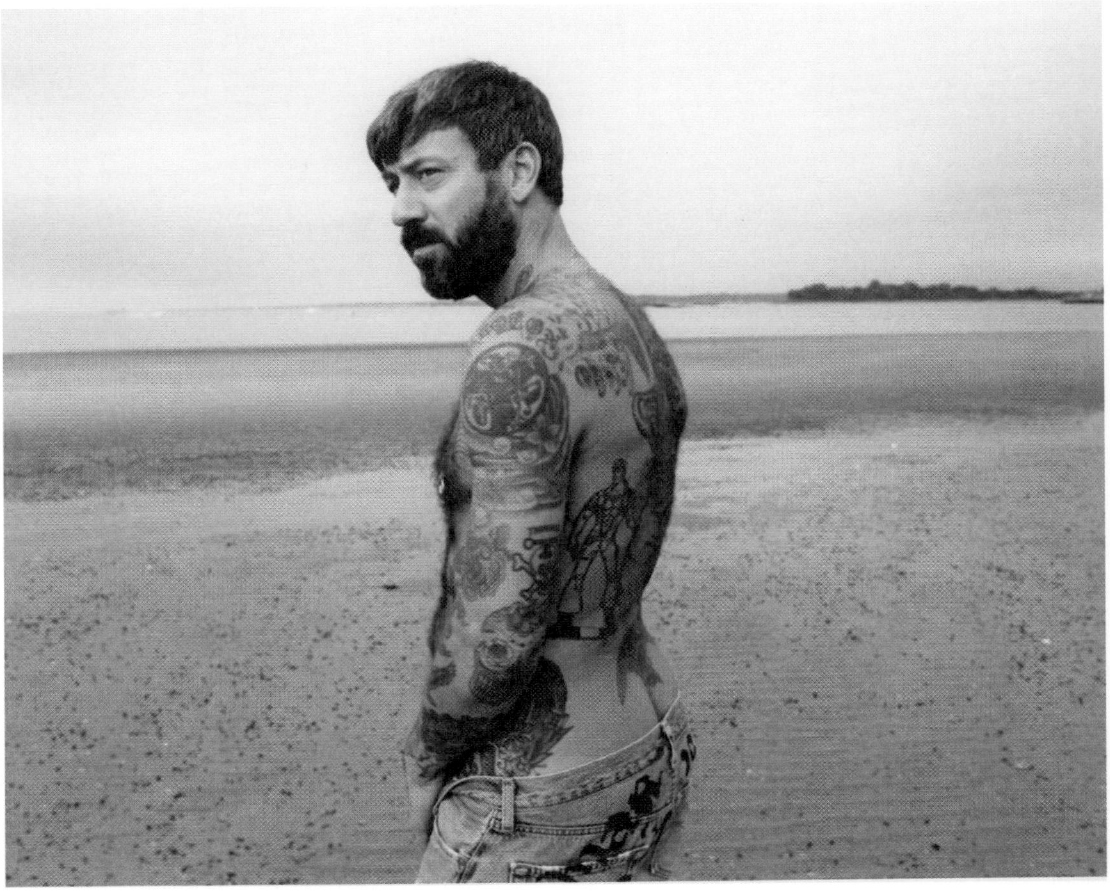

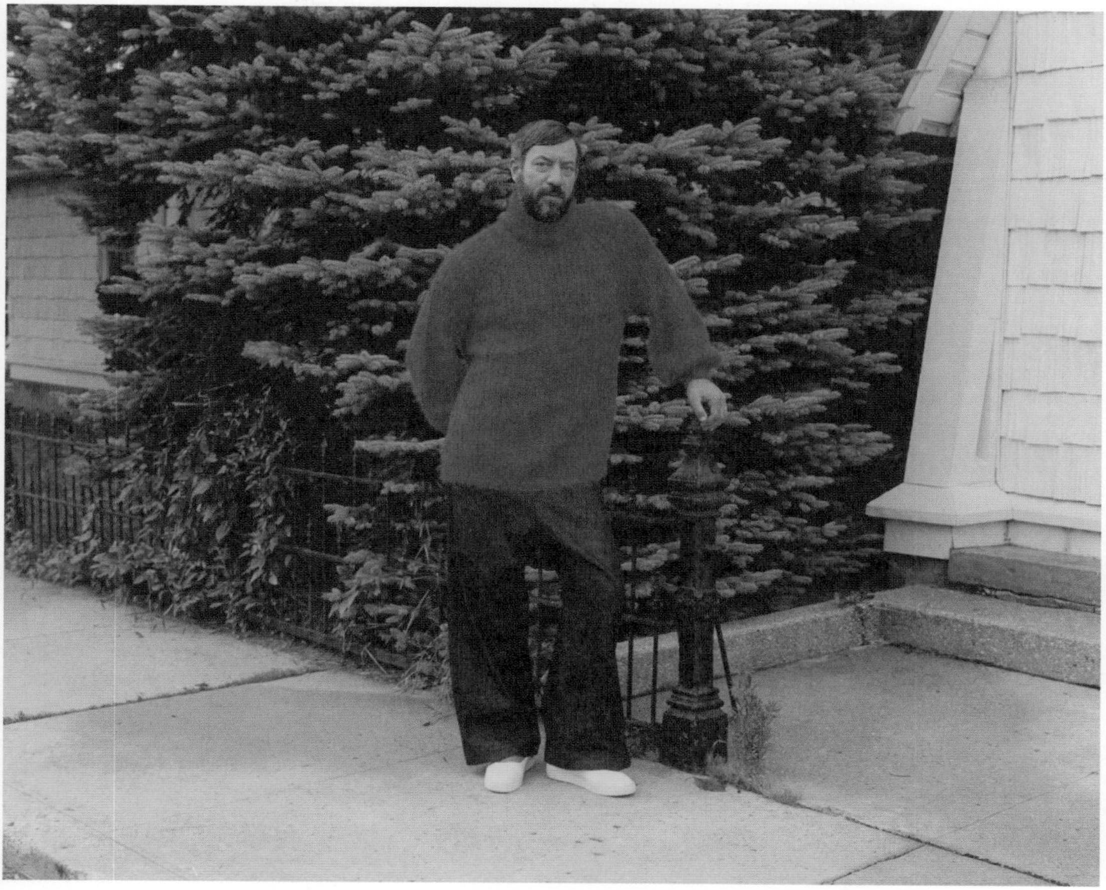

Who Conquers Who, or Surprisingly Good Airplane Food

Tommy Pico

We keep in touch phone stuff but what
do I *look* like in the cumuli
of your mind through the cold half-
sandwich of your lunch break–

I'm learning I don't always have to clean
my plate, but there's a saying about way–
about waste? Or is it waist . . . Anyway, it's morning
and I've already been so many people today.

Does the me you gather in my absence
match the *me* in my head, the mirror
the text snapchat face chat, the fat
kid wrapped in gummy memory?

Once, we didn't have the power to turn off–
deathless compass darting landward,
baskets woven to the gods. Now you,
you turn me on.

ORIGINALLY PUBLISHED IN *HELLO MR.* ISSUE 03 IN 2014.

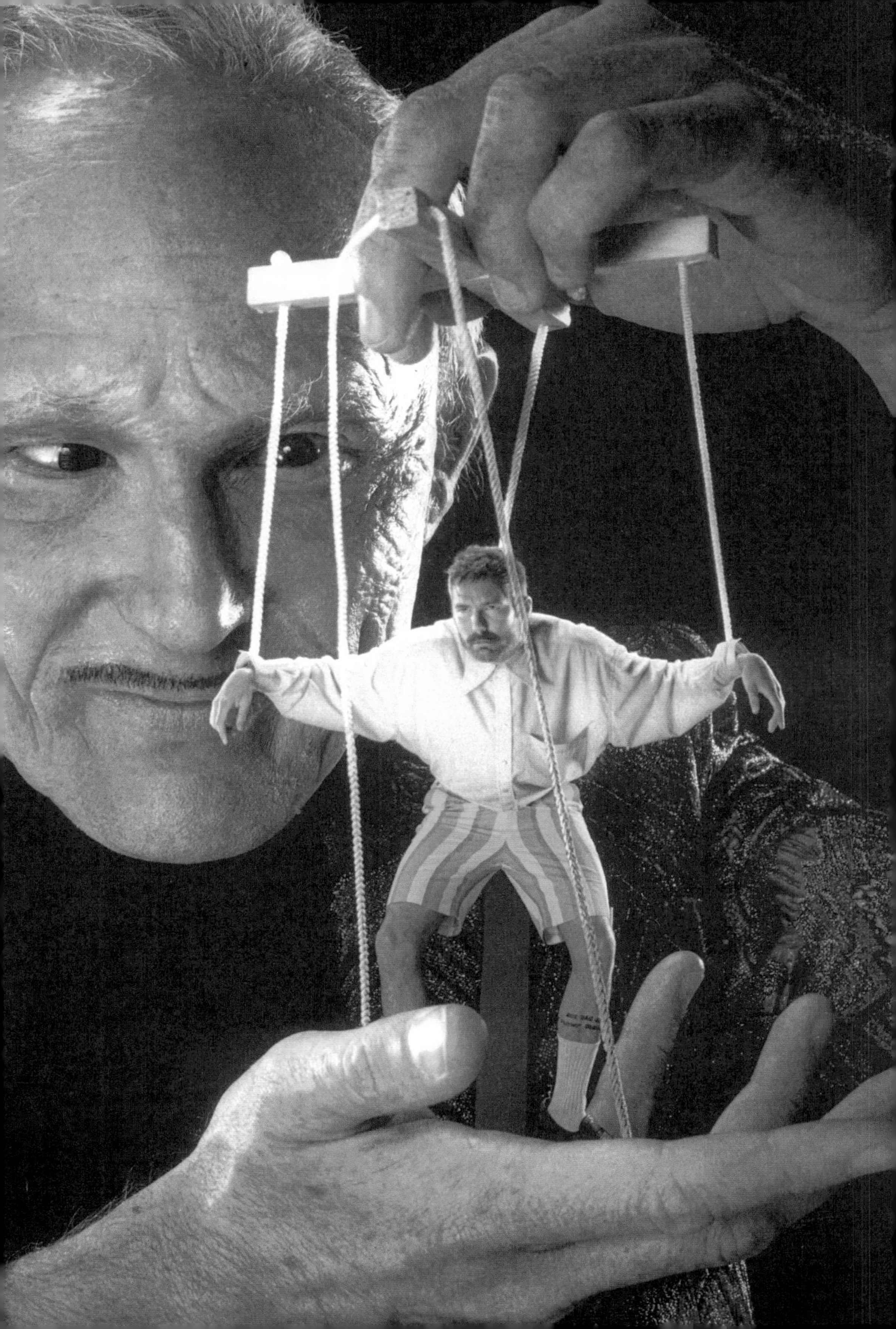

Shut Up After You're Thirty: Charles Rogers in Search of John Waters's Approval

Photos by Julian Buchan

"I know you don't have a lot of time. So first . . . I'm going to spit out my gum."

I wondered why I was saying this. I was stalling and it was only drawing attention to my uneasy hands and the fact that I knew there was nothing in my jacket to spit my gum into. My nerves were making me stupid.

As I fumbled for pretend napkins inside of empty pockets, I heard my artistic hero and all-time idol fill the pointless time that I was making us live in, "My mother was always so anti-gum."

"Are you anti-gum?" I asked, afraid that I might already be disappointing him. This was confirmed with a simple, "Yes." I apologized as my fingers dug through my wallet, finding the perfect FedEx receipt for tired gum. It rested next to an eight-year-old business card that had not left my pants since the day it was bestowed upon me by the man who I was now sitting across from: *John Waters*.

Eight years ago, I had tapped him on the shoulder at a gallery in Provincetown while a dozen gay men perused art made out of license plates. I invited him to a screening of my film at the festival that night. He declined, having already made plans, and handed me his business card as a parting gift. Had he known at the time that I would spend the next few years using that business card to persistently email him with requests to watch my feature, watch my TV show, be in my TV show, and to *meet with me, see me, know me, talk to me, and love me*, he might have thought twice.

The people who meant something to us when we were young will always be holy. When I meet a famous person today who wasn't on my radar until adulthood, they typically hold no magic over me. There is, however, a shortlist of giants whom I revered in my youth that deeply paralyze me should I find myself in their presence. John Waters is, was, and always will be my number one. And for that reason, I will never be able to prove to him that I can be funny or cool or fun.

I'm not delusional. I know John Waters isn't just mine. He's for everyone. His work has shaped the hearts and minds of thousands of queer kids for years and I am but one of them. I will say, though, that there is something extra special about having artistic idols for the kids who have dreams of going into show business. One day, they might even meet, work with, or *become* just like their idols.

My younger self knew one thing for sure: *One day, I would become John Waters.* And why wouldn't I? We have to be spiritual kin. We both love big characters. We both love exaggerating life until it feels more like life than life does. We both love making people feel uncomfortable to serve some personal and artistic crusade. We're both gay. We're both six foot two. And even our names sound kind of similar if you say them back-to-back over and over and over. Not that I have.

The *chicken and the egg* with having role models is that I'll never know how much of myself I owe to his influence, and how much is authentically me. All I know is that there is a lot of John Waters in Charles Rogers, and even though there is plenty about myself that I struggle to love, I know that I love that part, because I love him.

But here I was sitting in front of him in his Baltimore home as Charles Rogers. I was somehow still not John Waters. My life had taken turns I could never have expected. I had lived a lot of life since he handed me that business card almost a decade ago. I had moved from New York to Los Angeles at twenty-six, and by twenty-eight, I had created a television series called *Search Party* that was the lens through which I lived my entire life. Over the next chapter, I fell in big love, found a community of fun people that seemed to double by the year, traveled everywhere, threw parties, and took for granted that everyone was healthy. As my twenties closed in a flood of abundance, the tides gradually receded. The big love turned bad. The pandemic scattered my people. The fun changed. My show came to an end. My dad died.

My life is different now. The train arrived at the station after a years-long journey and now I try to make sense of the pain, glory, and chaos of the entire ride. I trust that another train is coming soon, but if I don't get to the bottom of who I am and what I want while my soul is still cracked wide open, then the pain will all have been in vain and I won't deserve a new train. I will die at this station, forever obsessing about that one ride.

I had come to my hero for advice, *real life advice about my own real life.* If the man who lives full-time inside my soul can't fix me, who can?

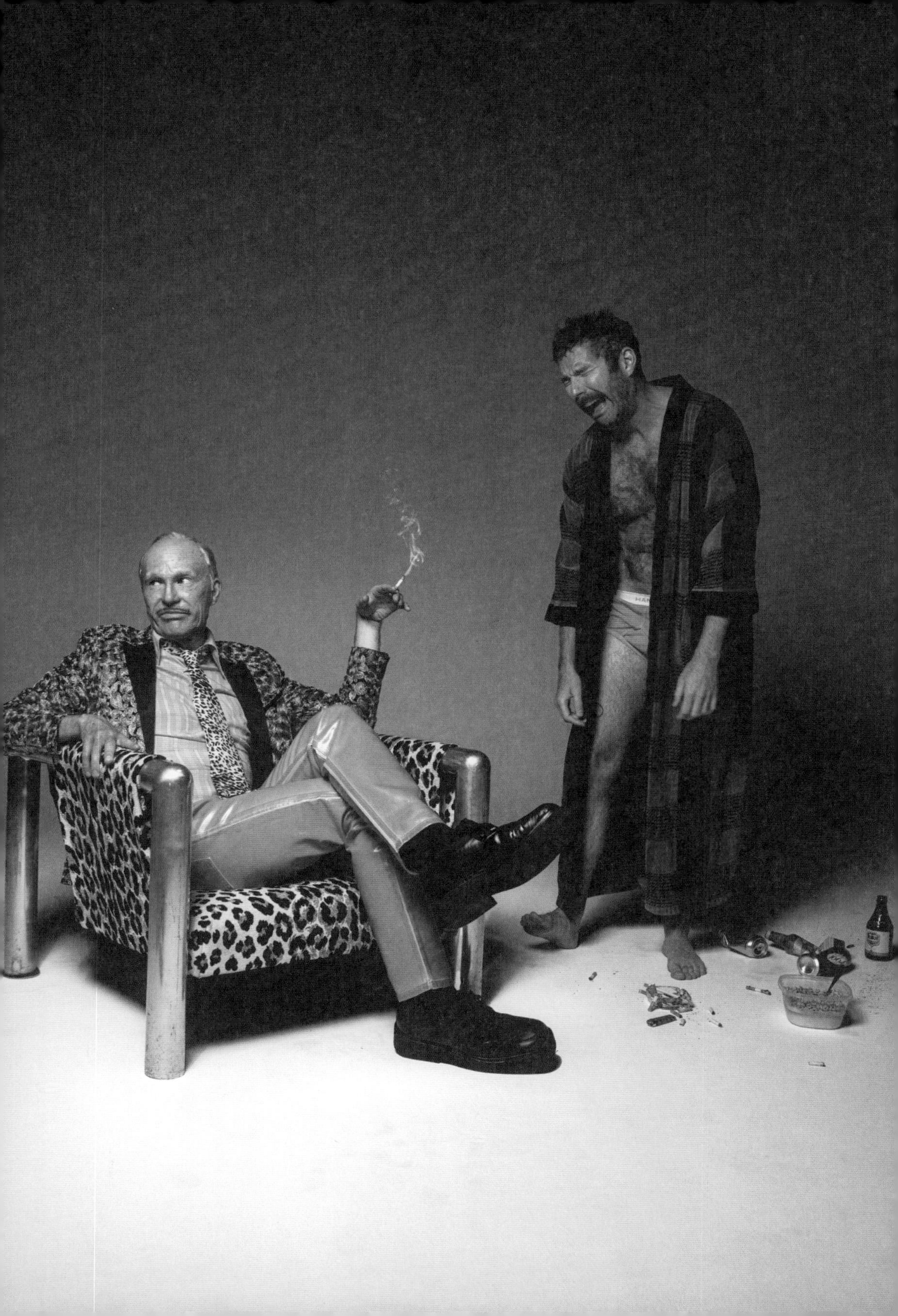

John Waters is someone who knows who he is. He knows what he wants. He is who I still wish I could become . . . and there's still time to try. So as I folded the FedEx receipt around my gum, I relayed the tired list of tragedies that shaped my last few years—the descent into madness that was the end of my last relationship, the dissociation and hysteria that was my dad's death, the fog that is my present, the mystery that is my future.

I wanted advice as loud and as ceremonious as the pain that delivered me here. I wanted a queer elder who could anoint me worthy of my next chapter. I wanted it so badly that I flew myself from Los Angeles to Baltimore to steal what little time he could give me, asking him questions in his own home. *I was in my idol's actual home.*

I couldn't even relish in the gravity of this fact—I could only focus on the difference in our homes. My house in Los Angeles is bright, postmodern, and circusy. John's house in Baltimore is sophisticated and cave-like. The lighting is warm, the art is real, and there are thousands of books for people who actually read. This difference was a red flag that I may not have become John Waters. He was doing Europe, and I was doing Hollywood. I would have to sell everything.

He absorbed my woesome bullet points; a sweetness in his eyes. For all of the devilishness of his persona, he's just as collected, intellectual, and empathetic. You can tell that he's a good person. He leaned in, seemingly ready to impart the wisdom that would finally deliver my soul unto itself, "I've gone through every single thing that you just told me happened."

I nodded along, prepared for a conveyor belt of answers and relief. He continued, "I've been in relationships that ended badly. I have been unable to get a movie made. I have made movies that failed at the box office. Both my parents died, but they were ninety years old. It wasn't tragic. I mean, it was sad. *But I wouldn't say that life was snatched away from them.* Half of my friends died of AIDS in the eighties. More than half, really. My brother sadly died of a brain tumor. So I've been through it. And you'll have *worse* happen to you, I just want to tell you."

Worse? No. My idol was mistaken. There was no *worse* coming. The point was that I was living through the worst of it *now*. There had to be better times ahead. I had earned that. Maybe John didn't understand that he was supposed to tell me what I wanted to hear. Was he just like everyone else in my life?

I softly switched strategies. "I feel like I know your point of view so well. But I'm curious about your relationship to yourself insofar as you feel comfortable sharing . . ."

John stared. "*Sharing what?*"

In truth, I wanted his soul laid out before me. But instead I asked for something that sounded more normal. "I'm curious about the journey of your life. How you experience—"

"*Journey*. I never say that." It was a dig. But he is allowed to make digs. He is good at them. It's an honor to be dug into by him. I tried a new word.

"The *shape* of your life?" But he was still thinking about my bad word.

"Whenever I have an actor that says the word *journey*, they don't get the part in the end. Or *humbled*." I was quick to assure him that I don't use the word *humbled*.

"*Rigorous* is another word. Or *surreal*." Fuck. I say *surreal* a lot.

I was beginning to realize that he may not want to be forced down a road of feelings. I thought we had counted down together at the edge of the pool but evidently only I had jumped in. This was not going to be *Tuesdays with Morrie*. Two gay men would never be so willing to meet in the middle like the two straight guys from that book were so happy to do. Morrie could have been bi, though. I remember him liking a good time.

I wasn't sure what exactly I wanted from the man who I had long ago appointed my god, but I knew that I was in search of a feeling. I've learned in my pursuit of self-actualization that there is a weird paradox with mental health. On the one hand, the only way to transcend your issues is to accept them, but on the other hand, the only way to accept your issues is to know them. You spend years trying to identify the entirety of all your blocks and hang-ups and patterns, and their many origins. It's endless work. And *on the third hand*, if you're someone who lives in the brain, you face the inability to ever experience epiphany. Epiphanies, they say, occur when new insight meets a wave of emotion, but all of my own self-discoveries feel at a dispassionate distance. So here I am, in an endless loop of dissection and inspection, unable to ever attain peace.

All the pain, all the thinking, all the lack of self-compassion, had made me phobic of the possibility that I'd lost touch with my instincts—and at the end of the day, my instincts are all that I have. I wanted to know if John had ever felt this way. I thought to disguise a conversation about feelings as a conversation about instincts. I could get him there through the back door.

"My instincts have always been about humor," he began. "The first thing I wanted to do was make myself laugh, and then my friends. We had a sense of humor that we obviously developed together, and I still have that. That's the main thing. That's what I'm trying to do when people see my movies: make them laugh. That's how you get people to listen to you, and how you get people to change their minds. And that's how you get them to keep coming back for more."

Interesting. Maybe I'd lost my sense of play. When I look at photographs of myself as a kid, my eyes were so alive. I was shining. Do I still shine? Are the only people who shine as adults mentally unstable narcissists clutching awards? Should I try to be *more* or *less* mentally stable? John shines. Is he insane?

"And you gotta make fun of yourself."

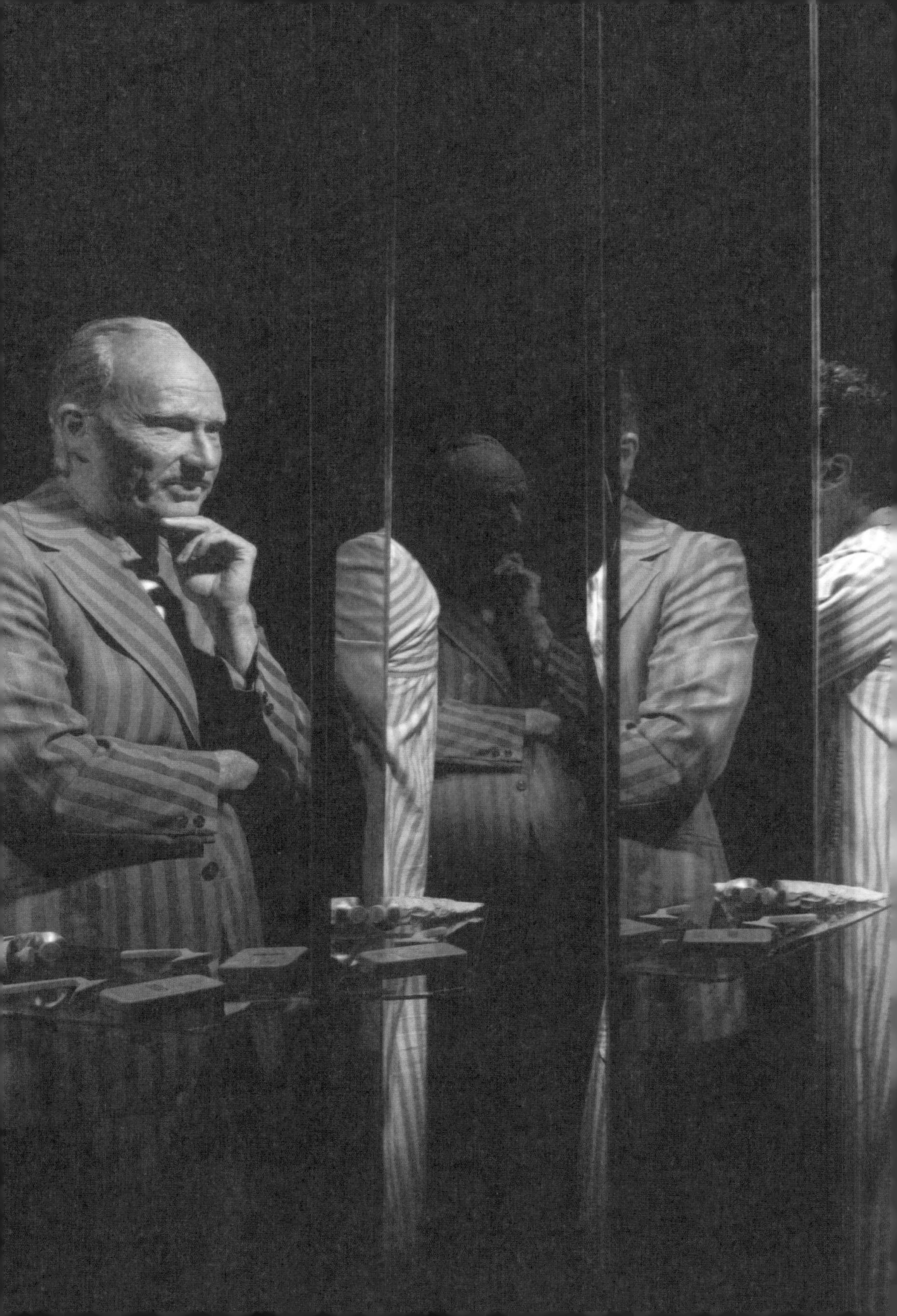

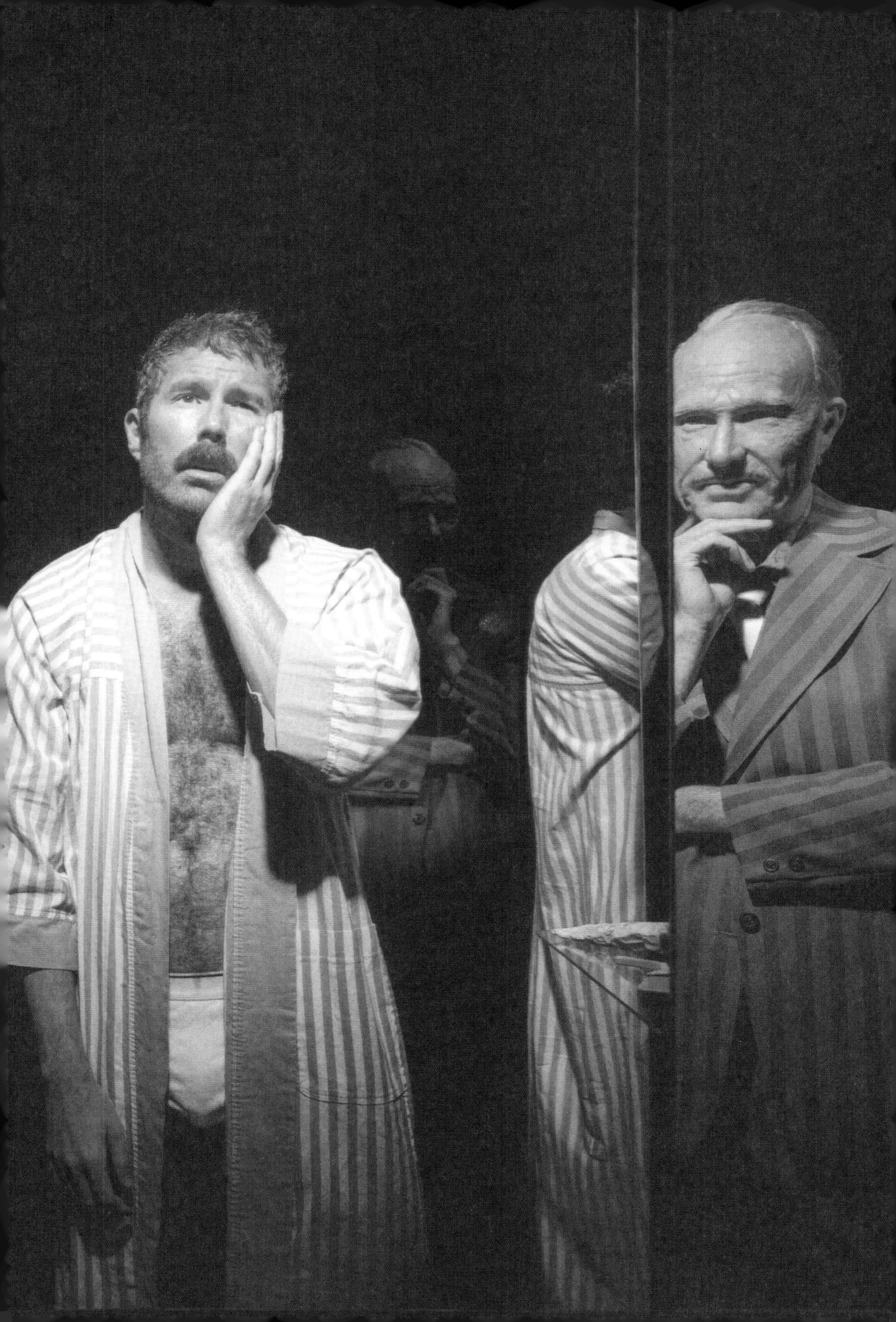

My heart sank. Making fun of myself is something that I'm very good at *pretending* to do well. But it still hurts. I'm good at acting silly, and I'm good at playing a character of myself. But I spend so much energy trying to prove that I deserve to be on this planet that I never feel powerful enough to portray myself as powerless. I had never realized before that John makes fun of himself. He went on, "I always use my self-image humorously. The Prince of Puke . . . all those things that people called me, they were said *nicely*. Nobody gave me those titles because they didn't like me. When William S. Burroughs called me the Pope of Trash, that was high praise. I went with all of it."

I wanted to understand how John had allowed himself to wear his own persona so loosely, while I was still triple-timing that I'm an adult man who people should believe in. I asked, "But did you ever feel like you were wrestling to prove something?"

I could feel him enjoying the question. There might finally be flow between us. "If I was, I wasn't conscious of it. I didn't ever really think about it. I was just trying to make the next thing that would make me laugh."

Why was someone I wanted to be just like so different from myself? Where was his sense of self-torture? Where was his fear of scarcity? *Where was his damage?* I needed to get it out of him. I needed him to be like me.

"I have this feeling that there's a lot that I need to do in my life."

"Well, you're only thirty-five. You've got plenty of time."

"Did you ever feel this way?"

He laughed. "Oh, people say, *why aren't you slowing down? You're seventy-six.* Because I believe you get one life, and this is it. And I'm trying to get as much out of it as I can. . . . I don't have to work right now. I have enough money, basically. So why do I drive myself so hard? It's a good question. All people in our business are basically very insecure, and they're trying to make up for something that they didn't get when they were young. And they never will. But they want the world—strangers—to tell 'em how good they are. That's insecurity."

I am insecure. But I knew that. It was a relief to be told that he was, too, even though he seemed more secure than I could ever be. Was that simply the wisdom of age? Or was it a symptom of having proved himself to the world more than I had? However he got there, I wanted it, and I wanted it *now*. "But now, on this side of your life, you've done so much, so I feel like people know you," I said.

He nodded, "They do."

"Has that put any of your insecurity to rest? Or has it changed your relationship with yourself?"

He mulled this over. "I think I'm reasonably content. But that sounds crazy, because I still battle with my emotions. Everybody does. It doesn't necessarily get easier as you get older. New emotions appear. You

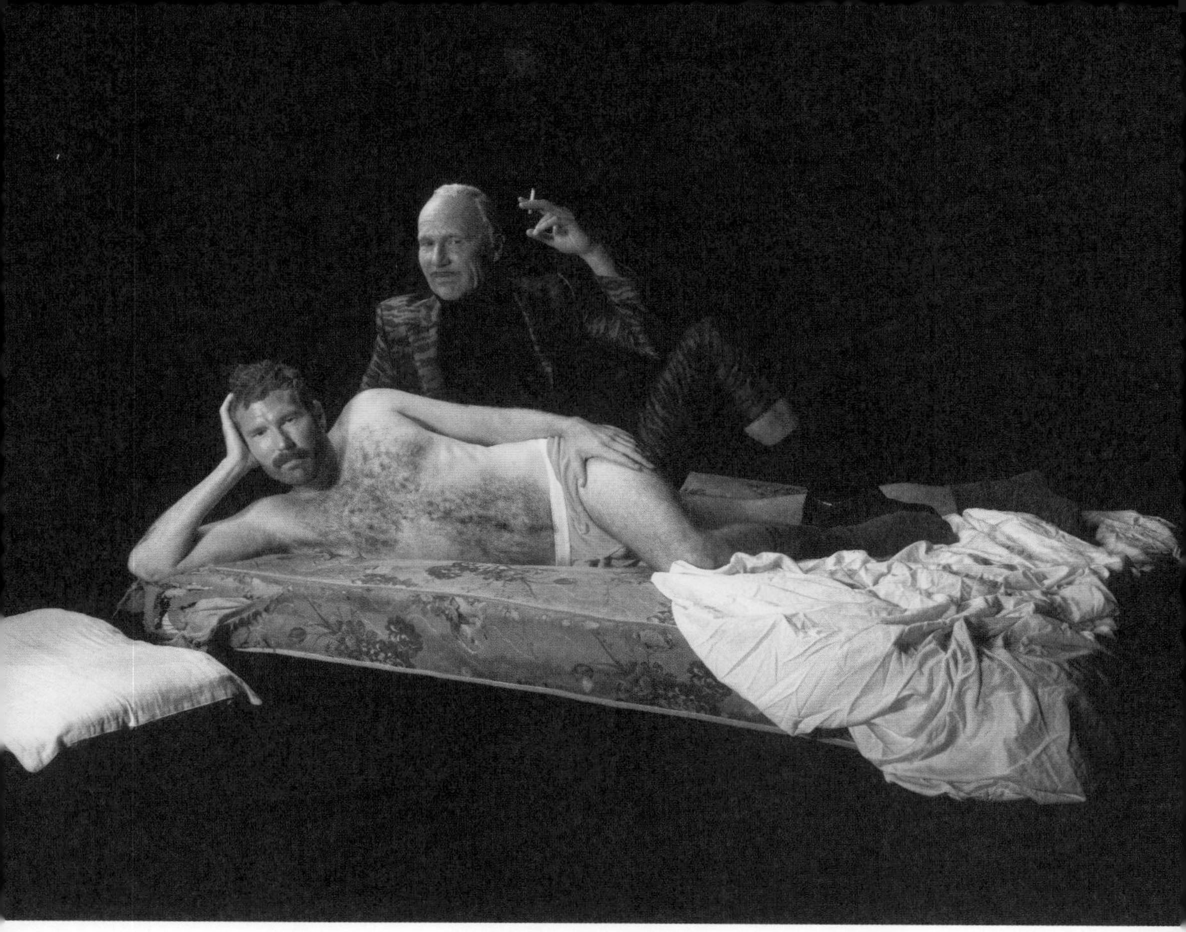

start to think, *well how much longer?* I can't say I'm middle aged. I'm not gonna live to be one-hundred and fifty-four."

John was undoubtedly part of a different generation. I was just under half his age. In a way, it was hard to remember this, because he is one of the few people on this planet who has aged the right way: He believes that provocation is virtuous; he gives the benefit of the doubt to the underdog and to the kids coming up. He never became bitter or close-minded, as so many people tend to do as they grow older. I want to do it his way.

He smiled. "So things are good. *Pink Flamingos* is being preserved by the National Film Registry. I'm going to get a star on Hollywood Boulevard. The Academy of Motion Pictures is doing something with me.... That's all great. I think it's all lovely."

The man sitting before me was neither bothered nor unbothered by the overwhelming and ceaseless nature of life itself. Maybe it was generational. For as much flack as my generation receives for whining and moaning, you have to hand it to us—we picked up tools that no one gave us. We needed to figure out how to talk about our own feelings as soon as possible. And just as we were begrudged for overindulging those tools, we begrudge the generations before us for resisting self-inspection.

John is timeless, though. And the ease with which he lives may have more to do with an innate grace than an unwillingness to see himself. He lives in a headspace that feels good to live in. What a concept.

I sat there, uncertain what should come next. Our conversation had taken turns because I had spent the hour skirting around one simple question. I was scared to hear it come out of my own mouth, because I knew I would sound ridiculous.

I floundered. He watched me. Then finally, I allowed it to happen.

"Do you think I'm going to be OK?"

John asked it right back, "Do *you* think you're going to be OK?"

No. It wasn't mine to answer: "Do *YOU* think I'm going to be OK?"

He took a paternal breath. He would give me what I'd come for. "I do think you're gonna be OK. But don't panic and don't put too much pressure on yourself about whether the next thing has to top *Search Party*, or be *like* it. . . . Just keep going. You have to keep going and things will change. There's always another chapter. Life ain't fair. I was born with a good hand with my family. And that is all it is. If your parents made you feel safe in any way, that's how you'll survive. If you didn't, you'll be fucked up your entire life. But don't blame them after you're twenty. I've always said that. After you're thirty, please stop whining."

Oh my God. I'm thirty-five. My eyes widened. "But I just started getting good at it."

It was true. I had spent the last five years of my life employing a team of therapists, energy healers, acupuncturists, self-help experts, and LA people to validate the pain I had spent the first thirty years of my life denying. Somewhere, early on in my journey (a word that I ultimately choose to keep employing), I felt victimized by aspects of my upbringing, as I imagine most queer people—*and maybe all people*—do. But my present isn't my past. I have so much to be grateful for in the life that I've created for myself, but I'm still somehow addicted to despair, even when most of me doesn't want to be that way. I suppose that when life stops hurting you, you start hurting yourself, just to stay in the game. It's hard to see. But it's what we do.

The pencil mustache crinkled under a half-smile. He liked what he was saying. "This is the hand that you were dealt. So shut up after you're thirty."

Should I have felt hurt by this? I wondered if he would have felt hurt if his hero had ever told him to shut up. I wondered if he would forever resist me after this meeting. I wondered what he thought of me, if anything at all. I wondered if I was ever going to arrive at this abstract feeling that I was so tired of scouring the earth for.

But none of that mattered. What mattered was that my hero had just told me to shut up. And maybe this is the key to how I finally become him so that I can finally become myself. It's worth a shot, given it's the one thing I've never even considered trying. It's a note that might even be worth passing along to an entire generation of people fighting a cacophonous and omnidirectional battle to have our pain validated at any cost. And ultimately, if we try it and in the end it doesn't work, what's to lose? We have a lot of life left. A lot of it will be great; some of it may be worse.

So, here I go. I'm shutting up now.

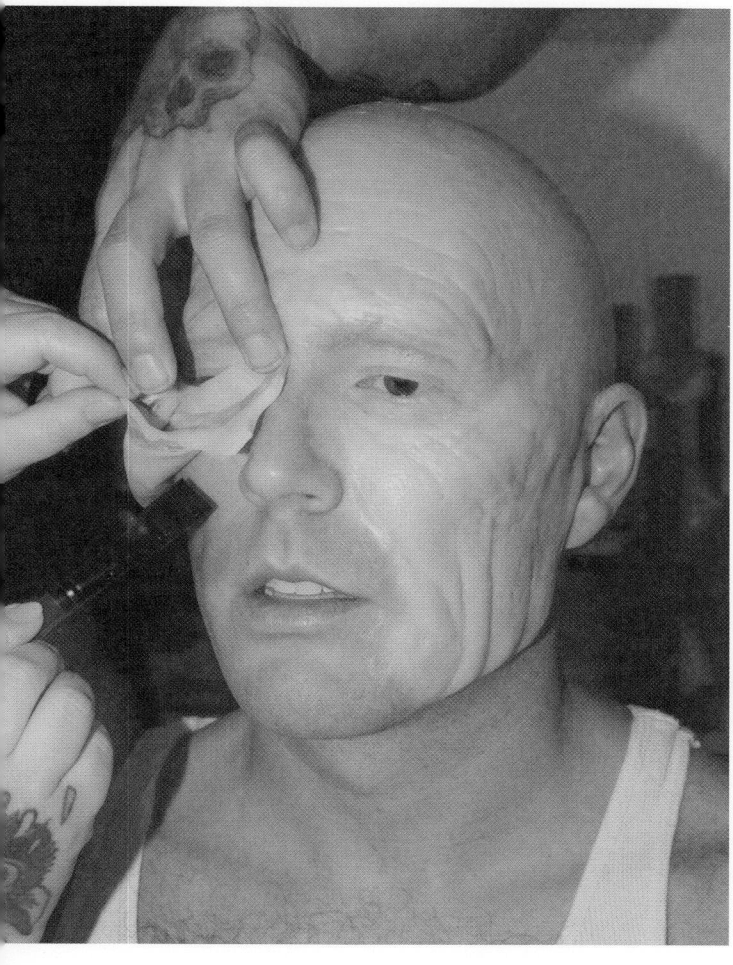

Makeup:
Ally McGillicuddy assisted by Lawrence Mercado

Styling:
Orchid Satellite assisted by Sailor Gonzales

Hair:
Amy Marie Wilson

Production design:
Megan Mantia

Digitech/lighting:
Taylor Galloway

Grip:
Rob Padilla

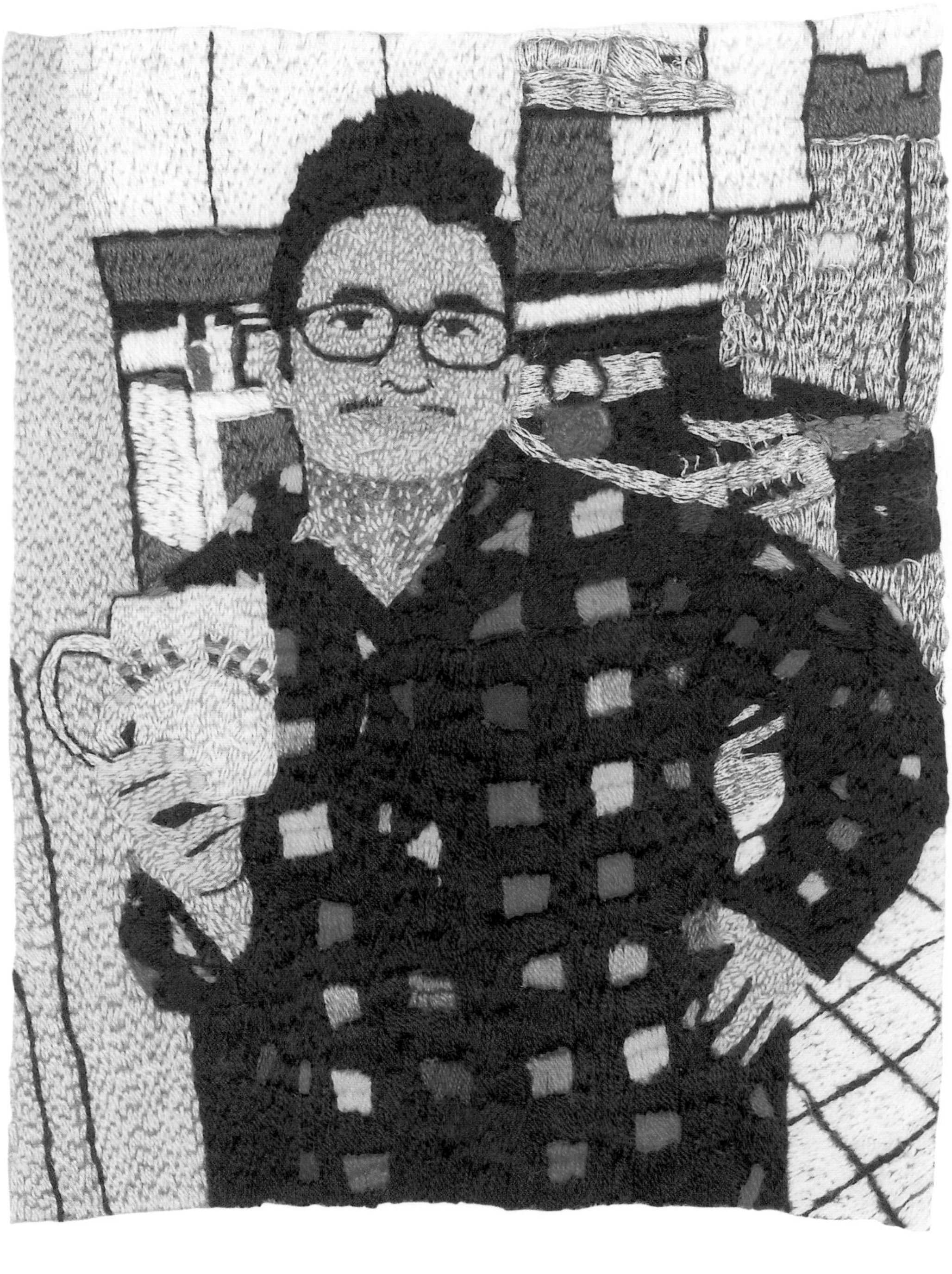

SANCTUARY

Jen Silverman | Art by LJ Roberts

She saw the first hornet against the window at night, just before midnight. It was the size of a thumb and the wings curved off its back like lace. It pressed itself against the glass, its face so close and large that she could make out the intricate machinery of its mandibles and mouth, its great blank eyes. She hadn't known hornets came out at night. She hadn't known anything about hornets, although the "murder hornets" were in the news lately, and when she called to Jacks, this was the first thing on her mind: "Jacks, come here, quick."

He came, compelled by her urgency, but he needn't have rushed; the hornet wasn't going anywhere. It sat on the exterior of the glass, spot-lit in the wide wedge of light from Tilly's iPhone flashlight. It seemed calm, attentive, nearly pleased. They peered at it.

"God," Jacks said. "She's giant."

"Is she a queen? Is she a She?"

"Could be." Jacks, like Tilly, was a product of cities, although his were midwestern and hers northeastern. "I mean, queens are bigger than the others, right?"

Beyond the queen, the night was thick and lightless. Catskill dark, mid-April, unseasonably cold, the last snow had melted but the ground was still frozen hard and in the mornings sometimes it crunched under their boots like gravel. Tilly heard strange animals at night, although she no longer woke Jacks up to listen. It had been three weeks since their arrival, and her insomnia had become a solitary one, in which she listened for hours to odd screeches and moans, high rageful shrieks followed by long silences. Once she had heard a series of low, heavy, bizarrely human grunts. Jacks slept easily and deeply and though Tilly resented him for it, she didn't mention her nightly vigils because she did not want to be the one of the two of them who could not cut it out here. Until the hornet. She hadn't meant to see it—her flashlight beam had glanced over the window and caught it out like an oversize brooch, attached to the screen and glittering—but now that she had, she couldn't let Jacks go unscathed.

"Anyway," Jacks said, as his awe ebbed. "It's outside, we're inside."

"It could come inside," Tilly said.

"I mean, not really. How?"

"There's holes, there's . . . gaps, I bet, there's—I mean, if we're finding spiders in here, they're coming in from somewhere, right? So things can get in."

"The spiders live here," Jacks said. "They were born here, they grew up here."

Tilly gazed at Jacks somberly across the light. He liked to make jokes and, more and more often, she tried to remember that she liked his jokes. "Jacks," she said. "If we wake up and this *giant fucking hornet* is in the room with us, I am going to go into anaphylactic shock."

"That's not going to happen," Jacks said. It wasn't even that he was trying to calm her, it was that, when Jacks looked down the road, he did not see the future. He never saw the future. He only saw an ongoing collection of present-tense moments, ones in which the hornet was not yet here, and so the hornet would never be here. Tilly looked down the road and she saw five years, she saw ten years, she saw fifteen years, she saw all the way to her own death, and although the nature of her death shifted, she never lost sight of it, like a glowing beacon unerringly ahead.

"Jacks."

"It's not going to *happen*, OK? Take a—take a gummy, c'mon, lie down."

Three nights later, the hornet was in the room.

The animals that were there: black bears, coyotes as small and tawny as dogs, bobcats, ravens, raccoons (the loudest screamers of the night), squirrels, mice, an entire community of groundhogs who had only recently emerged and begun frolicking nervously in the sun. And then the insects that had started to appear, although the full panoply wouldn't begin streaming out of the walls until June: centipedes as fat as baby snakes; flying ants; something shield-shaped and leaf-footed that Tilly had never before seen, that the internet revealed to be an assassin bug. "Known for its piercing, shockingly painful bite," Tilly read out loud to Jacks. "Also called a *Black Corsair*."

The birds disturbed Tilly the most, but only because of their deaths. The house had once been an old caretaker's cabin, but it had been renovated, and the small original structure now opened into a soaring modernist atrocity. As such, it was part low-ceilinged splintery wood and part double-height sheets of blinding glass. The sharp, heavy staccato of birds striking the house became a percussive loop that Tilly learned to dread. One day she drew big Xs on pieces of xerox paper with a red sharpie and taped them to the many-paned windows, as high as she could reach, but the birds didn't seem deterred. They kept flying and colliding and falling and then Tilly would go outside and stand mournfully over their small bodies, twitching piles of collapsed feathers. Some of them righted themselves within the hour and took off again, but some did not, and the bird bodies around the house began to accumulate.

“What are we supposed to do with them?” Tilly asked Jacks, at last. This was after the robin. They’d discovered it that morning, flat on its back, legs in the air, capsized in the center of the porch as if it had been elected to bring them a particularly blatant message. “Does Ella *bury* them, or like—has she ever *said* anything?”

“She’s never really mentioned birds,” Jacks said, frowning. “I guess I could text her?”

The house belonged to Jacks’s ex-wife, Ella, and she was not a person who gave directions, which was one of the foremost differences between herself and Tilly. The other was her phenomenal and punishing courage.

“I mean . . . would you? I feel like we’re perpetrating a bird massacre over here.”

“Well, *we’re* not.” Jacks was sipping coffee out of a drinking glass, because the mugs were dirty, and he kept scalding his fingers and having to put it down. “The house is.”

“Well, and we’re *in* the house, so.”

“Yeah, but we didn’t—we’re not the architects, we didn’t make this house.”

“Jacks.” Tilly heard her voice get thin and firm, the voice that was the opposite of how she imagined Ella had talked to him. She tried to iron it out, back into gentleness. “I just feel like, regardless of whose original sin it is, I would like to—you know, stop killing birds. Or stop witnessing their deaths. Or at least know if we’re supposed to bury them, and if so, does Ella have a shovel anywhere, because I haven’t seen one.”

Ella did not have a shovel, and she did not have advice about the birds. Jacks went outside to call her and spent a half-hour in the sunlight, walking up and down the dirt driveway where cell signal was strongest, laughing and gesturing, but when he came back, he said Ella hadn’t known what to do about the birds and they’d just been catching up. Tilly had watched him from the kitchen window, while he was on the phone. She wasn’t jealous of Ella, not really, not anymore—she knew that Ella and Jacks were good and easy friends—but Ella always made Tilly feel as if she should be more ambitious, more worthy of admiration, than Tilly knew herself to be.

Ella was effortless; Ella was an opera singer. When the pandemic had first struck, Ella and her new partner had been on a houseboat in Amsterdam. Ella had offered them the keys to this house with the ease of someone who was used to having things to give, who received gratitude in constant gentle showers. Five years ago, when Jacks had transitioned—for him, this had meant top-surgery and a legal name change—Ella had sent thirty-seven roses to his NYU Langone hospital room. Her note had read: *A rose for every birthday that got you here, and five for your first day as Jacks.* This had been two years after their divorce, a year after Jacks met Tilly. Tilly had been at the hospital with him, had been the one bringing him juice and soup and talking to the nurses. Tilly was the one who would take him home and, over the next most delicate weeks of healing, Tilly would help change out his bandages and drain his stents. But the exquisite extravagance of the roses stunned her. Who wants to remember your girlfriend helping you put on and take off your shirt without tearing your stitches? Who doesn’t prefer the memory of thirty-seven roses? Ella’s gesture would be what Jacks treasured of that day.

Tilly had been grateful for Ella's house as sanctuary, of course. She and Jacks had started to lose their minds in their cramped apartment, listening to the constant wet coughing that seemed to travel through the walls of every room, from upstairs and from below. They lived near a large hospital, and their ceilings were constantly painted by the rotating blue-violet of ambulance lights; often, when they glanced out the window, there was an ambulance parked on the sidewalk, siren off but lights turning. One night, as they watched, a series of EMTs had entered the apartment building across the street and begun retrieving bodies. Tilly had felt so frightened that her skin went numb, and it had taken days for the sadness to break through, after which she had started crying every time she showered—weeping and weeping, not turning off the shower until she could manage to stop. She hated her own cowardice, even though it didn't feel disproportionate to the situation, and she hadn't wanted Jacks to know. But after two weeks of showers, Jacks must have heard her anyway and called Ella, because it was during the third week that Ella had written with her offer of sanctuary.

The morning after Tilly glimpsed the queen against the glass, she went outside and circled the house, looking for the tell-tale gray paper lantern of a hornet's nest, but she saw nothing. She checked under the siding and gazed up under the gutters as far as she could see, but there was nothing to signal that the queen had begun making a home here. Maybe she had been on her way somewhere else. Maybe she was far away by now, in Vermont, let's say, or Maine. Did hornets fly north for the spring? Tilly didn't remember hearing about it, but then, she'd never before thought about a hornet as an actual animal, just as a piece of language—*mad as a hornet*, for example.

Jacks was in the little kitchen when she came back in, reading something on his phone. His feet were up on the edge of the kitchen table even though Tilly had asked him not to do that. "Find anything?"

"No," Tilly said, and hesitated before she said *Jacks, can you please not put your feet on the table, we eat off that table*. She had started making herself count to ten before she said these things, even though often, after ten, she said them anyway.

"Look at this," Jacks said, and held out his phone. A fat hornet, up-close; it could have been the cousin of the queen, or even the queen herself. "I was looking them up."

Tilly felt love swamp her, love and relief. She was not alone in this. She had been going to snap at Jacks, but really he was looking up hornets so that he could know what they were likely to do, whether they migrated like birds, if there was a danger. "And?"

"Doesn't it sort of look like a murder hornet to you?"

"Jesus," Tilly said, her relief draining immediately. "Does it? But they aren't here yet, right? Aren't they in Washington State, but not here yet?" She bent over Jacks's phone, studying a reflection of the tiny face from last night. "What kind of a hornet does it say this one is? Look up murder hornets, I bet they look different."

"This *is* a murder hornet," Jacks said, wagging his phone a little. "Doesn't it look like the one from last night?"

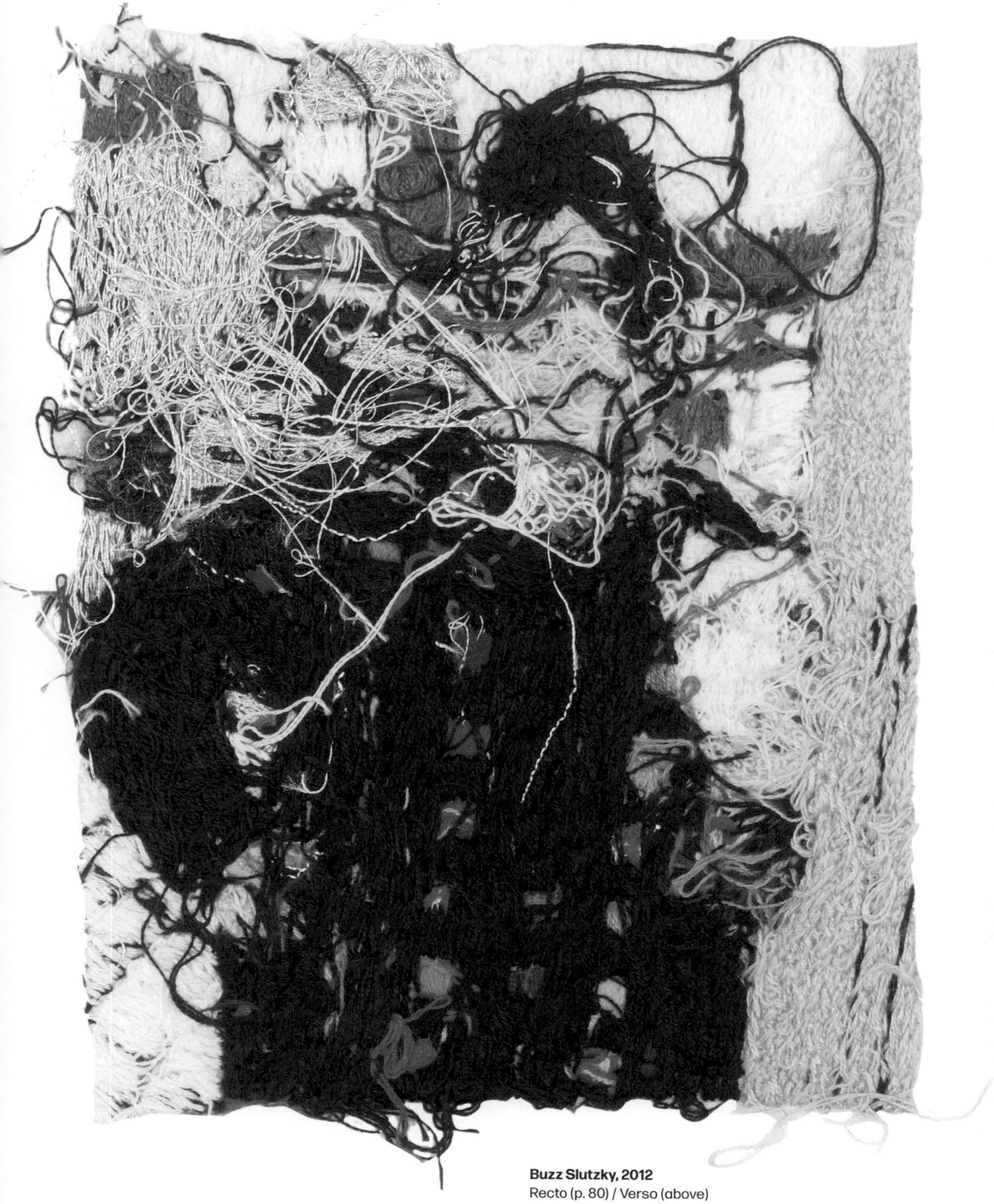

Buzz Slutzky, 2012
Recto (p. 80) / Verso (above)
(Embroidery on cotton)
Image: 15.6 x 12.1 cm / Framed: 27.9 x 25.1 x 2.5 cm
Courtesy the artist and Hales, London and New York.
Photo by Megan Martin

It did. Fuck, it did. Did it? Tilly squinted at the phone. Thumb-sized, the yellow-masked face. Yellow or orange? Orangey-yellow. The black stripes. But *this* had black stripes. "Oh my god," she said. "Jacks." Her voice thinned in panic.

"I mean, it still can't get in," Jacks said, hastily. "Also they don't really—like, *murder* hornet is, you know, an overstatement. People in Japan actually hunt them, did you know that? In some places people *eat* them, and there aren't that many deaths per year, I was looking up—"

"*Deaths*?" Tilly said. "Per *year*?"

"Yeah," Jacks said, his voice dwindling. "But only if people are very old, or very young, or—if they have allergic reactions sometimes—but generally you wouldn't *die* from a sting, it would just hurt. This one scientist said it's like being staple-gunned with a searing-hot staple."

"*Staple-gunned*," Tilly repeated, choked.

Jacks clicked his phone off. "It probably isn't even a murder hornet," he said. "I mean, they're rare."

She checked the windows that night, walking from room to room with her flashlight beam sweeping from floor to ceiling and from wall to wall, and she saw nothing. The next morning she did the same check, moving counterclockwise around the house—bedroom to bathroom to kitchen to library—and again saw nothing. The next night, the same, and nothing. On the third night, breathless and distracted, she performed her check more quickly. She reeled through the rooms, painting them briefly with light, and so she almost missed it. But something snagged at the edge of her attention, so she went back, and there it was: a darkness the size of a baby's fist, paused on the inside glass of the bedroom window, wings flicking.

Jacks was not in the house; Jacks had stormed out by then, and even though she called for him automatically—"*Jackson!*"—the sudden rush of silence after the name reminded her that she already knew he wasn't there. She was more alone than she had ever imagined being.

It had started, the third morning before the third night, with Jacks speaking the unspeakable. "You're just so *scared*," he said. "All the time, of everything! Til, we're out here, we're off the grid, there's nothing to be scared of. Bees are just *bees*, basically, you know? The stuff that's actually *scary* is—we've gotten some space from it, we've been lucky. Can't you just concentrate on how lucky we've been?"

In the silence, Tilly thought, in a wordless stream of images, about throttling Jacks. About throwing her cereal bowl at his head. About kicking him in the shins repeatedly. Tilly *was* scared of everything, but she didn't understand how anyone could be expected to be anything else. In general, yes, but especially now. And yet, she felt an instinctive flush of humiliation. Ella was in Milan now, Jacks had said, just the day before. Ella's new partner was in Doctors Without Borders, and Ella had accompanied him there, to the epicenter. Ella's bravery seared her, and so, when words came to her, they shot out like bullets: "OK, well, maybe your problem, *Jacks*, is that you're too *stupid* to be scared."

Jacks looked surprised, and Tilly felt equally shocked. This wasn't a way that they fought. They weren't name-callers; even when they disagreed vehemently, they barely lifted their voices. Jacks and Ella had done years of therapy before their divorce and so Tilly had inherited a relationship-language of generous listening, holding space, and "I Feel" sentences. Secretly, she sometimes felt like she and Jacks had never even had a chance to figure out how they liked to fight, because Jacks had already formed an unshakable conviction around what disagreement looked like.

"Excuse me?" Jacks said. Tilly opened her mouth to apologize, to say that she had no idea where that came from, that calling another adult *stupid* was a ridiculously childish thing to do, but then Jacks kept going, and his voice soared a few octaves into anger. "OK, well, first of all, Til, fuck you." Tilly's jaw dropped. "I am doing my goddamn best over here," Jacks said, his voice lifting in volume. "I am—I am disinfecting the groceries and wiping everything down and if there's a *beetle* I put the beetle outside and if there's a fucking *bobcat* in the middle of the night I wake up and tell you it's a bobcat and I am not *sleeping* because all I do is listen to how *scared* you are, so if that makes me *stupid* then . . ." Jacks hadn't thought through the entirety of this sentence ahead of time and he wavered and then found a crash-landing: "—then maybe I *am* stupid for always putting you first!"

He glared at her, having confused himself a little and feeling cheated of the bombastic ending he'd been heading for. Tilly had been on the verge of a whole-hearted apology, but Jacks's description of the nights pushed her back over the edge into rage.

"Oh, I didn't know you were losing sleep," she said acidly, "because when I hear you snoring next to me for eight hours a night, I guess I assume you're sleeping like a baby."

"And that's another thing!" Jacks yelled. The quieter she got, the louder he got, and this was another dynamic that was new to them. Tilly felt a thrill at the newness of it. "You're always *picking* at me, you're always, 'Don't do this,' 'Don't do that,' 'Do it my way,' 'Dry the cast-iron on the stove—'"

"If you don't dry it right away it rusts—"

Tilly began patronizingly, but Jacks ploughed over her: "Yes, but I can dry it with a fucking *towel*, Tilly; just because you dry it on a low heat that is not the only way to dry a fucking *cast-iron*. That is my point!"

"Well maybe another way to think about it is that if you took care of *anything*, at *any* point, without being *told*, then I wouldn't have to tell you!"

"I take care of *everything!*" Jacks roared. "Who got us this house?"

"Ella!" Tilly screamed back. "Ella got us this fucking house, and you may have been *married* to her but you didn't *invent* her, you cannot take credit for Ella!"

Tilly didn't track the rest of the fight after that, but it was exactly a fight, not an argument, and there was something glorious in the vicious messiness of it, the soaring strokes of illogic. Jacks screamed imprecations and Tilly screamed them back; they both used words that they had always found personally offensive; they leveled accusations that were patently absurd. Jacks called Tilly flat-footed and mean-mouthed, and then took a headlong leap and compared her to a rattlesnake; Tilly howled cutting observations about Jacks's increasing waist size and found herself chanting "Tubby Jacks" again and again until the front door slammed and she realized that she was alone in the kitchen.

She ran to the door and flung it wide, intending to scream *how dare he walk away from her*, but the car was already peeling out of the long driveway, down the hill, wheels churning and spitting up clods of earth, and then Jacks took a sharp left and the car was devoured by trees. In the echoing silence, Tilly felt winded, suddenly dizzy. She sat on the porch steps and put her head between her legs. A beefy fly whined nearby, and she got up abruptly and went inside, closing the door firmly behind her.

Across the long sunlit afternoon, she expected Jacks to return. She thought of the things she wanted to say to him, and sometimes she said them out loud, drifting from room to room, glaring at herself in the small, white-framed mirror hanging over the bathroom sink. She looked wild-eyed and a little unhinged. Hollows like thumbprints purpled the skin below her eyes; she hadn't showered that morning, and her hair was trying to escape her skull in all directions. At first the things were angry things about what he had said to her—"A *rattlesnake*, Jacks, really?"—and then they were angry things about having been left behind without a car—"I mean what if I slipped and fell and broke my *leg*?"—and then they were quieter sadder things—"I guess I just never knew you hated my *laugh*"—and then she had run out of everything it occurred to her to say, and she started wanting to make fun of the whole thing. If he came back, they could laugh at it together, how ludicrous and out of character it all had been. Maybe it would even bring them closer together. Perhaps he had never had this kind of fight with Ella before, and therefore had never had this kind of closeness. But it was early evening, and Jacks still wasn't back.

Tilly ate leftover stir-fry without heating it up. She sat at the kitchen table and then on the library couch and then on the reading chair where Jacks liked to sit. She put her bowl in the sink and walked away and felt liberated, and then the existence of the dirty dish started to stress her out, so she went back and washed it and placed it face-down on the terry-cloth bath-towel they were using as a drying rack. She checked out each of the windows, facing east, south, and west; she went outside for a few minutes and stood uncomfortably in the backyard. The birds were shrill and too loud. Beyond the birds, the silence was hostile. The sun set, slowly and then quickly, and tree-shadow devoured the yard and the house, and then night-shadow swallowed tree-shadow, and then it was dark, and Jacks did not return.

The baby-fist moved, it swooped suddenly from the windowpane to the curtain rod, and Tilly broke the silence with a scream. She flung herself backward, dropping her phone and with it the flashlight, and as soon as she was in the small hallway, she slammed the bedroom door with the full force of her body and stood, panting. An itch crawled in her skin and she flicked the hallway light on and brushed herself off sharply, checking the illuminated walls to see if the queen had escaped alongside her. Nothing. She concentrated, her ear pressed gingerly to the door. Could she hear it buzzing?

Her phone was inside. Fuck. She would have called Jacks, she thought, she would have swallowed her pride and asked him to come back. Maybe she would have ordered him to come back, but if he hadn't responded well to being ordered, she would have apologized. All of her rage had burned itself out. It was odd that he wasn't ready to return, but maybe he'd been much angrier than she had been, maybe he hadn't yet gotten to the point where he could see how the whole thing had been hilariously unhinged. Although that didn't sound like him—Jacks never really got angry.

Then, for the first time, she thought, *What if something bad had happened to Jacks*? and her fear, that constant background buzz against which her whole life played out, leapt to a roar. She saw the scenes as if she was watching the movie played back for her: car crash, leaping the highway median, spinning, sparks flying, engine exploding, Jacks, trapped and burning.

Or, before the highway even: Jacks, driving quickly and angrily on these narrow Catskill roads, a deer leaps out, Jacks swerves wildly to avoid it, the car plunges off the edge of its single lane and into the rushing river below.

Or: Jacks at a gas station, he is pumping gas into the car, a man gets out. Against her mind's eye, Tilly watched the dangerous looming figure of the man as he did multiple different things simultaneously: he coughed in Jacks' face and made him ill; he had a gun in the trunk and he shot Jacks on sight; he was smoking a cigarette and he dropped it near the open gas line and the entire gas station went up in black flames.

Tilly sat on the wood floor—old, splintery, *historic*, even—and she thought: *I didn't ask to be here. Did I ask to be here*? but within another few seconds, she wasn't even thinking about the house. "Here" was so large that it encompassed everything she hated about herself, every misalignment of her life with her wishes, and until this moment she hadn't known that the misalignments were so unforgiving.

She had always wanted to be brave. She had always intended to be brave. She had studied abroad in Paris, her junior year; she had spent the summer months afterward backpacking by herself, staying in hostels across Italy, Germany, Spain. People had told her repeatedly that she was brave to do this—a young woman, traveling alone—and she had believed them. In fact, when the summer had ended and she had returned to school, she had begun to think of herself as the brave one in her group of friends. She began pushing just a little further than anyone else wanted to go—one more drink, one more party, one more hour spent doing something that her friends were ready to move on from. "Come on," she would say, as if she were the embodiment of reckless abandon, "what's everybody so *scared* of?"

College had ended, and she had moved to San Francisco, because that felt like a brave thing to do. But eventually, even quickly, she had gotten a job in New York. And then she was in New York. And she didn't like the men shouting at her as she walked home from the subway at night; she didn't like the fat cockroaches, glossy as dates, that emerged from behind the stove or darted across the counters; she didn't like all of the chances to get mugged or stabbed or shoved or date-raped. She walked quickly, with her head down, and she jumped at loud sounds, and she started staying home on weekend nights because she was tired from the week and going everywhere was so arduous, it took so much time, it all started so late at night and if you didn't want to return home at unsafe hours, you had to leave pretty much as soon as you arrived. And so years passed, and there were fewer and fewer opportunities to think of herself as brave.

Despite the operatic tenor of it, the past year had been a relief, almost, that something terrible had finally happened on a level that drowned out her internal noise. Or no, didn't drown it out, but muted it. Made it easier to believe that whatever she didn't like about herself was only a product of the present catastrophe. But now, sitting in the little hallway on the other side of the door from the potential murder hornet, it was just her again. It didn't matter what else was happening all around the country, or all around the world, because it was still just Tilly here on the floor, and she was the sort of person who got scared, and Jacks was the sort of person who didn't.

Was that why she had loved him, at first? His immense and constant capableness? Or had she loved something else entirely—his messiness, his disregard for details, his belief that it didn't matter *how* something got done, as long as it got done—had these traits seemed freeing to her? Had they seemed to let her off the hook of her own exacting, precarious, anxious attention to detail? And then, as they built a life together, had she come to resent the fact that Jacks's baseline was so often cheerfully fine, and her baseline couldn't shift to meet it?

When she had first started dating Jacks, her mother had come to town for work, and the three of them had gone out to dinner. Afterward, mother and daughter alone in a cab, Tilly had pressed her mother for a first impression of Jacks. Really, she had been pressing for a benediction. Her mother had met a medium-size parade of past boyfriends and girlfriends and seldom had much good to say about any of them, and Tilly had never pressed her, but this start with Jacks felt different. She wanted her mother to know that this one would, if Tilly had anything to do with it, be serious.

"So Mom, what do you think?"

After some silence her mother had said, "Well, he's different, that's for sure."

"What's that mean?" Tilly asked, immediately on edge and ready to leap to Jacks's defense. But her mother said, "You always date depressives, darling, and this one seems . . . uncomplicated." And while it was a cutting remark in its own way, it also illustrated for Tilly what she liked about Jacks—he had an uncomplicated relationship to calm, to well-being, to joy even—and so she took it as a benediction anyway.

I'm going to go in, Tilly told herself.

This was after she had turned on every light in the house, checked and rechecked for additional hornets, marched up to the bedroom door, turned away, marched back, hand on the doorknob, turned away, pressed her ear to the wood, listened, listened, shivered, listened, took a lap around the small house, sat in the bathroom, stared at her wild, frantic face, told herself: *You are better than this, Tilly.*

Now she was sitting in the hallway again, a few feet from the closed bedroom door, her gaze fixed on it as if the hornet might itself figure out how to get the door open and address her: *Hello.*

"I'm going to go in," Tilly said, out loud. Her voice shivered the silence, but did not permanently wound it.

She reframed the sentence several ways to see if she believed it. *I'm* about *to go in. I* will *go in. I will* go *in, and I will* kill *that hornet. I will go in and open the window and wait for it to escape. I will go in and get my phone and call Jacks. I will go in and capture the hornet in a jar and let it asphyxiate and then it will be dead. I will go in, and I will take care of this situation.*

None of the sentences coalesced into belief. She tried a different approach: pure shame. *There is so much else to be scared of, always but especially right now, what is wrong with you? What is* wrong *with you? There are people who hunt and eat these insects, and you can't even go grab your phone? Just because there's a hornet in your bedroom doesn't mean that nowhere you go will ever be safe, that there is no sanctuary for you in this world, that you will live on this planet forever exposed, just waiting for the next disaster to strike. It's just a hornet!*

But something inside Tilly said that this, exactly this, was one step too far. Somehow, she had arrived at her breaking point. She hadn't known that she would find it here, but here it was: the cool clarity of the edge.

I hate that it's this, Tilly thought, *this is so stupid, there is no way to tell this later in such a way that I don't sound like a fucking idiot.* And then she thought: *This is what it's like to be a coward,* but instead of shame, she felt a tidal wave of relief.

If she was a coward, then she could just stop trying to be anything else.

The floorboard was oddly warm under her cheek. It had stored the sunlight all day, and even hours past sunset, it gave animal heat back to her. She lay on her side, and the slow boom of her heart made her knuckles tremble, her eyelashes shiver. Who was to say she couldn't sleep in a hallway? Who was to say you had to sleep in a bed? There was no set of standards anymore by which she had to do or be anything, there was no bravery because bravery only existed in opposition to cowardice, and there was no cowardice because Tilly was not being forced to muster courage. She was just lying on this floor; she was just going to lie here until the sun came back; she could smell the sun inside the wood and it was calming. Her eyes drifted shut. She was drifting, not sleeping. She was leaving her body. She was expanding, lifting, she was the air in the room. She wasn't even Tilly anymore. What was a Tilly? She was the hallway, she was the pine studded with knots, she was the wood beams striating the ceiling, she became the roof itself, she was quiet, she was empty, she was gone.

As for the hornet: It had been spring. Daytime, OK. The air like ice crystals, but once the sun hit, things thawed and you could smell the mellowness, the ripeness, right under the surface. Things waiting to rot and be eaten, sugar lurking, OK. The thick sweetness of summer, around the corner. Time to get busy, OK. An edifice? OK. Siding, wood, paint chips unfurling. A gap, a crack? OK. Crawl through, wings folded, drag through, OK. Whole rooms opening up, this much space, too much space, hadn't asked for this much space, but useful anyway, most things were. Space, OK. Then day ebbing itself, OK, hunting time soon. How to get back to the fullness of open air? Darkness, OK, flying, OK, now something firm, cool under the feet, solid air, OK. Hard to tell what divided the air from itself, you could see to the other side but never quite get there. Try again. Try again. Try again. Hmm. OK. Now something firm, cool under the feet, solid air, OK. Try again. Try again. Try again. Hmm. OK. Now something firm, cool under the feet, solid air, OK. Now try again. Try again. Try again. Hmm. OK. No. Try again. Try again. Try again, OK.

Jacks pulled into the driveway and even after he'd turned the engine off, he sat, feeling the car settle around him. Every light in the cabin seemed to be on, blazing from the kitchen, the library, even the bathroom, but he couldn't see Tilly. Only the lights in the bedroom were off. She must have turned on the lights for him and gone to bed. Was that an aggressive gesture, or a welcoming one? He wasn't sure. If he had done it, it would have been welcoming, but Tilly's aggression often leaked into gestures that Jacks had never before guessed could hold it.

This relationship is not going to work, he thought, and felt only vague surprise at being able to say the sentence to himself. The knowledge had sat heavy in him all day as he drove the back roads, as he took lefts and rights, as he meandered through small towns whose main streets turned back into farmland within seconds. The knowledge had sat in his stomach, undigested, and he had shifted around it, thinking for the first few hours that he had a stomachache. Then he had realized it wasn't a stomachache, it was clarity.

Jacks was never the one who ended anything. Even before Ella, he had been left by a series of women, and because he was always so understanding about it, because he never wanted to upset them by being resentful or angry, they had all stayed friends. They always said of him that he was such a good partner, that they just hadn't been ready, that probably there had been something wrong with *them*, not him. They emailed each other, they were on text chains together, they had long-running jokes about being a fan club made up solely out of Jacks's ex-girlfriends. After he transitioned, some of them had liked being his exes even more—it had conferred an extra kind of queerness on run-of-the-mill bisexuals and curious straights.

Jacks had thought he liked their jokes. He'd laughed, anyway. Sure, it had taken him a long time to get over them. He had Googled them late at night, re-read text messages and emails, stared at old pictures, stalked their new boyfriends or girlfriends online. Jacks had always felt the most sheltered within relationships, and every time one was stripped away, the exposure made him half-crazed with abandonment. But he'd still liked being their friend, he'd still liked that he was in some way special to them. He hadn't known that he was angry.

Now that he felt the fullness of rage, he was shocked to find that it didn't feel like a new sensation. Jacks hadn't known that it could be so sticky and corrosive, that it could have built up inside him over all these years, thickening his veins until a single spark had set the whole thing flaring.

He had felt for some time that he and Tilly weren't exactly doing *great*. But there was always a distraction, there was always a birthday dinner or a pre-planned trip or a work event. Everybody they knew was in couples' therapy, so there was always that as well—they hadn't done it, but they'd talked about whether, someday, they should. And then the world had fallen apart and then there was *that*, and that became everything. And now . . .

Sitting in the driveway, taking deep steadying breaths, Jacks's mind went to the pragmatic details. He would let Tilly stay in Ella's house. Maybe Tilly would rent a second car, or else she could drop him off at the Enterprise in Kingston and he could do it. He could go on Airbnb tonight, find another place. Or he could go back to the city, start packing up their apartment. He recoiled from that thought, and the step backward took him further back, until he was reconsidering, briefly, the entire endeavor. Maybe he could give it a week, see if things improved. They could start Zoom therapy, a lot of people had started Zoom therapy. But then he recoiled from that as well. He didn't want to fix things with Tilly, he wanted to extract himself from them. He wanted the clean slate of abandonment, in a new story where he wasn't the one who got abandoned.

He had never before wanted anything more than he wanted to be in a relationship. Now he wondered why. Tilly wasn't a terrible person. She wasn't even a terrible girlfriend. Ella had been much worse, to be honest; she had cheated on him regularly and, when caught, hadn't even had the grace to apologize. Instead she'd delivered a cool dissertation on how unnatural monogamy was for humans. And he had married her! Did he think that breaking up with Tilly would be a fresh start? Did he think it would make up for his past inability to find his own company fulfilling? Had he somehow made Tilly responsible for a vast slow suffocation that wasn't even her fault?

I don't care, Jacks thought, and that was new, too. He always cared about what other people wanted. *I don't care, I just want to be done.* But he was scared to face her, and his heartbeat began to rise in his chest, fluttering and arrhythmic, at the thought of confrontation. What if she cried? What if she started to shout again? What if he was making the biggest mistake of his life? *What if*, he asked himself, *what if after this nowhere you go will be safe, nothing will feel like home, there will be no sanctuary for you in this world?*

Jacks swallowed and swallowed again. His mouth filled, salty. His heart jumped like a fish. In front of him, the house churned out a steady glow, impossibly bright, hollow with light, holding nothing of value to him any longer.

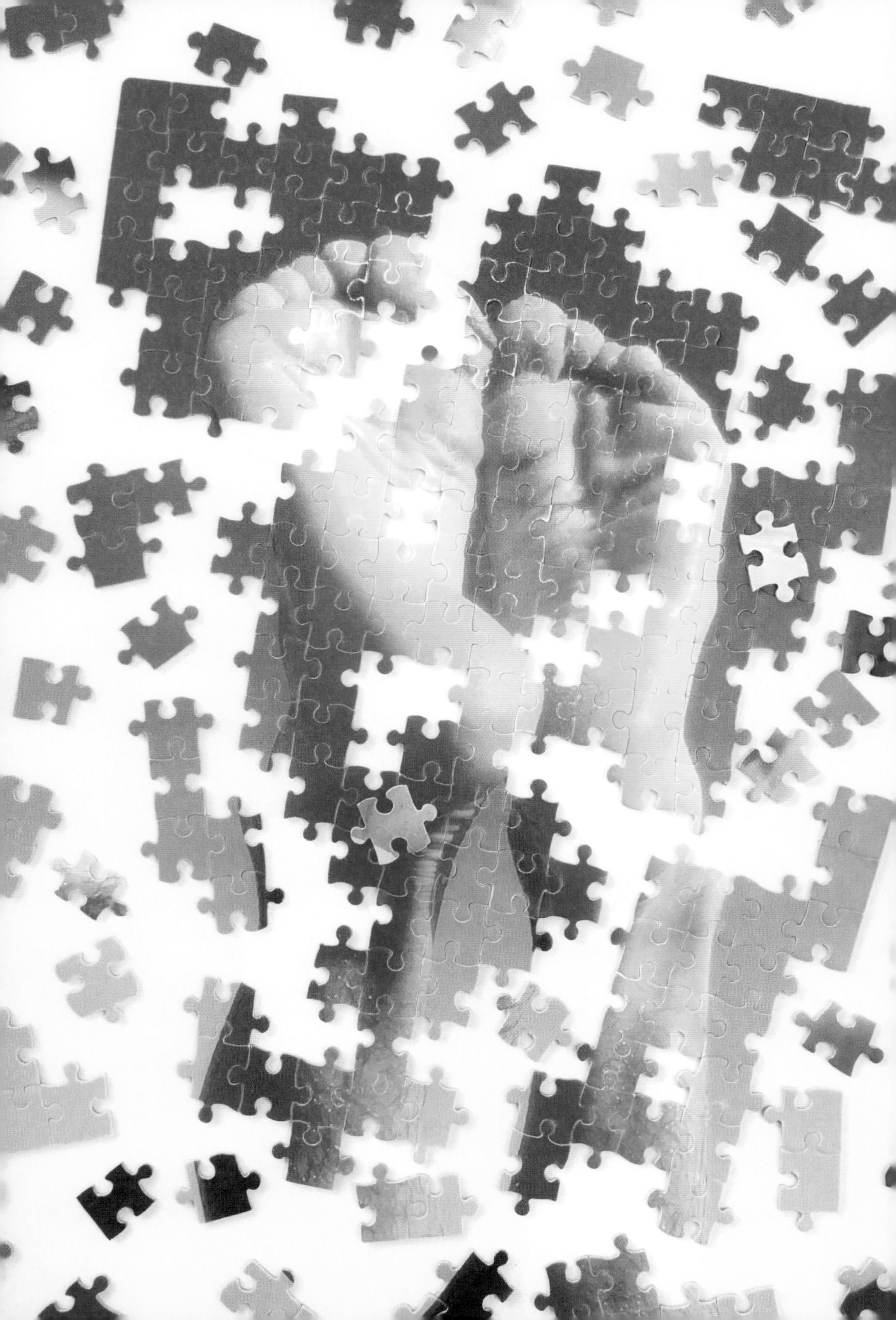

Blurry Soles

Mathew Rodriguez

Art by Mike Feswick

Once a year, my hot gay doctor asks me to remove my shoes and I comply like a good boy looking to earn a lollipop. After I tug off my socks and my heels hit the air, he bends below the examination table and rubs around my soles, asking at various points whether I can feel the pressure he's exerting. He's performing a routine foot exam to ensure that the vessels in my feet haven't atrophied and that warm blood is pumping from my heart to even my slight pinky toe. Sometimes, I imagine his mustache grazing over the stray hairs growing below my toenail. The last time my doctor tended to my feet, before I slipped my Adidas back on, he told me they were beautiful. I carried the compliment with me out the door, giggling on the inside. Something turns me on about my doctor—OK, technically a nurse practitioner—tending to my potentially bloodless feet with so much TLC.

I had a college roommate who would eat pre-packaged low-carb meals and half-joke about losing his foot to type 2 diabetes. *Gotta keep my toes!* he'd say, or *Do you want me to lose my foot?* What else can one do in the face of genetic fate but crack a joke? Even my own diabetes diagnosis came about serendipitously: I had gone to the doctor to get a prescription for PrEP because I was a young twentysomething living in New York who wanted to catch a load here or there. When I showed up for bloodwork, he told me I was diabetic and that he wouldn't prescribe me PrEP until I got my blood sugar under control. So I ate hummus for six months to qualify for Truvada.

In the years since being diagnosed, I get well-meaning nods from my mother to forgo another slice of cake so I don't end up like my dad. His diabetic neuropathy, a condition in a diabetics' feet, causes two opposite phenomena: one of intense pain and the other of numbness. In many cases, amputating a foot is actually preventative. A foot without blood flow cannot feel pain. Therefore, a diabetic with even a minor cut can get a life-threatening infection and not even know it. In this case, adapting a disability is a chance to live. And so from my father's own bodily trauma and my genetic predisposition was born this fear that one day a surgeon may slice his scalpel down on my foot and separate each digit, or maybe the whole thing, until it no longer resided below my ankle.

The prospect of losing your foot when you have a foot fetish is, I guess, nature's little homophobic joke. I learned I loved feet as a baby gay taking free tours of gay porn sites on Rihanna's internet before it was Rihanna's internet. Sean Cody's 2003 website sported a static image of a model with his legs in the air. My thirteen-year-old eye took a curious journey from the model's junk up to his thigh, his calf, and ultimately his foot: taut and pointed upward, toes curled in. I looked at his foot just as much as I looked at any other part of the image, and I wasn't sure if that made me a pervert. I was already gay and sneaking a look at porn in my family's computer room while my mom was asleep, so to imagine I was also destined to be some perv for eternity was too much for a thirteen-year-old honor student to take.

My thirteen-year-old eye took a curious journey from the model's junk up to his thigh, his calf, and ultimately his foot: taut and pointed upward, toes curled in.

The first person I met who had a foot fetish besides me was the boyfriend of my high school crush, Taylor. I met his boyfriend, Evan, at a carnival and later learned that when Taylor slept over Evan's house, Evan's father forced them to sleep head to toe, which Evan liked because he got to play with Taylor's feet. It was at that point I decided I had to become a homewrecker. (I ended up becoming friends with Evan, but nothing ever happened.)

My fat, brown, queer teenagerdom forced me to twist each of my differences into a burden. I had never been kissed, no one had even ever expressed interest in me, so let's just rack this up to one more sexual experience I'd never have, right? It's something of a small gift, even if you don't recognize the packaging, to find out sex can be more expansive than a blurry photocopy of straights banging. The gulf between what the men of *American Pie* wanted and what Sean Cody served was not wide. Sex was a strictly dick-in-hole affair, and most gay sex, even the scenes I snuck from *Queer as Folk*, resembled that, sans mention of fetish and kink. Most of that was otherized and felt like it was for extremists—those gays over there. Feet came into play only when a top would grab one and hold onto it for leverage when they were about to perform a graceless jackhammer.

When it comes to what causes a foot fetish, the answer is, as with most things, part nature and part nurture. As for the nurture side, if a person has a novel sexual experience with a foot, that can create a positive reinforcement. When it happens again, *boom*, you've got a neural pathway, meaning that your brain has started to meld the experience of a foot with the experience of pleasure.

Researchers in 1998 hypothesized that foot fetishes, and the expression of them, increased during times of health-related epidemics. In a study focused on heterosexual pairings—men interested in female feet—they found their thesis rang true in four separate times of epidemic in human history: the thirteenth-century gonorrhea outbreak, the syphilis outbreaks of the sixteenth and nineteenth centuries, and the AIDS epidemic of the twentieth. In the thirteenth century, it was paeans to women's soles. In the 1980s, there were magazines like *Foot Lickers*, *Foot Love*, *Foot Worship*, and *Under Her Toes*. Researchers also noted that, even in non-feet magazines, most editorials of models around the AIDS epidemic include at least one shot where she's showing full foot.

My discovery of this particular erogenous zone seems to be a mistake. I don't know how much intention went into the Sean Cody preview image—shot by a probably straight Sean Cody cameraman starring a probably straight Sean Cody top cramming himself into a probably straight Sean Cody bottom—but there could've been plenty. A friend of mine told me that every celebrity photoshoot where a random celeb is photographed with his bare feet propped up on a coffee table is really a ploy to get the sizeable foot freak population to shell out $20 to see his latest blockbuster. Maybe there was a conspiracy between a group of probably straight adults in the Valley in the early 2000s to get me to become a sole lover. Maybe it was a happy accident that now, every time I see a photo of a foot on my timeline, my day gets a little brighter.

There is something common yet shameful about foot fetishes. We can acknowledge that they are confined to sexual activity and yet that they can come about at any time. I can be on the subway or at a ball game or in line at the DMV and see someone in sandals, and that moment suddenly becomes sexual, as opposed to the kind of daddy-son role play or fisting enthusiasm that can really only be fulfilled in the bedroom or their imagination. The boundless arena of foot play is unnerving, like those early 2000s memes about how uncomfortable straight men get when ogled like they are straight women. The idea that an errant foot might turn someone on is powerful and scary to someone who doesn't want to be sexualized—and, in the case of blurred feet pics, even those who do.

I first learned to be ashamed of my love for feet in the summer of 2009, which was soundtracked by Lady Gaga's "Summerboy." Prior to that summer, I had my first non-breakup with my first non-boyfriend. Though we didn't have sex, sometimes while watching *Dollhouse* in his dorm room bed, I would take off my socks and rub my feet on his, the friction releasing shreds of dead skin onto his twin XL. He dumped me because I was a virgin, so I microwaved a plan to remedy this: get fucked by some OkCupid rando.

My first date was a bar crawl with a boy who lived in Carroll Gardens, where I'd never been. When we got back to my dorm room, drunk, we got naked and began to explore. After we had stuck our dicks in each other's mouths, I asked him if it was OK if I kissed his feet. He said yes and I planted the length of his foot over my entire face. The next time we met up on a date, I asked if he wanted to come over. He said yes, as long as we didn't do any of that "nasty stuff."

I sometimes wonder what he was thinking while I was tucked underneath his sole. For many people in their twenties, especially young gay men, I find—anecdotally, at least—that so many of our early sexual experiences barely register as pleasurable. I know I spent most of the time in my head wondering if I was doing the right thing, saying the right thing, sucking the right swatch of skin. A lot of sex is two people just trying not to look like they're bad at sex. That's the norm for people raised in a world that absolutely disrespects the butthole and abhors any sex that doesn't at least try to be a photo negative of a dick and a vagina.

I wish I were smart enough at the time to separate out what was his shame and what was my own. To this day, I don't know why he said yes, or if he thought it was gross that I was licking his foot. I just know that he said yes so that I would be happy, which is kinda beautiful. I often think about how far removed we are, in terms of kinks, from 2009, the year Grindr debuted in the App Store. I like to think of people around my age as the "Grindr Generation." The moniker is not just about the fact that we grew up with the ability to see who in an immediate radius wanted to fuck, but because of what it has meant for our own sexual self-image. My fellow Gen G's and I, the people between dial-up and GIF porn, became sexual beings in an age that empowered us to be our own pornographers. We've learned what angles complement us best, what parts of our bodies to show. We're no longer a number on a scale from one to ten; each segmented body part has its own score and a set of tricks to game the scale.

If my online foot JPEG story begins with a supposedly heterosexual cameraman just trying to get his money shot, it hits a snafu twenty years later, when foot-baiting is so common that I see friends, celebrities, and sex workers' soles in everyday scrolling. Just this morning, I retweeted an ad from an independent jockstrap maker who had his legs up, hole exposed, with the caption "Heard some of y'all like feet?" with the bottoms of his soles direct to the camera. It's true, many people do, and with that, people have had to renegotiate how they present their feet online.

Take Fernando. I can tell you what his dick looks like, but not his feet. I desperately want to fuck him. He has a centaur-like sturdiness. He supplies his alt account followers with so many photos of his girthy dick poking out from above the stretchy top lining of his briefs, or through their leg holes. Recently, he shared a full body mirror picture from atop his bed. From the direction of his leg, it was clear that his soles were pointed toward camera, but at the bottom of the photo, where his toes and instep should be, were a set of pixels. They looked like the set of stairs that Mario climbs in the original NES game. He had blurred them out.

It's happened a few times now, this odd meeting of the invitation to look and simultaneous deterrent to look *down there*. It's become something of a schtick. Gays in the comments reply, *Oh, someone's not giving the feet away for free!* These images leave me with a lot of feelings and more questions. I wish I could see the feet; why aren't they there? I hope this person doesn't think foot fetishes are weird; do people still think foot fetishes are weird? Thirst traps are about attention; why isn't foot attention part of the deal? I might lose my feet; why isn't he celebrating his?

Yes, sure, I am incensed by my own level of entitlement. Everyone should have the right to blur their feet. Their body, their choice. And many people with alts flirt with starting an OnlyFans. Knowing how many heel, toe, and sole lovers are out there, why give away the foot milk for free? But it also strikes me as singling out foot fetishes—and sexuality around the foot—as somehow different than the normal sexual attention that people often crave when posting thirst traps. Or from people who like pits or nipples or . . . ! It's an interesting tension; because foot fetishes are so common, it's easy to surmise that people will more readily fetishize feet than any other part of the body. But because it's so discussed, it can also be easy to stigmatize.

And yet we've arrived at the point in technology where feet are so readily available that someone might choose to blur them to deter unwanted attention, which, in my opinion, causes a kind of Streisand effect. I didn't know how much I wanted to jerk off to your feet until they weren't there. They must be stunning to hide them. I wonder about size, arch, whether the toes are more or less uniform in size or if the big toe overshadows the rest, how much the heel bulges out.

This blurred foot phenomenon speaks to a fundamental change in the understanding of our bodies and our own worth, a shift that began in many ways with Grindr. On Grindr, we became our own pornographers, leading others in a digital striptease by sending pic after pic to entice other people to consider having sex with us. In a sexual economy dominated by cropped photos, we had to learn the best parts of ourselves to stay competitive in the marketplace. We learned which angles complement, hide, and emphasize each square inch of our body. All this to potentially sleep with one of hundreds of strangers who live in our phones and reside down the street, in apartments we may never see but would love to if invited.

My favorite segment of a foot is its sole, the squishy plane that lands plush against my calves when I'm topping. But there is so much to love about feet: their salty smell, their shape, the way the folds cascade when the soles are curved upward. Even the euphony of the phrase "holes and soles" is intoxicating. Some of the best sexual terms have a great mouth feel. *Holes and soles*, like *cumdump*, gives you the joy of reduplicative rhyming, the kind of joy you hear when you say the words *higgledy piggledy* or *hocus pocus*. But the *and* between the words makes it feel like a phrase, more akin to a colloquial proverb like *go with the flow* or *snug as a bug in a rug*.

Thinking about my own desires helps me realize that it's not just the digital world that has made us segment our bodies into their best parts. Particular body parts hold special appeal to certain people. So our own portioning out makes sense in this particular marketplace. Technology

In a sexual economy dominated by cropped photos, we had to learn the best parts of ourselves to stay competitive in the marketplace.

hasn't created a novel sexual economy, but has changed how we navigate and interact in it.

In a way, the idea that we could pixelate our feet is an extension of the idea that we are becoming cyborgs. Most famous for proposing this idea is Donna Haraway, the philosopher who wrote that the categories between animal, human, and machine had been breaking down for centuries due to phenomena like Darwin's *Origin of Species*, which argued we were animals, and the Industrial Revolution, which ultimately argued that we were machines. Sure, she was writing about this in the context of rigid gender boundaries, but to extend this idea, it has a lot to say about how we approach our sexuality. Because technology allows us to edit our bodies, the pics that people like—including an edited photo of Kim Kardashian in a bikini or a full nude with an emoji-covered face—are really pics of cyborgs, beings that are sexual with the aid of technology.

How different, then, is the humble blurry foot pic, which acknowledges that we are carnal, and that rather than a foot at the end of our legs, we can choose to adopt a bundle of pixels or a blur. That foot is there, but it's not, and that's technology. It's a limb, both missing and present.

Which brings me back to my own foot, which is both there and could very well not be one day. The prospect of losing it frightens me not because of mobility or disability, but because of this scenario: I'm in my fifties or sixties, speaking to a man on Grindr or Scruff or Sniffies, whatever future technology exists for men to fuck. We meet up and his toes and soles are beautiful and I make love to him and to them. When I'm done, he asks if he can return the favor, and then I have to admit that I don't have all my toes, or that I'm even missing an entire foot. The scenario makes no sense: Wouldn't he know by then? Wouldn't my socks be off? Or I'm using a crutch of some sort? But, when it all comes down to it, the scenario that frightens me the most is that I might be a selfish lover, or be bad in bed, or deflate another foot lover's otherwise solid night. My phone right now is filled with random people I've never met who one day want to exchange foot rubs with me, and yet it feels like that exchange is in danger of not happening.

In many ways, my fear is not based in reality. It's based on an inherited sense of ableism, that having a body that doesn't function like most people's might make it less than. But that reality isn't true: I know many sexy disabled people who fuck using every inch of skin their body has.

It's also a renunciation of my own feelings on what makes gay sex great. I believe that queer sex is a test of the human body, asking us to embrace parts that other people might turn away. Gays have successfully reclaimed one of the most degradated parts of human anatomy—yeah, I'm talking about the butthole—and turned it into the hottest grotto since Plato's cave. When I sometimes watch and enjoy fisting videos, what I think turns me on the most is the capacity for people to derive pleasure from something that, if described to someone who had never heard of it, would sound extremely painful. No matter what, we make it work, Tim Gunn–style.

You see, the other side of the fear and trauma of my own diabetes diagnosis is a very macabre humor centered around my illness. I joke often about my own illness, maybe because I must use humor if I am to picture my diabetes and myself cohabitating in the same body. Freud even talked about this: People use jokes to triumph over their circumstances. In "Humour," he uses an example of a criminal who is about to be hanged on a Monday, who says, "Well, the week's beginning nicely." Freud says that there is "something liberating" about humor, and that in making a joke, "the ego refuses to be distressed by the provocations of reality, to let itself be compelled to suffer, in fact, that such traumas are no more than occasions for it to gain pleasure."

In a less funny, but more ironic twist, the doctor most associated with foot fetishes wasn't actually researching kink, but phantom limbs and body trauma. He found that the part of the brain most associated with genitals and the part most associated with feet live next door to one another and that sometimes, exciting one could excite the other, a form of neural crosstalk.

An alternate scenario of the one I worry about exists. I don't mourn the future memory of my foot. The man I want to fuck comes over and we've already swapped pics. He knows that my foot is gone and it doesn't bother him. In fact, when I take off my pants and roll up my socks, I say something like, *Well, I still have the other one*, or *Sucks you missed it, it tasted great*. We laugh and start to go at it. He goes down on me and just as I am about to finish, I feel a ghostly tingle; just as I am about to come, I look down and see my big toe extended at the top of my foot, just like that Sean Cody model's foot. It is arched backward, contorted like a marble statue, as if pointing back at my face.

Anal Fisting: A Case Study of the Mental and Rectal Elasticity of the Human Male

Sam Finkelstein

Art by Chris Williford

I'm scrolling through Grindr, looking for an activity. Sondra's quarantining because of COVID. Hillary's quarantining in Miami because of COVID. Wayne only wants to see me if I can take him to another party, which I'm not going to do while living with my immunocompromised mother. Anyway, all the sex parties I know about in the city have been shut down or postponed due to Omicron. Golden Boys, Inferno, even the Sniffies events are slowing down. I've watched every TV show available. I've exhausted Instagram and Facebook and Reddit. I've consumed as many pages of *NeuroTribes* and *X-Men* as my brain can withstand. I need something to fucking do.

I see a profile with no photos, just a display name, *BTTM4FIST*. What possesses someone to want a fist inside them? What's that process like? Do you kiss first? Do you file your nails before? How far can you go without injuring them? And how do you know when you've gone that far? I send a tap, the promiscuous gay equivalent of a Facebook poke. He's only about 1100 feet away. What is that, like five blocks? We get to messaging.

u like to fist?

never tried it, but im curious

ok

He sends a photo of the hottest ass I have ever seen. I've seen nearly every ass in Manhattan and can confidently declare this a perfect specimen. Normally, this is when I ask for a face photo, but this investigation is anthropological, not sexual, so that seems extraneous. Not like I was going to be face to face with his face, anyway. I start on the logistics.

im free later tonight. 3 hours from now sound good?

sure

any tips for me? I dont wanna fuck you up

fuck me up.

ill read an online guide before coming

smart

I don't remember what reason I gave him, or if I gave him one at all, but the truth is that I needed to play Tetris for at least an hour before going to do something this weird, plus I needed to wait for my mom to go to sleep. She always seems to get up for a late-night snack at the exact moment when I'm leaving for an excursion. I'm usually just going to listen to music and walk in circles for an hour or two. In the middle of the night while the streets are still empty, I can sing along to "Cyber Sex" by Doja or "Hallelujah" by Lenny C, make faces at the moon, and drum on any part of my body I like without distressing the human inhabitants populating the East Village during daylight hours. Fifteen games of Tetris, three articles on safe anal fisting, two dinners, and a half gallon of iced tea later, I embark on my journey downtown.

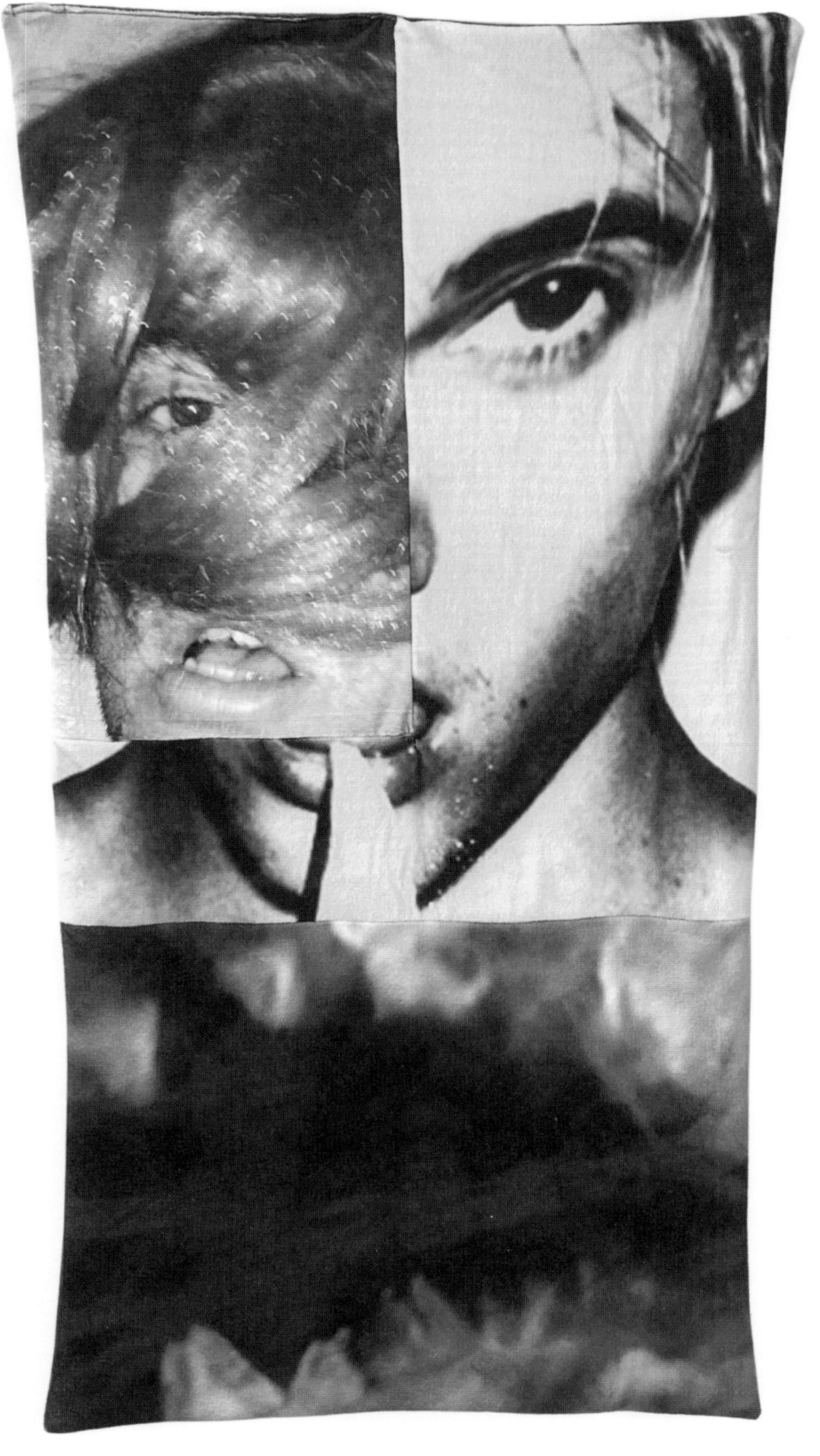

I put on my hood and lower my mask. I didn't realize it was raining when I made this plan. I briefly consider canceling and turning back, but I persevere in the interest of knowledge. I breathe in as quickly and deeply as I can, so the December air can cool the back of my mouth. If I press the blade of my tongue to the top of my upper teeth, and inhale through my nose, I can chill the passageway that connects nose and mouth, which feels especially nice. Music in my ears, I leave the apartment complex for the street.

I told him at 11 that I would need 15 minutes, but I arrive outside his building at 11:12. I decide to listen to one more song. The Bree Runway remix of "XS" by Rina Sawayama is sure to inspire scientific inquiry, so I pace in a circle contemplating the lyrics as rain patters on my head. I enter and tell the doorman which apartment I'm visiting. I can tell from his tone that I'm visiting a guy who gets a lot of visitors. His door opens and a good-looking face peeks from behind it at a 45-degree angle, the rest of his body hidden behind the door. *Excellent. He's already naked.* Human faces all look the same to me. I was in high school before I learned that Sandra Bullock and Anne Hathaway were not one person at different points in a single shared life cycle. All I can discern is that he's hot. I enter and see his mattress on the floor in the far right corner of the room, covered by a single sheet, pressed against a floor-to-ceiling window overlooking the city. *Blinds open.* Translucent panels line the right side wall, inlaid with lightbulbs about two feet above the ground. They form an array of glowing clamshells, illuminating the all-white room. A dog darts across my peripheral. My eyes make their way back to me, past the gray stools and white love seat, to the floor around my body, and examine the front of his body for the first time. He has thick muscular legs, eight bulging abdominal muscles, and as many inches. His pecs, separated by a near invisible tuft of hair, protrude, round. Perky, even. By the time I come to, he is looking down at his phone, scrolling silently. "You're incredibly sexy," I say. I consider my paralysis a compliment and see no need to apologize for it.

"Thanks. Now take off your clothes."

I take off my shoes and walk over to the bed, where I start to strip. Many people don't realize that men's evolutionary obsession with their partners' breasts manifests even in gay men. Of course, that itself was a co-opt of humans' egalitarian obsession with their partners' butts. All other mammals' breasts are flat outside of lactation, but in the four million years or so since they started walking on two legs, Earth's humans have evolved permanently engorged breasts in nearly half the global population to replace this lost fertility signal, butts no longer in their direct line of vision as they were when humans were quadrupedal. Why don't more men have boobs then? He joins me by the bed, placing in my hand what appears to be an open Crisco container. Without my glasses, I can't really tell what words or even colors are on the container, but I gather that it's some kind of industry grade anal lube. Wordlessly he gets on all fours on the mattress.

I'm impressed at how normal his body looks. Most guys who are into fisting, and many who are into other forms of extreme sex, have less of a rose bud and more of a bundt cake. I dip my right index finger into the Crisco canister. I was hoping it would be smooth and lotiony, but it actually has the texture of shea butter or cold coconut oil. Something between ground chalk and shaved ice, imperceptibly small particles held together by wet glue, in texture and in color. I'm inserting a single finger and already he's moaning. I can't decide if I should be flattered or worried about what's next. If a single finger elicits a moan, will a second cause a shriek? I work my way up to two and then three. *Oh yeah, in and out, in and out baby! Inenout!* Where else would I go? There aren't that many options. Every now and then I contort to reach my left hand across my body, my right still inside of him, to the container to the right of me to scoop out some more lube and smear it on the exposed portion of my right hand. This guy has been very thoroughly cleaned, but I still don't want to reach my hand directly from his asshole into his lube. I keep having a vision of him making a sandwich with this stuff after I leave, and I wouldn't be able to contain my laughter if I started picturing him dipping into his margarine and finding it to be tripe flavored.

I place my ring finger and index fingers over my middle finger, touching one another, my pinky over my ring finger, and my thumb at the top of my palm, resting in the crook of my ring and middle fingers, forming my hand into the head of a spear. With it, I impale him, but meet more resistance than I'm comfortable powering through. I'm not the one who will have to deal with the consequences of being overly eager. Can he tell that I bite my nails?

I repeat my process, removing my hand, reapplying Crisco as needed, pressing back into him, and gaining about a half centimeter on each attempt. I hear a sharp inhale and notice that the smell of poppers has been engulfing me. I wish that I had not.

One huff later and his hole is a spent rubber band. I finally get in past my knuckles, the widest part of the spear hand shape, so the contractive pressure of the sphincter inadvertently pulls my hand further inside of him. It's uncanny to see your hand disappear inside of another person. A finger, not so jarring. We put our fingers into all kinds of stuff, lotions, peanut butter jars, picking things out of a drain. The only time your whole hand is in something is a glove, but a glove allows you to continue believing that your hand exists and continues to be a hand. As I push farther into his body, he lets out a noise I don't think I've ever heard before, oscillating between a loud roar and wordless moans, interspersed with high pitched shrieks. I imagine torture victims might make similar noises upon losing a limb.

The inward pressure of his rectum envelopes my entire hand with a sensation of velvet, much like the inside of a mouth. I leave it there for a moment, allowing us both to acclimate to this new stage. Over a span of four seconds, I remove my hand from inside of him, and he growls in pleasure. There is a ring around my wrist, about two inches from my hand, of the frothed mixture of lubricant, sweat, and intestinal fluid characteristic of anal sex. He has a matching one around his hole. I reinsert my hand, slightly faster than before, and he tells me not to be cautious. He can take it. It's remarkable how much his body has adapted in just the fifteen minutes since I arrived. His cries of *fuckyesbaby* and *inenout inenout ohfuckohgod* encourage me to make a bear claw shape while my hand is inside of him. I press my thumb flat across my palm, place my remaining fingertips on my palm, and my knuckles pointing toward him, in order to avoid any abrasions from my fingernails. I'm shocked he didn't ask me to wear some kind of protection. No glove, no love, as they say. With my hand in this position, I pull it out of him and his high-pitched squealing is now accompanied by the percussions of simulated, or rather stimulated, flatulence. Somehow, he is able to regain command of his body just long enough to take another huff.

The odor is distinctly chemical, in a way that human language isn't equipped to describe. More than that, it is gross, like I'm drowning in a mop bucket full of cleaning fluid and vodka. Like I've been shrunken down and trapped inside the cap of a scented highlighter, unable to call for help as I choke back my own vomit. Subjects always offer me poppers, but I've only indulged once. Conventional knowledge says the rush from poppers only lasts a few minutes, but drugs almost always affect me in unpredictable ways. All that night I felt like I had just sucked the gas out of a bottle of Reddi-Wip, my naturally anemic iron levels compounding the chemically induced oxygen deprivation, resulting in a euphoric lightheadedness, my vision going white, and my sense of balance completely dissipating. Not unpleasant, but no good for field work.

I am experimenting with a number of techniques. I try entering as a cone, forming a claw inside, spinning my hand in circles, pushing my hand forward, pushing downward toward his prostate, forming a fist, exiting as a claw, leaving my hand in partially, removing my hand completely, in any and every combination. Any spinning or non-frontal pressure elicits an immediate *inenout inenout!* A more meaningful instruction than I anticipated. Right now, I'm entering as a cone, forming a fist, pushing as far into him as I can, and exiting again as a cone, as I find this causes the least amount of air to enter and exit his body. This has the dual benefit of reducing the very distracting noise, and also limiting the odor in the air. It's hard to explain the smell of anal sex, because it is a distinct odor from shit. Unfortunately nearly all human languages lack the concepts to describe odors objectively the way we can with colors and noises, relying instead on imperfect analogies. It is in the olfactory constellation of shit, but the metallic quality is distinctly intestinal. The geographic distance between the smelling organs and the smell-producing organs usually makes this a non-issue during anal sex.

I succumb to my success and begin to insert and remove my hand while formed into a fist. He is gripping his thighs, as though without an anchor he would be at risk of falling out of his own body. In the brief glimpses I catch of his face as he thrashes his head in every direction, he appears to be wincing, maybe even fighting back tears. Maybe even indulging them. Not because I'm hurting him, but because the human mind is not primed for this degree of sensation, especially in this location. I've read that the pleasure of fisting comes from the sensation of fullness, which a cynic will tell you entails a default of emptiness. I think the pleasure, however, is in the magnitude, not the nature, of feeling. There is nothing particularly pleasurable in feeling your stomach rise to your chest as you descend on a roller coaster track. Or in eating food so spicy your body turns red and you begin to tear up. Even children see the exploding head on a package of Warheads and know they want to experience that level of sourness, all sitting around a lunch

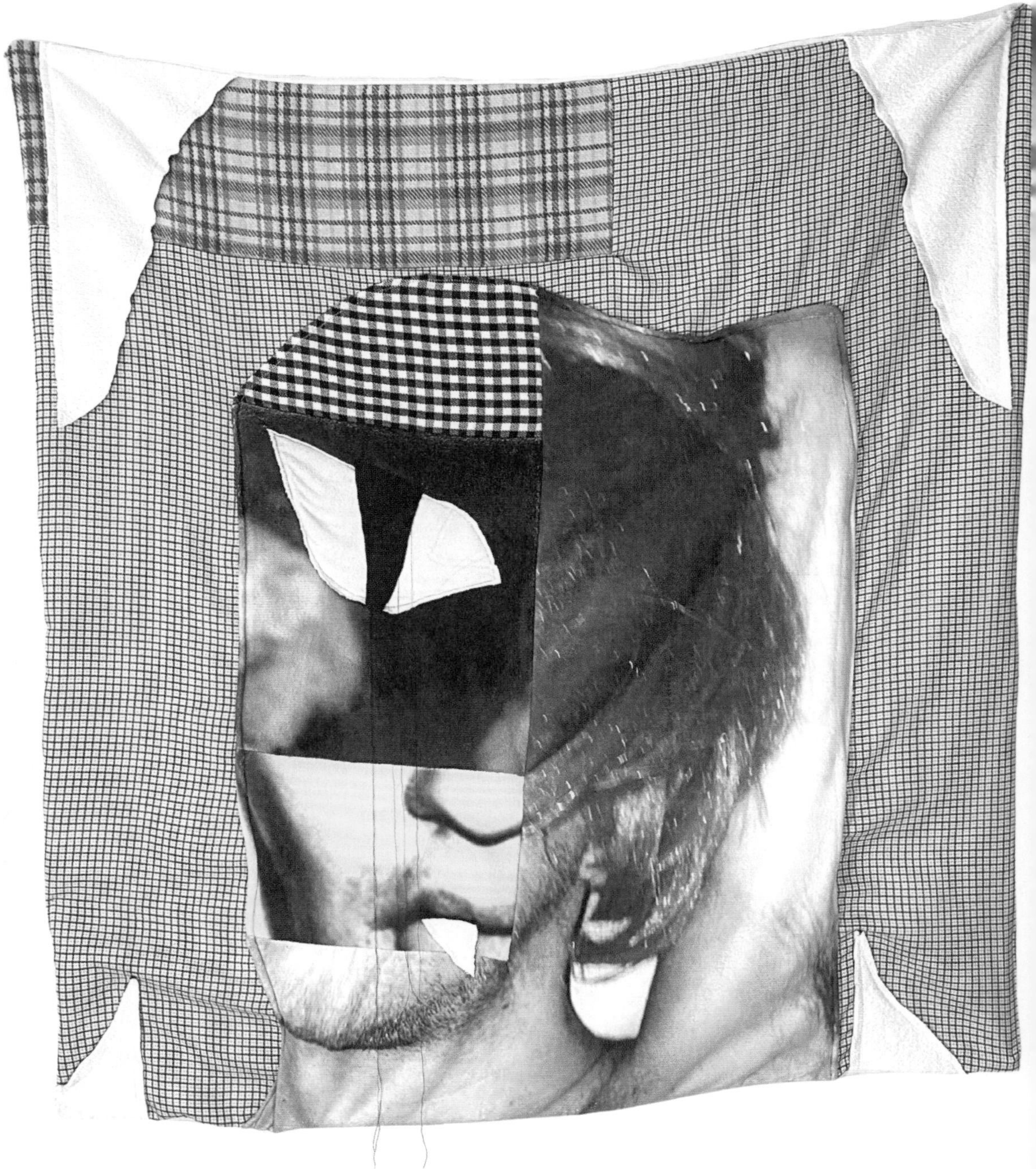

Exquisite Corpse Flag, 2014-2021
(digital prints on microfiber beach towels, bleach, embroidery thread)
29" x 60" (p. 105)

Homunculus (Living Doll), 2014-2022
(digital prints on archived microfiber beach towels, vintage wool, fleece, rayon, embroidery thread)
41" x 43" (above)

table, their mouths puckering and their eyes watering as they giggle at one another. It is the extremeness itself that is enjoyable. The act of approaching and surpassing our own limitations. Fisting is not anal sex for men who want impossibly endowed partners. It's not sex at all, actually. Anal fisting is Warheads sour candies.

His high-pitched repetitive wailing over the semi-regular racket of air escaping his body is the ultimate hyper pop track, a SOPHIE-esque cacophony. Just as I'm getting into the beat, it stops completely.

"Stevie, no! Go to your bed!"

When experiencing tension, humans tend to clench their buttholes. The pressure around my hand grinds my knuckles together. Do you think fisters are more prone to arthritis? His dog has come up to greet us and now my hand is stuck in a very uncomfortable position. If I re-adjust right now, I'll injure him, so I stay put. Finally his dog leaves us alone and he unclenches. It is a freaky miraculous sight, as it expands from a vice grip into an old scrunchy. The silky texture consuming my forearm is undeniably luxurious, and the ohfuckoooohfuckohfuckyesy-esyainenoutinenoutfuuuuuuucks are impossible to not find motivating. Should I tell him that the ring of froth around my arm is getting more and more red? Assholes bleed. It's part of the game. That really ought to be his call though. Hitting my stride, I'm mesmerized by the motion. I've long had a penchant for fitting things into other things. That's not an innuendo, by the way. I once traveled for a month with a single back-pack of clothes. I can make anything fit into anything. It's therapeutic.

For a moment, he overcomes his moans and asks me to take a video. My dominant hand is of course, inside of his body, so with my left hand I reach and grab his phone from him. My left hand, also of course, is covered in lube. It's my scooping and smearing hand after all. I am shaking, nearly tumbling over, as I try to lean back to get a good perspective for the camera, and simultaneously thrust forward to create some action for the shot. Looking at my own arm through the phone camera, the events of the night feel *hot* for the first time. I hand the phone back to him and stare at the thick paste on my arm and his hole. Opaque, muted red, like paint. It reminds me of the walls of the dining room in the house I grew up in. Raspberry, my mom called the color. It does sort of look like jam oozing out. Funky.

We decide the night is over, and he goes to rinse off a bit. "You know, sometimes after hookups, I'm so eager to get out that I forget to wash my hands. I don't think that'll be a problem this time." He produces a polite chuckle, a merciful act. It's the least he can do. He comes back wearing a towel and directs me to the bathroom. All white, except for the pervasive grout. I reach into the shower and grab the only soap I can find in the room. Rinsing and rinsing and rinsing. I need to get this disgusting fucking slime off me. No matter how hard I scrub there's still residue clinging to my hands and wrist. What's stuck has never made contact with his body or his bodily fluids, but the unctuous grime on my skin is making me sick. I scrape my hands clean on the shower curtain and try not to think about it. Now for the complicated part. Discussion.

I never know what's expected of me, and what level of unexpected can still be accepted. I start putting my clothes back on as he asks where I'm from. He's from the Bronx, he studied nutrition. He's only been fisted a handful of times, he says, as though that's a small number of times to be fisted. He tells me he started off as the fister, just thinking it's fun to try things. I'm not looking at him as he says this, but I imagine he does so with a grin. He was inducted by some older men who were career fisters, that he had met at the Eagle or some other aging sex club. Eventually one of them convinced him to get fisted himself and he's been practically addicted to it since. We share our shock at what a body is capable of withstanding, and what the mind is capable of deciding to enjoy. It's mentally exhausting, convincing yourself to ignore your every instinct. To overcome the urge to tense your every muscle, eject the hand as quickly as possible, likely rupturing yourself in the process, and run off to shelter. It is this conscious calmness that allows the body to leave such a violent experience unharmed, like sleeping passengers waking up to a crashed car and no broken bones. In a different person, this level of mental and body discipline could allow Tibetan monks to control their own heartbeat, or raise their body temperature to survive the Himalayas.

"This conversation is really interesting, I'd be happy to keep talking. But I'll let you dictate."

"Oh," he looks at me confused. "I actually have a really early morning tomorrow. You were really good at this though. I was impressed."

Truly I do not understand anything. I tie up my shoes. We kiss for the first time. He has a huge tongue. His name is Derrick, he says. I make my way out of the apartment, already contemplating how best to present my findings. The rain has passed, so I go for a stroll. Within minutes I have detailed the entire night in a public Instagram story, paragraphs upon paragraphs of anal prose superimposed on my expressionless face. I bet I could turn this into a standup set. I imagine walking away from the microphone and pantomiming being stuck in his ass, and consequently stuck on the stage. My specialty back in the day was the invisible lasso on the (equally invisible) cow, a nearly identical visual to fisting. Maybe in the middle of the set, I'll act out being clenched and unable to move. Better yet, I'll act out my arm motion, while I try to simulate all the noises. I'll alternate between whining for the sounds he made and beatboxing for the sounds I made him make. A twisted idea enters my mind. I record ten minutes of video, a play by play of the whole experience, all without so much as a quiver of my lips. I think I'll have to change *fuck yes baby* to *fuck yes daddy*. It's much easier to say a *d* sound than a *b* sound without moving your lips. To be clear, it's impossible to produce a *b* sound without moving your lips, but so long as you produce two discernible *d* sounds, you can fool a listener into believing one is a *b*. By pointing the tip of my tongue to the roof of my mouth and sliding it backward until its underside begins to graze my palate and I feel a slight stretch in my frenulum, I can enunciate a sound that captures some of the softness and echo characteristic of *b*, though the retroflex consonant is still unnatural in my mouth. I'll have to practice my Hindi before I publish. This research warrants a transdisciplinary representation. I text my next subject, or maybe collaborator. "Do you think it is possible to do ventriloquism in a way that is hot?"

Forgiveness

Christopher Soto

I shaved my
Eyebrows &
I pulled
Thin film
From my lips &
I gulped
Kerosene &
I struck a match
Against my face
Then lit the room
& I walked
Through prairies
Orange
Groves
Electrical towers
Wires humming
Like
Birds.
& I walked
Until dew then
Drunken night
Looking for
Forgiveness
But she
Wasn't around.
I called
Forgiveness
Forgiveness
Where are you?
A deer leapt–
From my chest
Into a cloud
Of dust.
This entire time
Forgiveness was
Inside me.

ORIGINALLY PUBLISHED IN *HELLO MR.* ISSUE 10 IN 2018.

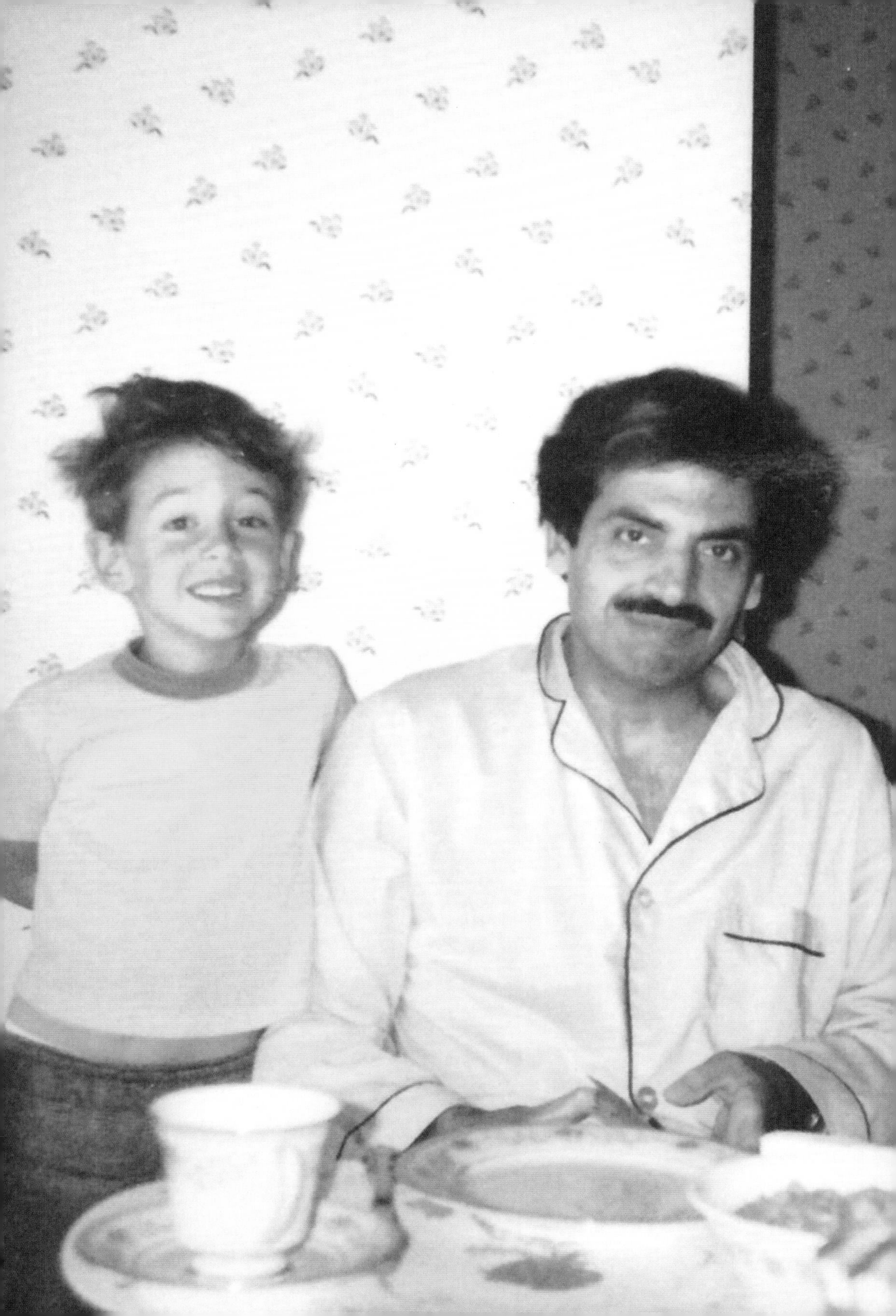

The Recording

Khalid El Khatib

I remember arriving at his house early to search his closet for a gun. I never, in the twenty-six years I knew him, suspected that my father owned one. I was even more certain that if he did, he wouldn't use it on me or himself. And still, my search—upending his walk-in closet, looking in shoes and behind picture frames, throwing open two safes—wasn't an act of hyperbole.

I didn't believe a gun existed, but I looked for a good reason: I didn't believe that we could exist beyond me coming out to him. Not just "us," but me and him separately. So much of my identity was tied to me not telling him I was gay. And so much of his identity was tied to pretending I was straight.

I kept my queerness from only him. I could go on national TV and say it, I could write about it in magazines, I could tell it to a new boss on my first day of work, but I couldn't tell my devout Muslim father. And once he knew, there would be nothing dark inside me I could cling to or aspire to purge—at least nothing tangible. Though I believed my dad knew I was gay, I felt that the narrative he had constructed and that I allowed to flourish was so delicately planted in his mind that when it was shattered, his brain would break, too.

When I told him, no gun appeared, but I felt death.

One of my most vivid memories of death is the passing of my maternal grandfather. He was a rural mail carrier in Iowa for almost fifty years and died in a freak car accident on the mail route he traveled daily. It happened just two weeks before his scheduled retirement. I was on the couch in our TV room when my mom got the call. I still remember her wail, her collapse.

My stoic father who practiced geriatric medicine knew death better than anyone; he was born into death in the West Bank in 1943, just before one of the region's most devastating wars began in 1947. He grew up a refugee in Syria and started his career in refugee camps in Jordan, which made him both empathetic to suffering and hardened to its eventualities. I saw him cry once, only briefly.

I came out to him on November 3, 2011, seven years after I came out to my mother, my sisters, and my friends. And I remember his wail, his collapse.

I think.

Or is that too dramatic? Was it just some tears and a rush through the stages of grief? Did he try to bargain with me to either take it back or to check myself into therapy? Did he argue with me until we both got tired and then did he dismiss me? Or am I right to equate what happened with death?

It's hard to remember what's hard. I've always struggled to remember trauma accurately—a breakup, a physical fight. There's astounding scientific evidence on how our memories betray and manipulate us so that we can keep going. And I feel it. So when I talk about coming out to my dad I qualify what I remember. I say, "I think I remember his devastation."

But I could know.

Just before I counted down from ten in my head and fought through broken breath to say, "I'm gay," I hit record on my phone.

Whatever happened taped for thirty-nine minutes.

I have memorialized trauma all around me.

In my living room, one whole wall has built-in bookshelves standing eight feet tall. And one full shelf is stacked with black journals

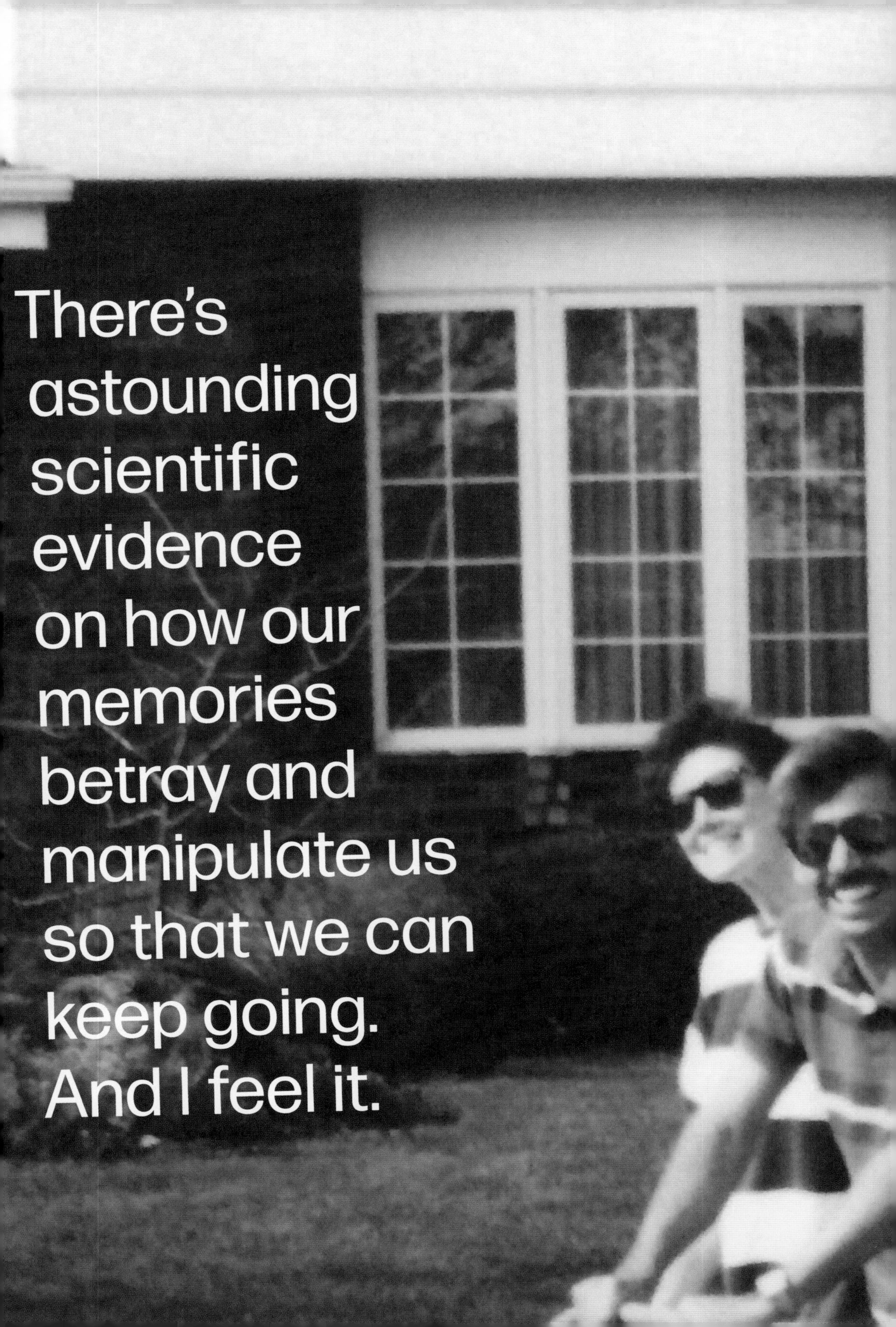

There's astounding scientific evidence on how our memories betray and manipulate us so that we can keep going. And I feel it.

documenting bad memories. Writing is how I remember trauma as well as how I process it.

The journal with the freshest ink is filled—long, rambling passages that are mostly manifestations of thirtysomething existential dread.

But the first journal in the collection is from sixth grade. It's spiral bound, with a hard black cover and an embossed metallic star. It's a meditation on bullying. It's hard to read.

The thickest journal on the shelf documents everyone I slept with and dated in my early twenties. I made the mistake of showing it to my ex-boyfriend, who used to call it my "burn book." But that's a mischaracterization, because more than anything it burns me. It's a detail-rich documentation of every time I failed, largely by not being enough for someone.

I reread one of many long passages about that ex-boyfriend, and I can pinpoint the exact moment it became nonnegotiable that I tell my dad I am gay. My ex had become a stand-in for all men; I realized that not being out to my dad might forever jeopardize my happiness. I couldn't sustain my relationship with my dad to have the life I was convinced I wanted.

I deleted a bunch of stuff from my phone recently and I saw our texts from the night before Thanksgiving. You were at a bar with friends on Macdougal Street. I was maybe 80 feet away and four floors up, in my apartment where my dad was visiting. He was dozing off to CNN and I was typing and deleting responses to you asking me to come down to see you. just say hi.

I couldn't do it with my dad 80 feet away and four flights up.

You replied, sometimes I feel like you don't love me.

I wish I would have had the courage to go downstairs and say to your face what I feel now: I love my dad, but I don't have to. And I won't if it means I can't love you. I won't, if it means I can't love me.

I remember the days leading up to my trip back to Iowa. I prepared for my coming out like a presidential campaign. I was methodical. I have always been obsessed with control. I have worked jobs—in crisis management and government affairs—where success was predicated on my ability not just to influence, but to control outcomes. And I believed that even if I couldn't control my dad's reaction, I could control my own.

I knew that the only way I'd remember exactly what happened is if I wrote it down after, and I knew that if it went as poorly as I expected, I wouldn't be able to.

I made a list of every possible outcome on a spectrum of extremity, from *he's fine and I've wasted fifteen years worrying*, to *excommunication*, to *honor killing*.

I dedicated three therapy sessions, at $150 an hour, to role-playing my coming out. My therapist and I would switch who played my dad because I hypothesized it would be easier if I could be as empathetic as possible.

I told everyone why I was flying to Iowa, from a first date three days before I left, to my boss, colleagues, and ad agency clients. I booby-trapped my life like the *Home Alone* house so that if things went wrong and self-doubt or depression started to take hold, someone—anyone—from my network would be there to lovingly slap me across the face and snap me out of it.

And then I boarded the plane.

The ride from Chicago to Dubuque is where my memory starts to shake like the puddle jumper I was aboard. I was the only person on the plane. The flight attendant awkwardly did her safety presentation just for me while I looked up from my "coming out notes" to validate her routine. But that doesn't seem right. I've taken that flight nearly a hundred times, and I've never been the only person on it. It strikes me that if I was, it would've been canceled. Why do I remember it that way?

I vividly remember the drive to my dad's house the night I arrived. My mom and dad, divorced for ten years, live four minutes apart—long enough to play one song. I was deliberate in my DJing: I buckled into the driver's seat of my mom's black Camry and put on Fever Ray's "If I Had a Heart."

After so much prep, I started to believe I might coast through my coming out. And maybe I was subconsciously worried that the moment I'd been dreading for years would pass by without so much as a tear. In effect, the song I picked to play for the drive was dramatic. A dull but eerie synth beat repeats and builds until a distorted voice moans with impassivity, "This will never end cause I want more. More, give me more, give me more."

Through my meticulous preparation, I recognized how my mind worked. I knew that the only way I'd remember exactly what happened is if I wrote it down after, and I knew that if it went as poorly as I expected, I wouldn't be able to.

The recording is on my old iPhone 4. The phone typically lived in a technology graveyard on the second-highest shelf of my closet, but for months I've kept it with me in my ever-present tote bag.

I've carried it to two countries and five cities, to cafés and conference rooms, to friends' homes and to hotel rooms. I charge it every few days after it dies, though I never use it. I've input my passcode just once, to make sure the voice note is still there all of these years later, that it's real.

Every night for many nights, I plan to listen.

I do everything to put myself in the mood. I light my favorite candle and take a thirty-minute shower to practice self-care. I pour a glass of wine, toast to my phone, and finish the bottle. I sit in a quiet West Village café at the bar and smile at the waiter who intuits to keep his distance; I take home a different waiter, we hook up, and I sit on my unmade bed holding my phone after he leaves; I sit alone holding my phone in the dark.

I can't create the mood because the recording isn't a song or a movie. It's a black hole.

It's Thursday night and the article was due weeks ago and I should've listened to this years ago, so I do what I did on November 3, 2011: I focus on stopping my hands from shaking and I count down from ten.

The recording starts when I'm getting out of the car, which I didn't expect. I hear the wind and the double beep of the car locking. I hear the swish of my coat as I pull it tighter around me, and the rustle of my pocket as I drop in my keys. The sounds build a clear picture of what a state of panic I was in.

The initial small talk is hard to listen to. My dad asks how I'm doing and I say OK. He asks if I took vacation to visit. He asks if my flight was cheap. I tell him I used miles. He asks how many. He is asking but doesn't ask *why am I there*? And I don't fill the long pauses between his questions.

Four minutes and thirty-five seconds of small talk awkwardly pass before he asks, "So do you want to go eat?"

"In a second, yeah."

I laugh.

Then I draw from my script, like the consummate media-trained professional I am. I tell him that I've been stressed and flew home to talk, "There's a conversation that you and I should've had a while ago. We're all growing up, and it's tough to have this conversation and it's time and—"

"You're gay?" He finishes my sentence. His voice is calm.

Five minutes and thirty-one seconds. I pause the recording, and I wish there wasn't any more because I remember.

After listening to the recording, I'm more sure that his mourning wasn't for me or us, but for some part of himself.

"Well, shit." His voice is calm.

"I don't know." I laugh uncomfortably, again.

He starts to cry. Not the quiet weep you see men do in movies about football or war. Loud, guttural sobs, that build into hysterics, and weirdly subside into something quieter and more high-pitched. He begins to sound like a child.

And then I apologize. "I'm sorry."

Six minutes and thirty-two seconds and I know I remember it all correctly: the bargaining—offering me money or therapy; the catastrophizing—that my sexuality is a disease and it will kill me; and the grief—that this was his fault, that he came to America to pursue the American Dream only to divorce from my mom and have me.

I remember how he mourned me while I sat across from him, while I stood over him, and while I followed him into the bathroom where he sobbed on the floor near the toilet, making himself sick.

I only listen for two more minutes. I can only listen to two more minutes. I remember it all correctly.

I sobbed on the drive home. I walked into my mom's house taking erratic breathes like a bike chain caught off gear.

My mom ran to hug me and I let her, but only briefly because I needed to be alone for a second.

I remember standing in front of the mirror of our laundry room with its tragic fluorescent lighting, looking terrible. I wiped at snot and tears and tried to catch my breath; I forced myself to smile.

When people ask about my background—a gay guy from Iowa with a Muslim-Palestinian dad—they almost always ask what it was like when I told him I was gay. They all assume I've told him.

"How'd he take it?"

"Not well," I demur.

When it's a full conversation I tell them my hypothesis: that my dad's emotional reaction was compounded by the fact that my telling him I was gay was like watching his American Dream crumble. I never tell people, "It felt like death," even though I think it. After listening to the recording, I'm more sure that his mourning wasn't for me or us, but for some part of himself.

He was among the first of his fourteen siblings to come to America from the Middle East. As one of the oldest siblings with a well-paid job, he led his big family. They never questioned his choices—moving to Iowa when everyone else moved to Chicago, where there was a large Muslim community, marrying a Caucasian Catholic American woman. During the thirty-nine minutes I came out to him, I watched his stubbornness fade and his confidence crumble as he questioned those decisions and every decision that came after it. Now that I'm a little older, and I've spent so much time thinking about it, I realize what I saw was a physical manifestation of regret.

After I listen to the recording, I call my dad. It's 9:49 P.M. and he is typically asleep by 10 P.M., but he seems happy to hear from me. I just saw him last weekend in New York and I'll see him again next weekend in Florida, where he is semi-retired.

I try to call him every week now that he's almost seventy-five with an excess of free time. I know he's lonely. Though single, I'm rarely alone in New York; I'm sometimes lonely for him—on behalf of him and for his company. Time—his age and mine—has muted our differences. And the destabilization of the world has steadied ours. Today's news cycle means we can speak without pauses lately.

I put my phone on speaker, set it on the coffee table, and walk away from it to get a glass of water while he talks. He's yelling about the president, who has recently bombed Syria, where today there have been catastrophic floods and famine.

I can hear him from the other room though I can barely make out the details of what he's saying. I close my eyes as he raises his voice—it somehow soothes me. I smile a little.

"Are you there? Khalid?" He uses the Arabic pronunciation of my name, which sounds nothing like how everyone else says it, but somehow I don't hear a difference.

I run back to my living room.

"Dad? I'm here."

ORIGINALLY PUBLISHED IN *HELLO MR.* ISSUE 10 IN 2018. PHOTOS COURTESY OF THE AUTHOR.

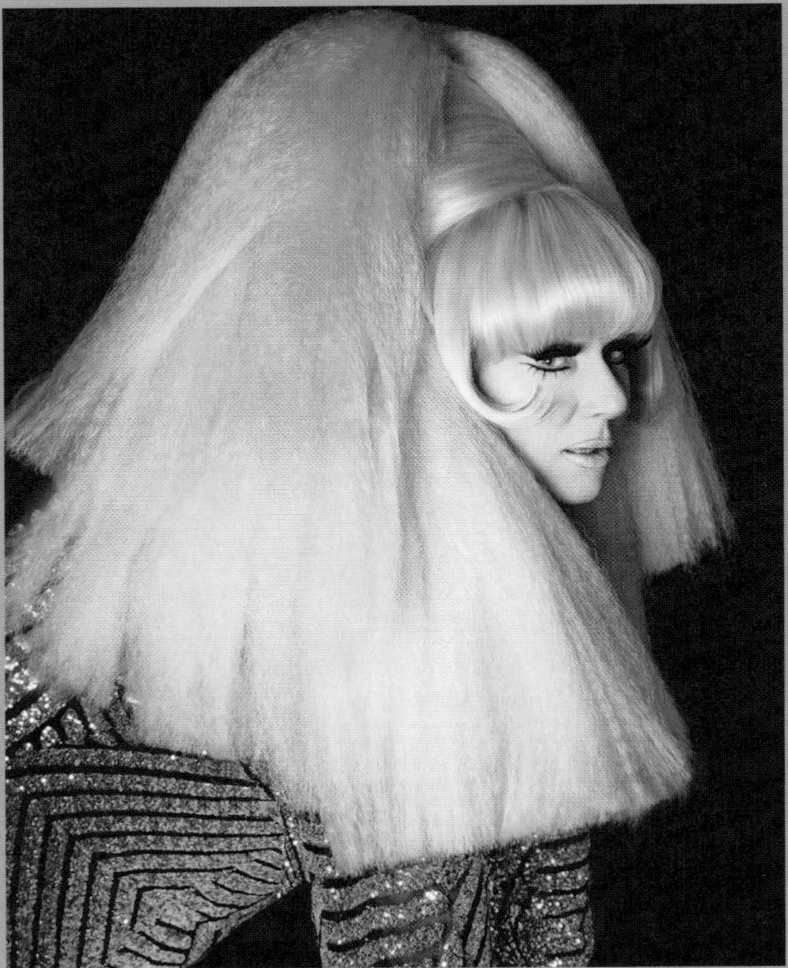

BACK TO START:

The "Lady" Bunny

Martin Belk | Photos by Billy Erb

The scene: a virtual diner, harking our younger days. Talking over veggie burgers, steaming mashed potatoes, sautéed spinach, and blueberry pancakes at three a.m. The plates are sticky. We've done this in New York, London, all over . . . late eighties, nineties, naughties . . . now.

Think: Stingy Lulu's café, Eighth Street and Avenue A, New York City. A block north of the Pyramid Club. Me, a club producer turned writer, and Jon, a.k.a. The "Lady" Bunny, a performer and now political podcaster, have been out all night. Now we're in for the morning. The coffee's gone lukewarm, the sun peeks over Tompkins Square Park. Inside—the pause, a daydream, the thirty-plus-year conversation percolates . . .

MARTIN BELK: Do you ever think of where we are now versus our slightly younger days? Like, what used to be able to happen culturally versus what can and cannot occur now?

Pause for the waiter, who fills our mugs.

LADY BUNNY: Back in the day, the community was really galvanized. If you wanted to do something, you just found a club or an open space, put up a poster, and invited friends. It either caught on, or it didn't.

MB: You mean you didn't start with an Excel spreadsheet and a business plan? What about Wigstock? How did that really start?

Sirens pass; glances out the window at a passing fire truck.

LB: Well, Wigstock started because I wanted to have a wider audience for the great drag performers and rock musicians who were regulars at the Pyramid Club, which only held about 200 to 250 people. I had just come to the city from Atlanta. I was in love with New York . . . it was full of action. It was like a much bigger version of Atlanta's few cool pockets during the early to mid-eighties. I was in heaven.

I've always organized things. Even as a ten-year-old kid in Chattanooga, I'd hang a sheet between two trees and perform these ridiculous plays I wrote. I'd basically be a ham and go 'round the neighborhood roping other kids in. I'm glad we didn't have cell phones. That type of person-to-person promotion probably wouldn't work by smartphone. But yeah, I had always been about putting on a show. So that's how Wigstock started.

Back then, it was very easy to get a fifty-dollar permit to use the Tompkins Square Park bandshell. It was also the right time, at the right place, but Wigstock was very much a product of the Pyramid Club and was funded by the Pyramid Club. It was a funky, underground club, billed as owned and operated by drag queens. It was a proving ground for people like Deelight, RuPaul, and even the band They Might Be Giants. The video director Tom Rubin, John Sex, Wendy Wild, Linda Simpson, Anohni—just tons of creative people.

Where we all felt part of something. If we wanted to try out some new act on stage, we were among our peers. Ethyl Eichelberger was a legendary drag queen who took me on and taught me how to put on fake eyelashes, which became an essential part of my look.

MB: So what's different? What's changed? What have we lost or gained?

LB: The whole process of sharing your work is different. Today people are making edited videos with props, high-quality sound, and maybe a cast and a set. Then, if you put it online and say it's not your best stuff? Well . . . you didn't really get that chance to workshop it. Because of that, a lot of work can just flop. It was very helpful for me to be in a community of performers—to see what went over well and discuss my fledgling act.

MB: There were a few places that nurtured this scene you're describing?

LB: Five blocks away was a club called Boy Bar, which featured more-polished lip-sync divas. A lot of great queens performed there. The Pyramid was like a home bar for many people, natives and new New Yorkers. And I'm not gonna, um, sugarcoat things: It was full of messy drunks on drugs, but for so many of us, it felt like we'd found our home, our community, and in some cases a job.

MB: So how does that compare, in your view, to now?

LB: Well, I think social media is an inferior form of community. Although it sure did come in handy during the COVID-19 lockdowns. But when you're in the company of others and can see people's faces, you can see the person. You can also take care of each other. If someone is too drunk to know what they're doing, you put them in a taxi home.

Back in the day we would see each other several times a week and even with the kind of "satellite people" who were only out every so often, we could look out for them. Now, I don't wanna paint us as a bunch of goody-two-shoes—there was plenty of reckless debauchery to be found—but I think it's important to connect with people in real life.

Social media is much more about "fronting"—like "here's the great vacation that I'm going on!" or "here's the fab new magazine article that I'm in!"

MB: *"Look at meee!"*

LB: I think that kind of social media posting can mask a lot of sadness, you know?

MB: It also masks a lot of expression. And nuance.

You do a wide range of gigs, from corporate at Bergdorf Goodman to tacky Pride floats, which aren't cheap. But you also go down and DJ at the Monster. Where does Lady Bunny, dare I say Jon Marc Ingle, situate himself between online noise, grass roots, or better still, the dirty curbs of Avenue A? And who's your audience? Social elites or working class?

LB: Well, "working class" as I think you mean it is more of a British term. In the US you would mean lower-middle class, or lower income-wise. My parents were solidly American middle class, not upper, not lower. My dad was a teacher, my mom was a nurse.

I've made different amounts of money at different times in my life, but I've always had a "working class" sensibility apart from my family.

MB: So by working class do you mean self-made? Self-reliant?

LB: Ish. My home has always been modest. Sometimes I make more money than what you might call working class. But living in the shadows of many towering elite cultural institutions that I find more neoliberal than liberal makes me feel more connected to the working class. But my work is expensive, a lot of overhead—and by that I mean WIGS ON MY HEAD!

Let's face it: I am self-employed, which is not that much different from a plumber, carpenter, waiter, hairdresser, or anyone else who needs to be with other people to make their living.

Drag queens can't really work from home like a lot of white-collar people can, so whether it's a lockdown or even another economic crash—*have we learned nothing since 2008?*—it hits home.

MB: I've heard that 2008 question raised in a lot of circles these days.

LB: Right? Another crash would mean people won't be going out to Lady Bunny shows—or anybody's. Longer term, you can't help but think about hardships as a senior, you know?

The waiter interrupts: "More coffee?" Bunny pauses, poised to continue . . . I may have struck a nerve.

MB: More coffee!

LB: *[inhales, not missing a beat]* I also feel very connected to the working class in that I don't mince my words and I have no time for political correctness: not in real life, not in my act.

MB: How do you define "political correctness"?

But my work is expensive, a lot of overhead—and by that I mean WIGS ON MY HEAD!

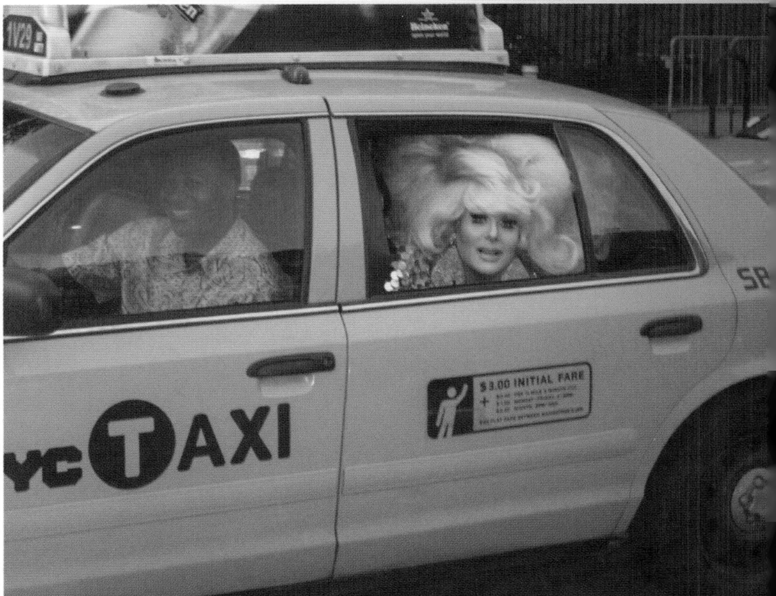

LB: Political correctness, in my view, is something that came out of elite universities, which I did not attend.

MB: There's a theory on that: Political correctness came out of a university system—whether expensive or not—that was running out of ways of attracting young people for liberal arts degrees. It keeps the student loan money flowing in . . . I think we agree that a lot of today's culture wars are a product of extreme neoliberalism and extreme neoconservatism, which are identified by many political scholars as two sides of the same violent capitalist coin.

If we rewind all the way back to twelve-year-old Jon, putting sheets between trees for a show, that indicates you have something to say. So, my question becomes: What if you put up a sheet between two trees down in Tompkins Square Park today—as the creator and producer of Wigstock that welcomed all—and these fractured people came, what would you say to them?

LB: I might ask a question. Something like: Are you not aware of which politicians want to cut Social Security, which is money taken out of our paychecks so that we aren't living in poverty when we're old? Most Republicans want to cut Social Security. Democrats are just as guilty on this front. Some regard Obama as a "saint." Others focus on wanting "the first woman president," or "first Black president," or "a president from my home state." People today can be wrapped up in a politician's identity—not their politics, policies, or their actual voting records. I didn't vote for Bernie Sanders because I'm a Jew. Or because I'm his age . . . or because I call myself a socialist. I voted for him because I do not want to see any politician undo the promise of Social Security, which I have paid into all my life.

MB: Is socialism the answer?

LB: We need a class awakening. I'm not a card-carrying socialist. I would love to have a more socialized approach to medicine, healthcare, and education. But instead, recently people have been voting for vague notions.

MB: Some of the 1960s counterculture hippies were criticized for making the mistake of forcing a scene, or "happening," just by getting a lot of people together—whether it be a show, festival, or whatever. On the other hand, a space that nurtures the soul, if you will, needs to be spontaneous. I think spontaneity motivates you—is that true?

LB: A lot of what I see today isn't spontaneous—it's people copying what they see on reality TV, and my thought is: You look great, you've spent three hours on your makeup, but you're not new or alternative. You're lip-syncing to Britney Spears or something on the radio. What's alternative or new about that? They seem to think that a Top 40 hit performed in a wacky outfit somehow becomes art.

I'm not going to put on a show that I'm not passionate about. I've had a few people tell me, "Oh girl, just cash in," but I've never wanted to showcase pedestrian drag. That doesn't need my help. That's already in every bar and every corner. Well, maybe not now, in Tennessee!

MB: Drag can be traced through Shakespearian times all the way back to the Greeks and beyond. Ancient Egypt looked pretty campy. What, say, since the age of modernity, is good drag?

LB: Drag can be *old school*, and drag can be *new school*, but drag has to have a spark and some imagination. I love Dina

Martina, who is just out of her mind and crazy. But I also love old-school, dynamite lip-sync acts. If you do it right, it can be a show-stopping act with a broad appeal.

MB: Win 'em over?

LB: If it's dynamic enough, a lip sync really can be show stopping. Of course, most drag queens lip sync because if they were to sing live they wouldn't sound like a woman.

MB: So if an old-school drag queen is lip-syncing to a popular song, what can make the appeal about the performance and not just the song? In other words, what makes a good lip sync surpass the popularity of the song itself?

LB: When I first started going to drag bars at fourteen in Chattanooga the drag queen's role was to introduce unfamiliar music. "Loving Is Really My Game" by Betty Wright was a lip-sync classic, but never a hit on the radio. Songs like "I Will Fight" by Gladys Knight, which was never really a popular hit, was big in the drag circuit because of its show-stopping vocals. Millie Jackson was another singer that was never really on the radio much, but was gold for the Black community. Queens who brought their own culture turned me on to Patty LaBelle, Melba Moore, Deniece Williams. . . . So through drag queens, I would learn dirty songs like that pussycat song I would go on to do live in New York for many, many years. We were exposed to an array of music that was not homogenized Top 40.

MB: And now?

LB: Well, the drag queens used to educate. But now, especially with the more mainstream brunch audiences? I mean, hey, an audience is an audience. The gays sit on hookup apps, and so the drag queens have got to perform something. But when you perform for a mostly straight audience at a drag brunch, the material is newer to that audience. They'll go wild tipping you if you do "Proud Mary" by Ike and Tina Turner. Now you and I both know that that number was tired, what, forty years ago?

MB: But this supports your point that the drag queens introduced you to something. And I'm adamant about the fact that when someone discovers something for the first time, it is the first time *for them*. Friends used to make each other cassette tapes as gifts, of music that spoke to them, and they shared it.

LB: *[inhales for a crescendo] HOW*-ever: there's the flip side of it.

Recently I went to a drag show in DC, having a great time with all the girls backstage, when I suddenly heard tumultuous screaming and cheering. I thought, "Oh my, this performer must be absolutely murdering this song!" So I ran out to watch.

The queen was performing a big-hit Nicki Minaj song. And she wasn't murdering it. She just had on a pink wig like Nicki and an outfit like Nicki, and she didn't look that much like Nicki. She was walking around collecting dollars. It was like seeing a drag queen become a jukebox.

MB: So that's not drag, that's costume performance?

LB: Back when MTV came out, it became a "thing" to mimic the choreography in Janet Jackson's "Rhythm Nation," or Robert Palmer's "Addicted to Love" videos—even at typically weird and eclectic places like Boy Bar. When I saw it I was like: "Wait a minute!

I don't wanna copy videos!" The drag performers I knew and liked were much better dancers and performers than in those videos. . . . *Please.*

MB: Something strange happened in the late eighties and early nineties. The "spark" you mention that came from dance music, soul, punk—voices from the aforementioned working classes—seemed to shift from "being heard," and expressed a desperation for fame. Like Dorian Corey said in *Paris Is Burning,* it was a shift from "what you can create, to what you can acquire."

LB: Well, one example comes to mind. . . . Hip-hop celebrated a fifty-year anniversary at the Grammys. Everyone was dressed in Louis Vuitton. The messages of old-school hip-hop artists like Run DMC, Nas (not Lil Nas X, but Nas), and Tupac Shakur used valid social commentary. KRS One, Public Enemy—they were protesting social situations and conditions. And then came the shift to the P Diddy ilk: *"All eyes on me in the V-I-P we're drinking Zi"*—messages of success and excess, and living the high life.

MB: If we agree this alludes to authenticity, what then grabs your attention?

LB: In Chattanooga, my favorite drag queen is a Black trans woman called Taisha Khan. She performs the Pointer Sisters' country song "Fairytale." She acts out the melancholy story of the song about leaving your love on a gut feeling.

This bitch came out in full drag, with a whole suite of luggage and just sat there on her suitcases and did this song. In CHATTANOOGA! *That* was theatric! I would rather see a queen's personal brand of creativity any day.

MB: Well, you and I sat through a couple of little off-West End plays in London recently. Was it something I really wanted to do? No. Would I go back? No, but I'd rather sit and watch a good, original effort with promise any day than to watch something totally predictable.

LB: Right. If you just copy something that everyone has seen, the audience can see how well you *copied* it. Copying things you've seen isn't imagination.

Waiter interrupts with the bill.

MB: If you think back to doing the first Wigstock, what did you come to say?

LB: It was really a simple message: Come and be entertained by me and friends; my very talented, or just insane, friends.

It was a dark time, and I was aware of all of the important work that groups like ACT UP and people like Larry Kramer were doing. I was twenty-one, and I didn't think that I had much depth or much to say, other than offsetting the grimness of AIDS, the grim days of having to fight the government, with a day of celebration. I wanted to say that we are here, we can still enjoy life, and we can still use a theme as silly as wigs to get together and have an end of summer blowout. There are people who said that it was a political statement, but honestly, that never crossed my mind.

MB: Do you ever get nostalgic and miss the days of the old Pyramid when September would cool off and you didn't have to worry about a sponsor to throw a party? Would you go back for a minute, or even start all over?

LB: Of course! Over the years, it's been amazing to get people like Dorian Corey to come down and perform, or to get some of the queens from Escala to perform alongside the crazies from the Pyramid, like Baby Gregor, Wendy Wild, Mr. Fashion, and the Broadway Queens who performed at Don't Tell Mama. Our last party was sponsored by HBO and it was wonderful to showcase people like Tabboo!, Justin Vivian Bond, Bianca Del Rio, Jinx Monsoon. And I'm so grateful a lot of queens forfeited a lot of wages just to be there. . . . Bianca cohosted the show until she literally had to jump in a cab to the airport and catch a plane. [*pauses for a look out the window*]

[The Brooklyn drag festival] Bushwig's success shows there's an appetite for a new drag festival, but because I travel so much I'm not as in touch with the New York City drag scene as I used to be. And global warming has made late August and early September difficult for outdoor festivals . . .

MB: Climate change killed the Wigstock star?

LB: Yeah . . . [laughs]

MB: If you could book a table for ten at four A.M. for a late supper and invite absolutely anyone, who would be on your guest list?

LB: Well, I would book the Cowgirl Hall of Fame, which can't be beat. I would invite Ethyl Eichelberger; Lee Bowery; Baby Gregor, who may have been a mess but embodied rock 'n' roll drag; Octavia St. Laurent; Donna Giles, a singer with an amazing set of pipes–

MB: Anyone, ya know, *living*?

LB: OK, you can come. And let's see: Dina Martina, who is just hysterically funny; Grace Jones, who is truly iconic; Gottmik; Miss Vanessa Vanjie Mateo; Briahna Joy Gray, Bernie's former press secretary and doing some of the best journalism I've seen; Nina Turner; Chris Hedges; and Glenn Greenwald. And Bianca Del Rio as the waitress.

MB: That's fifteen.

LB: I have a very big guest list.

MB: What are you watching, reading, seeing these days that you want to recommend?

LB: *Ain't No Mo!* by Jordan E. Cooper and produced by Lee Daniels, who also produced *Precious*, and which RuPaul supported. I hope it'll get revived soon. "There for You" by Monét X Change. Movies . . . *Queen Bees* with Ann-Margret, the animated film *Coco*, and *The Time of Their Lives* with Joan Collins. My all-time favorite is *The Killing of Sister George*.

I did see a great show recently about Eartha Kitt and the incident where she was invited to the White House and she read Lady Bird Johnson to filth over Vietnam. . . . It was so good to see Eartha being praised for her bravery.

I see what I can, but I think in the ongoing days of the pandemic, it's all about managing risks. This is a time for introspection; working on my own act. I guess I'm just doin' my own thing. . . .

MB: Like you always have.

FAG SCHOOL
#6 ½

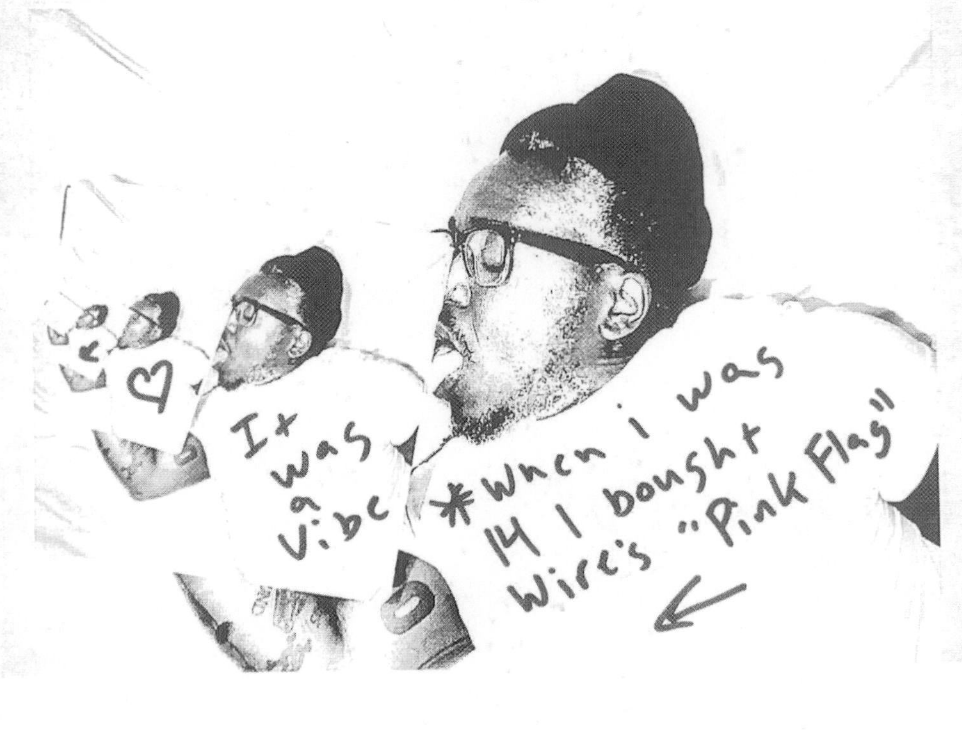

JABOUKIE

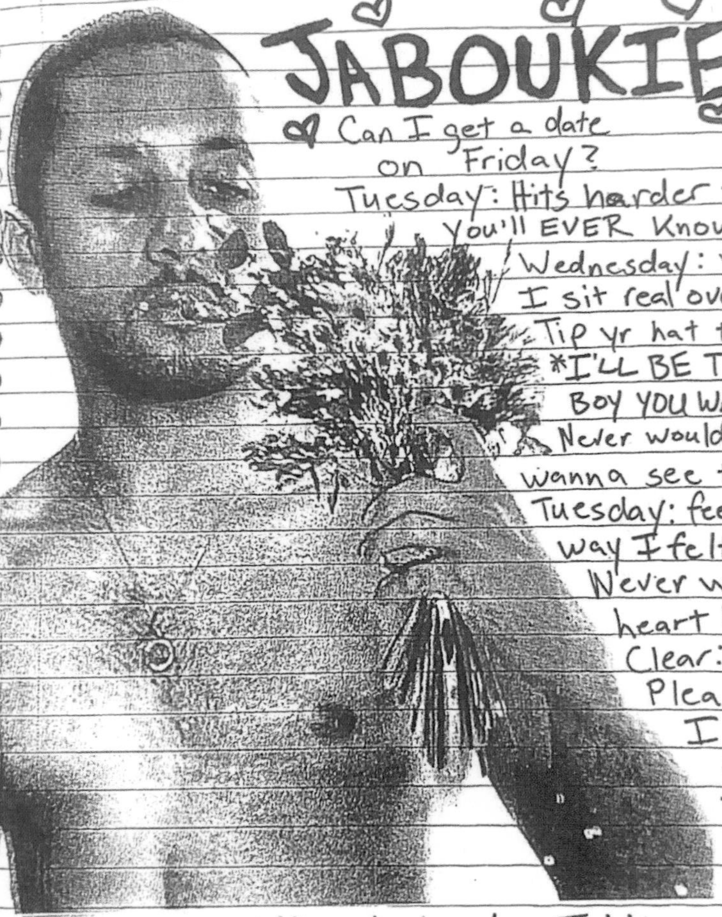

Can I get a date
on Friday?
Tuesday: Hits harder than
you'll EVER Know...
Wednesday: Yeah
I sit real over it
Tip yr hat to me
*I'LL BE THE
BOY YOU WASTED*
Never would I
wanna see the day
Tuesday: feel this
way I felt
Never would my
heart beat
Clear: so far
Please
I would
tell him
Beware:
my ♡

Beware: my Kiss. As hard as I hit some boys
I break in two. AYO- I'm yours tonight
I'm yours tonight. DO WHAT YOU WANT TO ME ♡

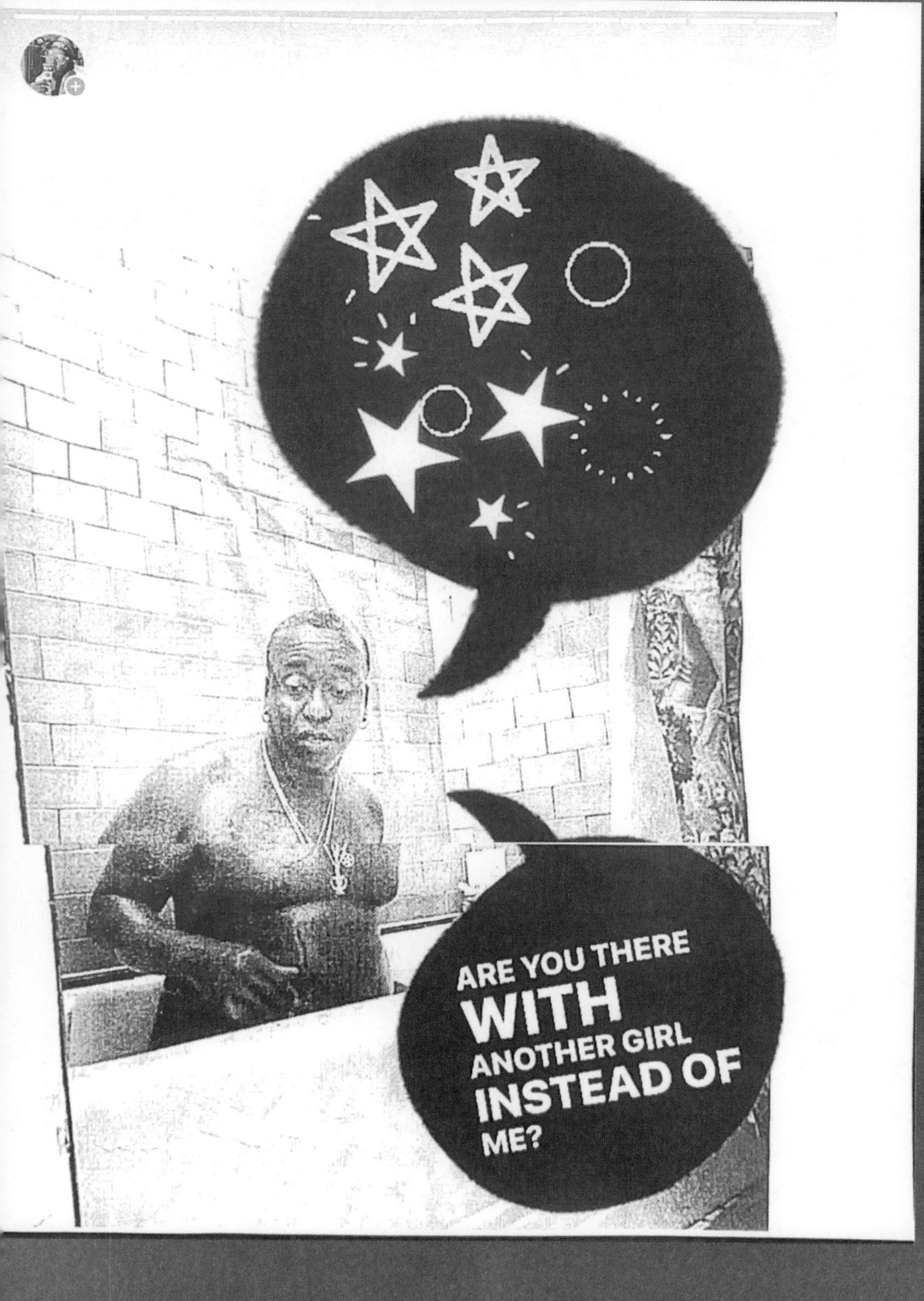
ARE YOU THERE WITH ANOTHER GIRL INSTEAD OF ME?

2:55

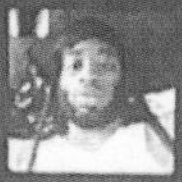

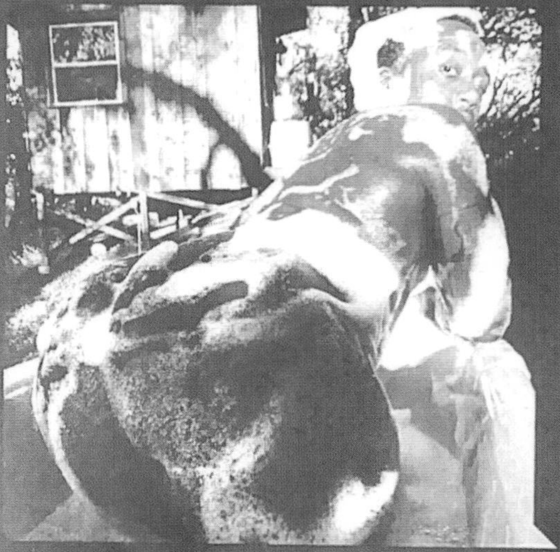

total dl here

Delivered 2:55 AM

Say something...

Aa GIF

Zine Review

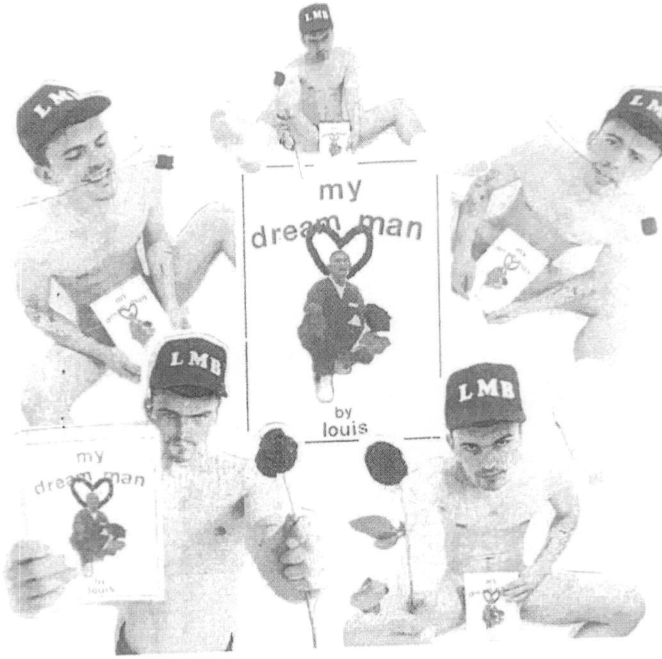

Louis is a Downtown*IT* boy & zine maker. His new zine My Dream Man" is written from is 14 year old alter ego and explores hrough found images his poetic enderings of "the perfect boyfriend" We asked him about it..

Brontez: So I'm gonna start by asking you what's your sign and how do you feel it affects your work.

Louis: I'm a Leo and I'n into the Leo fantasy Fantasy because I'm all about a um. I do believe that it kind of like rings true that Leo's like to be the center of attention. But I do think so. There's this other element of it that like isn't talked about as much about Leo's where they're very like, compassionate and like sort of thoughtful, empathetic people. And I think um. in that sense, it makes me a little bit more like romantic and in tune to things and kind of like, I romanticize like um little moments and I'm very like, um I don't know, very in small moments mean a lot to me and I can really feel them. So I like the star quality of a Leo, but I also like the sort of empathy that they also have. And I think that reads in the work.

Brontez: What was the last zine called and what was the inspiration?

Louis: it was called My Dream Man. And it was about uh basically me sitting and envisioning what it would be like for me to be 14 years old again, envisioning sort of my dream man at that time, only knowing like the world around me and sort of um. an idealized version of love and romance without any real tangible experience with relationships. So it's like the fantasy of young love

Brontez: and you explore it through kind of found a lot of sound image, right?

Louis: yeah, totally. I spent a lot of time kind of going through the thralls of the internet and kind of and googling places like the mall where I grew up and things that were um that felt like at that age when I was like 14 or like a young teenager or Tween were very sort of like um. very like, what's the word? It's kind of like, um it's like. they felt very like real to me, like text messages, fake text messages between like a boyfriend and a girlfriend that are like, I love you baby and I'm never gonna leave you no matter what happens and these things felt like they were what represented a relationship when I was young and they're just sort of like delusional ideas of what love and romance is kind of blind, you know? Oh my God. I think that, uh, my idea of what love is has completely shifted and I think that happens with a lot of people. Like, once you have some real world experience, it's obviously like when you're, when you're dreaming about it as a child, you don't understand the harder parts of it and the parts of it that maybe aren't so um. that aren't so like savory or like so fun and great. And I do think as I've gotten older actually, within the last two years. this is the first time in my life that I've gotten more attuned to like who I am as a person, I would say like in a sense, um. I'm not my own dream man, like in a, in a perfect world. I'd like to believe there is still some sort of fantasy man who's gonna be everything that I ever want. But I know that probably won't ever exist. But I've learned very much to be ok with being on my own and not try to find like purpose or identity or like meaning through somebody else. And now I know that there's not gonna be anybody who will ever complete me. But I would like to find somebody who can. accentuate the person who I already am. You know what I mean? Like I feel like I have learned that I am my dream man in the sense of like um. like I'm the one I need in my life and then if I can find a hot guy to come along with it, that's fierce, you know.?

Malcolm Betts

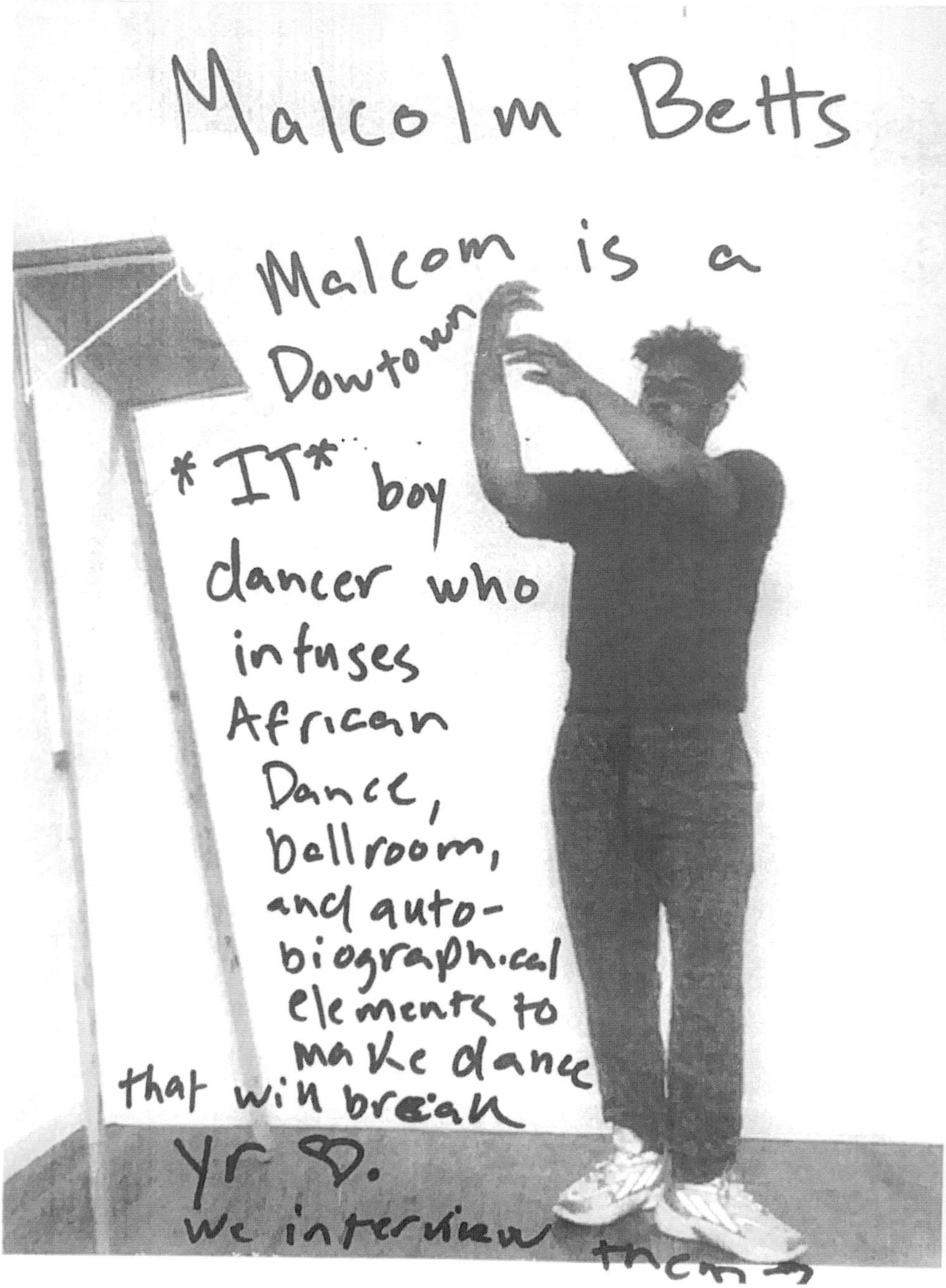

Malcom is a Dowtown *IT* boy dancer who infuses African Dance, ballroom, and auto-biographical elements to make dance that will break yr ♡.

We interview them →

BRONTEZ: OK. Can you hear me? Hello? Can you hear me? Yeah. Yeah, I hear you. Ok, cool. Um So we're gonna jump right into it. What's your sign and how does it affect your work?

MALCOLM: Um I'm a Virgo. Um I think now it affects my work of like trying to show up on time and I guess some sometimes like having to um. yeah, I guess how I'm intention of facilitating space and my practices and. yeah, also, yeah, in ways like open to things but also like close in other ways. I hear that.

BRONTEZ: How did you start dancing?

MALCOLM: Um I started like, I like my love of dance. It started out like dance. I'm from Harlem. So like kind of like dancing with block parties and like, I guess just my earlier memories of like connection with dance like was kinda under this like social dance of just um yeah, like social dance and kind of like the collective of block parties. Um. And then I started. um I was on the hip hop dance team also, like, but afterwards I took like a break and I started doing West

African. and then um I think that's when I started making my improvisational work. um more like improv, but it's always like, in this like context of like, I guess, challenging hypermasculinity within my body of life that like, kind of shows up, I guess as far as like, um I guess being inspired by those like hip hop movements and how I can, like, break out on the phone somehow and like it improvisational practice. Um. But yeah, no, I'm just like a improvisational dancer or. um tell me about your last dance show as a Judson. um That was *** at sundown. So um. I guess I was like, interested in um Yeah, I guess I'm just always interested in like, visibly being visibly black and also, like, creating um like, I like research, like Ash Crowley is one of my favorite authors and like, I was like, playing with his tech for like two years about um it was called the Black Pentecostal Breath, but he talks about like. creating like other world possibil otherwise possibilities of like um. just alternative modes of like um being violent and like being a system of violence. Um So I'm always like, thinking of that. So I guess now I'm like, interested in um. I guess kind of like lively critiquing the institution or kind of like, um. yeah, just like, I know a lot of my, I guess entry points come into like, these like, forms of like childhood play and like humor. So, like, kind of like, I would say, thinking of like a stand up act but like kind of like critiquing who's in the room and playing off that. And then um. yeah, again, it was like, he like physically wise, physicality of like kind of just like moving through these very, like hyper, I mean, hyper masculine like movements and like investigating that. Um I like to call it like experimental Crump thing. Um I guess it was also like a clothes design element where like, I kinda like imagine that the costumes um that I like die in pain or like kind of like scores or like traces in the body. Um But there's like, yeah, so that's what I was like, kind of like thinking about it and I guess like the intimacy among like a duet and like two black men is always just like um. I guess something that like, I always like rub it against are like, I guess trusting their consent or like trusting that no one's gonna get hurt or injured or. um. but yeah, I guess I called it like *** at sundown me because I guess I was like, honestly like thinking about like sundown towns and like the history of that and how like, I guess most. um queer men are like, not, I'm not speaking for a queer men but like most like our um points of liberation and freedom is in this night life. So kinda like playing with that also with the, like, slow in the dark and like the lighting. What does it? Yeah. What does it mean to? Yeah, just shift those and play with those different things. Um. But yeah, I'm always, yeah. Did I answer your question? I feel like no, you completely did.

NEW YORK

DREAM BABY PRESS

DREAMBABYPRESS@GMAIL.COM

ALL THESE CATS HAVE AIDS

Jason Villemez

The story of Hugo and I, as much as the world might wish it different, is this.

We met in 1973 at a bar called the Monster, when I was twenty-five and he was twenty-nine. He loved that my name is Winston because Churchill was one of his idols. I'd moved to New York the previous year, eager to see what the burgeoning gay movement was all about. Hugo had been in the city for five years and loved every minute of it. He laughed every chance he got, and I found his joy mesmerizing. He told me stories about the sanitation strike and mountains of garbage, about the Pride parades that stretched down Fifth Avenue as far as the eye could see. I told him that he made the city sound magical, and he said that was the highest compliment I could give him. We fucked when we got back to my place. It wasn't my first time with a man, but it was the first time I thought it was OK, the first time I felt no need to jump in the shower after. He fell asleep in my bed so quickly, I could have sworn he was my brother, or my child.

Hugo was stubborn as hell. I liked that about him. One summer afternoon, years after we'd moved in together, we were listening to records in our apartment on Avenue C. We put on the portable fan because it was vengefully hot and our landlord refused to replace our window unit. He said we must have broken it, so we should fix it ourselves. We knew gay people who'd been evicted for the most ludicrous reasons—having mildew in their bathrooms, keeping flower pots on their balconies—so we didn't push the issue. The fan puttered even on the strongest setting. I told Hugo to splash some water on his face to make the air feel cooler. Or I could kiss him all over. He always liked when I did that.

He said he had a better idea and went off to the kitchen. I stuck my head out the window, searching for any hint of a breeze. A minute later Hugo returned with a metal bowl filled with ice and placed it under the fan. The air bounced off the bowl and hit him in the face, blowing back his curly brown hair. "Like a January wind," he said.

We took sleep when we could. Sometimes we'd go days without a solid few hours. The worst was when the phone rang early in the morning and we had to greet the day with the news that someone else had died. It was always cruel, not knowing who'd be next. We had lists in our heads of the people worse off, the ones who'd been sick the longest. We lived in the land of the worst-case.

We had our own problems, too. Hugo had prolonged bouts of diarrhea. At night he'd moan hollowly, his voice hoarse because of his dry mouth, and it wouldn't be until morning that he'd exhaust himself enough to drift off for a few minutes. I always made sure to slip out from the covers as smoothly as possible, to avoid the creakiest floorboards, and keep my belt buckle from clinking when I put on my pants.

My main goal back then was to hold it together at work, then let it all out at home. After I got fired from the insurance company, I found a job managing the office of a nonprofit that gave free legal services to LGBT people. They'd tried to help me get my job back, but when that didn't pan out, they hired me instead. Most of the time people called because they'd been entrapped or discriminated against at work. I helped keep their information organized and assigned lawyers to each case. My salary wasn't much, but I didn't need a lot since Hugo made enough for the both of us. When he was in college he'd wanted to be a lawyer, but his gift for friendly discourse led him to advertising sales, and then, when he learned it was more interesting selling people than selling objects, to public relations. I didn't care for such glitz, but I loved that he loved it.

The lawyers at my job worked at liberal firms, but even so, I was always surprised that they were allowed to do their "pro-homo pro-bono." A few of the highest earners covered the office expenses and salaries for myself and the office assistant, Janice, a gentle woman who could coax even the most shameful secrets out of people. She and I would often joke that one of our clients would eventually make it big, really big, like Freddie Mercury, and they'd take care of us. They'd buy us a place to live and provisions to last a lifetime. We'd never have to work again.

The other day, I received a letter from a high school student doing a book report. He'd come across an old article about Hugo in *The Advocate*, and he wanted to write about gay militants. The boy said he'd never written to a prisoner before, and as he was writing he felt a newfound excitement.

It's been thirty years since we did it. I've gotten a lot of letters in that time, and I respond as often as I can. I answer people's questions and debunk the untruths, but mostly I just tell them who I am and who Hugo was. Somehow, the news reports always seemed to miss that part. The boy said that writing to me felt forbidden and secretly fun. None of his classmates would be quoting someone like me for their projects. He asked if Hugo and I knew we would alter the course of history, if that was what drove us. I told him that we were not gay militants. We were not liberators; we were not ones to be celebrated. When we did it, we didn't know what would happen in five, ten, twenty years. All we wanted was not to die, and we did whatever we could to make that happen.

The first year HIV/AIDS was reported in the media, nobody knew what to call it. GRID, CAID, ACID, AID. The gay plague. Even in 1987, as we sat sweltering in our apartment, long after the illness had an actual name, most media still called it gay cancer. The younger gays who thought they were invincible called it that. And that pissed Hugo off to no end.

We needed to grab people by the scruff of the neck and hold them in front of us. My first idea was a giant art installation of works painted with HIV-positive blood. Then I read in *National Geographic* that cats have lived with a similar virus for centuries, so I thought we might set up a petting zoo with the banner *All These Cats Have AIDS*. Then I wondered why we couldn't just get someone famous to speak out for us, someone who could convince the masses that we weren't a threat. Hugo looked at me like I knew nothing of the world.

According to him, we needed to be aggressive. We needed to get the publishers and TV producers on our side. We needed to seduce them, get their blood beating at the inhumanity of it all. We needed to remind them that all people, men and women, gay and straight, were susceptible. It wasn't just us. He said this to me every night as he got dressed for his fundraisers and black-tie galas. One night, he returned around ten, perfectly sober, a bounce in his step.

"A friend of mine said Mayor Koch is finally going to come out. Do you know what this'll do for the community?"

"I'll believe it when I see it, darling."

He gave me a quick kiss and went to change into his jogging clothes.

I could rarely keep pace with him when he ran, but I needed to tell him what had happened at work. He told me how glad he was that I'd chosen to tag along. It was so rare he got a running buddy. He had a colleague who often joined him on weekends, but when Hugo asked him, one afternoon, what he thought about Reagan's AIDS policy, the man looked at him strangely and then never accompanied him again.

We ran up the West Side Highway, past the piers, past the meatpacking district and the homeless enclave of street kids and drag queens. We'd seen some of them before, hustling at the bars, hoping to get lucky with a closeted man because discretion came with a surcharge. We turned onto 80th Street and headed into Central Park to avoid the cars and red lights. I told him about the call I'd received at work that day.

A gay man named Desmond Morris was assaulted by a pair of cops. They'd halted him on Bleecker Street and asked for identification, and when he said that he'd left his wallet at home, that he was just going to the corner store to buy a sandwich, they laughed and said he must be dying for some sausage. It wasn't until after they beat him, after he'd been carted to the hospital and treated for a fractured skull, that the cops discovered he had HIV. The pair of them, straightlaced Irish boys from Red Hook, went into hysterics, stalked him outside his home, cut his phone line, until they were convinced to launch a criminal lawsuit, assault with a deadly weapon, and advised to stop talking to the press. One of our lawyers had volunteered to take the case, but his boss played golf with the chief of police and forced him to withdraw.

Hugo ran faster. It was impossible to keep pace, so I relented after a few yards and stopped at a water fountain while he sprinted down the path. *Good*, I thought, *get the rage out now, when nobody was watching.*

"Show-off," I said when I caught up to him. He bent down to re-tie his shoelaces.

"I want to speak with this guy Morris myself," he said. He often donated his PR services for community events, but he'd never taken on something as controversial as this. "Screw the lawyers. For now, let's show him someone has his back."

As we ran out of the park, we passed a trio of cops outside an office building. They shouted something at us, but we didn't stop to look back. A few blocks later, they simply weren't there anymore.

A week later, Hugo and I visited Desmond Morris at Rikers Island. A bruise prickled under his left eye and he had stitches down the side of his cheek. He sat up straight. His build reminded me of all the football players I'd crushed on in high school but never had the nerve to speak to. He had a deep voice. He looked like he could fight. Why the cops chose him, out of all the people in the West Village, was perplexing.

"I *wish* they'd gotten infected," he said from across the table. "I could have taken them, if I'd just fought back."

"How'd you get those marks on your face?" Hugo asked. He wore one of his best suits. People probably thought that he was a lawyer and I his paralegal. We took notes on yellow pads that I'd swiped from the office.

"Oh, you know, bricks, lead pipes, toothbrushes."

Hugo cringed. Unlike most of us, he had never been beaten up. Not even a schoolyard brawl. His charisma shielded him from most trouble. He could have won over anyone, varsity players, class presidents, prom kings. Yet Hugo looked at Morris with such tenderness, as if he'd gone through the exact same thing. He'd stepped into Morris's boat and was using all his limbs to plug the holes.

"I know a guy who's friendly with the warden," Hugo said. "We can get you into solitary confinement."

"Absolutely not. I don't want special treatment. I won't give them another reason to single me out."

"Morris," I said, "we'll get you a good lawyer. But you have to take care of yourself until then. You need an ally in here. If people see that, they might leave you alone."

"And I'll talk to the press." Hugo's voice was calm, measured, as if he were holding a pack of cutthroat reporters at bay. "But for now, you have to keep yourself safe."

Morris scoffed at us.

"Doesn't matter what cell I'm in. People keep saying I'm a child molester." He stared at the floor. "I can stand up for myself, but there's not much room when it's five on one."

I looked around at the other inmates. Most were talking to women, their wives or girlfriends or mothers. They all wore the same beige jumpsuits. I wondered what a straight man would do if he found himself in a prison full of angry gays who wanted him dead or, worse, infected. I would have watched that TV show. Hugo jotted something on his pad, but when I looked closer it was only scribble. He always kept a pen with him to take down phone numbers, but oftentimes he merely used it to doodle, to give his hand something to do while his brain mulled things over.

Suddenly, Hugo reached across the table and took Morris's hand, just held it tight like a friend would do. One of the guards came over and hovered near us, but Hugo didn't let go. That's all it would take, I thought, a single handshake between someone important and someone like Morris. Put that on the front page of the papers, and we would have had a tide of goodwill, an unflappable burden of proof to those nurses who refused to draw blood, those caretakers who refused to nourish the enfeebled, the parents who refused to hug their dying sons. Imagine if the President had shaken the hand of an AIDS patient. It would have buoyed us for years.

We left the prison and took a taxi back home. Hugo had meetings and I had cases that needed attending. But something about that ride stuck with me, something about Hugo, the way he smelled, the way he held my hand tighter than normal in the space between our legs. Frustration, desperation, hope. I wondered what he'd concocted in those heavy moments of silence.

There's an advocacy group that keeps sending me letters. They want to represent me and try to get my sentence reduced. Even if they got one life sentence commuted, there's still the other one. I don't bother writing them back. Some of what they write is true. We were trying to protect our community, and it's true that I wasn't anywhere near the ballroom at the time. But the idea that I'm not as culpable as Hugo is a lie. I was just as angry and just as desperate; I wanted revenge on those who hurt us. And I did nothing to stop him, which, in my mind, is the real reason I deserve to be here. I could have done any number of things that night. I could have locked Hugo in our bedroom. I could have called one of the civil rights groups to talk some sense into him. I could have told him, simply, please, don't do this. I love you.

Morris was killed a week after Hugo and I spoke with him. Pushed down the stairs or knifed or hung from a rafter. Take your pick. We never learned the real cause. The newspapers reported only that a fight had broken out in the jail yard. I'm sure the people who did it knew Morris had HIV. They probably thought he deserved to die like that, alone on a cold, dirty floor. Hugo was the one who told me. He came unannounced into my office, dabbing his eyes with the cuffs of his shirt. Janice poured him a cup of tea and sat with him by the windowsill. I returned to my desk to finish up a phone call about a bribery case. Hugo held the mug to his lips, hands trembling. I'd never seen him so unsettled.

The two cops spoke at a press conference and said that while they would have liked Morris to have his day in court, they felt safer knowing that such a dangerous person was no longer a threat. They smiled, waved to the crowd, and that was the front-page photo on all the papers the next day. I tacked it to the wall and we doodled all over it. We drew a dick in one of their mouths and gave the other one a giant swastika tattoo. Then we burned it and sprinkled the ashes out the window, a little black snow for the summer day.

This was around the time that Hugo got a cough he couldn't kick. We spent a few weeks thinking he had a summer flu and I'd catch it soon. But I never had anything wrong with me. We'd shared so many fluids that we thought that as long as I was OK, Hugo was OK, too. But when his coughing turned bloody, I told him that he needed to see a doctor. I knew of a few clinics that had continued to treat gay men even as the crisis worsened. People often called my office asking for referrals. As we looked around in the waiting room, at men who were more bruise than skin, Hugo whispered to me that if it were him, he would never leave like that. He would die beautifully, without a smudge. I promised to help him with the makeup.

We resumed our lives as best we could. Hugo kept a cadre of black handkerchiefs in his suit pocket and got good at wiping his lips without giving anything away. To all his straight friends he had only a terrible cough. They told him it was fine, that something was going around and he shouldn't worry. They offered him lozenges.

People forgot about Morris. We put up a memorial in Sheridan Square but it got rained on and ruined after a week. The flowers were pilfered and put in people's hair or redistributed to the other memorials dotting the streetlamps. Hugo tried to get the *Village Voice* to write an obituary but got turned down by the senior editor.

"They're all homophobes," he said, "they're no better than the *New York Post*."

"Why don't you write something," I said. "We could print it up and distribute it around the streets like they did in the early days, before Stonewall, before faxes. We could give copies to a motorcycle gang and offer free beer for every twenty fliers they hand out. They'd plaster the village in no time."

He laughed and pinched me. We put the plates in the sink, switched off the lights, and made a quick retreat to the bedroom. We put on a Cat Stevens record and shed our clothes, making a silent pledge to not let anyone or anything ruin our evening. We held each other and danced skin to skin, and when I put his legs up onto my shoulders, he requested we stay that way forever.

When I woke the next morning Hugo wasn't in bed. He wasn't in the apartment. He'd left no note. It wasn't unusual for him to leave earlier than me, but he always kissed me goodbye or, if I was still asleep, left a message on the counter. I wondered if I'd get a phone call from the precinct and have to bail him out as I'd done many times for friends who got too friendly with an undercover cop or had their pants down during a bathhouse raid. But when I got home from work there he was, sitting on the couch in his suit, legal pad on his lap, hand covered in ink.

"I'm going to do something," he said. "And I need your help."

Hugo always was the brave one.

I grew up in a conservative Catholic town. My general fear—of retribution both earthly and divine—compelled me to follow the rules. I attended Bible school every Saturday, church every Sunday. I remember the priests and their booming voices, their achingly good gifts for manipulation. I remember them shouting that bad things happen to those who do bad, and even the smallest offenses were damnable. I didn't want to be thrown into the abyss. But, as Hugo told me his plan in between fits of coughing and holding his ribs in pain, I realized we were already there, swimming around in a cold, dark hole.

The Joseph Clark Memorial Dinner was, and still is, an annual white-tie gala for Catholic charities. The ballroom at the Wortham Hotel is dolled up with red and white flower arrangements. The mayor, the chief of police, and the publishers of the major papers all attend. The Archbishop plays host. A church secretary arranges the place cards and a massive stage is erected for the notable guests to look down from their perch. Invitations are difficult to come by, and they were always expensive, so I wondered why Hugo took such sudden interest.

"The cops that attacked Morris are being recognized. They'll be sitting at the head table, right near the stage." He handed me a copy of the press release. His hands were sweaty, his fingernails chewed down. I skimmed the paper.

"Sounds perfect for ACT UP," I said. "Maybe they can lay on the floor in protest, like they did in that church."

"Come on, sweetheart. We've got to go bigger, bolder." He waved his fingers like the falling embers of a firework.

"How about let's figure out what to have for dinner before we change the world."

He laughed, kissed me, and went to the bedroom to find something more comfortable to wear. I took a closer look at the press release, at the sentence "In recognition of their work protecting Americans against the gay plague," and reminded myself that people had gotten it all wrong. We were not the enemy. We were nothing to fear. And yet, we still received such vast, misplaced hate, as if we were an army that had slaughtered millions without prejudice. I told myself, on particularly hard days, that it was all beyond my understanding. It was easier to not even try to comprehend.

After dinner, we needed to get out of the house. It was a Friday night, still hot as hell. Hugo suggested we go to the Duplex. We hadn't been to Christopher Street in a while, and a night out with drinking and dancing sounded like a perfectly civilized form of release. My office had been flooded with calls that week about people being dumped in the street because morgues wouldn't store them and funeral homes wouldn't bury them and crematories wouldn't burn them. Their passage had been denied. There was no ferryman in sight. I was exhausted.

Hugo spent an hour searching his closet for an outfit. He'd lost thirty pounds in a month. He came out and modeled a pair of bell-bottoms I'd never seen before. "Wore these when I was twenty-one," he said, "before I discovered pastrami." The pants still swallowed him, but I took two butterfly clips and pinched the sides like clamshells. We could cover them up with a long shirt or a belt or whatever struck his fancy. He plucked an army-green denim jacket and draped it over his shoulder, James Dean-style.

"Dashing," I said. "Now you've just got to slick your hair back and find a criminally fast car. Let's go, partner."

I put on a plaid shirt and jeans. Most of my clothes came from thrift stores like Goodwill, and I enjoyed the idea that they had been worn by others before me and I was adding to their history. I didn't pay attention to the latest fashions. I cared only for comfort. Unlike Hugo, I didn't have to worry about what people thought of my appearance. I didn't need people to remember me.

At the Duplex, the entrance hallway spilled out into a large area, like the state of Oklahoma. Near the door you got all the smells of the city, whatever happened to be wafting by, but in the main space it smelled like polished wood and perfume and dried gin. Oftentimes a bartender or another brave soul would stand at the window and perform Donna Summer, The Bee Gees, the latest show tunes. Sometimes the Broadway crowd showed up after work and gave impromptu solos. I knew some of them through work. Several shows were forced to close when their actors and crew died of AIDS. We tried our best to get them new work, to point them toward people who wouldn't flinch at their touch, but most of the time we failed.

Hugo got us seats across from the piano and I brought us some whiskeys. His stomach did better with whiskey than gin or vodka, and he sipped so slowly that by the time he finished he was drinking mostly water anyway. We said hello to a few people we'd known from the neighborhood. A few times we marveled that so-and-so was still alive, like a far-removed uncle who sends Christmas cards every five years.

A man walked to the microphone. His face was pale and he had heavy black liner around his eyes. He wore a motorcycle jacket and carried himself with the confidence of a performer. He didn't say his name. After a dramatic silence, the man hushed the piano player and started to sing alone, and then I remembered who he was: one of the actors in *Cabaret*. We hadn't seen it. Friends of mine had loved the movie, loved the novel it was based on. But I couldn't bring myself to imbibe anything that rang too true to life. No James Baldwin, no Edmund White, no Armistead Maupin. The gay guys so rarely wound up happy, and I already knew enough about loss. When the man finished his number he took a seat at the bar. I walked up to him and touched his shoulder. I said I loved the song. It must have been fun to star on Broadway.

"It's a routine," he said. "Like any job."

"You're in a hit show. You get applause every night. How many guys can say that about their job?"

"True." He stared at the floor and lit a cigarette. "People love watching a good genocide."

"But do you think they would have fought back if they could?" I asked. "The characters in the show."

"An uprising of deviant whores? Not a chance. They wouldn't fight."

"You mean they're not strong enough?"

He shook his head. "You miss the point. They don't care enough about themselves to stay alive. Deep down, they believe they deserve it."

I didn't say anything, and without looking at him again I walked back to Hugo. I couldn't acknowledge what he had just said. I refused to allow it any more air.

We watched the next singer, and the one after that. When Gloria Gaynor came on the speakers, we stood up and sang along. Around two thirty the bar emptied out. We ambled down Tenth Street, past the NYU kids smoking weed from their windows, past the Fifth Avenue condominiums and neon-lit bodegas, past the drunks splayed on front stoops and the lovers sitting on fire escapes with their feet dangling down. We paid them no mind. We had nothing more to say.

Somebody had to write the story, Hugo told me.

I'd begged to accompany him, but he shot me down without hesitation. Somebody needed to tell people what happened, to explain why. But we agreed that when the time came, I would walk him through the hotel lobby, stay with him until he went upstairs, and send him off with a smile. That was non-negotiable.

On the day of the memorial dinner we played a record in the apartment. We picked at the loose threads on the couch and we talked about the night we spent riding the Staten Island Ferry, staring at the lunar eclipse and making fools of ourselves as we howled at the sky. We were always different at night, more fun, more free. It was easy to become someone else, to slip through blackened doors and emerge among friends, to get a rush from a bare fingertip grazing your body. At night, we knew who we were.

If someone had told me that eight years later there would be drugs that could keep people alive for decades, that there would be evidence showing our touch was harmless, that people in real power would be rallying for us—if I'd known all that then yes, of course I would have told Hugo not to do it.

He'd gotten a few sarcomas on his neck and one on his forehead. They looked like islands, like New Zealand or England or Japan, and every week it seemed a brand new country bubbled up atop his flesh. They made him appear suspicious. People would look at his skin and wonder what was wrong. It was plausible that someone in the audience would know he had AIDS and call him a demon. We'd already bought him a smaller suit to wear because of the weight he lost. Now we needed to cover him up.

I got some makeup and an applicator at Macy's. The salesgirl thought it curious that I was buying different skin tones. She said my wife couldn't possibly be that many colors. I laughed and told her that we all change. The truth was that I didn't know which shade would look the most natural on him, so I bought ten. We couldn't have him looking patchwork. In a ballroom of white-tie tuxedos and thousand-dollar gowns, he needed to blend in completely.

Hugo sat on our bed and I dabbed the foundation on the sponge like children's paint. I lined up all the different colors and searched for the one that matched, the stripe that would render the best camouflage. We decided on 25C, cool beige. I traced around his eyes, down the ridge of his nose and the circumference of his lips, across his neck. I glammed him up like a rock star headlining Webster Hall. Hugo didn't speak the entire time. He just sat there silently, smiling, moving only when the pressure of sitting was too much for his tailbone. When I finished he looked happy and bright, as if no time at all had passed since our first date. He was twenty-seven again, chatting with me in the bar of the Townhouse, full of joy.

"Remember to do what I told you," he said while he checked himself in the mirror. "Get out of the hotel as soon as I head up to the ballroom. Leave the city, lay low for a while."

I came up from behind and held him. I kissed his ear. "Of course, darling," I whispered. "Sly as a fox. Stealthy as a ninja. They'll never find me."

I put my head on his shoulder. We stayed like that for a moment.

"Be honest," he said. "Do I look believable?" He turned and reached out for a handshake, like he was meeting a new client. His hand was cold, too cold, even for October. I rubbed it like I was rolling dough, like I was trying to light a fire with twigs.

"I'll keep them in my pockets," he said.

"You'll be all right with the vest on. It'll warm you up." It was on the bed next to a pack of cigarettes and lighter. It took us a month to secure all the materials, then a week to sew the pockets in all the right places. Remember, this was the eighties. Nowadays I have no doubt that we would have been caught in a few hours. But if we'd been planning this today, that would have meant we'd both survived, and I would serve any sentence if that were true.

The lobby of the Wortham smelled like verbena. Tourists walked the hallways, staring up at the chandeliers and the carved ceilings. Women carried their purses in one hand and their drinks in the other. Men smoked cigars at the bar. I saw a family of four walking side by side, the boy in blue and girl in pink.

Hugo's cheeks glowed as he passed under the chandeliers. We didn't hold hands as we walked and I'm glad we didn't. I have no idea what he was thinking. If it were me, I would have wanted to be alone with my thoughts. I would have pulled my body along while my mind drifted elsewhere. I wouldn't have wanted a long, tearful goodbye. I'd want to make peace with my decision and do it quickly.

A few people waved at Hugo and he waved back, said hello, and did everything he could to be charming. He always liked conversations and simple pleasantries, so I'm sure he felt at ease. Through all of this—the illness, the fear, the hate—he still loved hearing stories about people who'd made it big in art or business or politics. Even more, he loved the stories of the people behind the celebrities, the kingmakers we never knew existed.

More guests arrived. We didn't linger. We didn't want anyone to have a chance to talk with Hugo at length, to appraise his suit coat or his cufflinks or his shiny shoes. We couldn't chance someone seeing a flaw in the makeup I'd applied, or the four stitches I'd added to the top of his shirt to help the vest fit underneath. It would be a success if he simply got into the room, took his seat, and faded into the background. If that happened, we'd be home free.

I couldn't kiss him goodbye; I couldn't hug him like a friend at the airport, a friend I wouldn't see for a long, long time. But nobody we knew got a proper goodbye. It felt right that we wouldn't get a grand farewell either, nor did we have the time to worry about our end. So all I did when we got to the elevators was turn to him, smile, and wave as if I'd passed him on the street but had no time to stop. He took his place in line, behind a woman in a lush taffeta gown, and I continued down the hallway, looking for a place to sit, willing myself not to turn back.

When I was nineteen, I got a draft notice. Many of my classmates had already died in Vietnam. Men my age were among the first to get called. I didn't believe in the war, but I wasn't about to spend my life in Canada as a traitor. I would do what I was told. I went to my appointment as scheduled. I spoke with a gray-haired officer about my life. I told him that I grew up in Virginia Beach and my father was a fisherman. I said I'd known plenty of soldiers and I respected their heroism. I said I was proficient at violin and at the typewriter. I didn't play any sports, but I could run as fast as anyone in my gym class. The officer led me into a big room sectioned off with white curtains. I sat on an exam table and stared at the vision chart across from me. A while later a doctor entered and asked that I undress. When I was younger I always felt shamed at disrobing in front of the pediatrician. I thought that I needed such cover to maintain the boy I pretended to be, the boy who flirted with girls, the boy who did nothing wrong. I thought that if someone looked at me naked, I wouldn't be able to hide.

The man shined a flashlight on my face. Fine. He pressed his hands hard against my lower back then reached around and prodded my stomach. Fine. He asked me if I felt any pain and I said I felt nothing. He placed the stethoscope on my ribs and asked me to breathe deeply, then normally, then to exhale and hold it. He asked me to do it again. He wrote some things down onto the paper and said I could dress. When I returned to the officer he said I was free to leave. There had been an erratic beat in my chest, an abnormality that refused to behave. He gave me a pamphlet and said there were other ways to serve. There would be no war for me.

I stood on the street, feeling for my pulse and trying to understand what I'd done wrong. It started to rain. I took shelter under a bus stop, but with no money in my pocket and no end to the deluge in sight, I gave up waiting and walked back to my dorm room. I toweled off and began my lessons for the week, resuming a life that was, as I always learned, completely out of my control.

I wish I could have seen the ballroom. I'm sure people experienced different things. To one person in the crowd it might have been a Molotov, another might have seen a crashing stage light, a table buckling. If a person had knowledge of demolition, or coal mines, or a war zone, perhaps they could have correctly gauged that it was an explosion caused by dynamite. But I'm sure, in the heat of such a moment, that even the most battleworn among them had trouble finding the truth.

I don't know exactly how much time passed between leaving Hugo at the elevators and the security guard sprinting down the lobby. I told Hugo I'd immediately return home, but I felt compelled to stay, to have at least a glimpse of what he'd done. The stairwell doors flung open. People emerged, shouting at each other, tripping over the carpets, holding tight to the nearest sturdy object. A woman fell in front of me. She opened her mouth but no words came out. Her dress had been ripped at the bottom so it looked fringed, like something Josephine Baker would shimmy in. I helped her to her feet and told her not to worry. I went to the door. The crowd was running in all directions away from the hotel, east on 48th Street, north on Lexington, south to Grand Central. People sped around me as I made my way down 47th. I walked and walked and walked. I walked the perimeter of the island, until the sun came out and men began shouting for ice at the Fulton Fish Market. Every time I heard a police siren or an ambulance, I wondered if they were going to the hotel.

When I returned to the apartment I took an hour-long shower. I didn't watch the news. I drank coffee and ate the last of the fruit salad in the fridge. I sat on the couch and went through old photo albums of Hugo and I. I fell asleep with our greatest hits on my lap, our Christmases and New Years, our Fourth of Julys and Labor Days.

Sometimes I couldn't believe that Hugo and I had ever met. I couldn't believe we'd been together for fourteen years, that we danced to Sylvester at Studio 54, that we shacked up on Fire Island three summers in a row and made blueberry pancakes on Sundays. How lucky we were.

When I woke up the next morning, I wrote the story out on notebook paper. I listed all the materials we used, where we purchased them, the lies we told the salesmen. I described how we sewed the explosive into the lining of the vest. I told them how Hugo wanted to wait until the end of the night to set it off, but I convinced him to do it as soon as everyone had arrived, before the evening's speeches. I wrote why we did it, though I knew people would fabricate their own reasons. It was no use trying to change their minds.

I tidied the apartment. I put the photos of us into boxes along with any paperwork that seemed important. I gathered up our vinyl and books and left a note for them to be donated to the Oscar Wilde Bookshop. I threw the food away. It would rot before too long. Mid-afternoon, as the East Village traffic crawled along, I stuffed the letter into my pocket and walked out the door.

So many articles were published about that night. Historians wrote books about it. I remember a feature in *The New Yorker* around the one-year-anniversary, the ramped-up security at hotels, shopping malls, train stations. The author interviewed a woman who was sitting at a balcony table. She didn't notice Hugo in the crowd. Everyone had just gotten their salad. When it happened, the man next to her screamed. They all looked down at the stage and saw two tables burning and a gentle red mist floating in the air. The author showed photos to the woman, images of the aftermath, the fire, the hole in the stage. As she thumbed through them, she fainted.

One of Hugo's acquaintances was there that night, a Columbia professor who often took the 9 train downtown for unsavory fun. He and Hugo had slept together back in the day, but Hugo found the sex to be uninspiring, so they remained strictly platonic after that. His table was toward the rear of the ballroom, so he was one of the first to escape. He did interviews. Later, he wrote a book about what happened. He believed that Hugo had surrendered to a misguided impulse for revenge. He suggested that the evening had set the gay rights movement back fifty years, and caused more harm than AIDS ever did. Things would have righted themselves eventually, he claimed. People would have come around.

From all the coverage, I learned something new about Hugo. Amazing that you can spend a decade and a half with someone and still not know them fully. His hometown paper published an article about the bombing, and they sprinkled in bits of his early life among the vilification. He graduated from high school in 1964. I knew that. But I didn't know he was the class valedictorian and that he gave the commencement address. I still wonder what he spoke about, if he bored people or made them laugh or mesmerized them. I wonder if they remembered his words. But mostly I wonder why he never told me. After all these years, I haven't been able to track his speech down, even though he's the most famous person ever to come out of Laurel, Mississippi.

The two cops died in the ballroom. People often forget that they were the reason behind all of this. I said as much when I gave my statement in court. My lawyer warned me not to say anything, but I wanted people to remember how those men beat Morris for no reason, how they'd rendered him guilty without evidence or even knowing his name. I suspect, though it's never been proven, that Hugo was right next to those two men in the ballroom. Maybe he spoke to them. Maybe he even smiled. They got the most publicity of the five killed. People put up memorials in Brooklyn. A middle school in Bay Ridge was named after them. Nobody remembers what they did to Morris.

Hugo did what he wanted. Everyone knows his name now. He set the course for as many lives as those cops did. And yet, I can't put them in the same breath. I can understand the horror in what Hugo did, but I can't see him as a symbol of death or hatred. I see him only as he was when we were together, when we were friends, lovers, young and unmoored and free. Most people believe that Hugo blew up that ballroom out of revenge, and I'm sure that was part of it. But I think the most pressing thing on his mind, as simple as it might seem, was a frustration that he could no longer bear: After six years of watching us die for no reason, people still refused to recognize us as human, as worthy of kindness rather than contempt.

I told him that it would be so much more effective if we could just turn those two men gay. One morning they would wake up, look at their wives, and find themselves as limp as week-old flowers. They'd go to work and have to hide their erections in the locker room showers, to suppress the urge to stare at their colleagues from behind. They'd have no idea what to do. Perhaps they'd seek help. They'd find us at the Stonewall, at the Duplex, at the Monster. They'd tell us that they've never felt so adrift in their lives, and we'd say that everything would be all right, that the distance to shore was not as great as it looked, and we'd bring them back, safe and sound.

I've been in here for thirty years. I wake up every morning to the slate gray of the walls, the sliver of light that looks like a line on a tennis court. I'm served all my meals inside my cell. I read books. Once a week, under the eye of a guard, I can check a pre-approved list of websites: *The New York Times*, *CNN*, *The Advocate*. I read the wedding announcements and look at the photos of Jerry and Zack, Omar and Thomas, Sarah and Jess, and I wonder whether that could have been me if I'd just done nothing. If I hadn't come out so soon. If I hadn't been brave. Maybe I would have never known Hugo. Instead, I would have been sitting in a house far away from New York. I would've seen the news on television and pitied what happened. I would've been thankful for my unremarkable life, thankful that it wasn't me who'd gotten blown up. And after a few moments I'd resume my day, mow the lawn, have a drink with my wife, and lounge in the shade.

At three in the afternoon I'm allowed to go outside for forty-five minutes. I talk to a few people, but most keep their distance. I don't know what sort of mythos has clotted around me, but it's palpable. Other inmates glance at me as they pass my cell. I get line after line of puzzled looks. How could a person possibly survive with the weight of the world's anger on their back? Yet, I've never been touched. They're scared of me, though I can't pinpoint a reason why.

Now they have pills to prevent HIV, pills to render the virus moot. It still infects people, but it's no longer the danger it once was. I've never taken them. After Hugo, I figured it would be a few years for me, that I'd die like so many men I knew. I waited for the bruises to appear, for my mouth to grow dry and my bowels to cannibalize themselves. Every time I woke with a new scratch or bruise I thought: *This is it, I'm ready*. Knowing that I would quickly follow my partner, that we'd see each other soon, was one of the reasons I agreed to help him. But nothing happened to me a month later, a year, ten, twenty. I'm fine. I don't know why.

The kid wrote to me again, the one who did his book report on Hugo and me. He sent another letter saying that his teacher applauded the breadth of his research. She said he should look into a career as a historian, though he had his sights set on law school someday.

He said I could write him back if I wanted. He wasn't sure if I had any friends, considering what had happened, but he could tell from my handwriting and from the way I described the past that I wasn't a bad person. But, if I didn't want to write back, he'd understand. Sometimes he got so lonely that he didn't want to do anything. He wouldn't be surprised if I felt like that, too.

I retrieved my pen and notebook from under my pillow, and when the first morning light came through the windows, I wrote down all that I could see. The cracks in the concrete, the pillbug crawling up the rail, the rustle of my neighbor in the cell next door.

Do I regret what we did? I know I'm supposed to say yes. I'm supposed to say that if I had known there would be medicines, that fifteen years later most people would survive on a daily pill, I would have told Hugo to wait. But even if I had tried to convince him to endure, maybe it wouldn't have mattered. Maybe those cops would have kept beating people. Maybe I still would have had to watch my love disintegrate, bit by bit. Maybe I'd still be in this cell, staring at the wall, writing a slightly different ending to the same story.

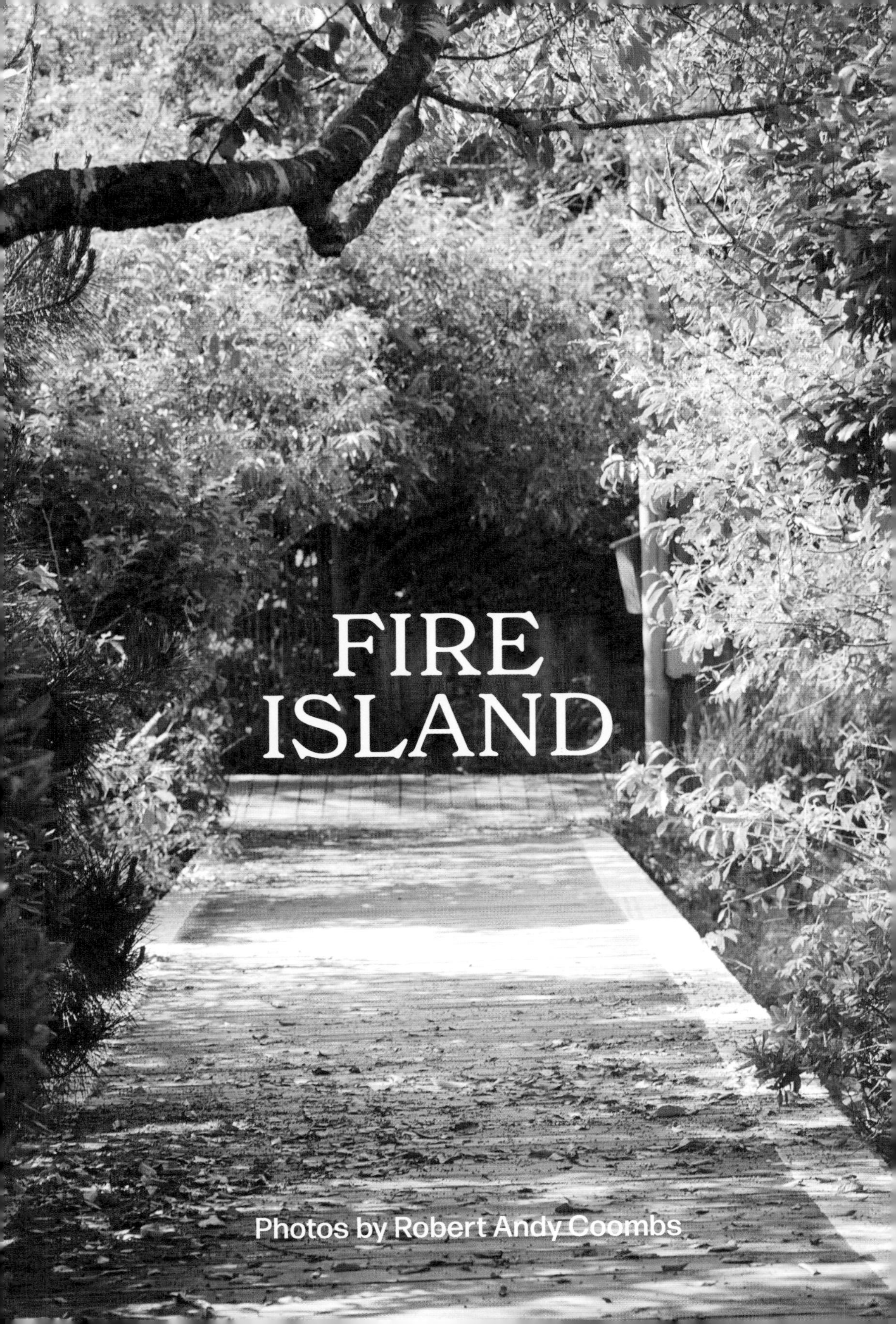

FIRE ISLAND

Photos by Robert Andy Coombs

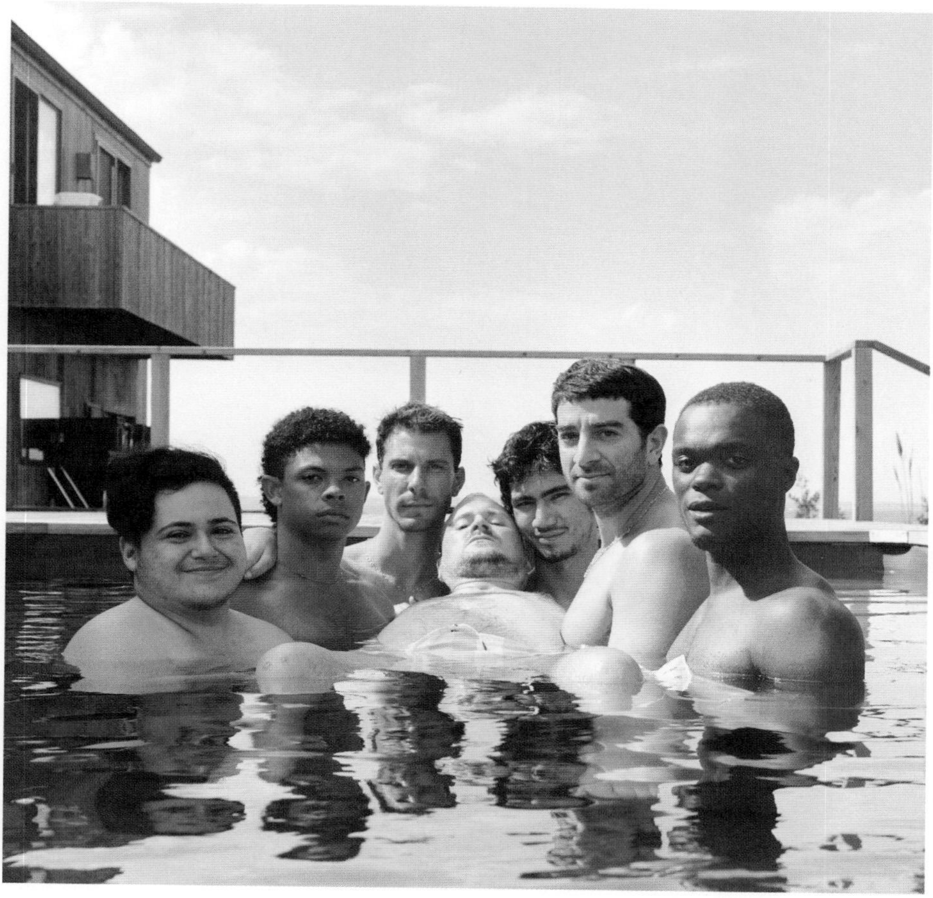

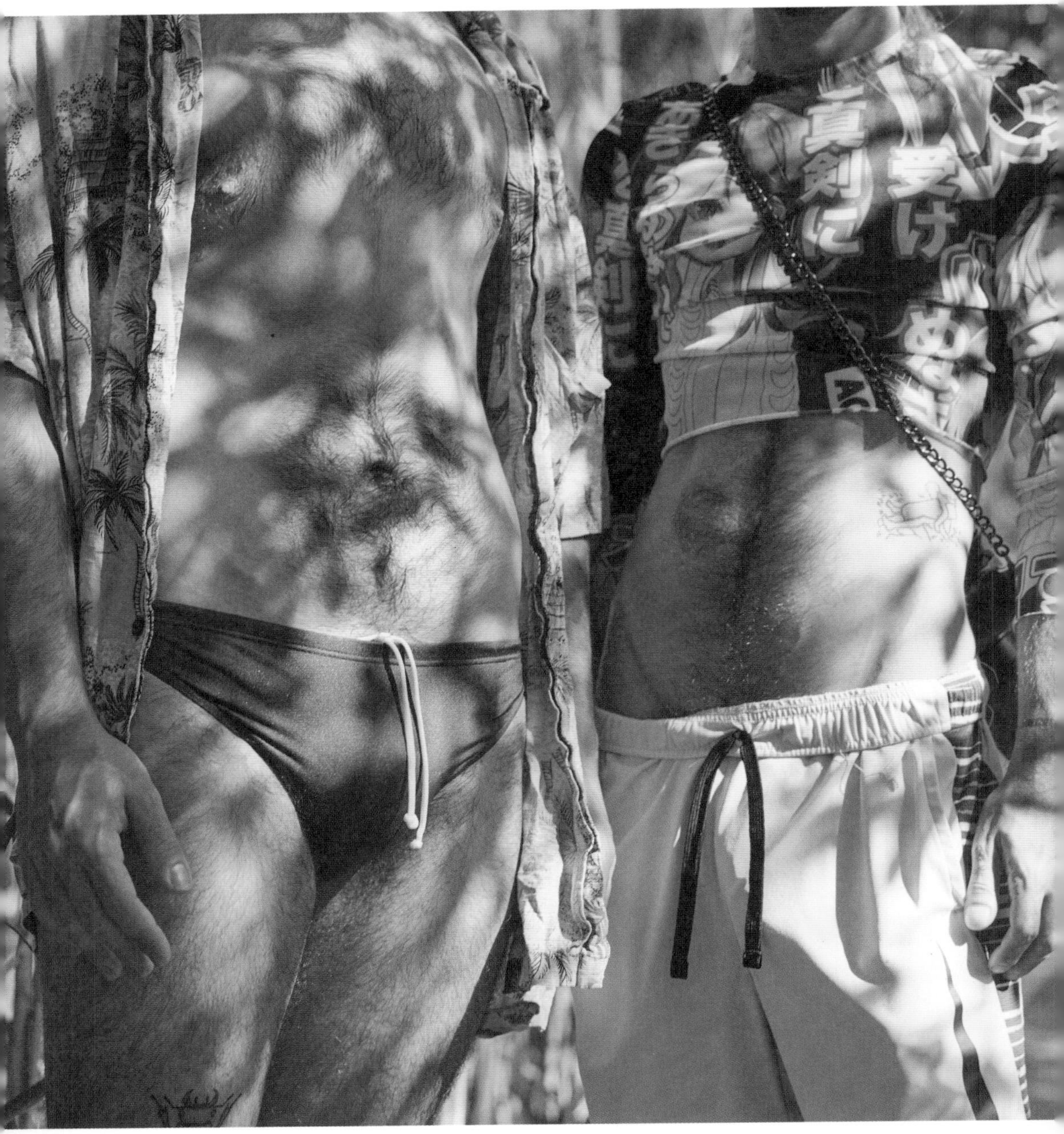
真剣に
受け

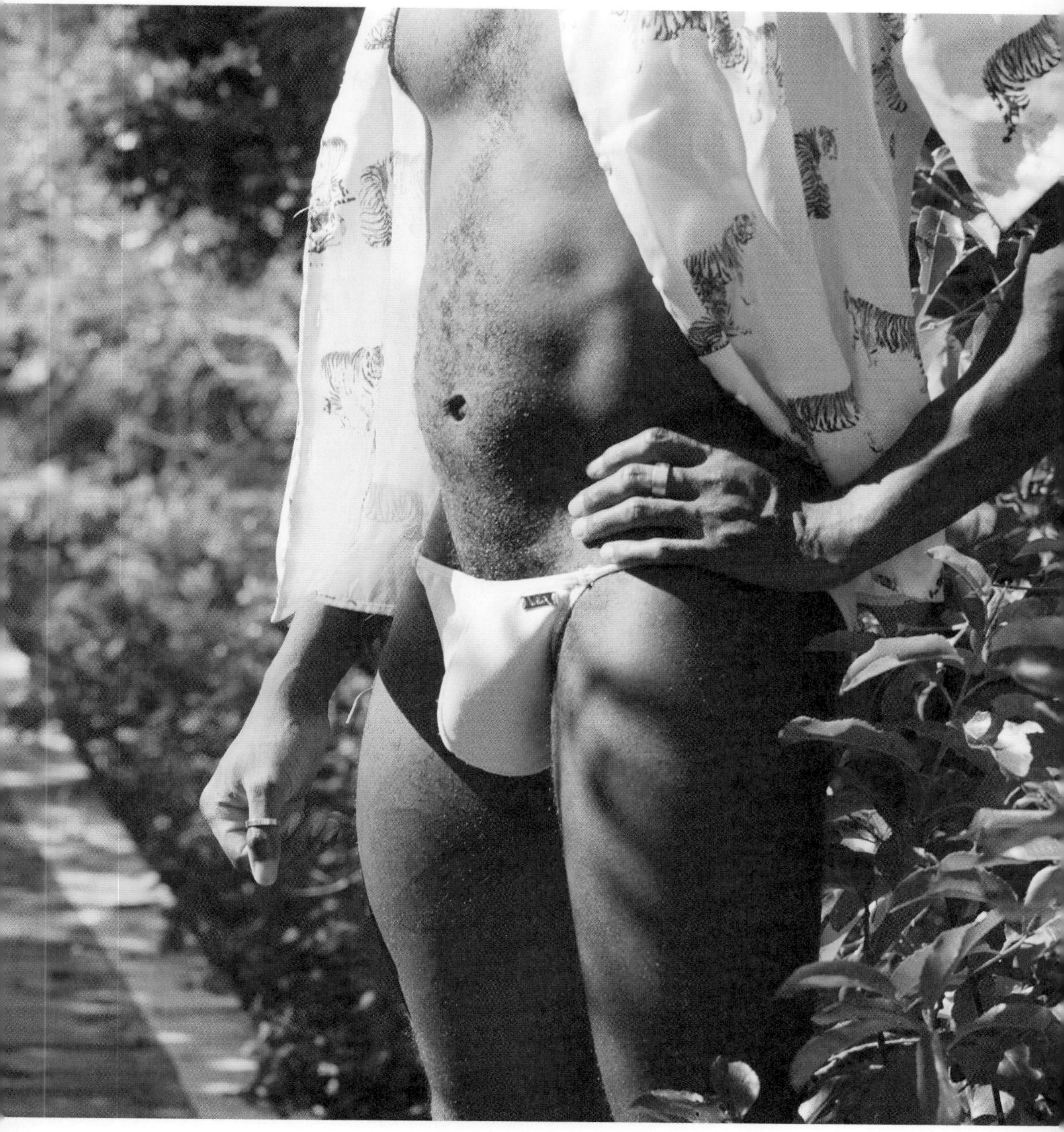

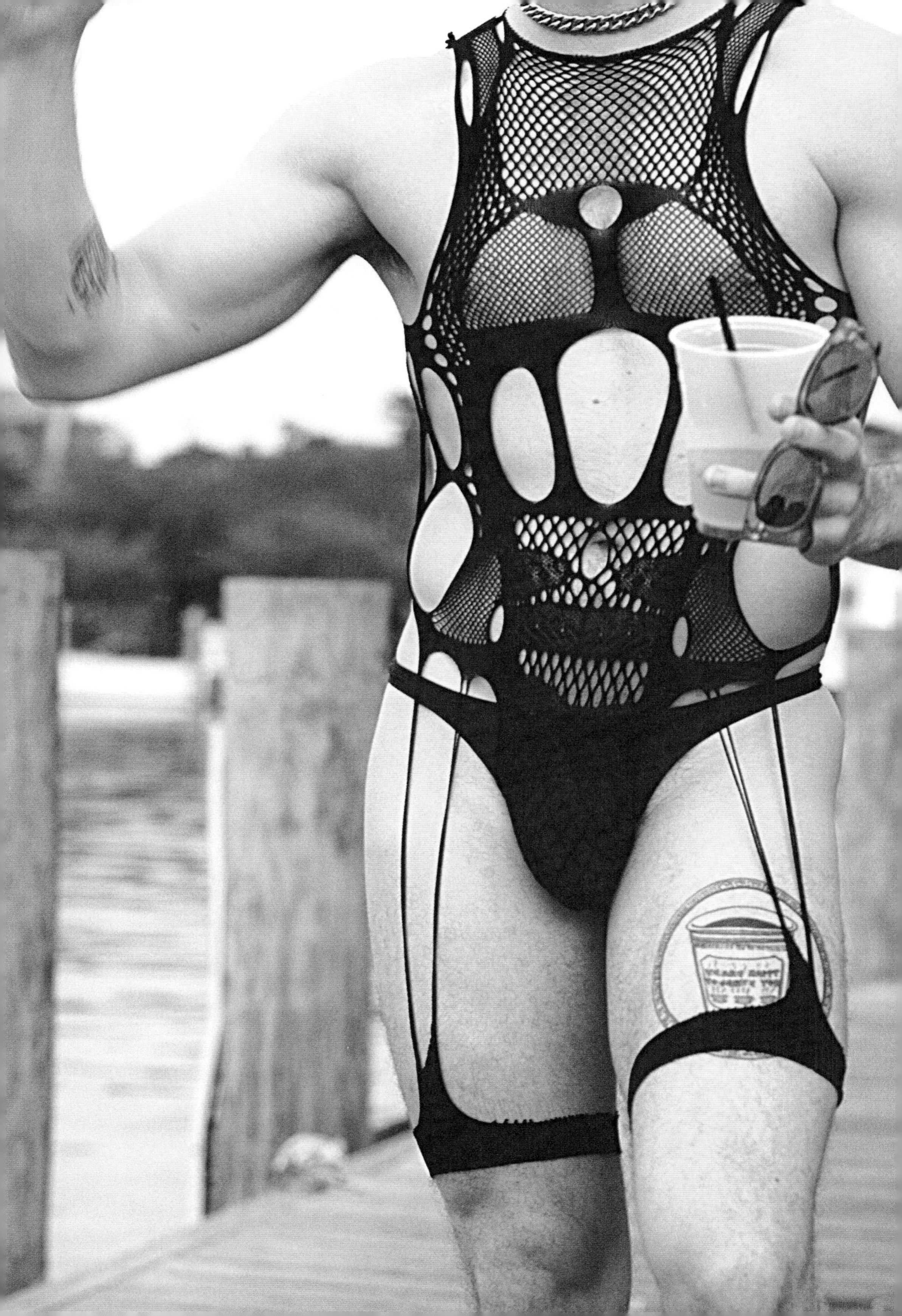

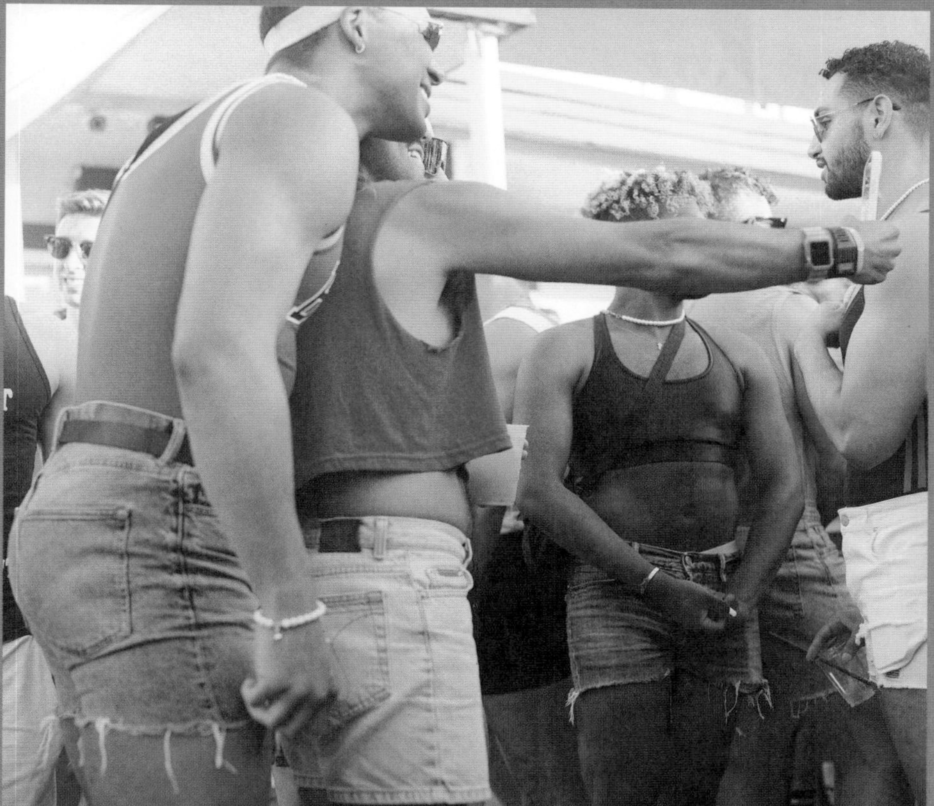

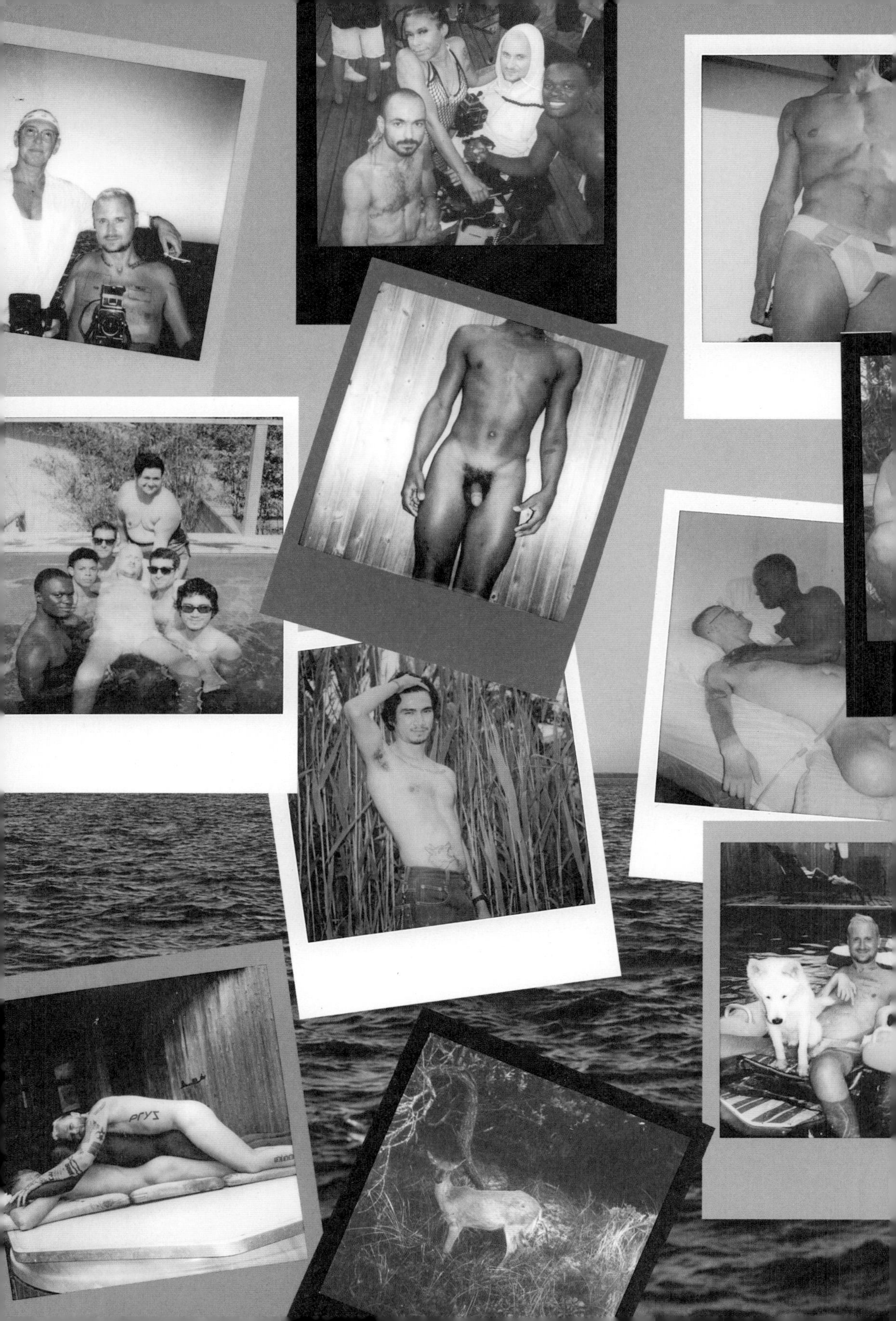
prys

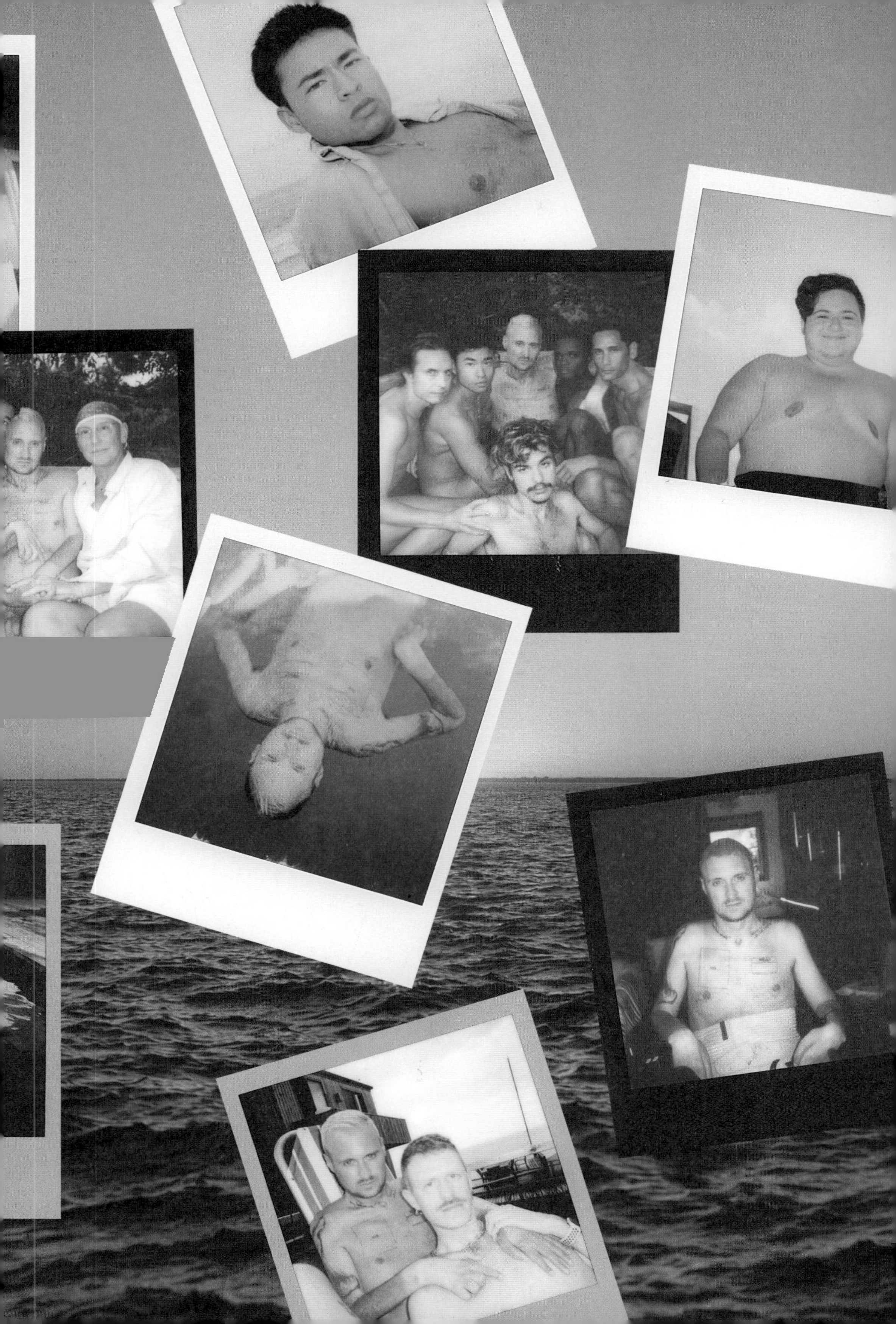

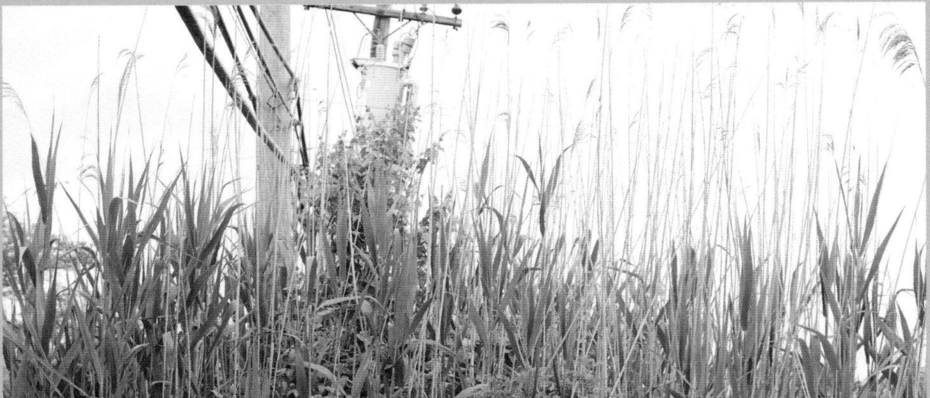
GROVE
BOARDWALK
ENDS
USE
ROADWAY

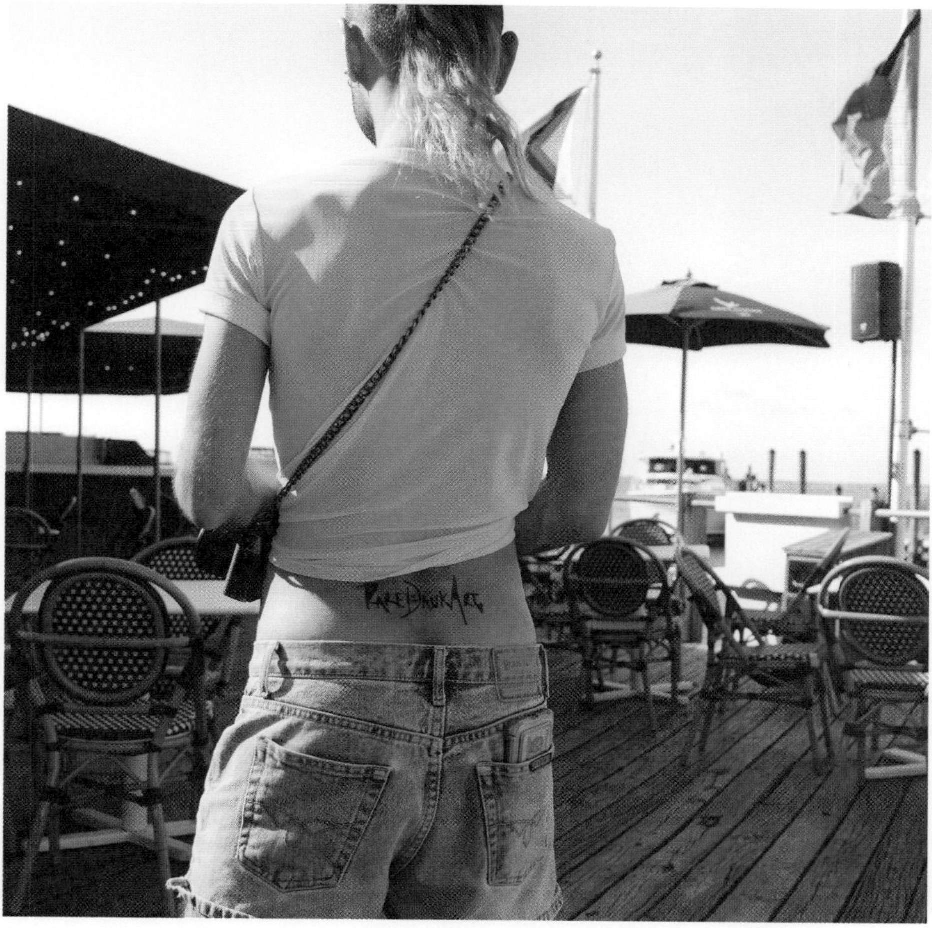

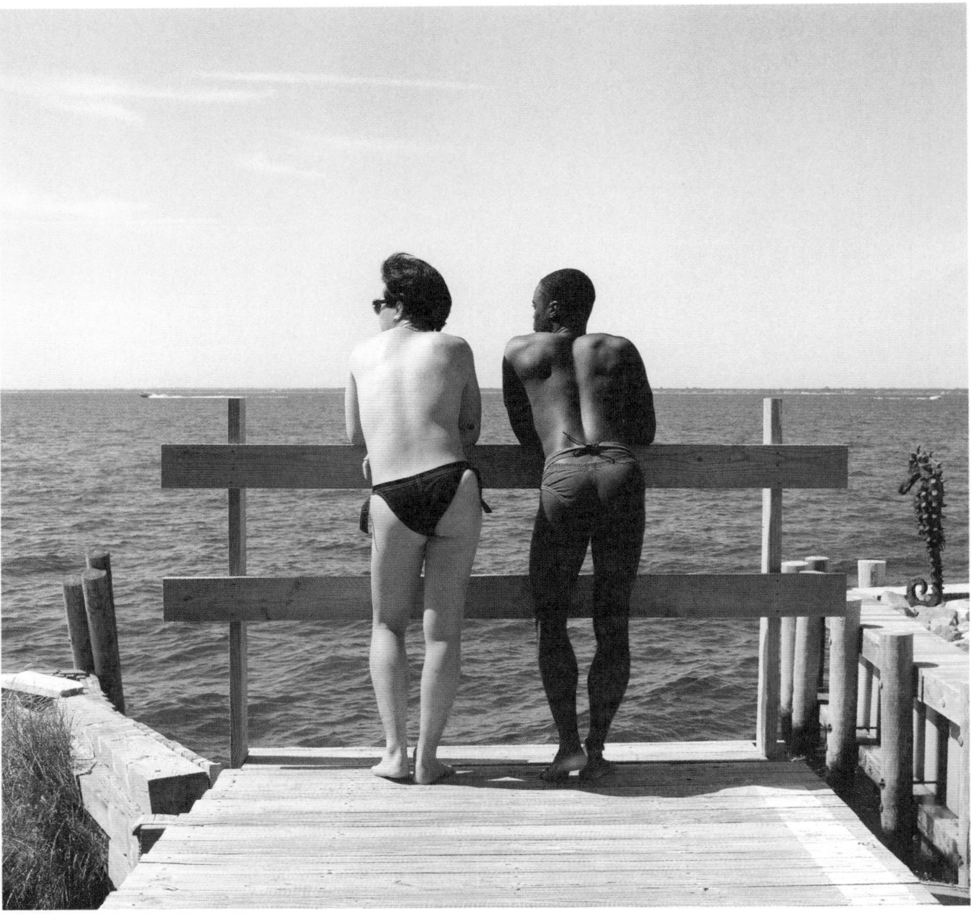

CREATED WITH SUPPORT FROM BOFFO RESIDENCY FIRE ISLAND

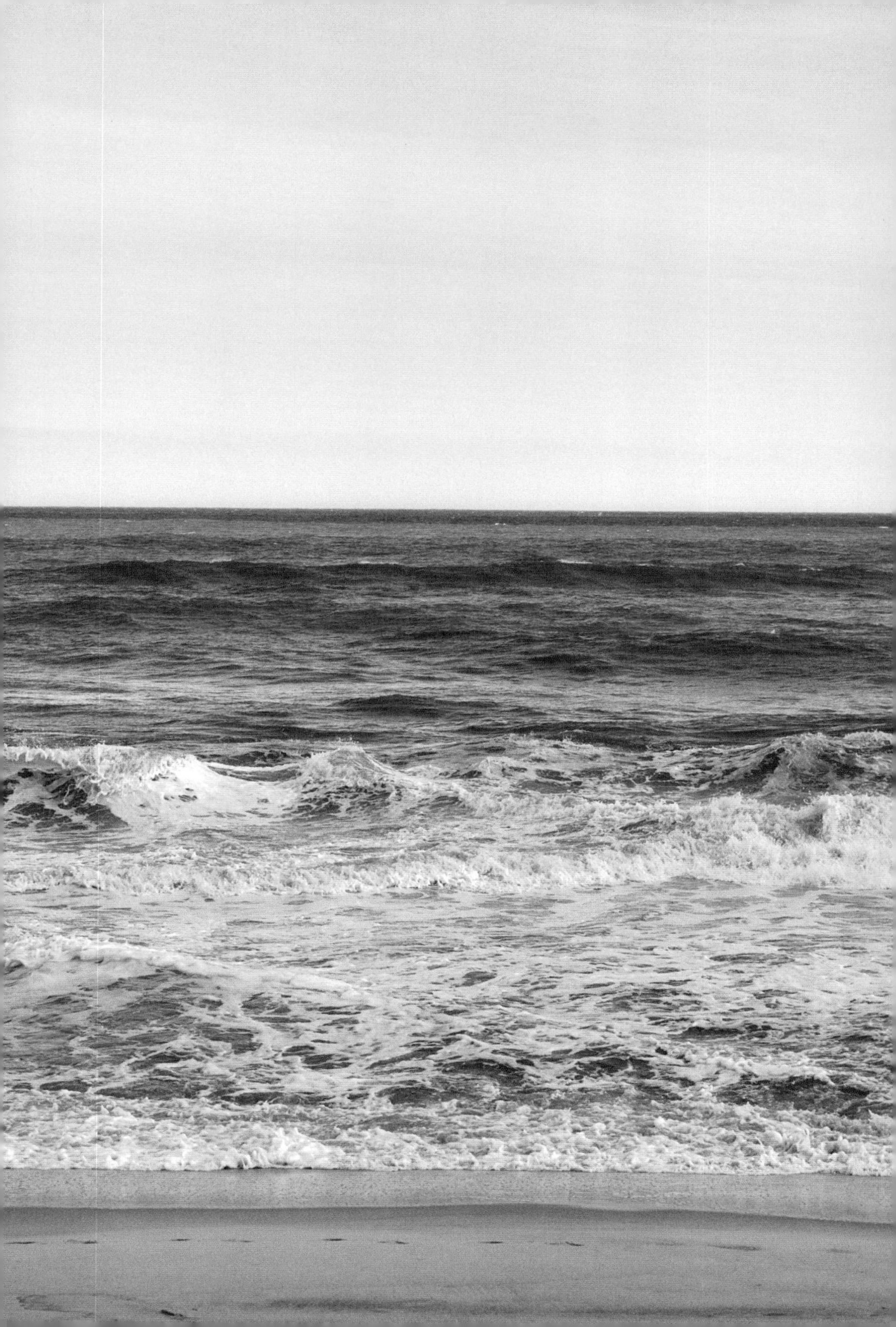

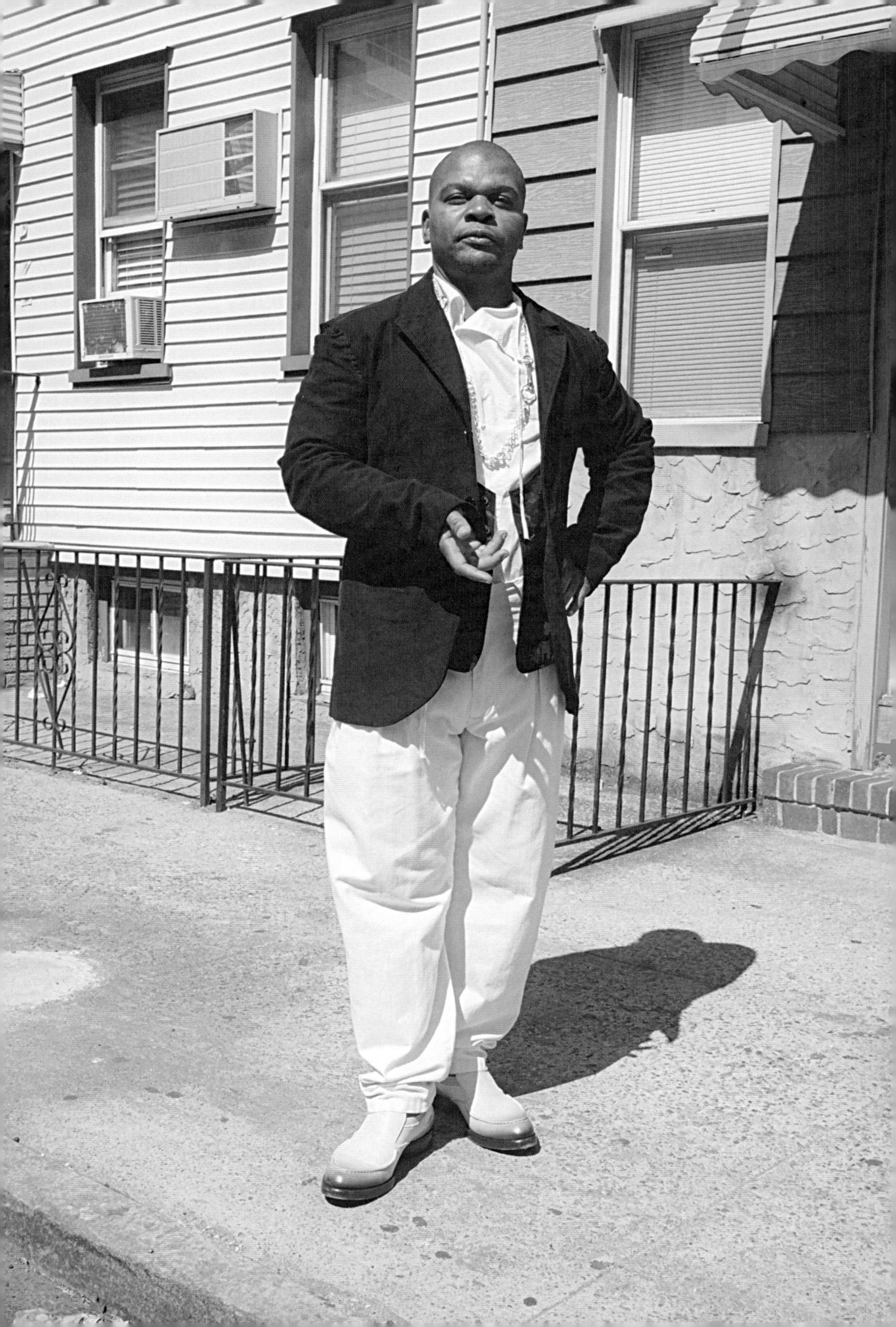

KEHINDE WILEY IN 3D

An Artist's Quest to Unflatten Black America

Antwaun Sargent | Photos by Amber Mahoney

For most of the history of art and movies, magazines and books, all objects that document western visual culture, Black people have been missing. There's a visual language we inherit from white supremacy about the way we should see Blackness sexually, physically, and psychologically.

Kehinde Wiley, among other artists, is trying to explore and reconfigure "how Black identity is constructed, consumed, and manufactured." He has broadened his approach to include an international set of people of color, who share a similar quality to the Black folks he first went out to take pictures of (which eventually turned into paintings) in Harlem and his native South Central Los Angeles. Embedded in every picture are the complications of the lives his subjects live.

Take *Officer of the Hussars*. In the naturalistic painting, a young Black model he street casted in Harlem (as he typically does) replaces a military official first seen in the eponymous 1812 Théodore Géricault work. Wearing Timberland boots, blue jeans, and a white tank top so tight you can admire his physique while he rides a horse, wielding a sword, the Black male is fully human on the canvas. The picture transfers the power and spirituality historically reserved for depictions of whiteness to an unassuming Black Harlemite, allowing him to ask a simple question of us: When you look at me, do you see me? The query has proved to be a matter of life or death for Black women and girls, boys and men and trans folx.

Born in Los Angeles to a linguist mother who raised Wiley and his five siblings alone, he has spent the last decade and a half living in New York and Beijing, prolifically painting ordinary people of color from all over the world. His grandiose portraiture found in places like the Met and the Studio Museum mix the stately conventions of traditional European painting with the contemporary vernacular of its hip-hop, gay, and female Black subjects. As he documents the unseen, his pieces are truly like nothing art has ever seen.

The first time I saw Wiley's work in person was in 2015 at the Brooklyn Museum opening of the traveling retrospective *Kehinde Wiley: A New Republic*. The art that floored me was not his paintings of the hardly seen Black or brown gay men, like me, but his representations of Black women. In a series of works entitled *An Economy of Grace*, he painted Black women from Harlem and the Bronx in white Givenchy dresses designed by Riccardo Tisci. I remember standing before the painting *The Two Sisters* for a long time. I looked at the ways they were caressing each other, gazing directly at me, so self-assured it was hard to find in my mind a competing image in popular culture. So powerful, so beautiful, so free. I wondered, if it had affected me this much, what it must've meant for Black women to see these reflections.

In person Wiley appears like one of his paintings: Black and heroic, in custom-made suits patterned in the ornate, decorative textiles found in the backgrounds of his art. Here in conversation, we talk about Kehinde's memories, his art, and the legacy of *Paris Is Burning*.

ANTWUAN SARGENT: One of the things people say, mostly young queer Black men, about your work, is that this is the first time they've seen themselves reflected in art. What was your experience? When did you remember first seeing yourself reflected in art?

KEHINDE WILEY: One of the most striking images I remember seeing was the barbershop painting by Kerry James Marshall. Seeing it in LACMA [Los Angeles County Museum of Art] specifically—having that ivory-tower, elite institution housing a painting that has this kind of familiar Black American scene in the barbershop—it busted open a new set of possibilities for me. It made me feel as though the walls of the institution were accessible and permeable, rather than alienating.

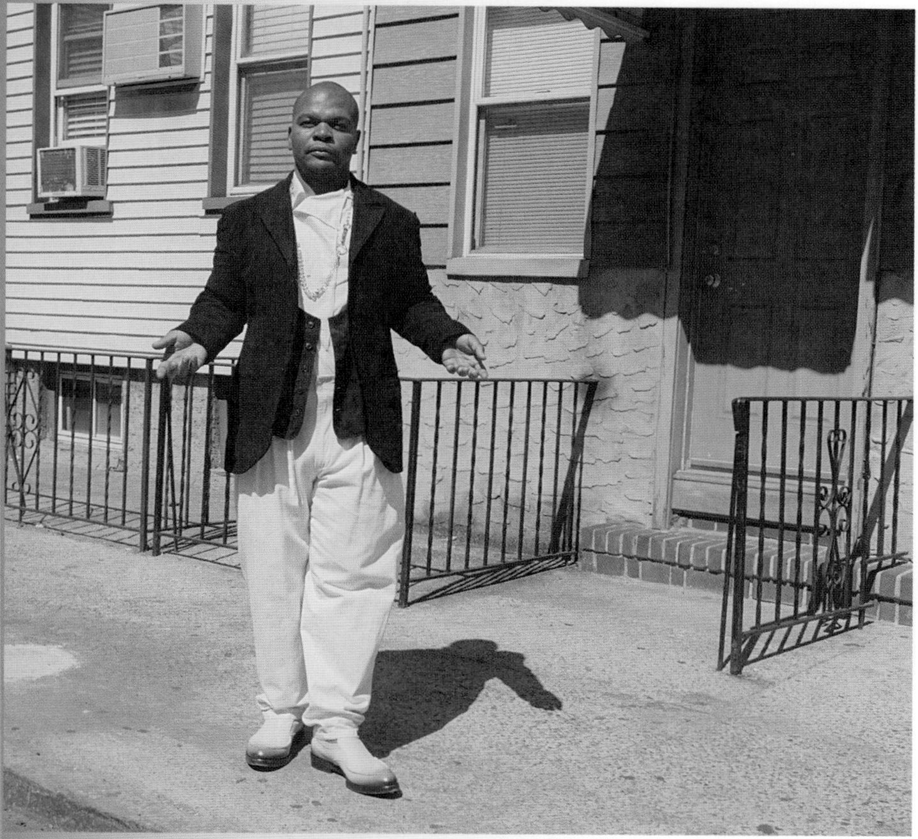

AS: I love that work in the same way. As you talk about Kerry, who are some other influences?

KW: Early on I was really interested in this sort of à la créme painting style that had this interesting factuality to it. It made it feel as though these guys, at the twist of a wrist, could create these amazing brush strokes that approximated reality. Artists like John Singer Sargent and John Paul. It's actually illusion, because if you read Sargent's notes and if you look closely at his paintings, you'll find that he would make a stab and if it wasn't quite right he'll wipe it off and start over. It was this illusion of mastery that I was thrilled by—the burden of influence that every artist feels. The idea that you stand on the shoulders of all of those who've come before you, yet you're expected to somehow come up with authentic statements, this pregnant moment that hasn't existed before. In so far as my own work is concerned, I turn that burden into the subject matter of the work. I fold into the anxiety as the place where I start.

AS: How do you cast models? Most of them—all of them really, are young, Black and brown people who don't really get to have a relationship to an art institution. From Jamaica to India, and local places like the Bronx and Harlem—that decision

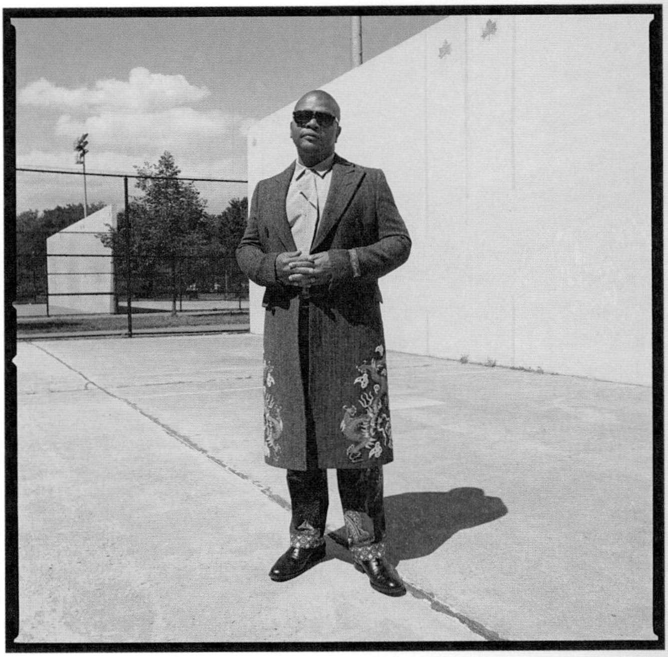

came early on in your craft. Can you talk about why that's important?

KW: I'm an LA boy and driving culture is in my blood. I still drive here in New York. I like the relationship between public space and the mediation of your vehicle. When I got to New York, I was thrust into the Harlem of pre-9/11 America where people were parading around 125th Street competing and peacocking. That sense of staring and desire and passion was all on the streets. I wanted to somehow wrap my practice around that, so in a very direct manner, I just started stopping people and asking them if they wanted to be the subjects of my work. It was mostly "NO" [laughs]. It's New York City, and people have their guards up. But in a sense, these paintings are about those people who say yes. A certain self-selecting type who responds to the provocation. As I've expanded this process out into the world, in the Congo or places like small village Tunisia, there is this fear of the camera—the sound, the lights, the white people—that level of attention in their communities is associated with an oppressive state or the police. And so they're like, "Get out of here and leave me alone."

AS: So what would you do in that situation, how do you get them on your side?

KW: I think it's about slowing down. Showing them examples of my work so they can imagine themselves in it. And I mean the cynical and cold reality of it is that most of the people participate because they are compensated for their time.

AS: Is the gaze so much different than, say, someone in power and a subject of disadvantage? Is the gaze different enough from the European painters who influence your hand?

KW: I think the trouble is that people are unprepared to allow the complexity that exists in the work. People are unable to view an urban Black subject with the

> **But my job is not to slow down so that others can get it, my job is to continue to wrap and grow new fields of providence.**

level, the verve, and the complexity that you would view, let's say, a John Currin painting. There's an assumed narrative and an assumed level of humanity and depth that exists when you're looking at a scene with forty-year-old white American social life. Whereas if you're looking at the picture of my Black and brown boys and girls, there's a flattening-out that happens. Whereas, in my work, there's the religious gaze that starts off in some of those early paintings. There's the homoerotic gaze that's assumed as one finds a male subject attractive and worthy to be the subject of the painting. It's a reaction against the very two-dimensional view that Black American men are placed under. The propensity toward sports, hypersexuality, antisocial behavior. These things run in direct response to the kind of softness and intimacy that the body is placed under in my paintings. There's the tension in the risk and the tear between the body language dress code, the way that one displays power in relationship to the body and the hips, and the posture and what was once the sort of height of masculinity now sort of comes across as vague. And then there's the transference between the economic realities and the global superstructure. But oftentimes because of the urban Black and brown bodies, they're unable to see it. But my job is not to slow down so that others can get it, my job is to continue to wrap and grow new fields of providence.

AS: Can you talk a bit about your personal art collection?

KW: Yes, it's usually just my friends. I'm just not one of those people who puts their own paintings on their walls. I don't like to spend hundreds of thousands of dollars, I just trade. It's something that will inspire more people to do more. I really do like when I see other creative people engaging and collecting. That's what collecting is: a very personal thing.

AS: What women artists do you look up to?

KW: I like Jennie Livingston. I like the sense that she is able to be a fly on the wall yet infuse important films like *Paris Is Burning* with her own personal aesthetic. A type of empathy and charm is there. She's a great filmmaker and a revolutionary.

AS: Speaking of Jennie, what's your favorite scene in *Paris Is Burning*?

KW: Let me see. Oh god, there's just so many. I literally teach that film when I'm doing lectures as a means to talk about the multiplicity of identity, performance of desire, and subjugation. And not just sexual desire, there's also class desires, too.

AS: That reminds me of one of the things you said earlier about the ways in which Black and brown people are not given the full humanity as whiteness. There is a connection, at least in my mind, between your work and hers.

KW: I would love that.

AS: So, what do you do for fun, outside of painting?

KW: I travel. I learn languages, I cook, I fish. I love fishing.

AS: Yes, the fishing. You just got back from—

KW: Guyana. We were on a school boat and went camping every night deeper and deeper into the forest. It's a way of disappearing from your headspace. And from the New York scene or the Beijing scene or the Dakar scene and it's like just about slowing the fuck down.

AS: What did you catch?

KW: Massive fish, like the size of a couch. I would release them, since there's only so much fish you can eat. It was amazing. But also scary as hell—there are jaguars out there, spiders, anacondas.

AS: Can you describe your first artist memory?

KW: By the time I was eleven, I'd started off in art classes. I'd been surrounded by antiques and tchotchkes. My mother essentially ran a store that was similar to Sanford and Son. We would go around collecting people's old furniture, old clothes, old appliances, and sell them secondhand. That was a means for her to pay her way through graduate school while raising six kids alone. And so one of the things that occurred to me was that there definitely was this kitschy, granny fifties-style furniture that I was surrounded by as a kid. [I'm] heavily influenced by the almost garish and overly sweet.

AS: What other things inspire your work? What inspired your show, *Trickster*? Were you tired of doing the globetrotting?

KW: As I mentioned earlier, anxiety is the overriding subject matter of my work. And one of the most anxiety-inspiring things any artist can do is consider himself in relation to his peers, so instead of making an abstraction, I made it an actuality. I started pivoting exactly to the people I'm surrounded by, who I came up with. I also wanted to use the metaphor of Blackness in a very different way. This ubiquity, this type of invisibility, yet this overriding and overwhelming presence is something I wanted to explore within Blackness. The fear of Blackness, the fear ultimately that is your most reptilian sense of just being eaten. There's this notion of Blackness as a kind of literal and figurative field in which you can explore the Black bodies of the writer. It was incredibly successful in the sense that it scratched the itch that I was trying to get to.

AS: We always think of you as this incredibly successful—it's hard to sort of imagine Kehinde Wiley as being unsuccessful—but are there moments where you're like, "Yes, I put this painting out but I don't know if it works." Moments of vulnerability?

KW: That's a *yes* for every artist. I think at its best you want to make that your friend. You take that fragility and roll it around in your hand and try it on for size and see what the contours are because that's your guiding light. People love my work because I decided to go in a direction that I feared myself. When I was having my first exhibitions at studios in Harlem, I had this notion I was going directly into my childhood and going directly into the Black bodies and the fear of art history and it was all there in a very honest way. Vulnerability has been my friend, and should always be my true north, my guiding light.

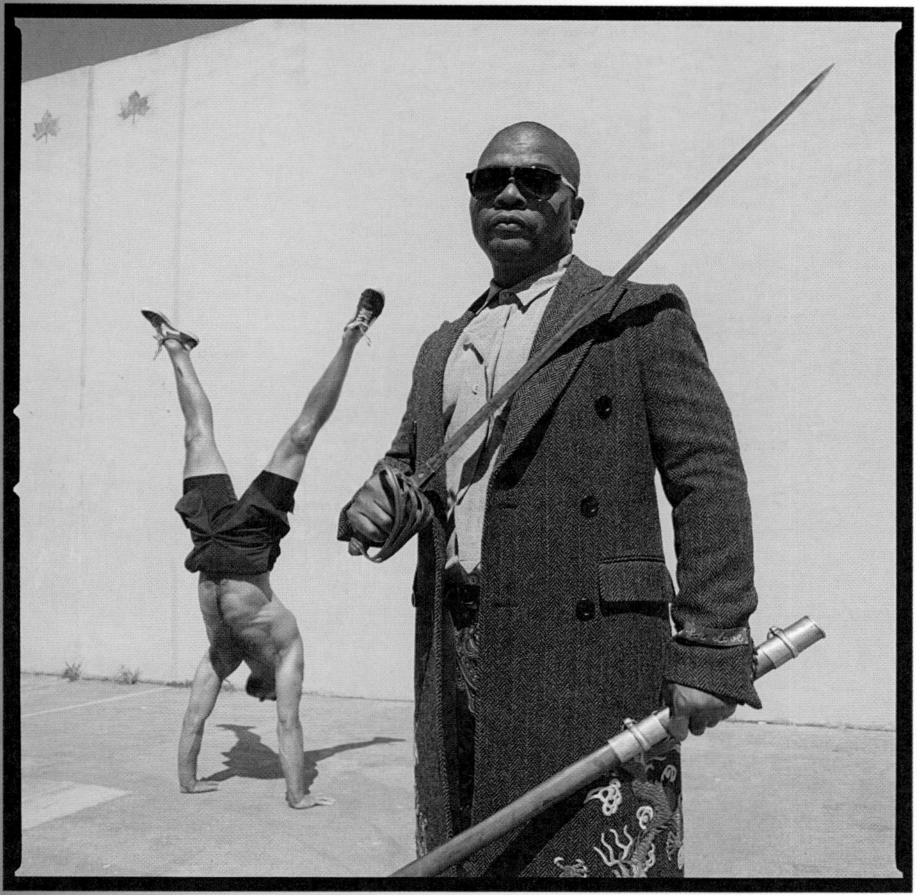

ORIGINALLY PUBLISHED IN *HELLO MR.* ISSUE 09 IN 2017.

AS: And, as we're at such an interesting time politically, how does this affect your work? How do you see your art affected by the moment?

KW: I thought Trump was going to win about a year before he got the nomination. I remember I told everyone at a dinner party in London, "I bet all of you five thousand dollars that this man is going to become the next American president." I just know the depth of American depravity, and I know the resentment that lies in the end of a Black president. I don't know. There is no destiny. We are the young magicians, we are the ones creating and contributing to the broader evolution of culture. I want it to continue to be a free radical that surprises and delights.

AS: Oh, I have one last question, if you weren't an artist, what would you do?

KW: I like farms. I'd probably have some kind of massive gardening thing going on. I know it sounds boring, but it's just the way I am.

AS: So you'd be a farmer?

KW: I would be a farmer.

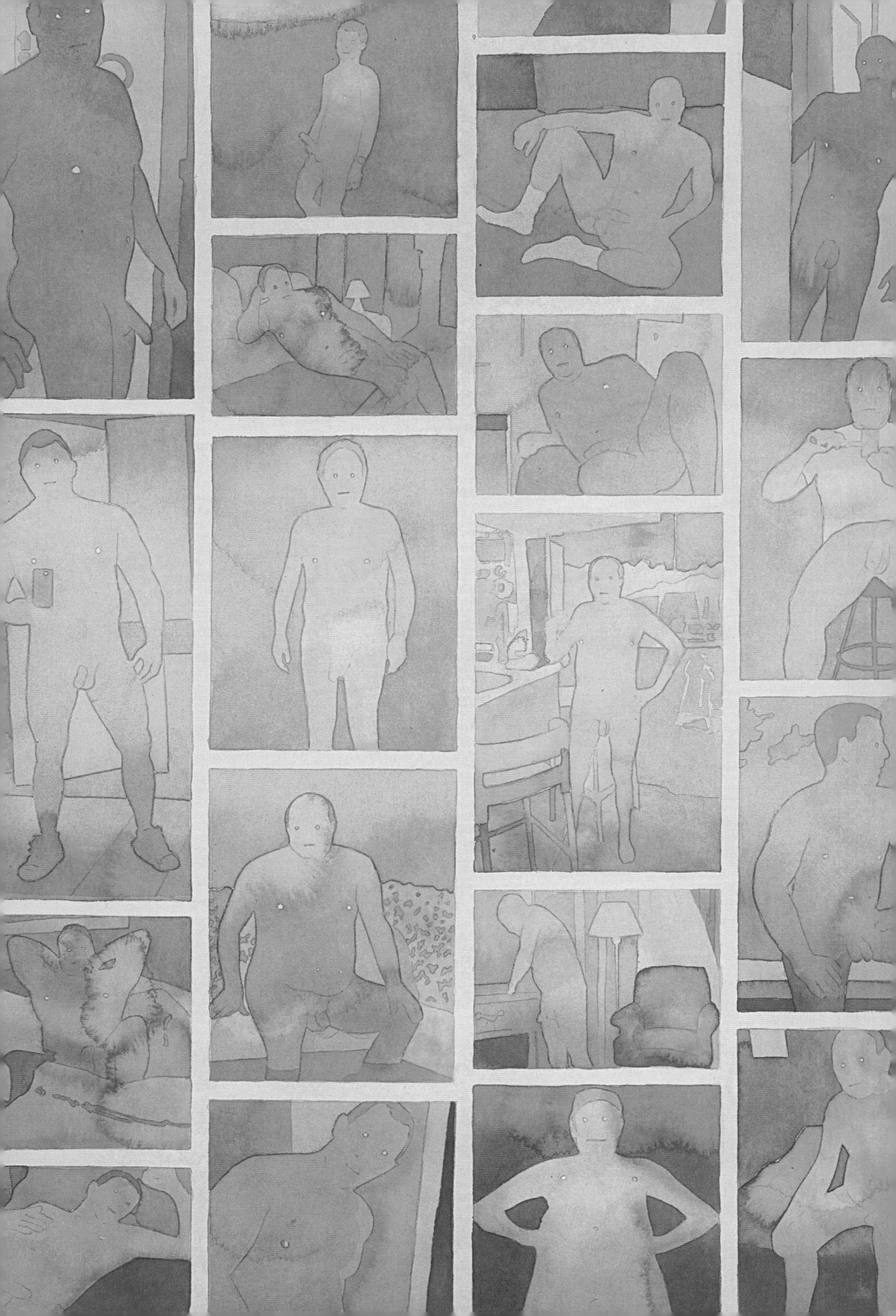

The House of the Sleeping Beaus

John Better Armella

Art by Dan Gluibizzi

It was around the beginning of June 2004 when I arrived in Bogotá. I woke up freezing and was wandering aimlessly along the city's grand avenues, trying to forget the bitch of a night I'd just spent under a clothing store awning. Carrying a huge duffel bag on my back, I dragged my exhaustion to a gas station. I didn't know exactly where I was, but the mass of people and the Torre Colpatria in the distance suggested downtown. I asked to use the bathroom at the station, took a long leak, a brief shit, washed my face, brushed my teeth, and filched the roll of toilet paper.

I left without knowing where I was headed. After a few blocks, I stopped at a newspaper stand and with the last of my coins bought a paper, scanning it for options.

An English-style house with a neglected rose garden welcomed me.

"I'm here about the ad," I told the woman who came outside to greet me.

"Follow me," she replied, showing me in. Her name was Ginet.

"No, no, no! That name won't do for this business. From now on your name is Adriano. Say hello to the others. He's Ángelo; that's Javier; this precious thing is Sergio; and the oldest over there is Byron," Ginet said, pointing to the posse of boys who were sitting on a black sofa in a sort of waiting room with a huge charcoal painting of a nude sailor.

"Hey, guys!" It was as if I were talking to a pile of trash, because none of them responded; instead they went on with what they were doing without even looking at me.

"These are the rooms where we attend to the guests," Ginet indicated.

Three air-conditioned rooms, all the same: a large bed, a nightstand with a lamp, a color TV, a reddish wood armoire, carpeted floors, and heavy curtains that blocked even the slightest beam of light.

"This will be your room, Adriano."

Behind the house was a smaller house with six small rooms, separated by wooden dividers, where the boys like me were housed—that is, those of us who came from cities other than Bogotá. We were "the live-ins," as La Medina liked to call us. La Medina ran the business and was Ginet's right hand. Ginet was the owner of this summer house just beyond the hills of the capital city.

Business? Guest rooms? Live-ins? What was this all about? The business: a brothel; the guests: the house's potential clients; and the live-ins: us, the hustlers who gave up our asses for whatever the clients wanted, including spankings by whatever crazy fuck was introduced as a "very special" house guest.

2.

As the days passed, I began to break the ice. My room became the meeting place for all the sleeping beaus, as I called them. Whenever we had free time, we'd hole up and smoke, play cards, or drink aguardiente until La Medina's ugly voice yelled from the parlor: "Introductions!" That casting call meant that someone had arrived. One by one, in single file, we'd go to one of the rooms where, as a rule, a guy in a dark suit was waiting for us, whom we were tasked with convincing that we were the best little whore he could find in a city full of whores. Each of us had fifteen seconds of fame to introduce ourselves:

I'm Adriano. For fifty thousand pesos, I'll take it out; for one hundred thousand, I'll put it in; for two hundred thousand, I'll make you see stars; for more, I'll pull them down and make them beat in your hands.

That wasn't the first guy I'd gone to bed with since I'd set foot in the city. When you're new meat, everyone wants to touch you, smell you, use you, put their fingers in all your orifices. I was still wearing the "new meat" tag, and in this business that translated to cold hard cash.

"You're new, right? I haven't seen you before. Not here or anywhere else. I like that. It's sad when I see the same boys who go from one place to the other. Tell me, what city do you come from?"

(What city do I come from? Well, I'll tell you, you fucking son-of-a-bitch, from a filthy, ugly city, a shit hole, full of rats that immigrated years ago and turned that cloud of dust on the banks of the river into their lair, with their supermarkets and country clubs, boutiques and fusion restaurants. But we also built a city, out of sticks and rocks, and even if they try to hide it, even if it doesn't have a zip code in the telephone book, it's the city where I'm from, my dear friend.)

"I'm from Barranquilla, Señor. They call it the golden door; it's very pretty."

"Ah, yes, yes, I agree with you. It *is* a beautiful city. I went to your carnival years ago, what memories! How many boys did I take to my hotel back then? Four, five, fifty? Anyway, they all start to look alike. . . . Well, now to what we 'came' for."

People "come" into the world for lots of reasons, some of them very unsavory: presidents, clerics, and policemen are all proof of that. But do you believe there's anything worse? If so, I invite you to spend about an hour alone with some pig you've never seen before, that you're not even sure brushes his teeth every day, just so he can unload the rancid cum he's built up during a stressful week at work. Go ahead, try it, and then we'll talk.

"I see you're a boy of few words, Adriano. You should try being a little nicer."

Nice? What could I say to a guy like him? I could say: *Thank you, Señor Son-of-a-bitch, for giving me money in exchange for the nausea caused by your cheap cologne mixed with your rancid humor.*

"I hope you come again. We're here to serve you," was all I said.

3.

Bogotá in August is freezing. The wind blows colder than usual, and when they rise in the morning the ripened peaches are prone to shrinking on the patio of the house of the sleeping beaus. It's the month of calla lilies: a beautiful flower that looks like it's made of wedding cake icing. In spite of La Medina's warnings, I cut one from the front garden and take it to my room. I put it in a vase of water and throw myself onto the bed with a hangover from hell. It's barely six in the morning. Everything is quiet, everyone is asleep after last night's party. It was one of the boys' birthdays, and we pumped him full of aguardiente and blow. Everyone's asleep now, except for me; at times like this I can't sleep no matter how hard I try. I take a drag of a cigarette and follow the trail of smoke rings as they stretch out in spirals that escape through a crack in the ceiling. The sound of a car pulling into the house's parking lot causes me to sit up instantly.

La Medina comes in. "There's a client in the parlor, and you're the only one up, so go take a cold shower, and get a move on," she says in a queenly voice.

I chew some cardamom seeds to mask my prehistoric bad breath, and I put on underwear. I go out and cross the small patio that separates me from the house: the prickly grass feels like a fine carpet of needles that bury themselves into my feet. I go inside, and there's no one in the parlor, so I assume the guy must've gone to one of the bedrooms. I open a random door, where some of the beaus are lying naked, their bodies wrapped in a deep, pleasant sleep—a beautiful image. I pick up a bottle that's lying on the rug and take a long swig that brings tears to my eyes. I leave quietly so as not to disturb them. When I open the door of the adjoining room, La Medina's horrified to see me in my underwear, with the bottle of booze tipped back, as I take an even longer drink than the one before.

"Ginet will hear about this," the old queen says, and she leaves the room cursing. I lock the door and hand the bottle to the new arrival.

"It's too early for me, but I'll have one on you, for this entertaining encounter."

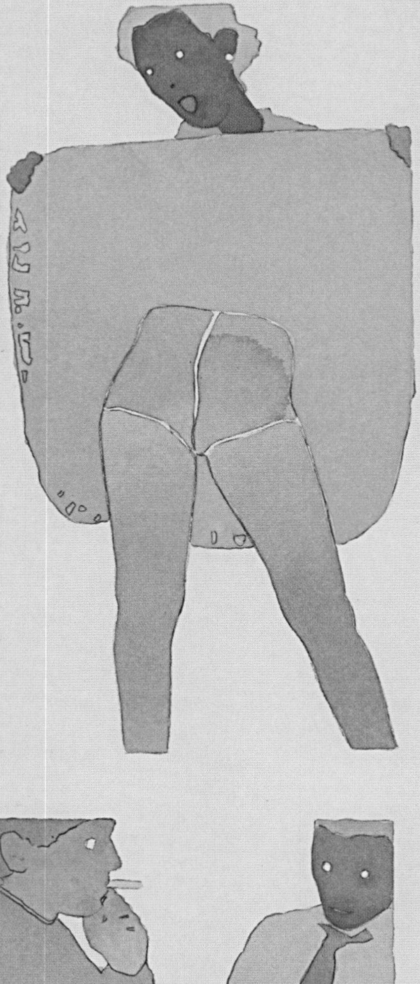
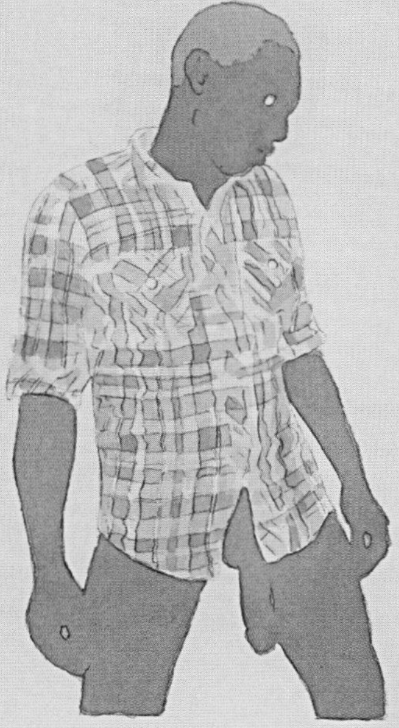
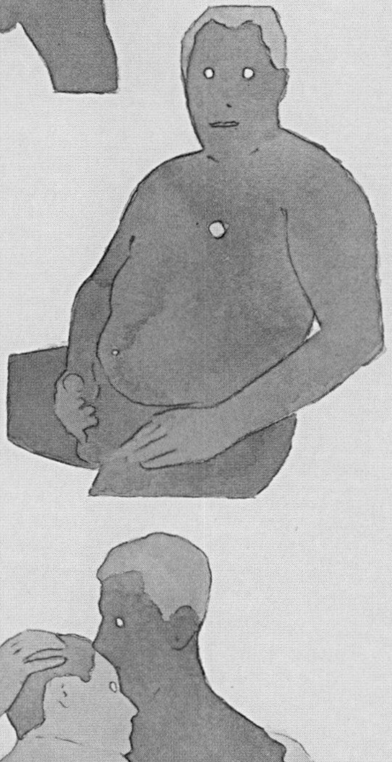
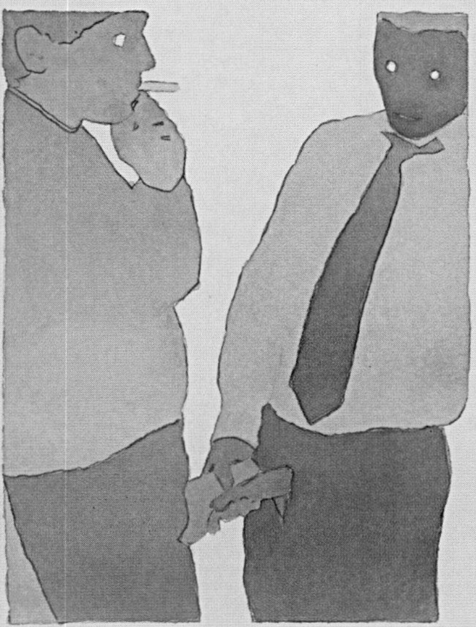
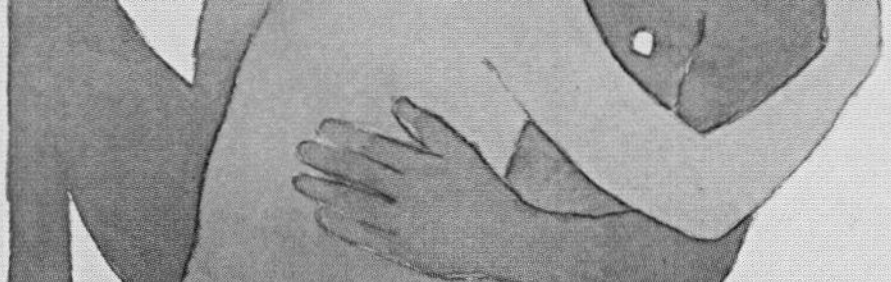

4.

Not everything in the house was bad, not everything reeked. There were beautiful, fleeting moments, like Esteban.

"We've been fucking all morning; you're going to cost me a lot of money, chico."

"I think you should go now," I answered.

"Or we could . . ."

Esteban left about noon, and I went back to my room. La Medina didn't say a word. I went to sleep and didn't wake up until the next day, or rather Ángelo woke me up when he and Sergio came into the room. They'd just attended to one of the so-called "special clients."

"It was fabulous!" Ángelo said.

"Maybe for you. You like to have your ass spanked. Look at this," Sergio said, showing me the throbbing bruises on Ángelo's buttcheeks.

"One day, one of those assholes is going to show up and want to shove a hot poker up our ass, and as long as he has the cash, that bitch La Medina will put a gun to our head so we'll let him fuck us," I said.

"We'll talk later; we're going to take a bath," Ángelo said.

And they got in the shower together. I could hear them from my room, first laughing, playing in the water like little boys, then whispering and moaning: "Do you like that? Aw, you like it?" I heard one of them ask the other. I started to jack off, thinking about Esteban, and about Sergio and Ángelo fucking in the shower. I got up and stood on tiptoes to make myself come faster; a gush of hot semen exploded against the wall. I felt more relaxed, took a bootleg CD of Alaska and Dinarama out of one of the chest of drawers, lit a cigarette, and starting singing: "*con tu tacón de aguja, los ojos pintados, dos kilos de rimmel . . .*" ["with your stiletto heels, your painted eyes, two kilos of mascara . . ."]

5.

There were quiet days at the house of the sleeping beaus, when no one came to fuck up our lives or our asses. We'd all sit around the fireplace and talk about the world, about our families or unrequited love. That's not just girl stuff; boys also succumb to such trivialities. I'd gotten a letter from Esteban, saying he was going to Barcelona to take care of I don't know what. In the letter, he sent me some money that I'd already blown on booze and the pile of bootleg CDs that we were now listening to, as we passed around a bottle of cheap wine. And because we didn't have firewood, we stoked the fire with pages from old phone books.

Six months had passed since I arrived. Things had noticeably changed; I was no longer the new meat. There was a new beau, Felipe, so my income declined considerably. The outlook was grim: I owed a few months' rent, and there were the run-ins with La Medina. The smartest thing, I thought, would be to get out of there as soon as possible.

I left the house of the sleeping beaus at the beginning of December of 2004, late at night and without making noise, leaving a pile of debts and taking the month's profits that I stole from La Medina's secret hiding place—that is, under her mattress.

Now here I am in a hostel in central Bogotá. The guy in the bed who's snoring like a pig is Aníbal—at least that's what his ID says. I met him last night at La Oficina.com, a bar in the posh Chapinero district, where I go a lot. It's easy to hook up, and there are boys that pay a butt load for a night of sex, and others like this guy Aníbal who don't even cough up enough to pay for one night in the cheapest hostel downtown—which is why you have to spike their drink with a tiny pill so they'll fall into bed like a felled tree. With the money I pinched from his wallet, I'm planning on buying that ceramic cat I saw in a store in the north of the city. It'll add a touch of class to this pigsty I'm living in now. Yep, that's what I'll do. Oh, one last thing: My name's Alejandro now. I like emperors' names best.

Good Dick Is a Myth

Mack Rogers

good dick is probably a bot
good dick always forty miles away
good dick sure as hell better be hosting
good dick will block you on your way out
good dick always visiting for the weekend
good dick say *let's do this again sometime*
you know i only leave the house
for my vitamin d & this address
better be right cus i'm outta data
& outta my mind speeding 2 towns
over for some of that unattainable
dick that veiny hooded chew-on-it
dick that i follow you on onlyfans
dick that i like all your pics on twitter
dick & fuck me like you fucked your
friend last wednesday dick that fuck
the condom dick that tell all your
friends dick that don't tell a soul
dick that take pictures but don't
post that shit dick that i know ain't
worth half a tank in this economy
but good dick don't come free & you
best believe imma get my vitamin d

hello mr.

We Meet Again: Familiar Faces of *Hello Mr.*

Ernesto Macias

Revolutions lead to change, and in some cases, growth. Revolutions, too, have context—a war oftentimes sparked by mounting unconformities affecting a specific group or community. I think of the (alleged) liberation of countries from their oppressors. I think of Stonewall, and the queer liberation in America. I think of the feminist movement. I think of the growing challenges ahead. And I'm reminded of Latino labor heroes Dolores Huerta and Hugo Chavez's simple yet effective words: *Sí, sí se puede!* It's hard to think about new realities without considering the impacts of those who came before me, so that I could grow up in a world they envisioned, and in many cases, never got the chance to enjoy themselves. I am reminded of the many revolutions my self-identity has experienced—the many coming-out moments, the knowledge passed on from past and current lovers, finding a community, experiencing mentorship. All these fractals make me the person I am today, unafraid of occupying spaces that are unwelcoming for people that look like me and with a seething thirst for expressing myself and protecting our future. When the opportunity came to be part of the making of *A Great Gay Book*—revisiting the work and men profiled in the pages of *Hello Mr.*—one idea prevailed: to push progress forward. Our community relies on the collective defiance and progress of others. There's an embedded nostalgia in our community that moves us to examine the past and the paths of others in order to forge new ways forward. These stories, our stories, embody revolution. At a time when our mere ability to exist is in peril, it feels important and necessary to have an acute understanding of our collective and individual power to make change happen. Each of the subjects featured in the pages ahead creates reactionary work, pushing against the world's obsession with obstructing our visibility, while always respecting what came before as they lead us into an unapologetically queer future.

Nic Dorward

Issue 01, 2013 | Photos by Adrian Tuazon-McCheyne

The story behind the first *Hello Mr.* cover is loaded with emotions: tender, crushing, and inspiring. In order to understand the magnitude of the first-ever issue, we have to go back to Australia in 2012, when *Hello Mr.* was a buffering dream. In the midst of producing the first issue, a letter found its way to the magazine's founder, Ryan Fitzgibbon. The excruciating and heartwarming letter, written by Nic Dorward, was the story of a gay man telling his best friend that he is HIV positive. The cover image—eyes closed, evoking warmth—was chosen because it felt inviting for people to engage with the inaugural issue. That letter has turned out to be, nearly a decade later, more important and impactful than ever. In 2020, Ryan reconnected with Nic to share the news of his own HIV diagnosis. The steps outlined in the original letter, and the accompanying emotions, helped the very same person who once felt inspired by its contents. Their conversation harks back in sentiment to a line from the first-ever editor's letter: "By lowering our guards and exposing ourselves to scrutiny, I believe we've created something as true-to-life as the genuine individuals who have generously contributed to it." Such is true for Nic. As a co-founder of The Institute of Many (TIM), his activism over the last decade has changed the way Australia talks about HIV and how people living with HIV feel about themselves. His work continues to ignite social change and inspire others to build new futures for their respective communities around the world. It always goes back to the community. Always.

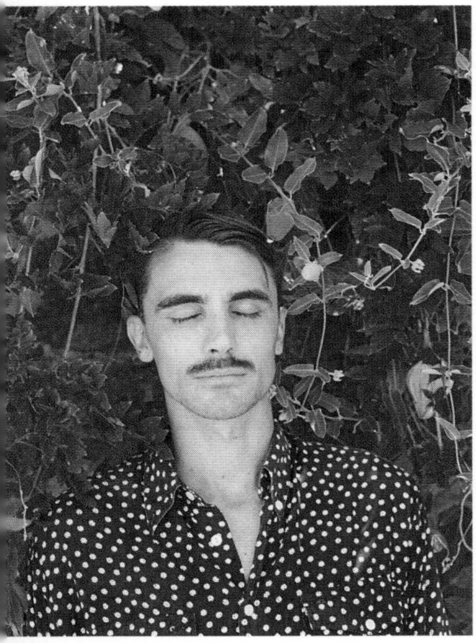

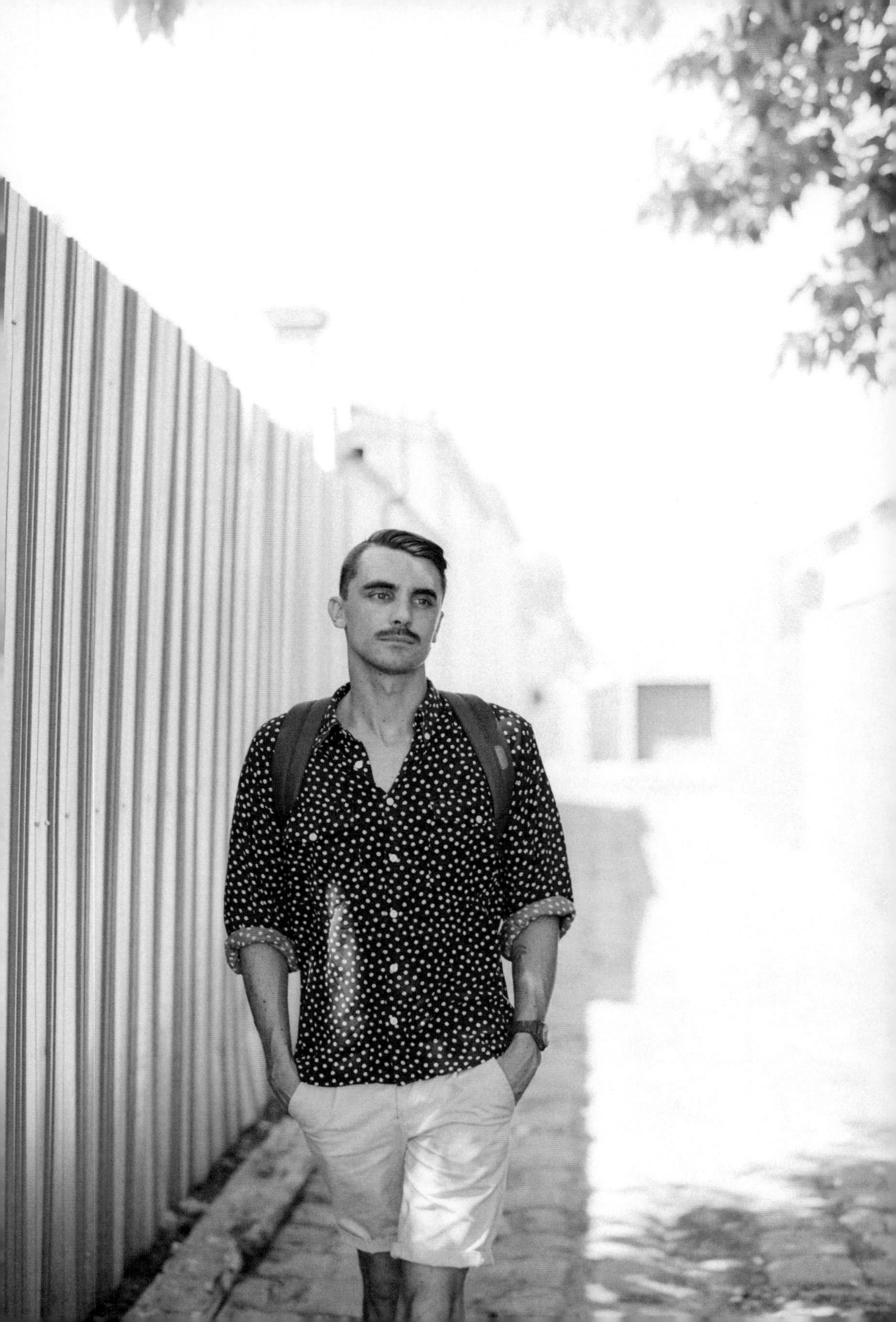

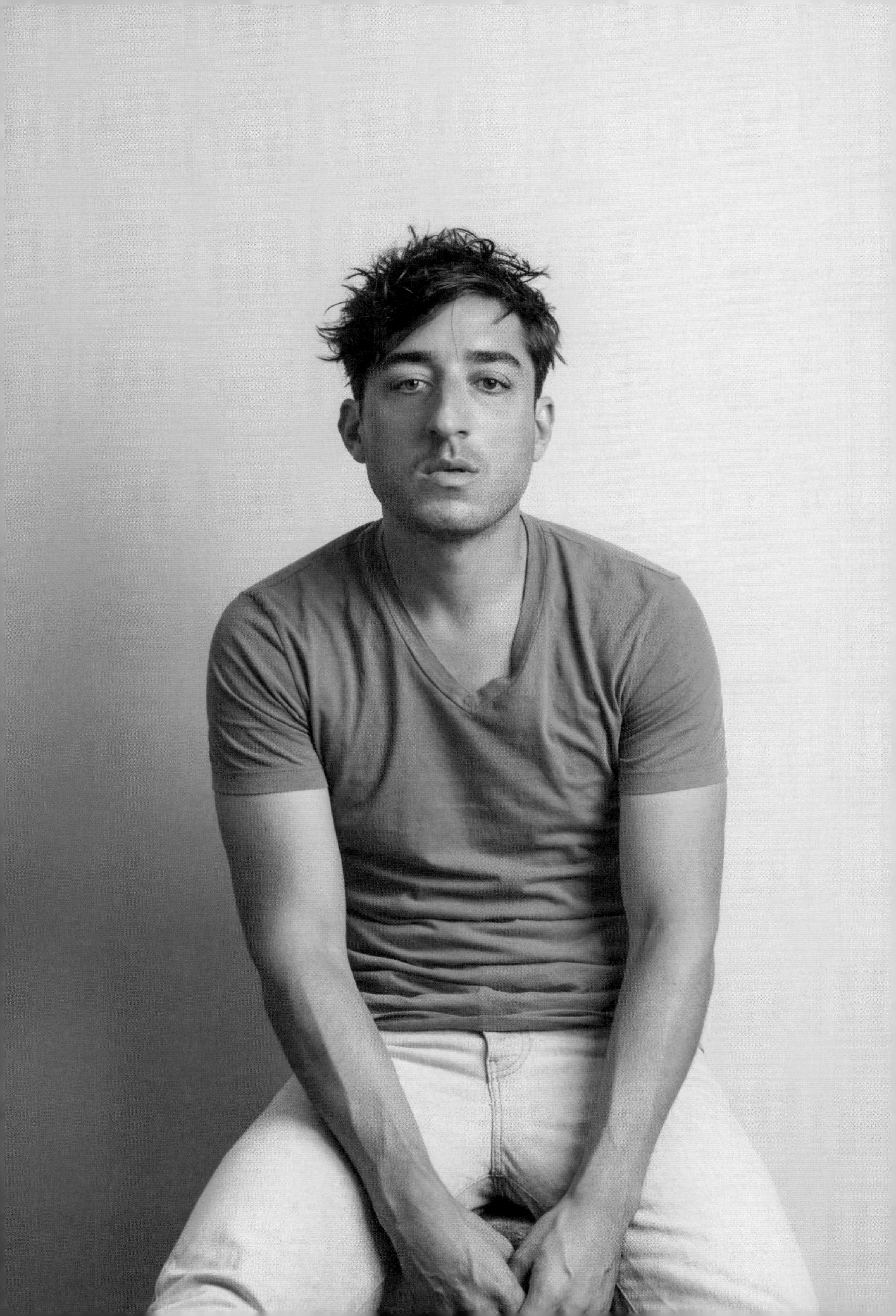

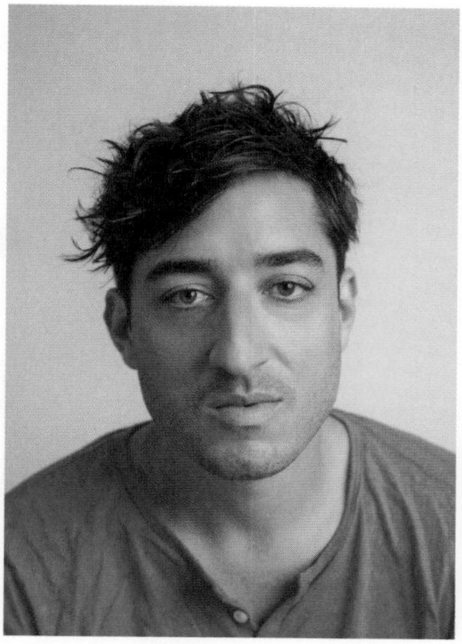

Ed Droste

Issue 02, 2013 | Photos by Daniel Seung Lee

On the cover of the second issue of *Hello Mr.* in 2013, Ed Droste talked about leaving New York City in search of less chaos and more peace. In those years, he was the poster child for indie culture—melancholic, drum-filled music, unique style, and an inner circle formed by quirky creatives and *it* folks. The former lead singer of cult favorite band Grizzly Bear, Droste had recently relocated to Los Angeles, enamored of the sunlight and the landscape, not to mention the ease of California living. Droste built a world in which his lived experiences served as inspiration for his music. The musician hosted an infamous yearly Cape Cod escape with thirty of his closest friends, which he once described as "summer adult vacation." The gatherings brought together Droste's personal world—childhood and life friends—with some of the era's hottest culture shakers and movers like Alex Hawgood, Busy Philipps, and Rostam Batmanglij, who all happened to be part of the safe haven the musician built around him. All of this, as he explained during his *Hello Mr.* cover interview, was in the pursuit of peace, growth, and clarity.

Now forty-three years old, Droste is off the grid, not active on any major social media. In 2020 Droste announced, via a podcast episode of *Lunch Therapy*, that he was leaving the ebbs and flows of the music industry to pursue a career in therapy. His music career, creating and performing anthems of high emotional wattage, now seems a fitting prelude for his current gig.

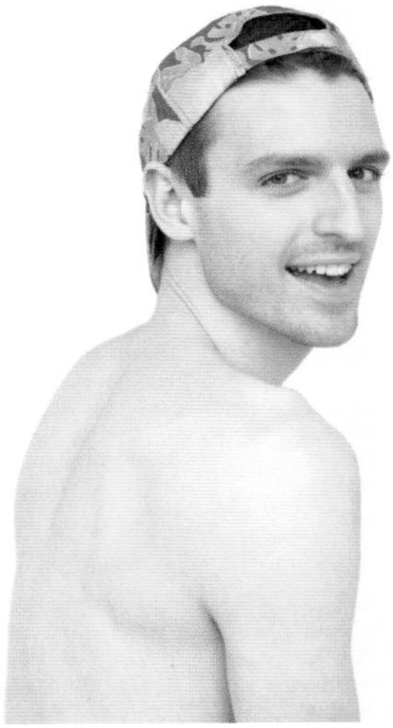

Dan Donigan

Issue 03, 2014 | Photos by Marcus Morris (above) and Zhang Qingyun (opposite)

With his appearance on *RuPaul's Drag Race* season 6, Dan Donigan, known on stage as Milk, embodied on television a new era in queer culture–opulent identity expression, the resurgence of the camp aesthetic, and nostalgic chaos inspired by the likes of Michael Alig and Leigh Bowery. Who better to represent a new wave in queer culture than Milk on the cover of *Hello Mr.*'s third issue in 2014? "Camp is simply looking like a joke while being in on the joke," he said during the interview. Following in the footsteps of Club Kids before him, Milk has dedicated his life, both personal and professional, to coloring outside the lines–even ignoring the lines at times–broadening the frontiers of drag, one bald, sequinned, pregnant look at a time. In recent days, Milk remains active not only as a pop artist and drag performer but also as an internet starlet. His website, bigandmilky.com, showcases design elements reminiscent of the early days of the internet and immediately points to a YouTube channel filled with cooking videos, makeup tutorials, and other wacky content. The website feels like performance art, equal parts homage and critique on the current state of internet culture. It's all so very Milky.

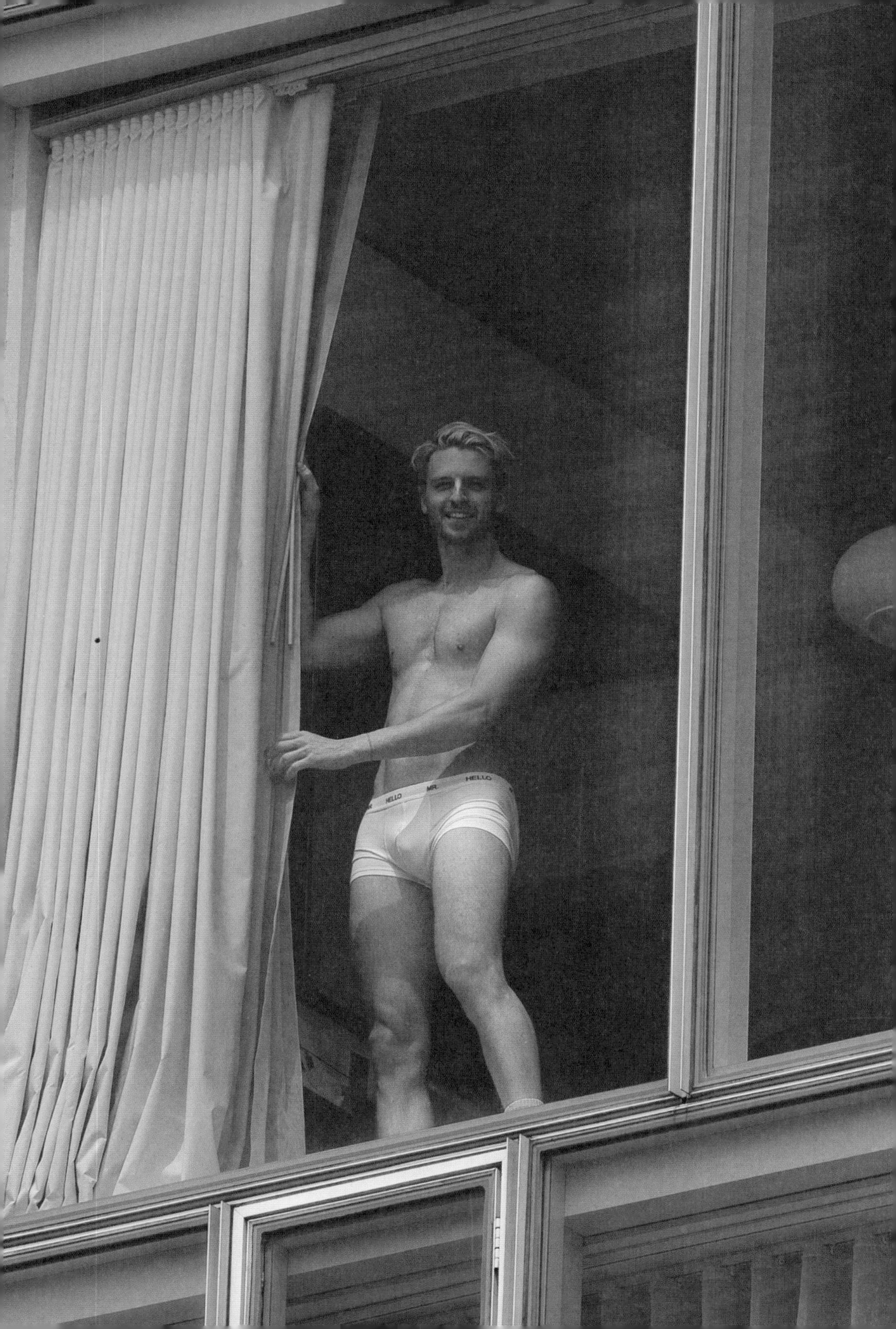
HELLO
MR.
HELLO

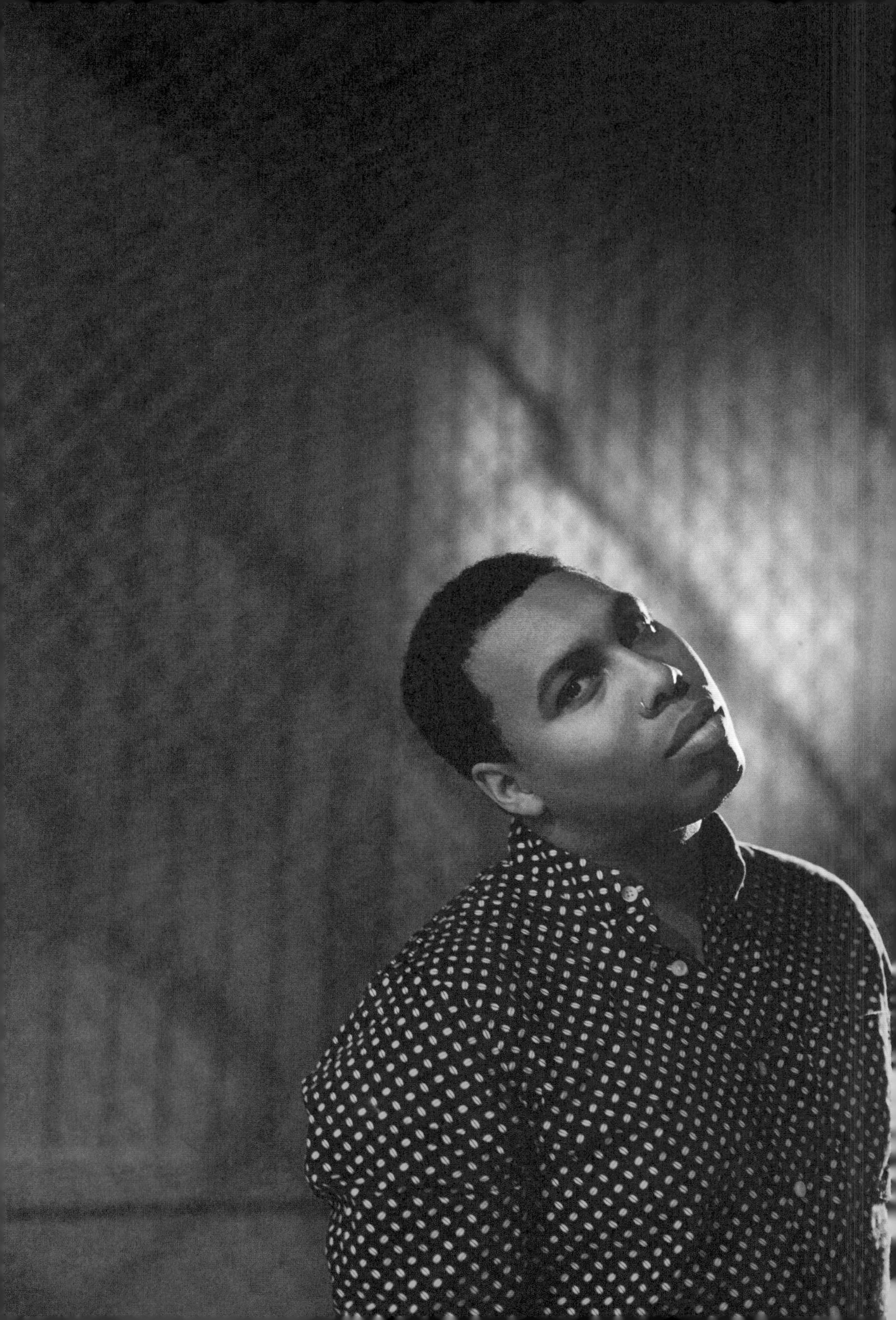

Saeed Jones

Issue 04, 2014 | Photos by Michael George

At the time of his 2014 *Hello Mr.* cover Saeed Jones was emerging as a leading force in culture: a hot up-and-coming poet and the founding editor of Buzzfeed's LGBT vertical. During his interview, the Memphis-born, Texas-raised poet went to great lengths describing the wild nature of his now award-winning poetry book *Prelude to Bruise*, the result of a reclusive time in New York City. The book went on to become a finalist for the National Book Critics Circle Award for Poetry. In the time since the publication of Jones's first book, his writing has appeared in *The New Yorker*, the *New York Times*, and *GQ*; he's also accumulated awards left and right. Jones published the memoir *How We Fight for Our Lives* in 2019, which earned him the Kirkus Prize for Nonfiction. Now a fully formed poetry supernova, Jones published his second book of poetry, *Alive at the End of the World*, in 2022 while launching a culture-centric podcast, *Vibe Check*, with Sam Sanders and Zach Stafford. The poet and culture commentator continues to share his self-proclaimed, unapologetic, and very queer thoughts on Twitter. Some things just don't change. And we love to see it.

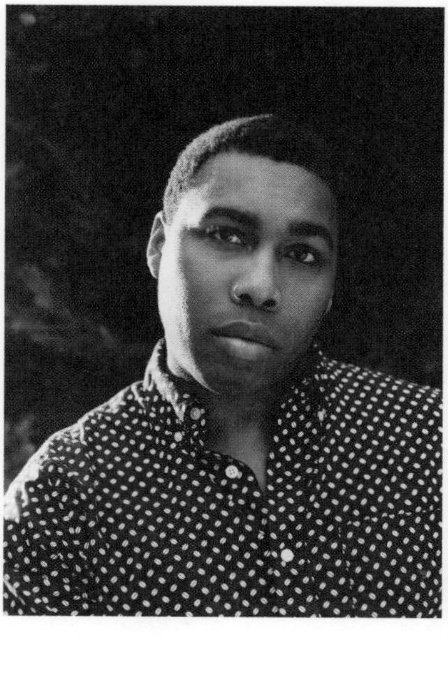

Mike Hadreas

Issue 05, 2015 | Photos by Kathy Lo

After the release of his third album, *Too Bright*, Perfume Genius, born Mike Hadreas, was experiencing a sort of renaissance in 2015. Going from internet idol—we described him as "queen of sad boys, art kid weirdos, and all the cult-classic horror films you've never heard of"—to celebrated and often imitated queer musician. Even years after becoming our fifth cover mister, Perfume Genius has maintained and reimagined a work (and fan base) that began on MySpace into a blue utopia where queerness overlaps with cinematic depictions of love, anger, fear, pain, and joy. During the cover story interview he discussed moving away from New York City and practicing habits that enriched his life and ultimately his art—like not smoking cigarettes. After six studio albums, including *No Shape* (2017) and *Set My Heart on Fire Immediately* (2020), two profoundly deep and flamboyant albums, he's not only a critically acclaimed and loved musician, but also a rebellious queer idol. Now in his forties, with his most recent album, *Ugly Season* (2022), Hadreas continues to explore and expose the many, often beautiful caveats of living life as a queer person in an oftentimes difficult and chaotic world. Not bad for an internet sad boy.

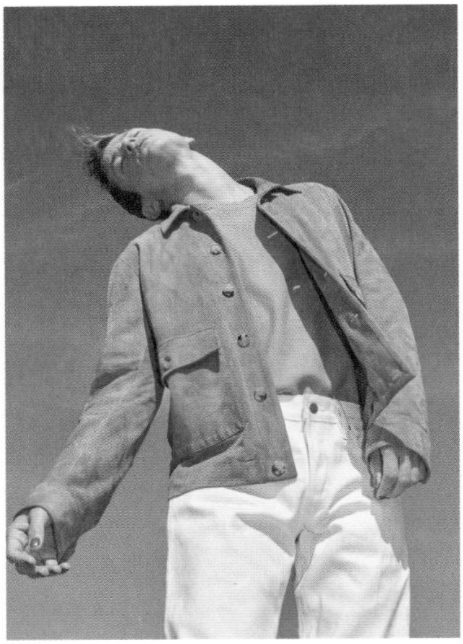

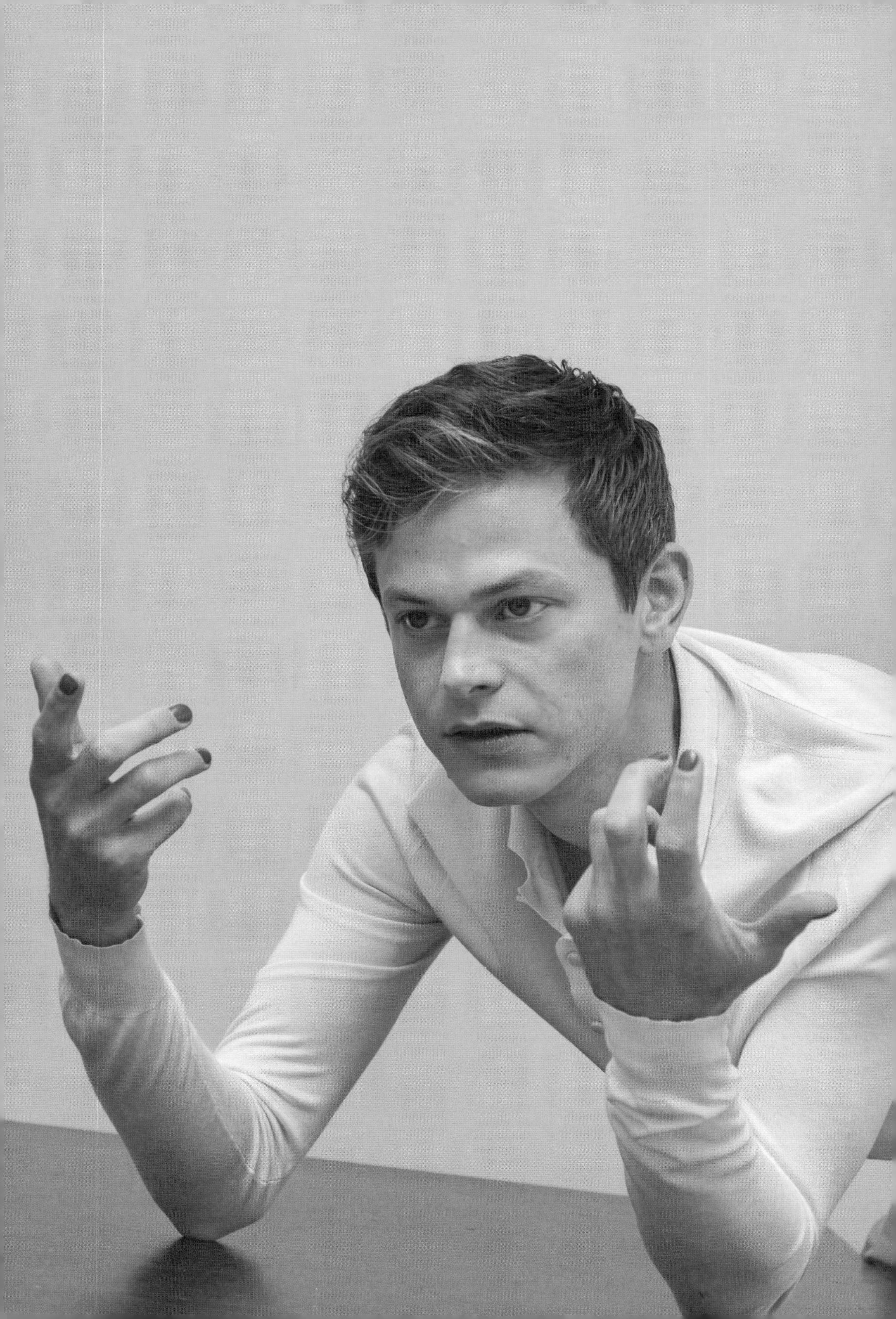

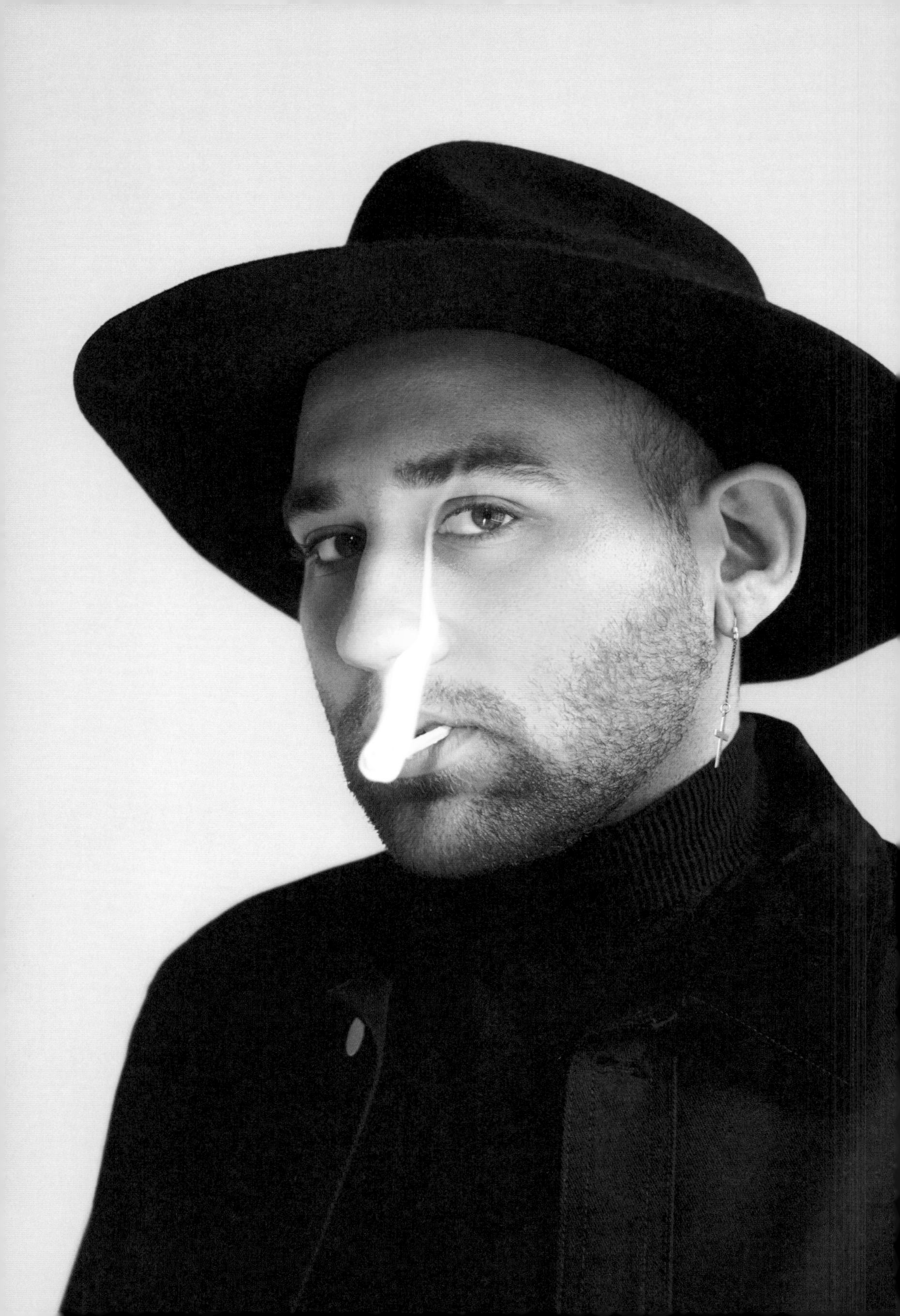

Parson James

Issue 07, 2016 | Photos by Peter Ash Lee

In 2016 when Parson James was featured on the cover of *Hello Mr.*'s seventh issue, signs—red flags, in fact—of the United States' (and worldwide) unraveling were shining bright. Movements on all sides of the culture wars were developing at lightning speed, much like the career of Ashton Parson (his birth name) of Cheraw, South Carolina. At the time of his cover, the singer-songwriter was stealing the show, quite literally. His song "Stole the Show" with Kygo was a meteoric success worldwide. It was all happening. As a biracial gay man from the South, Parson embodied the success and liberation many dream of achieving. It made sense then that his story be shared in an issue inspired, in the words of *Hello Mr.*'s founder, "by those who challenge the ideals of others." In his conversation with writer Fran Tirado, Parson opened up about being "a human being, discovering love, my darknesses, the energies within myself," in order to write his album *The Temple*. That itch to learn more about ourselves often leads to new, unexplored territory, or as the editor's note of the seventh issue states: "It is this desire and need for more, after all, that pushes us to succeed." Parson continues to create music. He's worked with JoJo and continues to party with Kygo. Many things have changed, but not his love for wide-brimmed hats and honesty.

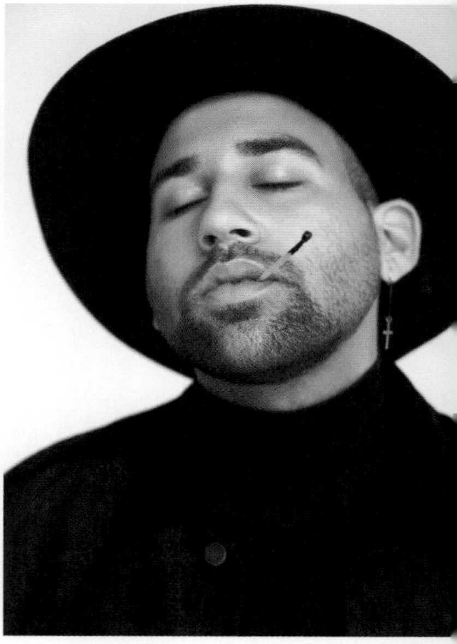

Stephen Galloway

Issue 08, 2016 | Photos by Jody Rogac

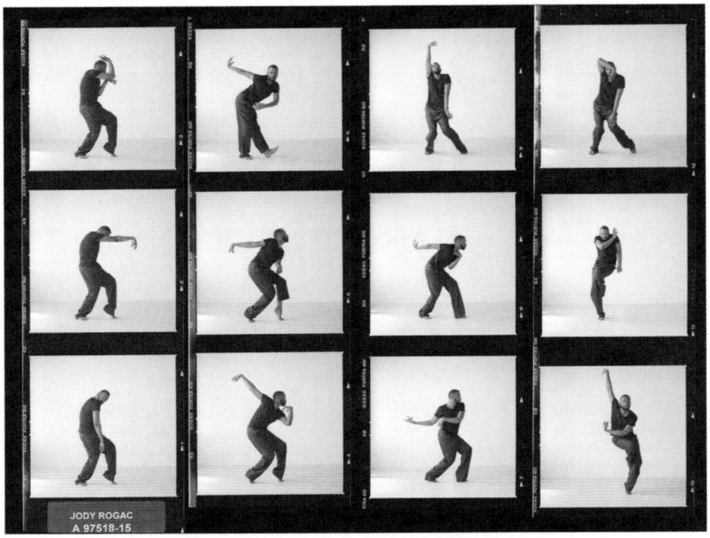

In order to achieve one's dreams, a dash of delusion is essential. "To not be governed by opinion," as the editor's note of issue eight of *Hello Mr.* states, allows creative minds to bloom. Take the life and work of Stephen Galloway—the prolific American movement maestro with more than two decades of experience in ballet dance theater, which has been as free flowing and thunderous as the many fashion images he's become synonymous with directing. It makes sense then that in the wake of the tragedy at Pulse nightclub in Orlando, Galloway's story of resilience and endurance took center stage in an issue celebrating the actor and HIV activist Javier Muñoz. Oftentimes life's hurdles stall individuals with star power like Galloway, but it is their ability to trust the process and adjust to their environment that allows for the magic to happen. As the multi-hyphenate confided to writer Teddy Tinson during their conversation for the issue's feature, his mother knew he was meant to be an inspiring and groundbreaking presence in the world, offering him words of advice when he faced adversity. "My mom used to say, 'When people are looking at you in a strange way and for long periods of time, it's because you're so beautiful. They've never seen anyone like you, so you should stand up tall, look them in the eye, and smile.'" Today, Galloway continues to create beauty while staying true to himself. "I simply do my best to align myself with the universe, and the art happens around, or in addition to, that."

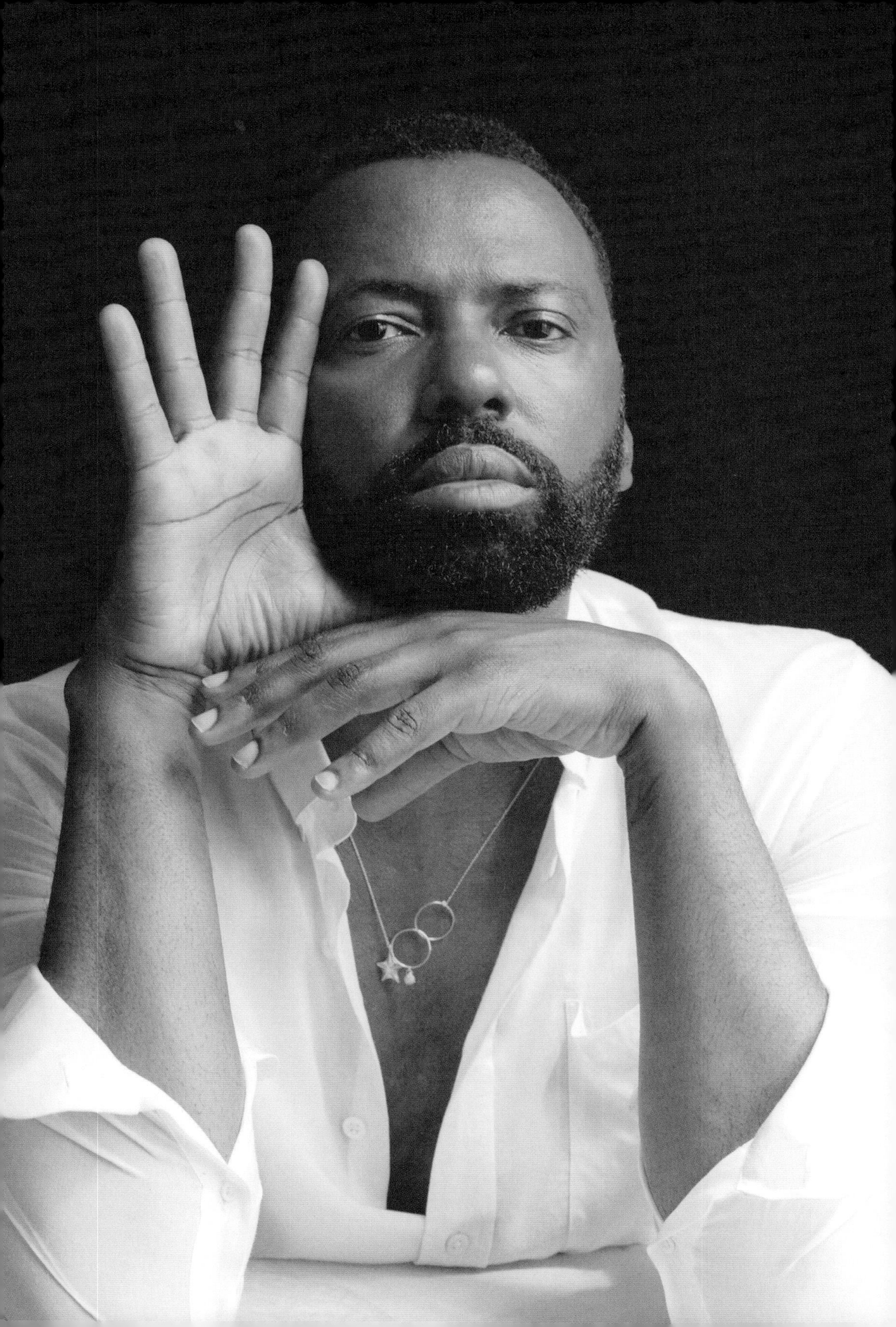

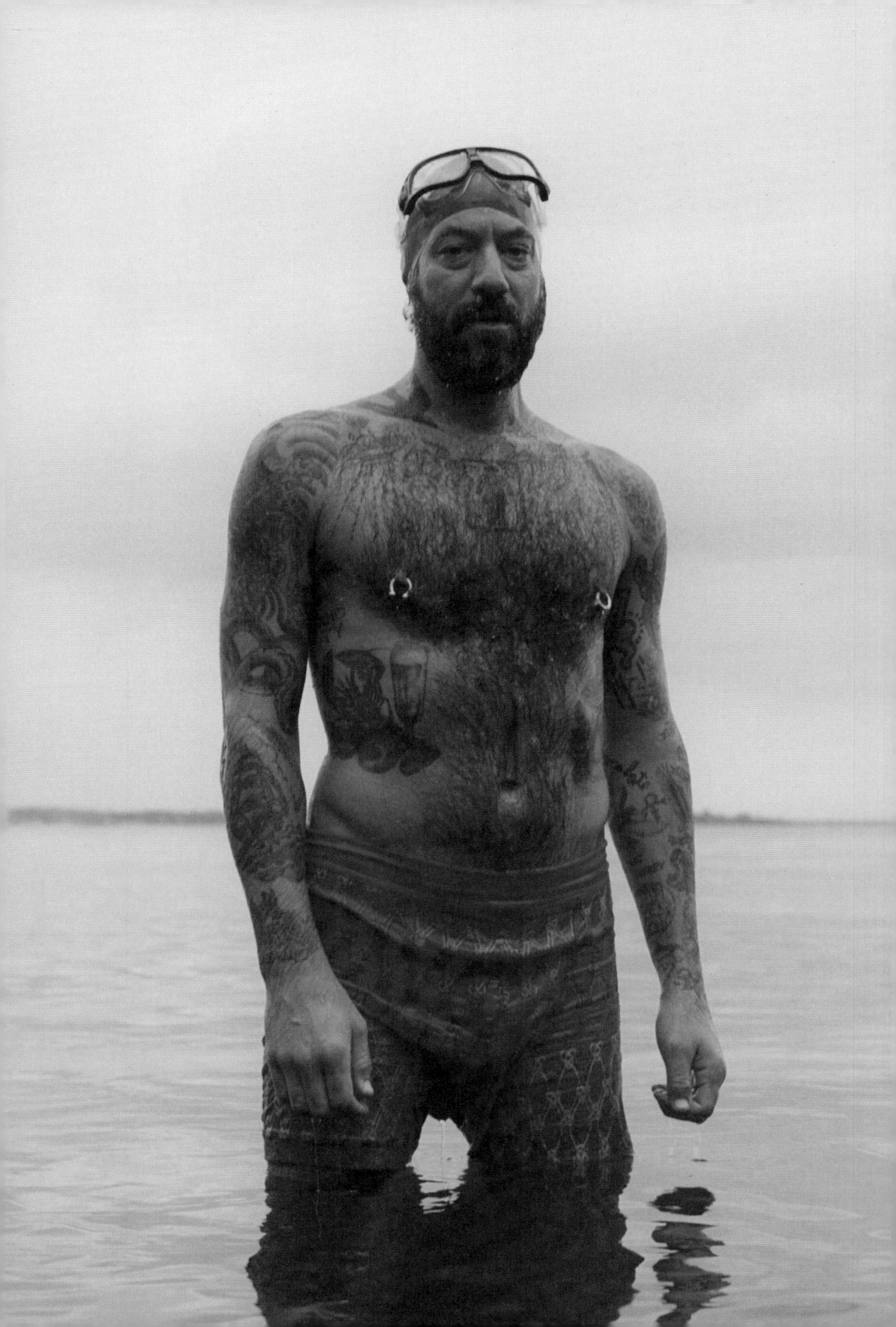

Brian Anderson

Issue 09, 2017 | Photos by Samuel Bradley

"Pursuing something that challenges expectations requires a lot of personal sacrifice." These words, from the editor's note of the ninth issue of *Hello Mr.*, encapsulate the essence of Brian Anderson, the pro skateboarder from Queens, New York, who single-handedly rattled a sixty-year-old sport industry at the expense of his own coming-out story, and privacy. After spending a lifetime building a career and reputation in the skateboarding world—he's a World Cup champion—Anderson risked it all in 2016 to tell his story, in his own words. In the wake of Trump's election, defying established standards, especially in cis-hetero dominated spaces, carried a lot of weight personally and culturally. By coming out publicly, Anderson busted doors open for many generations of skateboarders to come, and by proxy pushed the LGBTQIA+ community to reexamine its oftentimes contentious, ageist, and toxic understanding of the coming-out narrative. He reminded everyone that there is no timeline to learn to be ourselves, and getting there takes time. And as our fierce founder reminds us, again, in his editor's note for the issue, being our true selves is always worth it: "The work we create to help ourselves, will always find a way to be a guide for others." Today, Anderson continues the hard work of leading by example, pushing the limits of the sport (and our culture) to become even more welcoming and diverse. He is still six foot three and handsome.

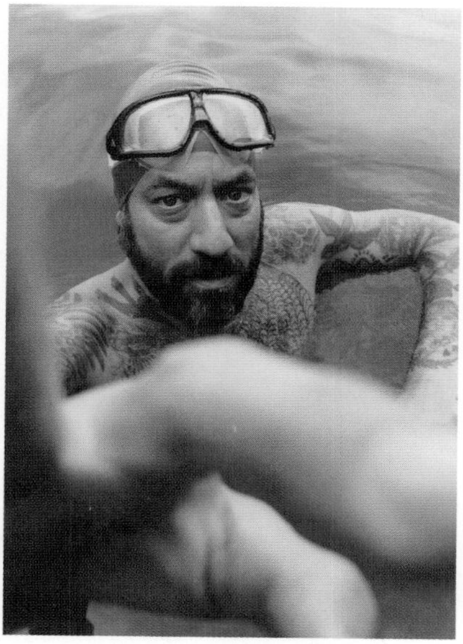

John Early

Issue 09, 2017 | Photos by Stanislaw Boniecki

John Early has always been a funny guy. His talents rose to prominence during a time in American history when evil in the form of Donald Trump as the United States president reigned supreme. The looming presence of the unknown instilled fear and caused many to seek shelter. That was not the case for Early or *Hello Mr.* In fact, the actor caught the eye of *Hello Mr.* and the comedy glitterati with his role in *Search Party*, a character he explains as archetypal yet critical during the conversation that accompanied his 2017 *Hello Mr.* cover. Early's breakthrough was imminent as he combined his social media presence, unfiltered gayness, and humor largely aimed at poking fun and flipping off the Trump administration. "It's clear why so many of the most powerful cultural forms are the product of turmoil, heartbreak, or pain," read the editor's letter of issue 09. Early's career is in a way a product of that era. His career has since seen a meteoric rise without losing his true essence. Today he continues to share jokes and memes, but to many new fans and through larger platforms—his debut HBO special, "John Early: Now More Than Ever," premiered on June 17, 2023. Early's work, then and now, can be best described by this quote pulled from his interview: "Do your anal jokes, give people a break."

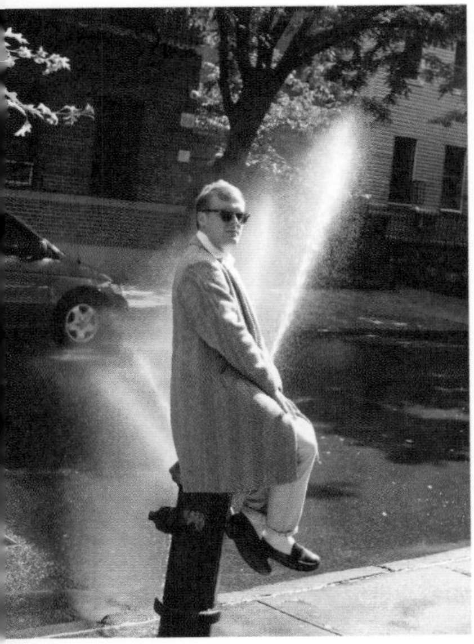

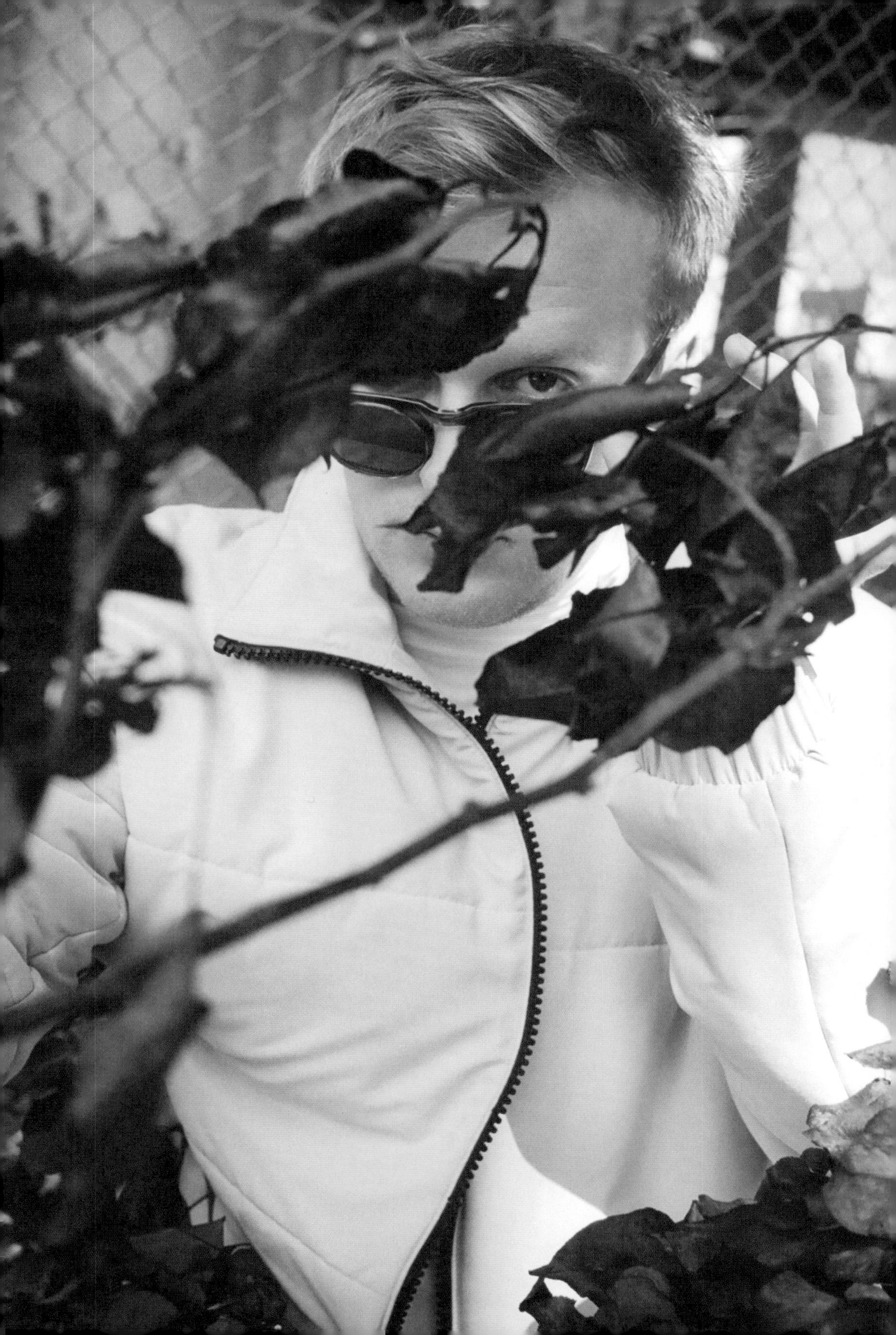

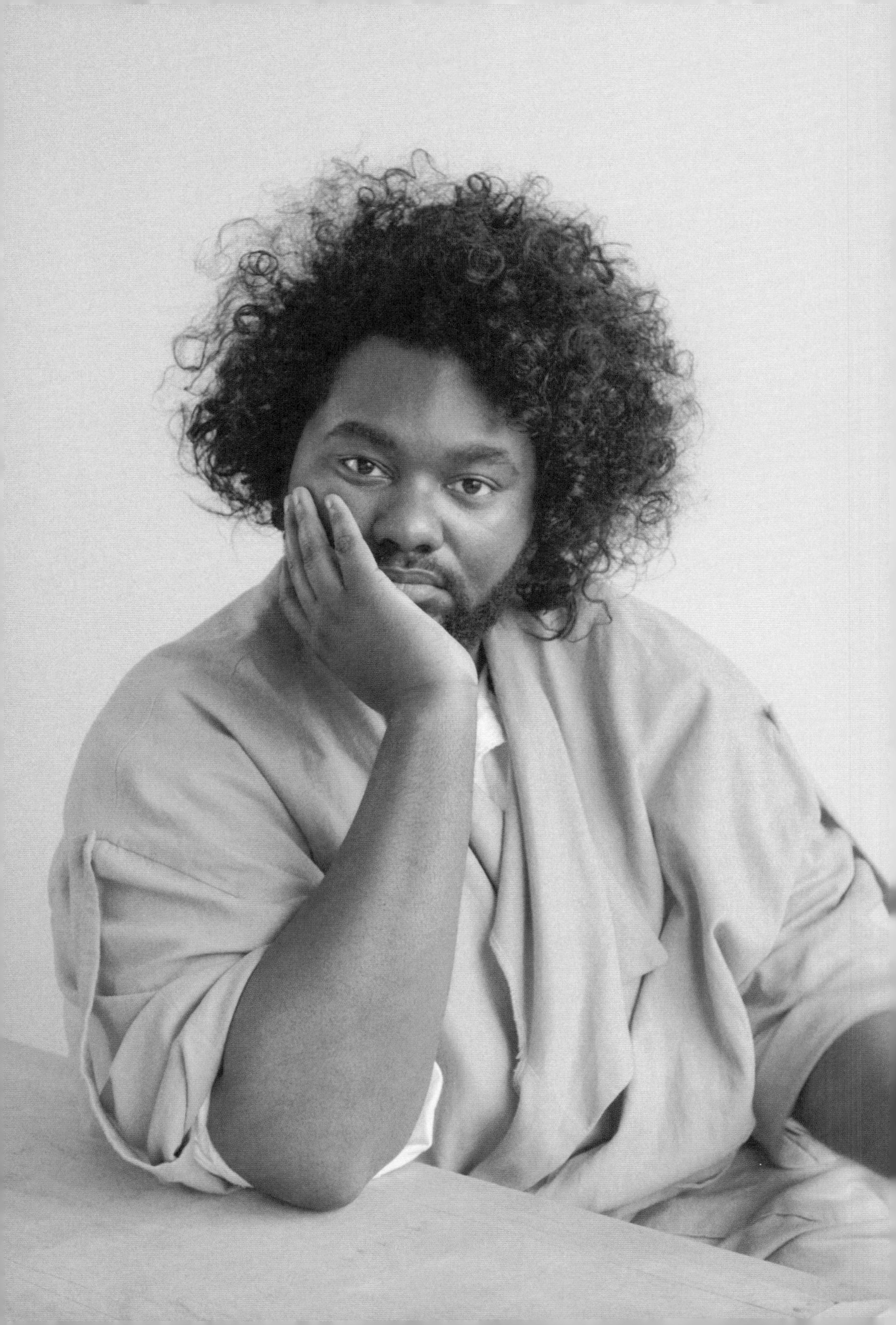

Tunde Olaniran

Issue 09, 2017 | Photos by Landon Speers

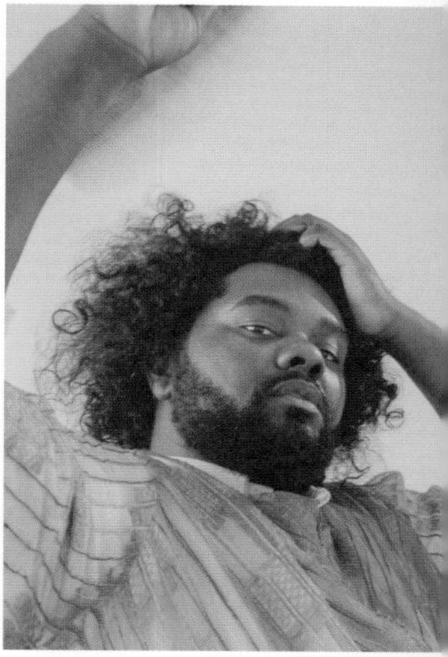

When our humanity and identity are threatened, our innate reaction is to fight back. In 2017 it was made clear to women, queer, Black, Indigenous, and other people of marginalized identity that even after decades, centuries even, of fighting the good fight, America was still subservient to its racist, abusive, and xenophobic ways. Vitriol spilled like flood waters through our culture, exposing the visible cracks of our fractured systems. Tunde Olaniran grew up in Flint, Michigan, and like many of us, they probably recited the words "With liberty and justice for all" at school every day. Those divine rights, which we were promised applied to all, proved to be reserved for only a select few. "Can one really transgress by simply living, by pursuing a life uninhibited, unsymbolized?" ponders the founder of *Hello Mr.* in his editor's note for issue 09. The answer for the then twenty-nine-year-old singer-songwriter was simple. Sometimes being ourselves is enough to rattle a space. Olaniran's music hit chords with the culture at the time of their feature in the magazine. Life is not necessarily fair for a gender nonconforming Black singer-songwriter from Michigan. It has never been, and that's the point. To many, Olaniran's anecdotes of oppression and racism drenched in sweet musical notes and lyrical prowess exposed a new, terrifying reality in America. They were labeled as a transgressor when in reality their music was and continues to be about "dealing with the simple subject matter of everyday life." Unlike many, Olaniran's reaction when faced with imminent threat was to bask in the glory of their own identity. A simple act with infinite resonance.

Olly Alexander

Issue 10, 2018 | Photos by Scott Gallagher

The tenth issue of *Hello Mr.*, published in 2018, came at a pivotal time in culture: Gay was going mainstream. With the impact of the popularity of *RuPaul's Drag Race*, the arrival of new shows like *POSE* and the 2018 *Queer Eye* reboot, and three years after the ruling of *Obergefell v. Hodges*—the yassification of culture was well underway. But below the surface where things usually begin, a nascent movement was forming in the queer community. Extravagant self-expression accompanied by a deeper questioning and understanding of *the* community opened the floodgates for a reckoning. During that time, many faces emerged as leaders of the movement. Olly Alexander is one of those faces. In fact, the actor, singer, and pop star had been waiting for this moment. At the time of his *Hello Mr.* cover Alexander was entering a new era in his pop journey with *Palo Santo*, an in-your-face futuristic queer musical project. At the same time, Alexander was reintroducing himself to fans, critics, and the internet as nonbinary. In the years since, culture has evolved through revolutions few of us could have imagined. And so has Olly Alexander's career. He starred in the 2021 seminal HIV/AIDS series *It's a Sin* and released the dance album *Night Call* as Years & Years. He has collaborated with the likes of Kylie Minogue and Elton John, continuing his mission of creating worlds; as he told us back in 2018, "societal constructs and hierarchical forces that have governed us for thousands of years, don't exist anymore—that's a queer imagination."

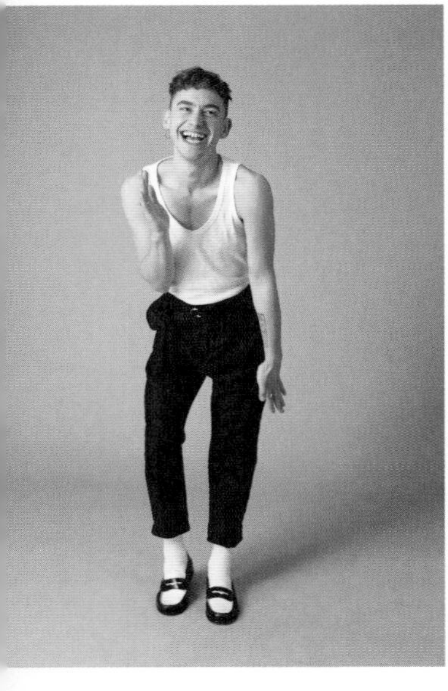

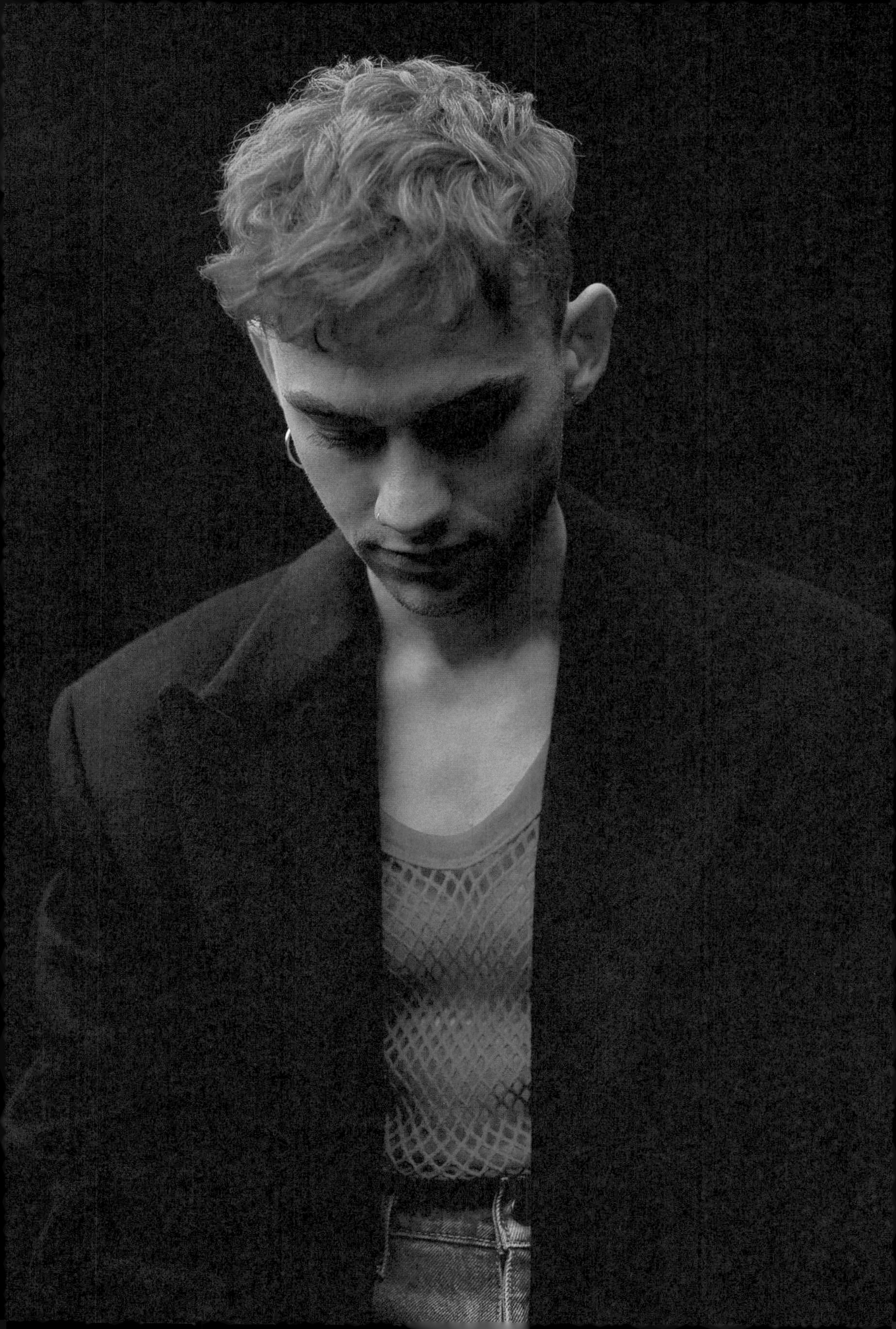

History of My Blood

Mason Pippenger

Daniel's café has the ugliest green carpet and it always smelt like old cigarettes. My parents say that they have gone to Daniel's since they've adopted me and my brother. Mondays through Thursdays, the café serves undistinguished American food. Rubbery hamburgers, cold Pepsi products, and the like. But on Fridays, Daniel prepares his domestic specialty: Ethiopian food.

My parents have always tried to surround me and my brother with our heritage as best as they could. The living room of my childhood home had shelves lined with African twine art alongside the family portraits and my great-grandma's china. They kept our traditional Ethiopian baby clothes hung up in their closet long after we had outgrown them. I remember when I was five, sitting down on the family room floor and watching old VHS footage that my dad had taken while they were at the orphanage, seeing us for the first time in person, readying to take us on the twenty-three-hour flight back to America with them.

Ancient Greek historians first used the word *Aethiopia* to describe the people who resided in the horn of Africa. *Aitho* meaning "I burn" and *ops* meaning "face." People often ask when I figured out I was adopted. With two white parents and three white siblings, it was kind of obvious to me which of us were the ones with burnt faces. But that didn't mean much to me. I was taught that blood is only sort of thicker than water. I knew what a metaphor was before I could read. But family is family, and that's all I've ever known. And as much as my parents tried to connect me to my African roots, they never could understand the weight of Blackness. But they tried and I love them for that. Going to Daniel's café was just another way they tried.

On the occasional Friday night, my parents would call my grandma and tell her to meet us at Daniel's. It was a thirty-minute drive to Ligonier from our house and I never understood why we made the long trek there when we could have a perfectly good Happy Meal right down the road. But I'd roll my eyes and crawl to the backseat of the van, waiting for the night to be over. Daniel would come back from the busy kitchen and greet us when we arrived, giving my father a firm handshake and hugging my mother. He'd squat and give me and my brother fist bumps and smile ear to ear, showing the gap in his teeth. He was a kind man. Too kind. Like when my parents would insist that I eat the Ethiopian plates they would order, but all I wanted was the chicken strips and

French fries, Daniel would tell my parents that I was young and could enjoy the spicy beyainatu when I got older. He'd punctuate this with a wink. Sometimes he would give my brother and me quarters for the gumball machine outside the restaurant. I always felt like he understood something my parents didn't, like maybe our African blood tied us together.

In the corner of my room, the old Ethiopian flag hangs down from two hooks. It depicts the Lion of Judah striding confidently, long golden mane hanging low. In its paw, the lion holds a cross with the country's flag draping down its stem. In Genesis, a father blesses his son, telling him he will be praised by many, a leader, a lion. Ethiopia is one of the two countries in Africa that was never colonized. Italy tried to take the land, twice actually. White men flocked to the continent, thirsty for Black blood and their land. European powers took country by country like picking fruit from trees. In 1896, 120,000 Ethiopians unified to defeat the impeding Italians with a mix of rifles and spears. It is known as the worst defeat ever inflicted on a European power in Africa. Three decades later, the Italians tried again, and failed. History shows that white men don't like to be humiliated by niggas. In 1935, Benito Mussolini and his troops invaded. Using sulfur mustard, an illegal chemical warfare agent, Italy was able to defeat the Ethiopian army and occupy the capital of Addis Ababa. Years of violence ensued between the Italian government and Ethiopians until 1941 when emperor Haile Selassie returned from exile and claimed his rightful throne in Addis Ababa, driving out the European troops and avoiding colonization of his country. This is my history.

For my twentieth, my brother got me one of those DNA tests where you spit in a test tube, mail it off to some billion-dollar company, and they send you back all this information about yourself so you can connect to your distant relatives across the world. It's strange how the science knows more about me than I do. But I've grown used to this, and I shipped my saliva to California. There was something ceremonial yet taboo about me and my brother sitting around our dining room table sending bits of our bodies out into the unknown. My brother, Matthew, is the closest thing I have to a biological relative. Many mistake us for twins, but I believe our differences to be obvious, knowing that he comes from the Amhara region in the northern region of Ethiopia and how you can tell because his body is short and muscular and his face rounder. Only four months older than me, we've gotten to experience much of this life together. I know that sometimes he shares the same burdens, yet we've never really talked about them. Still today, I wonder the weight of the things he holds and the things he's let go.

I didn't know what to expect, but I was nervous about getting the DNA results back. Like maybe they would reveal I had a biological sibling out in the middle of Alabama. Then I would have to fly to Alabama to meet this stranger and make awkward small talk over coffee while our parents live-streamed the whole thing. I didn't want to do that. It sounded too much like the Hallmark movies my father likes to watch. The results came back with scientific gibberish. Stuff about maternal haplogroups and Neanderthalic ancestry composition. I didn't know what that meant. But I now knew I had around fifty-five DNA relatives. Distant cousins and relatives were scattered around the globe sharing .04 percent of my DNA. The closest relative to me was estimated to be around an eighth cousin, from Egypt. Matthew's results were similarly useless. I breathed a sigh, one of equal parts relief and disappointment. As much as I was satisfied with my life and my adoptive family, a sliver of my mind occasionally wanders to a place where Hallmark movies are true and the chase for a long-lost sibling is intoxicating. This is the truth of abandoned children.

People often ask if I would go back. The simple answer is yes. The evasive answer asks how do I return to a place that I've never known. How do I be someone I've never been? When Daniel serves me homemade injera on a Friday night, are we at my table or am I a guest eating his food? And am I wrong for turning it away?

A white man messages me on a hookup app. He asks me where I'm from. He can tell that I am from Africa, it's in the facial structure: the elongated oval shape, the thin then wide nose, the sable eyes. "Ethiopia," I type back. "Oh, so you're a real black." "Hm?" I say, even though I know what he means. I know that he means that I am pureblood nigger. From the motherland. I know that he means by some miraculous and divine interaction involving prideful burnt faces and chemical bombs, my ancestors were able to avoid being taken by his ancestors. I know that this man means it's time for me to pay up. Pay up for the sin of pride. I know that real Black means untamed Black. History shows that white men don't like to be humiliated by niggas. This man makes me sick and I feel like a traitor when we fuck anyway. I wanted to watch him suffocate on sulfur mustard and see his neck curl back, red, begging for forgiveness. But instead, I watch this man take what he wants and call it his and repeat his history.

Before the continental diaspora, but after the shifting of tectonic plates, scientists say that the earliest signs of modern-day human beings can be traced back to Africa. The buried skulls and teeth have carefully determined that the start of our civilization was over 75,000 years ago in the jungles of central Africa. Scientists also found evidence that early homo sapiens migrated from Africa up north to the Middle East, parts of Asia, and even Europe. I can imagine them, naked and Black among the trees, walking to an open field, spreading like pollen, without guns or gas. Just their bodies.

I am everywhere. The blood of my mother's mother sinking into the earth. My father's father's tears dispersing into sky. I was here in the beginning and I am here now. As a result of migrations, and adoptions, and fallen armies, I am here. My burnt face being swallowed whole by the freedom of tomorrow. Like sand, my past and future are scattered.

Every few months, I log on to that ancestry site and look at my new shared (but still very distant) DNA relatives. Occasionally people message me saying they are also in the Midwest or that they found the last name of our third great-grandfather. Recently, I received a message from a lady named Hanna from Sweden. She told me that she was adopted from Ethiopia soon after she was born and now has a husband and four kids of her own. Sometimes they ask about her ancestry and she said she has tried to fit the pieces together, but she doesn't know much. I don't want to disappoint her and tell her that I don't know any more than she does. I do want to tell her that even though I haven't been to Daniel's café in years, I like Ethiopian food now. My tolerance for spicy food had an exponential increase sometime around middle school. I want to tell her about the sulfur mustard and Mussolini, which she might already know, but I want to remind her.

And I want to tell her that I don't have any pieces to the puzzle, but that there is a map that always leads back to us. But I don't. I don't type anything back. Instead, I think back to Daniel and his gapped smile. I don't know his story or how he ended up in a small dying town in Indiana only thirty minutes from me, but I knew that he was my miracle. I don't believe in coincidences, but I have no choice but to believe in the history of my blood.

Notebook Fragments

Ocean Vuong

AN INTRODUCTION

I lost my virginity earlier than most people I know. The one line in my journal mentioning it simply said: "I lost it today." What strikes me, looking at that entry now, is the cold factuality of those words, that nothing else I could have written would have been that true, that exact. Yet I am pulled, also, to how myriad the phrase is—both in its literal sense of losing one's virginity, but also as a colloquial claim of having lost one's mind, one's self—all of which were faithful to how I felt.

"Notebook Fragments" works as supposed entries in a journal, something I had always wanted to do—the journal having an innately queer quality to it. For me, as for many queer people, the journal, the diary, the notebook, whatever you want to call it, is a place where we can store the parts of ourselves the world (including at times even our loved ones) might not know how to understand or accept. To render my experience into language, even for no one else's eyes but my own, can be a liberating act, albeit a small one. But I think it's the small acts, as small as letters on the page, that add up to saved lives, saved ideas of selves. My entry from today, July 26, 2016:

"11:35 A.M. Umbria, Italy. Two hours ago, before writing this, I fell from my bed and woke up on the tiles of this hotel room. My head hit the laptop, which I stupidly put on the floor when I got tired last night. Glad the screen did not break. My elbow and hip hurt a little. I think I'm okay. For now the light looks like it won't change. See you later."

With this poem, I wanted to insist that this notebook form, as it encompasses the mundane language and images of quotidian life, is still worthy of a poetic project in the same way the sonnet or sestina or haibun are. This idea of making a piece of art not as elevated life, but simply more life, excited me. The notebook is a place where we can lose ourselves and still be held, if only by language in language, which makes it rare and worth it, I think.

A scar's width of warmth on a worn man's neck.
    That's all I wanted to be.
Sometimes I ask for too much just to feel my mouth overflow.
Discovery: My longest pubic hair is 1.2 inches in length.
Good or bad?
7:18 A.M. Kevin overdosed last night. His sister left a message. Couldn't listen
    to all of it. That makes 3 this year.
I promise to stop soon.
Spilled orange juice all over the table this morning. Sudden sunlight
    I couldn't wipe away.
My hands were daylight all through the night.
Woke at 1 A.M. and, for no reason, ran through Duffy's cornfield. Boxers only.
Corn was dry. I sounded like a fire,
    for no reason.
Grandma said *In the war they would grab a baby, a soldier at each ankle, and pull . . .*
    Just like that.
It's finally spring! Daffodils everywhere.
    Just like that.
There are over 13,000 unidentified body parts from the World Trade Center
    being stored in an underground repository in New York City.
Good or bad?
Shouldn't heaven be super-heavy by now?
Maybe the rain is "sweet" because it falls
    through so much of the world.
Even sweetness can scratch the throat, so stir the sugar well—Grandma
4:37 A.M. How come depression makes me feel more alive?
Life is funny.
Note to self: if a guy tells you his favorite poet is Jack Kerouac,
    there's a very good chance he's a douchebag.
Note to self: if Orpheus were a woman I wouldn't be stuck down here.
Why do all my books leave me empty-handed?
In Vietnamese, the word for grenade is "bom," from the French "pomme,"
    meaning "apple."

Or was it American for "bomb?"
Woke up screaming with no sound. The room filling with a bluish water
    called dawn. Went to kiss grandma on the forehead
just in case.
An American soldier fucked a Vietnamese farmgirl. Thus my mother exists.
    Thus I exist. Thus no bombs = no family = no me.
Yikes.
9:47 A.M. Jerked off four times already. My arm kills.
Eggplant = cà pháo = "grenade tomato." Thus nourishment defined
    by extinction.
I met a man tonight. A high school English teacher
    from the next town. A small town. Maybe
I shouldn't have, but he had the hands
    of someone I used to know. Someone I was used to.
The way they formed brief churches
    over the table as he searched for the right words.
I met a man, not you. In his room the Bibles shook on the shelf
    from candlelight. His scrotum a bruised fruit. I kissed it
lightly, the way one might kiss a grenade
    before hurling it into the night's mouth.
Maybe the tongue is also a key.
Yikes.
I could eat you he said, brushing my cheek with his knuckles.
I think I love my mom very much.
Some grenades explode with a vision of white flowers.
Baby's breath blooming in a darkened sky, across
    my chest.

Maybe the tongue is also a pin.
I'm gonna lose it when Whitney Houston dies.
I met a man. I promise to stop.
A pillaged village is a fine example of perfect rhyme. He said that.
He was white. Or maybe, I was just beside myself, next to him.
Either way, I forgot his name by heart.
I wonder what it feels like to move at the speed of thirst—if it's fast
as lying on the kitchen floor with the lights off.
(Kristopher)
6:24 A.M. Greyhound station. One-way ticket to New York City: $36.75.
6:57 A.M. I love you, mom.
When the prison guards burned his manuscripts, Nguyễn Chí Thiện couldn't stop
laughing—the 283 poems already inside him.
I dreamt I walked barefoot all the way to your house in the snow. Everything
was the blue of smudged ink
and you were still alive. There was even a light the shade of a sunrise inside
your window.
God must be a season, grandma said, looking out at the blizzard drowning
her garden.
My footsteps on the sidewalk were the smallest flights.
Dear god, if you *are* a season, let it be the one I passed through
to get here.
Here. That's all I wanted to be.
I promise.

Camp

Michael Huey

Photo by Phil Balyeat

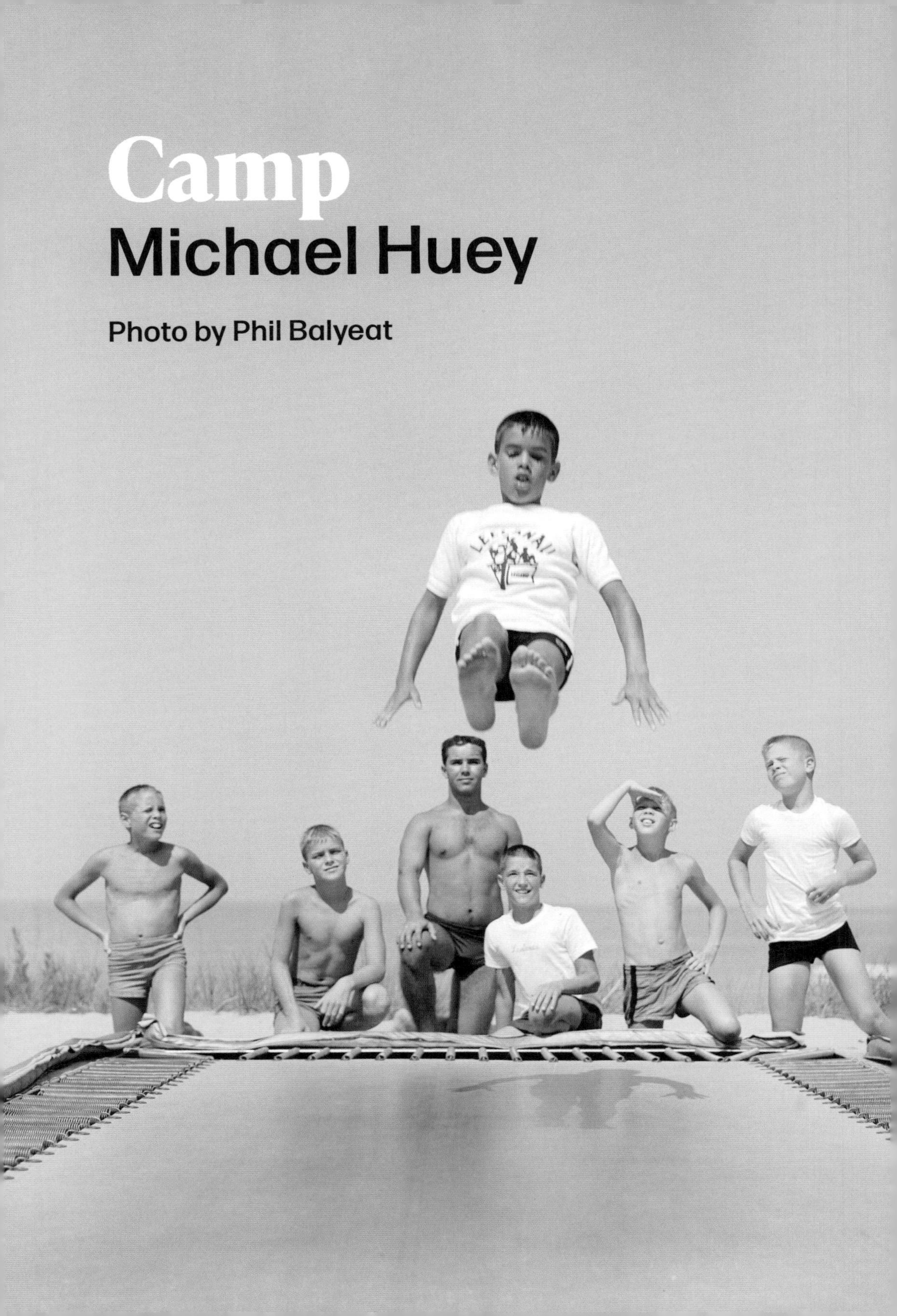

1.

The penis was big, the boy looking at it small. The big penis belonged to a much bigger boy who was a counselor-in-training. The small boy, closest to it, regarded it with curiosity. Later, when he was himself big, he would no longer be able to reconstruct just how it happened that he and the four other campers had assembled in a loose semicircle facing this seventeen-year-old stripling or how the CT had framed his offer to display such a wonder. Were wet swimming trunks involved, on the floor at the CT's tanned feet, Lake Michigan water issuing from them and pooling on the scratched floorboards, the way this event was slowly seeping into the small boy's mind? He would never forget the fabulous erection of the CT, or how it pointed due north, like the stalwart trembling needle of a compass.

The boy was not yet six and too young to be there at all, really, even among the littlest campers, who were a year older. Because of family connections, however, an exception had been made. Still, even as the youngest, he was the one to ask politely if he could touch it, which the CT kindly permitted. The boy poked the side of its bright head with a forefinger as he might poke at a dead bird in the driveway with a stick.

The boy's parents' outrage, had they learned of this, would, like the CT, have been muscular, tumescent. The boy's mother, known for her lavish, friendly smile, would have transmuted into a fury, enraged at the boy, too, for his complicity. Had the news reached his desk, the boy's grandfather, who had owned the camp and many other things, would have dismissed the CT out of hand and held confidential meetings with the head counselor. The authorities—had they gotten wind of it, had this been another era—would have started an investigation. But this was not that era and the grandfather was busy in his office and the parents were naïve and trusting, as the boy was naïve and trusting.

So the sun shone down through the oak leaves and the breeze blew in through the screens and the boy touched the penis that had been proffered and, remarkably, he was not damaged; he had made his first memorable acquaintance with the openness of his own being, and with his own nerve, both of which served him well that day, and in the future.

2.

In any case, it was by no means the most shocking occurrence the boy met with in the summer of 1970. It was brazen, yes, but other latent encounters frankly alarmed and preoccupied him more. The boy recognized in them clues and codes, invisible, it seemed, to many of the others in his midst; at certain moments it was as if the world intentionally switched to a different language, the way émigré parents will, in the erroneous supposition that they can outwit their own children. But the boy was already alive to abstract thinking, and quick to piece together the meanings of the other language.

Enclosing the bay at the forward edge of his property, the grandfather's vast private coastline stretched its arms for a mile in either direction, grasping, it appeared, always for more. For the camp, days began here, with calisthenics on the beach, chill and damp in the absence of the sun, whose view to the proceedings was blocked by the high wooded hill behind, the west each morning briefly keeping its inconsequential little secret from the east.

From their cabins amongst the junipers the boys came yawning to the shore, stubbing toes on the uneven planks of the white pine boardwalk, made slippery by fine quartz sand. Many appeared to arrive straight from suburbia, in colored terry cloth bathrobes, towels on their shoulders. The boy wore printed cotton pajamas and beaded leather moccasins from the souvenir shop in town.

Briskly and in unison, the campers and their counselors absolved a regimen of sit-ups, windmills, and jumping jacks, led by a twenty-two-year-old posing as drill sergeant atop the lifeguard stand; his preposterous military bellowing echoed out across the peaceful bay, agitating the waterfowl. The maneuvers he commanded—unrecognizable in the supple and seductive fitness schemes of a later generation—provoked the skittish, mechanical movements of wind-up toys. Finally, and while running in place, boys and men alike disrobed for a ritual dip. The plunge was brief as a baptism, for by dawn the water had grown cold and still, having waited in darkness through the night.

The boy had never encountered nakedness on this sweeping scale. He had frequently seen his elder brother undressed—only slightly more than a year apart in age, they lived together in great intimacy and near-perfect celibacy, in the manner of an old married couple—and he had even once seen his father naked, which had been a kind of thrill, like coming unawares upon a magnificent stag in a field at dusk.

Here, though, was a veritable catalog of unclothed males: theoretical versions of himself in years to come, some still hairless at genitals, chests, and underarms, others smooth and easygoing in their post-adolescent nudity, yet others hirsute or with perplexing and frightening dark patches of hair at their bodies' structural crossroads. From behind, at some distance, their identical tan lines might have suggested a cadre of prep school swimmers in matching white suits. (Yet even then it was clear to the boy that they were not, as the saying has it, all playing on the same team.) Marking their skin like ghostly tattoos, the pale zones delineated and addressed what was taboo of the body.

It was a spectacle that begged examination, though somehow he understood that he must not appear to examine it. He must observe this display, if at all, only out of the corner of his eye, and pretend that it meant nothing. Nothing to him, nothing to anyone. It was an early brush with the peculiar constitution and broad possibilities of fictional realms.

He Opened Up Somewhere Along the Eastern Shore

Jason Hanasik

Steven and I arrived at Patrick's house in Rochester, New York, at around one A.M. We had been on the road since six that morning and were running off the buzz of surviving the drive and knowing a bed was within reach. By then, the snow was falling lightly, and I asked Steven if we could make two pictures before bed—one by the tree in his brother's front yard and one directly in front of his brother's house.

"Sure," he said, but only after we had a beer and unloaded our gear.

Before I flew back to the East Coast for the holidays, Patrick and I discussed the possibility of getting together at one of our favorite hangouts: Pinboys, a bowling alley near Lynnhaven Mall. Patrick was working during the week for a company in Virginia and commuting to Rochester on the weekends to be with his new wife and her family. Finding a job in the greater Rochester area had been tough since Patrick had retired from the Marine Corps, so he returned to our hometown, where a large military installation sustains the local economy.

As I was approaching the bowling alley, Patrick sent me a text that said he had secured our lane and that I should just grab some shoes at the desk and come find them. *Them?* I wondered.

I rented a pair of bowling shoes and found my way to Lane 13. As I was tying my laces, Patrick's younger brother, Steven, walked up beside me with a thirteen-pound bowling ball in his hand and a shit-eating grin on his face.

Our conversation was stunted and awkward. There was some banter about military politics, where everybody was living, and who else we had seen from high school, but mostly we just drank beer and flung our bowling balls down the long lane in front of us.

That night was the first time I had seen Steven since he'd stood guard next to Josh's casket. Josh had been Steven's best friend, and they'd enlisted in the Marine Corps the same day. Like Patrick and me, Josh and Steven had been inseparable throughout high school. But unlike Patrick and me, they'd enlisted together and helped each other endure the rigors of boot camp. They even found a way to be stationed together at the same base in Hawaii.

Although the four of us were always passing each other in the doorways of our family's homes, we never consciously spent any time together as a group. Patrick and I agreed that one of the reasons was because

It was like the myth the military had fed him had disintegrated the moment he looked down at Josh's body.

Steven assumed I was gay and wanted to stay as far away from me as possible. Truth be told, I wanted just as little to do with my sexuality at the time, too. Since then, I had come out, confirming Steven's suspicions. And though others who had issues with my sexuality grew to accept it, Steven never seemed to come around.

At the end of our evening of bowling, Patrick suggested that we spend New Year's in Rochester with him and his new wife. Caught in the rush of the reunion and, more importantly, the aftereffects of our third pitcher of beer, I looked at Steven and said, "I'm game if you are."

Seemingly drunk, it took Steven a second to register the offer. He paused, then smiled. Patrick beamed, and we started discussing the logistics of renting a car, and if we should make a stop to see other friends in New York City.

I met Steven at six A.M. at a car rental shop close to the Hampton Roads Bay Bridge Tunnel. We split the cost of a basic compact car and contorted our six-foot-plus frames into its small interior. It had been a week since we had seen each other at the bowling alley. Sober and without Patrick as a jovial buffer, the conversation was focused on directions to Rochester and whether or not either of us wanted the heat turned up. Once we were on our way, we both fell silent and let the radio fill the space.

Somewhere along the Eastern Shore, I broke our unspoken pact, turned toward Steven, and asked him how he was coping with Josh's death. He deflected the questions with a series of short answers, "I'm fine," and, "You know, OK," as the car entered a corridor of tall pines. I nodded and said, "Oh, OK." I could feel that he wasn't telling me the truth, so I went silent and closed my eyes.

A few minutes passed and Steven—staring straight ahead—said, "Actually, I am not OK."

With little more than a quick inhale, Steven started to seemingly vomit all of the viewpoints surrounding the controversy of Josh's death. At that point, all I knew was that Josh had died because his chopper crashed in a lake in Iraq. The family was told that he had drowned with all of his gear still clinging to his back. Steven countered this claim saying that something wasn't right considering the circumstances. I pressed for clarification and he went silent. Having been around the military my entire life, the dance of small revelations followed by immediate withdrawal was not new to me, so I just let it be and continued to look out the front window at Route 13.

At some point during our short discussion, I subconsciously turned the radio down so we found ourselves coasting in silence for a few minutes. An odd tension hung in the air, the way humidity can almost suffocate you after a rainstorm in a large city. Finally, I looked over at Steven and said that I was sorry. He winced as if he was disgusted so I quickly looked back at the road.

The car was still bathed in shadow from the trees when Steven silently let go and started to weep. He swerved a little in his lane, so I asked if he needed to pull over.

"No, I'm fine," he said.

The corridor of trees ended, and the car was once again full of the bright, mid-morning sun. As Steven regained his composure, I turned toward him.

"I'm sorry. I shouldn't have asked you," I said.

Steven winced again and then his face quickly settled and he told me that he had not told anyone how he felt about Josh's sudden death. He said that he just shut down. He had never expected to stand watch over his best friend's body while it lay in a flag-draped coffin. More so, he was terrified when he boarded the plane for Iraq immediately after Josh's funeral because he didn't feel safe anymore. It was like the myth the military had fed him had disintegrated the moment he looked down at Josh's body.

I looked forward and thought, *Fuck, what do I say?*

A moment or two passed and then I finally thanked him for sharing how he felt. He nodded and looked at the road ahead.

I turned the radio back up. We let a Top 40 station fill in the car. Shortly after stopping for dinner at a Burger King just over the state line in Pennsylvania, I received a phone call from my father that a bad snowstorm was moving through the state.

The mood had shifted, and our conversation about death had transitioned into one about Steven's various girlfriends. As predicted, the snowstorm met us a few miles up the road, and we both reminisced about how long it had been since we had driven in a whiteout. My father warned that it would be rough, but we didn't expect visibility to drop as quickly as it did.

The opening bars of a familiar song came on the radio, but, for the first ten seconds, I couldn't place it. Right before Whitney Houston began singing, I remembered the first line and joined her: "I believe the children are our future . . ." Steven looked over at me and laughed. I immediately stopped singing but Whitney continued on.

I was so focused on the snowstorm in front of us that I missed Steven's inhale ahead of the second stanza. Suddenly, Steven took the mic, "Everybody's searching for a hero . . ."

For the next three and half minutes, we took turns singing the song for each other, screaming out sections in full-chest voice and vocalizing over Whitney's melody. By the time the song finished, we had decelerated to ten miles per hour and I could no longer see the brake lights of the car in front of us. We coasted in a haze of pop songs for what seemed like hours. As we crossed the New York state line, the snowstorm subsided and I took a nap.

We arrived at Patrick's house in Rochester around one A.M.

Over the course of the next week and a half, Steven and I grew closer, and I shot a few pictures of him. The best ones were taken those first few days when I had no idea what I was doing. I was not sloppy as much as I was naïve and searching for a picture that would describe this new space that had opened up between us. Watching Steven perform in front of my viewfinder felt right. He was a familiar foreigner. He seemed to be as curious about me as I was about him. Our sessions were like the first few dates of a promising relationship. We each offered ourselves up wholly to the other person without concern or mediation. It was the safest I had felt with another man in a long time.

On New Year's Eve, after Patrick and his wife had gone to bed, Steven and I were out in the garage drinking a few beers. Stories of Josh started to surface again, and I watched tears gather in Steven's eyes. Drunkenly, he swayed back and forth a little bit and I walked toward him. We were uncomfortably close, even for me, but he didn't back away. We were both crying at this point, and I reached out my arms for a hug. He relaxed into the embrace, and we continued to sob.

In the middle of our hug, I realized that it had been a while since I had held and been held by a man. It felt so good, and I flashed to endless nights of cruising online, looking for someone to hold and hold me, not caring if we ever hooked up. In retrospect, it makes sense—the only other times I had been that close to a male my age was on the dance floor of a gay club. I didn't have a script to go by, and I started to confuse our intimacy as a sign of sexual possibility on his part.

I didn't have a script to go by, and I started to confuse our intimacy as a sign of sexual possibility on his part.

Our hug ended, and Steven said he needed to head to bed. I stepped back, swayed a little bit and told him I needed to as well.

The next morning, I wondered why, like many men I know, I perceive male vulnerability and intimacy as a code for homosexuality.

We left Rochester two days later.

During the ride home, Steven asked me what I planned to do with the pictures of him. I couldn't tell if he was nervous about what the images might reveal or if it was just a way to make more conversation during the tiresome ride back to Virginia. I hesitated to tell him that I thought I may have stumbled upon a way of visually dismantling the myth of the impenetrable (straight) American male. The same myth he had watched crumble when Josh died. In my eyes, Steven had finally shed that skin a week and a half ago, in a dark corridor of tall pine trees somewhere along the Eastern Shore.

When I finally stopped analyzing why he asked the question, I said, "Oh you know, I'm just playing around at the moment. You remind me of your brother, the best parts of him—at least the parts I consider to be the best." I explained that I had been trying to photograph the friendship between his brother and me for the better part of five years and that the images had failed. Not because they were bad, but because there was not much at stake in them. They were just lovely photographs of a man. At their worst they verged on very tame homoerotica, and at their best they were simply pretty. The problem was that all of the images lacked the emotional intimacy that the two of us shared in our day-to-day friendship.

Steven was puzzled and asked why they had to be anything more for me than a picture of my friend. I asked him to remember the moment in the car on the Eastern Shore when he finally opened up. He grunted, which I took as confirmation that he was back in that headspace.

I floated the question, "Why did you decide to finally tell someone—and why was that me?" He said he didn't know. I told him I didn't either, but that there was something magical in that moment and that I wanted to better understand it.

Steven was silent and stared out the car window for a moment, and I thought, *Perhaps Steven's arrival and our process of accepting each other is a second chance at capturing that magical space men can occupy together?*

With a devilish grin on his face, Steven turned toward me and said, "I'm game." I didn't quite know what he was game for, but I knew a sports reference was a good sign.

Steven and I met up once more during my trip back to the East Coast. The energy was different, and I struggled to take a "good" picture of him. Although he was excited and willing, whatever space that existed in the car and in Rochester was gone. He seemed distant. He certainly had not returned to the same guy I knew before the trip, but he was not nearly as open as he was the week prior. Maybe the return to the familiar sent his guard up. Perhaps, while remembering the time we had spent together, a red flag had been raised in his mind and he now thought that something was not exactly "normal." I don't know, because I never asked.

In this moment, he had regressed to the men who loomed large over m youth—the impenetrabl ones who wouldn't let me in, wouldn't open up.

During our shoot, I could tell that the images were not great. Hoping that we'd break through to the emotional space we cocreated in his brother's basement, I continued to photograph him for about an hour. I thought, *If only I could figure out a way to make a picture of that complicated embrace we had on New Year's Eve.*

"Let's move on to something else, somewhere else. You don't seem to be as excited about these pictures. It's almost like you're working too hard," Steven said. I guess he could tell that things were different between the two of us, too.

I lowered my camera, and we started wandering in an area of overgrowth, an area that the park system had seemingly forgotten. Steven pushed through the brambles and a path finally opened up in front of us. We realized that the area had, in fact, not been forgotten, but instead was intentionally left wild to hide a series of substations or power generators.

I raised my camera up to my eye as I followed Steven through the maze of green boxes and underbrush and found myself continuously pulling focus to keep him sharp in the frame.

Walking around with a camera to my eye is something I rarely do because the camera blocks my peripheral vision and makes me feel incredibly exposed.

When I pulled the camera away from my eye for a second, I realized that I felt completely safe with Steven. In fact, I feel protected when I am with him or his brother. Maybe it's because they are trained to kill people with their hands. Or maybe it is because we have an unspoken understanding that we will protect each other no matter what, a sort of brother's pact.

A cloud moved out of the sun's path, and I asked Steven to turn around. The wind picked up and smacked him as he turned toward me. He scowled a little, and I snapped the shutter button. The camera clicked, I closed my eyes for a second, and the image I had just made started to appear on the back of my eyelids. The harsh noontime light flattened him, and it appeared as if he was a cardboard cutout—one-dimensional against a field of trees and bushes. As I looked at the scowl on his face and the side-eye he shot me over his sloping shoulder, I couldn't find the man who sang "The Greatest Love of All" with me in the middle of a snowstorm. In this moment, he had regressed to the men who loomed large over my youth—the impenetrable ones who wouldn't let me in, wouldn't open up. The result was a cold and uninviting portrait of masculinity.

The temperature seemed to have dropped ten degrees during our time together, and I heard storm clouds approaching. I opened my eyes, looked down, and realized that that was my last exposure.

ORIGINALLY PUBLISHED IN *HELLO MR.* ISSUE 05 IN 2015.

A Compendium of Loss

Thom James Carter | Art by Elliot Stokes

ON LOSING YOUR INNOCENCE

You'll forget the name of your first best friend. He was half-Greek, half-American, and ten years old, but he spoke as if he already knew everything the world had to offer. He looked like a finished puzzle, colorful and complete. He told you that his mother was a psychic, and that she knew what other people were thinking, so you would try to stop thinking in her presence so that she could not hear you. Your name is Mark, but in her thick accent, she declared you "Muck." You hardly went round to your best friend's house because of her, and took him by the hand and went to play outside instead. You'd eat each other's lunches underneath the maple tree and watch boys trade football cards and girls trade secrets. You'd do cartwheels across the grass until your elbows gave in and your knees bent backwards. You'd see who could hold their breath the longest both above and below water. You'll lose these memories one day to make room for remembering recipes, addresses, and birthdays. Eventually, you will forget those, too. You'll wonder if you will pass him on the street and still recognize his face, the outline of his body, or the deep grooves that lined his forehead when he frowned. You will. You'll bump into him on the tennis court and lose all six games of the set. You'll stare at him, looking better in tennis shorts than you do, his legs like thunder. He'll have no excess weight and no receding hairline, but you will notice that he has a tattoo on his forearm: the name of a man, the same name as your husband. You'll say that you both must have great taste.

ON LOSING YOUR LAST NAME

You'll divorce your husband. You'll lose the final and last argument, then you will lose both him and his last name in one fell swoop. It'll feel like a soap opera. He'll curse at you and accidentally call you by another man's name. It is then that you will remember what your best friend was called. From that moment on, your words will not be spoken, but shouted from across the room. You'll wonder how to reflect your hurt back onto him and scan the kitchen for utensils. What about salt in his eyes? Or a laxative in his coffee? How about bludgeoning the back of his head with a ladle? Give him an excuse why you have gone quiet when he asks. Realize you would not be able to do enough damage as you would like.

You'll argue over who gets the cat and who gets the television. Which will benefit you the most? This is what you will be told to do, to think about yourself for the first time in years. How did you wear your clothes, how did you wear your smile, and how did you feel fulfilled before you met him? You'll try to remember. You'll try to remember how to be Mark. Perhaps your best friend's mother called you "Muck" due to your passivity, your willingness to be treated like dirt.

You'll remember your first date together at an Italian restaurant in the middle of town. As he ate and as you watched your waistline, Dean Martin's voice rattled through tinny overhead speakers, but before he could insist *that's amore*, the music stopped. The owner rammed the speakers with a wooden broom and swore at them in English, Italian, and through body language as he thrust his middle finger upwards. Your husband ordered dessert, you paid the bill, and then you both walked to the subway with Bolognese sauce around your mouths, though you

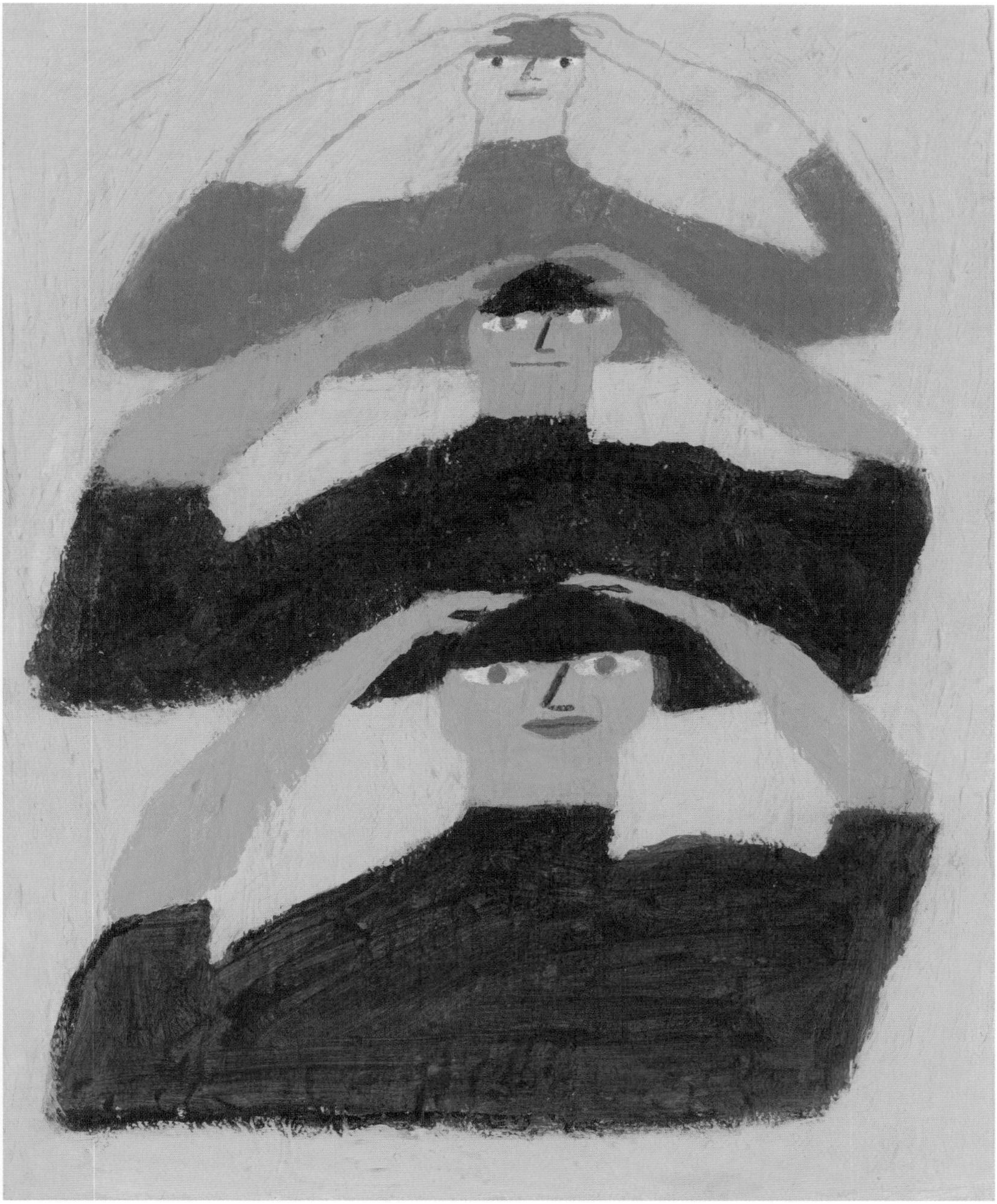

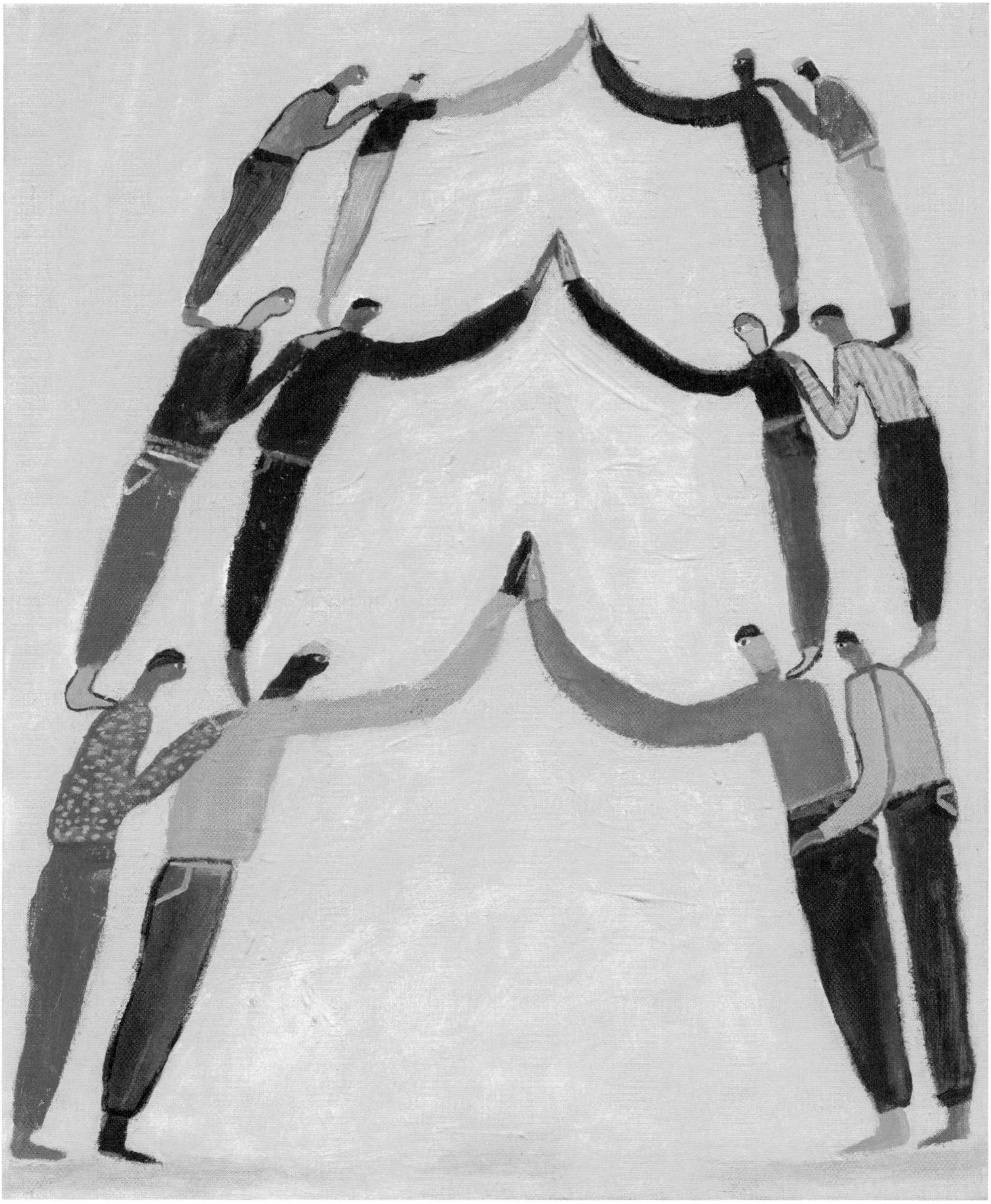

only ate salad. You'll remember much more of your lives together and your appetite will fade. You'll quickly learn that the most effective diet is a divorce.

ON LOSING YOUR CLOTHES

You'll find a smaller place to live. You'll pack your things and try to leave as soon as possible. Collect the keys two days later. You'll walk from your new apartment door to the back of your car to fetch your boxes, but you will feel as if the neighbors already know what has happened to you. You'll feel small, like the last Russian doll in the set.

You'll lose your clothes. The denim and the cotton will fall off you and make their way down to the bathroom floor. You'll turn towards the mirror and whisper Bloody Mary three times under your breath and expect her to unveil your future and give you some sage advice. She will only tell you that she is fully booked for the next three months. You'll step inside the bathtub as the shower hisses and spits. It'll be hot, comforting. You'll stand still and only think about moving when you realize that you will have to pay the water bill by yourself. You'll step out of the shower with your skin like almonds and your hair like rope, and you will wonder, *Why is there nobody around to hang me up to dry?*

The next morning you will wake up, walk to the kitchen with no clothes on and begin to make yourself breakfast. Two eggs, over easy. Across the street an elderly couple will spot you through the window. You'll all laugh and you will shrug with a spatula in your hand. This is what it feels like to start over. You'll turn the eggs. You will put them on a plate, add some salt, some pepper, and then take it to the bedroom to eat. Afterwards, you will feel full.

ORIGINALLY PUBLISHED IN *HELLO MR.* ISSUE 06 IN 2015.

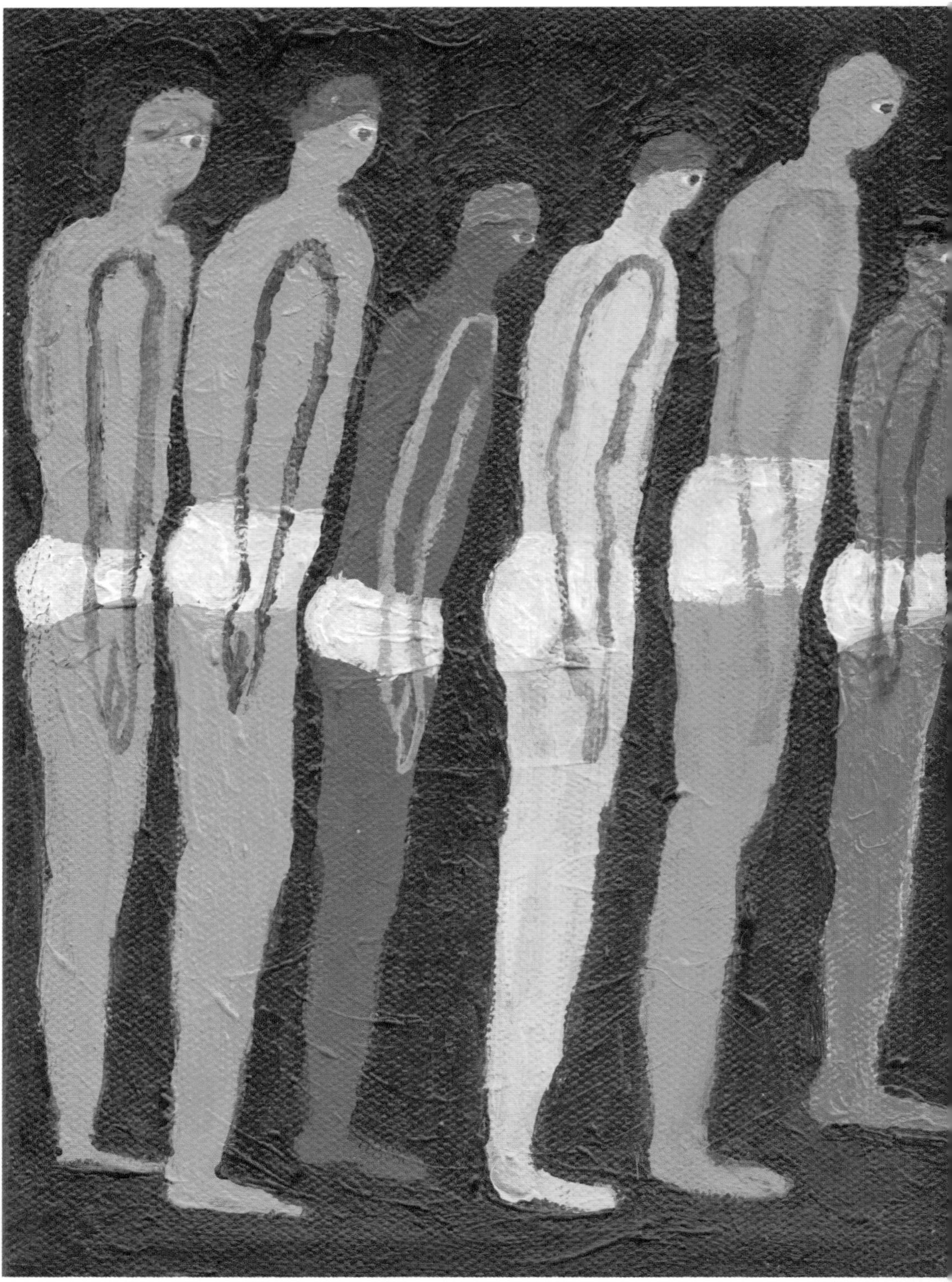

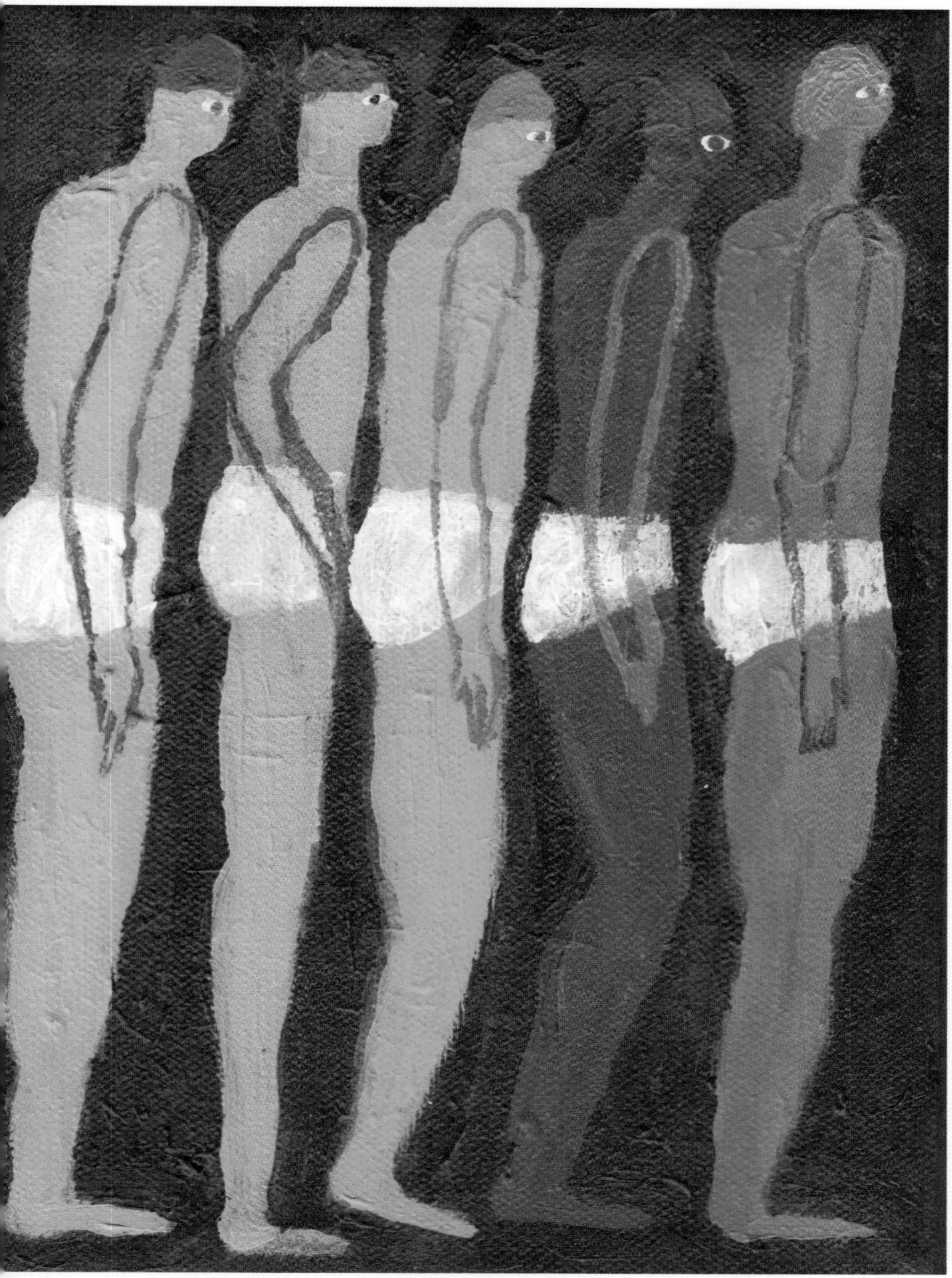

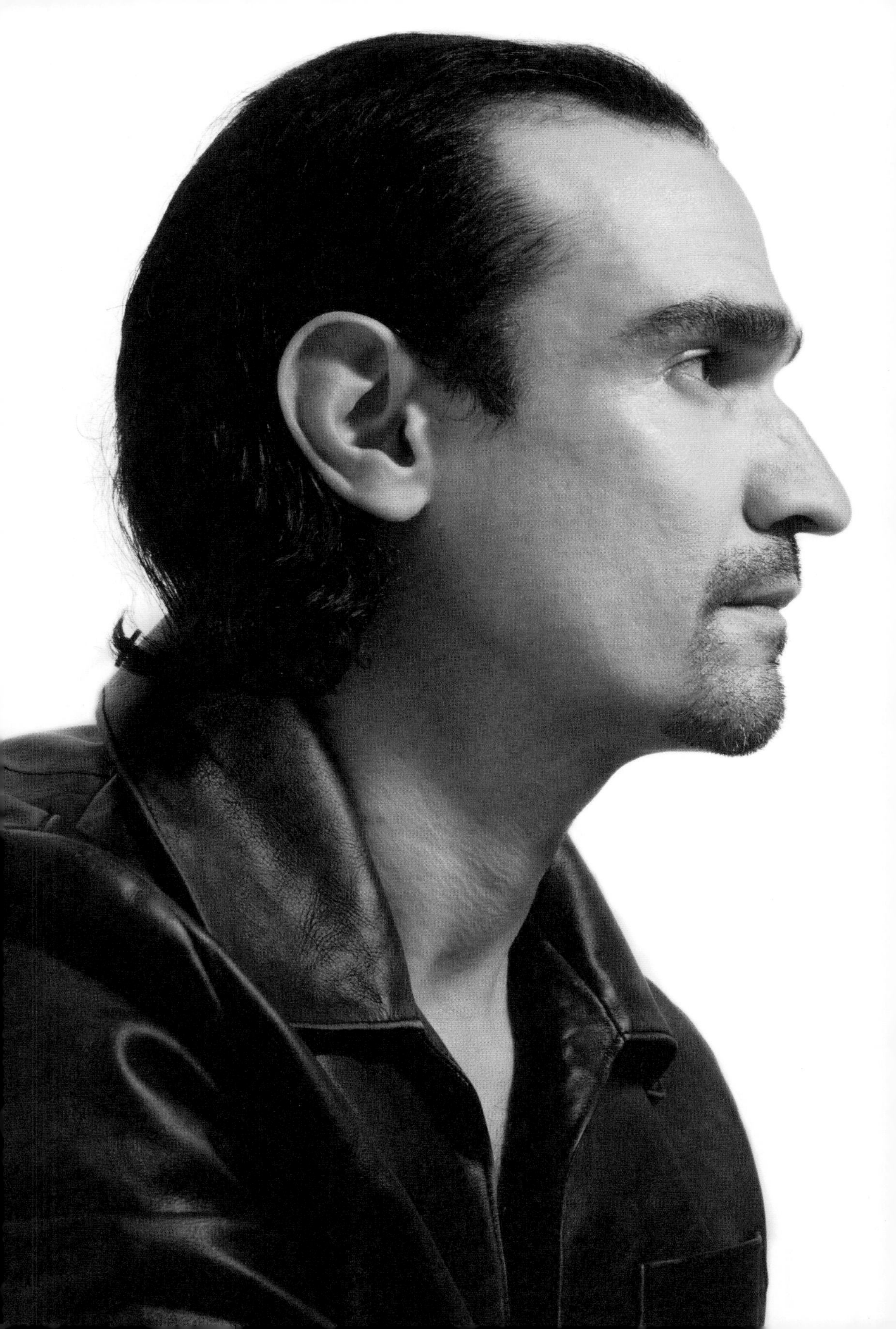

Javi Muñoz: *Hamilton*'s New Hamilton

Scott Bixby | Photos by Matthew Tammaro

"Hardly anyone calls me Javier." He's *Hamilton*'s new Hamilton, the title role in the paradigm-shifting Broadway musical that has transcended its medium to become what everyone, from theater critics to the first lady to Beyoncé, has deemed one of the greatest artistic achievements of the modern age. The show has garnered a Pulitzer Prize, a record-setting number of Tony nominations, stratospheric-bordering-on-intergalactic ticket sales, and, in the year of #OscarsSoWhite, featured a cast almost entirely composed of actors of color.

"No pressure!" he joked.

He grew up in the Linden Houses projects of Brooklyn, the youngest of four brothers in one of the city's roughest neighborhoods during the opening salvo of the crack epidemic. For a shy kid with an artistic sensibility, East New York was a dangerous place to be.

"It was very violent and very aggressive, so I didn't have a lot of friends in the neighborhood or at school," Javi said. Being Puerto Rican didn't help. "I was too 'white' for my neighborhood, and I was too 'dark' for where I went to school."

A self-described "unapologetic nerd-geek-man-one-hundred-percent extraordinaire" who spends his time off-stage live-tweeting genre shows like *Game of Thrones* and *Stranger Things*, Javi chalks up his gravitation toward story-telling to the escapism that beat in the heart of a lonely kid in a tough neighborhood.

"I was fat as a kid," Javi said. "I spent a lot of time alone, so I had space to let my imagination grow. That's really where the artistic and creative parts were born, playing with my toys, watching TV, or writing stories that I wanted to make into movies and cartoons and stuff."

Javi's creative streak found a home in performing arts at Edward R. Murrow High School in Midwood, Brooklyn, a magnet school where he initially flirted with studying astrophysics before taking up theater, "the first community I ever felt a part of, socially." He called the not-entirely-obvious transition between the two disciplines "sort of a marriage of everything I loved."

"I'm happy to say no to something because it's beneath me, and it's beneath me to play a stereotype."

"The process of putting up theater makes sense to my science-brain, right? When you're working on a character, it's sort of like the experiment process," Javi explained. "What's the hypothesis, and what's the formula to reach the answer I'm looking for, and how many attempts can I make in this experiment 'til I get it right? It was very scientific, in my brain, but it was also very powerful."

And powerful Javi was. After numerous starring roles in school productions, he signed with his first agent one month before graduating high school and set his sights on professional training at New York University's ultra-competitive Tisch School of the Arts. Fellow alumni include Philip Seymour Hoffman, Idina Menzel, and Felicity Huffman.

In theater, a putatively progressive industry where many casting directors, writers, and producers hold a narrow definition of who can make it as a male lead—queue up straight, white guys taller than five eight—Javi knew that being Latino would make the already steep climb to success as an actor steeper still.

"I was always cast in roles that fit me and had nothing to do with my ethnicity, so I found myself playing a lot of leading men in scene work and class assignments," Javi said. "I found that I could transcend all that and still portray these characters with absolute integrity, fullness, and richness."

Most actors in Javi's position—talented, handsome, and Latino—would graduate into professional theater facing down a long line of ensemble tracks and stints as a Shark in *West Side Story*. But Javi, encouraged by his family and buoyed by faith in his talent, never cosigned the industry's bullshit assertion that a gay Latino man couldn't be a leading man, even if it meant turning down a paycheck.

"I'm happy to say no to something because it's beneath me, and it's beneath me to play a stereotype," Javi said. The problem isn't the roles—*Hamilton* is positive proof of that—but the people filling them, for whom Javi has little patience.

"You should be better at writing, you should be better at casting, and it's not on me—it's on you," he said, of writers and

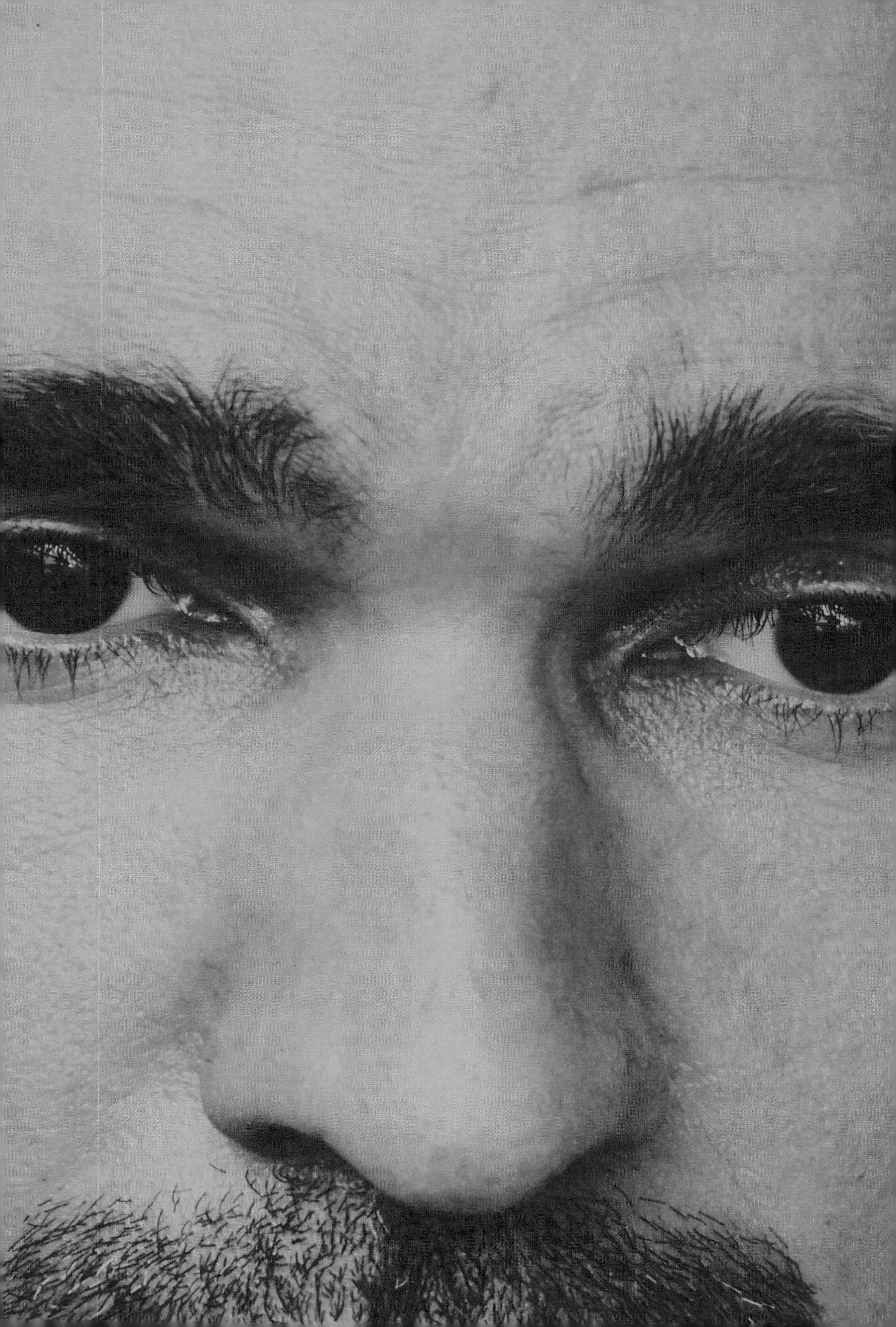

casting directors who see Javi's résumé as the makings of a drug dealer on an episode of *Law & Order*. "Maybe it was a chip on my shoulder, but that's exactly how I walked into every situation. I have a lot to offer, and if you can't see it—bye, where's my next audition?"

Javi, who put himself through NYU, knows what it means to work and knows that there's more integrity in bussing tables than in taking a role that reduces his skills.

"I worked a forty-hour work week on two part-time jobs, I always had eighteen credits a semester, I was always in a show—I knew how to work hard," Javi said. "It did not scare me to turn down an acting job and go back to my restaurant or work four other jobs to pay the bills. I knew how to make that work."

Even after his first starring role—replacing Lin-Manuel Miranda as Usnavi in *In the Heights*, Javi had trouble finding the right work, putting that work ethic into practice. "When I wouldn't get hired for things, I went back to a restaurant," he said proudly. "And did people recognize me when I went to seat them at their table? 'Ohmigod, were you Usnavi in *In the Heights*?' 'I sure was! Right this way.'

"There's no shame in wanting to put food on my table and pay my rent—I was gonna do whatever I had to do, and that was it, and it was going to be according to my integrity and my worth," Javi said emphatically. "I'm worthy to be cast in these roles, and I'm going to keep fighting until I'm cast in these roles."

Then there was the other consideration: How much of his personal life would remain personal? Even on ostensibly queer-friendly Broadway, openly gay actors are more likely to play the funny friend than the leading man, and the choice to come out has long-reaching career ramifications—doubly so for minority actors. Javi saw the issue as one of integrity.

"I decided in 2005, three years after being diagnosed with HIV, and absolutely sickened by the hypocrisy that I was seeing in the gay community regarding HIV, that I was going to live my life completely open and own every aspect of who I am, and no one was going to be able to hold anything over me to make me feel small or bad," Javi said. "That's who I am—*that's who I am*, and that's what I'm bringing to the table. If you don't want me at your table, I'll go find another one."

Fear of losing out on casting because of his sexuality or HIV status was countered by the support of Javi's family and friends. "They said, 'We love you, no matter what—we love you.' And if these people in my family, who I loved and admired, could say that to me and give me that love, the problem was not with me, the problem was with someone else."

That support went from abstract to dead-real after Javi's diagnosis.

"On my worst of days—and I mean where I had allergic reactions, hives, and pustules covering my back, in the dead-heat of summer I'm wearing a long-sleeve shirt 'cause my skin is covered with an allergic reaction to medication—I had friends I could go to when I couldn't even look at myself in a mirror.

"It's that exchange with people that reminded me I was still worth something, and it was worth fighting whatever I had to fight," Javi said, growing emotional. "It was worth it because these people believed in me and loved me, and this was not going to be permanent. This allergic reaction was gonna pass, this depression was gonna pass, this anger was gonna pass. And they helped me find the strength for that."

After this came Javi's biggest break: getting cast as Miranda's alternate in *Hamilton*, the story of how "a bastard, orphan son-of-a-whore and a Scotsman dropped in the middle of a forgotten spot in the Caribbean by providence, impoverished in squalor, grew up to be a hero and a scholar." (It's also about the founding of the National Bank, which is much more exciting than you think it is.) Javi performed once a week on Sunday matinees, waiting in the wings during the seven other performances every week in case he was needed to take over at the last minute. Miranda, a famous workhorse, seldom gave Javi the opportunity, although he did perform in the title role for President Obama during one of Miranda's off days, an opportunity Javi called a "whoa" moment.

Although Miranda is unquestionably the show's godhead, inspired to write the show he would eventually headline, based on Ron Chernow's 2004 biography of the nation's first secretary of the treasury, Javi was with *Hamilton* almost from its conception, participating in nearly every workshop and reading of a song cycle called the *Hamilton Mixtape* that would eventually become the biggest Broadway show in twenty seasons. Ownership over the character of Alexander Hamilton—the "young, scrappy, and hungry" immigrant who rose to the apex of American political power before dying in a duel with Vice President Aaron Burr—is shared, Javi said, not just between himself and Miranda but with every member of the show's creative team.

"It's absolutely extraordinary to have that kind of trust with another artist. I'll get into the trenches with Lin any day, any time, for anything. It's that kind of absolute trust."

"I was allowed to make it my own, but I was also in the room to help marry my choices to Lin's, as well," Javi said. "It's absolutely extraordinary to have that kind of trust with another artist. I'll get into the trenches with Lin any day, any time, for anything. It's that kind of absolute trust.

"I still marvel at the kind of relationship that Lin and I have—it's extraordinary, and I've never shared that kind of trust with someone, as far as the creative process," Javi said. "Two people can't just do that out of nowhere, out of thin air—you can't just put two actors together and say, 'Share this

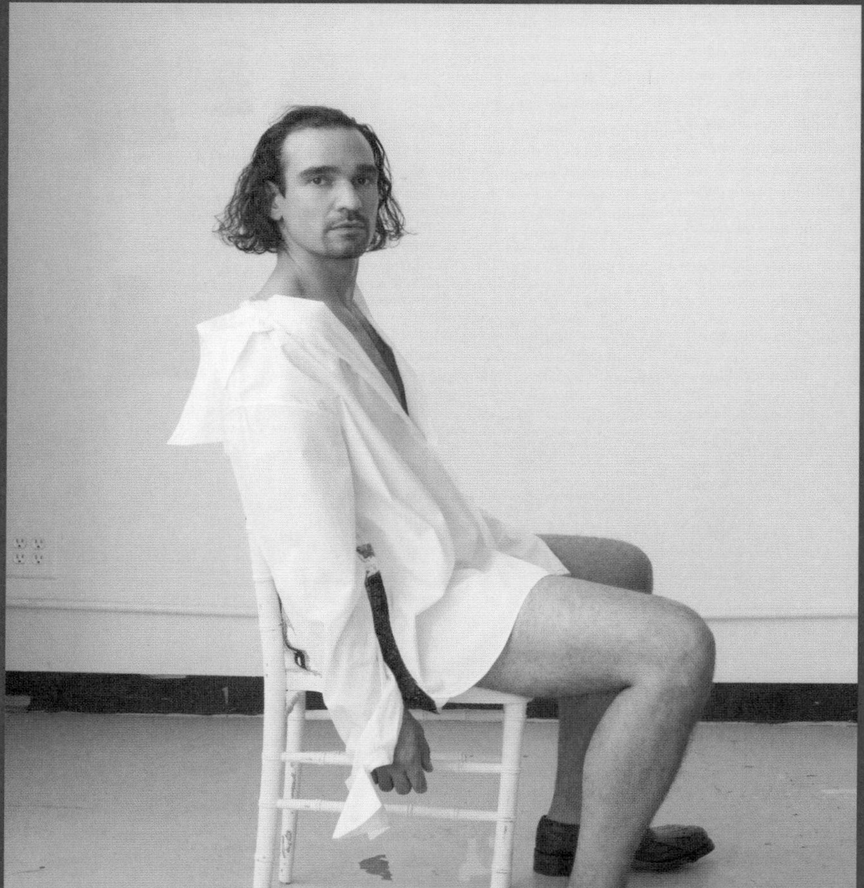

role'—that's not gonna happen. It really has to be invested in and nurtured."

And then, at the moment of his greatest success as an actor, Javi was dealt another body blow: He was diagnosed with cancer. Javi, who had cleared hurdles with every step since he left East New York, was afraid for the first time.

"*Jarring* is such a minimal word to describe what it felt like. It derailed me in every way," Javi said. "I consider myself someone who doesn't get scared very often, of anything. And I know what fear is now, after that."

He underwent surgery and radiation treatments, missing months of performances while *Hamilton* graduated from hit Broadway show to bona fide cultural phenomenon, his spot as Miranda's alternate held for him as he fought cancer with his family at his side. His parents were both cancer survivors diagnosed six months apart, and Javi gave up work at the time to be nearer to them. They and his older brother David were instrumental in Javi's return to health and to the stage.

"My family loved me so much and supported me so much," he said. "That was where I fit in. That was the safest place I could be."

With their encouragement, and that of castmates who organized food runs when he was too weakened from radiation treatments to leave his apartment, Javi went into remission—then started champing at the bit to return to *Hamilton*.

"I knew it was within my power and my ability to go back to the show. It was a question of how, and it was a question of when," Javi said. "I had to treat it like I would treat anything, and just say, 'What does today feel like?'"

His determination to get back to playing Alexander Hamilton was occasionally an obstacle in itself, one that had to be tempered by members of the show's cast and crew who gave Javi one job: to get well first.

"I get so stubborn, and so über-focused, that the blinders come on and I want to get to the prize and accomplish it. I just wanted to get my body back in shape and my endurance back to peak level, and I wanted to be back in the show, yesterday," Javi said.

But "there's something to be said for being stubborn, sometimes," Javi said, pointing to his successful return to the Richard Rodgers Theatre just three months after his diagnosis.

"I was so uncertain walking into that first performance as to whether or not I was gonna have the breath control or the stamina, in spite of the fact that I had been back to the gym and I'd proven to myself, outside of the theater, that my body was ready to do this. I was uncertain—but with the amount of support that I had, always focusing on the fact that I knew I could do it, that was enough for me to say, 'This is possible.'"

In remission, Javi took over for Miranda full-time, stepping into the brightest spotlight on the Great White Way to rave reviews for Javi's seductive, sensuous iteration of the title role. The good looks and magnetic stage presence that pegged Javi as a leading man at NYU prompted infamously captious *New York Times* theater critic Ben Brantley to call him "the Sexy Hamilton," an appellation the actor takes as more than just encouragement to up his reps at the gym.

"I love it. Not because of anything that has to do with *Hamilton*—I love it for the fact that I am very out and open about my story," Javi said. In an industry where being gay, being a person of color, being HIV-positive are seen as disqualifications for sex-symbol status, Javi sees the #SexyOnSundays phenomenon as proof that an artist's integrity can transcend the small-mindedness of both the queer and theater communities.

"That says a lot about where audiences are and people are, in general, to still consider me 'The Sexy Hamilton.' That's a very powerful combination of things. It helps inspire other people living with whatever other health conditions that they're going through, to say, 'Yeah, you are sexy. You are someone. You do matter. You have power. You're not just your illness. You're not just a thing.'"

With tickets to the Broadway production sold out into next year, Javi plans on his tenure as Alexander Hamilton to be equally resilient. "I'm gonna be there a good long time," Javi said with assurance, calling *Hamilton* "a way to help someone else maybe embrace parts of themselves" that are hidden from view.

"He's such a flawed character—he's neither good nor bad, and I'm hoping in every performance that holding up that mirror to an audience is allowing an audience member to say, 'I'm capable of both good and bad, too, and that's OK.'"

A large part of *Hamilton*'s phenomenal success has been due to its use of art forms long derided as inferior—rap, hip-hop, R&B—to convey the rich, complicated, occasionally contradictory story of America's creation. The end result is the articulation of the young immigrant voices that shaped the country's future in the musical language most popular with America's youth. There are 3,522 lines spread out over *Hamilton*'s forty-six songs (minus the unrecorded third reprise of "The Story of Tonight" that many purists don't consider a song proper), each of them pushing forward the story of a young man—and an even younger country—that braved known obstacles and unexpected calamities to reach a more perfect union.

Asked which of those 3,522 lines he connects with the most, Javi let out a long whistle.

"Holy moly," he said, taking a beat.

"I recently hit a point with all my health issues I've faced where I really felt at peace," he said, after a moment. "So when I say in the show, 'I imagine death so much, it feels more like a memory,' my answer, every time is 'Yes.' It couldn't be more true. That's truth."

ORIGINALLY PUBLISHED IN *HELLO MR.* ISSUE 08 IN 2016.

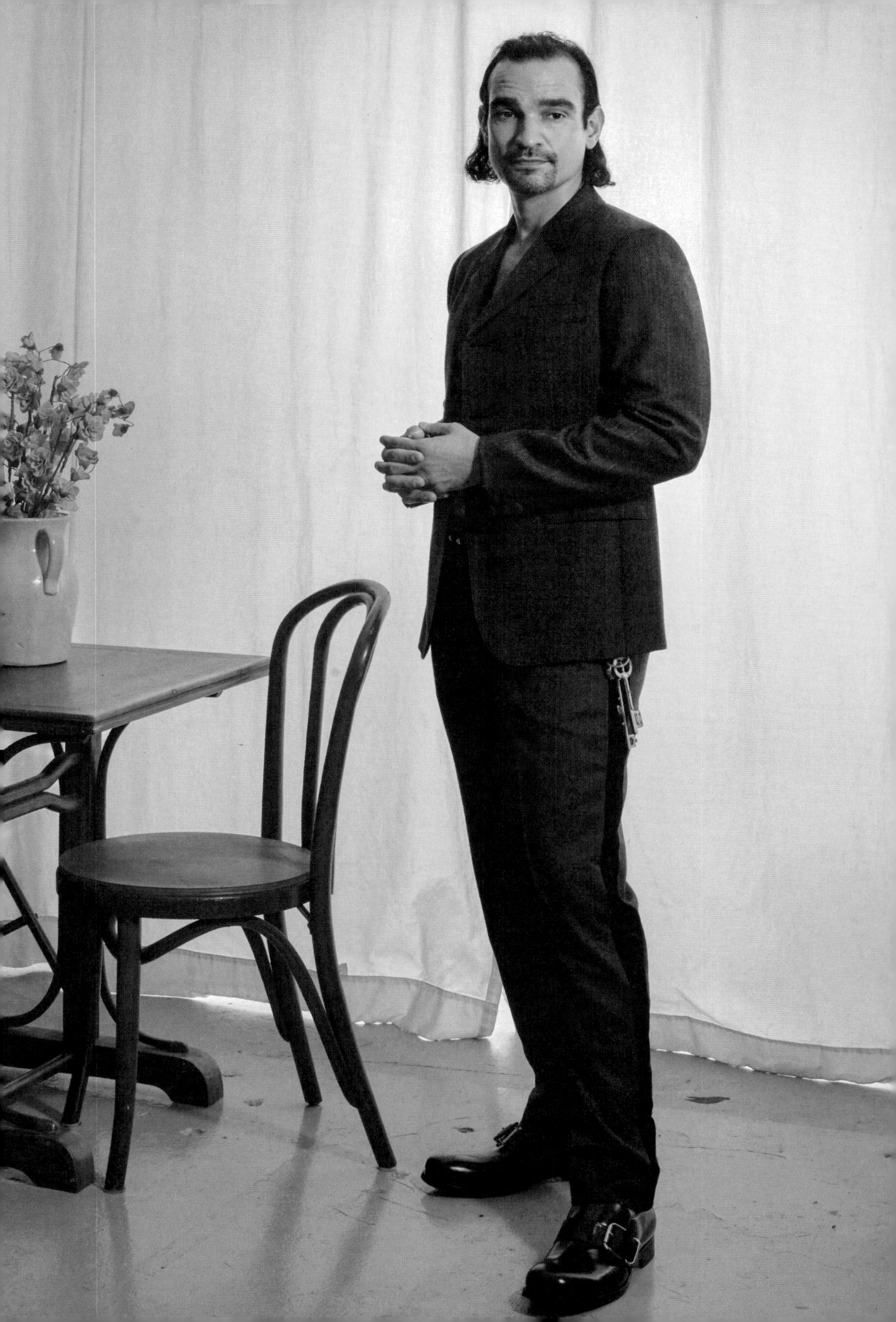

Close Encounter

Noah Michelson

For B

Lately, I keep thinking back to when
you told me you were almost certainly
taken that late summer night when
you were riding your bike through
Bushwick and saw that funny, fizzing
light dangling above you in the sky—
and then its sudden, deliberate propulsion,
and then its hopeful dive.

I don't know how they held you when
they first held you, or what flooded through
you when their tractor beam hit you, if
you resisted when they held your breath
for you, or if you only noticed how
blue and beautiful and terrible
the earth finally seemed as it shrank
beneath you.

I don't know where they took you when
they took you, which icy planet they
flew to, or how many light-years it took
you, or if, impatient to make their
way inside of you, they pulled their ship over
and parked in the middle of all that
imperfect black nothingness and
immediately turned their attention to you.

I don't know what it feels like to be inside
of you, or the intergalactic precision of the
tools it would take, or the mess it would make
breaking into you, or how still you begged your
heart to stay, or if you found yourself praying
or crying or singing as they made themselves
at home in the few clean holes you couldn't
keep closed.

I don't know why they took you when they
took you, or where you went to, or what you
went through—I only know if I were them
and suddenly you were mine, I would never

give you back.

ORIGINALLY PUBLISHED IN *HELLO MR.* ISSUE 04 IN 2014.

CLEAR CONSTELLATIONS:

Mapping the Cultural Pinpoints of Critic Wesley Morris

J Wortham

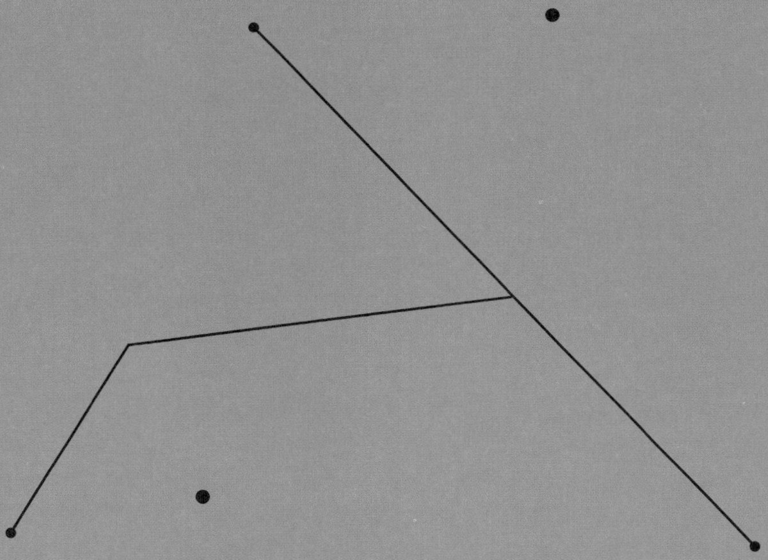

Culture is one of those words that loses its meaning if you say it too many times. There are so many permutations of the subject. We use it to describe conduct at a corporation, as well as vast genres of art and entertainment. It is a changeling, shape-shifting, expanding and contracting to fit human needs. It can go high and go low, it can encompass entities Black, brown, American, and all of the above. It can be something defined as "counter" or "mainstream." Culture is a tricky subject to talk about and elusive to nail down, yet somehow, you know it when you see it. Vivian Ward wasn't cultured until she learned how to eat a snail without sending it sailing across the room. The way society has normalized sexual assault and abuse is as much of a culture as Netflix's attempts to seduce employees with unlimited vacation. A series of paintings by Kerry James Marshall can capture the culture of an entire group of people at a moment in time.

Conversations with Wesley Morris are always an adventure in culture, because he loves it all, the good and the bad. He can easily talk you into loving a confusing, new synth-trap Gwen Stefani song, or tell you the best place in Manhattan for androgynous Japanese clothing, or even somehow, when you least expect it, find a way to espouse the misguided aesthetic of a painter like Dana Schutz, and the underappreciated brilliance of Barbra Streisand—all in the same breath.

As a cultural critic, he is also an autonomous algorithm for connecting the past to present: He will remind you that before Aretha was the hilarious auntie on your favorite meme account, she was the greatest vehicle for American hope, a medium for the largeness of Black angst to metamorphose into something perhaps even larger than itself. So it comes as no surprise that in 2012 at the tender age of thirty-five he won a Pulitzer for criticism, or that he hasn't stopped since.

But that's one of the great things about Wesley Morris. In his current role at the *New York Times* as a writer-at-large, and as cohost on the podcast we make together, *Still Processing*, he is less interested in defining what culture is. He is more invested in the pursuit of it. He is entirely interested in culture as a question, as a vehicle with which to understand life, and what we're saying about it, as we all collectively live it.

J WORTHAM: What do you think of, when you think of "culture?"

WESLEY MORRIS: I think about how one of culture's responsibilities is to make life clear, but also make life livable. Either by showing us who we are or who we wish to be, by surprising us and freaking us out. Obviously, it's allowed to do anything and everything. My relationship to culture is to find what it's doing to me, and what it's doing to us, and where those moral boundaries are and finding surprise when things do the unexpected.

JW: What was your first understanding of popular culture as a way of understanding the world?

WM: My mother was in a Book of the Month Club, so when she was done reading something, I would read it. I grew up reading really weird shit, like Judith Krantz and Barbara Taylor Bradford and stuff like that. I read a lot of books about sisterhood and camaraderie [laughs].

And I read enough about them to know there was this whole world that existed where adults did and felt things that we just never did. If you watch enough older movies you also get that sense. I became used to not having color in my culture, watching all of those old movies. They were all old black-and-white films, but there were also no Black people in them so there was literally no color.

JW: [Laughs] Literally, no color.

WM: And I was OK with it, in the sense that, I wasn't thinking about it. But at some point, your relationship with culture changes as you are able to figure out what taste is. I don't think I had any taste when I was a kid, but as I became a teenager in middle school, you figure out all of that "culture" and develop taste.

JW: And you were thinking about this in middle school?

WM: I always wanted to know why I loved Cherrelle as much as I loved Cherrelle. Why wasn't Luther Vandross as interesting to me as, like, fifteen other people? If you had asked me in the eighth grade who I liked more, Aerosmith or Luther Vandross, I would have said Aerosmith in a heartbeat.

JW: And that makes sense, too. I mean, what's a child doing listening to all this panty-dropping music, music for when you want to be in a convertible with the top down on a beach. Music is the soundtrack to a fantasy.

WM: Then you realize that taste is telling a story about you and that culture is telling a different story about the country, and society, and other people's taste. But that sort of took me a while to figure out. For the most part, it was just my mother exposing me to all this stuff that I would not have otherwise known. I listened to a lot of musicals back then. I heard Barbra Streisand, Stephanie Mills, Gloria Lynne, and Nina Simone. I'd heard all of those people by the time I was nine or ten.

JW: You did grow up before this period in time when a burgeoning young cultural critic would experience so much of this [via the internet]. Now there are Instagram stories and GIFs, [which could] maybe lead you to a movie. You came into culture at a very different time, encountering versus looking. I think when we are encountering something our brain is doing something different than if we are just absorbing, looking. Our brain has to fill in so many more of the gaps. Do you think of that at all?

WM: I do wonder what my taste would be like if I was starting to figure out this stuff now. I wonder what my relationship would be like to all of this if I were growing up now with the internet with all these wormholes to go down. That said, VH1 and MTV in the early days had a lot of wormholes and even though they didn't play videos all day there were strange commercials, which felt like what the internet does now in some ways.

JW: Like when Nickelodeon was really weird in the early stages. There was a lot of storytelling that was vivid and a little grotesque and that can be really appealing to people online.

WM: I remember being really upset when Nickelodeon started to change.

JW: Was there a pivotal moment when you saw something that made you decide you wanted to be a cultural critic or something adjacent to it?

WM: I think somebody told me it was a job.

JW: That's always how it goes.

WM: I had a great social studies teacher who decided I had written a great book report on the movie *April Morning*, which I hated. We had the option to read the book or watch the movie. I didn't like the book but I hated the movie, so I wrote a review

I think when we are encountering something our brain is doing something different than if we are just absorbing, looking.

as to why the movie was so bad. And he told me there was a line of work associated with this type of writing. I started writing for the high school paper and then my college paper and then the *Philadelphia Daily News*. I wrote for a section called *Yo Fresh Ink!*

JW: [Laughs] *Yo Fresh Ink!* sounds like a *Saturday Night Live* skit. That's not like a real thing.

WM: It was real and spelt just like that—*Yo Fresh Ink* exclamation point.

JW: Was the idea that someone was going to pay you to put down your thoughts on paper a preposterous idea for you?

WM: Oh yes, especially back then. But I didn't even know being a full-time cultural critic was a real job during senior year in college. I really had no idea what I was going to do. I got really lucky because a few of my friends from college started an online publication and I edited the cultural section. But even after that I still never thought this would be a real job. In my wildest fantasies I thought I'd be thirty-three or thirty-four by the time I was doing this. And I got my first real job at the *San Francisco Examiner* when I was twenty-four. I couldn't believe it. It was a real professional job. I worked really hard to make my mom proud. I wanted to make sure she didn't have to hang her head in shame when she goes to a family gathering.

JW: And so, you won the Pulitzer.

WM: I know, I know. Some people decided it for you on your behalf. You don't really ask for it. You don't campaign for it. You don't interview for it. It's something that just happens to you. I just got a phone call one day. I'm glad that I was recognized but I'm really self-conscious about what comes with it. It follows you around. Journalists are weird because they know what goes into winning something like that. It's held against you in jest—"Well what do you care, you already have a Pulitzer."

JW: That's so rude. It's a way of stripping you down.

WM: You know how it is.

JW: Was there a film or soundtrack or artifact that is tied to a coming-of-age moment for you?

WM: The year 1987 was that for me. That was the year I figured out I was not an adult but I had interesting interests. I read *Lolita* and saw *Fatal Attraction* ten times.

JW: Not a boy, not yet a man.

WM: My parents didn't seem to care about me seeing these films. No one was enforcing the rated-R policy at these theaters. But I think 1987 was the year. That was the year Michael Jackson's "Bad" came out. I also figured out what it was like to be attracted to someone, like William Hart. He was like, my first boyfriend. I also remember seeing *Broadcast News* for the first time that year. I remember thinking *These are my people*. I wanted to be around smart people who were emotionally fulfilled.

JW: I remember that I was always impressed with *The L Word*. Back then, it was the only template for female queerness, Black queerness, POC queerness, that wasn't totally offensive. I remember hearing about lesbians and not wanting to become one and then I watched *The L Word* and was like, "Oh this is something I want to become."

WM: Well, I can tell you that since I worked at a movie theater from fifteen to eighteen, I also had a horrible image of lesbians from the movies. And it's not like the lesbians themselves were bad people, but like why can't lesbians be in good movies?

JW: Where did all of the lesbian films go?

WM: For one thing they became commercialized. People like Todd Haynes are making movies like *Carol*. And I'd much rather watch *Claire of the Moon* or any other shitty lesbian movie before I watch some shit like *Carol* again.

JW: What? You didn't like *Carol*??

WM: I hated *Carol*. It's so uptight. It's worth a conversation about appropriation, the artist's relationship to their subject via empathy. My question, for artists who live in the present day and are choosing to go back in time: What are you expecting to find if you are Todd Haynes, a gay man in 2017? What do you expect to find in the 1950s? Those movies are about denial of pleasure, the denial of self, a denial of happiness, and it gets on my nerves. It's not that it's not true, but *Carol* is a movie that should have come out thirty years ago on ABC and we could have all learned a lesson about female repression. And the entire point of the 1990s films was to say "Fuck that, I'm not going to hide myself." There was a movie called *Jeffrey*.

JW: 1995. I just googled it.

Let's see a movie about gay men who live well-adjusted gay lives out in the world and go on healthy dates.

WM: I remember thinking it was a perfectly stupid depiction of men's sexuality. Then there was *Wild Reeds*. And even that one was fraught with the politics of being openly gay. There really wasn't a lot going on in the mid-nineties. But what little you got felt so electric. I don't know if I learned about what I wanted my life to be like during this period. There were also no Black people during this time, at least not Black men.

JW: So what would be your ideal gay love story? Is it *Moonlight*? Did it already happen?

WM: I just want to see two Black men in love and being normal and live a life on screen. That never happens. I would love to just see that. I would love to just see any type of gay men—not a boring life—just having a normal life. No drama. No coming out. No "I need to tell my wife." Let's see a movie about gay men who live well-adjusted gay lives out in the world and go on healthy dates.

JW: *Looking* on HBO was that.

WM: Well, *Looking* was the closest we have ever gotten. That show was trying to build a world. I'm sad it ended. But I knew it wasn't going to last. Even gay people were like, "It's so normal. I don't like this show." People either want Harvey Milk or *Queer as Folk* twenty-four-hours a day. I don't know. There's gotta be something between revolutionary politics and activism and sex slaves.

JW: I think this goes back to marketplace

Hearing Nina Simone for the first time—I will never forget. That voice? You didn't know someone could sing like that.

demands. Like who are we putting this life on the screen for? Is it for the people living it? What do they want to see when they watch themselves? Is it educational? Is this award-show bait? It goes back to the economics of why a show is made. Look at the movie *Girls Trip*, that is for a particular audience. Look at *Milk*, it's for gay people but it's also for everyone else to say: "Look, gay people have been struggling, guys. It's been rough."

WM: I'm not saying I don't like *Milk*. But it's kind of the same thing with Black people. It's like you get a slavery movie or you get, you know, whatever Kevin Hart wants to do. And it's really hard to find a normal, middle ground. August Wilson was supposed to be that, given there are so few movies about Black people doing much of anything interesting. So you don't want to treat it like an event, but it really is. One of the greatest Black actors—or actors in general—is sort of an event within the context of so-called "Black movies," so then *Hidden Figures* starts to look extra good. On one hand *Hidden Figures* is like, "Oh I'm going to tell you something about American history you probably didn't know." But all of those scenes with women hanging around the BBQ and being normal, those scenes were great—they were excellent.

JW: And those scenes were really amazing and the best in the movie. It's like, "Yeah, I'm super here for this nerd shit. But sometimes I want to see them drinking corn liquor in the living room while making a cake." That's the stuff we don't see. We always see Black women struggle; struggle to find love, struggle to be mothers. But at the end of the day I just want to see Taraji, Octavia, and Janelle Monáe getting into trouble. And no one is going to go to jail. There's no tragedy here. This is what I want.

WM: Exactly.

JW: If you had to name the most influential pieces of culture that have shaped you as a person, what would they be?

WM: *Broadcast News* was one of those things. I think reading *Beloved* for the first time was important. From 1993 to 1995, I tried to read every single thing that a Black woman had ever written and it unlocked a lot for me. And I read *Invisible Man* and that was very important for me. I read a lot of poetry, like Audre Lorde, Gwendolyn Brooks—which all Black kids get shoved down their throats. There's Thylias Moss.

JW: Who's that?

WM: Thylias Moss. She's the best. She's a poet and she also makes films, which I've never seen but you should see them.

JW: I'm on it. Let's have a screening.

WM: There's something about seeing slavery, like in *Beloved*, from the point of view of a woman that has lost, but hasn't lost everything. She still has her womanhood and her sexuality and everything they tried to rob her of. And I think if someone like Margaret Atwood tried to write about that, it just wouldn't be the same thing.

JW: I have a new copy of *Beloved*, but I'm worried to read it. It's so devastating. I mean the brutality of this time is different than the brutality of that time, but there's still violence and pain and Black women are fighting in a way. Also, slavery wasn't that far removed from us. We can point to our families.

WM: Hearing Nina Simone for the first time—I will never forget. That voice? You didn't know someone could sing like that. With that voice and all that pain, but it wasn't just the pain. She was fun, she could sing, but the blues in her voice was so powerful. I remember I bought a double album of *Wild Is the Wind* and *Four Women*. I think you got like twenty-four songs and I listened to it every week until I graduated college. But, yeah, a lot of things are important to me.

JW: I know, that's one of my favorite things about you. Hearing you talk about these important cultural reference points, I can map more of a clear constellation of the types of things that interest you. You're able to make these amazing connections. So many brilliant artists were, and are, looking at what you're looking at and it's easy to forget that. And it helps us understand the arc of culture and why culture today looks the way it does, how the past is speaking to the present and the future, and there's so much to look at, and so much of it is in conversation.

WM: I mean, there are also a lot of people who make really bad shit.

JW: That's very true. You like a lot of bad stuff.

ORIGINALLY PUBLISHED IN *HELLO MR.* ISSUE 9, 2017.

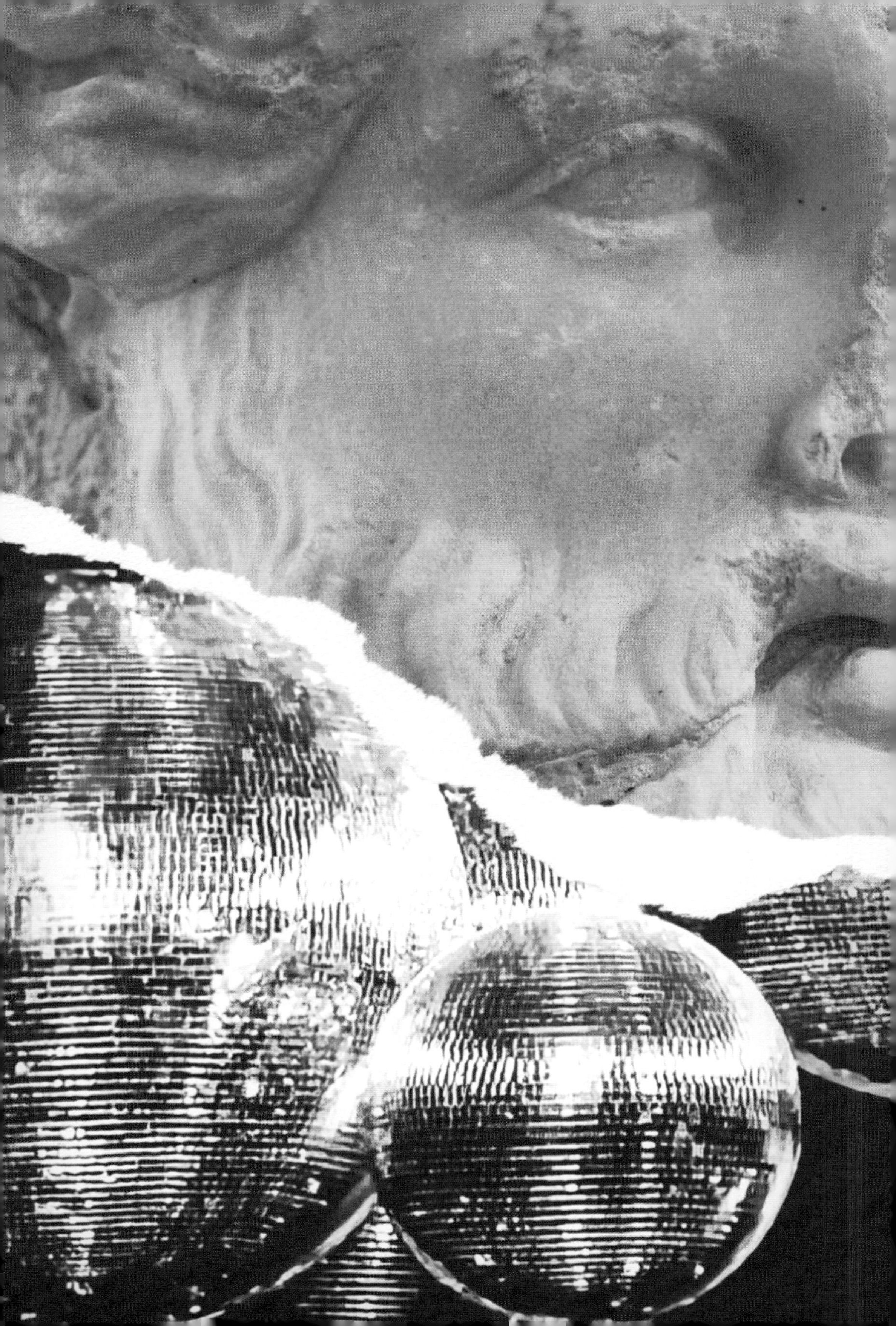

FALLING PREY

Fran Tirado | Art by Benjamin Edeline

[Ganymede] was the loveliest born of the race of mortals, and therefore the gods caught him away to themselves, to be Zeus' wine-pourer for the sake of his beauty, so he might be among the immortals.

– THE ILIAD

It was nearing last call at Olympus.

"Ladiessss," a staticky shrill from a drag queen named Urethra Franklin echoed through the bar, "a little birdy told me it's somebody's birthday tonight."

A generous chuckle from the crowd—the night's theme was "birds of prey," so everyone was incentivized to dress up as either a bird or their prey. Dim light refracted white and purple around a packed, ivory room. From the ceiling hung thousands of heaven-sent pearls draping just above the heads of men scantily clad in feathers and fur, slutty interpretations of the night's theme.

Olympus was New York's premier gay club, a chichi hotspot in a sea of piss-smell dive bars buoyed on the choppy waters of a dying industry. It was stationed perfectly downtown for Manhattan- and Brooklynites and offered fairly priced drinks. And that night, the club's owner was the bird of the hour.

"Zhuuuuuu," a gaggle of partygoers in large beaks chanted from a velvet sofa.

"They'dies and gentlemen," Urethra said, throwing a boa of black ostrich feathers over her shoulder. "Can we get a little music for the man, the myth, the king, Mr. Zhuuuuuuu."

Rihanna's "Cake" played as the crowd bumped a bit. A spotlight pulled over their heads and landed on Zhu Reyes. Zhu perched over the dance floor in the club's VIP section, a mezzanine high above the crowd. Referred to as "Mr. Zhu" by even his inner circle, he was reclined in a large velvet chaise and surrounded by an entourage of prey. Gorgeous men, a mix of some his age (fifty, today) and other modelesque boys who looked recently of drinking age.

Mr. Zhu was dressed like an eagle, in a brown feathered kilt bearing his tan thighs as big as Christmas hams. His chest was bare and took up the width of the chair under a Usekh collar of feathers. Staged on either side of him were two Adonises dressed as doves, rubbed head to toe in body oil. Bearing enormous white plumes, they fanned the birthday boy like a god. Though the top half of his face was covered with a macabre plague doctor's mask, Zhu's chiseled jaw broke a smile. He's always loved a little theater.

"OoOoOOoo, daddy. The eagle has landed!" said Urethra, to another tired laugh from the audience.

"OK, kids. It's twink time." Hera, Olympus's front-of-house manager, was at the other end of the venue surrounded by a procession of toned, hairless men (and a few enbies) dressed in identical mice costumes. "Gianni, I'm putting you in front. You're my sacrificial lamb—er, mouse."

"That's him, right?" asked Gianni. The pack-leading bottle boy lit the sparklers atop the champagne bottles he had in either hand. "He's kinda hot."

"Kinda?" said an eavesdropping mouse. "Zaddies aren't your type, are they? Mr. Zhu is a perfect specimen. His Zaddiness should be studied."

"He's so exotic," said a problematic rabbit. "Like, where is he even from?"

"I've heard no one really knows," said another mouse. "He just appeared one day with all this money and took over downtown."

"He's a mix," slurred a white guy in a pink mesh tank top, backward baseball hat, and Chromatica jockstrap. "His dad was Chinese, his mom was Puerto Rican."

"You're all being kinda racist," Gianni said, eyeing the jockstrap. "Wait, what are you even supposed to be?"

"I'm a flamingo," said the Little Monster, sipping a vodka tonic with five tiny straws.

"I can't see his face." Gianni squinted. He felt hot and uncomfortable in his costume: thigh-high white stockings held by garters on a pair of high-waisted latex panties and a tail to match. Though Gianni was twinky, his ass pushed the latex taut with just enough cheek peeking on either side. A petite nose and whiskers were drawn lazily to go with the ears on his straw-blond buzz cut.

Gianni sighed. How did he end up here? Moments like this felt utterly humiliating, like watching the tragic ghost ship of his life sail away. Moving to New York was one of the hardest things he'd ever done, and for what? No real friends, no real job. All that ambition lubed up and squeezed into rubber Spanx for minimum wage and three nonconsensual gropes per hour. And when things felt like this, when he wasn't in control of his own life, his own body, it felt good to concede. He was floating, things just happened to him. He wanted this night to be over so he could go home to *America's Next Top Model* rewatches.

"Shall we all sing Mr. Zhu a happy birthday?" said Urethra, drunk. "And a one, and a two—"

"Go, go, go," said Hera. The crowd erupted into an annoyingly on-key "Happy Birthday" as the twink mice ascended through the crowd up to the mezzanine with a cake so large it required the support of four. At the head of the procession was Gianni holding the champagne sparklers over his head. He snapped into his bimbo character with a toothpaste-commercial smile, swinging his hips the way he knew how.

They placed the cake in front of Zhu just as the crowd reached its harmony for "tooo youuu." The mischief of mice dispersed and Gianni leaned over to pour the boss a drink, his butt tooched with great intention.

"Champagne, Mr. Zhu?" he said with a porny coo. God, he hated this. He poured the champagne into Zhu's glass, but the bubbles quickly overflowed, spilling onto his crotch.

Zhu jolted. A few members of his posse gasped. He was precisely the man you did *not* want to spill a drink on.

"Oh, fuck. I'm so sorry, Mr. Zhu, I—"

"Just," Zhu's voice was deep but sweet like molasses. The twink peered through Zhu's mask to his deep amber eyes, "clean it up."

Mortified, Gianni took a bar cloth and mopped up the champagne. His mind racing, the mouse fumbled the cloth across Zhu's lap, grazing the largeness of his bulge through his kilt.

"Oop, sorry, I—" Gianni quickly pulled his hand back. Zhu's chest heaved and Gianni noticed Zhu's dark nipples were hard. Terrified, Gianni scurried back downstairs with his head down. Fuck. That could not have gone worse.

"Can I go home early?" he asked Hera, toweling the bar to keep himself busy.

"Yeah, right. You're closing, kid."

"I'm actually not sure I can handle the embarrassment," said Gianni. "I'm an Aquarius."

"And I don't give a shit," said Hera, glancing over at two ass-bare bluebirds heading into the bathroom. "Can you go make sure they're not doing heroin?"

Gianni was humiliated but also aroused. Zhu's bulge. Was he even hard? Gianni was sure it was flaccid, but it felt big, and Gianni wasn't even a size queen. If anything he preferred an average penis. It was ergonomically correct.

Lusting after Zhu felt problematic. He'd heard about the mogul but wasn't completely clear on how he made his living. Surely something evil and imperialist—like real estate? Or was it venture capital? As the night died down Gianni was doing everything to keep out of the mezzanine's eyesight, but he felt Zhu's gaze.

"Kid," Hera barked down the bar to Gianni, who was counting cash. "Zhu wants to see you."

"Me?!" Gianni almost fainted. He was about to be fired. "What does he want?"

"You're mistaking Mr. Zhu for someone who provides context for his demands." Hera grabbed the cash from him. "Get up there, Timothée."

When Gianni came up to the mezzanine Zhu's entourage was mostly gone, save a murder of ho-ey crows gossiping in the corner. A large man without costume, presumably Zhu's bodyguard, stood by Zhu, who sat like a statue. It almost made Gianni feel bad for the titan. An adoring crowd, yet so alone.

"Zhu, I really am so sorry about the champagne. I don't know what I—"

"What's your name?" The eagle cut him off so quick, Gianni felt it in his stomach.

"Gianni."

"Johnny."

"Um, yes, like Johnny. But 'Gee-ah-nee.'"

"I prefer Johnny." Zhu picked up his empty glass, his bicep curling into the size of a cantaloupe. This guy knew the power he had and reveled in it, but Gianni didn't want to suffer any longer.

"Listen, if you're going to fi—"

"My champagne needs a refresher," said Zhu. "I was hoping you could make it up to me."

For a moment, Gianni was stuck in time, his head spinning with all the various outcomes and disasters this current shit-uation could get him into. This man's raw, vibrational power alone could very well ruin his life.

"Of course, sure thing, Zhu." He reached for the champagne.

Zhu grabbed Gianni's forearm, firm but not rough.

"You can call me *Mr.* Zhu. Or *Sir.*"

Gianni's face warmed. This was a mindfuck. Some psycho game Zhu was playing before Gianni was undoubtedly blacklisted from New York nightlife, all for a fucking champagne spill. Sweat trickled from forehead to nipple as Gianni wondered where he could get a job next. Maybe Zara was hiring. He pulled a bottle from its chiller and popped the cork off.

"Yes, sir."

Just before Gianni started to pour, Zhu stopped him. From the DJ, "Pull Up" by ABRA played.

"Ah-ah-ah," Zhu sing-songed. "You're doing it wrong. Let's not have a repeat of last time."

Zhu took off his eagle mask. Under the mystifying amber of his eyes was a beautiful, aquiline nose and a set of lips that jutted from his pronounced chin. His complexion was dark, his hair in loose salt-and-pepper curls. The breath left Gianni's body. He was gorgeous. The mogul cupped Gianni's champagne hand as he grabbed the bottle. Heat trickled over Gianni all the way down to his cock.

"You tilt the glass like this," Zhu turned the glass at an angle so the bubbles filled slow, "and voilà."

To Gianni's surprise, Zhu poured a second glass, then gestured to his bodyguard. Without a word, the mezzanine was quickly cleared. They were alone on this velvet balcony—with champagne.

Gianni had been in the industry long enough to understand what was unraveling before him. This was his boss's boss, after all. Gianni had no place being here. He wondered if he'd be fired for rejecting Zhu's advance, or if he'd merely be hazed at work—getting shittier hours and fewer tips. He wondered whether Hera helped set this up in some sick, complicit game. How many bottle twinks had been sent up here before? Did he just want a little fondle, or something more? This man belonged to a certain class of people who got what they wanted in every sector of their life, and that made Gianni feel quite gross. And then, an even grosser intrusive thought: Would it be so bad to get on this guy's good side? This could be Gianni's ticket to something better. And even simmering resentment and moralistic spiraling didn't change the fact that Zhu was *hot*. My god, those thighs. Gianni wanted to be crushed between them like a Pepsi can. All this swirled in the great soup of Gianni's mind in the few seconds he stood dissociating on this mezzanine in a slutty mouse costume.

Zhu smiled. "This is Dom Pérignon, my favorite," Zhu said. "My favorite champagne, at my favorite bar, on my birthday. Do you know what could make this moment even more perfect?"

Gianni breathed harder. They were close enough Gianni could smell him—probably Aesop. Leathery like vetiver and crisp like a forest.

"What's that?" Gianni asked.

Zhu held out the second glass. "If you were sitting in my lap."

Though he wished it weren't true, power turned Zhu on. It'd been that way ever since he was a kid, even before he had money. Money was fake after all—a myth of humanity to construct illusions of authority. Power, though? Power was real.

And though he wished it weren't true, Zhu loved to have power over an unassuming twink, especially ones with pouty Caravaggio lips, flushed cheeks, youth still dewy in their eyes. A constellation of pink freckles trailing perfectly down their neck, shoulders, the small of their back, a delicate canyon leading to the ass, supple and jiggling ever so slightly. This was the kind of twink who didn't know his own beauty or the power it possessed.

But by his own rules, Zhu always waited for reciprocity after he made the first move. Waiting for the twink's answer, he felt his cock grow under his kilt just at the thought. He wondered how old the kid was. Old enough to work at his bar at least. But these days it only took one wrong move before someone deemed him a predator or something. But that wasn't Zhu at all, so he thought. He just liked twinks. Especially coy, bottle-service twinks with fat asses. Fuck.

For a few more seconds, they stayed in a stalemate and Zhu wondered if he would be rejected. He needed enthusiastic consent, or it was over.

But without a word, Gianni took the glass out of Zhu's hand and gently placed the fullness of his ass onto his lap. The weight of it sank in, reclining back into the chair of Zhu's chest and stomach. He felt his cock curl tautly under his own kilt as he was sure Gianni felt, too.

"Well, cheers then," Gianni cooed.

"Salud," Zhu said. "That's a good boy."

Gianni downed the glass before pouring another. He was difficult to read, this twink. A smirk on his lips and fear in his eyes. But then his hips started to gyrate in a slow circle. Pressing his ass down onto the meat of it, he clutched Zhu's thigh and arched his back.

"Happy birthday, Mr. Zhu, sir."

"Mmm, fuck," groaned Zhu. Enthusiastic enough. His underwear was so tight now it might rip. No underwear fit him properly. He had to buy it custom. Zhu started to fiddle with his waistband, but quicker than anything, Gianni turned around and got on his knees to grab the kilt's clasp.

"Ah, ah, ah," Zhu said again. He could tell this twink liked to be told what to do. "Kiss me first."

Gianni complied. Soft met hard. Gianni's lips were tender and wet, Zhu's plump and scruffy. Champagne swilled in their mouths with the taste of Zhu's overpriced mouthwash, the cigarettes on Gianni's tongue. Suddenly, he was ravenous; they both were.

Gianni then kissed his way down Zhu's chest, brushing his tongue along the recess of his armpit and finally, finally around his nipples. He wrapped his mouth around as much of Zhu's pec as he could before biting, hard.

"Ahh," Zhu gasped. "That's my favorite."

Gianni swirled his tongue around the nipple, hard and protuberant. He pinched the other before ripping the feather collar from his broad shoulders to reveal Zhu's canvas of trimmed chest hair. He bit harder—so hard Gianni seemed to break the skin of his pec, though no blood drew.

"Fuuuuck." For the first time, Zhu squirmed. This twink could really pack a punch.

Gianni opened up the clasp of Zhu's kilt and pulled it off; his bulge mountained through black briefs. He pressed his face into the length of his cock and smelled it sweetly. Gianni sighed again, drawing his mouth around the circumference of it over the fabric, then his teeth.

"Can I have a taste, Birthday Boy," Gianni asked.

"Ah, ah, ah . . ." Zhu teased.

"Can I have a taste, *sir*."

"Yes, you may."

Gianni pulled his king's waistband down and his cock flew out like a great snake released from the tension of his briefs. The mouse moaned just looking at it.

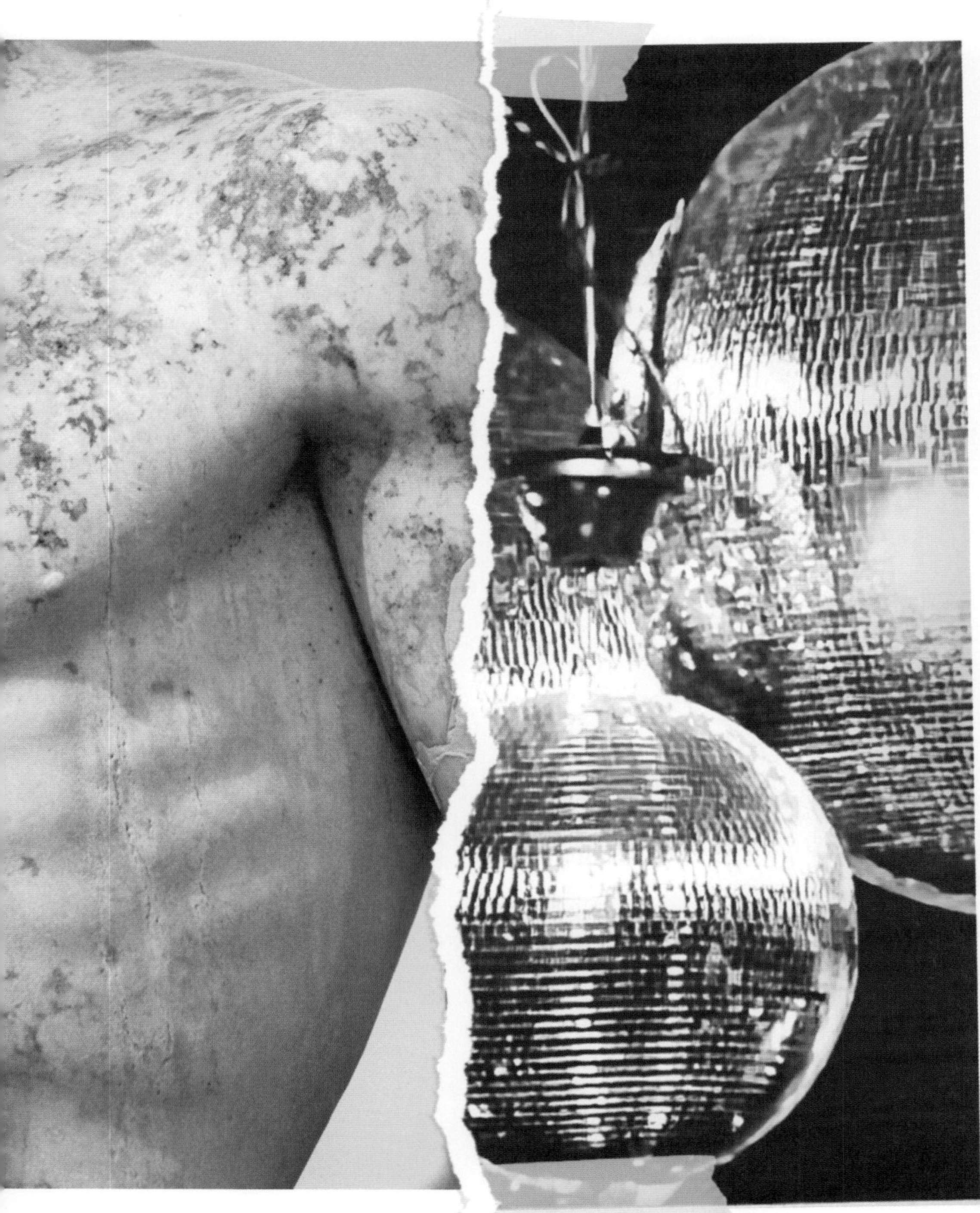

Starting slow, Gianni kissed Zhu's pubes, then his inner thigh, up and down to make the mogul squirm once more. Gianni's tongue traced down to his balls, taking one, then the other, gently into his mouth. Zhu let out a hissing exhale, another moment of weakness earned.

The pipe of Zhu's cock dwarfed Gianni's tongue as he sucked along the shaft with a slow rhythm. To the eagle's surprise, they locked eyes as Gianni wrapped his mouth over the head of Zhu's cock, taking the shaft with both hands. He could feel his own energy slipping from his body. Gianni was way too pleased with himself.

Zhu yanked a fistful of blond and slid his cock slowly to the back of Gianni's throat. Even then, Gianni still had inches to go. Up and down, Zhu put ginger pressure on Gianni's head, forcing him down more, a challenge. Gianni's eyes watered and his face went pink. Gasping through his nose, Gianni pulled in another inch of cock with ease, another. Gianni inhaled through his nose as a tear fell from his eye. The mouse choked, pulled his mouth off the cock, a thread of saliva connecting the two.

"Good boy," said Zhu. "You're pretty when you cry."

The mouse wiped the precum from the corner of his mouth and licked his finger.

Gianni got up to reveal a full erection under his latex. He straddled over the chaise and perched himself on all fours, wiggling his ass gently in Zhu's direction. With anyone else it would look so stupid, but Zhu was absolutely entranced. He resisted standing up. Zhu made the orders around here, he would not concede to the "come hither."

But then Gianni reached back and peeled the latex from his ass, slick with sweat. His cheeks spilled from the rubber along with his plumped perineum. Pulling it down to his thighs, his erection finally sprung from the panties, swinging heavy. My god, Zhu thought, and suddenly he was on his knees.

His mouth clamped onto Gianni's perineum like a forbidden fruit. Sucking vigorously, Zhu buried his nose into Gianni's ass before sticking his tongue in deep, sliding up and around the inside of him as Gianni's fingers curled into the velvet. Gianni tried muffling his moans into the velvet but it was useless. He wrestled Gianni's tight little hole open, trying to get as deep as he could with his tongue. Too tight still. Grabbing Gianni's neck and pulling his face up from all fours, Zhu hooked his index and pointer fingers into the twink's mouth roughly before returning them to his beautiful little hole, a hole that could ruin him quite honestly.

"Fuuuuuck." Gianni's body melted as his hole gaped. Zhu twisted the fingers, then pulled them in and out with increasing speed. Gianni started to moan more, shuddering his breath as Zhu used his massive hands to fuck him.

"Someone might see," Gianni whimpered, peering through the thin veil of pearls to a crowd still dancing below.

"Good," said Zhu. He put his tongue back inside, and this time he was looser, wet with saliva. Then he stood up and took Gianni's ass with him. Gianni gasped. Without effort, Zhu lifted him almost entirely from the bed and threw his legs over his shoulders, holding Gianni upside down. Licking deeper and deeper, there was an energy pulsing through their bodies, like static, like the way your foot feels when it falls asleep. Gianni's cock fattening onto Zhu's chest, having no other option but to suck off Zhu upside down.

A thumpy little techno beat dropped.

"Do you want me to fuck you?" Zhu said, with the boy upside down.

"Please, Zhu."

"What's that?"

"Please, Mr. Zhu, sir," Gianni said.

Zhu flipped Gianni back onto all fours with ease, pushing Gianni's chest into the bed so his ass was straight into the air. Licking his palm, he smacked Gianni right on his little hole, pink and raw. Gianni whimpered with delight. Opening his palm, Zhu smacked it again, then once more on the right cheek, leaving an imprint.

"Please, sir," Gianni whimpered again. This was what the mouse came for.

He slid the head of his cock up to Gianni. Pushing in slightly, the mouth of Gianni's hole wrapped around him and tightened. Zhu felt something prickly, something unnatural. He felt his lightning travel all the way down his spine and into Gianni, who finally let out a satisfying yelp. Gianni wanted to be filled by him, he could tell. Filled with his lightning all the way to the brim. He clutched Zhu's forearm from behind, a plea.

He placed his palms on Gianni's ass and rested the full weight into its cushion. He slid in an inch, then another. Gianni was wet and warm, his hole gripping Zhu's cock with a tenderness. He sucked air through his teeth.

Gianni's back was wet with sweat funneling down its groove. Another inch, another. Most guys couldn't take it, but Zhu was astounded to see Gianni writhing his ass onto Zhu in a circular motion, deeper. Leaning back, Gianni sat back onto Zhu's lap, riding his cock from behind. The only thing he loved more than having power was not having it.

"Ah, fuck," Gianni said, another inch.

"Ahhh," Zhu said, another inch. Zhu let out a howl and rammed the rest of himself into Gianni, who yelped again.

"Oh, my god," Gianni moaned, and little did he know, he was right.

Zhu smiled and wiped the sweat from his brow before taking Gianni for the ride of his life. He pounded the boy like a piece of meat, sweat beads jumping off the drum of his ass fat like crystals. Staying inside him, Zhu picked Gianni up again and plopped him on his feet so he could clamp Gianni's throat as he leaned on a nearby banister. Zhu felt Gianni's pulse as he slid in and out, faster and faster, giving the boy all of his heaven. He took his mouth to his mouth, breathy and wet, tonguing each other through staccato moans until they were in perfect unison. Gianni's cock flopped to the rhythm of Zhu's ramming. He tried to grab himself but Zhu smacked his hand away. Ah, ah, ah.

"I'm getting close," Gianni said.

"I know," Zhu said. He wrapped his giant fist around Gianni's cock and gripped it tight. "I'm gonna fuck the cum out of you, cup-bearer."

"Oh, my god," the boy said, right again.

Zhu let out a roar, a sound that trembled Gianni's whole body. Zhu's yell made Gianni yell, too, so loud the eagle clamped down on his mouth right as he came. Gianni's moan was muffled, his pitch getting higher, his cock red in Zhu's fist. He was coming too now, Zhu could feel it dripping down his fingers, so much of it, too much of it. Then Gianni shot more semen full force, glistening as it landed among the pearled ceiling, and then more—Gianni couldn't stop—onto a small puddle on the ivory floor. Zhu rammed in one more time for good measure and shuddered. They collapsed into each other, arms, legs, cocks, sweat. They lay there for a long while breathing heavy. Over the murmur of the crowd, Janet Jackson played softly.

"Am I gonna have to clean up this mess," teased Gianni as he sat up. Looking down, he gasped.

The puddle of his cum was luminous, silver and glowing in the darkness of the club. Looking closer, it almost seemed to shimmer, refracting light just like a star.

"What the fuck," said Gianni. He reached down to touch the liquid, pulsating with light. "Are you seeing this?"

But of course, Zhu saw. He reached for the champagne and took a swig straight from the bottle, a dribble sliding down his neck. He was wearing nothing now but his Prada loafers, his cock hanging heavy. At the end of it, Gianni spotted the same glowy liquid glistening on Zhu's tip.

"I feel dizzy," said Gianni. "I feel like I'm flying."

"You are," said Zhu, handing the champagne to the mortal. He smiled. "Are you ready to live among gods?"

Jello Boy
Calvin Gimpelevich

Midnight and I'm circling the club in briefs and sneakers, balancing drinks on a tray. Drinks in the sense of being alcohol, not a liquid; plastic cups of green and red and blue jello spiked with vodka and frozen and stuffed into trash bags and brought here. I have acne, but it's dark, it doesn't matter. There are scars, but people can't tell in this light when they look at my chest. I'm passing and nearly naked, which is intoxicating; the briefs are built for women, nothing bulges, no one comments, I'm surrounded by sweating, dancing, drinking gay men. The older ones—meaning forties, fifties; I'm twenty-four—buy shots, pat my ass, and give a generous tip. It's so rote they don't seem to notice the fondle. If I was a dyke I would have clocked them. When I was a dyke that kind of grabbing meant *FIGHT* but now it's friendly, the battle ended, we're in a queer club, the touching equivalent to hello. I've spent the last years in a subculture so specific that even though I live in this city, I don't know anyone here. *Gay* might be the better word for this night at this club, while the space I know better is *queer*. My last event—the one that got this gig started—was a benefit for a friend of a friend of a friend in the wider community. Insurance doesn't cover surgeries yet and there are constant cycling fundraisers for double mastectomies and new vaginas, for the expensive, painful process of zapping away facial hair. Some are depressing house parties where the recipient and maybe their partner sell Rice Krispies treats to the same dozen people making their usual circle of friends; at least some of whom will be making and selling their own bake sale goodies to sell to the same people, for the same reason, in less than a year. This one was better connected: a venue with DJs and quasi-celebrities judging a pageant for trans men. More than a hundred people came, all paying the cover and buying jello shots that pushed from comically oversized fake syringes, their "needles" as thick as my finger, with open blunt plastic ends. Not a specifically transgender crowd, but trans- and queer-dominant, politics twining with party: the organizer making a speech about all the trans women, that year, murdered; buttons available saying He/Him, She/Her, They/Them. The winner of the Sexiest Trans Man contest was a twink who kissed everyone leaning in. Some of the contestants were women, because gender is a construct, and another trans guy was hitting on me, buying syringes, getting on his knees so I could shoot in his mouth, telling me to get on stage and compete. I'm not a performer. I don't like alcohol. I don't like sugar. When I do this, people buy me shots that I fake drinking and put back onto the tray. At the end of the night, the jello shots left are subtracted from how many I had when I started, which are calculated into the money I have, dished back to me as an hourly wage plus my tips. I do social work as a day job, teaching, massage, other hustles. I'm trying to build enough savings to quit and write for a year. The benefit happened in a realm of normalcy and comfort. I counted the money I left with and told the club that I'd be around whenever they wanted me selling again. I get on some kind of gig work gay world roster, plugging t-shirts, checking IDs, and taking cover. The best is jello, which feels like work, but also leisure, like I'm dancing my weekend away as part of the usual crowd. Darkness, smoke machines, light beams; sticky drink-encrusted spillage; condoms left on the floor. It's Halloween and someone's dressed like PrEP, which has just been released and my friends are calling gay birth control. A shirtless man with a werewolf head and leather harness tells me I wouldn't be interested in him with his mask off, that the mask brings all of the boys. He's looking for someone to talk to. I'm interested in his wallet. People are buying and then they aren't, it's getting late, the costumes familiar, I'm tired, sales-per-hour are going down. Someone is dressed like a diva, someone is in horror-goth drag. Someone is happy and huggy on Molly; someone is chanting in the bathroom "you're OK, you're OK," taking a toilet stall. The werewolf wants my number. I am unwilling to give it to him. He leaves, huffy. Another party gets out and gives us a surge. The other shot boy is pocketing tips, but I'm stupidly, rigidly honest, and put mine in the general bin. The organizer is a guy I don't know who stiffs me at the end of the night, keeping most of my tips. I had been making so many tips. There is no preparation in me for intra-community betrayal, which suddenly seems a utopic vestige of a tighter network. All my defenses are set on outside, but the attack is coming within. There is no recourse. My friend is texting, drunk and sad in a park after running into his ex. The party is humid with bodies; my briefs are tacky, sweaty, clinging uncomfortably to damp skin. Then I'm outside in October, freezing with coat and hat and long pants, walking through the sloppy remnants of costumes in bar-hopping crowds, through candy wrappers and evidence of trick-or-treating children, with my briefs still damp under the cold weather clothes, feeling as translucent and sticky as jello, which is made of gelatin, which is collagen, which comes from tendons and animal skin and their bones.

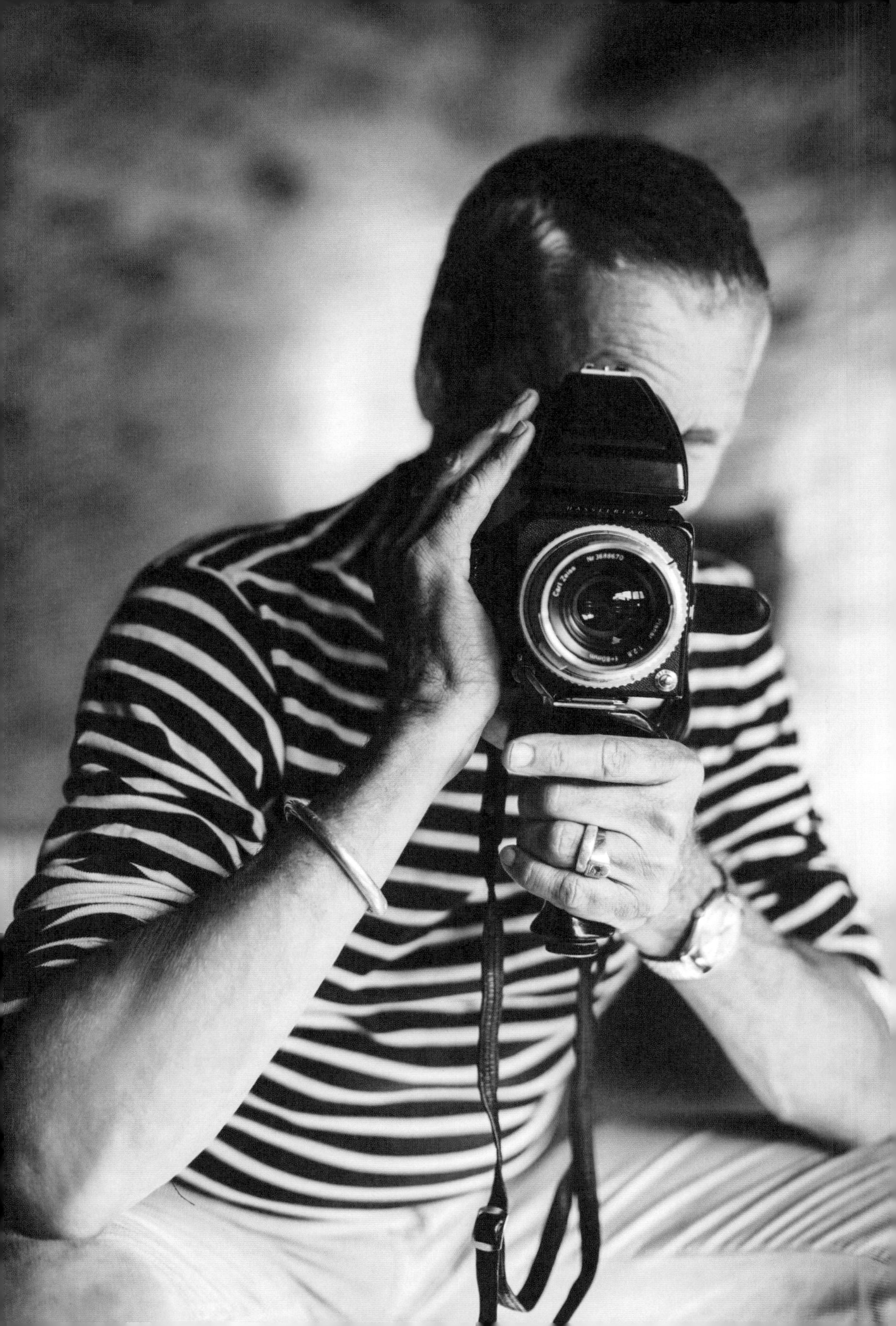
HASSELBLAD
Carl Zeiss

WHAT'S LEFT OF MARCUS LEATHERDALE?

Martin Belk | Photos by Jonathan Daniel Pryce

Years ago, I conceived of a photo-biography project, which Marcus and I gave the title *What's Left of Leatherdale*, based on an off-hand joke he'd made during one of our marathon, hours-long phone calls. Now, "what's left" is all there is—and wasn't that always *the point*?

Mythologizations aside, Leatherdale was by far, not the most prolific photographer-*célèbre* of the New York City scene from the 1970s to the '90s. In retrospect, I'm not sure he *really* ever wanted to be, knew how to be, or possessed the rapacious drive required. The Leatherdale I knew, while always remaining a Warholian luminary, was a proponent of human rights, animal rights, and fairness. During his New York City years, art and artists were aplenty. But in spite of himself, some A-list tastes, and the raptorial scene from which he emerged, Leatherdale's body of work and the stories it contains are important. They capture human subjects, moments, and vibes that the star-chasers missed.

I recall one day reading an article in a back issue of *Interview* at our friend Barney Johnson's living room on East Sixth Street (which held a massive self-portrait print entitled *Grace* c. 1985 that Marcus had given him, one of the few that seem to have eluded the internet). The piece was a lighthearted indictment on the unquenchable social-climbing of the club scenes. In essence: *The doorman anoints you and lets you in. There you discover a DJ booth that you ingratiate yourself into. Then you discover a secret VIP room behind the giant speaker, and socialize your way inside, where you see a door leading to the manager's office, which a friend pulls you into. In the manager's office, you see another door. You await the right moment, push it open and quickly rush through before anyone notices. The door slams shut behind you, and the rush of cold air greets you as you realize you're in the alleyway, beside the trash cans.*

I like to think it's a lot of the candid, alleyway moments Marcus managed to capture. He was no commercialist; the people he photographed didn't have to be on guard with him. The images are posed, yet there's intimacy. To paraphrase Roland Barthes, from *Camera Lucida*: "What founds the nature of photography is the pose . . . a *real thing* happened to be motionless in front of the eye . . . something *has posed* and has *remained there forever.* Even the corpse is a *living image* of a *dead thing*. Someone has seen the object in *flesh and blood, in person*. By attesting that the object *has been real*, the photography surreptitiously induces belief that it *is alive*, and makes us attribute eternal value."

To me, this, not celebrity, association with fame, scenes, gossip, or marketing agendas will earn Marcus Leatherdale some pages in the contemporary canon. A record—just as most of the "Hidden Identities" series images he contributed to *Details* magazine—of who he and his kind, according to Barthes, *are*. A contemporary of Marcus's once told me, "All the broken people come to New York." Perhaps, but not by accident. Not by chance. Marcus seemed to capture the phenomenon. As his closest confidant Claudia says, Marcus's work is "a celebration of why we moved to New York City in the first place."

Another friend, Jorgé Soccorras, who was born and raised in New York City, curiously noticed that most of Marcus's subjects, just like Marcus, were indeed from far beyond the walls of Gotham. Perhaps the identities he obscured for other people were, on some level, symbolic of an obscured identity within himself?

Pop-hysteria, drugs, one-night stands, guest lists, and tabloidy-things aside, why would Warhol, Mapplethorpe, or Divine indulge a fledgling young French-Canadian art student from San Francisco? Why would Madonna wear his ratty old jeans for a photo? Because that's how it used to work. Time travel perhaps. Finding the way, together.

—MB, JANUARY 2023

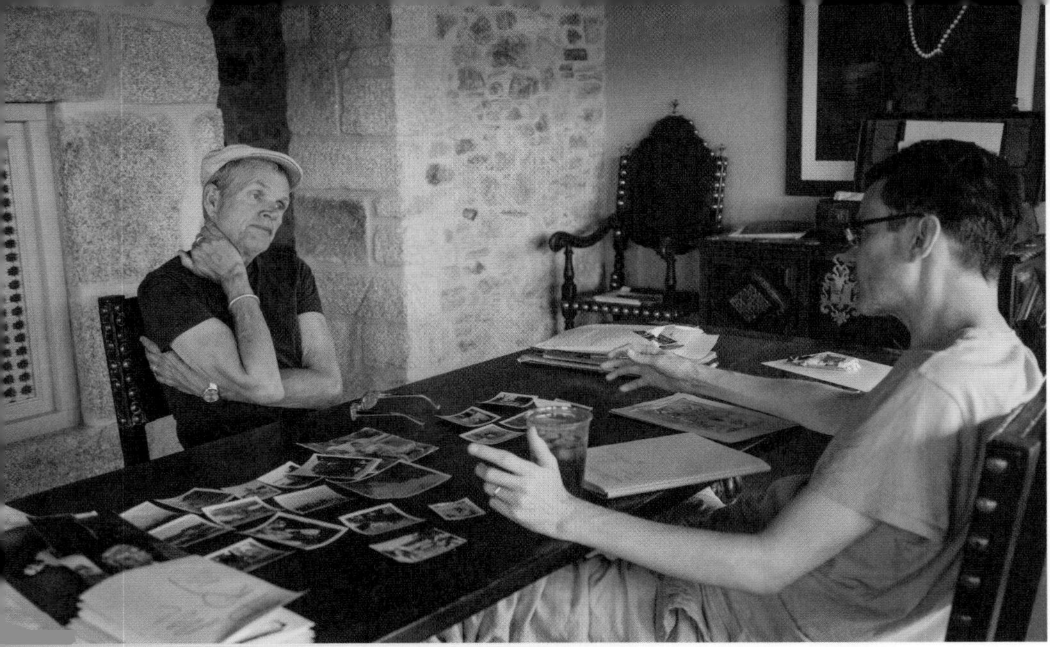

PORTUGAL, JULY 2015. One by one, the boxes, portfolios, and dusty address books emerge, filled with snapshots and fragments of another time. It's fascinating to observe the ways in which a photographic and creative legacy can inform the present. Images and stories surface of Jean-Michel Basquiat, David Burns, Quentin Crisp, Divine, Keith Haring, Iman, Grace Jones, Liza Minnelli, Issey Miyake, Jack Nicholson, Andy Warhol. The list goes on.

The images and clippings are from the archives of Marcus Leatherdale, a friend for over twenty-five years, who I met on the downtown New York scene—our family of choice. If you use nightlife as a historical marker, that era encompasses Studio 54, Area, and Mudd Club through to Pyramid, Roxy, Beige, and SqueezeBox! Over the last ten years we've been in conversation about bringing forth Leatherdale's past, making sense of leaving New York City for Europe, his annual sabbatical in India, and what it means to maintain a creative edge in today's global village.

It occurs to me that looking back is one thing; staring back nostalgically is quite another. Leatherdale's story is one of connectedness through the creative commune. And though in recent years the internet has strengthened and extended the possibilities of this beyond the ghetto, it's remarkable to realize that shaking hands with Leatherdale, one experiences several degrees of separation to the hands of Tennessee Williams, Christopher Isherwood, and Truman Capote.

As we began to unpack his life on that hot afternoon, some original notions are confirmed: age doesn't matter, relevance does. Here, Marcus talks to me candidly about some of his most poignant memories so far.

MARTIN BELK: Where did you grow up?

MARCUS LEATHERDALE: I was born in Montréal, Canada. My father was a veterinary surgeon, my mother a gorgeous housekeeper.

MB: What was it like as a child?

ML: I had wonderful parents. We were privileged and well-off, and I had an absolute terror of an older brother. We moved around a lot, so I was always starting at new schools. School was hell. There was a stretch from third grade to ninth grade where I actually had stability and exactly three friends that I hung out with, which helped a lot. Otherwise, school was absolute hell.

MB: Do you think there's anything about being bullied—it being hell—that sort of makes you . . . stronger? Like what doesn't break you makes you stronger?

ML: No, I think I could've done without it. I don't think I needed to know how unique and different I was by constantly being bullied for it. I think I could've figured that one out without it being smashed in my face [laughs]. I guess, it did make me stronger, but it got pretty intense—I mean, I was taken out of school for it. I remember my father marching me out of school to a psychiatrist because they were afraid I was going to get my ribs broken.

MB: Were you supported creatively growing up?

ML: Absolutely. My father never expected me to be a veterinarian, nor did he encourage me to. My mother used to paint and sing, but she gave all that up—apparently she was on her way to go and become a singer in Europe, but then she met my father. They always assumed I was going to be an artist, and they were very encouraging. I knew I'd go to art school—I didn't have to fight to not be a lawyer.

MB: And within that, did you always know it was going to be photography?

ML: Ha! No. I didn't even know what photography was. In 1969 I went to École des Beaux-Arts, as a fine arts major. Within a year the dean introduced photography, animation, and film—so I took a course in each of those. In fact it went from painting forward. With painting I realized I was impressionistic, and didn't have the skills to do detail—and when I realized detail was a big issue, I thought, "Why in hell should I spend so much time and energy learning to do detail when I can capture it in a photograph?" So I shifted.

Later, in 1977, at the San Francisco Art Institute—where I went for film—I switched to photography, even though I was an honors student as a painter and actually won an award for my painting that year. My teacher, who was himself a successful artist, kept encouraging me to stay and paint, but I didn't listen and switched over. I still kept a drawing class every day, and I was the only photographer at the Institute that would turn up to photography class covered in charcoal—they just didn't do both then, but to me it was always as though both were the same thing. So I've always approached photography as an alternative artistic medium, not as photography versus art. I never thought of photography as commercial. I never wanted to be a

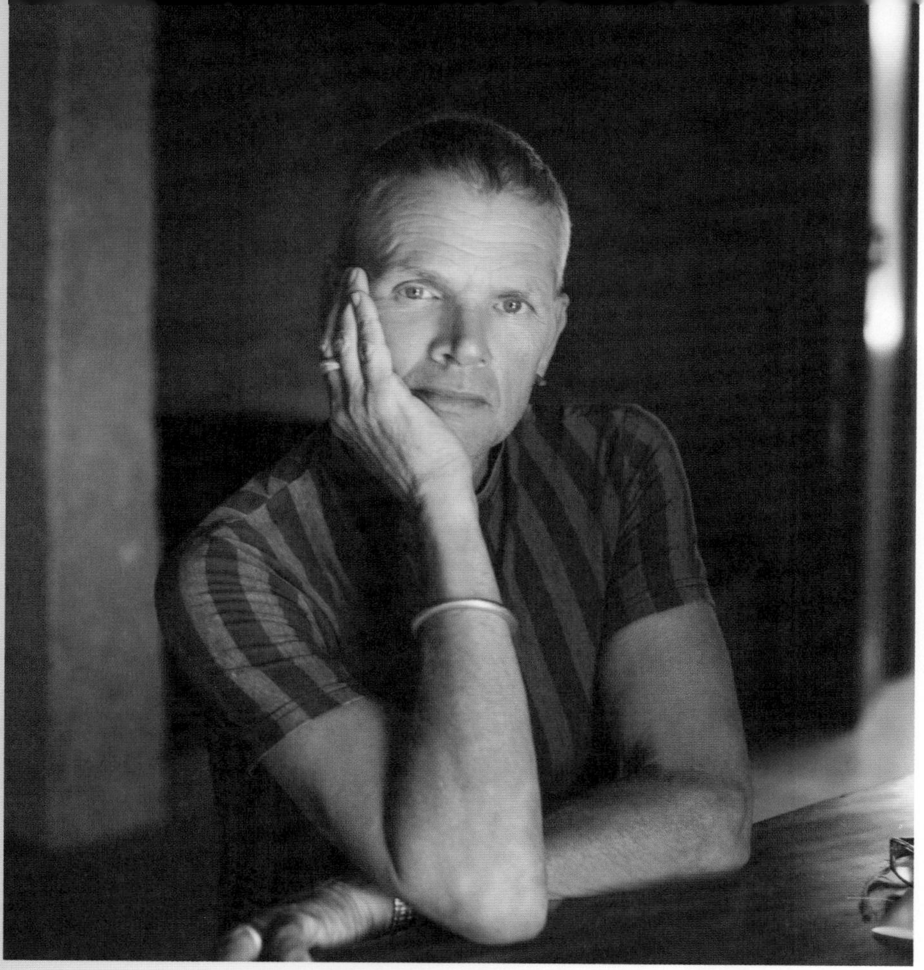

commercial photographer, and didn't want to work for *Newsweek*, or be a *Playboy* photographer. That was not what photography was about for me. Except for *Interview*, but that was an Andy [Warhol] thing—keeping one foot in fine art, and one in the commercial world.

MB: In that period of time it all sounds so organic and natural. Did you consciously talk about work, creating shoot ideas, or did it just flow?

ML: Nothing was preconceived. This was a time for me when my student fund ran out, and I had to get a job. I first met Robert [Mapplethorpe] at his 1978 show in San Francisco, and through him Sam Wagstaff, who had the largest photography collection in the world—and both hired me to manage their studios. I never discussed things with Robert in detail, unless I had to assist him on a rare occasion on location, like when we shot Truman Capote at the United Nations. Working with Sam was amazing. All of a sudden all the slides that were flashing in front of me while I was at university were now sitting in my hands. Images from Irving Penn, Alfred Stieglitz, Richard Avedon. I had to organize them with little filing cards, all placed in a flat drawer—it was a very privileged position.

MB: How did they influence your own work?

ML: It gave me a sophistication—a reference point to where things originated. My inspiration always came from painting and not photography. Although I've always loved Sanders and Penn, it was really Rembrandt, Caravaggio, and Modigliani that impressed me—their use of light.

MB: A lot of your story is about this incredible world you lived in—the famous people, the places. How did these early experiences change you?

ML: It humanized celebrity. When I met Truman Capote, I had read everything he'd written, and then I met him and he was this sad, little lonely person in a tiny apartment that reeked of hard-boiled eggs. It made things more real and easier for me not to get starstruck. Celebrities can spot an ass-kisser a mile away, and they'll never become real friends.

MB: Is there a particular memory of New York that really made an impression on you?

ML: I remember one time Yves Saint Laurent threw a party for the launch of Opium on a Peking yacht, and it was sat in a harbor with a long runway. I went with Robert, and I didn't own a tuxedo, so I went black tie from the waist up and leather pants from the waist down. I'd also just shaved my head which was unusual at the time. It was amazing—we walked down a runway with rose petals all over the place and ended up hanging out with Paloma Picasso and Saint Laurent. That was impressive. I was a punk then so when everyone started to dance I began to pogo dance. It caught the attention of an artist named Larissa, who became a very close friend. She was head to toe in gold lamé and gave me my first experience of a limo that night. She took us to Studio 54, and we stayed all night.

MB: And how did Robert Mapplethorpe figure into all this?

ML: Well, while I was in San Francisco, Peter Berlin, another gay icon, introduced me to Robert. And then I got a postcard from him inviting me to New York even though I was already on my way. I was housesitting his studio while he was away in Amsterdam, and when he returned we became friends. I wasn't rich. I wasn't famous. I wasn't even "gay" at the time, and all the S&M stuff just didn't interest me. I wore a leather MC jacket to be like Marlon Brando in *On the Waterfront*, and I didn't get the other connotations. I guess to some I appeared like packaged meat in the right attire. I never intended to have a sexual relationship with Robert, it just kind of happened as a result of everything else. Robert seemed to only have room in his life for money, fame, and sex—you can figure out which category I fit into.

MB: Was it, as they say nowadays, "complicated?"

ML: Perhaps. But don't get me wrong, I loved Robert and still consider him one of my best friends. I could've skipped the other stuff and just happily been the best of friends.

MB: What about you and Andy Warhol?

ML: Robert introduced me to Andy initially, but after that, Andy and I became friends. He was one of the first to truly take me and my work seriously. He insisted I sign everything I did, absolutely everything—this really encouraged me. There were lunches at the Factory and dinners out. Andy sat for me several times and got me work with *Interview*. I'll never forget, one night after leaving Mick Jagger's house for Jerry Hall's birthday party, we were in a taxi with Tina Chow and were passing a hospital, when Andy looked out and said, "I'll never go into a hospital, because I'll never get out again." That was the last time I saw him. Tina died of AIDS not too long after—women got it, too. I guess I'm the lone survivor of that cab ride. There were a lot of those back then. The scary thing was that people would be perfectly healthy one minute, gone the next. There's a photo of me with Andy at the Metropolitan Club with Henry Post, the editor of *New York* magazine. He was one of the very first in New York City to die of AIDS. That was in the early days when they made you wear a hazmat suit to go visit and say goodbye to your friends.

MB: Are there any misconceptions about these scenes, the time period, the notorious reputations?

ML: I think the biggest misconception is the myth that people just went out all the time and did drugs constantly—which could be true, but it wasn't the rule. A lot of these people, myself included, would go out and play for a while but would leave and go back to their studios or apartments and get back to work. There was an incredible amount of hard work, effort, and dedication that went into what was one of the most creatively explosive periods New York City has ever seen. This gets missed a lot of the time when people are telling the big party stories.

MB: How did your series for *Details*, "Hidden Identities," come about?

ML: I was upstairs at the Mudd Club when I ran into Stephen Saban, who was then the downtown chronicler for *SoHo Weekly News*. My first picture ever published was a picture of Mary Lou Green, artistic director of Vidal Sassoon. Stephen had seen it and asked me if I'd like to do some profile photographs to illustrate his weekly articles. It paid thirty-five dollars a week, or something like that, and continued for about a year until the paper was sold. I still didn't consider myself a commercial photographer, but later he started *Details* with Annie Flanders and asked me to contribute. There was a Dada night called "Underground" at that time and I took the gogo cage and made it into a studio for unidentifiable portraits—Dada has always spoken to me. After that, Stephen came to me and suggested "Hidden Identities." There was an understanding that I didn't get told who to photograph, and when it started there was a sense that if you didn't know who it was, you weren't cool enough. As time went on, names would start being revealed in the next issue, and eventually the subjects' names were written in the back of the magazine with more recognizable names like Jodie Foster. It ran from 1982 to 1990. Everyone wanted to be a "hidden identity." I turned down the likes of Grace Jones because I knew she'd arrive three weeks late—she was notorious for it.

MB: Did anyone in particular stand out for you as a subject?

ML: Leigh Bowery turned up in full drag in the middle of the day. He wore a beaded mask, a bustier, silver boots, and a merkin—butt naked otherwise, in broad daylight. He

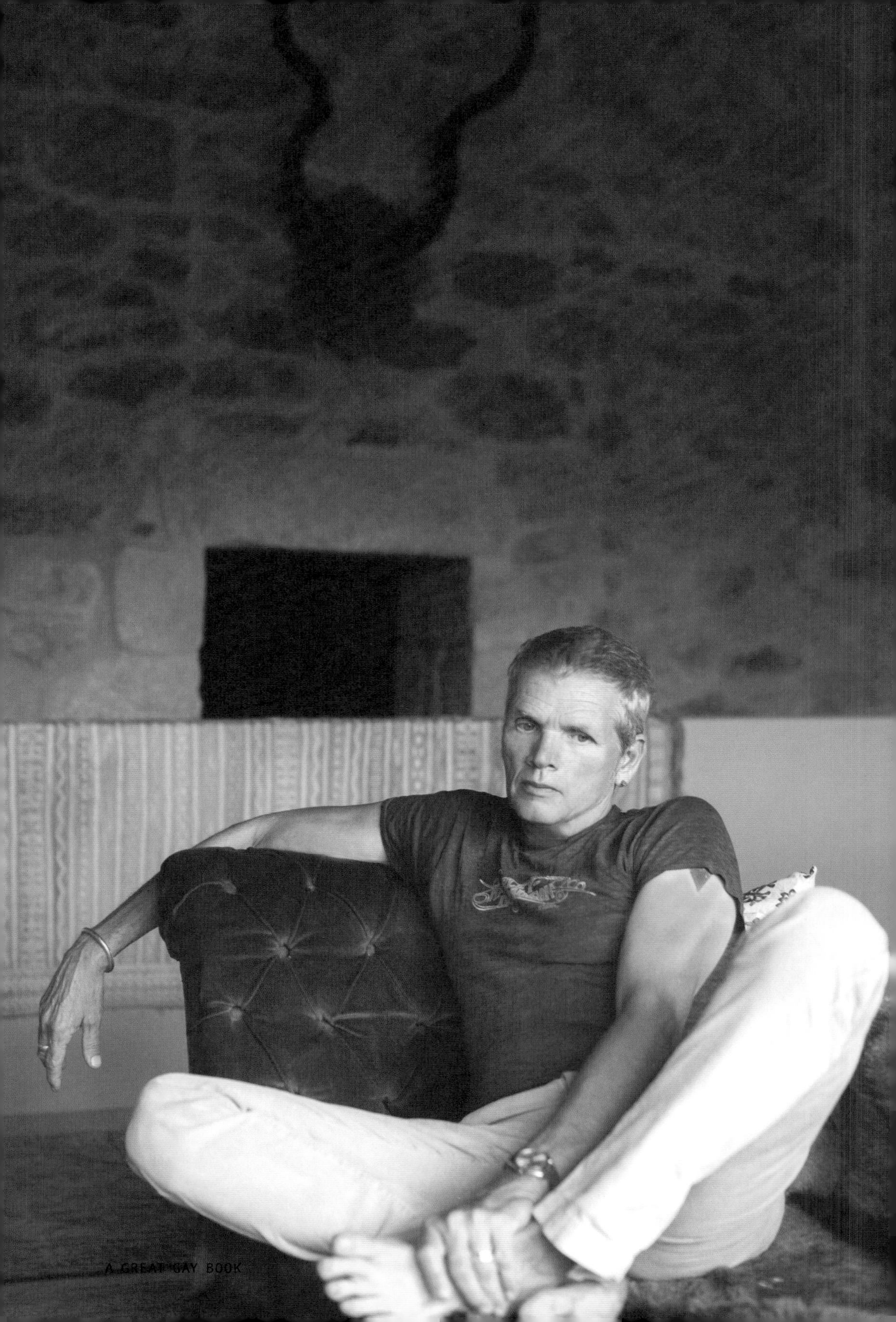
A GREAT GAY BOOK

turned up at my door and I actually never met him without a mask so at the time I didn't even know what he looked like. He couldn't have been more courteous. After I shot him we left together and went down to Broadway to get him a cab. Two or three went past but one finally stopped. Hailing cabs for these people wasn't the most fun thing.

MB: Did anyone not make it into the magazine?

ML: We shot hundreds. Madonna and Debbie Harry didn't make it in because *Details* was sold unexpectedly and became a men's magazine. It's too bad, too: There was a lot of funny stuff that happened along the way. When Madonna showed up I put her in my denim vest and posed her in the lotus position, way before all her yoga, and before I ever started shooting in India—who knew? They're all in my extended collection now though.

MB: How many frames do you take in a session?

ML: About three to six rolls of twelve per roll. That would just be a warm-up for a digital guy. I use a Hasselblad 500C/M. The only one for professionals.

MB: What do you think makes a great photograph?

ML: An internal dialogue. Showing, touching, or saying something. It's art to me. If I had to pick five favorites out of my own portfolio, they would likely not be the famous subjects. It doesn't have to be who is in the picture.

MB: What do you think makes you skilled as a photographer?

ML: I think the true talent is in the printing. It took me years and years to learn. When I take a photo it's not just the flash—it's dodged and burned. I finger paint with light. That's the skill element. Otherwise I'm not interested in wading through the technology to get to the image—that's just the gesture line in paint. People should just get lost in the image and discover what it says to them.

MB: What did you want to be as a child?

ML: I didn't have a particular goal. I knew I wanted to be an artist of some sort. I was actually suicidal at fifteen because I thought there was no future for me. Luckily my mother had a hunch something was wrong. She left the hairdressers with curlers still in her hair and came home to find me overdosed on sleeping pills. I could never see myself as an adult, but now I'm stuck.

MB: Any words of wisdom?

ML: Enjoy the trip. Enjoy the process. Chances are the destination is not what you're going to expect—and that's not a negative thing. I learned that from Robert. He was one of the most discontent people, but one of the most successful. If you live in the past you'll live in remorse, and if you live in the future you'll be a worrywart, so live in the moment. That's what I'm trying to do right now.

ORIGINALLY PUBLISHED IN *HELLO MR.* ISSUE 06 IN 2015.

On Watching MormonBoyz Porn as a Gay Ex-Mormon

Craig Mangum

Art by Hayden Davis

The first time I wore garments, my entire body broke out in hives.

It wasn't enough that I had just promised to wear the highly unflattering underwear for the rest of my life. It wasn't enough that I had to throw away the clothing I owned that couldn't cover them up. It wasn't enough that I couldn't tell my non-Mormon friends why my remaining clothing suddenly fit so poorly, why I constantly tugged on my jeans to stop the fabric from bunching up in my crotch. No. God, in His infinite wisdom, decided to send a plague to accompany my introduction to His favorite type of underwear.

God, famously, works in mysterious ways.

At the time, I thought the rash was divine retribution for unworthily participating in the ritual to receive the garments only a month after I had "accidentally masturbated." But in retrospect, I wish I had recognized the sores as a sign, a voice shouting down from the heavens as though to say, *"Girl, are you sure about this?"*

But I was sure. At least I was back then.

Religious clothing is hardly exclusive to Mormons. And like most religions, there's a ceremony that accompanies the investiture. My *endowment* (not a pun, just the name of the ritual) took place in a small Mormon temple in Columbus, Ohio. I was nineteen and a few months away from being sent to Bolivia as a missionary. As part of the ritual, I put on a "loaner pair" of garments and entered a brightly lit room divided into four quadrants by long white curtains. I moved from section to section as men anointed me with oil and water and proclaimed blessings on each part of my body. It was the same blessing with the same words that six generations of my ancestors have been given when they received their garments, a rite of passage I only vaguely understood. Like them, I promised to wear the garment every day of my life, removing it only to shower, swim, or exercise. And like them, I was told that if I dutifully wore the garment, it would be a "shield and a protection to [me] against the power of the destroyer until [I had] finished [my] work here on earth."

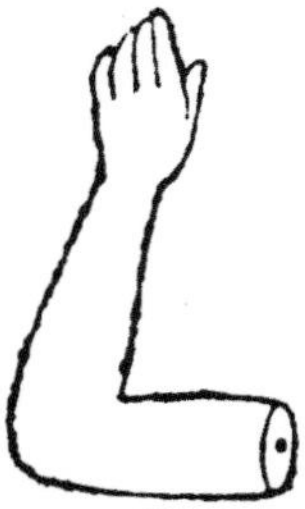

d

And I believed it. So I wore it.

I wore the garment every day as a missionary, growing accustomed to the way the fabric would grow wet and heavy from my sweat as I walked through the sweltering Bolivian countryside, clapping my

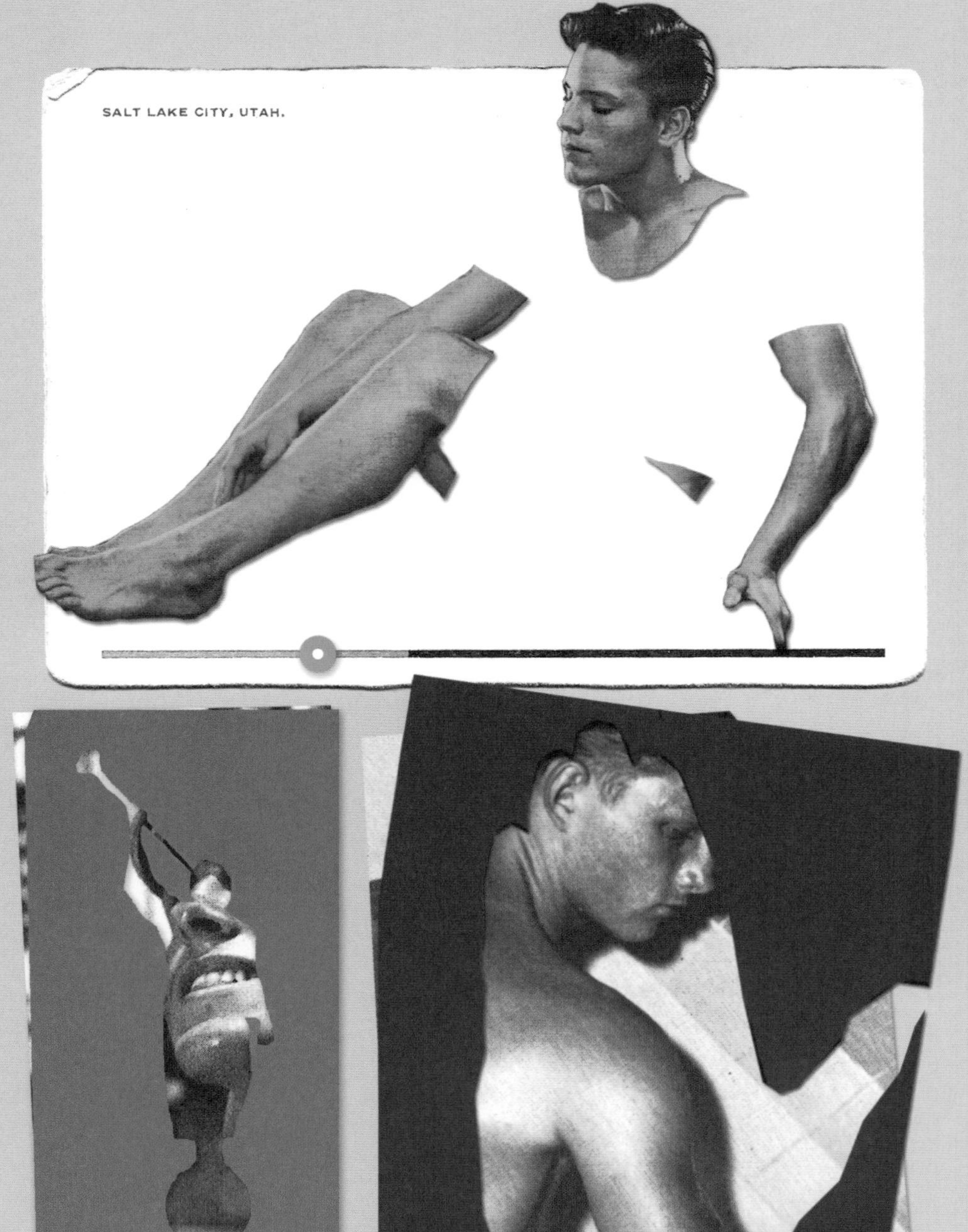
SALT LAKE CITY, UTAH.

Eventually, you take them off. You just do. And that's when the real work begins.

hands outside people's houses because you can't knock doors where people don't have doors. I wore the garment when I returned to BYU post-mission, determined to marry a woman who also wore those same garments. I even wore those garments as my faith began to fray and fall apart. I was wearing garments the first time I kissed a boy.

Eventually I took them off, like all ex-Mormons do at some point.

So I was not wearing garments the night I discovered the MormonBoyz. I logged onto Pornhub to peruse the algorithm's offerings. And there, hiding in plain sight among the thumbnails, was my old underwear. I don't remember the exact title of the video. Probably something like, "Elder Barebacked in the Temple" or "Bearded Priest Fucks a Rebellious Missionary's Tight Ass." I clicked. A pair of garments concealing an erection that redefined the meaning of *VPL* filled my screen.

I could have broken out in hives.

In the pantheon of porn, specificity reigns supreme. And as a gay ex-Mormon, few porn categories feel more targeted, confusing, and complicated for me than that of MormonBoyz.

MormonBoyz is just one brand of many that falls under the larger category of Mormon-themed pornography. It's a strong yet mighty subcategory within the larger world of religious-themed porn. (Non-Mormon examples would include Catholic nuns, priests, or, as I discovered while researching for this piece, the highly specific category of "Passover porn.") But when typing *religious* into your favorite porn tube, the results will most likely be overwhelmingly Mormon. Mormon missionaries, apparently, have knocked enough doors to produce widespread sexual fantasies about the lives they live when they aren't at your doorstep. An entire cast of characters, young boys in white shirts, ties, and black nametags, doing everything I was too scared or too shame-filled to do when I dressed like them.

The history of the company responsible for the deluge of Mormon-themed porn is almost as lurid as the videos it produces. MormonBoyz, as it was launched in 2009, no longer exists. The original creators were forced to relinquish their MormonBoyz site to a company that subsequently rebranded as Missionary Boys in 2018. Legrand Wolf, the creator of the original MormonBoyz, went on to relaunch a site called MasonicBoys.com under the banner of his company Carnal Media in 2021. Unfortunately, these behind-the-scenes business dealings seem to have caused some confusion for the storylines. Though Masonic in name, the "boyz" all wear Mormon garments. And though dressed like Mormon "elders," the boys are now called *apprentices* while the older men who oversee the sexual gauntlet that constitutes their induction into "The Order" are called *grandmasters*. They participate in sexualized rituals named after very real Mormon rituals (i.e. *ordination*, *the sacrament*, and *the second anointing*), but there's no reference to the various levels of Freemasonry.

This Mormon/secret society splice is somewhat surreal for me as an ex-Mormon. Seeing the dynamics I originally believed to be exclusive to Mormonism semi-seamlessly projected onto Freemasonry definitely ruined some of the mystique. But it also made me aware of the themes present in MormonBoyz videos that grab the attention of outsiders.

Porn, lest we forget, is not real life. But fiction always orbits something true.

At its core, the world of MormonBoyz/MasonicBoyz explores older male/younger male dynamics. This doesn't seem to be a proclivity exclusive to MormonBoyz, but rather, a point of view shared among all of Carnal Media's offerings (which includes sites such as "Fun-Size Boys," "Boy for Sale," "Twink Top," and "Gaycest"). Mormonism, it seems, isn't the only scenario of older/younger dynamics that have been sexualized by gay men, but rather, a highly specific flavor profile of a dynamic as old as time. Essentially, "Bishop" seems to be the Mormon version of "Daddy," and a barely legal "Elder" is just a more religious form of "Boy."

Porn, lest we forget, is not real life. But fiction always orbits something true. While it's easy to dismiss pornography as some seedy, inconsequential means to an end, I think it's enlightening to use pornography as a reflection of our collective erotic consciousness; a searchable treasure trove of the endlessly diverse scenarios, topics, and dynamics that we complicated, horny human beings find hot.

Which is what makes the prevalence of Mormon pornography so fascinating to me. When and why did we (or should I say "they"?) become the leaders of the "religious porn" category? What exactly is it that people find so hot about door-to-door proselytizing? And what does this say about Mormons and Mormonism?

One of the perks of being ex-religious is that I really don't have much of an opinion about whether Mormon-themed pornography is *good* or *bad*. Instead, analyzing Mormonism through the lens of the pornography produced about it brings into stark relief additional themes about my former faith tradition I hadn't seen while I was in it.

Like many kids from the Midwest, one of the best days of my life was when I took my high school grade card to Blockbuster to check out a one-day, non-new movie rental. We all cope with the closet in different ways. If my preferred method was cleaving to familiar forms of success and academic achievement, so be it.

The last time I cashed in my report card, I checked out *Latter Days*, a 2003 *sort-of* romcom about a Mormon missionary who (spoiler alert) discovers he's gay after falling in love with his hunky next-door neighbor in West Hollywood. Their romance is discovered and the missionary is sent to conversion therapy. He leaves and returns to his lover, apparently cured of any residual religious trauma syndrome by the sheer magnitude of their love. The movie features a delightfully homophobic Joseph Gordon-Levitt and British actress Jacqueline Bisset performing a role that is essentially a living mood board of Lisa Vanderpump. Frankly, I'd love to see a sequel.

I went to Blockbuster with my friend Emma, whose Christian upbringing essentially ensured she'd never heard of the film. When I found it on the shelf, I picked it up quickly, making sure she couldn't see the cover art of the missionary and his soon-to-be-boyfriend.

"What'd you get?" Emma asked.

"Oh, it's this movie about Mormon missionaries I've been meaning to see. Thought I should do my research given that I'll be one in a year."

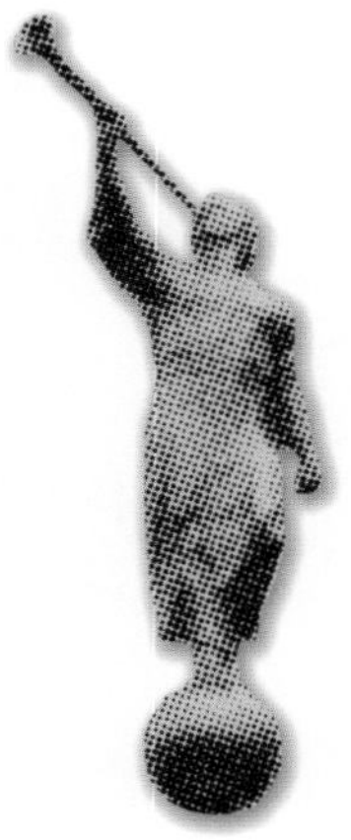

She laughed. Her evangelicalism prevented her from really engaging with the fact that I was a member of a church her pastor labeled a cult. While I knew I managed to get the film past Emma, I had not accounted for who would be working the counter of Blockbuster that night. The only "out" gay person at my high school: David.

David and I had worked on our school's literary arts magazine together. In our high school, this was pretty much the equivalent of saying *we came out to each other without saying the words*. But I had a cover: I was a chaste, naïve Mormon boy. Emma handed David whatever Julia Roberts movie she had picked out and I slid mine under hers. We both showed our grade cards, which was, in and of itself, a fairly demoralizing experience, watching David inspect our academic performance for the year against his high standards. Luckily, our grades passed Blockbuster's standards (though probably not his) and he began to check out our films.

And then he saw the title.

"This is about two gay Mormon missionaries," he said bluntly. I felt his eyes like daggers, expecting some sort of explanation.

"Oh, really? Well, I guess I should know about that, too."

David totally knew what I was up to. But in an act of gay-on-gay kindness, he moved on. Emma, always a tad oblivious, just smiled.

I took the movie home and watched it late at night after my parents had gone to sleep. It's a brilliant disaster of a movie. I laughed. I cried. I fantasized. When the star-crossed lovers finally confess their feelings for each other, they steal away to an airport motel near where the delinquent elder was about to be sent home. They make out, strip down, and after a brief moment of hesitance, the missionary commits the cardinal sin of garment wearing and takes them off (for a non-approved form of exercise: gay sex). It was, essentially, a softcore version of MormonBoyz, but it was my intro into a new awareness: garments . . . could be hot?

The movie devastated me. Seeing it all play out felt like a weird fast-forwarding of my own life. Around three A.M., unable to sleep as I thought about the movie, I sat up in bed and said, "I'm gay." It was the first time I had ever said the words aloud. Regardless of how good the movie may or may not be, it certainly did the trick.

A *fetish* is an attraction to an object for the purpose of sexual gratification. There are widely known fetishes (feet, for example), but also fetishes that are more obscure, like the man in the UK who was arrested in October 2015 for having sex with more than 450 tractors. Police later discovered more than 5,000 images of tractors on his computer, noticing a special preference for John Deeres.

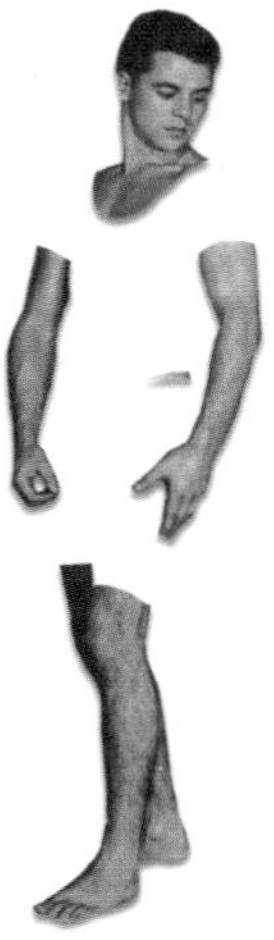

Most MormonBoyz videos begin with an almost unending ritual of undressing. The Elders start in their missionary outfits, and then they are stripped down only to their garments. Most MormonBoyz wear the infamous mesh version of the garments, the fabric of which is slightly see-through and thus inherently suggestive. The Mormon version of a tease. But eventually, they are told by their leader(s) to remove those, too. And then they are just skin, stripped of their costume.

I wondered if garments were the key to understanding the allure of the MormonBoyz. Perhaps all of that content was just a way of accessing the strangeness of our underwear. It wasn't shocking

I've committed the very sin I didn't want to commit when I began writing this piece: I've taken porn too seriously.

to me but definitely ironic since garments are designed to be patently unsexy and function as the main enforcers of Mormon rules around modesty.

But the crux of a fetish is the *object*. And in the world of MormonBoyz, garments are not the main meal but simply an appetizer. Which led to a more uncomfortable realization: If a *Mormon festish* exists, it rests on the perception of a Mormon body as an object, not a person. Something unthinking that fulfills a function. Some*thing*, not some*one*, that does as it's told. And if Mormons are *objects* of desire, garments are simply our packaging.

While it makes me uncomfortable to reckon with a past version of myself being perceived as an object, another part of me thinks: *not wrong*.

A Mormon mission, despite how it's portrayed in the *Book of Mormon* musical, is best understood as a religious pseudo-military boot camp. But instead of "cadet," you are called "Elder." You wear the same uniform as the Elder next to you. You maintain the same precise haircut. And for two years, the biggest expression of your identity is the tie you choose to wear each morning. This slow but steady whittling away of one's identity facilitates a much larger process of being re-created into a dutiful servant of Mormonism, a more thorough conversion for the already converted. And this process, in which a person becomes an object, a *thing* that performs a function, is what I actually believe the MormonBoyz fetishizes. Because once you are an object, you will do whatever you are told.

And I did.

When they told me to baptize children because it would boost our mission's numbers, I did it.

When I was told to go to a police station to pick up a Mormon missionary who had been accused of inappropriate sexual contact with a child so that his crimes could be dealt with inside the church, I did it.

When they told me to break into another missionary's bedroom to search through all of his personal belongings to find some evidence, any evidence, that he had slept with the bishop's daughter, I did it.

And of course, when they told me to hate the gay part of myself, which is to say, all of myself, I did it. I did that really well.

When I think back on all the things I did when I was Mormon, "fucking a leader to get into the highest order of the priesthood" is not on the list, but it might as well have been. What wouldn't I have done? At what command would I have said, "This is too much"? "*Enough*." "*Stop*."

I don't think I would have. I don't think I could have. I certainly never did.

This is where the MormonBoyz stop being hot for me. Mormon porn doesn't celebrate us, but rather, it celebrates our lack of selves. The conceit of the scenes is consistent: One day they were good MormonBoyz, innocently serving the Lord as though unaware that sex even exists, and then, suddenly, they are getting railed by their Bishop with bottoming skills that, frankly, make me jealous. But in the lived experience of it, our supposed innocence is actually ignorance. Our naivete, fear. Our willingness to do as we're told, desperation to be told we are good and worthy because we do not believe we are. I look back now and think how selfless I was. How wholly and completely theirs. How conquered. Like putty in their hands, begging to be given form.

At its core, this points to the harshest truth of all: In order to be Mormon, you must, in essence, allow yourself to be exploited in order to belong.

One of my favorite questions to ask fellow ex-Mormons is what they did with their garments once they stopped wearing them

Eventually, you take them off. You just do. And that's when the real work begins.

One of my favorite questions to ask fellow ex-Mormons is what they did with their garments once they stopped wearing them. Most simply throw them away and leave the past behind them. But I'm gay and love dramatics. So I drove to southern Utah on the cusp of Zion National Park and found a campground and built a fire. One by one, I took my entire collection of garments and burned them in a cathartic ritual of goodbye. It didn't involve men in rooms with white curtains, anointing my body to protect me from a supposed destroyer. Just me, my rage, and a smoldering fire, hungry and hot.

Though that took only a paragraph to write, the lived experience took years. Years to take them off and then more years to feel comfortable to leave them in the past. And since then, more years of therapy to slowly deconstruct the programming I was saturated in. To learn how to say no. To salvage a self from the object I was reduced to. I worked so hard to take that garment off. Which makes it annoying when most people's fantasies around my upbringing almost seem to want me to put it back on.

"So, did you ever hook up with another missionary? Did you fuck your companion?"

It's a question most gay ex-Mormons have heard before, especially within the context of a first date. When they only know us as MormonBoyz, it's a fair question. But it makes me keenly aware of the baggage I carry into the room when I choose to tell someone I grew up Mormon; that amalgamation of innocence, gullibility, and eagerness they've been led to believe I possess. Would they want me if they knew the truth? Or would it kill the mood if I confessed to them that my Mormon mission was one of the most sexless times of my entire life. Perhaps they'd like it if I went into detail, to explain how I only masturbated three times during my entire two-year mission. Perhaps they'd get off knowing that within twenty-four hours of each of those three orgasms, I had to meet in person to "confess my sins" because I felt so unworthy I couldn't even knock a door. Does my shame get you going? Is my trauma still sexy to you? Do you want to know what it feels like to feel unworthy of your own underwear? Is that thing I've built a life around *not* being the very thing that makes me most desirable?

You tell me. I'm just a MormonBoy. I do as I'm told.

I've committed the very sin I didn't want to commit when I began writing this piece: I've taken porn too seriously. I've analyzed it too much, squeezed the fun out of the carefree world of fantasy. Porn, lest we forget, isn't real life, remember? And I have no interest in labeling Mormon-themed porn as *good* or *bad.* Because ultimately, MormonBoyz capitalizes off the work of the Mormon Church, which is to say it sexualizes the objects (formerly people) branded and produced by Mormonism. And in this sense, I don't blame MormonBoyz for the content they've created. They simply took advantage of something created by another entity. And in the hierarchy of exploitation, theirs feels like much less of a crime. At least, in the make-believe world of MormonBoyz, there's consent. There's pleasure. And someone's fucking instead of everyone getting fucked over.

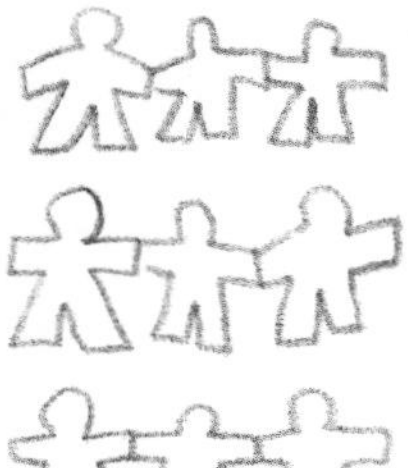

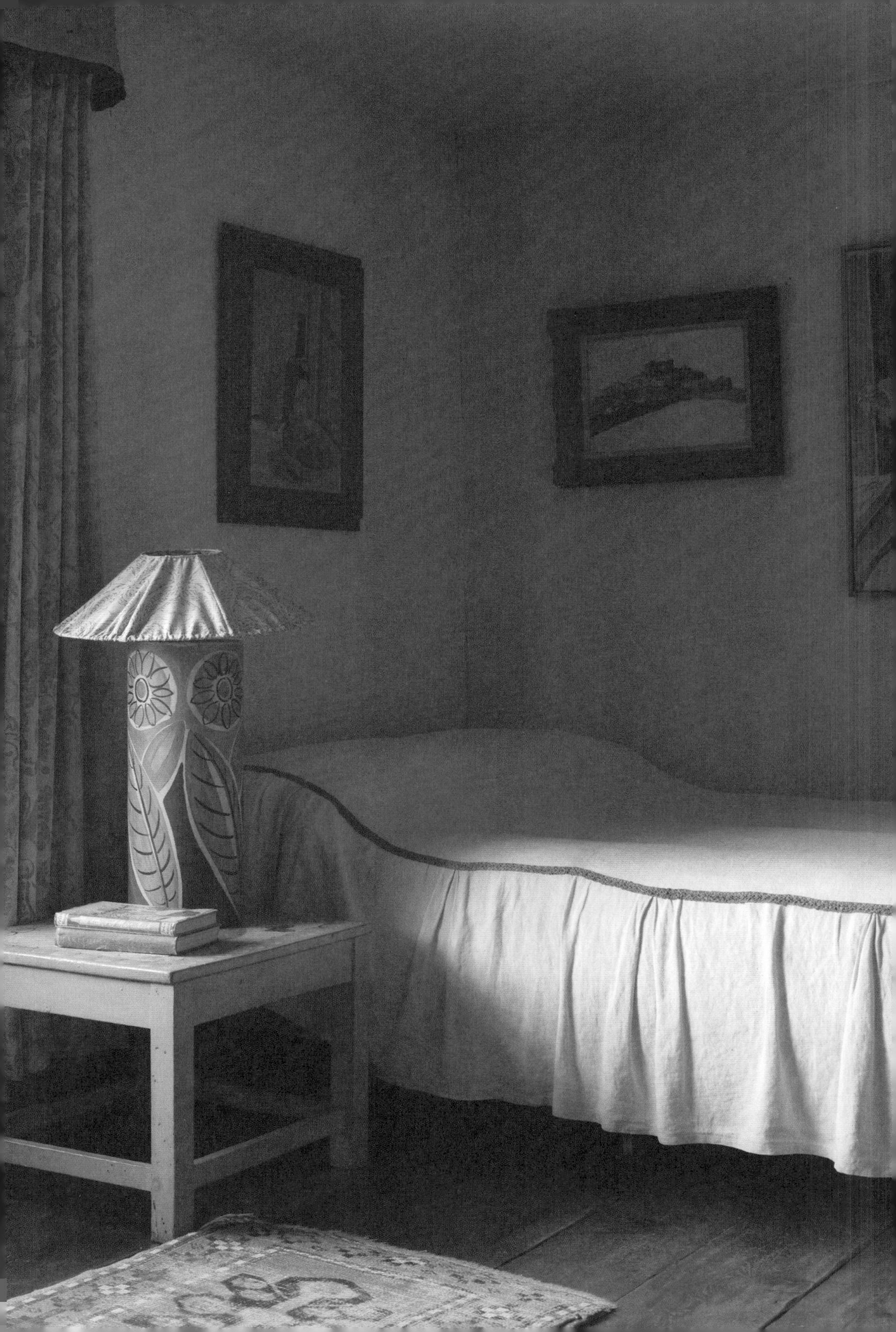

QUEERING SPACE

Davy Pittoors

As a child, I could often be found cutting, gluing, and decorating giant cardboard boxes, turning them into elaborate Wendy houses, complete with furniture, lighting, and soft furnishings. Walls were painted bright colors or plastered with drawings, and I'd pester my older brothers to help me engineer doors and windows. My parents owned an electronics business, so with our endless supply of TV and hi-fi packaging my "designs" became ever more elaborate. I have fond memories of playing inside these cardboard dwellings, fully immersed in my own creation, protected from the outside world.

Even as an adult, objects, space, and homemaking have been my way of expressing my identity and finding shelter from the norm. I eventually settled down with my partner in our own home in East London, where I'm always finding ways to display an ever-growing collection of art, objects, and flea market finds. In 2020 I started my own business selling and curating queer art and objects, staging immersive exhibitions in domestic spaces, opening a pop-up gallery on the English coast, and most recently, helping brands, museums, and other creatives who aim to blur the lines between queer art and the domestic.

As I've come to realize through reading and research, my attraction to homemaking and collecting is neither unique nor novel. Throughout history, LGBTQ+ people have always found ways to fulfill a need for nurture, safety, and pleasure in what are often hostile or dangerous environments. To truly flourish, however, queerness requires a sort of supportive ecosystem, which is why protecting queer spaces, both public and domestic, is so important. One of my first encounters with such an ecosystem was at Charleston, the former residence and studio of artists Vanessa Bell and Duncan Grant, who occupied the home in 1916. Their many-roomed, centuries-old house provided a safe haven for Grant and many other members of the Bloomsbury group, most of whom were queer. At Charleston social convention and law were left at the door. Here, they forged alternative ways of living.

I'm fascinated by Grant and Bell's radical approach to art, domesticity, and community. I was eager to dive a bit deeper into their lives, looking at them alongside contemporary LGBTQ+ experiences. I sat down with Darren Clarke, head of collections and research at the Charleston Trust, and three inspiring creatives with similar values to discover what impact their identity has had on their living spaces, and how the sometimes traumatic ideals of traditional domesticity can be overcome through the use of art, objects, and space.

DAVY PITTOORS: What does *queering space* mean at Charleston?

DARREN CLARKE: It's very much about trying to make both the historic house and the contemporary spaces feel welcoming for all our visitors. One of our leading ideals, especially recently, is that this space was specifically the home for Duncan Grant and a queer household. Also, the space itself is interesting in that there's no traditional structure; there is no primary bedroom so there isn't a dominant domestic space designed for a man and a woman. There's also a round dining room table, so there isn't a head of the table or a hierarchy. Whether that was intentional or an aesthetic choice, these equality ideals are there in the ethos, in the air, in the fiber of the building. There isn't a patriarchal, heteronormative lead.

Darren Clarke is the head of collections and research for the Charleston Trust. He trained as an artist but now prefers looking and talking about other people's work, particularly that of the Bloomsbury artists Vanessa Bell and Duncan Grant, though he does like living artists, too. Instagram: @charlestontrust

DP: That sounds quite radical for the time, and I understand that a lot of the interior choices, and even their Omega Workshop project, directly challenged Victorian standards. Are there any aesthetic choices that stand out for you at Charleston?

DC: Yes, with its Post-Impressionist interior, Charleston is a great example of challenging Victorian standards. In Charleston we see the influence of Omega and the whole Roger Fry project of championing and even naming Post-Impressionism and bringing over those artists to the UK, sort of en masse for the first time. Post-Impressionism is a lifestyle; it's not just something contained by a picture frame, but an attitude that can enter into every aspect of your life in a very domestic way, in the colors you paint your walls, the textiles you use, the ceramics you eat off, and the furniture you sit on. It's kind of the first lifestyle, branded experience. Gays love that!

DP: Haha, yeah I know what you mean, why do we love it so much?!

DC: [Laughs] Yeah, it's about creating a whole environment, an environment that you can control. With Duncan Grant and Vanessa Bell, if you lent them your house for the summer holiday, you'd return and they'd have decorated, moved stuff around. They wanted to make spaces their own, even if they were only staying for a short time. With Charleston, there was no expectation that they were going to be there for fifty or sixty years when they moved in, in 1916. It was very much a necessary move because Duncan Grant and his lover, David Garnett, were conscientious objectors. So they made a political stand against that macho, patriarchal, warmongering attitude of the government and society. So while the move was political, they decorated as soon as they arrived. They had the whole house whitewashed, creating an almost blank canvas. They wanted control over a space within a wider world where they didn't have control.

DP: Would you say creating such an environment encouraged them to live more openly?

DC: They lived as openly as they could. There was this sort of polyamorous relationship between Duncan Grant and his two lovers, Garnett and Bell. But even within their own home, they had to be careful about what they did and how they acted in front of the servants and the wider world. There were several different social and financial constraints, restrictions on their personal freedoms. So they'd find ways to express that freedom in decoration and curation.

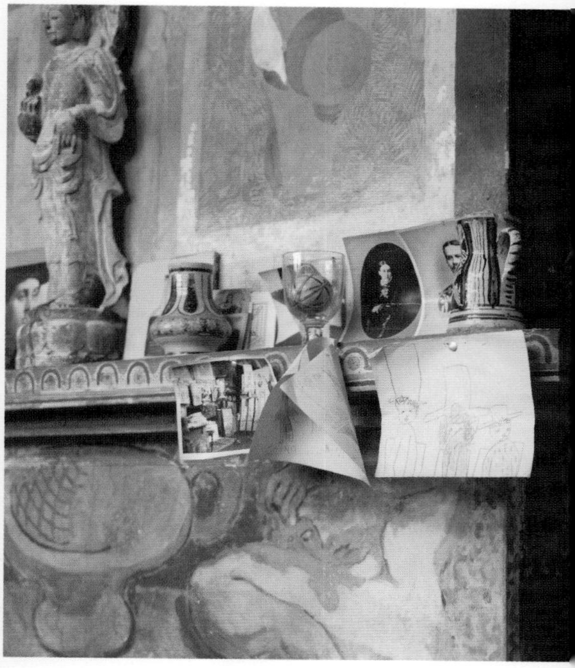

DP: How would you describe a typical day at Charleston?

DC: Gosh, it was very much a space for work, so if you were coming to visit, you'd be expected to bring something to do. Everybody would meet in the dining room and Grace Higgins, the housekeeper, would make breakfast. Then you'd go off and work. Artists would go to the studios, writers to their rooms, and they'd all come back together again at lunchtime. In the afternoon there might be a country walk, but life was very much centered around mealtimes and communal eating. In the afternoon there would be tea and then an evening meal. I mean, it sounds like a really nice life!

They wanted control over a space within a wider world where they didn't have control.

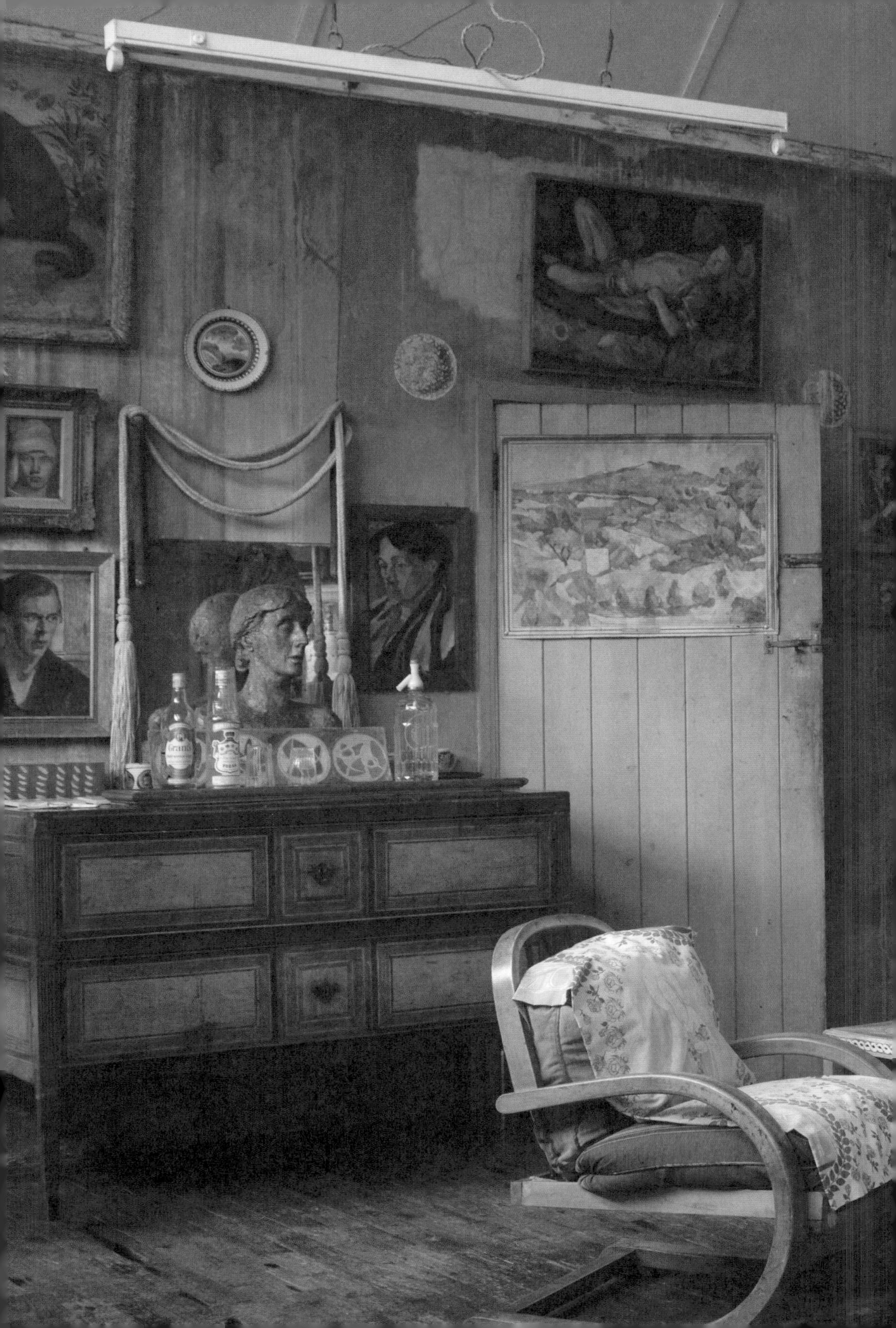

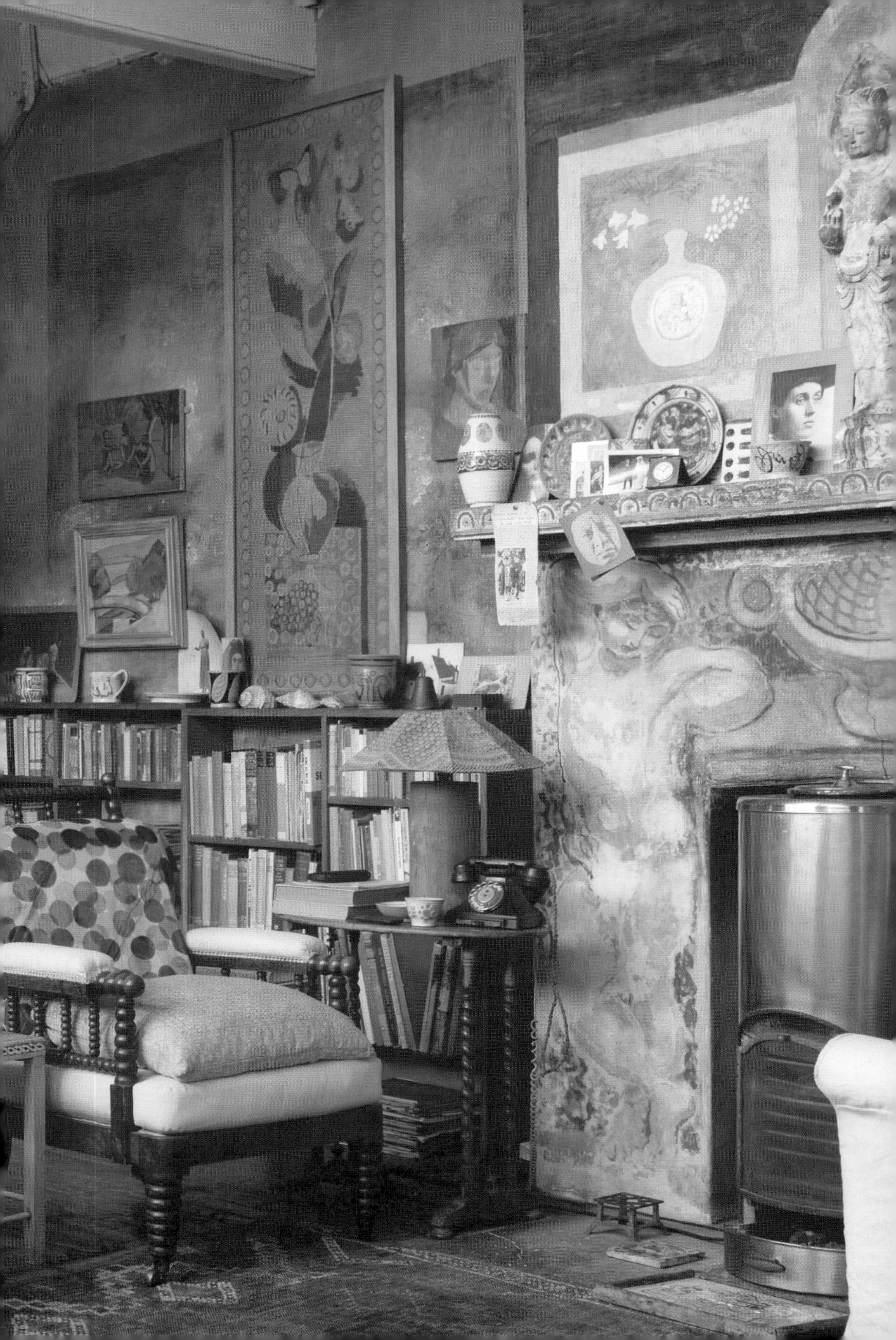

Martha Summers is an architect, artist, and leatherworker living and working in London. Key themes in her artistic and architectural practice include queer domesticity, self-fashioning, and butch identity. Instagram: @marfsummers

DAVY PITTOORS: What does *queering space* mean to you?

MARTHA SUMMERS: I think it has multiple meanings: As a queer designer and architect, it's about making queer spaces or reading existing spaces in a queer way, finding queer readings of spaces that maybe seem quite normative. But then there's also spaces which are canonically queer in a way due to their history or use. For me it's mainly about non-normativity; there's no specific aesthetic, I think. It's not necessarily possible to look at a space and say: This is a queer space because of what it looks like. It's more about a process and partly about purposeful choices that are queer in dimension, for example, thinking about the design of the space having a camp aesthetic, or a sense of humor, or ornament, frivolity, and artifice. But it's also about spaces not being fixed. I think a space is an extension of the self or an extension of a community, and there's a blurry line between the two.

DP: What advice would you give people when they are occupying a space?

MS: I often apply a methodology I have for architectural design projects. When working with an existing space, you begin by doing a queer appraisal. The first step is finding the little irregularities and strange moments, the nooks and crannies. When you're renting, you often end up with a weird set of things that you wouldn't necessarily have chosen, but there's opportunity within that. It's about trying to find the moments in a space that you can identify with and finding ways to draw more attention to them.

As a gender nonconforming person, I'm used to existing in a world that isn't designed for me; for example, the clothes I wear were not made for my body. Having all the various tools at my disposal, be that leatherwork, a sewing machine, woodworking tools, I can fashion a shirt or make a set of curtains. Fashioning a home is like an extension of that exact same practice.

There's also this idea of not fighting against reality, and the power of acceptance. There are so many ways to transform meaning through juxtaposition. If you divorce your brain from binary ideas of gender, you start to look at spaces as they are and build from there, rather than

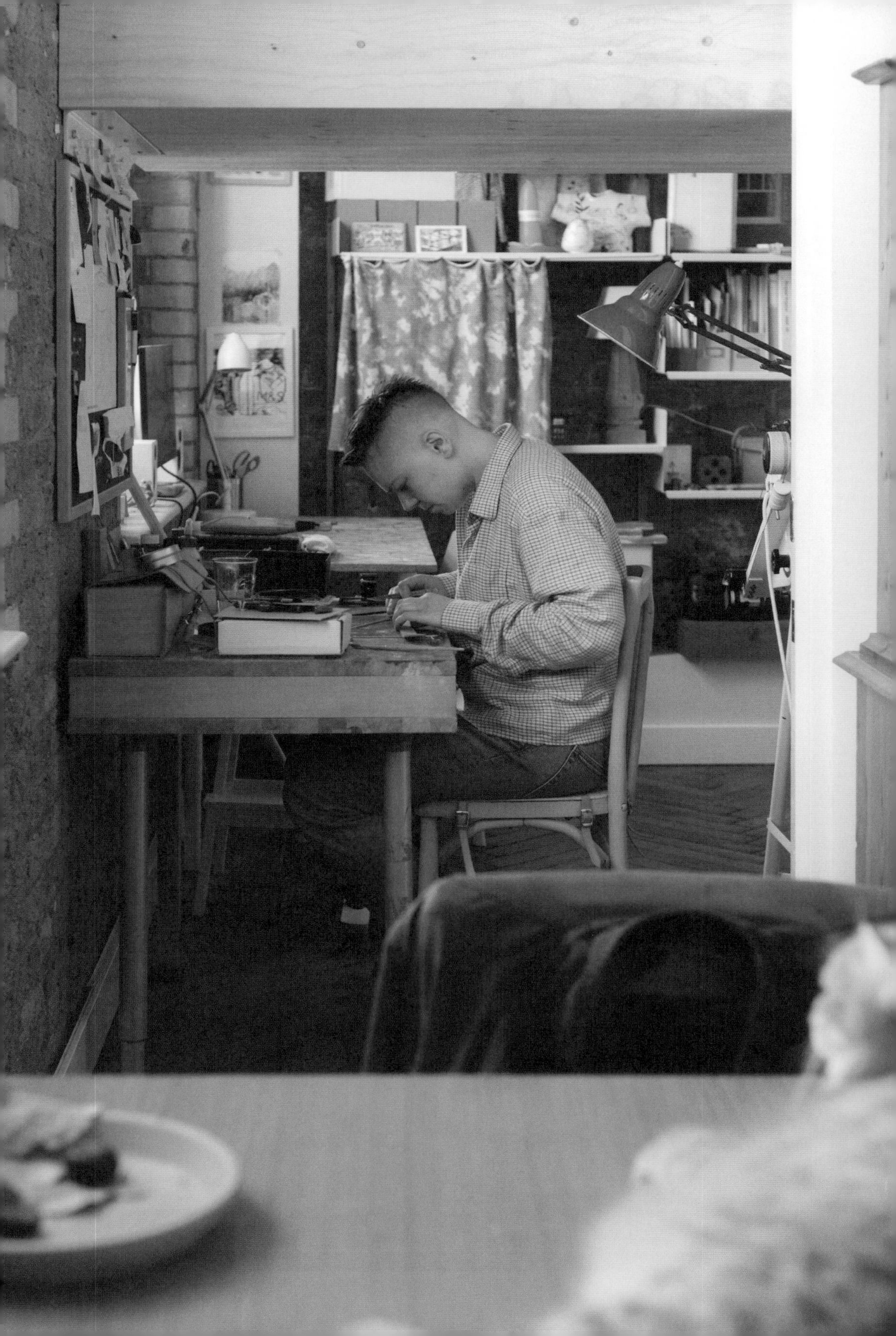

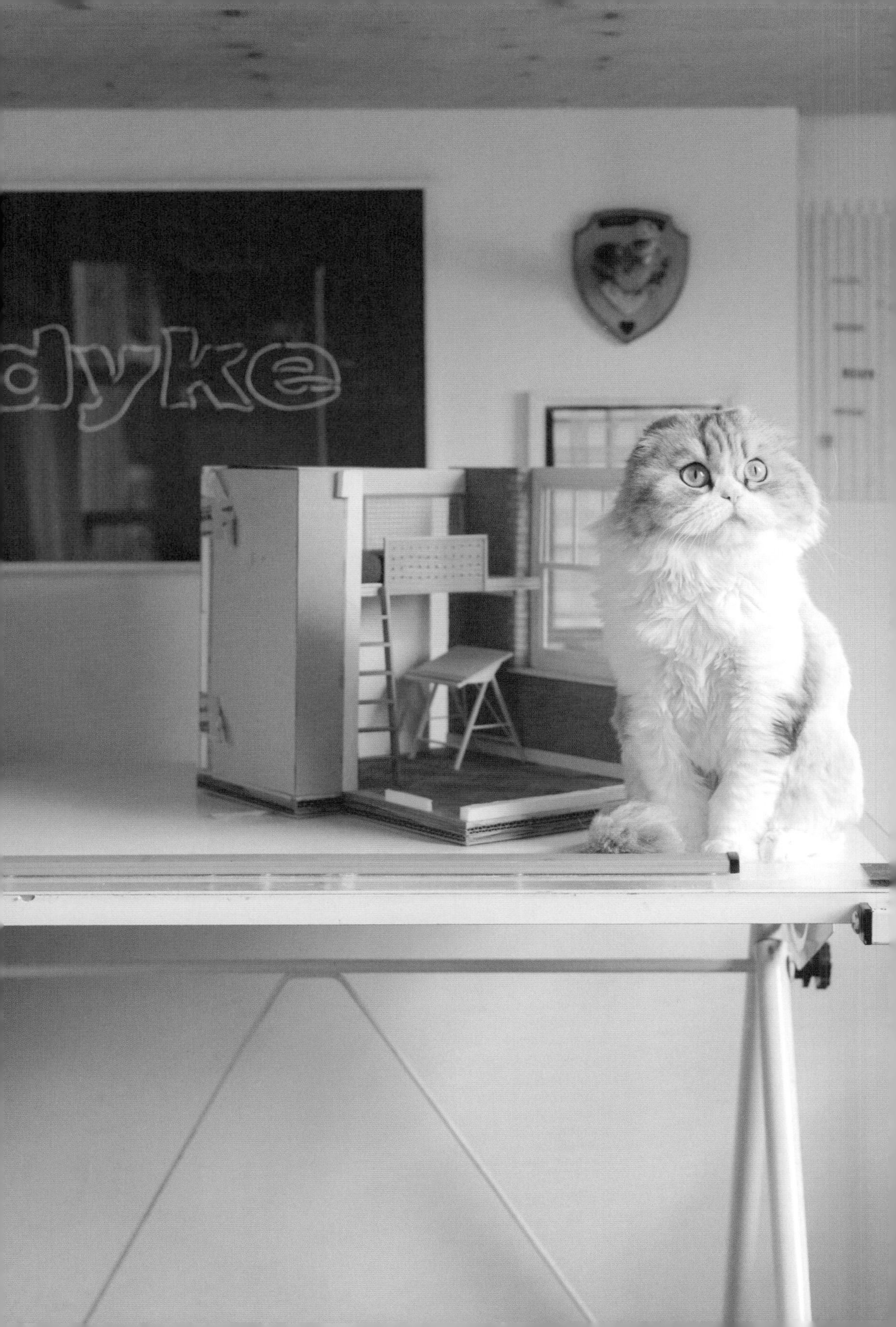
dyke

having these preconceived notions of how a space should be, act, or arranged. Rather than parachuting in this idea of what a queer space would be, it's about asking what that means for you. Because queer life varies greatly, and I think that's the point: In the range of queer homes and what they can look like, there's no visual spatial consistency.

Fashioning your space and your home becomes an extension of the self, you can't really separate the two. I can certainly say, having now moved and creating a new space from scratch, I don't think I've ever been more aware of the importance of that, but also how incredibly affirming and comforting it can be to actually take that time to create a home that is non-normative.

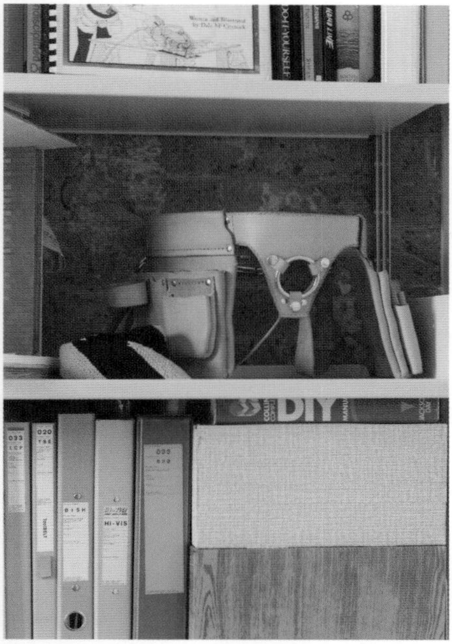

If you divorce your brain from binary ideas of gender, you start to look at spaces as they are and build from there, rather than having these preconceived notions of how a space should be, act, or arranged.

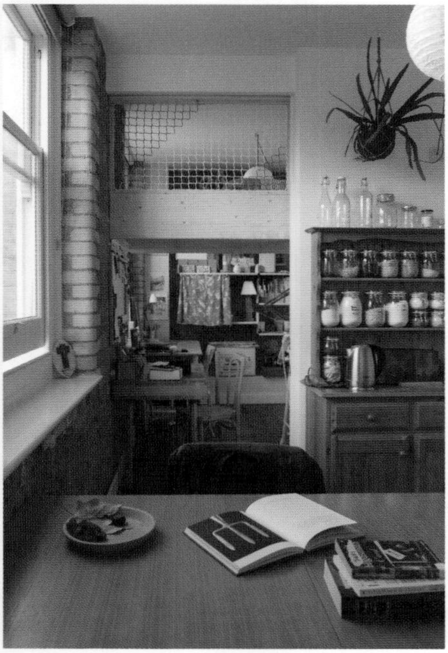

Peter Ibruegger is a London-based German/Hong Kong Chinese artist and yogi. In his art and design work he explores themes of hybrid identity in multiple layers, being a biracial man, yoga teacher, and queer artist. Instagram: @peteribruegger

DAVY PITTOORS: What does queering space mean to you?

PETER IBRUEGGER: For me, it's an authentic expression of myself and that just happens to be queer. I identify as a gay man, and part of my experience as a child was very much about creating my own world as an alternative to the norm. At that time in the eighties, my world consisted of female action figures like She-Ra; I collected all of them. There's a notion of creating families and tribes with these figurines, but at the same time I was also interested in how to create sacred spaces, almost like altars. I was always trying to find ways to curate items to have meaning together. Even as a child and teenager I was inspired by the Bloomsbury Group, Freud, psychoanalysis, and symbolism in art. As an adult, I've got a bigger space to play with and can combine my different interests as a designer, yoga practitioner, and artist. Not excluding sexuality from spirituality, not necessarily in a pornographic way but more in a symbolic way, I think, is my take on my queer experience.

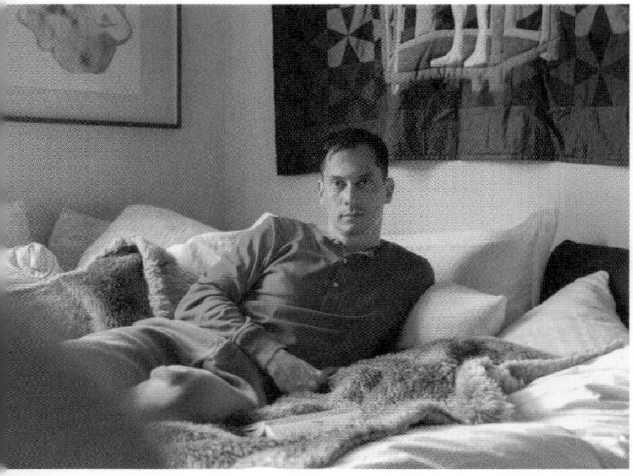

DP: I really see that reflected in your home, the fact that you feel quite confident in having queer objects and art on display, for example.

PI: I've been quite uncompromising about that, and it's interesting having builders around sometimes, you know, and witnessing how they keep their composure. They're mostly respectful, in my experience, even quite complimentary. I find it quite liberating to just be up-front about it.

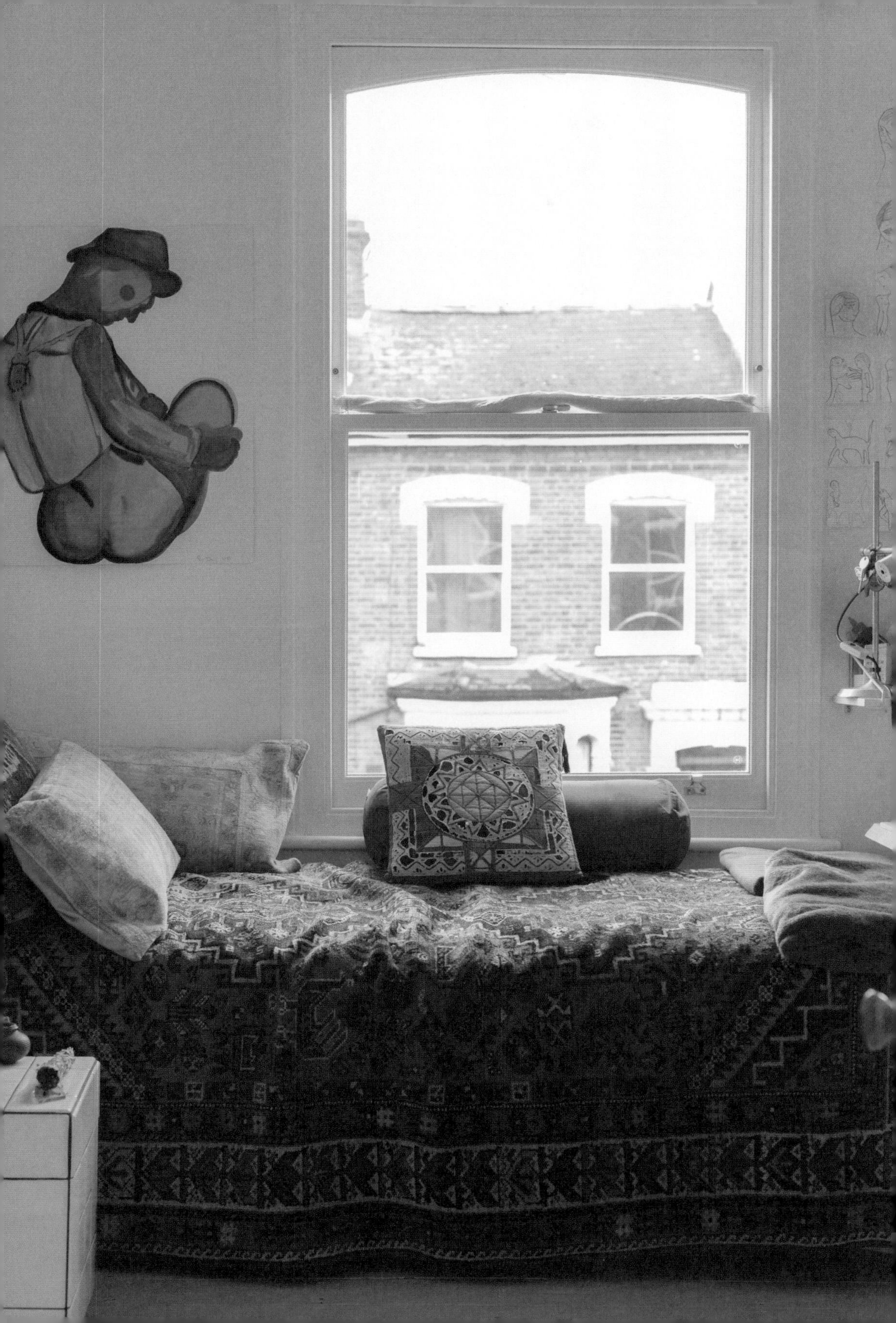

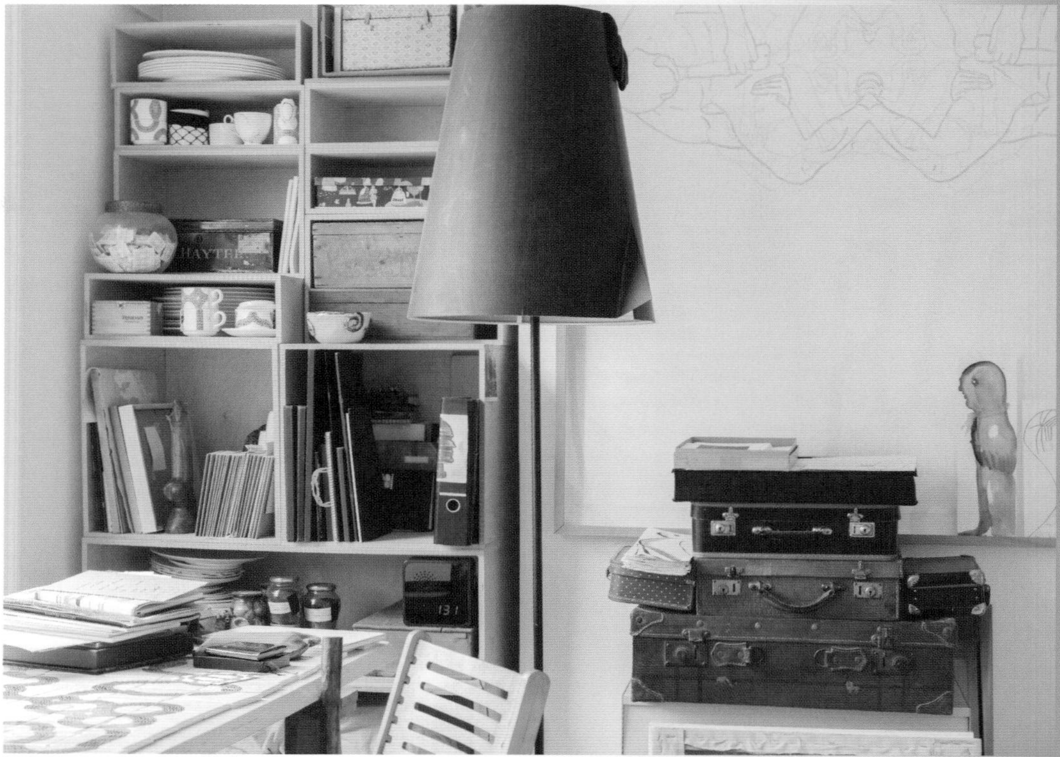

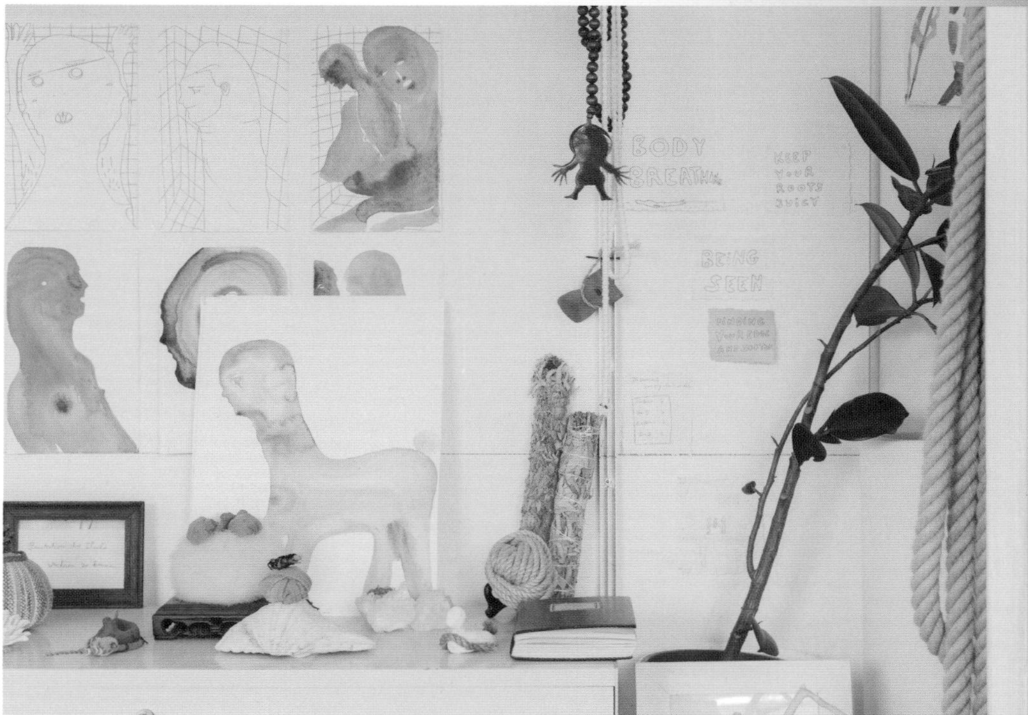
BODY
KEEP YOUR ROOTS JUICY
BEING SEEN

I wanted to fuse everything together and create a space in which I can host, invite people, and hold space for other people.

DP: It's also really great seeing it in contrast with your grandparents' furniture!

PI: Yeah, my paternal grandfather was German and an industrialist in the fifties and had this big Bauhaus-style villa filled with beautiful Danish furniture. So that's where my design knowledge and affinity come from. I live in a Victorian terraced house, so I'm respectful of that while creating harmony, but without compromising my queer life. I try to make it a very comforting, homey place, but at the same time quite sensual, and conceptual.

DP: That's really interesting because Victorian terraces often have very heteronormative layouts built around family life. You really went against that and untangled some of those ideas, putting your own twist on it.

PI: I remember when I was house hunting, some of the worst places I looked at were the ones that were specifically designed for that, and didn't offer possible, easy changes. As an artist I knew exactly what type of space I needed, so in my current home it made more sense to use the primary bedroom as a functional studio space rather than for sleeping. Then downstairs, the layout has the sitting room in the front and dining room next to it, traditionally separated with double doors. I had the doors taken out and created my office space in the dining area and kept the sitting room as it was.

Also, choosing this house was very much about accommodating the furniture that I grew up with, creating that link to one part of my history while queering it up. I wanted to fuse everything together and create a space in which I can host, invite people, and hold space for other people. This is where spirituality comes in, too—I teach yoga one-to-one in my studio, so I can really offer an immersive experience in the space, which is very important to me.

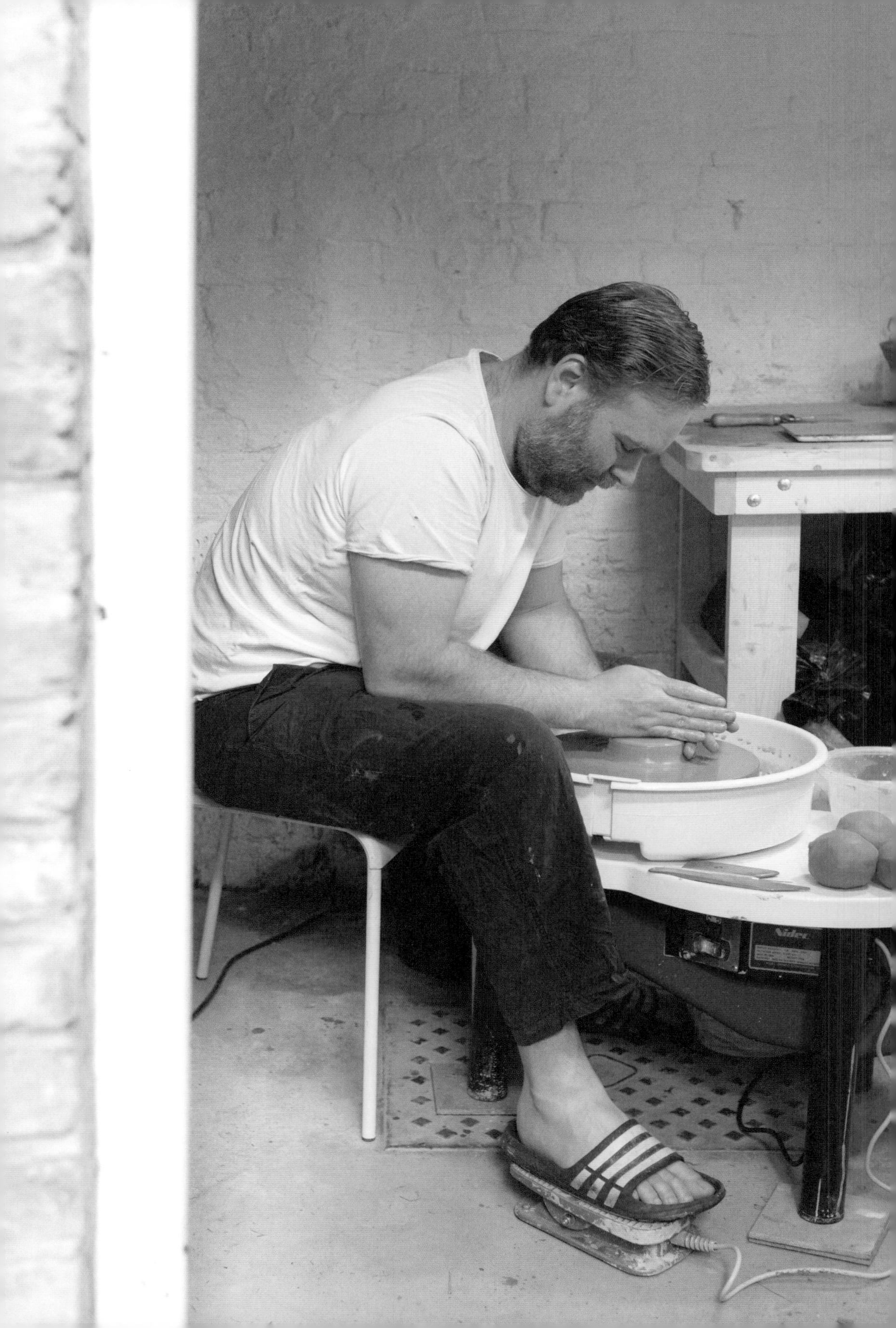

Will Martin is a South African artist and potter based in London. He is known for his narrative supper clubs and immersive ceramic installations. Instagram: @will.martin

DAVY PITTOORS: What does *queering space* mean to you?

WILL MARTIN: I suppose I'd have to break that question up into what I consider to be domestic and how one might queer it. I think that I'm currently in this search of domestic space without necessarily having had a very immersive experience of it previously. At the moment I'm trying to make a home, but I've been trying to do that for many years, and I don't know if I've necessarily achieved that. Don't get me wrong, my parents obviously made their respective homes very well. But what I've taken from growing up is that mealtimes were when I felt most at home. We moved house quite a lot and it was usually rented. There was never a sense of a permanent family home and I don't even know if that's possible for me to have. I've been living in my current place for about four years and I'm getting itchy feet; when I first got to London, I was moving every six months. I've always been much more comfortable in studios or semi-industrial spaces than in actual homes, which have always felt a bit cloying and claustrophobic. But when I do have a domestic space at my disposal, I'm constantly rearranging it because that's kind of what you do in studio spaces—constant tweaking for what you need at that moment.

DP: Yet, all your art feels very domestic?

WM: Yes it is; I do room installations, make domestic ceramics, functional ware, decorative objects, the cooking and supper clubs came in more recently, too. My work has always been very craft oriented and maybe I've traditionally been associated with the domestic and feminine, which was intentional when I was growing up in Cape Town to challenge that hyper-masculinity I saw growing up after apartheid. So I started making pottery and embroidery instead.

DP: What would your dream home look like?

WM: My ambition is to create a more permanent domestic environment somehow, but again, I think it would always revolve around the kitchen. I imagine an open-plan space, maybe a loft or warehouse conversion with one big, long table for everyone to sit around.

DP: But for the time being the supper clubs and meals provide a great alternative!

WM: Yes, definitely. I actually suffer from quite severe anxiety attacks, and one way I take care of myself is by creating these community moments that make me feel safe. Hosting is a way of feeling like I'm in control of my environment; it's a benevolent control that everyone participates in. It's like setting a scene for negotiating ourselves amongst each other, and maybe that's a form of queerness because it's not hierarchical. It's about providing a space for people to just do and say what they want, within reason of course. But because I also welcome people who might identify as heterosexual or normative by default, this is a space where they can act a bit outside their comfort zone. I'm not forcing them to, but they can perform a different version of themselves that they might normally not.

DP: I want to home in a bit more on your magic formula, what is the thinking process behind building an evening or an afternoon with food?

WM: Well, one thing that's come up in recent meals is trying to strike the right balance between being served, serving yourself, and serving other people. There are three options there in terms of exchange. I usually do a served starter and the main in sharing bowls and again a served dessert. So, in serving people the starter, it allows them to feel looked after, but in asking people to serve themselves the mains, they regain some agency and can give themselves what they want and what they like. The most crucial part about that is that they can recommend things to their neighboring guests, too. For me, that's the feeling that really brings the whole thing together. You've all eaten the same thing, now you're all friends and you can actually just relax. I also like to swap places and move around the table. If I see someone get up, I generally jump in their seat; if I just do that two or three times, the table shifts organically without us having to play actual musical chairs.

DP: Finally, what advice would you give other people when throwing a dinner?

WM: So for instance, issues around control make me anxious. You don't have to be in control of the dinner, you're *facilitating* the dinner, and once you take the role as a facilitator, it removes the pressure. There's this social contract: you're giving the diners space to exert themselves socially and that takes pressure off from you controlling their behavior. Guests feel more comfortable because they're not afraid of doing something wrong. They're co-creating the event with you, whether they're aware of it or not. I think it's about using what you have, and I'd use a similar approach with conversation and with food, you know, encourage guests to participate, bring food or ingredients even. It's in the participation that you queer a dinner, because you're creating a dynamic narrative.

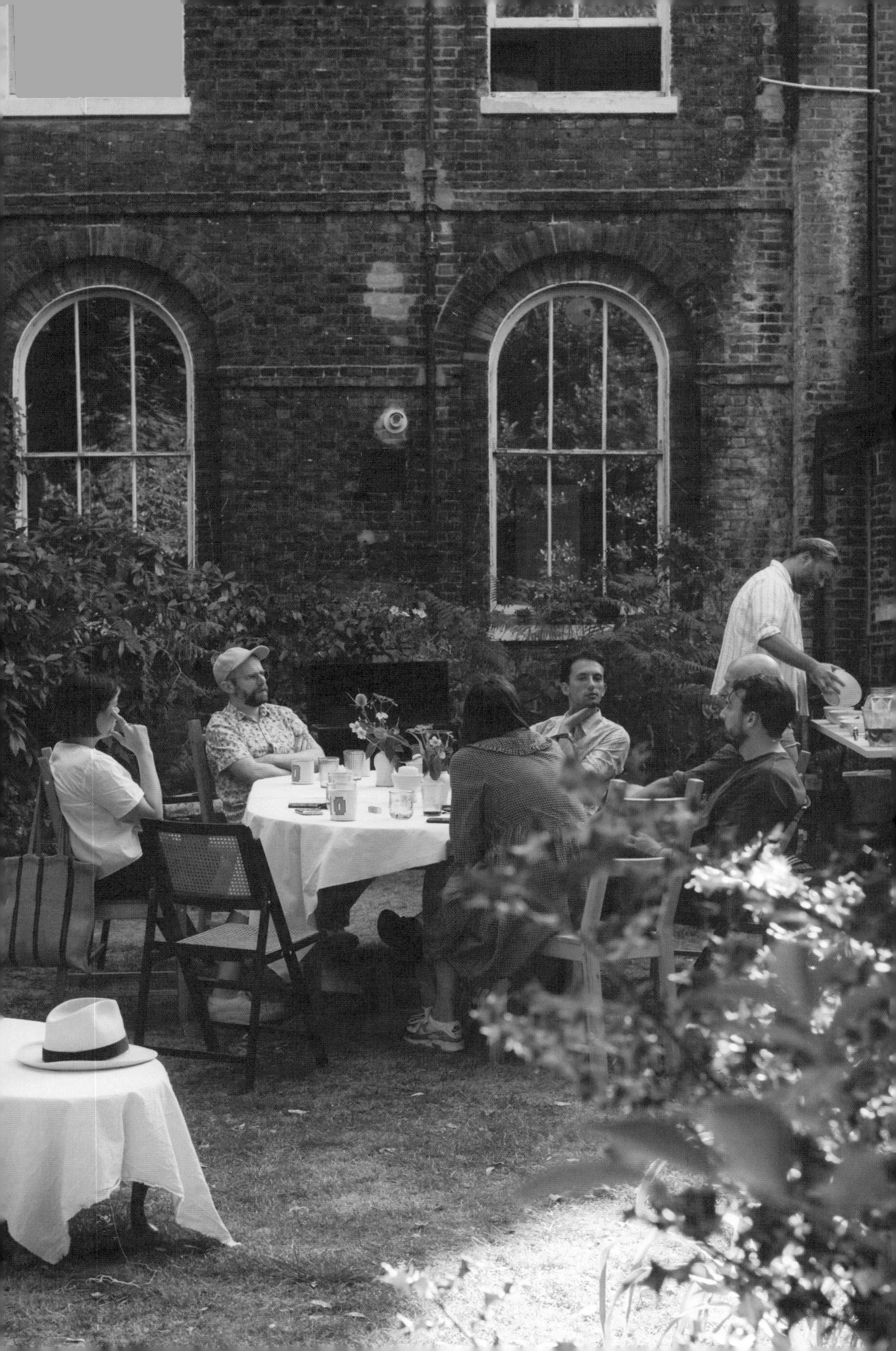

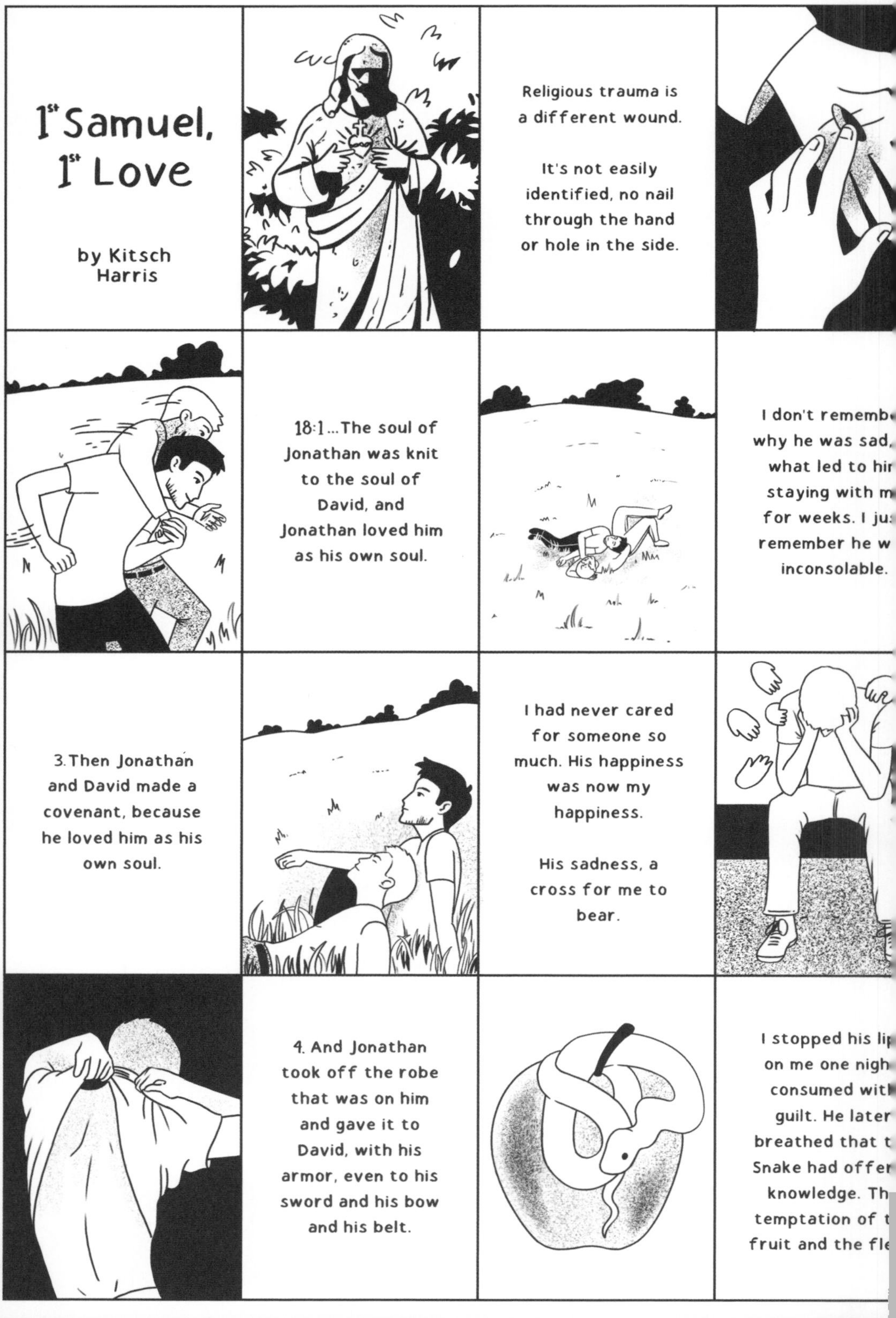

1st Samuel, 1st Love
by Kitsch Harris
Religious trauma is a different wound.
It's not easily identified, no nail through the hand or hole in the side.
18:1 ...The soul of Jonathan was knit to the soul of David, and Jonathan loved him as his own soul.
I don't rememb why he was sad, what led to hir staying with m for weeks. I ju remember he w inconsolable.
3. Then Jonathan and David made a covenant, because he loved him as his own soul.
I had never cared for someone so much. His happiness was now my happiness.
His sadness, a cross for me to bear.
4. And Jonathan took off the robe that was on him and gave it to David, with his armor, even to his sword and his bow and his belt.
I stopped his li on me one nigh consumed wit guilt. He later breathed that t Snake had offer knowledge. Th temptation of t fruit and the fle

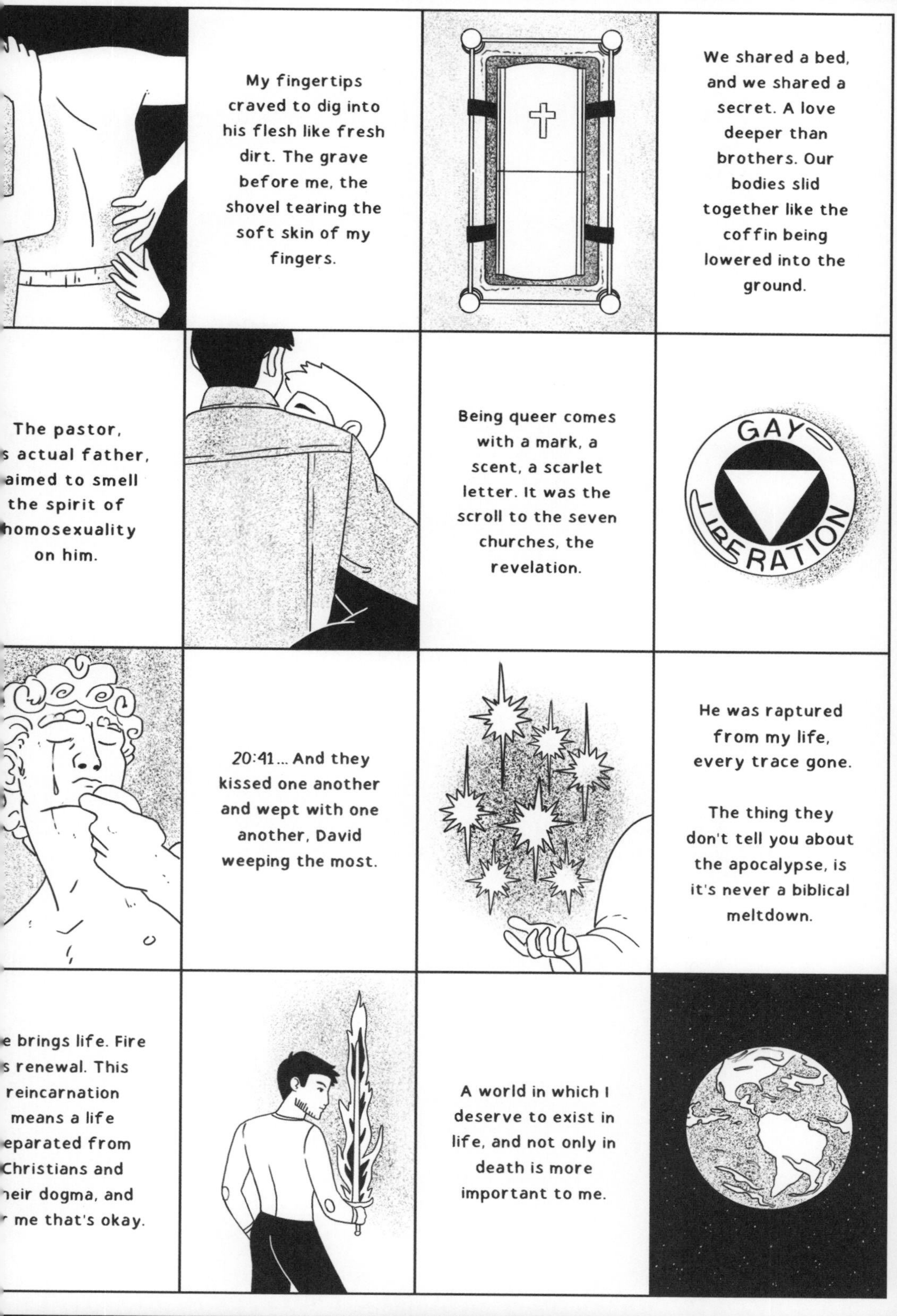

My fingertips craved to dig into his flesh like fresh dirt. The grave before me, the shovel tearing the soft skin of my fingers.
We shared a bed, and we shared a secret. A love deeper than brothers. Our bodies slid together like the coffin being lowered into the ground.
The pastor, s actual father, aimed to smell the spirit of homosexuality on him.
Being queer comes with a mark, a scent, a scarlet letter. It was the scroll to the seven churches, the revelation.
GAY LIBERATION
20:41... And they kissed one another and wept with one another, David weeping the most.
He was raptured from my life, every trace gone.
The thing they don't tell you about the apocalypse, is it's never a biblical meltdown.
e brings life. Fire s renewal. This reincarnation means a life eparated from Christians and heir dogma, and me that's okay.
A world in which I deserve to exist in life, and not only in death is more important to me.

How to Unerase Yourself with Garrard Conley

Scott Bixby

Thirty-one years after the American Psychiatric Association removed homosexuality from its list of mental illnesses, Garrard Conley and his mom walked into Love in Action, an ex-gay Christian ministry located in a Tennessee strip mall.

"I can no longer remember if there were any signs in that foyer of what was to come, any paintings on the wall, any rules posted," Garrard would later write of that first step toward, he thought, "recovery" from same-sex attraction. "The foyer exists for me now as a blindingly white waiting room, the kind you see in Hollywood depictions of heaven: a blank space."

Many authors working in the memoir space find that, at the end of the grinding process by which a memoir comes to be published, their memories—hard-wrought, painfully recalled, and carefully rearranged for reader and page—have been flattened into buzzwords: "coming-of-age"; "tell-all"; "survivor narrative"; "priv-lit." *Boy Erased: A Memoir of Identity, Faith, and Family*, Garrard's story of his time at Love in Action, has itself been sorted into a relatively new sub-category: the conversion-therapy memoir.

But *Boy Erased*, first published in 2016 by Riverhead and now a mainstay of queer shelves, chafes under that restrictive label. Interwoven with Garrard's experience at Love in Action are recollections of his father's growing religious fundamentalism, the dashing of his high-school girlfriend's hopes that they might marry, his mother's increasingly untenable attempts to bridge the divide between her Missionary Baptist preacher husband and her only son, and Garrard's outing at the hands of his rapist—the inciting incident behind his family's attempt to cure his feelings toward other men. The result is a rich (and richly told) tapestry of youth in the Ozarks; of the collision between faith, politics, and identity; and most of all, of coming to terms with horrible things committed in the name of love.

It was a story, Garrard told *Hello Mr.* during a meandering springtime walk through Brooklyn, that he wasn't always sure he was qualified to tell.

"It was like, 'Who am I to tell this story?'" Garrard said. "Other people have bigger stories, more epic stories, more intense stories . . . and yeah, my family gave me this really shitty ultimatum in which love was no longer unconditional, but there were so many people that were in it for longer, and there were people who killed themselves from it."

Garrard—pronounced, with some difficulty, *Gare-urd*—spent two weeks at Love in Action's "The Source" outpatient program, following months of one-on-one counseling in the hope of alleviating his same-sex attraction. Others spent months, even years under the group's tutelage in search of a cure.[1]

"Can I be a good cypher for that experience? I struggled with it," Garrard said. But he found that, in addition to the decade of distance he had put between himself and his time at Love in Action, Garrard's relatively clean escape from the ex-gay ministry helped him approach it with a more critical eye. "The fact that I wasn't as traumatized meant that I could write a little more objectively about the experience, and that I could speak to the families who are very gullible, and even the counselors who were affected, in their own way, by bigotry in their childhoods."

Conversion therapy stories have long been thick on the ground in queer pop culture—the first gay movie I muled out of my local Blockbuster as a teen was *But I'm a Cheerleader*, concealed inside a *Zathura* DVD case—but many of those narratives, Garrard pointed out, prioritize lampooning conversion therapy's manifest absurdity over combating the practice itself. "People are still shocked when they hear about it," he said. "They think, 'That's just a crazy place that you're from where they do that.' And I'm like, 'No, these places are all over.'"

The ubiquity of campy jokes about lispy, light-loafered counselors "praying the gay away," Garrard said, make it harder for the straight and powerful to see conversion therapy for what it really is.

"No one else was writing about it in a way that was sophisticated, in my mind—there were a lot of really good articles, and there were a lot of really good investigations, but everything in pop culture was flippant," Garrard said. "I wanted to write something that was very counter to that easy joke thing. I love a good catty gay tone, but I didn't want to do that; it's too easy."

The ubiquity of campy jokes about lispy, light-loafered counselors 'praying the gay away' makes it harder for the straight and powerful to see conversion therapy for what it really is.

The book's potential to clarify the conversation around conversion therapy was one of Garrard's motivations to write about his experience as a memoir, despite the tempting option of fictionalizing his account (and thereby avoiding a few uncomfortable conversations with people who appear in *Boy Erased*, including his high-school girlfriend).

"The political value of this book is that it's nonfiction," Garrard said. "You can read *The Miseducation of Cameron Post*, which is a beautiful novelistic description of conversion therapy, and that feels important for development of identity, but this felt like a book that was needed to help stop conversion therapy" as a real-world practice.

Many of the tactics employed by self-styled conversion therapists, many of whom are largely unlicensed and untrained, would traumatize even the most resilient patients. In one 2016 civil trial, in which former patients of ex-gay conversion therapy provider JONAH contended that the group violated consumer fraud protections, the clients testified that the group's methods included stripping nude with clients at weekend retreats, duct-taping men together, and telling clients that the gay "deathstyle" would lead to high rates of "bowel disease."

For Garrard, the insistence that his sexual attraction to men was "satanic" came only weeks after another trauma: his rape by a fellow classmate during his freshman year of college.

Afterward, Garrard wrote in *Boy Erased*: "Everything else that led to my enrollment in Love in Action felt like a deserved punishment. . . . I believed that God was punishing me physically for my mental transgressions."

A few weeks after he was raped, the classmate, "out of his own desperate guilt," phoned Garrard's mother and outed him.

"He's disgusting," Garrard's rapist said to her. "He's a monster."

"Added to all of this shame was the knowledge that I had secretly pined for the opportunity to be this close to another man," Garrard wrote. "It was extremely difficult after my experience to consider gay sex as anything other than rape."

Garrard's mother picked him up from college, and his father—then an aspiring Missionary Baptist pastor—told him that if he were to ever act on his feelings again, he would never be welcome in his own home.

The threat of being disowned, compounded with the trauma of his rape, shook Garrard enough to obey his father, who was pointed in the direction of Love in Action by the Bellevue Baptist Church of Memphis, Tennessee.

"He saw this hope from what they said at Bellevue," Garrard said. "I always call them out on this: They said, 'Here's the place that can cure him.' And Dad wouldn't have done it otherwise."

Following a months-long intake process intended to weed out people who might be too skeptical of Love in Action's program—as well as journalists or activists seeking to shed light on the group's mission—Garrard entered a two-week, $1,500 "assessment program" intended to gauge how long he might need to be in therapy to be cured of his homosexuality.

"Anything," Garrard thought, upon his father's ultimatum. "I'll do anything to erase this part of me."

Every day, Garrard, along with other patients who would "be homeless, penniless, excommunicated, [or] exiled" if they turned their backs on Love in Action, made a moral inventory of misdeeds, physical and spiritual. Garrard was barred from listening to almost all music—even Beethoven was deemed un-Christian—and ordered to avoid practically all public spaces.

"There was a map on one of the facility's walls that listed the few areas in the city without any malls, restaurants, movie theaters, secular bookstores, or porn shops," Garrard wrote. "Every part of the city was forbidden except for places with the word 'Christ' in it, really."

But Garrard, as bright and engaging in person as he is introspective and circumspect on the page, grew increasingly suspicious of Love in Action and its mission.

"LIA was telling me on a daily basis that a loss of self meant a gain in virtue, and a gain in virtue meant I was drawing closer to God and therefore closer to my true heavenly self," Garrard wrote. "I came to therapy thinking that my sexuality didn't matter, but it turned out that every part of my personality was intimately connected. Cutting one piece damaged the rest."

Love in Action's operating thesis is that homosexuality is a result of intergenerational sin—Deuteronomy 5:9: "For I am the Lord thy God, a jealous God, visiting the iniquity of the fathers upon their children unto the third and fourth generation"—a tactic that often further alienates patients from their already estranged parents. Neo-Freudian understandings of psychology are the bedrock of ex-gay therapy, particularly the psychodynamic "triadic relationship" of a distant father, an overbearing mother, and a sensitive child as the recipe for homosexuality.

For Garrard, whose loving, deeply intellectual relationship with his mother is one of *Boy Erased*'s most well-realized motifs—at one point, they were reading works by literary critic Barbara Johnson and gay wit Oscar Wilde at the same time—an attempt to force a wedge between himself and his parents was the moment he decided to walk out on Love in Action for good.

"They listed off activities—watching rom-coms, shopping, just very gay stuff that you might do, but it wasn't coded that way—as something we had to 'watch out for'; I thought, well, that's mine and my mom's entire relationship."

For Garrard's mother, whose warmth and fear and love radiate equally from the pages of *Boy Erased*, Love in Action forced her to confront the damage her faith had caused her son.

"Coming out, no matter what the story is, forces other people to come out that they care about you," Garrard said. "And in my mom's case, she actually had to. She made a decision that was totally against what my dad wanted, and she had to justify it, and justify it by saying who she was."

"She had to say, 'I don't want to be a mom who almost kills her son.'"

In the years since, she also chipped away at Garrard's father, now a full Missionary Baptist pastor.

"I'll never know what she had to go through, because she doesn't like to talk about it, but when she went home, it was not easy," Garrard said. "She had to make that decision, and that's the moment when she realized that this patriarchal dynamic was not going to be their thing anymore."

Garrard describes his relationship with his father as "complex," but has found common ground in the pastor's unexpected fondness for poetry.

"After we went through the basics, I was like, let's try Walt Whitman. And he loved it!" Garrard laughs. "He was like, 'Man that guy's weird, but he's great!' So that became our language for a little while."

Writing *Boy Erased*, Garrard said, helped him come to terms with a common truth of parent-child relationships; namely, that actions done in love or ignorance can leave deeper scars than neglect or abuse—and that finding peace with those actions comes not from resolution, but acceptance.

"I knew that my parents had done this really fucked-up thing out of a place of love, which is hard to wrap your mind around," Garrard said. "But after interviewing them and seeing what they really thought, they obviously didn't want to destroy their son."

With the success of *Boy Erased* and increased national attention on the issue of conversion therapy, Garrard has become adept at discussing even the rawest aspects of his memoir. The forthcoming adaptation into a feature film starring Lucas Hedges, Nicole Kidman, Joel Edgerton, and Russell Crowe, however, has pushed Garrard to confront his past in a new medium.

"I was in such excruciating discomfort that I couldn't even see it," Garrard said. The lion's share of Garrard's discomfort was rooted in seeing a version of his younger self remake the same mistakes that he had made. For Garrard, seeing Lucas Hedges "go along" with his parents' plan was like living a mortifying memory all over again.

"My husband was sitting next to me, having emotional reactions, and I was like, 'How? This is just BAD,'" Garrard said, of his screen-self's decisions. "At the time, I was like, 'How was I so fucking stupid?' In the book, you get to do this great interiority, but the movie is just like, Lucas is just agreeing with this right now—he looks insane!"

It was only after his third viewing, when he could see *Boy Erased* beyond his own past mistakes, that Garrard felt he could appreciate the film as a film. Part of that credit, Garrard said, goes to Hedges, who he said manages to translate pages of narrated text onto his face.

"He had already read the book three times" by the time they met, Garrard said, underlining passages that he loved. "He said, 'I'm only doing this because of your book. I don't know about the rest of it, but I love this book, so I wanna do it.'"

"It just felt very beautiful, and right."

The casting of an actor with a private personal life in such a high-profile queer role—even an actor with an Oscar nomination at nineteen—prompted understandable consternation from queer cinephiles who have grown weary of seeing our stories told by straight, cis men. But Garrard defended the casting as valid—after all, he said, it's his story to tell.

"Coming out, no matter what the story is, forces other people to come out that they care about you."

"I get it—it's high-stakes for a lot of people," Garrard said. But Garrard notes that cinema has plenty of queer stories told by straight actors and directors that ring true (*Moonlight*, *Call Me by Your Name*, *Brokeback Mountain*), and others, told by queer directors and actors (*Stonewall*) that . . . well, don't.

"Anything I was precious with, I definitely told them," Garrard said. "There were a few, what I felt to be false resolutions, with some of the characters, and they changed it. It became a more unusual film, in that it doesn't offer an easy answer. That was exactly what I wanted to do."

ORIGINALLY PUBLISHED IN *HELLO MR.* ISSUE 10 IN 2018.

Learning I'm Susceptible to Cults

Andrew Ketcham

In this dream tender is only a bruise. A purple
diner smudged against the endless desert
horizon. Conditioned air. Flies in the pie case.
A booth of laminated grease stains. In this
map, I'm unfurling. All our borders drawn
incorrectly. Hometowns swallowed up by
water or the men we know in them. The diner
is a metaphor for places we always talked
about. Itineraries sketched on napkins over
a plate of fried eggs in west Nevada. Every
word you speak pulls a trigger in my gut. *I'm
in a series of missed turns with the wrong
kind of man* I say to the waitress. I say to
anyone close enough to hear it. A week later,
we're in his car. Your feet wet all day. When
he says the destination is something more
permanent than your body. Fist against
chest, fingertip to fingertip, and light shining
through our thinnest parts. How you never
meant to go this far.

Maggie and Olivia, or: Flickering In and Out of Many Things

Erin Riley

In an interview filmed in 2016 at the London Review Bookshop, the nonbinary author Olivia Laing is in conversation with author Maggie Nelson about her book *The Argonauts*. Their immense brains are beautiful and conversation flows. At the beginning of the interview, Maggie takes a moment before reading a passage from her book to highlight her admiration for Olivia's writing, their "overlapping points of kinship."

It's true, they have many threads of overlap. Especially how they write about gender, power, freedom and how bodies can be. I read *The Argonauts* when it came out, and again more recently, after Olivia's book *Funny Weather: Art in an Emergency* inspired a reread. Both writers have this beautiful capacity to weave together stories of the everyday while questioning the world and its structures—how people and systems and words (and the context in which these are spoken and understood) can be stifling or liberating or a combination. Nelson and Laing's works reckon with power, queerness, the body, art, capitalism, and the limits of language, especially when it comes to speaking about gender and its possibilities. Both are interested in opening imaginations to the fullness of humanity.

I was experiencing a sort of deep kinship with Maggie and Olivia and disappeared into YouTube and podcast wormholes, devouring whatever I could find. I dived first into Maggie's 2021 interview with Olivia on the release of their book *Everybody: A Book About Freedom*. After reading Olivia's *The Lonely City* a few years ago, I was obsessed with everything they had ever written.

Olivia's writing is the kind that stops the world, bold and wandering, curious and spacious. Words that weave ideas together effortlessly and inspire you to borrow more books, read more. Words that introduce you to new people and open up worlds. Their work is a nervous-system experience, its reading simultaneously intellectual and bodily. It is hard to capture this kind of pleasure in words. For me it is akin to how a dip in the ocean brings more glimmer to a day, the way a fleecy jumper sits on the skin afterward. A micro moment of tiny pleasure.

In the 2021 interview, Maggie thanks Olivia for hosting one of her favorite interviews of 2016. I quickly traced the links back in time to the bookshop in London and a role reversal. The duo is nestled behind what looks to be the front sales desk, as if working on an audit late into the night. The desktop computer almost obscures Maggie's face. A collection of multicolored Moleskin notebooks lines the wall behind

Olivia's head. Olivia's hair has a soft and voluminous quality to it—loosely tied up high, light and airy, full of ideas.

Toward the end, Olivia references a press interview Maggie had done for *The Argonauts*, in which the journalist was annoyed that Maggie hadn't been more specific about her partner Harry's transition, "wanting a concrete paragraph explaining who Harry was/is/became." Olivia uses this example as a microcosm of society's obsession with categorization, especially as it relates to gender, as if gender has become (or has always to a degree been), as Maggie deftly notes, the "ultimate category of 'what it is.'"

Olivia views *The Argonauts* as a book that captures the spirit of "reparative reading" as described by queer theorist Eve Kosofsky Sedgwick in her essay "Paranoid Reading and Reparative Reading, or, You're So Paranoid, You Probably Think This Essay Is About You." Both authors agree they still don't quite fully understand what Sedgwick is getting at in this piece—its academic thickness near impenetrable. The essay is essentially about how we approach meaning-making, how we understand the world around us.

Olivia suggests that the journalist's grasping for certainty is defensive, concerned with information-gathering, identity, categorization, and the need to "know." Olivia:

> It struck me, the interviewer's desire to have that clarified. To have a sort of before-and-after notion of what somebody's gender transition is is a paranoid reading, and it's a paranoid reading that we're culturally obsessed with right now—the . . . bathroom bills, the stuff about if somebody is biologically female, this sort of horrific language that seems very invested in finding out the truth of what a person is . . . as if genitalia will tell you.[1]

Olivia talks of long being obsessed by Sedgwick's essay, by what the academic's trying to get at. For Olivia, the concept of reparative reading is "to be fundamentally more invested in finding nourishment than identifying poison. This doesn't mean being naïve or undeceived, unaware of crisis or undamaged by oppression. What it does mean is being driven to find or invent something new and sustaining out of inimical environments."[2]

I loved Olivia's obsession with queer culture, especially that of gay men, such as their delight in the work and life of artist and activist David Wojnarowicz, whose biography, *Fire in the Belly*, I'd read twice years ago.

I have long held a rich fascination with gay men, and Olivia's penchant for this topic of central importance to my own identity was wild to encounter. Someone with the name Olivia was writing about their obsession with faggots. I have always felt like a faggot, a queer man who is not a man, but sits close-to, in a body that is read as not quite. Many things and none at all. To the world, I looked like an androgynous woman and my fagginess was a mostly internal experience. It sat mostly invisible to the world, understood by queers on the fringes. An identity indulged and affirmed via the porn I consumed, the art I liked, the sex I enjoyed, in the language of lovers. I realize, to a degree, that there is a pain in invisibility but also in a paranoid reading—both my own and that of the world external to me. A paranoid reading (one of course sitting inside a larger cultural capitalist hetero-patriarchal big-*P* paranoia) of faggotry has not often had much space for the body that cannot be classified so neatly.

I have always felt like a faggot, a queer man who is not a man, but sits close-to, in a body that is read as not quite. Many things and none at all.

When I chanced upon, in Olivia's recent work, their definitive faggotry, I felt warm affinity:

> At the time, my own gender was like a noose around my neck. I was nonbinary, even if I didn't yet know the word. I'd always felt like a boy inside, a femme gay boy, and the dissonance between how I experienced myself and how I was assumed to be was so painful that often I didn't want to leave my room and enter the world at all.[3]

Recently at work, I received an email, one directed at my colleague and me. "Hi Ladies," it began. Out of all the possible collective nouns to choose from (this list, to me, seems endless), this one has been a favorite lately among the people at work. I have also several times been addressed as "girl," as in "hey, girl" but with that elongated *urrr* sound in the middle—as if, subconsciously, they have a drive to just squeeze out the most discomfort from words that do not fit me. It is punishing, and yet my workmates hold no malice as they scrape burnt cheese off the sandwich press in the staff kitchen, smiling at my face full of mustache. "Girl, how was your weekend?"

I look like Kurt Russell in *Escape from New York*. I wear button-up corduroy shirts, I dye my mustache, and sometimes I wear earrings with a dangly silver chain. I do not look like a lady, in a binary sense, in the way I know they mean it.

I want for *lady* to have little baggage—to be genderless and whatever one would like it to mean for them—but we do not live in that place at the moment. And so I viscerally crumple, another moment in which this body, its gender, is unrecognized, to a point of it literally vanishing in conversation.

There's this bit in *The Argonauts* that speaks so accurately of the dissonance of such cultural obliteration:

> Soon after we got together, we attended a dinner party at which a (presumably straight, or at least straight-married) woman who'd known Harry for some time turned to me and said, "So, have you been with other women, before Harry?" I was taken aback. Undeterred, she went on: "Straight ladies have always been hot for Harry." Was Harry a woman? Was I a straight lady? What did past relationships I'd had with "other women" have in common with this one? Why did I have to think about other "straight ladies" who were hot for my Harry?[4]

There is something quite magical in a reparative positioning, I think, especially as it relates to the body and to gender.

I'd had my pronouns in the signature of my work email for a while, in the hope that including them might do the trick, maybe clear some of the semantic scrub out of the way. Nothing changed. The latest "Ladies" left me so aggrieved that I mustered the courage to try to shift this narrow and paranoid reading. I penned an email to all the people I had ever had contact with at work with the subject line: "I'm Trans/a request."

I began my email with "Hi Favorites" because these work people are both profoundly decent yet so deeply problematic, ensconced in what I like to think of now as a paranoid reading of everything. They are victims, too—of the limits of both language and the cultural obsession with categorization, the needing to know.

Olivia Laing wrestles with this issue, too: "What I wanted as a trans person was to escape the binary altogether, which seems so natural if it includes you and so unnatural and violently enforced if it does not."[5]

For those who have not been lucky enough to have been born queer, these are not ways of living and thinking that come easily. In my workplace, I overhear women having conversations about babies. "What is it?" someone asks the newly pregnant one, a question once posed to Maggie Nelson, to which she responded, confusedly, "Ah . . . it's a human baby!?"

In my email I pointed out my gender, as well as the harm that can stem from not thinking about how heavily language is gendered. I assertively asked people to use my name or *they* as a pronoun, sent out some resources, and thanked them in advance for their efforts to affirm my gender at work.

Sedgwick's idea of reparative reading is also, maybe at its most simple—which is mostly all I can garner from it (which is absolutely enough!)—about the interplay of reading and language. It is not only about how we approach the world, but also in how our approach influences how we choose to speak about it. A reparative reciprocity. A circular motion, in which curiosity about language leads to a curiosity about, and openness to, what it is attempting to make and create meaning of.

I like the idea of placing a reparative lens on the body and am curious what it might mean to come to bodies and gender from a less paranoid positioning. (I think of the paranoid position as a default cis-heterosexism with a stubborn drive to categorize people as man/woman.) If we come to people and the world with a more curious outlook, instead of giving in to the urge to categorize, we create a space of openness where reparative work can be done.

Much like talk therapy, there is a lot of benefit in being able to accurately notice when we are dysregulated, because we can learn to respond in ways that align with our values—to be less defensive and have compassion for the parts of us that have been primed to respond in these ways. When we're in an activated state, triggered by our nervous system's hyper-speed responses to cues of danger, we haven't much capacity for curiosity, because our system gets too overloaded. The paranoid positioning is akin to living in this constant fight-or-flight mode. We are quick and reactive; we are seeking safety from danger (the unknown)—and sometimes it's unsafe if we cannot categorize, know, and control.

There is something quite magical in a reparative positioning, I think, especially as it relates to the body and to gender. It can impact how we see the world, who we see, what we see, and how we understand ourselves. A curious approach to gender, a reparative approach, is one that challenges the crippling and oppressive edges of words and makes space for them to be refashioned anew.

Maggie, in the opening to *The Argonauts*, writes that: "Words change depending on who speaks them; there is no cure. The answer isn't to just introduce new words . . . one must also become alert to the multitude of possible uses, possible contexts, the wings with which each word can fly."[6]

I affirmed my gender long before I ever took hormones to help bush-ify my mustache. Actually that is not the fullness of it, because it was not really all my doing, I realize. It was in the reparative positioning of others that affirmed my gender, too. It was in the words whispered into my ear by lovers, "Your dick is so hard." Like when I call my partner my boyfriend, when I say "good boy" and when they say it back. Language gave to me the body I knew was mine and brought into existence so many possibilities for what my gender can be. My partner's reparative positioning to my queer body, less concerned with definition, certainty, binary—an openness to the reality of surprise—affirming the inside out. The reparative reading of my body has been, come to think of it, one of the greatest gifts of my queer life.

Sedgwick in the erudite essay speaks to the idea that because the reparative reader "has room to realize that the future may be different from the present, it is also possible for her to entertain such profoundly painful, profoundly relieving, ethically crucial possibilities as that the past, in turn, could have happened differently from the way it actually did."[7] She goes on to ask: "Where does this argument leave projects of queer reading in particular?" With the relative deemphasis of the question of "sexual difference" and sexual "sameness."[8]

I take this to mean that reparative reading is a trans reading, one less concerned with binaries and definitions than it is with playing a role in the expansion of queer understandings and possibilities. Like Olivia, I had no language for the middle ground of gender in which I have always found comfort. Although holding a reparative positioning in this regard is exciting for a future in which binaries are less important and our gender is valid, I'm saddened that these reparative readings were not available to our younger selves, since their omission from cultural possibility and understanding impacted how lives were lived.

Carving out spaces for the likes of Olivia and me—faggots on the

I affirmed my gender long before I ever took hormones to help bush-ify my mustache.

spectrum—has always been limiting, so insufficient. Sedgwick answers her own question: "I think it will leave us in a vastly better position to do justice to a wealth of characteristic, culturally central practices, many of which can well be called reparative, that emerge from queer experience but become invisible or illegible under a paranoid optic."[9]

Sitting on the couch recently, my partner asked me about what my aim might be, in terms of affirming my gender. We had not spoken much about it in a while—the changes are so slow and subtle day to day that it's mostly not a topic of conversation. They asked what I had in mind and if I had a goal of how I wanted to look and feel in my body. If I went ahead with top surgery, did I think I might want to continue toward a more binary transition. Or if I still felt the same desire to find the middle space that has always been home to me.

I had started hormones to find a more ambiguous physicality, though remain on a full masculinizing dose. What this means is that if I do not reduce it, I will in a few years be read socially as a man. I am still misgendered in the world—at the shop, at the dog park, at the café, at work, at social gatherings, generally at most places. My answer to my partner's question was that my aim was not to be misgendered and that maybe I would continue the dose until fewer people called me "lady."

"That might never happen," my partner said, reminding me of transmasculine friends, even those who had undergone a full binary transition, some even with flourishing beards, who still experienced being "ma'amed" at the shops.

My outlook, I realize now, was a paranoid one, when I think of things in the way encouraged by Olivia and Maggie and Eve. Perhaps I have it all wrong and may well have bastardized her beautiful academic ideas. Even if I have (sorry, Eve), this idea of the reparative versus the paranoid has at least got me thinking. I have, for a long time, wanted the world to see me as I know myself to be—a queer faggot, not a woman, not a man. I appreciate that this is a tough ask of a system that is completely paranoid and predicated on containing, naming, and finding out the "truth." Gender is fluid, whereas paranoia is stuck in the mud.

It is not a stretch to think that queers might be susceptible to such readings, for we too are members of the paranoid external world, constantly battling against and within structures around us that contribute to the pains in the first place—namely patriarchy (with its attendant misogyny), power, language, gender norms, and how these factors play out daily.

I wanted hormone replacement therapy (HRT) to change me in ways that might mean some people would not be so quick to call me a lady, and also to feel more connected to my body. However, I did not want my faggotry middle ground to be rendered invisible, to be later mistaken for a man. Indeed, if the system is mostly paranoid and forces us to live in black and white, my partner is right, and my desire to be "properly" read may never truly be achieved.

In reviewing *The Argonauts*, Olivia reminds us that Maggie is bent on using these kinds of experiences—in her case, partner Harry's constant experiences of being misgendered—to pry "the culture open, of investigating what it is that's being so avidly defended and policed. Binaries, mostly: the overwhelming need, to which the left is no more immune than the right, for categories to remain pure and unpolluted. . . . Individuals migrating from one gender to another, let alone refusing to commit to either, occasions immense turbulence in thought systems that depend upon orderly separation and partition."[10]

Maybe a reparative positioning of gender and the body is one in which curiosity about what a body can be, both in language and in physicality, is made possible. In maintaining some kind of transitional turbulence. Perhaps it is achievable by not making life easy for the paranoid system—which, in my case, I was trying to do when using its limited vocabulary to try and signal to it. There I was, waving madly across the dog park: See me as I am, as my boyfriend does when they turn to me in bed in the morning and say, "Your mustache looks so beautiful today."

I have held tight to the idea that interactions with other people were a way to gauge my own gender expression, as if somehow it is not legitimate unless it is recognized by everyone. (That said, of course, we know ourselves through relating with others, and not being affirmed for a long time can be very painful.) As if, when someone at the dog park finally looks at me and umms and ahhs and fumbles over their words, and cannot box me in, then I'll know it's time to go get a new script, get off the full dose. This will signal that I'm finally "there" at my destination. As opposed to, I fucking live here already and have always been here. A paranoid system is one in which people reach for the category that lives closest to what they know—it is a reality of a system that is not big enough for fringe dwellers, yet is nevertheless expanding. I realize, in trying to signal within its narrow remit, with its limited language, I deny others the opportunity for reparative reading, or to be a body among others, like Olivia's that can be part of a reparative movement toward the body and to gender in this dreamy moment.

In *The Argonauts*, Maggie writes that before meeting Harry, "I had spent a lifetime devoted to Wittgenstein's ideal that the inexpressible is contained—inexpressibly—in the expressed! This idea gets less airtime than his more reverential 'Whereof one cannot speak thereof one must be silent,' but it is, I think, the deeper idea. Its paradox is, quite literally, *why I write*, or how I feel able to keep writing."[11]

Perhaps a reparative positioning of the body and gender is that expressability comes into being via people who, by somehow unburdening themselves of the paranoid lens (resisting the outside paranoid pressure of needing to help people "know," which, for me, remains very difficult), bravely continue to exist in bodies and genders like Harry and Olivia and mine with the understanding that words are not yet good enough.

Toward the end of her interview with Olivia at the bookshop, Maggie speaks about her experiences of doing press for the book. Many times she had this sentence in her head, gifting it finally to Olivia: "It's not *The Crying Game*, OK . . . I'm like, do you get out much? . . . because a lot of people live in a world where you might fuck somebody when you're not totally sure what their gender is—it happens, you know."

In some ways, the nonbinary trans body is a reparative object (a hot one), and by just existing, it can pry open the space Olivia speaks about, to allow for Eve's dream of doing justice to this "wealth of characteristic" that was simply invisible under the paranoid gaze.

Maggie reminds the audience at the bookshop of the good news that it's possible to be shifted from one optic to another, and that one of the things that can get us there is "being close to people who flicker in and out of many things." There's something quite poetic in the idea of gender as a constant flickering, a shining in and out. Not static but constantly on the move, bright and luminescent. It feels full of possibilities, drained of paranoia. My new pronoun, at the bottom of the email, reads *Them*, that one flickering in and out.

1. "Maggie Nelson and Olivia Laing: *The Argonauts*," London Review Bookshop, 2016, https://www.youtube.com/watch?v=s-Yxhc2nNxo&t=2751s.
2. Olivia Laing, *Funny Weather: Art in an Emergency* (London: Picador, 2020), p. 4.
3. Laing, *Everybody: A Book About Freedom* (London: Picador, 2021), p. 284.
4. Maggie Nelson, *The Argonauts* (Melbourne: Text Publishing, 2015), p. 10.
5. Laing, *Everybody: A Book About Freedom*, p. 284.
6. Nelson, *The Argonauts*, p. 9.
7. Eve Kosofsky Sedgwick, "Paranoid Reading, Reparative Reading, or, You're So Paranoid, You Probably Think This Essay Is About You," in *Touching Feeling: Affect, Pedagogy, Performativity* (Durham, NC: Duke University Press, 2002), p. 146.
8. Ibid.
9. Ibid, p. 147.
10. Laing, *Funny Weather: Art in an Emergency*, p. 263.
11. Nelson, *The Argonauts*, p. 3.

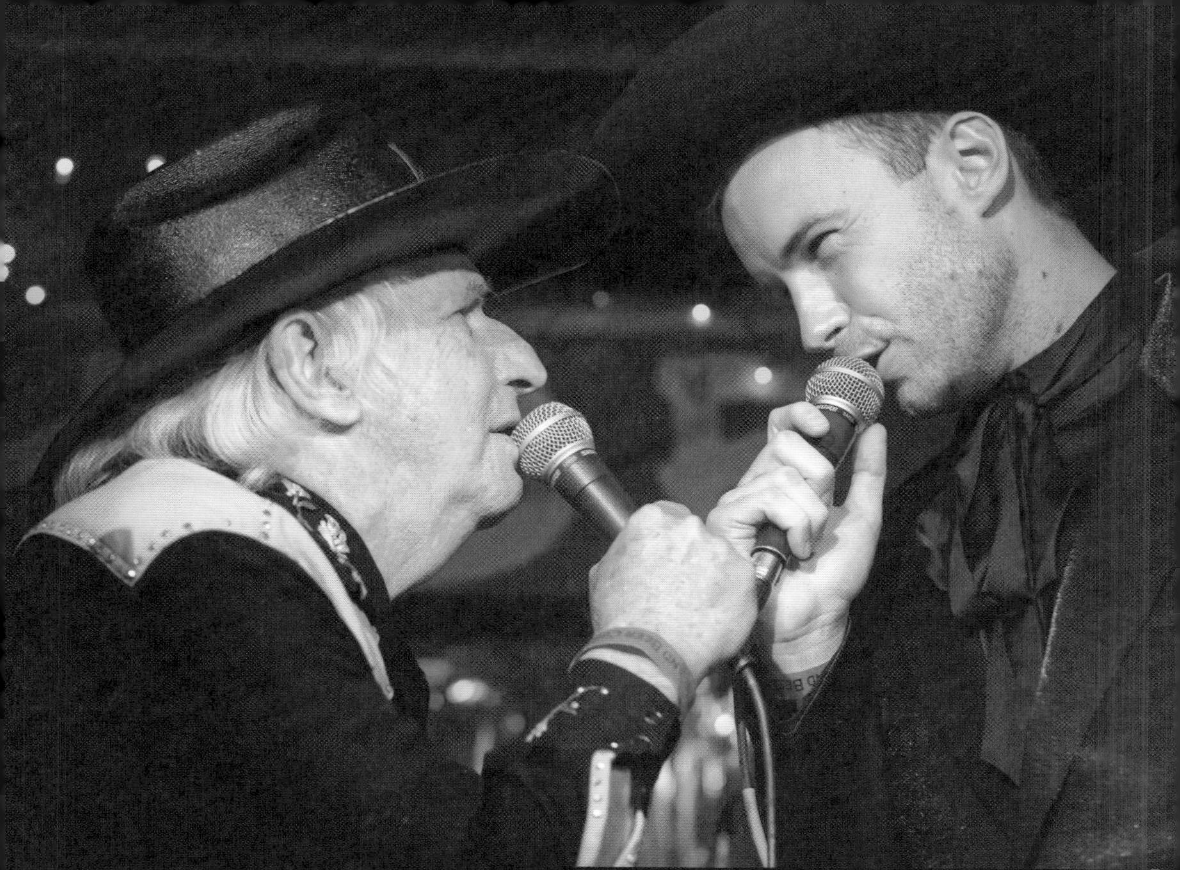

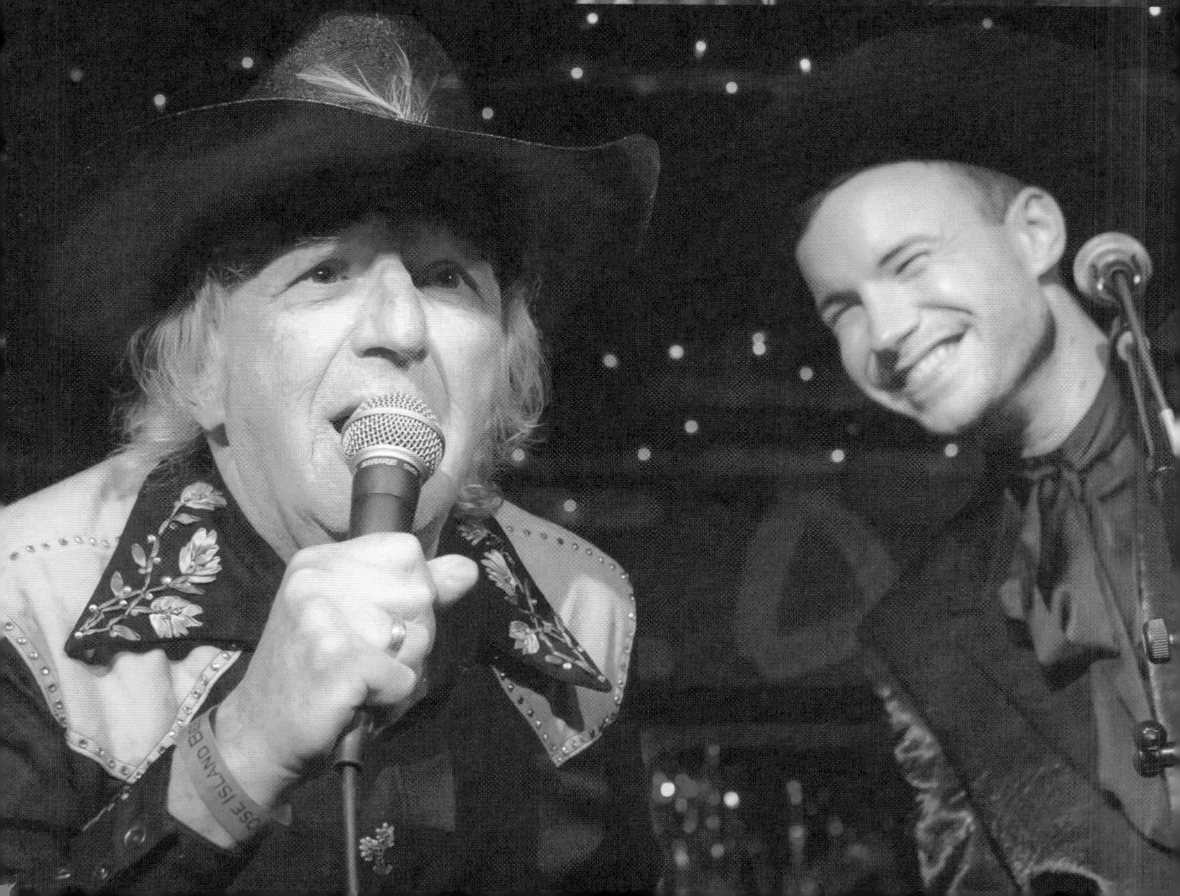

Cryin' These Cocksucking Tears: Remembering My Friend, Patrick Haggerty

Andrew Sa | Photos by Sarah Elizabeth Larson

Patrick Haggerty was a pioneer of modern gay country music. Born in 1944, he's even called the first by some. For certain, he was the "queen of bathhouse sluts" who "got kicked out of the Peace Corps for suckin' dick!" Oh, and he was a "screaming Marxist bitch!" He would proudly exclaim these words at his band Lavender Country's every performance, which I was fortunate enough to witness several times.

My folk-leaning acoustic band, Andrew Sa and His Blue Boys, first opened for Lavender Country in April 2018 at the Hideout Inn, a snug but beloved Chicagoan music venue, known for their progressive politics and communal support. His performance that night changed me. I'd never witnessed someone with so much command of a stage. He had everyone in the room in the palm of his gentle hands.

He wore fringed purple cowboy boots, "Lavender" written in cut leather on the left and "Country" on the right, and a matching lilac hat with a hand-painted rainbow and little daisies on the front. Like the gay grandpa I'd always wanted! He had the room rumbling with laughter one moment and unable to hold back tears the next. The entirety of his set was a condensed life story, winding in and around his equally provocative songs.

With a little help from some whiskey, I approached Patrick at the merch table after the show. I gushed over his performance and tried to express how moved I was. He thanked me and said he would *kill* for my voice—something he'd sweetly repeat many times during our friendship. I'd covered "She's Got You" that night, which got us indulging in our mutual love for Patsy Cline, which led to Loretta Lynn, and pretty soon we'd already planned a show together, to cover Patsy and Loretta.

From this night on, Patrick had given me permission to be the faggy little country boy I'd always been. My sad gay cowboy persona, Lonesome Andrew, was finally and fully out of the closet.

Everybody in town knew he was a sissy, and still he could've been president of any club he wanted.

Raised near the rural Canadian border of Washington state, Patrick was the sixth of ten children born to poor dairy farmers Asylda Mary and Charles Edward Haggerty. Unlike other queer kids in similar circumstances, even today, his parents were very accepting. His father particularly encouraged him to have pride in himself and his talents. He would often recall his father's love, referring to him as a saint. At Port Angeles Senior High, Patrick was both head cheerleader and senior class president. Everybody in town knew he was a sissy, and still he could've been president of any club he wanted.

Being discharged from the Peace Corps in 1966 moved him to spend the rest of his life fighting for gay rights, Black liberation, and socialist politics, starting with coming out of the closet in 1969. In 1973, he formed his band and released the first known gay country album, self-titled *Lavender Country*. Going fairly unnoticed, selling about 1,000 records total, Lavender Country played around the Pacific Northwest at various LGBTQ+ events, including the first Seattle Pride in 1974, until they disbanded in 1976.

On March 25, 2014, more than forty years after its initial release, the North Carolina label Paradise of Bachelors reissued *Lavender Country*, giving Patrick's music career a second wind at seventy years old.

In April 2019, Patrick came to play the Hideout again. As if it were tradition, they again booked me to open. We shared the bill with Patrick's friend, touring buddy, and manager, Paisley Fields. That night, there was a huge snowstorm in Chicago and the show was lightly attended. It was still a great time. I had written a lot in that year between shows and had more originals to share. Patrick stood in the audience and watched my full set. He approached me after, squeezed my elbows, and pulled me close to say, "Last time I didn't see you, but I get you now. I *see* you." What a precious affirmation.

I arranged for the band of eight to stay in my two bedroom apartment in Andersonville for the couple days they were in town. Patrick and his husband, JB, shared my little three-quarter bouncy bed. They were getting situated when I asked if anyone wanted to smoke some weed. To my surprise Patrick said yes.

When I pulled out my dirty little pipe, Patrick laughed. He smiled mischievously, a signature flirt. He pulled out his own rolling papers, dumped everything from my grinder, and rolled a perfect joint in seconds. The man was a professional pothead. We walked to Hamburger Mary's and when the drag queen approached our table, lip syncing her heart out, Patrick was still face deep in his menu. She was annoyed he hadn't noticed her and said, "Well who the hell is this, the mayor?" He only responded with a smile.

We invited him back to Chicago to join the Cosmic Country Showcase set in April 2020, but it got postponed due to the COVID-19 pandemic. During that year and a half, our friendship continued to blossom over Facebook Messenger. We'd try to lift each other when spirits were low. In August 2020, he sweetly wrote, "Right now my goal is to live through all this so we can do at least one more show at the Hideout. You and me, darling."

He got his wish a little over a year later, when Lavender Country headlined the revived Cosmic Country Showcase. The show hovers somewhere between the *Outer Limits* and *Hee Haw*, with a few Chicago comedians and a roster full of local indie starlings singing spacey country tunes with our supergroup house band, including Sima Cunningham, Liam Kazar, and Spencer Tweedy, alongside the producers of the show, Sully Davis and Dorian Gehring. Hosting with me, our anti-host if you will, Mary Williamson puts on creature drag as our rodeo clown to round the night out.

As the headliner, Patrick led the band with a set of Lavender Country tunes to close out the show. I was the host of our three-show run (two nights in Chicago and one out of town at Cactus Club in Milwaukee, Wisconsin) and played other gigs the same week. My plate was pretty full.

When he asked me to sing backup for his set, I graciously declined. "Oh babe, you don't need me up there with you. I don't wanna upstage you!" I joked. He loved that, smiling that glimmering smirk of his and said, "You couldn't upstage me if you tried, doll. I dare you."

He wouldn't take no for an answer. I later found out I was a very important part of his act. I played the "straight man" for his storytime stage banter. He would say something shocking, like how he'd counted his lovers up to the thousands "stacking 'em up like cord wood," he'd turn to me, my blushing face as his punchline.

I had my fun with him, too. On the night of our first show, halfway through his set I asked the audience, "Is it hot in here?" and pulled off my sharkskin suit jacket to reveal a slimmer suit jacket, blanketed in rhinestones like fresh fallen snow. After all, he had dared me. He loved it, and was truly without ego. As he'd often say, "I am your stepping stone, to lift you up."

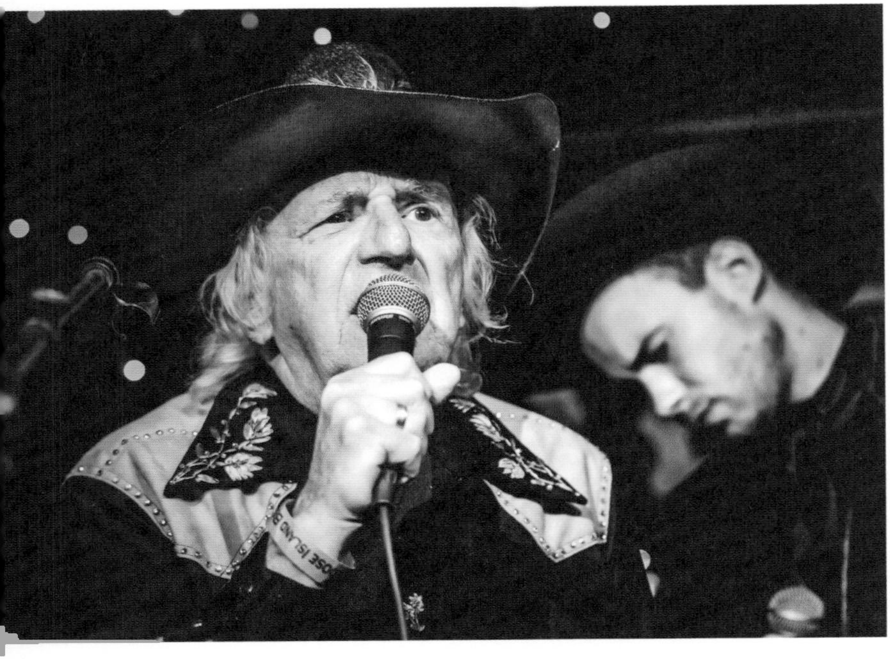

The next year we played SXSW. At a sidewalk show on a sunny day catty-corner from a pair of Bible thumpers on megaphones, he responded to their proselytizing with the legendary crowd favorite, "Cryin' These Cocksucking Tears."

He was heading back on tour the next day, so we decided to get breakfast. Patrick loved a greasy spoon. Over pancakes and bacon, we reworked our plan for a Patsy and Loretta cover show, this time imagining a studio album. Over the next few months, we spent a lot of time on the phone ironing out the details. We playfully fought over one song in particular, "I'll scratch your eyes out for 'Crazy'!" he snarled.

We brought him out in July to play the Cosmic Country Cookout, a day-long summer festival edition of the Showcase, and booked Foxhall Studio to record the first half of the record. The session went on without a hitch, with Dorian Gehring playing most of the instruments and engineering. We also brought in Patrick's close friends, guitarist Jack Moriarty, bassist Lyn Rye, and Sophie Sputnik on backup vocals. I cried hearing his crackling rendition of "Crazy" (he'd won the fight) and he cried while I belted Loretta's "Love Is the Foundation"; two queens crooning the highs and lows of love. Those three days of recording I'll cherish my life long.

As he'd often say, "I am your stepping stone, to lift you up."

The last time I saw Patrick was the night he flew out. We shared a Thai dinner with Jack Moriarty and Patrick's husband, JB, relishing the last three days and dreaming of the future of our album. Patrick said, "I haven't had a hard-on in two years, but... hope is on the horizon when I think of this project."

We planned for him and JB to come back for Thanksgiving, spend three more days in the studio, and finish the record. As a parting gift, I gave him my copy of *Me & Patsy Kickin' Up Dust*, Loretta's book recounting her friendship with Patsy. He's holding it and smiling in the last photo I took of him.

When I got the call on Halloween that Patrick had passed, I'd just arrived in Milwaukee on tour with the Cosmic Country Showcase. I sat on the curb and took a moment to cry, remembering that it was exactly one year since we shared the Cactus Club stage. Patrick influenced me like only an elder could. Bravely shining his light, he paved the way, encouraging me and many other country queers to lift our heads and brightly shine our own. His legacy will live on through us and will never go back in the closet again. As our finale that night, we pulled the cast onstage and took turns singing Patrick's inclusive anthem, "Lavender Country," enlisting the whole room in the chorus:

Y'all come out, come out my dears to
Lavender Country
Y'all come out and make yourselves to
home
It don't matter here who you love or what
you wear
'Cause we don't care who's got what
chromosomes

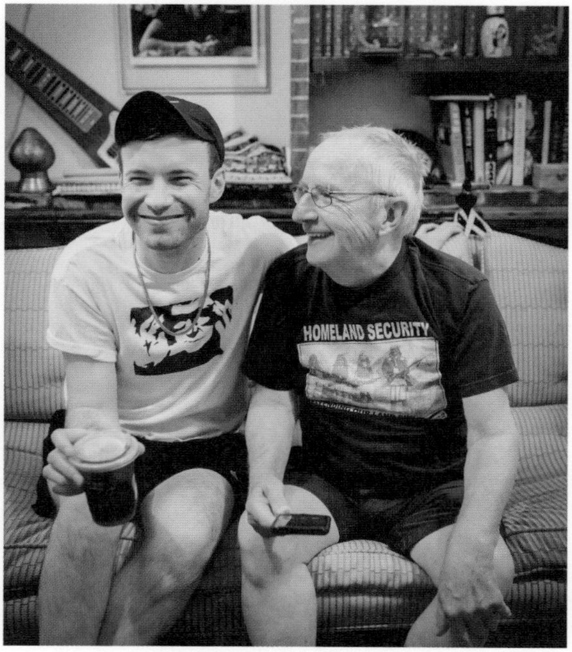

Nature Poem

Tommy Pico

A couple years ago, I spent the summer writing a book called *IRL* in an office space in Greenpoint. I spent every day from May through August bent over a desk writing a 98-page poem while all my friends were at the beach, on rooftops, or in the Catskills (thanks, Instagram). When I finally finished, I booked a trip to Portland with one intention and one intention only: to do nothing but sit on my friend's porch petting kitties and drinking prosecco. The night before I left, I had goodbye drinks with friends and my bff was talking about how, as a Black woman, she made a point of not eating watermelon or fried chicken in front of white people. I told her that similarly, as an American Indian, I consciously didn't write about nature because that felt so expected and stereotypical. A white guy in the peanut gallery said that was bullshit, that I could write anything I wanted to, why couldn't I write about nature? I didn't argue with him because I wasn't getting paid to educate this man, and I believe labor should come with a check. But I left New York with what he said ringing in my mind. Indeed soon I was on a porch petting kitties and drinking prosecco for about two days, before I started to get antsy. Full disclosure: relaxation makes me nervous. Before long I found myself again writing a book-length poem, in response to that white man at the bar. *Nature Poem* itself is a nature poem about why I can't write a nature poem. It resists the idea of nature poetry, expands what "natural" means, and cracks a ton of jokes along the way. It me.

AN EXCERPT I

The stars are dying

like always, and far away, like what you see looking up is a death knell
from light, right? Light

years. But also close, like the sea stars on the Pacific coast. Their little arms lesion
and knot and pull away

the insides spill into the ocean. Massive deaths. When I try to sleep I
think about orange cliffs, bare of orange stars. Knotted, glut. Waves are
clear. Anemones n shit. Sand crabs n shit. Fleas. There are seagulls
overhead. Ugh I swore to myself I would never write a nature poem.

The sand is fine. They say it's not Fukushima. I feel fine, in the sense
that I feel very thin—I been doin Tracy Anderson DVD workouts on
Youtube, keeping my arms fit and strong. She says reach, *like you are
being pulled apart*

I can't not spill. Sometimes it, sometimes what you see is what you
glut. There are sometimes insides.

AN EXCERPT II

WHAT'S YR NATIONALITY!?!? This guy shouts at me during drag
queen karaoke at this gay bar two stops down the line.

In order to talk about a hurricane, you first have to talk about a
preexisting disturbance over the ocean, so you have to talk about mean ocean
temperature, so you have to talk about human industry and sun
rays, so you have to talk about helium, so did you know helium was
named for the sun god Helios and was defined by a gap in the solar
spectrum so literally not itself but what surrounded it, so of course
we have to talk about the solar system, the milky way, the networks of universe
and the Big Bang.

How far back do you have to go to answer any question about race?

UM, AMERICAN? I say

or

KUMEYAAY. I say I'M FROM THE KUMEYAAY NATION.

which are both technically true, but I know that when he says NATIONALITY he's saying *you look vaguely not like a total white boy* plus I'm trying to get lucky, so I put on my face that's the opposite of a tall can tipped over and glugging out onto the floor

I'M FROM AN INDIAN RESERVATION NEAR SAN DIEGO I burst back, over the drag queen sort of singing the Michael Bublé version of "Feelin' Good."

AN EXCERPT III

Like poison oak or the Left Eye part in "Waterfalls"
you become a little bit of everything you brush
against. Today I am a handful of raisins and abt 15 ppl on the water taxi.
When my dad texts me two cousins dead this week, one 26 the other
30, what I'm really trying to understand is what trainers @ the gym
mean when they say "engage" in the phrase "engage your core"
also "c4ore"
restless terms batted back and forth.
Rest is a sign of necrosis. Life is a cycle of jobs. The biosphere is alive
with menthol smoke and my unchecked voicemails. I, for one, used to
believe in God
and comment boards
I wd say how far I am from my mountains, tell you why I carry
Kumeyaay basket designs on my body, or how freakishly routine it is to
hear someone died
but I don't want to be an identity or a belief or a feedbag. I wanna b
me. I want to open my arms like winning a foot race and keep my
stories to myself, I tell my audience.
Grief is sneaking cigs from the styrofoam cups on the tables next to the
creamers and plates of Mary's pineapple upside down cake, running off
to the playground behind the schoolroom trailers to (try and) smoke them
We were supposed to grow old together, hold down food, run for cover,
give birth.
Body the job was to keep breathing.

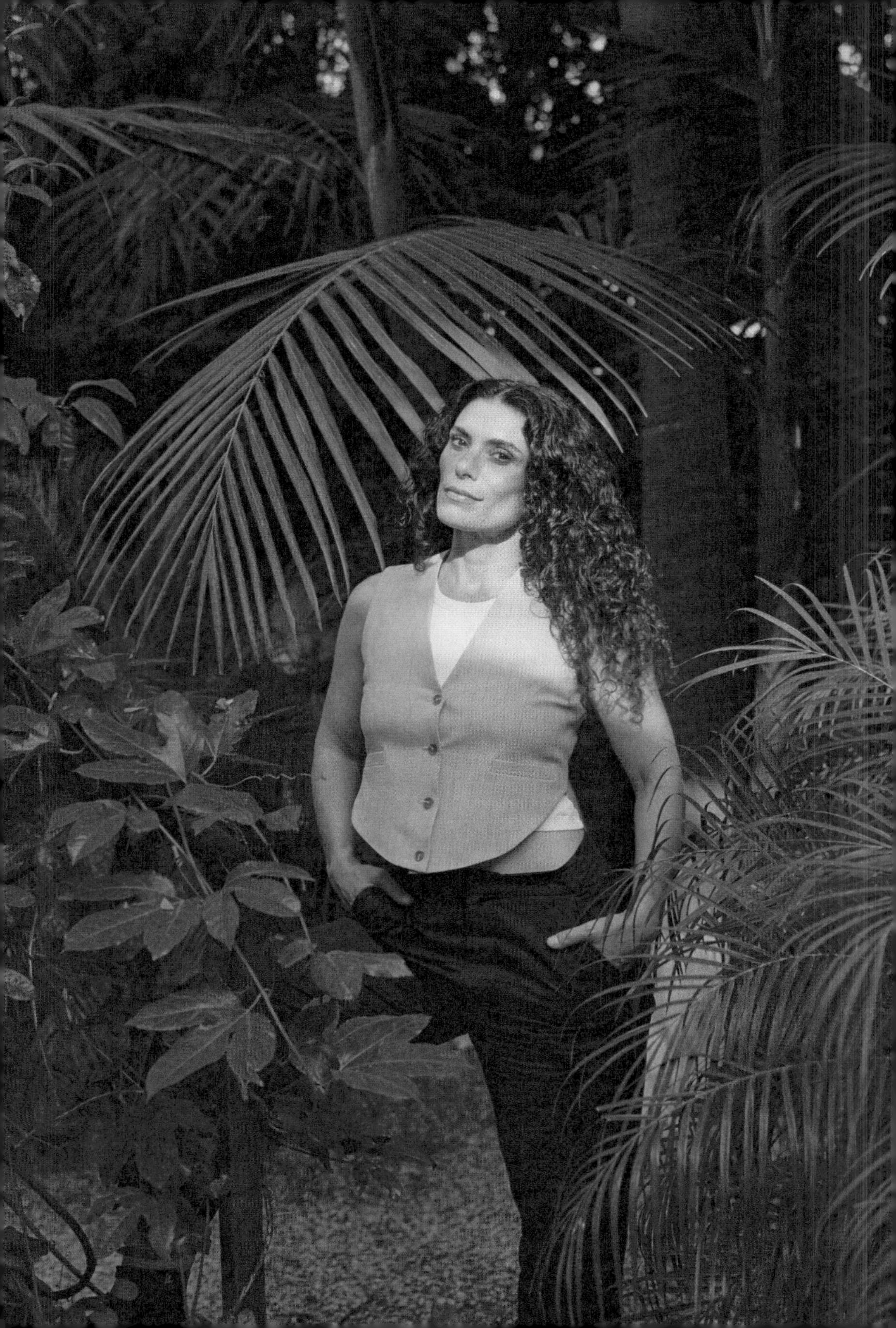

CHANI NICHOLAS IS IN YOUR HOUSE

Alexander Chee | Photos by Liam Woods

Chani Nicholas is an astrologer who writes the kind of horoscopes you want to read to your friends over the phone or share on social media. The urgent connection you make with her horoscopes makes you urgent about sharing them with others. I first found Chani Nicholas's horoscopes through my friend, the writer Kaitlyn Greenidge, who swears by them. And I was instantly a fan. The voice of her writing comes through like the bullshit detector in the back of my own head, and it was true with that first horoscope. I didn't just add her on social media when I discovered her—I read her Twitter feed back about a month, read her blog, and bought some workshop materials from her website. I basically went to her website and threw money at her like it was the end of a drag show she had just slayed.

It's easy to become a Chani evangelist quickly. And her audience—over half a million followers on Instagram and more than a million readers on her blog—shows this. She's been the subject of a number of recent profiles, and much of the press surrounding her focuses on her left politics, present in all of her horoscopes, and her willingness to let readers leave her rather than change her overtly political stance—weirdly shocking to the mainstream press—as well as her history as a former actress. But I really wanted to hear about her focus on queer astrology, her much-awaited new book, but also, I wanted the Chani Nicholas origin story—what set her on the road to becoming the astrologer she is now.

I met up with Chani in the West Village, near the West Side Highway, on a recent visit she made to New York City. In a café of professionally looked-after people, she gave off the air of someone who just showed up looking the way they hope to: casually cool in knee-high boots and jeans, her brown curly hair charmingly adrift. When she looks at you, she has that perfect Susan Dey smirk, like she's going to laugh at you but you'll laugh, too. And as I found out, this is exactly what happens.

We went for a walk over to the piers and talked about her first teachers, the give and take of giving a reading, her path to being the force for change she is now, and the ancient sources for her vision of queer astrology. And, of course, her first book, *You Were Born for This*.

ALEXANDER CHEE: When did you first get interested in astrology? Did you read your own horoscopes as a kid?

CHANI NICHOLAS: Two events in my childhood. When I was around eight years old, I was taken along to this . . . [chuckles] illegal activity. My caregiver was selling stuff, and the person they were selling to asked for my date of birth. And I remember her pulling out this book—this was the eighties, no computers—and she looked at it, and then looked up at me, and said, "You're very judgmental." And I thought, *Yes. I am. Thank you.* And I didn't know what it meant, but what I felt that it meant was that she was distinguishing me from the situation, in a sense, saying, *You have certain opinions about things.*

I grew up in a situation where there wasn't a focus on me at all, and to have someone home in on me, and this part of me—I was like, *Yes, I like this.* I felt she was throwing me a little shade also, but that was my first moment of astrology, and I thought, *That is fascinating.*

My second moment of it, I was twelve, with a newly formed part of my family structure: my father, my new stepmother, stepbrother and sister—her children. Her mother was a Reiki master, and she got us all an astrology reading. And even though it was a new part of my family structure, I had known my stepmother since I was four, knew my new siblings since they were born—we grew up together—so I knew them all really well. I was a twelve-year-old trying to figure out how all of this was going to work.

And the astrologer sat down and dealt with each one of us as separate beings, and why we functioned the way we did. It really just blew my mind. I needed to understand how I was separate, how we might come together as a family. And because we had all come from really extreme situations of violence and addiction, come together out of so much trauma, separately and together, the reading just really talked about how each one of us would deal with that emotional baggage. She didn't use those words but that's how I understood it.

I always felt like I was doing everything wrong, but for an astrologer to be like, *Oh no, that's the way you're built, that's how you do you,* it was really helpful to understand, to know that was a tendency in me—even how I might be creating more self-harm. And with the added stuff of our life experience, how those specific parts of your personality can get exacerbated.

Plus, when she started speaking, I felt like she was speaking a language that I knew, but no one had ever spoken to me before. It immediately made sense to me and was familiar to me. She had written a book, and so I sat through all of the readings and listened to everything she said to everyone, and then I got the book and I devoured that, and I've just been reading and studying since.

AC: So you read that first book, and that put you on your path?

CN: Yes. And my stepmother's mom had this incredible library of astrological books. I had heard of my stepmom's mom before I met her. As a young person I was really searching for some sort of adult mentor in my life, someone who had some connection to themselves and some way, some system of moving through the world.

AC: Someone who just wasn't lost?

CN: [Laughs] Someone who had matured and grown up. Her name's Anita, and when I met her, I had one of those experiences where this voice that I hear, that I've come to know and trust, it rose up to me and said: *This woman will show you the way, she'll show you how to get from where you are to where you wanna be. This is it.* It was an *ahhh* moment. She's incredibly beautiful, stylish, and a very powerful presence. Meeting her was like a spiritual experience in a way. Anything she said, I hung on to her every word. So when I was told we were going for an astrology reading, I was like, "Great."

AC: Right!

CN: So the thing about getting a reading and giving one, right, is that we're sitting with strangers and we're telling them something that is confirming something very deep and personal. I think what readings do is that they give us back a little bit of faith. That there's something bigger than us, and maybe we're going to be OK. Maybe there's a meaning, maybe there's a purpose for all of the pain and all of the trauma that we've come through, maybe there's something holding experiences in the present in its entirety.

AC: So do you think that was a successful strategy for the way that this new family unit was put together?

CN: For me, it was. I was the one in the family who would hold that knowledge. People in the family would be like: "What am I, Chani?" I'd be like, "Well, you have a Scorpio moon, so you know . . ." [laughs]

AC: [Laughs] You sort of became the reading for the family, in a sense, the voice, or the archive. The living voice of the archive.

CN: I immediately retained it. [Laughs] For me, it's like the mark of the chart gets etched into my mind or being or

Maybe there's a meaning, maybe there's a purpose for all of the pain and all of the trauma that we've come through, maybe there's something holding experiences in the present in its entirety.

somewhere, so if I give somebody a reading and a couple years later they come back, I won't remember their name and I might not even remember their face, but as soon as I see their chart, I remember the whole thing. So it is burned into me somewhere.

I sense that now when I'm looking at family charts—the parents' chart, the kids' charts, the siblings' charts, everyone's holding a different piece of each other. The children will have a very different parent. Like in their chart, one child has a devouring mother, another child will have a distant father, so they're experiencing the parent in their own unique way and still there's this theme that's being worked out.

My stepmom's mom—the one who had a library of astrology books that I could go into—she was the one that took me to my first real astrology class. It walked me through how to put a chart together in that system, and then about four years later I started working with Daniela George, who is a master astrologer, scholar, and historian. I started learning traditional, more Hellenistic-based astrology.

AC: The ancient system.

CN: Yeah, kind of the origins and the roots, and that completely changed the way I look at charts.

AC: How would you say it changed the way you look at a chart?

CN: It was like, well I love rules, because I'm very judgmental [laughs]. I love rules and structure because if I have that, it then gives my intuition somewhere to land and go from.

AC: Are you a Virgo?

CN: No.

AC: Look at me trying to guess your sign. What sign are you?

CN: [Laughs] I don't talk about it. I'll totally tell you, just not in the interview. I have a very strong Saturn influence in my chart and so I feel like if I have rules and structure and boundaries, then my intuition and the fluid creative muse can then move through that structure—that's what I dig. Modern astrology is much more about the observation of the psyche, and the persona, in that sense, and the ancient one, is like quality of light. Quality of light in everything, in the sky and the ways.

AC: More scientific, less impressionistic?

CN: Yeah, or because astrology and astronomy were the same thing until they separated. So through observation in Mesopotamia we got like seven hundred years of astronomical, but also astrological, observation documented in cuneiform tablets.

AC: Wow.

CN: A seven-hundred-year history of documenting what happened, how Mars moved, how the sun moved, and then what happened. Very rudimentary. It's clunky. It's strange information. We're constantly observing the natural world, how it worked and seeing what kind of correlations there were. It's much more about the observation of what heat does, what light does, what cold does, and what moisture does, in a sense. Also what planets have what temperaments and what that means when it lands on a human life.

So if my temperature is hot and dry, I might get really angry and things might break, because when things are hot and dry they break. Some people call them the humors, but there's these qualities for when the Sun moves/lives by the fixed star Regulus in the sky, that's like a marking of a king's lineage or royalty. So looking at the markings of things and denoting the quality of life, more than the type of person you are.

AC: So this movement toward the ancient for you happened around the same time of the movement of queering of astrology for you, would you say roughly?

CN: Yeah, roughly.

AC: Can you talk a little bit about the queering part?

CN: I am queer [laughs] and I do astrology [laughs]. I mean I'm interested in humans, and humans as the lens of astrology. I think that the cosmos is super queer—like totally gay—because there's all these different iterations of moments. Every moment has its own unique stamp and every moment humans are born.

In each astrological framework there's a totally unique energy, so how could that not apply to our ways of expressing everything, including gender and relationships and how we're functioning in the world? I really honor all the work that was done before me, and also in that honoring I'm allowed to go back and say the way that this is taught or said is actually problematic and can be harmful to folks. We've learned and we've grown so let's restructure things in a new way. So in 2013, Astrobarry and I did a course called "Queering Mars and Venus." Just a night, a talk. We wanted to talk about how astrology has been used against queer folks in a lot of ways. I think that the teachers, astrologers, and authors that wrote what they wrote most likely didn't mean to be harmful, but because they're writing from a heteronormative place, it is.

AC: It was exclusionary.

CN: Yeah, and it made queerness problematic.

I was involved with two queer astrology conferences that happened after that. We're trying to reenvision this without losing astrological structure: How do we counsel as queer folks to other queer folks, what's our addition to this lineage of astrology?

AC: So your personal path between, like, the class of your step-grandmother and the "Queering Mars and Venus" panel, you're sort of going along that path, but in fits and starts it seems, right? But I'm curious about your other teacher—the dreams.

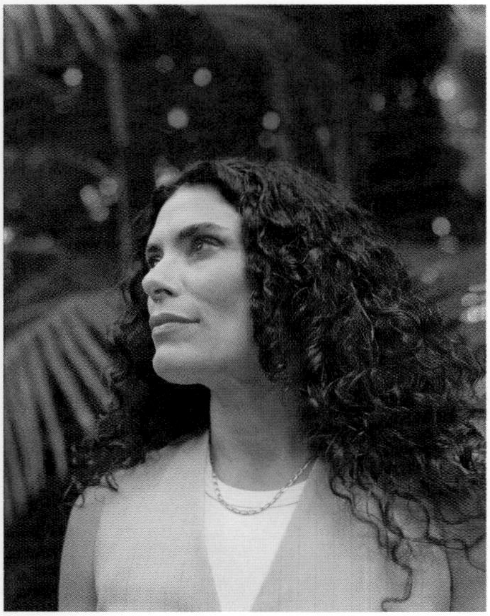

CN: Oh, yeah, yeah [laughs]. So when I wasn't doing astrology professionally and when I had big moments of doubt around it, I had these teaching dreams about a planet or a configuration, either in my chart or just in general. That happened a lot in my twenties. I remember telling my aunt about it and she was like, "You know that not everybody has those dreams." I was like, "What?" and she told me that it probably meant something [laughs].

For all of the disruption in my childhood, I had access to very alternative communities, so I've always had queer folks in my life, I've always had people that were into dream analysis, therapy, and spirituality. We talked a lot about dreams and all of that, so I knew that got implanted somewhere.

But I never thought astrology was a profession. I always thought, *Well that's not professional.* I wanted to be something—but I didn't know what.

OK I'll heal. I'll do what I need to do to heal this shit so that I can seek what I might be able to be in the world.

AC: You wanted to draw some lines around your life [laughs].

CN: I was very judgmental about astrology. I disrespected it for a long time. I didn't find it to be something that was worth putting my life energy into. It was just something that I knew how to do. And so the dreams would come and they would come really forcefully and they weren't always nice. They were jarring a lot of the time, but they would tell me things I needed to know. It was like a shock, like a psychic shock, reconnecting me to that thing that I knew, and I'd go to therapy and talk about it and my therapist would go, "So when you talk about astrology, energy comes off you, you come alive. So I just want you to know that." [Laughs] "I just want to show that that's where the energy is in you." And I'd be like, "OK, but I still don't know what I want to do for a living."

AC: So was it the case then that you had a Saturn return that put you on the path to be an astrologer?

CN: Kind of, but it was more like my Saturn first quarter, which is like mid-thirties. I moved to LA during my Saturn return. I needed to live out a different type of my artistic life, which was acting at the time. I was in a repertory theater company. I was doing that which I loved, then I felt like I exorcised it out of my being.

AC: Exorcised the acting out of your being, and then you were like, "OK, now astrology."

CN: Then I was into healing. I was initiated into Reiki when I was fourteen. I begged her [Anita], and she decided I was old enough. I studied that with her for twelve years along with astrology. I'd do all of her workshops and then work on people. Reiki was also part of my professional life in a sense. So I went into yoga teaching. I taught yoga for a long time.

AC: So what was it that brought you to finally commit professionally, to being an astrologer?

CN: I was brought to my knees [laughs]. Nothing else worked. I dropped out of three grad programs in a row, the last one cost me $14,000 and it was such an awful experience. It was so stressing—grad school is really stressful—but that particular thing was so heinous and so costly. I learn lessons usually through expense, physically. I was like, "You know, what if I stop trying to search for this piece of paper that, I think, will give me some legitimacy and pour all that energy and passion into my business, what would happen?" So I gave myself a year to do that and said fuck it. I was living in San Francisco at the time. I moved back to LA. and I just put it all there.

AC: And what year was that?

CN: It would've been like five years ago [2013]. And then I met my wife and things just sort of exploded.

AC: Professionally? Did she help you professionalize? Is she that kind of person?

CN: Mmm, yeah. She is my boss [laughs]. I work for Sonya Passi. What the relationship did for me is it gave me a home that I'd never had. It gave me a place to be and it gave me support and love in a place that I never had it. Then everything kind of flourished.

I was in my mid-late thirties, had been single for a really long time so I was very much Fuck Monogamy and needing to have a relationship and all of that. I was very into my single persona, having relationships however they came, but when we got together, it was like I found gravity or gravity found me and I got to drop in. She was also my editor so that helped a lot, and my business partner—she just held everything with me and held me in a place I'd never been held. It was immediate, that thing that I'd been waiting for my entire life, that I've been working on since I was twelve. I was like, OK I'll heal, I'll do what I need to do to heal this shit so that I can seek what I might be able to be in the world. If I hadn't spent all those years in therapy, in Reiki, in yoga, and in healing, I would've fucked it up or burned it down.

AC: What do you think people don't understand about astrology, or get wrong most often?

CN: I think that people want it to tell them what they want it to tell them.

AC: And they're not prepared when it doesn't.

CN: Right? [Laughs] I have friends that ask, "Well, what does my chart say?" and I'll tell them, and to me it's like, "That's so you" and they'll be like, "That's my life purpose." It's so deep and profound and people want it to be this big fancy thing.

Sometimes when I look at a chart, I'll see an event that happened in someone's life and it'll be so intricately woven into the purpose of their life, but it might be like a really difficult event, and oftentimes it is. But how that event shapes us, what we do with it, how we work with whatever—that's so much of the time our purpose. Of course there's the career trajectory and the family and all that stuff, but it usually goes back to the central theme that we're trying to work out for our life. So it's not very fancy often, but it's a portal into something that, if worked with, meditated on, leads to everything else. People want to be told that they're Cleopatra in a past life, you know? All these fancy things.

AC: It's a type of self-rejection that they're engaged in. They do want that. Hoping for glory isn't the same as hoping to learn about yourself.

CN: And It's not the same as leading a meaningful life. I'm very Jewish in that kind of way. I'm like, OK, there's a lot of suffering, so where's the healing? How might we derive meaning from the things in which we feel so bitter and are so burdensome and are such a struggle. Also, where are my gifts? And where is that grace in the chart that says, "Maybe you don't even deserve this, but here you go." You know there's a goddess of fortune—Fortuna—and she comes along, like the Wheel of Fortune, and you know, no one deserves it, but all of a sudden we're graced with something, blessed with something. We can blow it or we can use it.

AC: My experience as a teacher is that the gifted student doesn't always value the gift. And that's always their trajectory. Part of why they don't value it is that it allows them to do something easily that other people have to struggle for. So they'll go off looking for something that they can struggle with, because they think the struggle is the value and they don't even understand what it would be to struggle with a gift.

CN: Right? To struggle with what it is we have, instead of wanting something different. I mean that's, like, the bottom line of every horoscope I've ever written. It's . . . you're stuck with yourself, you might as well love it [laughs]. This is it, you're going through it. How can you be in a relationship with it?

AC: Which, I'm realizing, is the title of your new book. So what was the inspiration for the book? Was it just, this is the thing that I need to tell all of you . . .

CN: [Laughs] Listen! Stop fucking asking me these questions. I don't know, buy the book! It was publishers that started to ask about "the book," and I thought, I guess there's a book. I had a lot of stuff happening, and I feel like it's a kind of exorcism, you know you compile a bunch of something and then you have to put it somewhere, structured, so I feel like I need to do that: put it on paper and I feel like I can get on with my life. It's a thing that wants to happen, so I said, *Yes. It's happening.*

AC: So it sounds like you were approached about the possibility of writing a book and you thought, *I'm going to write a book, this is the book*.

CN: Yeah. I had a different book in mind and I thought, *Well, there's a million astrology books; they've already been written.* And the publisher said, "We don't have one in your voice. It's the reason why I'm coming to you." So I'm writing a book for non-astrologers about traditional astrology. I think I'm that bridge. The people I study with, I learn from, they are very intense academics that are putting together very dense material that's incredible and takes me a long time to get through, and my teacher's like this, too: She's able to translate that in a digestible way.

I wanted to put together a book about how your chart tells you your life purpose, and if you follow these simple guidelines you'll get there. You won't get there immediately, but if you work with it and have a relationship with it, it will unfold and you will be affirmed by all of your hopes in your heart. Your entire life experience is here in this map in the sky. God knows why it works, but it does.

AC: I think that's a great place to end. Thank you! I cannot wait.

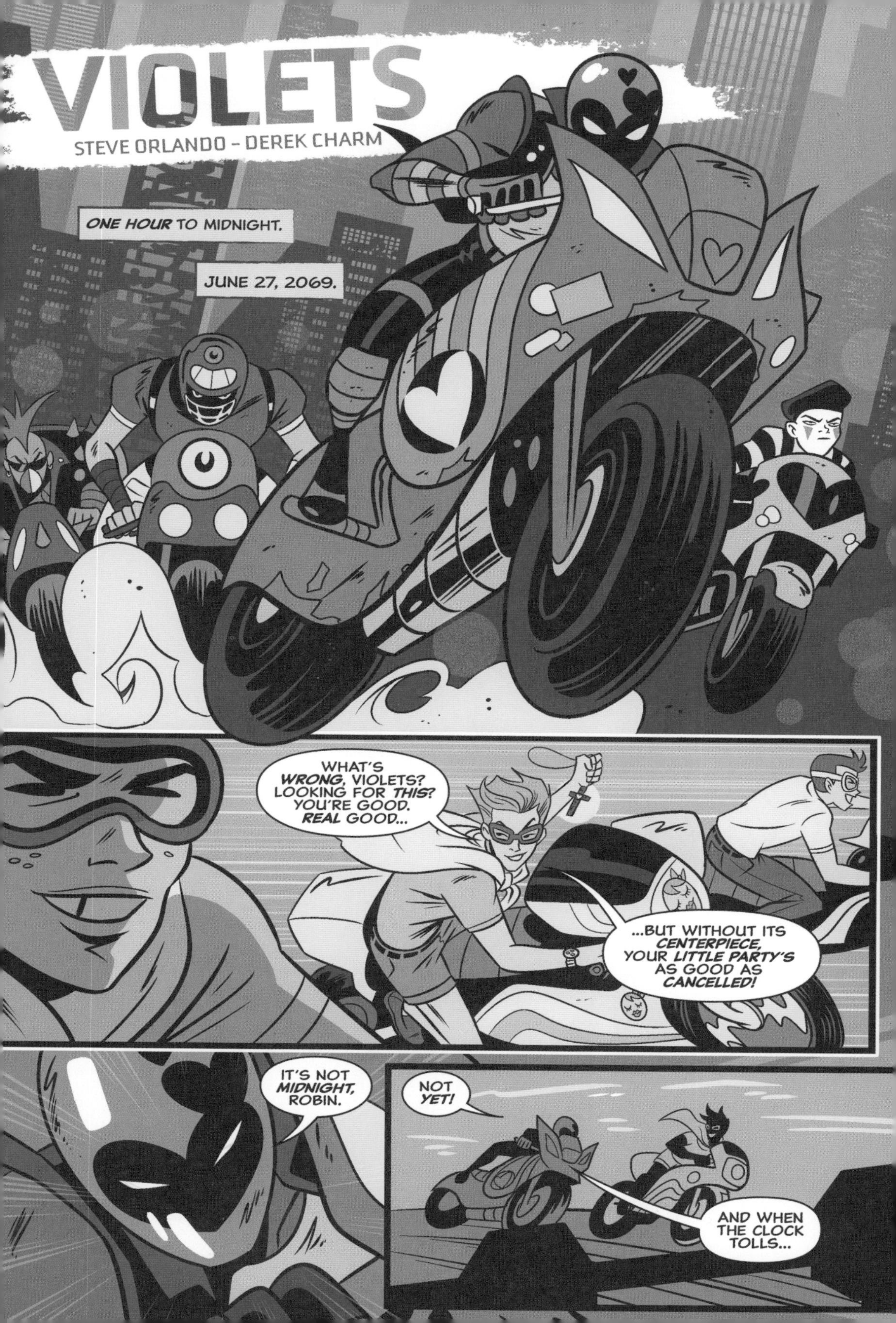
VIOLETS
STEVE ORLANDO - DEREK CHARM
ONE HOUR TO MIDNIGHT.
JUNE 27, 2069.
WHAT'S WRONG, VIOLETS? LOOKING FOR THIS? YOU'RE GOOD. REAL GOOD...
...BUT WITHOUT ITS CENTERPIECE, YOUR LITTLE PARTY'S AS GOOD AS CANCELLED!
IT'S NOT MIDNIGHT, ROBIN.
NOT YET!
AND WHEN THE CLOCK TOLLS...

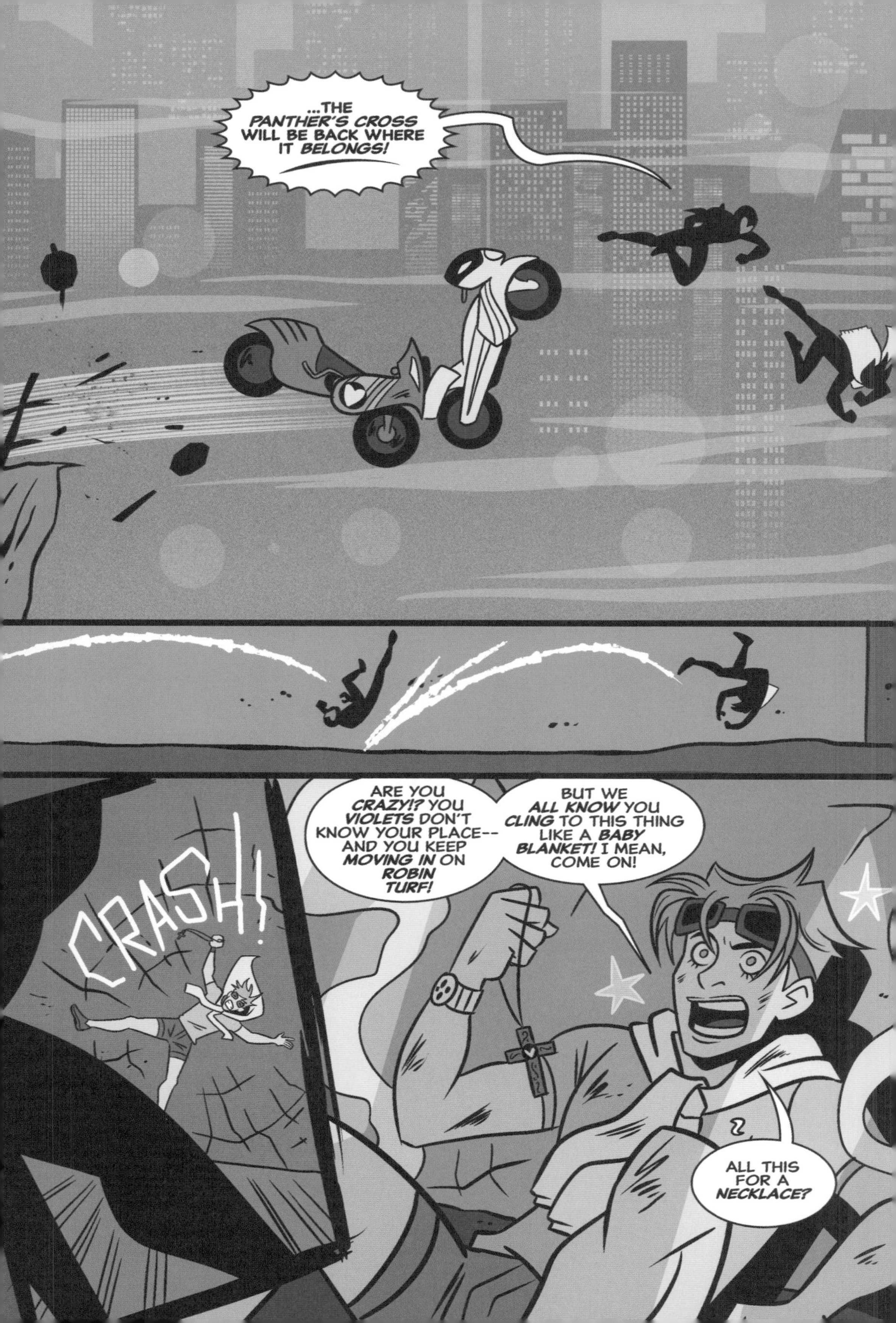
...THE PANTHER'S CROSS WILL BE BACK WHERE IT BELONGS!
CRASH!
ARE YOU CRAZY!? YOU VIOLETS DON'T KNOW YOUR PLACE-- AND YOU KEEP MOVING IN ON ROBIN TURF!
BUT WE ALL KNOW YOU CLING TO THIS THING LIKE A BABY BLANKET! I MEAN, COME ON!
ALL THIS FOR A NECKLACE?

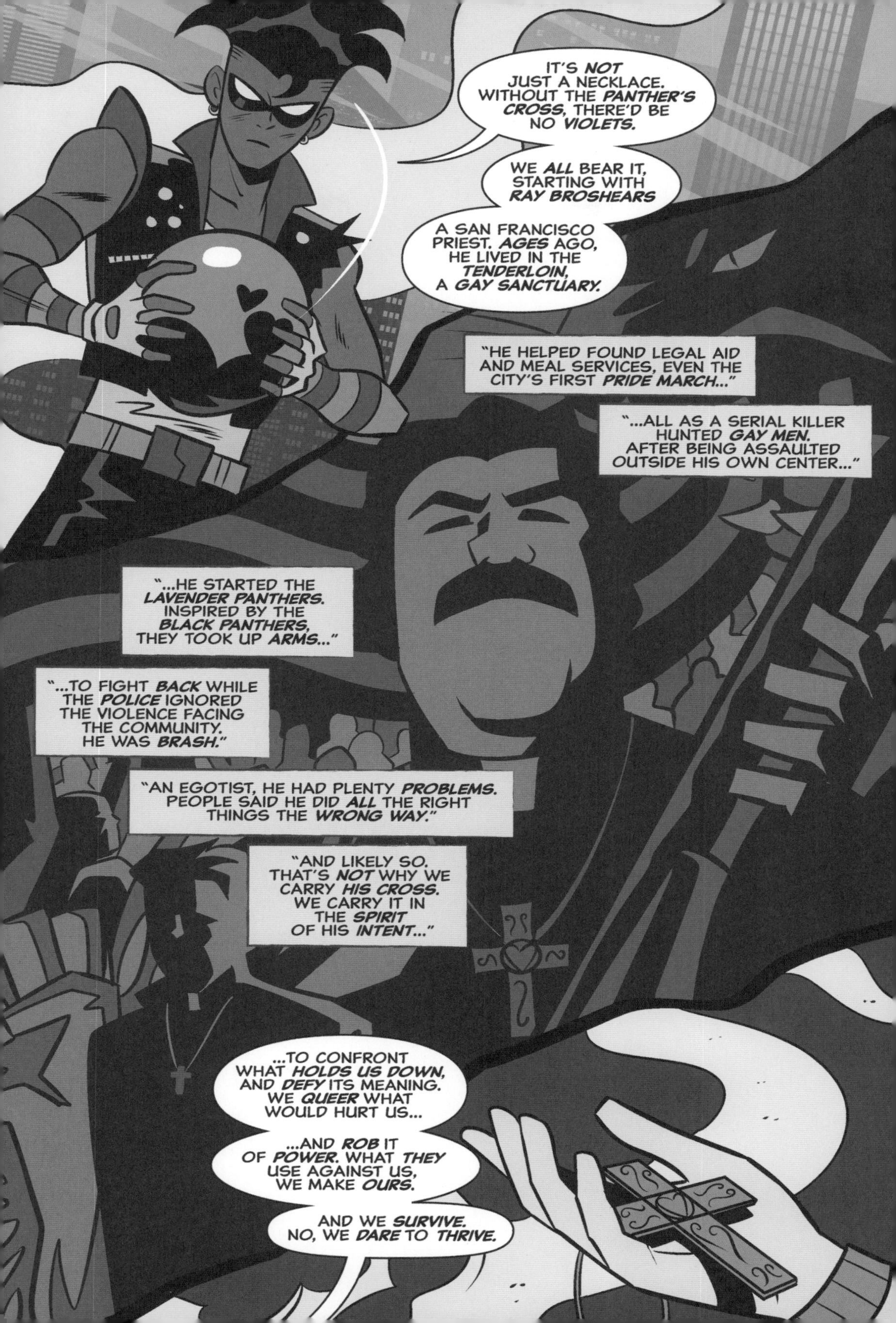
IT'S NOT JUST A NECKLACE. WITHOUT THE PANTHER'S CROSS, THERE'D BE NO VIOLETS.
WE ALL BEAR IT, STARTING WITH RAY BROSHEARS
A SAN FRANCISCO PRIEST. AGES AGO, HE LIVED IN THE TENDERLOIN, A GAY SANCTUARY.
"HE HELPED FOUND LEGAL AID AND MEAL SERVICES, EVEN THE CITY'S FIRST PRIDE MARCH..."
"...ALL AS A SERIAL KILLER HUNTED GAY MEN. AFTER BEING ASSAULTED OUTSIDE HIS OWN CENTER..."
"...HE STARTED THE LAVENDER PANTHERS. INSPIRED BY THE BLACK PANTHERS, THEY TOOK UP ARMS..."
"...TO FIGHT BACK WHILE THE POLICE IGNORED THE VIOLENCE FACING THE COMMUNITY. HE WAS BRASH."
"AN EGOTIST, HE HAD PLENTY PROBLEMS. PEOPLE SAID HE DID ALL THE RIGHT THINGS THE WRONG WAY."
"AND LIKELY SO. THAT'S NOT WHY WE CARRY HIS CROSS. WE CARRY IT IN THE SPIRIT OF HIS INTENT..."
...TO CONFRONT WHAT HOLDS US DOWN, AND DEFY ITS MEANING. WE QUEER WHAT WOULD HURT US...
...AND ROB IT OF POWER. WHAT THEY USE AGAINST US, WE MAKE OURS.
AND WE SURVIVE. NO, WE DARE TO THRIVE.

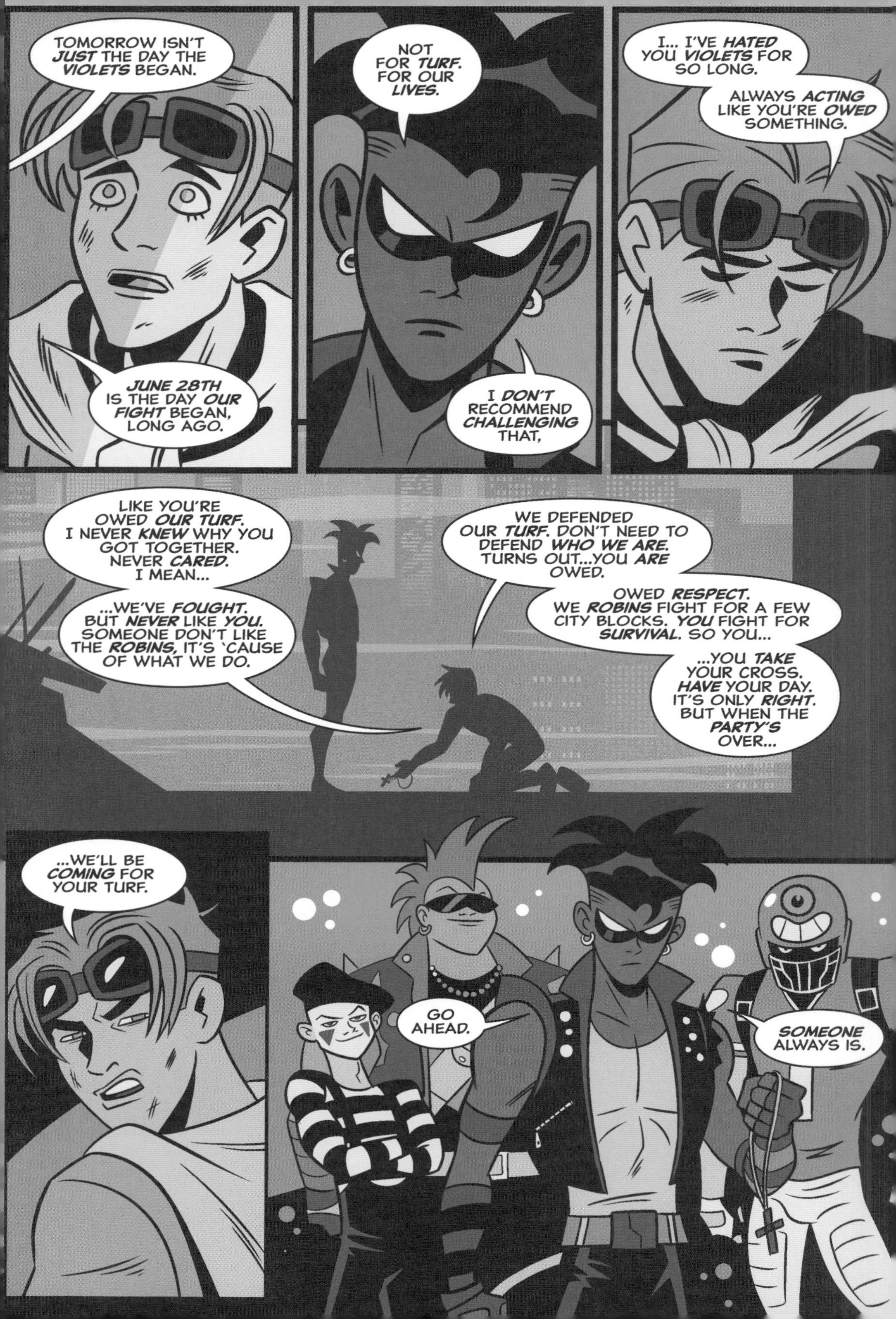

TOMORROW ISN'T JUST THE DAY THE VIOLETS BEGAN.
JUNE 28TH IS THE DAY OUR FIGHT BEGAN, LONG AGO.
NOT FOR TURF. FOR OUR LIVES.
I DON'T RECOMMEND CHALLENGING THAT,
I... I'VE HATED YOU VIOLETS FOR SO LONG.
ALWAYS ACTING LIKE YOU'RE OWED SOMETHING.
LIKE YOU'RE OWED OUR TURF. I NEVER KNEW WHY YOU GOT TOGETHER. NEVER CARED. I MEAN...
...WE'VE FOUGHT. BUT NEVER LIKE YOU. SOMEONE DON'T LIKE THE ROBINS, IT'S 'CAUSE OF WHAT WE DO.
WE DEFENDED OUR TURF. DON'T NEED TO DEFEND WHO WE ARE. TURNS OUT...YOU ARE OWED.
OWED RESPECT. WE ROBINS FIGHT FOR A FEW CITY BLOCKS. YOU FIGHT FOR SURVIVAL. SO YOU...
...YOU TAKE YOUR CROSS. HAVE YOUR DAY. IT'S ONLY RIGHT. BUT WHEN THE PARTY'S OVER...
...WE'LL BE COMING FOR YOUR TURF.
GO AHEAD.
SOMEONE ALWAYS IS.

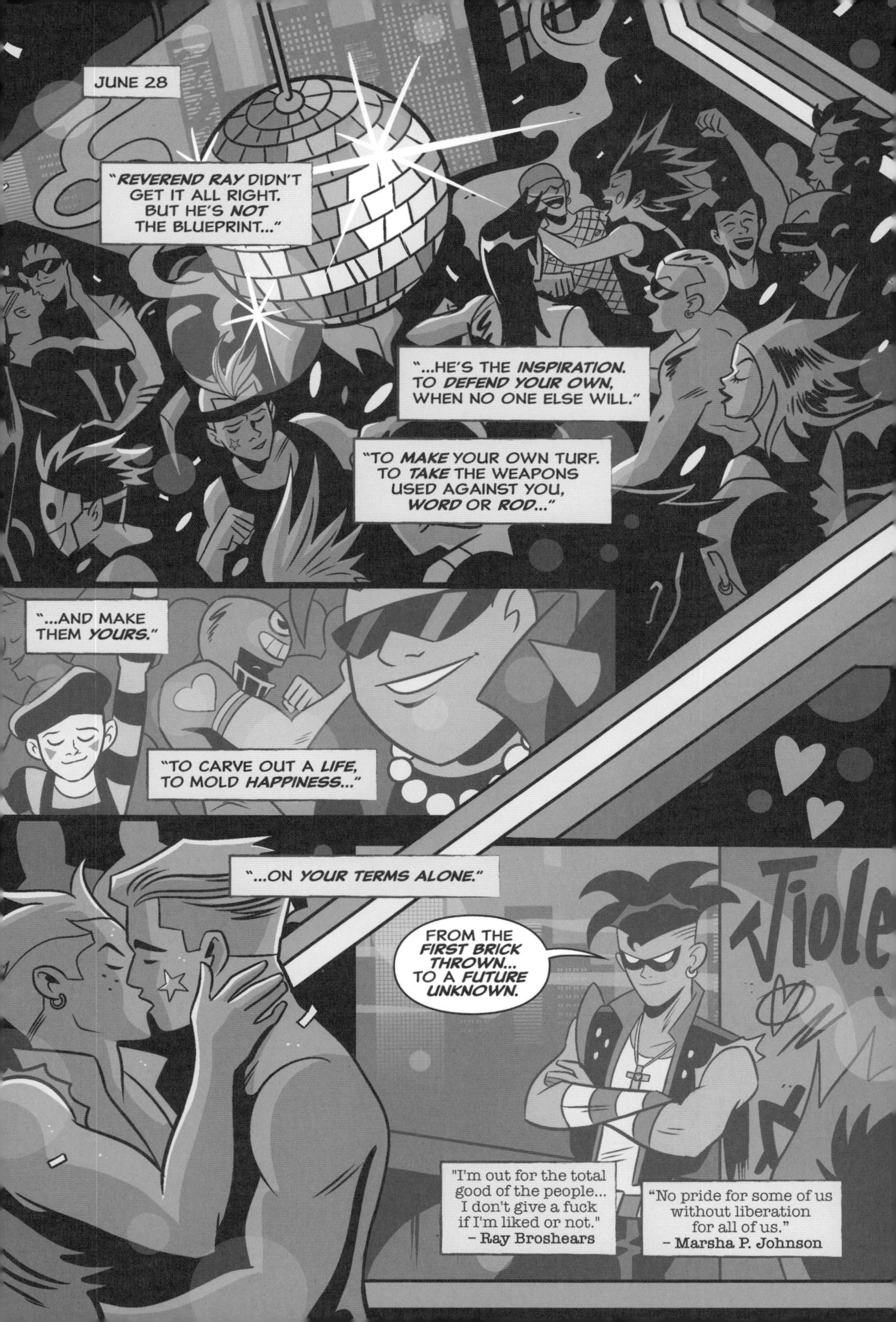

JUNE 28
"REVEREND RAY DIDN'T GET IT ALL RIGHT. BUT HE'S NOT THE BLUEPRINT..."
"...HE'S THE INSPIRATION. TO DEFEND YOUR OWN, WHEN NO ONE ELSE WILL."
"TO MAKE YOUR OWN TURF. TO TAKE THE WEAPONS USED AGAINST YOU, WORD OR ROD..."
"...AND MAKE THEM YOURS."
"TO CARVE OUT A LIFE, TO MOLD HAPPINESS..."
"...ON YOUR TERMS ALONE."
FROM THE FIRST BRICK THROWN... TO A FUTURE UNKNOWN.
"I'm out for the total good of the people... I don't give a fuck if I'm liked or not." – Ray Broshears
"No pride for some of us without liberation for all of us." – Marsha P. Johnson

Just Be Cool

Matthew Harris

Art by Lie Dirkx

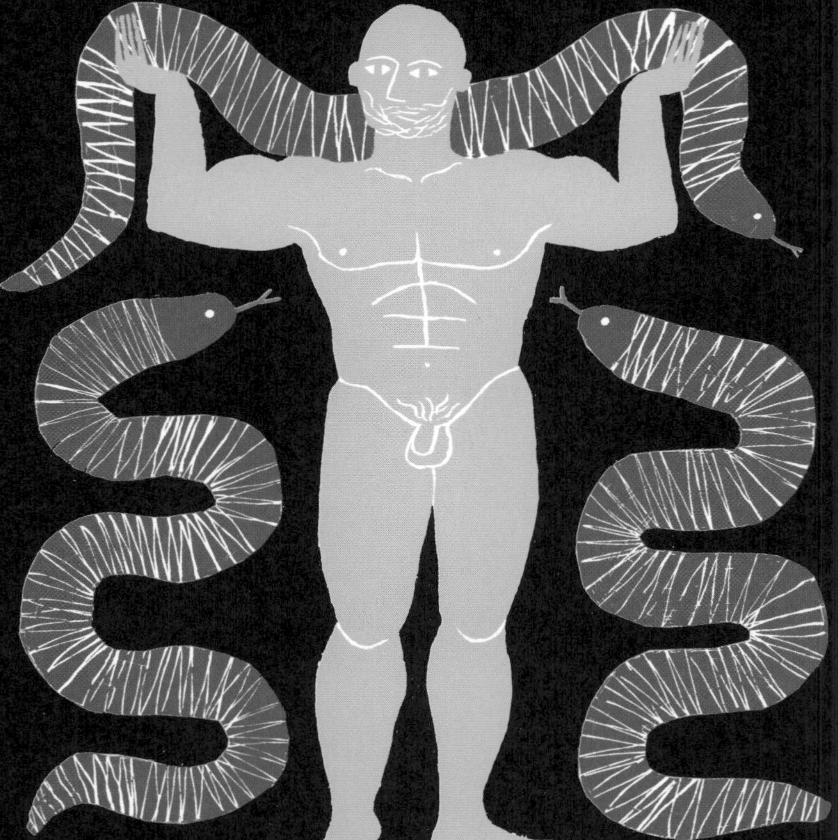

Randy Hunt had snakes.

Randy Hunt wasn't his real name—it was his name on Gmail. But I only realized it was fake after we slept together a couple of times. He told me his real name, but I forgot it. We usually just called each other *you*. "You and You"—I believe this was Shakespeare's original title for *Romeo and Juliet*.

After we had sex, he'd tell me about his work, his parents, his snakes. Or, about losing them.

"I was at Pride," he said. He'd gone to a club on Church Street to show off his sixteen-foot python. The boys passed around his snake while buying him shooters. It is very hard to tell this story and not make it sound like I'm talking about his penis.

After an hour, Randy drunkenly stumbled down the bar's steps. "My first clue that something was wrong was when I noticed my shoulders were weirdly . . . light." Back at the bar, the muscle queen bartenders were clutching each other. They pointed behind the counter. Amid boxes of empty bottles, there was the python, coiled up like a thick yellow lasso.

Our snake chats were thanks to Craigslist. This was back when I was too poor to have a phone with Grindr on it. I was incapable of Grinding—I could only do some Craiging. I had also just come out of a long-term obsession with this guy Adam.

Adam was basically my teen dream. He was mysterious, well-dressed, and had a raging coke problem. I'd read his Facebook status updates as if I were close-reading a Shakespearean monologue. I ached to figure out why he'd posted, "It's really hot out." (Was it code? It didn't feel that hot. Was he actually telling everyone that he was really hot for me?) I guess my frenzy showed because after a few of my more gushy messages, I finally got a genuine, heartfelt response. I don't remember the other five hundred incredibly pleasant words of his email, but I do remember the line, "Matthew, I'm sorry. I never said that I liked you."

After Adam, I resolved to be cool. Cool guys were always busy looking fit, feeling bored, and sampling awesome boners. They didn't worry about something as uncool as having their feelings hurt. (I guessed—I was basing all of this off porn.)

That's how New Matthew often found himself Craiging after getting very drunk at bars. With enough alcohol to forget that I looked like a rumpled muppet, I'd mash out ads for guys. They were usually short and filthy—the ads, not the men. Well, not *always*. My main focus was that the guy was nearby. There was a drunkenness countdown: after twenty minutes, drunken Cinderella would go from refreshing herself at the Craigslist ball to collapsing into a snoring pumpkin.

One of these nights, Randy contacted me. His photos were cute—suspiciously so. I was a thirty-year-old graybeard who was too embarrassed to send shirtless photos. He was an adorable, dolphin-like twink—you could probably roll marbles down his cum gutters. What was his story?

That first time Randy came over, he brought only one Smirnoff Ice—for himself. He was also so drunk that he kept apologizing as we kissed. I practiced my new laissez-faire attitude while dodging his breath, "Don't worry about it. That's totally cool."

In bed he lay perfectly still, like an antique landmine, waiting and hoping I'd figure out how to make him go off. His body was fantastic, as porpoise-like in real life as in his photos, and despite his planking style of lovemaking, I could tell he was largely happy to be there. I set to work and got the job done. Randy sighed, lispily. As I finished myself off, I thought, *I might be in love.*

At no point during this first encounter had Randy voluntarily touched me, but I didn't see that as getting in the way of our eventual marriage. There was something magical about this cool new habit of not revealing my feelings. My whirligig of emotions could go spazzing about my head, and it didn't have to knock our fuck-buddy relationship off track. This was a revelation! I was freed from a lot of worry. I could love a guy and not give a fig what he thought about me. Who needed reciprocation? *Vive l'amour!*

Even if he didn't love me, Randy must have liked something, because he returned every so often with his bottle of Smirnoff Ice. After some sex, he'd usually tell me more about his snakes.

He had lost his yellow python again, but this time in his apartment. "Snakes are smart—smarter than people," he told me. He had looked behind the TV, under his bed, everywhere you'd look for a sixteen-foot python in a four hundred-square-foot apartment. Randy was terrified she had escaped his building and would soon swallow some nearby child. "Then, the other day, I reached down for the TV remote, and I felt something scaly." We were so close in the dark, I could almost hear his heart rapidly beating. "I can't even tell you how happy I was!"

"I'm glad you found your snake," I said, slightly terrified that, in his drunken stupor, he might have lost a snake in my apartment. "I'm sure she missed you."

I could hear Randy grinning in the dark.

"You know what?" he said. "Why don't we go on a real date?"

That's how we found ourselves in a Vietnamese restaurant under cafeteria-strength lighting while steaming bowls of broth and noodles whisked by our shoulders. The first half of the meal was charmingly awkward—almost as if we had never had sex. I ordered pho, and he ate vermicelli. I asked him more details about his family and their snakes in Niagara Falls. He was from a family of snake charmers. (His were the biggest, obviously.) He looked bored whenever I spoke about work.

After dinner, we ordered beer. When the waitress dropped our bottles off, Randy said, "Oh yeah, it's no big deal. But I should tell you. I've been arrested."

"Oh?" I said. This was it. The strongest test yet of my newfound chillness. I couldn't let genuine alarm and fear mess everything up. I slid a metaphorical pair of Ray-Bans onto my face. "That's interesting." I sipped.

He smirked as he told me the story. He said his relationship with his ex-boyfriend had been rocky. One night, they got into a fight and his boyfriend called the police. Randy was arrested for assault. He was only in jail for a few days, but when he got out, their shared apartment had been cleared out. While the charges were dropped, Randy was left without money and possessions.

"One of the first things I saved up for after my arrest were my snakes," he said, now actually laughing. "I love them."

I was speechless. He was playing with his coaster, spinning it on the table. I grabbed his hand. How do you console the arrested? *I hope you aren't mistakenly brutalized by the police again?*

Instead, I blurted: "I really like you, Randy."

He pulled his hand away to drink the rest of his beer. "We should probably go, Matthew," he said. He dropped some twenties for the bill. "I have to work tomorrow."

"Yeah." I nodded, not even really thinking thoughts. "Got to buy more snakes!"

We kissed goodnight on the street corner, and his lips were even cooler than usual. On the streetcar home, I tried to type out something non-crazy to text to him, something to erase my words. Unfortunately, humanity has not yet discovered a way to do this. Nor did I text him the next day or the next week. Over-emotional Matthew had scared another one away. I tried to forget about our date.

Occasionally on GChat, I would see his name pop up with a green dot next to it. I would think about typing him a question, "Why was my liking you such a dealbreaker?"

But as the weeks without our hookups went by, I wondered if I had gotten him wrong. I imagined losing all of my possessions because of the person I loved. And how personal this story might be, and how telling someone about it might be a huge gamble. You might want your story to excite the person hearing it, to make them angry and upset, to make them *feel* something.

I was trusted with a secret. Randy wanted to make a connection. And what had I offered this person who had gone to jail over his lover? A bland "I like you," and a name that was not his name.

I was only trying to protect myself. I can't think of a more cold-blooded thing to do.

ORIGINALLY PUBLISHED IN *HELLO MR.* ISSUE 06 IN 2015.

Selected Poems from *The Walt Whitman Reader*: An English-to-English Translation

Paul Legault

One's Self I Sing

I'm into myself, but so am I.

As I Ponder d in Silence

My favorite thing about war is the men in it.

In Cabin d Ships at Sea

I want to be read, slowly, on a boat, by the sailors of the future.

To Foreign Lands

My name's Walt Whitman, but you can call me America.

To the Garden the World

Gardens should be designed to have sex in them.

To a Historian

The future of history is the future. In the future, what I'm doing now is historical. In the future, pay attention to what I did do. Always pay attention to what I'm doing in the future. Thanks.

To Thee Old Cause

I feel like dying for a good cause. Who's yours?
My ideal man is a sexy ghost.

Beginners

How they are the first ones. How they love it that way.
How it fucks them up. How love is how.

For Him I Sing

Shout-out to my boo.

To a Certain Cantatrice

You can have all of the birthday presents I was going to give to those dying soldiers, because you are Beyoncé.

I Hear America Singing

One of my superpowers is the ability to hear the soundtracks to other people's lives. I can hear all of the background music of America's mechanics, carpenters, masons, boatmen, shoemakers, deckhands, woodcutters, and ploughboys. My favorites are the ones from when they're having gay sex with each other.

Me Imperturbe

I want to be as ready for the world as an animal. Luckily, I am one.

Savantism

I want to always be like—wait, wait. I got this. Don't worry. I got this.

Shut Not Your Doors

Every library should be a 24-hour library, with my book in it.

To You

Why shouldn't we talk to strangers? Hey, you.

Starting from Paumanok

Look at me now, Mama Paumanok. I can see you reading me. I'm looking at you, everyone. Have I told you how much I like locomotives, yet? Life gets me hard. Life can be very hard. Don't be an idiot when you are young, or know that's all you'll ever do. Wrestle with me naked and maybe I'll bless you. Look. It's just the two of us now. Hurry up and reach out and touch me.

Thou Reader

Reader, I can tell you're turned on, because I am too.

Song of Myself

"If you don't love yourself, how in the hell you gonna love somebody else? Can I get an amen?" —RuPaul

ORIGINALLY PUBLISHED IN *HELLO MR.* ISSUE 07 IN 2016.

The Mother, the Son, and the Holy Spirit

Dany Salvatierra

Art by Matheus de Simone

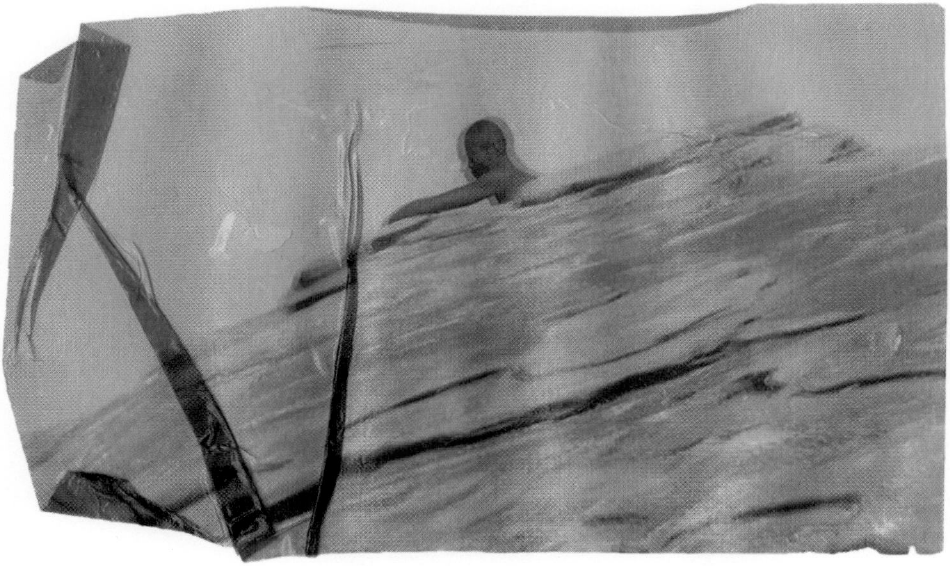

There is no one to greet me at the airport. I drag my broken suitcase through the international arrivals area and exit the terminal, still buried beneath my gigantic coat. The Florida climate strikes me like Satan's bathhouse, forcing me to strip my outer clothing, the remains of a South American winter I'd left behind. The other exiting passengers glare at me in silence, waiting for me to pull something out of my bag, possibly a bomb.

My head is pounding from the seven-hour flight from Lima and the extensive customs inspection. As the officer stuffs his gloved hands inside a pair of packed shoes, he asks what I do for a living. Instead of mentioning my usual day job, I reply that I am a writer to avoid the likely salary questions as advised by friends who had gone through the same ordeal.

Two hours later, following the commuter train ride, the local Metrorail, and two additional buses, I finally set foot at the corner of her apartment building. She lives in a predominantly Latino, residential area in the far suburbs south of Miami. The female busybodies glue their faces to the windows, examining the bearded muchachito traipsing through their parking lot with his wet hair plastered against his face, consumed by the early July humidity. I try to memorize their faces and even wave in case I run into them later, only because my mother, who knows every single family in the building, has already told them about me.

Her door is decorated with the King Jesus International Ministry official sticker, featuring a banner that reads: *Este es un hogar cristiano*. After three knocks, she finally opens the door, her bifocals balanced over her chest, attached to a silver chain, fresh from a recent Bible reading. She smiles politely but not warmly. Or not as warmly as I would hope given my recent odyssey. I can see a slight smirk indicating she's already starting to regret my visit.

"Hola, Hijo," she says.

Not *hijito* (my baby), not *mi amor*, not even *mi vida*.

"Hola, Mamá," I say.

Not *mami*, not *mamita*, not even *ma*.

She holds the door open, displaying her bright red and perfectly manicured nails. I pause for a moment before taking the initiative and give her a small kiss on the cheek. She smiles again politely and steps aside to let me in.

No kissing back, no pat on the shoulder, not even a hug.

I set my suitcase in the living room by the couch, my makeshift bed for the next four days. While still standing, I feel her eyes burning on my back. I close my eyes and hear in Spanish.

"That shirt is too tight on you."

I'm too exhausted for a counterattack and use one of my prepared phrases for this very topic, which always happens the first day of any visit with her. "I need a shower."

"That's good, because my friends are about to arrive at any minute."

"What friends?"

"Just some friends from the temple. We've prepared a little welcome party for you. Nothing big, but wear something that meets my approval."

Whether the first lies were to herself or to her church friends, I don't know.

The party news is not as shocking as the fact that she refers to her church as a "temple" (*templo*), which makes me think of a cult conducting elaborate ceremonies in the Everglades. As she steps into the kitchen without asking about my trip, I open my suitcase and find the outfit I'm forced to bring for these situations: a plain, light blue short-sleeved shirt and a pair of oversized Old Navy jeans she bought for me two years ago. I lock myself in the bathroom and undress, taking note of the various objects next to her sink. These belongings from her former self include perfume bottles from two decades ago, night creams, an amusing liquid soap container shaped as a transparent high heel with quartz stones. All traces of the life she abandoned in Lima more than fourteen years ago when she divorced my father, moved to Miami, and left everything and everyone behind. The only little inconvenience was that she, on top of it all, found the Lord.

It wasn't that I was a nonbeliever. She raised me as a Catholic and taught me how to say my nighttime prayers, although at the time of my First Communion she was more worried about her dress than shedding any tears as I received the holy wafer. Her faith matured and accelerated when she settled in Miami by herself, working as a caregiver in a posh Coral Gables hospital and grieving over my father's estrangement as she watched her patients die. Over time she was slowly led into the "temple" by the other nurses with whom she worked during long, overnight shifts. Some months later she started questioning my lifestyle, my clothes, and my physique, and when she failed to pass on her rediscovered faith to me, she started lying. Whether the first lies were to herself or to her church friends, I don't know.

I can't blame her for the constant meddling of her social circle. It's inevitable that an independent lady will have inquiries about the anonymous young man whose portraits and newspaper interview clippings are displayed on her living room walls. Especially if that fellow has no recorded history of chasing women, flirting with secretaries, or false paternity claims. My mother will summarize their doubts in a single sentence, "Oh, I'm sure he's dating someone, but he is way too focused on his work." And when her friends claim that a single male over thirty with no children should be living with his mother as God intends, she responds, "Oh, he travels so much that he can't settle down anywhere, but I'm sure he'll buy us a bigger apartment once he lands a book deal with a major publishing house here in America." Her story has stayed remarkably consistent over the years, so much so that I wonder if she's truly come to believe it herself. Occasionally, interviewers ask me where I got my talents for storytelling, and I have to tell them from my mother's side.

I come out of the bathroom wearing my ill-fitting clothes, yawning from my relaxing fifteen minutes under the warm shower and longing for an extended nap, when suddenly the doorbell rings. My mother runs toward me to conduct a final inspection on my appearance, commenting on how beards are only worn by "homeless and homosexuals." I fire back citing a selection of bearded Hollywood actors and she responds, her neck red with anger, "But they're fit, muscled, and masculine. You're too skinny, and you don't look masculine at all."

The door then opens to four well-coiffed ladies carrying a guayaba cake, a small plate of mini empanadas, and a box of chocotejas. I greet them with my best smile and wonder at the same time what I could do to get rid of all that food. My mother's colleagues are certainly more lively and colorful than she is. They wear high strap-on heels, white tight pants, and tons of jewelry, certainly very un-church-like for ladies on their "spread the Word and tell the Good News" mission. Two of them are named Úrsula and Amaranta, and when I try to joke about how those are also the names of two characters in García Márquez's *One Hundred Years of Solitude*, my mother informs me that those very ladies are just this moment working to ban that depraved novel from the local high school because it celebrates the unnatural love of an adult man with a thirteen-year-old girl.

As we sit in the living room, my mother brags about my writing career and "the girl I'm dating back in Lima." I smile wearily and look out the window, gazing at the salmon-colored buildings, palm trees, and the rest of the deep rain forest throughout the apartment complex. Amaranta mentions that I will probably dump my Peruvian girlfriend for one of those nice corn-fed American gringas. Suddenly they are discussing where the wedding will be held, and after half an hour of answering their inquiries with a head bow, I rise up and excuse myself, mentioning that I'm going to get some rest and that I need to edit a chapter of my manuscript by the next day. Úrsula is the first to hug me goodbye, taking my hands in between hers and saying that they are praying that I'll soon start writing for the Lord, and that my forthcoming novels will help readers around the globe prepare for the Second Coming. I don't have the heart to tell her that my manuscript is about a fugitive Peruvian terrorist who also happens to be a child molester.

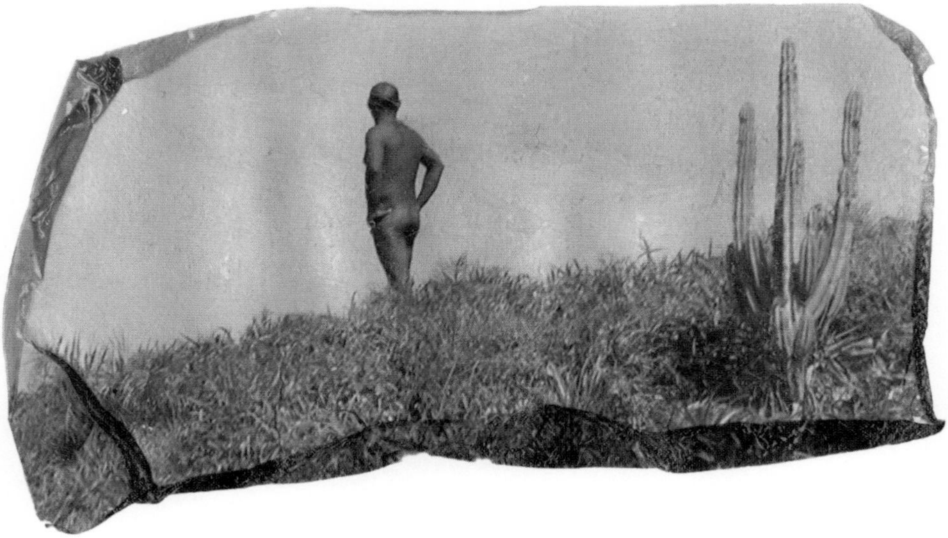

I retire to my mother's bedroom, clutching the remote as I search for prime-time Telemundo telenovelas, just as I did as a kid. Later that night, while mouthing heroine Kate del Castillo's dialogue, I hear the ladies chanting Bible verses in the living room, invoking Jesus's name and adopting spooky deep voices that don't sound like their normal cadence. *The Exorcist* instantly comes to mind. Why does this simple Christian ritual sound so sinister? Wasn't this supposed to take place deep in the Everglades instead of my mother's living room? For a moment I'm afraid they will try to kidnap me and send me to a gay conversion camp. But when sneaking out for the bathroom a bit later, I realize that, thank God, their worship is over. I find my mother sitting alone in the dim light, reading her Bible, munching over the remaining mini empanadas.

The heavy rain wakes me early the next morning. When it clears, I prepare for a day at the beach, packing books and a towel in a tote bag. My

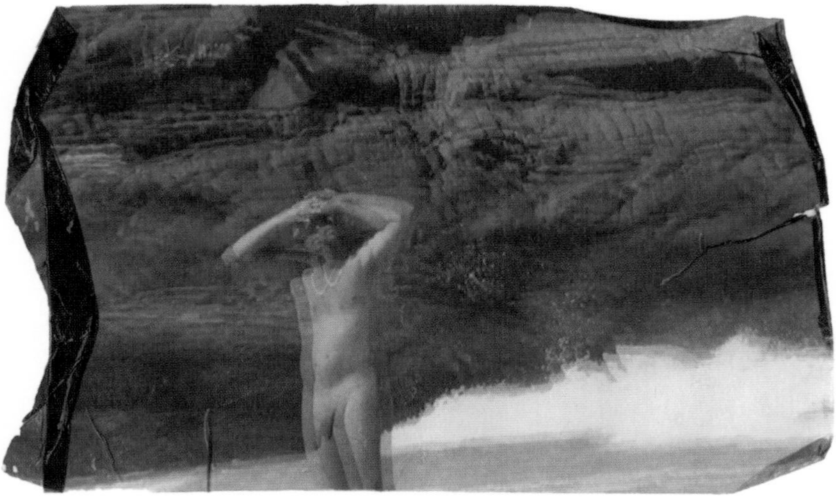

mother is already up and has even made breakfast for me, since she has to be at the hospital by nine. As I try to kiss her on the cheek, she extricates herself from me and stares blankly, in horror.

"Why are you wearing that tank top? I've told you: when you're under my roof, you're under my rules and under my control. And you're not leaving my house in those shorts. Would you please wear the normal clothes I bought for you? You can change later when you're away from my sight."

"Mamá, I'm thirty-four years old."

"That's no excuse. Can you imagine what the neighbors would say if they saw you?" she fires back, her eyes teary with remorse and authentic fear. "The last time they found out about your condition, I had to move out to avoid their constant gossiping. Nobody would even give me the time of the day. Now, several people from the temple live nearby." She dries her eyes with the back of her hand and immediately points a finger to the window, exasperated: "Do you want that to happen again? Don't you love me at least a bit? Please, do it for me."

I sigh, go to the bathroom to change my clothes, and leave the apartment stoned-faced, declining her offers to drive me to the train station. One of the biggest tragedies of my failed efforts at being a cosmopolitan globetrotter is that I never learned to drive, and in order to get to South Beach from Kendall I have to take two buses, then a local train, and then walk twenty minutes before reaching the gay beach on Sixteenth Street, an hour-and-a-half trip in the best of cases. The first bus drops me at Dadeland Mall where I change back into my summer clothes in the restroom and manage to buy some vodka that I mix inside a bottle of cranberry juice, Lima-style, to drink on the ride over. The booze lifts my spirits, and by the time I take the train to Government Center in downtown Miami, I'm tipsy enough to miss my connecting bus.

Once I get to Ocean Drive, I finish the remaining vodka and finally settle on the white sand beach near Sixteenth Street, unable to read any of the novels I brought. I try to relax, feeling good for the first time since I arrived in Florida, when I notice a handsome, long-haired, bearded guy sitting nearby who is giving me the eye. He's sitting with another good-looking friend, chatting and laughing as he throws the usual deep stare in my direction from time to time. A moment later, as I lose myself in the beautiful sight of the waves, I perceive the unmistakable scent of pot drifting over from my neighbors. Buoyed by the vodka still coursing through me, I leave my blanket and swiftly approach them. I mention that I'm going for a swim and ask if they don't mind watching out for my belongings. The one that keeps looking at me smiles broadly while exhaling a prodigious cloud of pot smoke and says, "Sure, no problem." A sparkle in his eyes gives me the sense of assurance I'm looking for, and I ask if I can have a toke. He laughs and almost chokes on the fumes.

"Please, go on" he says, his eyes always on mine.

"Gracias, *guapo*," I say after accepting the joint and confessing that I'm Peruvian, currently on vacation. They invite me to join them and immediately start asking where I'm staying. Already feeling a rush of exhilaration from the smoke and enjoying my newly acquired self-confidence, I scrap my initial plans to unburden my heart on these two handsome, stoned gentlemen. Instead, my lips part and out comes the story of a mother named after a European capital, who dyes her hair blonde and who's taken half a day off to drive me to the beach in her vintage 1967 Corvette.

The boys sitting next to me are all smiles and nods, and they offer me yet another toke. Suddenly everything becomes surreal, the three of us in Speedos, enjoying the sea breeze, and laughing about absolutely nothing. At the same time, I'm struck by the realization that my story was hardly any different than my mother's own fabrications. In fact, I had been describing the main character of my first novel, though before that moment I'd never made the connection.

After that, the hours pass quickly. At some point we hit the waves and later they tell me they're both students at the University of Miami together. They tell me UM's radio station is possibly the best in the country, a claim I've yet to assess but am inclined to believe. By five the stash is exhausted and they ask me to join them for sunset happy hour. I politely turn them down, saying that my mother is taking me to dinner at Gloria Estefan's restaurant to introduce me to her latest boyfriend, a recovered ex-Christian who might be the inspiration for a novel. Walking back to Collins Avenue, I write these ideas on my notepad knowing my latest lie could be a good pitch for future development.

That night my mother is astonished by my appetite (the inevitable *bajona*, as my friends call it). Over the coming days, I begin to informally study her daily routines, from home to hospital and hospital to church or weekly prayer meetings, and try to understand her motivations for putting a mask over my real life instead of being honest with those who know her. It's not easy being with a stranger I hardly recognize and who criticizes every move I make, even during mealtime. If I cut my steak too slowly she shouts that it's a shame that I'm not manly enough, and when I rise abruptly to excuse myself from the table, she hisses that I should do it more slowly because "the neighbors can hear."

I discover that she keeps a little shelf with all my books and everything I've published on her nightstand.

I discover that she keeps a little shelf with all my books and everything I've published on her nightstand. I grab a copy of my second book and find her King Jesus International Ministry cardboard bookmark on page 47. The page opens with a paragraph at the end of which there's a brief and educated mention of a blowjob, and I know that she's put an effort into reading the novel right until that point, where she doubtlessly decided it was too much for her, although it meant the world to me that she at least tried.

Aside from a second trip to South Beach, I fail in my efforts to find a used bookstore in Miami and end up at Barnes & Noble. I spend my remaining days lying on her couch, devouring tome after tome, until one night before bedtime my mother surprises me with a chaste kiss on the top of my head. "I love you," she says.

I'm prepared to say I find her words questionable. *You don't love me*, I'd like to say, *you love an idea of me, you love the image of someone you want me to be, but you don't love me.* That's what I want her to hear. Isn't the Lord supposed to be all about love?

Instead, I turn a page on the book I was reading and recite, without looking at her, "I love you, too."

On the last night, she cries. She claims that during my short stay she has gotten accustomed to my presence, and that she likes seeing me on the couch when she arrives home from the hospital. But she still won't take me to the airport, even to the Miami airport, admitting that she can't drive at night due to the cataracts starting to develop in her eyes. Instead, she's hired one of her church friends to drive me to the airport, a gesture I tell her I appreciate, and I do. Still, I don't have the heart to tell that I'm flying from Miami to New York that night to see my editor, and I don't tell her that my journey back to Lima will bring me back to Miami, where I'll be spending several days with a friend. This visit has reached its end, and I don't want to see her again until the next one.

Her friend honks from the parking lot at 5:30 A.M. sharp. My mother hugs me, still wearing her nightgown and slippers and her hair messy from sleep. In my mind I think about all those school trips that started similarly, back when she was a different woman who didn't cry but simply told me to be careful, over and over. This time, my mother cries because she knows she's wrong. Because she has to live two different lives, for me and for the church. That sacrifice, in the tradition of the Hispanic self-punishment-based upbringing, is a cross she'll carry until she decides to accept me in full. A fact that I (yes) pray will happen before it's too late.

ORIGINALLY PUBLISHED IN *HELLO MR.* ISSUE 06 IN 2015

She hugs me one more time and stifles her sobs with a tissue. Inside the car, her church friend is watching us and she silently sobs too, probably imagining how painful it is for us to be apart. I try to imagine how Telemundo could shoot this scene as it is and consider all the income I'm missing out on from screenwriting.

My mother doesn't tell me to be careful. She says, "Don't forget to put your life in the hands of King Jesus," and waves goodbye. The lady who drives me to the airport, whose name I'd forgotten because it wasn't Úrsula or Amaranta, comments on how hard my absence will be for my mother. I know she's right, in a way. My mother keeps sight of us as we exit to North Kendall Drive, and I'm sure she would remain there, staring at the highway, with her eyes fixed not on the image, but on the real me that is now gone.

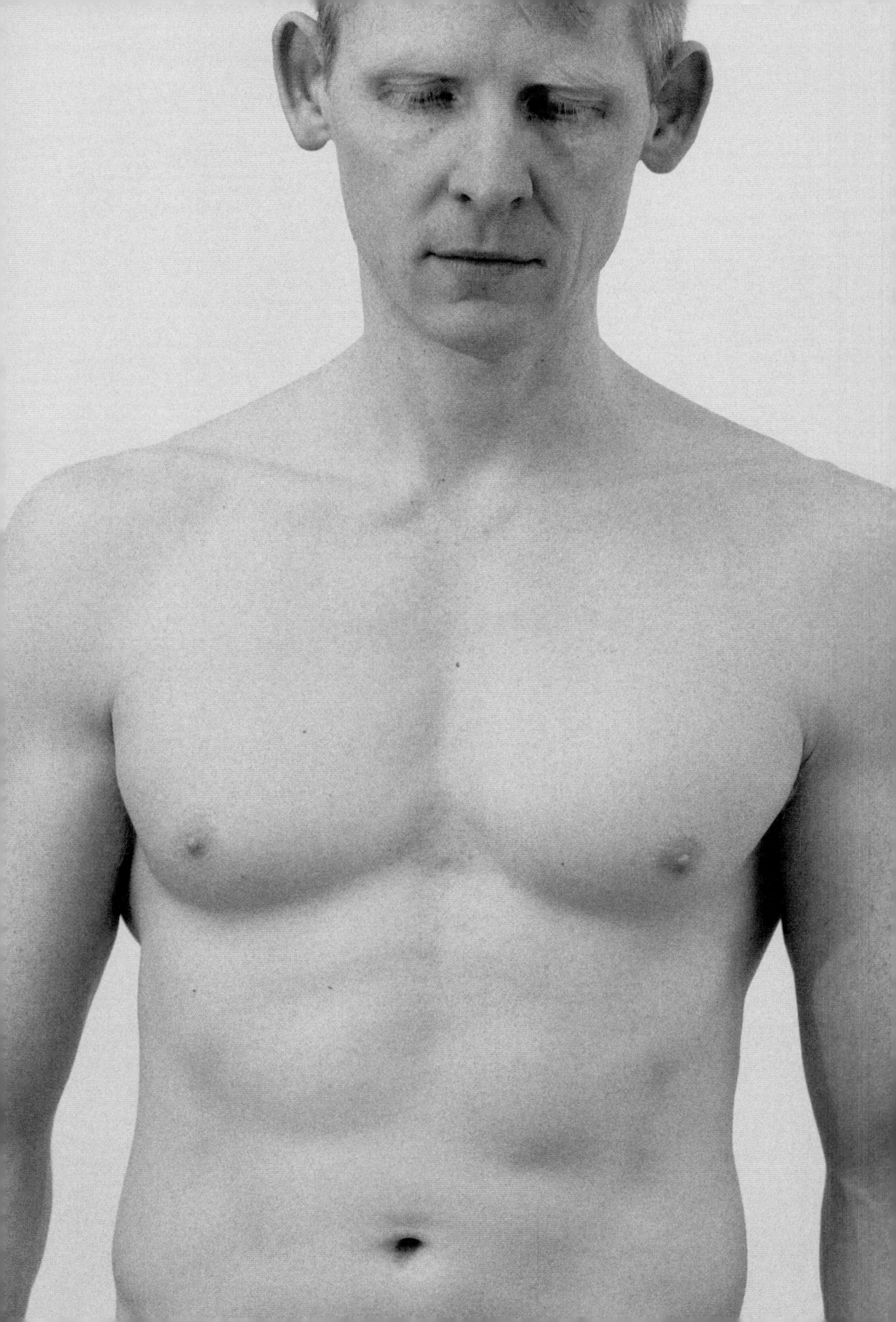

Screen Test

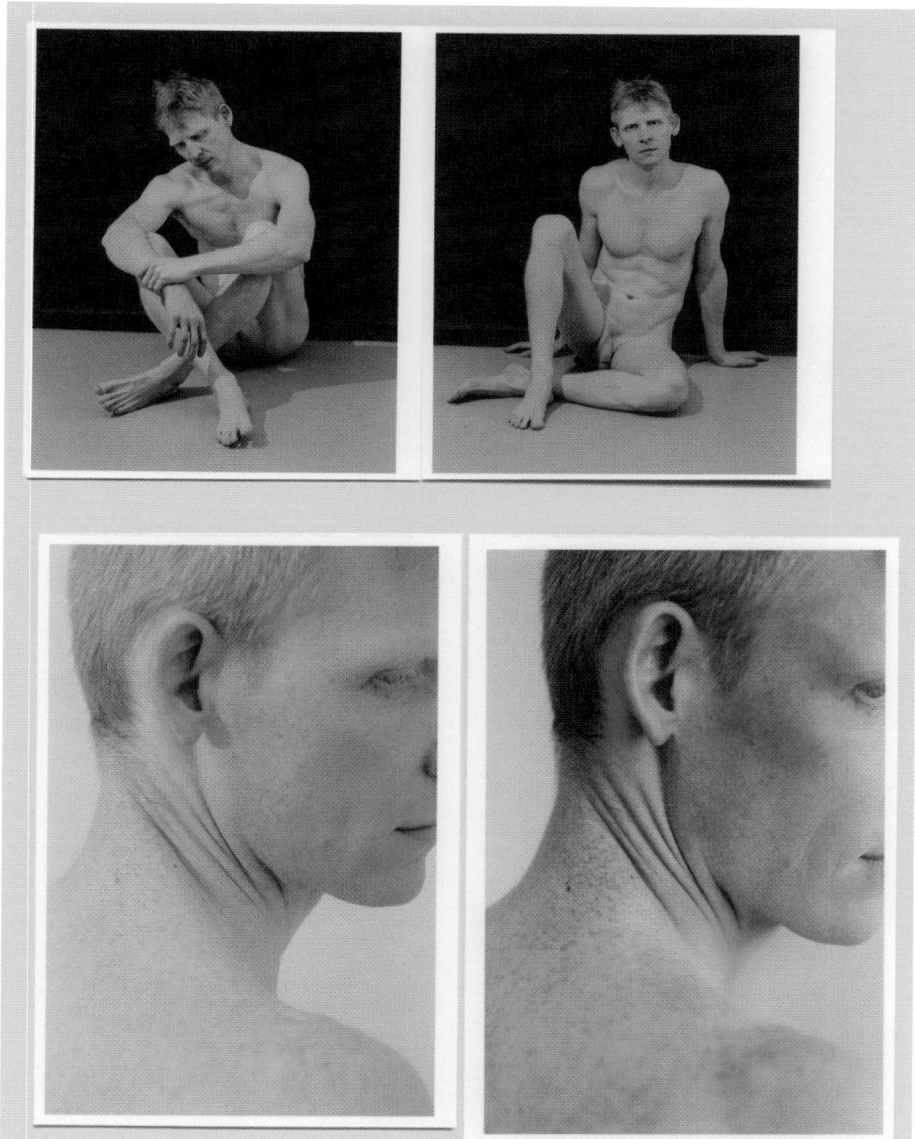

Photos by Daniel Shea

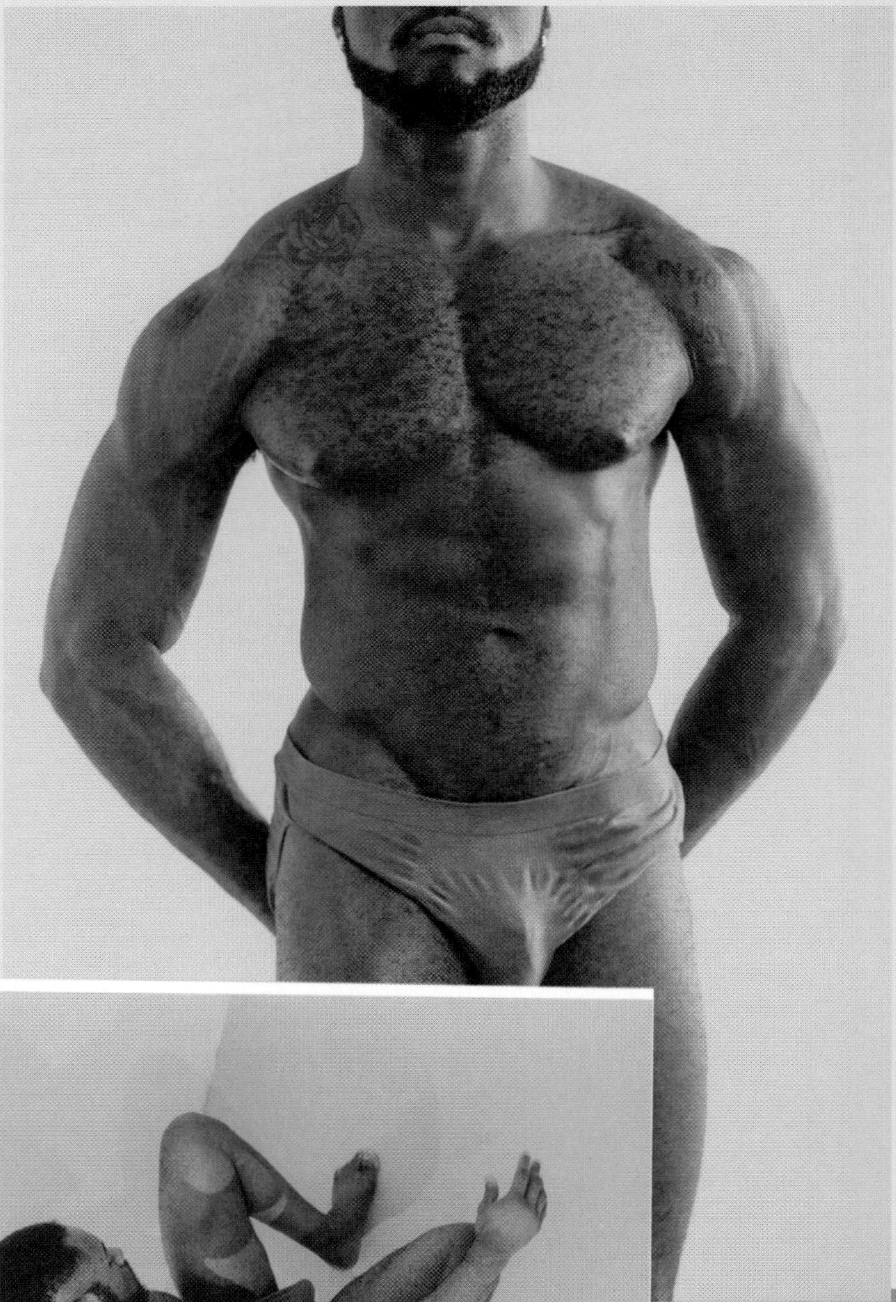

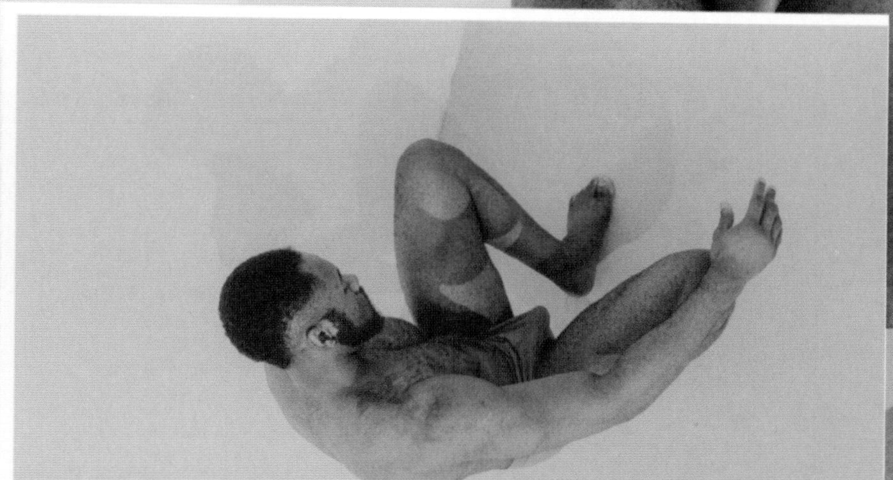

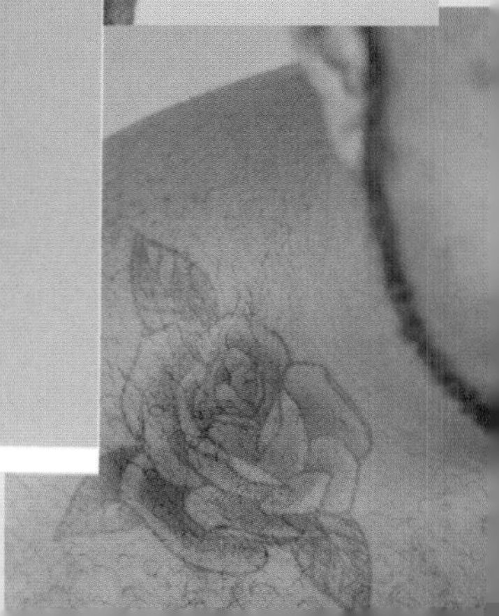

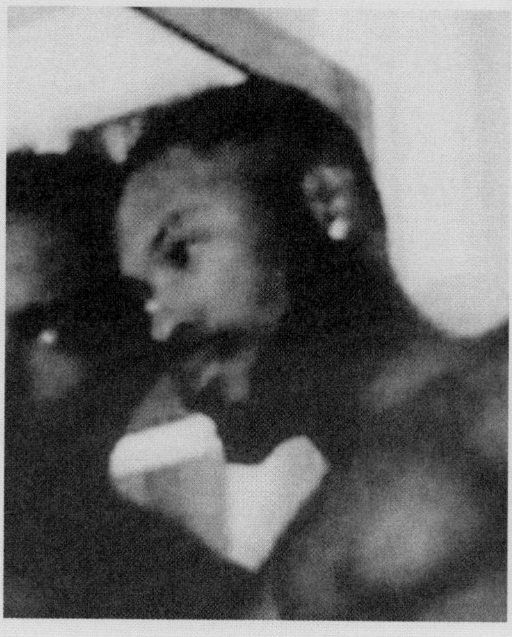

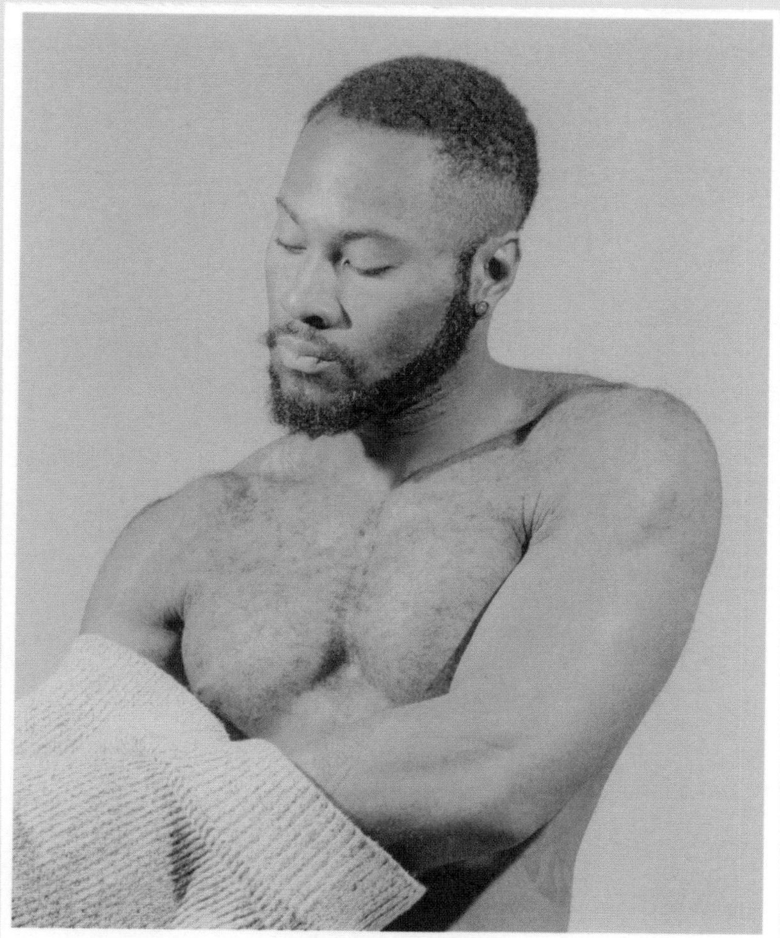

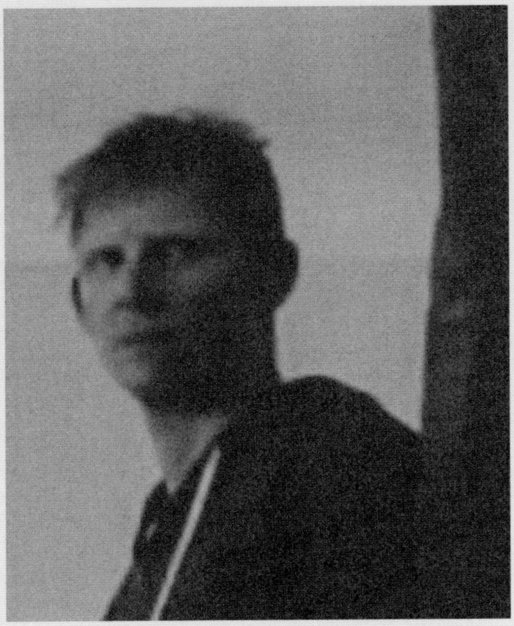

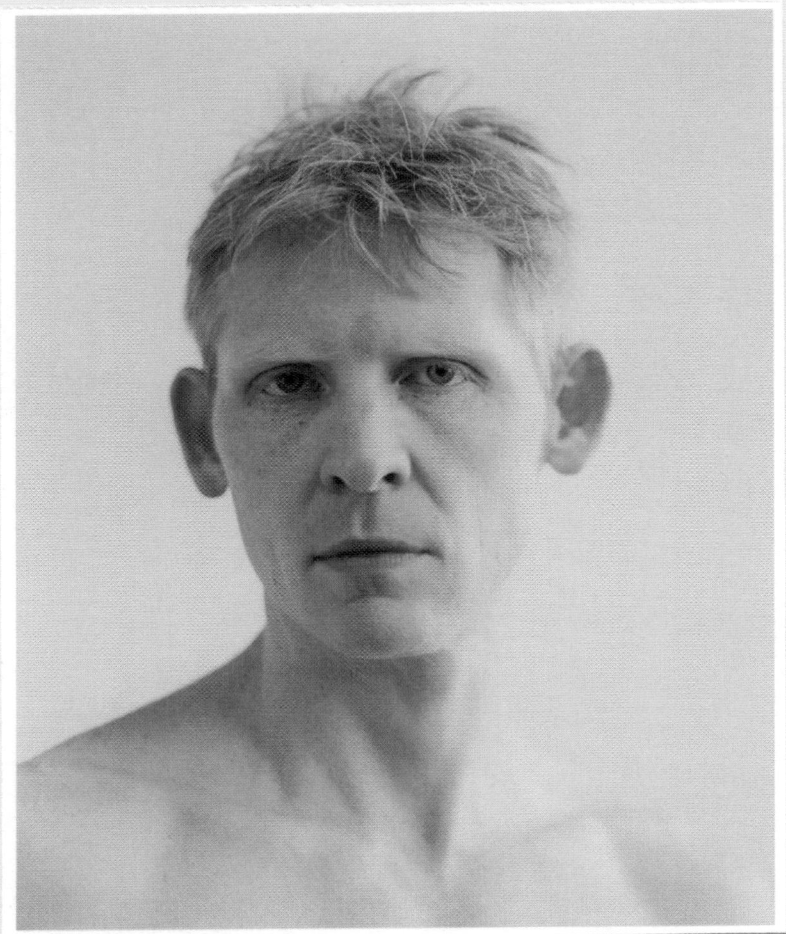

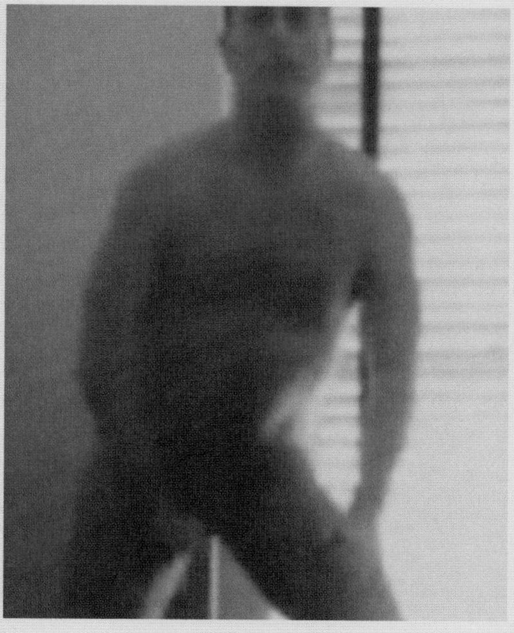

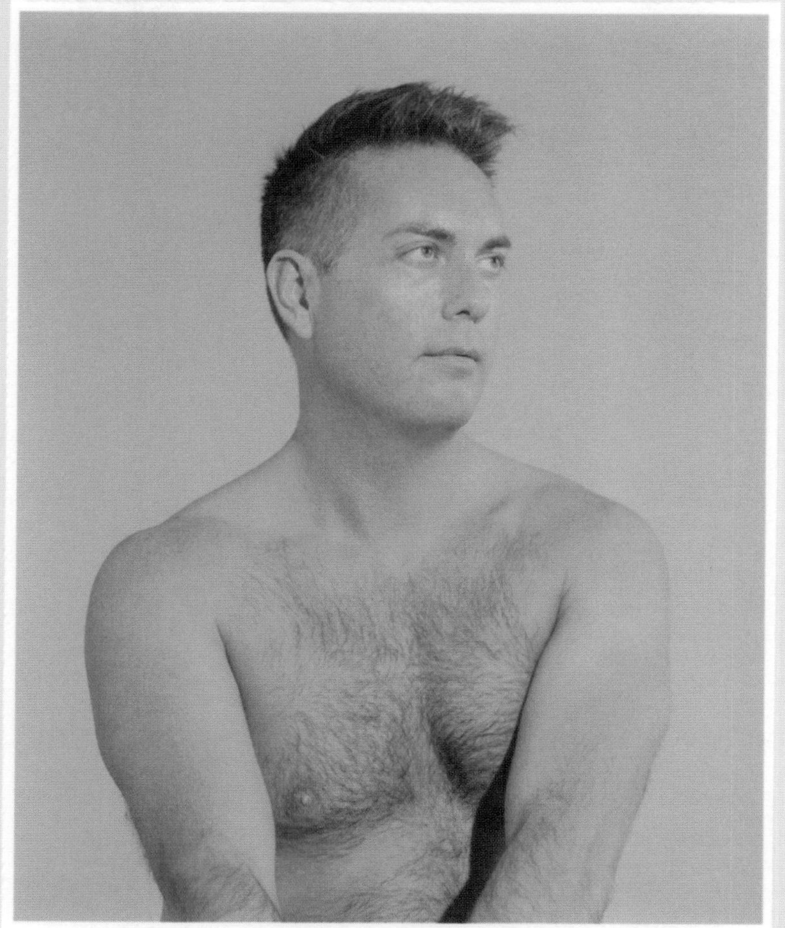

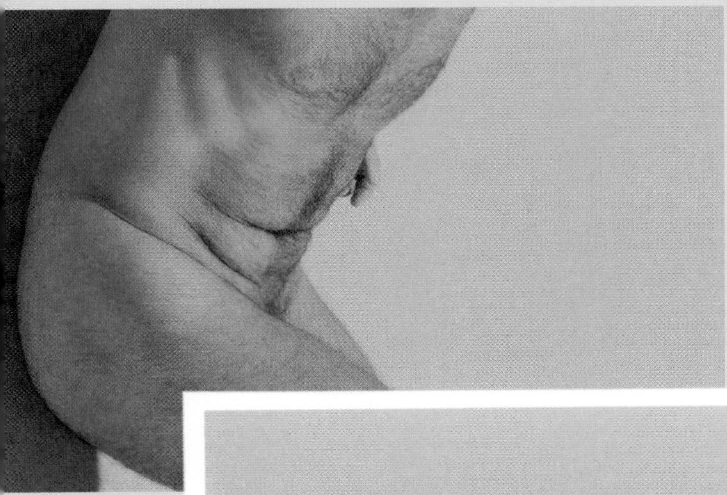
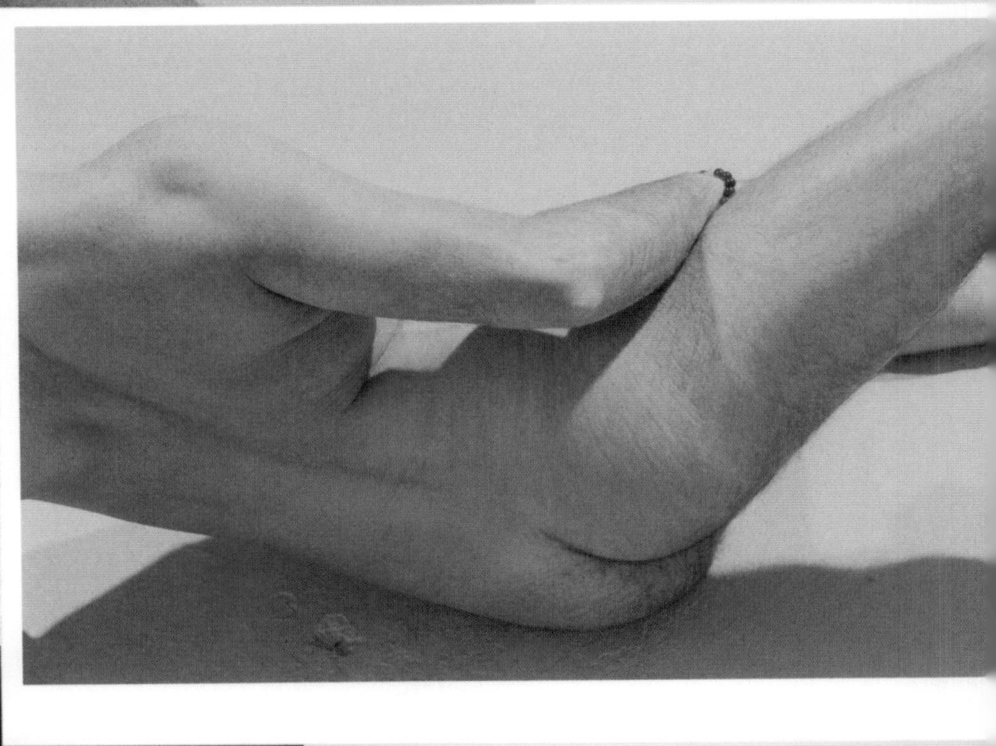
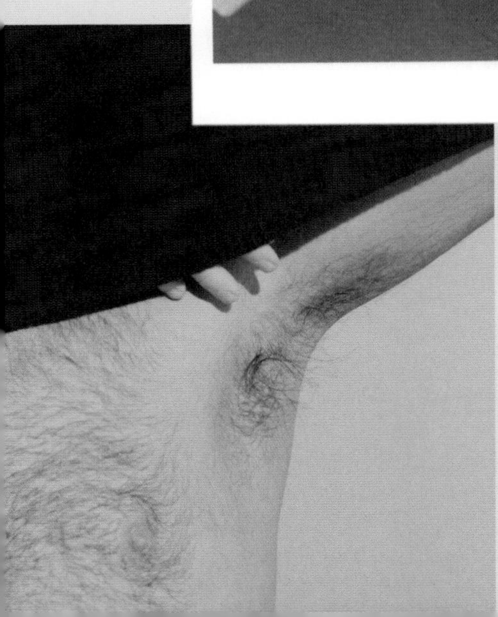

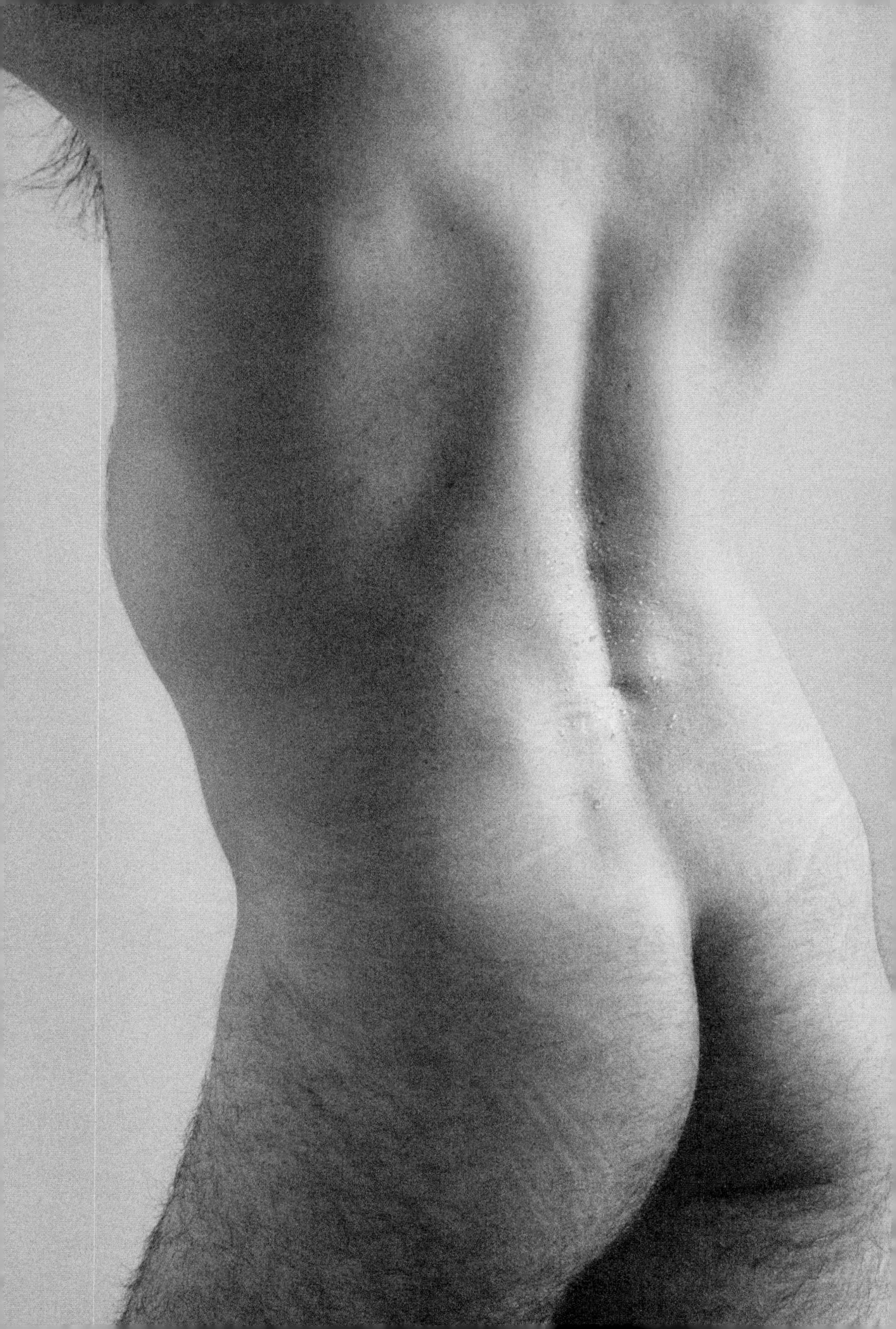

SAYING HELLO TO NEW QUEER VOICES

Colby Anderson in Conversation with Yezmin Villarreal

In 2017, Issues, a zine-in-residence initiative started by *Hello Mr.*, transported Colby Anderson and Yezmin Villarreal's visions for a queer alternative publication from an idea into a possibility. *BRUNCH CLUB*, Colby Anderson's publication, exclusively highlights trans and queer people of color. *Dyke Queen*, Yezmin Villarreal's project, is a magazine about QTPOC literature, style, and art.

This twelve-week residency for creatives looking to develop a queer magazine concept provided support from editorial to event planning, with mentorship from media industry professionals. Each resident's completed publication was distributed exclusively as an insert in *Hello Mr.*

As queer people, we're often tasked with trying to survive the present moment, and we don't always have the capacity to imagine a queer future for ourselves. Issues was a portal into the future, where the legacy of *Hello Mr.* will continue to live on.

Dyke Queen and *BRUNCH CLUB* editors/creators indulged in a phone chat to discuss the residency, queer zines, and why queer community is a vital and nourishing force of life.

COLBY ANDERSON: *BRUNCH CLUB* was launched in 2017 from me reaching out to [*Hello Mr.* founder] Ryan [Fitzgibbon] for advice, wanting to know more about the industry. Which led to the creation of *Dyke Queen*. The title has always screamed "confidence" to me. Where did the idea for *Dyke Queen* come from?

YEZMIN VILLARREAL: I moved to LA in 2014. I really wanted to break into journalism, and I actually wasn't out publicly. Nobody really knew that I was gay. I'm from Phoenix, Arizona, and when I moved to LA, part of me thought, Oh, if I move to Los Angeles, I can go be gay and free. My family won't know, people I grew up with won't know.

CA: Yeah, that's a similar reason as to why I moved to New York.

YV: One of the first gay stories I covered as a freelancer for *LA Weekly* was about Maricón Collective. They were a group of queer, Latinx creatives. They threw parties to create community for queer Latinx people. It was the coolest thing—I had never been around queer spaces at all before coming to LA, really. The funny thing is, when I interviewed queer subjects like Maricón Collective, they didn't have any idea I was gay. I'm pretty sure I said, "Oh, I'm just doing this because it's interesting."

CA: You said you weren't out. Were you just cosplaying a straight person?

YV: I was definitely ambiguous. I've always looked queer so people never asked, just assumed. I was never open about it, never said anything. I wrote a gay story, then more gay stories, and it led up to me applying for a job at the *Advocate*, arguably the most famous queer magazine in the world.

At the time I thought, *How hilarious would it be if I get hired at a gay magazine—and I'm not even out; my own family doesn't even know.* When I got the job, the company told me they were starting another publication called *Pride* and asked if I'd help launch their website, which of course I did. I told my family I got a job at a magazine, but no other details.

CA: They never asked?

YV: No. My family, my mom and my dad, aren't too comfortable speaking English. It was easy to obscure because they weren't looking for it, you know? Magazines, especially in English, were kind of a foreign thing. I was an editor at *Pride* for a while, then went back to the *Advocate* and was there during some significant times in queer history: marriage equality, Pulse, the Trump election. Around 2017, I got the idea for *Dyke Queen*.

I attended the LA Printed Matter Art Book Fair and was blown away, absolutely in heaven. But I was kind of disappointed that most everything queer was for gay men only. I was frustrated and thought, what about us? I wanted there to be cool art magazines for queer women. Some exist I know, but not as many. I pulled out my phone to write a reminder to myself in my notes app and wrote, *Dyke Queen—a dyke mag I wish existed*.

CA: We had the idea to create our publications in the same year. That's pretty cool.

YV: never heard the story, what gave you the idea for *BRUNCH CLUB*?

CA: I moved to New York in 2016 after college with just two suitcases and no job experience. I worked many temporary roles until I realized I wanted to create something that set me apart. Lots of queer people in New York do that: create passion projects that will help them get where they want to be.

I messaged Ryan, told him I admired his work. I wasn't expecting a reply! He invited us to his office and we talked about *BRUNCH CLUB* as more than just a lifestyle. He had started a residency that taught people about publishing. *BRUNCH CLUB* became the first zine-in-residence! We created it for queer people of color. Queer media had mostly been run by white gay men, and we wanted to find ourselves

Having these magazines allows us to give people opportunities to tell their stories and as a result, uplift many.

and our community within the landscape.

Sometimes *BRUNCH CLUB* doesn't get a ton of engagement, but a white queer account will get much more. It's hard to not pay attention to or care about that.

YV: Totally. It's all celebritized. It often feels like straight media props up queer people for their own entertainment, you know? Queer culture has become more mainstream, but also not.

CA: Definitely. It's usually the same familiar faces being promoted. Unfortunately, there is plenty of gatekeeping within queer media. We all love talking about community, but sometimes the queer community does not feel very communal.

YV: Yeah, that's what inspired me to start *Dyke Queen*. Wanting to shine a spotlight on all kinds of queer people of color, women of color—filmmakers, artists, all kinds of creators. There are few platforms that embrace QPOC artists without exploiting them—turning us into clickbait.

It's important to create spaces that exist outside of the white gaze. A space of beauty and respect; of opportunities for queer women, nonbinary people, and trans people to share their amazing work in community with each other.

CA: Agreed. Having these magazines allows us to give people opportunities to tell their stories and as a result, uplift many. Giving someone a chance to be a cover star, telling them they're important. It's similar to how Ryan gave me this opportunity. I like to invest that energy back.

YV: Yeah. It's cool putting an issue together, connecting all these people who maybe wouldn't have gotten a chance to collaborate in a publication, you know?

CA: Definitely. It's my favorite part of the process—finding creators and sparking conversations. Spending months creating and watching it come to life. Those collaborators become friends and feel like a community.

YV: Being a part of the *Hello Mr.* residency feels like family, so does *Dyke Queen* and *BRUNCH CLUB*. We are all building separately, but also together. I'm excited for us both to keep growing and see where it goes.

CA: Definitely. Zines have been around since the beginning of mainstream or public queerness. I read that Langston Hughes had a zine in the 1920s called *Fire*.

YV: Growing up, I didn't know anything about queer history. There were some queer courses at my college but I didn't take them. Really, I started learning about queer history for the first time through Instagram accounts such as @lgbt_history and @h_e_r_s_t_o_r_y.

Their feeds show an archive of queer people from the seventies to early 2000s. I fell in love with the photographs and zines they shared from back in the day. I used to look at their vintage images and think about all the queer people that came before us and how we still have a strong connection to the generations before us, even if it doesn't feel tangible. I felt their presence, but instead of looking towards the past, I wanted to show the queer present and document queer community as it's happening today. I thought, *Will it all be forgotten if we don't archive it in our own way?*

CA: I don't know where I would be without the connections I've made online. Had I met them sooner, I probably would have come out much earlier. When I moved to New York, it was the first time I'd ever witnessed people calling themselves "queer" and totally owning it. Being from small-town Texas, it was hard to own it. I do now.

YV: Yeah, online communities have been so important for the development of queer culture. What feedback about *BRUNCH CLUB* has moved or surprised you the most?

CA: I struggled with imposter syndrome. When we have magazine events, I feel really seen and also simultaneously surprised by the compliments. Trying to learn to accept love and let *BRUNCH CLUB* do exactly what it's supposed to do.

YV: Right? It reminds me of this quote by Eileen Myles. They say that when you put out creative work into the world, it becomes a magnet—drawing the right kind of people toward it. The people that need to find you, find you.

Will it all be forgotten if we don't archive it in our own way?

CA: That makes sense. Through *BRUNCH CLUB*, everyone I've met feels like they're meant to be in my life, or that I've known them forever.

How should queer people be supporting independent queer media?

YV: I think it's important to support each other—especially when you find a project that really aligns with your values personally. When we reach out to new people, we have no idea how our lives will be changed.

CA: Crazy to think that if I didn't reach out to Ryan, I wouldn't even know you!

YV: And I wouldn't be here either! Thank you, Colby. Independent queer media relies on community for support. If you find a publication you like, attend their events, buy their newest issue, reach out and ask if they need help. Or just like their page, share it with a friend, subscribe to their newsletter.

What's the hardest thing about keeping your platform alive?

CA: Having funds to create it all! Working a full-time job definitely teaches you time management. I find myself needing a lot of breaks, but the challenge is fun for me. During the week, I'm at my day job. On the weekend, it's *BRUNCH CLUB* time.

YV: It takes a lot of intensity to push through to completion. My passion for creating a publication for queer people of color is what motivates me on the hardest days when I don't feel like working. It's tough managing a full-time job with a passion project, but I think as long as you're taking care of your mental health, it's just the most amazing experience ever.

CA: Was there anything that you learned while creating *Dyke Queen* that surprised you?

YV: Creating the third issue was as equally rewarding as it was difficult. The pandemic was tough for everyone and caused the beginnings of many new chapters in our lives. I saw it as an important period to spend time on projects that truly energize me. I knew I needed to dive back into *Dyke Queen*.

During the pandemic, I left my queer bubble in LA and moved back to Arizona. When our issue was ready to go to print, I sent all our files to a local printer here in Phoenix, thinking I would have the issue right away. But, to my surprise, the printer came back and told me they were so offended that I thought they would publish our work that they refused us service. They said we had to find another printer because not only was "Dyke Queen," the title of our publication, offensive, but so was all the content inside the issue.

It was emotionally draining to have someone reject publishing our issue because of our LGBTQ content, but it also cost us time. Ultimately, we were able to publish the issue with another printer, and I was so happy once it was out, but it was a stark reminder that homophobia is alive and well.

CA: Is there something that you learned or would have done differently?

YV: I let myself be sad for an entire weekend, then moved on. The upset struck a chord with me because it felt like I was a teenager again, closeted and afraid of the rejection I would experience if I was fully my gay self. In this case, the rejection was real. What did I learn?

CA: Just be a bad bitch! That's what you learned. If your hometown is conservative, visiting home can feel really jarring—like you're being asked to lessen your queerness.

I also think it's been cool to build a connection with you and *BRUNCH CLUB*, too; we're like sister publications.

So, what's next for *Dyke Queen*?

YV: I love print, but I want to try something different. I've been experimenting with audio and the idea of starting a podcast of immersive, queer stories. I'm taking it one step at a time, since it's totally new to me. I don't know anything about the process!

Where is *BRUNCH CLUB* going, or where do you want it to go?

CA: People frequently ask this question and I have to be honest, I really don't know. At the end of the day, it's a fun project that created a community and enabled me to redistribute some of the funds I've made to amazing queer and trans organizations. Not knowing where a creative project is headed is totally fine. When I'm home for the holidays, that's when new ideas start brewing. I just want people to continue to feel seen.

I want to ask you about queer representation. Do you think it's equal and just right now?

YV: In the media? No. Just because there's representation doesn't mean there's been a significant cultural shift. You know? There are still mostly straight people everywhere I look.

CA: Totally. It's changed a lot since we were kids. I compare myself to Gen Z, the representation they have in media, for dressing however they want, etc. I think about how much happier I would have been.

YV: Yeah, when we were in high school there wasn't a lot for us to go on. I remember when Lindsey Lohan started dating Samantha Ronson. To me, that was *so* iconic. I'm happy for kids growing up in today's world—they have so much more than we did. When we were in high school, it was still *so* scary to be out.

CA: I remember being in middle school, watching *Queer as Folk* super close to the TV. Just in case my parents came into the room, I could change the channel without them noticing. There was still not much representation of queer people of color, though. Then *POSE* came out, but that was incredibly dark content. So, there's still not much representation of queer people of color who are happy.

YV: Right? We grew up with gay hate crime movies. All the gay people were dying. But when *Glee* came out, it was wild to see openly gay characters on TV. Now we have some queer representation with happy endings. Like *Carol*! One of the first lesbian movies with a happy ending, or at least that I know of. I loved it so much that I saw it five times in theaters.

Just because there's representation doesn't mean there's been a significant cultural shift.

CA: We need more happy endings. It's time to start writing other stories.

YV: What's some advice you have for queer creatives seeking motivation on taking the next steps in realizing their goals, or telling their story?

CA: Connect with people you look up to! Don't compare yourself to others. Everyone's different.

YV: Yeah, I would say, if you get a cool idea, run it by your people and get confirmation that what you're dreaming of is, in fact, really cool. Instead of getting all in your head about it. We need all ideas.

CA: Yes! Having a support system leads into another good question: how do you define community?

YV: Making others feel important, included, and invited.

CA: Yes. Community is being lifted up and held accountable; protected and mirrored. When friends know about your dreams, it's easier to be redirected when you move off course.

YV: With the current political climate, it's so important to protect one another and create spaces where queer people feel safe and understood.

CA: One last question. Is there a queer leader, writer, or someone you really look up to? It doesn't have to be a famous person. Could be a queer person in your close circle.

YV: So many people. It feels like there are millions. I'll think about it, you start.

CA: V, my co-editor from the last issue of *BRUNCH CLUB*, is an icon to me. I've learned so much from them: to be confident in my work, trans rights in general. They're a mentor and a very bright light to me.

YV: I love that! Okay, I thought of mine. Melissa Ramirez, who is a huge part of the *Dyke Queen* origin story. I met her, actually, because we both played for the same queer feminist basketball team in LA. Shout out to LAFABL.

CA: You're an athlete?!

YV: Yeah, I play basketball. I'm really obsessed with it.

CA: Oh, the more you know!

YV: When I moved to LA I thought she was the coolest person for running her own video zine project, *Stumble on Tapes*. She's Mexican and queer, like me. She's not that much older than me, but I looked up to her because of how she led a queer, creative life. Coming from a conservative Mexican family, I didn't meet a lot of people like Melissa. Seeing her live her life so passionately made me want to live out my dreams, too.

CA: That's really cute. I think it's cool that even as adults, as queer people, we are always somewhat going through a sort of puberty. Always growing and learning. We sometimes have experiences as adults that we should have had as teens.

HOW TO TALK TO STRANGERS

Bryan Washington

Be white.

If you're not white, be well-spoken. Enunciate. Have a bachelor's, a master's, an engineering degree in progress.

Spend the time you aren't using to pursue an engineering degree in record stores, bookstores, taquerias. Buy books regularly, but never at full price. Use the money you save on an online dating subscription.

Find a coffee shop in midtown. Walk there daily. Observe the occupants behind a novel you'll never read.

Tip well.

Spend the money you still haven't tipped with on more coffee. When the stranger across from you looks up from his *Wise Blood*, his *Fader*, his *One Hundred Years of Solitude*, run a hand over your brow. Keep the other one on your coffee.

Come back to this coffee shop daily, around the same time. Wait for the aforementioned stranger.

Learn little things about him.

Learn that he's attending the college up the road.

Learn that he treats himself to pastries on weekends.

Learn that he's familiar with the ginger barista, the one you haven't tipped, the one who fucks your name up. Imagine said ginger walking over to your table and asking for a synopsis of the book in your hands.

Learn that your stranger screens his calls.

Learn that your stranger's Spanish is poor.

Learn that your stranger is lactose intolerant, that he smokes Camel mints, that he is at least casually interested in Manchester United.

Spend your tipping money on streaming services. When the connection at your place breaks down—the way everyone's connection in your complex breaks down because the super knows his Latins and Blacks won't phone the boss to straighten it out—don't let it ruffle you. Wait an hour, maybe two.

Find poorly written romantic comedies and watch them on your laptop, in sweatpants, in the evenings.

Watch Jennifer Love Hewitt and Jennifer Lopez and Jennifer Lawrence fall in and out of love with dark-haired strangers. Note how similar they are to your stranger. Do not compare.

When your mother calls to ask about your extracurricular pursuits, your appropriation of her monthly allowance, your decision not to dabble in fluid dynamics, politely redirect the question.

When your mother asks why you haven't sent your sister, your father, your cousins across the border any money, politely redirect the question.

When your mother asks if you're seeing anyone, politely redirect the question.

When your mother insists on an answer, imagine what she'd think of your stranger, briefly.

Imagine you and your stranger at home—not home here, but home home. He's been there before. On a boat, with his parents. Exhaust the joke about how this is something you have in common.

Imagine the two of you walking downtown, a speck in the sea—except for once you aren't the speck, you aren't the thing in the picture that is not like the others.

Imagine him with your family at dinner, around a meal you grew up with, the type of meat your stranger's only seen on the Discovery Channel, at full speed. And when your stranger speaks to your mother, imagine him gurgling her name like mouthwash, the same way she gurgled his, and though neither of them know it, think that in this way they are the same. Imagine your sister sitting across the table, smiling amiably, stepping on your toes, and imagine your father—he's not at the table, he's out pulling fruit or driving a cab or screwing a neighbor or just standing behind the screen door, cheek in one hand, smoking a cigarette because what would he be doing sitting at the table with your stranger? You cannot even imagine it. It is unimaginable.

When your mother insists on an answer, politely redirect the question.

Cancel your online dating subscription. Pledge to keep it canceled for the rest of the year, the rest of the season, the rest of the month. Until next week.

Pledge to use the money on a latte for the stranger.

See yourself actually approaching the stranger. What you'd say. The face you'd wear.

See the stranger rejecting your latte.

See the stranger accepting your latte, only to choke on it.

See the stranger accepting your latte, only to burst into flames.

See the stranger accepting your latte, shaking your hand, smiling. He gurgles your name, but only the first time. You'll take his hand, or he'll take yours, and when he asks you out for dinner act like you're honestly considering saying no. And after dinner comes and goes, and you're lying on his sofa, under his body, over his mattress, think that it's all very nice, really. But don't get too attached.

Don't get too attached when his nose brushes your ear, negotiating the smoothie of your bodies.

Don't get too attached when he comes to your apartment, and he touches everything, asks where all of it's from, what it all means, and you have to tell him that sometimes things are just things and nothing else.

Don't get too attached when he introduces you to his friends, and their eyebrows always, always, always rise before they speak.

Don't get too attached when he asks about your sister, or when you visit his parents. Don't get attached as he sways to your music, orders your favorite drink at the bar, rubs your shoulders when you call your mother.

Don't get attached when he asks you what's wrong, and you don't know what it is, just what it feels like—like a shattered Christmas ornament in the center of your chest.

Spend the winter seeing these things. Imagining maybes. Dreaming them up.

Allow your stranger to remain strange. Try not to chastise yourself for it.

Watch the leaves fall, the sidewalk turn. Apply to the college up the road.

When your mother calls, screen it.

When your father calls, screen it.

When the college up the road calls you back to inform you that you're not eligible, hang up. Do not try again.

When your sister calls, answer. Tell her this country's so bright, so shiny. Tell her that you've applied to school. That she will love it here, that everyone in this country's in love.

Watch the election, watch the ball drop, watch Jennifer Lopez.

Tip, eventually, meagerly.

Google "JUNIOR COLLEGE DOWNTOWN CHEAP TUITION." Try again in lowercase.

Resubscribe to the online dating service, before unsubscribing, just to resubscribe again.

When you return to your coffee shop months later, on your lunch break, with an ear-marked textbook, and the stranger knocks on your table to ask if they've changed the Wi-Fi password, keep an expression that is both muted and all-knowing.

Smile.

Say you aren't sure. That you can find out.

When he thanks you, don't stutter.

When he gives you his name, breathe.

Shake his hand when he offers it.

Talk to the stranger.

ORIGINALLY PUBLISHED IN *HELLO MR.* ISSUE 06 IN 2015.

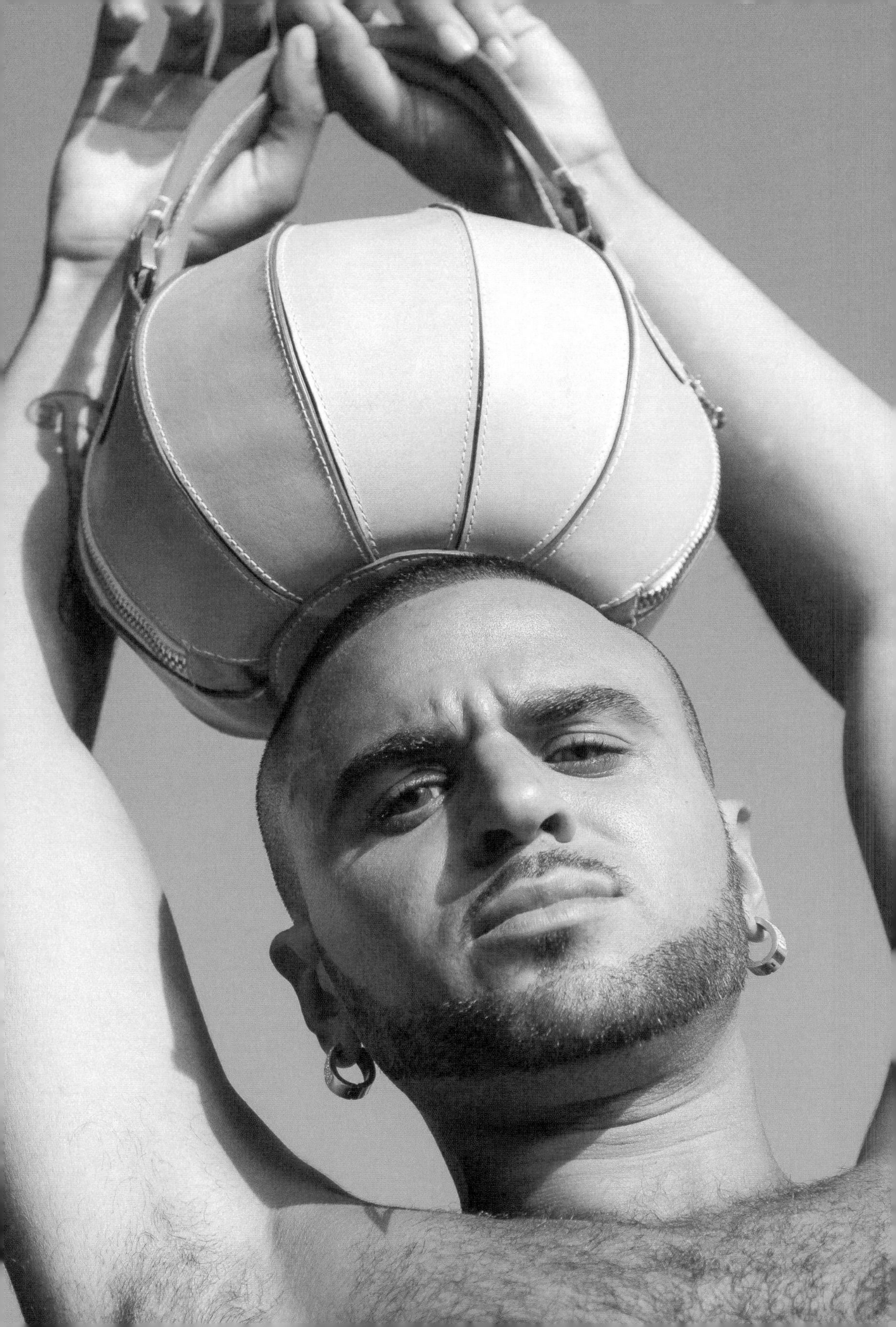

THE PERFECT IMBALANCE OF RAUL LOPEZ

Ernesto Macias | Photos by Delwin Kamara

One day, while I was scrolling through memes, thirst traps, and other gay internet things, a tweet jumped out. It simply said: "imagine having a body." This thought-provoking statement, hiding in plain view among mundane jokes and GIFs, sent me on a spiral of thoughts and questions, the same feeling that meeting Raul Lopez, the face behind the boundary-pushing—scratch that—boundary-*breaking* brand LUAR (Raul spelled backward), evoked in me when I met him at his studio in the garment district of New York City.

I knew of Raul and his work before our first encounter, but seeing him work next to his team, switching with ease between Spanish and English while draping white fabric cut on the bias ("It creates this beautiful butterfly-like pattern," he explained, as he signaled for me to move closer and inspect his work in progress), was sort of magical and confusing.

Knowing the work that Raul produces, as seen on icons like Rihanna and Solange, it was an odd feeling to see his soft side. But after speaking with him about his upbringing, understanding of fashion, the body, and gender, it began to make sense. Raul is a rebellious New York kid who loves to adorn and embellish the body. His clothes are more like a sparkling armor, one that beautifies and redefines the body.

Although he designs for men and women—his creations are not gendered—his work questions the behavioral, cultural, and psychological traits assigned to a body and its gender. But why should anyone care? Isn't every designer and brand embracing this moment? Isn't fashion the most understanding and queer-embracing industry?

Maybe, but not for a brown kid who grew up in Los Sures—now famously known as Williamsburg—who got punched in the face, hid his Versace and Coogi from his family, and fell in love with fashion after watching a Christian Lacroix runway show.

Raul is no fashion rookie. A former designer for Hood By Air, his creative direction for LUAR is fresh and doesn't play by or even look at the rules. His designs reflect his life: a perfect imbalance of the femme, the masc, and loving "everything everyone else hates."

ERNESTO MACIAS: Before fashion, before LUAR: Tell me about Raul . . .

RAUL LOPEZ: Well, I was always interested in fashion. My mom actually worked in the Garment District, so I grew up with an industrial [sewing machine] in my house, always. I guess the majority of Dominican immigrants worked in factories; it was the only trade they had. So my grandmother had a sewing machine, my aunts, everybody. I was always around industrials and my dad went to school for engineering and architecture, so I was around a lot of construction sites and all that. A lot of that plays into my day-to-day design life. My dad was trying to make me go with him to the construction sites and I was like, "*Nooo*, I have a stomachache." [Laughs] I always loved watching my mom make stuff: I thought it was way cooler. I always gravitated toward that stuff as a kid. In kindergarten, my mom had to buy me a suit every week. I would go to school every day with a tie, they used to call me *chalinita*, which is like the slang of "tie" in Dominican culture. So they called me "little tie" because I wore one every single day of the week.

EM: How old were you?

RL: Kindergarten!

EM: That's so cute.

RL: Ain't that crazy? My mom was like, "I knew it!"

EM: You grew up in New York, right?

RL: Yes, born and raised in New York. In Williamsburg, which was called "Los Sures" before.

EM: How can you explain that experience, growing up in Los Sures and seeing it transform into what it is now?

RL: I mean, it's crazy because when I was coming up it wasn't OK to be gay, it wasn't OK to be flamboyant, it wasn't OK to be any of that. I wanted to express myself and I think that's something that has, subconsciously, inspired me to always make people uncomfortable because I couldn't find comfort in my own surroundings. I would put my clothes in my backpack and get dressed on the train platform, because I couldn't leave my house like that. I tell my friends now, a lot of the people that live here now, "Honey, it's not the same." You were not gonna be able to walk around like this here. You probably would have gotten bashed, for reals. Do you know how many times I got punched in the face? I had to fight.

EM: That's rough and even hard to imagine now.

RL: I know, it was crazy. I mean, it was bad, but in a way it was good because it helped me build tough skin and it made me think in a sort of way: "OK, since you don't like it, I'm going to do it even more." This old queen, back in the day when Christopher Street was like the street to be at—I mean that's the only place we could actually feel kind of comfortable—he told me, "You know, you're fab." He was an old, old queen. He was like, "You know why? Because you don't look like everybody, and that's fab. When you stand out, you make people uncomfortable, and when you make people uncomfortable that's when they learn to respect." I was like, damn, that's kind of true.

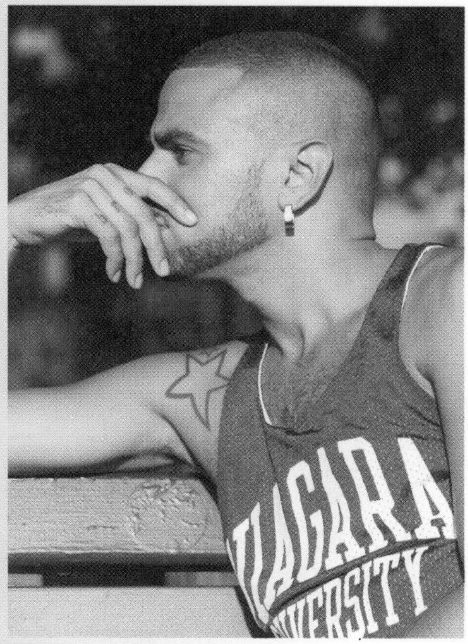

EM: Oh wow, wise advice for a queen to pass down. Has that helped you understand yourself and the things you create?

RL: Yeah, he was like, "People need to understand and they need to get it. Because they don't get it and they don't understand, so if you don't rub it in their face they're never going to understand." Like when I came out to my family, I mean they already knew, but I was trying to hide it my whole life even though I could've probably came out. So many people were like, "Just come out." My reaction was, "Excuse me? I'm not gay, no. I'm Dominican, I'm a dude, whatever." But I kind of just, when I came out to them I said, "I'm bi." I didn't want to say, "I'm gay."

EM: That's interesting—so before coming out, what recollection do you have of your first interaction with fashion?

RL: Well, in New York back in the day, they used to have a channel called FashionTV.

EM: Oh yes, I remember watching FashionTV.

RL: So, you know, I wasn't allowed to watch it. All the shows would come out at night and my first show that I saw that I was *Oh shit, whoa, this is so major* was Christian Lacroix. I remember doing it when everybody was asleep because I could get in trouble. It was a taboo to watch. I was like, "Whoa, oh my god, I want to be this guy." As the internet progressed, AOL, dial-up, and all that stuff started coming in, I would go in the chat rooms.

EM: And talk fashion?

RL: I would see people talking about designer stuff and all that. I realized, "Wait I can actually talk in here and nobody knows who I am." Know what I mean? Mind you, my name was LUARZAPO112119@AOL.COM [laughs].

I'm inspired by what everybody hates. If you hate it, I love it. I probably love everything everybody else thinks is ignorant, ugly, and trash—literally.

EM: So LUAR has been coming for a long time.

RL: Yeah, well, I used to tell my teachers in school: "I'm going to be a designer, I don't need to do this. I don't care about algebra." If you ask anyone who I went to school with or my family, they all say the same thing, they always make fun of me because of what I used to tell my teachers.

EM: What are your inspirations, do you look at social media? I tried looking you up everywhere and I found nothing besides your LUAR Instagram.

RL: No, no, no, I don't have none of that. I always tell people, "If you're going to research go to a library, actually do research." Once it is on Instagram, Tumblr, or anything else—it's done. It's been watered down and everyone has the same essence.

EM: That's quite interesting, I mean especially in the age we live. Designers, photographers, and creatives in general become names using social media—some, not all—and you don't have any of it.

RL: Everybody has the same thing nowadays, no one is doing anything special. I'm inspired by what everybody hates. If you hate it, I love it. I probably love everything everybody else thinks is ignorant, ugly, and trash—literally.

EM: Where do you think that comes from?

RL: Maybe it is because I was born and raised in New York and we didn't have all the luxury and nice stuff that goes around today. I just always been that kid, trying to stand out. So I tried to find inspiration in the weirdest things and places. If you see all my images on my phone, a lot of them are of people in the streets, bums.

EM: A sort of validation?

RL: To me it's like check, check. I feel like me and my circle of friends are cut from the same chain. Like Shayne Oliver, Akeem Smith, we all think alike. Our process of thinking is definitely different than most people. I feel like that's why we're all best friends and we get each other, the way we think and look at things.

EM: Looking at your designs, the things you create, it makes sense that you take in everything that's around you.

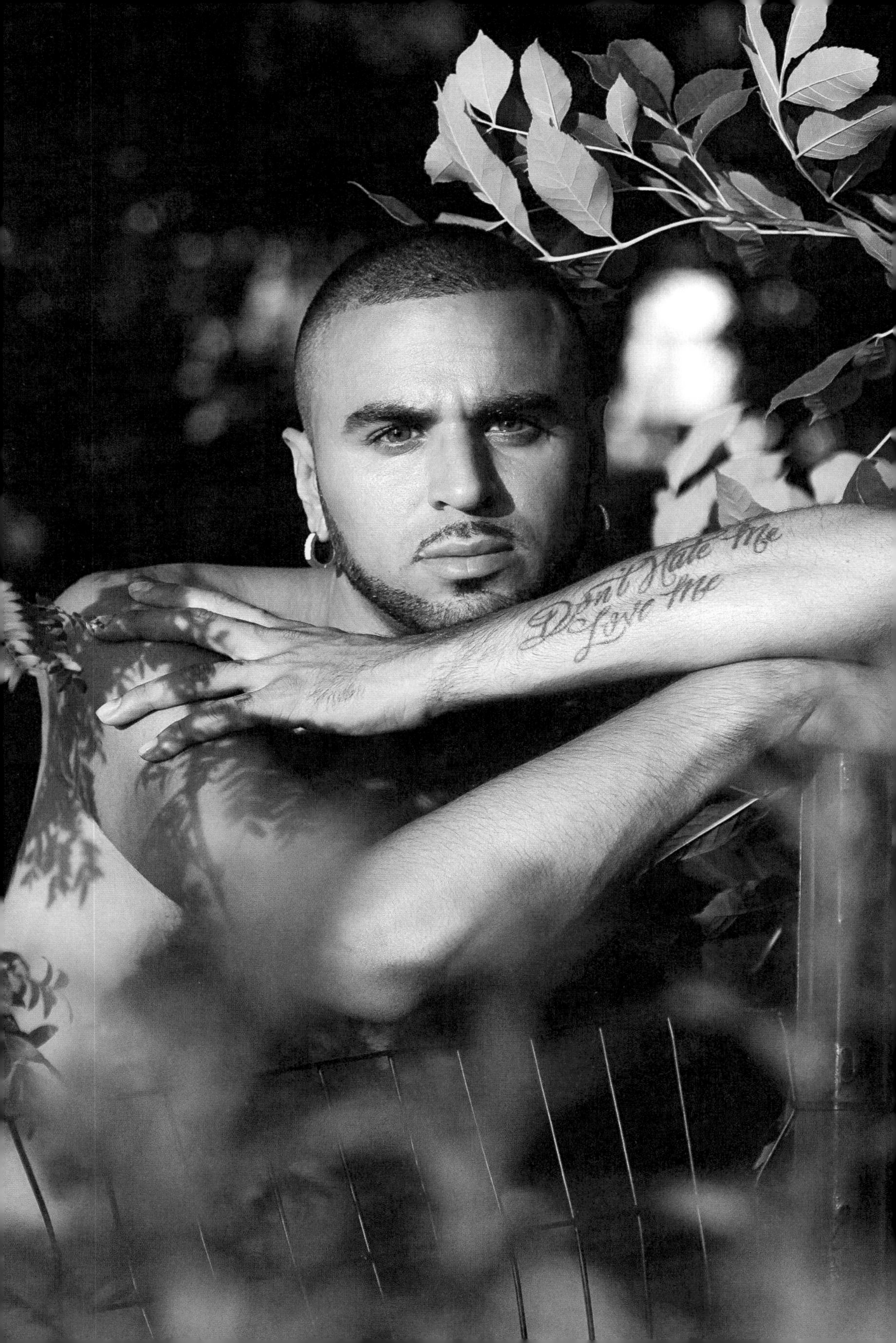
Don't Hate me
Love me

RL: Everything is made here in New York. It reminds me of my upbringing and seeing my family members doing stuff here. It's a little nostalgic and it makes me feel like I'm paying homage to everybody who came before me, but taking it to another level. Which is what I normally do, I'm so inspired by Dominican culture. Going to Dominican Republic and coming back and seeing them [my family] there and seeing them here, is just so inspiring.

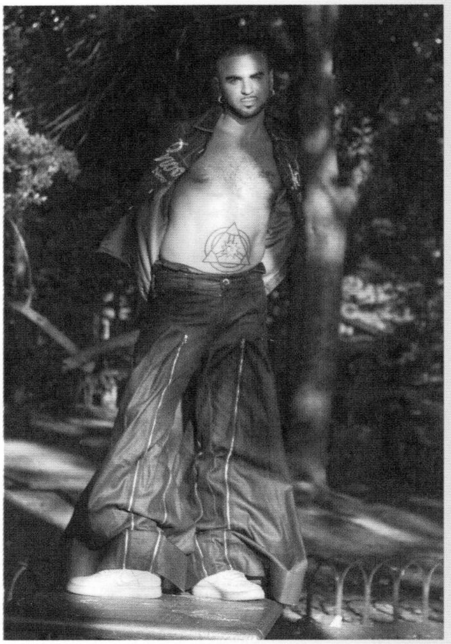

EM: So your clothes have been described as radical and futuristic, because of how they look—

RL: That's just me, it's a product of me.

EM: So what is your design philosophy? I see now that LUAR and Raul are one in the same, but explain it to me.

RL: It's just a reflection of me—that's why it's backward, LUAR is just Raul. It is a reflection of my life, my upbringing, who I am. I want everybody, when they wear something of mine—from a T-shirt, to a bag, or whatever—that it takes a piece of my life with them. I don't make clothes for queer, straight, gay—I make clothes for people who wanna step out the house and make a statement and be known and be seen, not anything to do with gender.

EM: What do you mean?

RL: I'm a person that, before all the gender stuff, I always thought about living in the future. I thought by this time we would be flying. That was me as a kid. Imaging the future, and I infiltrate that into my designs.

EM: That's a good philosophy to live by.

RL: That's how I feel everyone should be. Mind your business, wear whatever the hell you want to wear, go in your husband's closet, take his clothes and wear them to work—or wear a dress if you want.

EM: Speaking of gender, and that cultural movement that's happening right now. In fashion it's always been there—do you think it's possible for designers to create clothes without thinking about gender?

RL: I think it is moving slowly more in that direction because of the new era of designers and the internet. For example these viral rappers, music and fashion influence each other, it goes hand-in-hand. I feel like men are starting to experiment more. Mainly because the Young Thugs and Lil Uzis are making it "OK" for you to wear pearls, wear a chiffon Valentino blouse.

EM: Even though, in reality, people have been doing it for so long.

RL: Absolutely, but the mainstream needs to see it certified by people in music or some type of presence, so they can justify it. It's like *Why? For What?* Sometimes I'm dumbfounded by this way of thinking—this male or female way of thinking. For what? It's crazy.

Sometimes I'm dumbfounded by this way of thinking—this male or female way of thinking. For what? It's crazy.

EM: You find the separation absurd?

RL: I feel like they're doing this thing to our community—making us segregate within our own community. I respect everyone with their pronouns, their sexuality—always. I mean, I grew up around transexual women, as opposed to my immediate family. My second family was gay men and transexuals. But when I was growing up, there weren't so many pronouns. I respect it, but sometimes I feel like [the] hetero lifestyle and the government push for us to fight about this and divide us. So we can fight each other and we don't focus on them. They sit back and watch us bash each other online. Everybody just needs to chill and just be you. I don't want to feel like I'm making people feel uncomfortable. It is so hard now.

EM: Do you think that when designers don't think about gender, the fashion they produce is different?

RL: Not really. It's just about how the person, the designer perceives it—it's just not my way of design. But when I do make women's, I want to make women's-women's because I feel like a woman loves her body. Doesn't matter if you're skinny, fat, whatever, a woman always wants to look good. So I feel like looking at old designers and how they cut stuff and how they construct, is how I make clothes for women—in my understanding—which could be a trans woman, hetero woman. To me a woman is whoever feels like a woman.

EM: When you think about the future—fashion, your brand, culture—what does that look to you?

RL: I just want everybody to be equal, to be the same. In my way of making clothing that screams, "Mind your business," I want people to feel like that. In the future, once we understand gender, people will start drifting to the mindset of not caring. The more they see it, the more they'll get it.

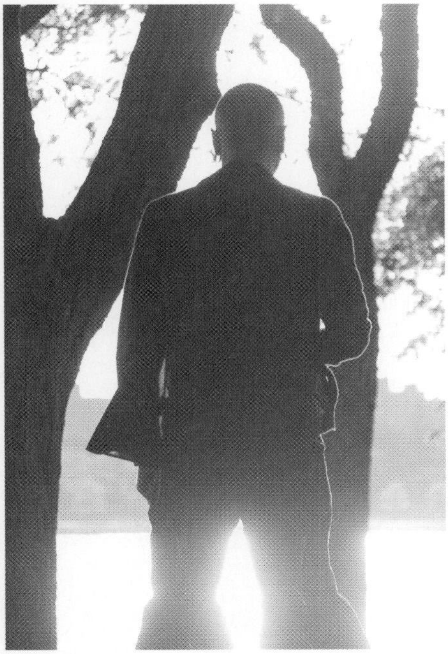

ORIGINALLY PUBLISHED IN *HELLO MR.* ISSUE 10 IN 2018.

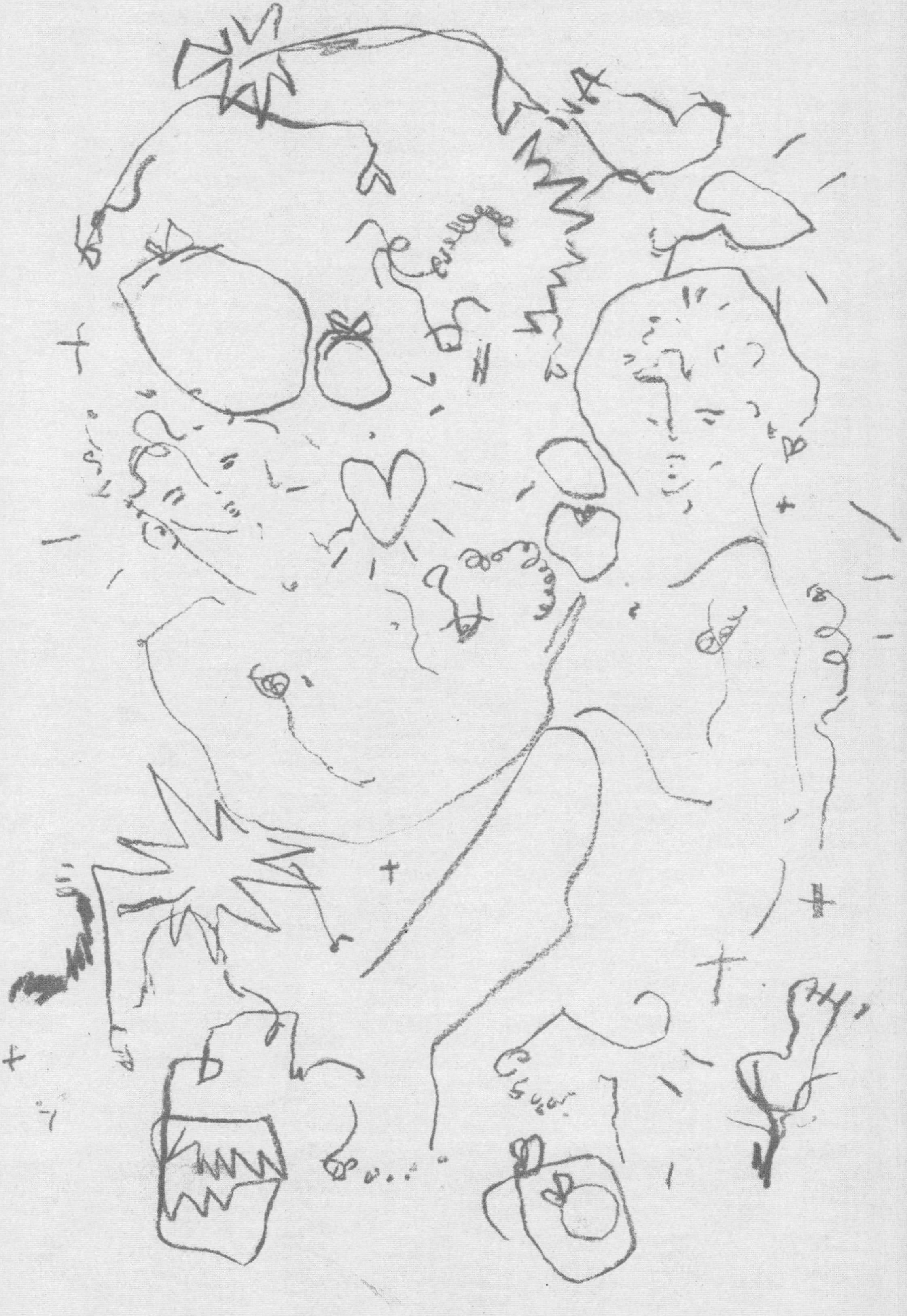

The Wound

Riley Yaxley

Art by Jack Taylor Lovatt

There is a dime-sized hole in my chest. Its edges are jagged and pink, and it smells like an overused, souring dish rag. If I crane my neck far enough, I can see the circular face of the bullet where it's buried in the damp, burgundy muscle of my heart. Despite my exhaustive efforts, I don't remember being shot. I know I've carried the bullet since I was a child, rarely mentioning it to anyone. I naïvely believed my injury was unique, that I shouldn't speak about it to anyone in order to avoid becoming defined by it—afraid that others might only see my wound. I was unnerved to discover that strangers had nearly identical wounds and was even more stunned to realize that they were also able to recall and describe early memories where they became aware of the projectiles nestled between their ribs. The Spanish writer Paul B. Preciado recounted a similar experience, "I was three years old when I felt the weight of the bullet for the first time. I knew I was carrying it when I heard my father call two girls walking hand-in-hand in the street 'disgusting, dirty dykes.'"

I was fifteen when I felt the weight of the bullet for the hundredth time. I was riding in the backseat of my father's Jeep Wrangler, my father driving, and my uncle sitting in the passenger seat. We were on our way to the office of the automotive robot repair business they started together. I cleaned the office bathroom once a week for some money. It was the day before my birthday, and I was trying to decide between having my parents take me to Outback Steakhouse or Red Robin for dinner. Fox News was playing on the radio. The host criticized President Obama, who had reversed course and announced he supported same-sex marriage in the face of reelection. The host condemned the move, insisting that marriage is a union between a man and woman. My uncle scoffed and said, "I think we should send all the gays and lesbians to a remote island. The men are all effeminate, and the women are masculine, so they would be a perfect match for one another. That or natural selection will run its course and they'll all die." He enunciated each word so forcefully that spit flew from his mouth and landed on the dashboard. I stared out the window, nervous that my uncle might catch my eye in the rearview mirror.

I worried that he might somehow know how often I fantasized about being a girl, the hours I spent in my room wrapping my bedsheets and tying them in a tight knot around my chest, walking back and forth with a gentle sway in my hips. I would pretend to be Drew Barrymore as Dylan Sanders in *Charlie's Angels* when she volunteers to spend the night with Eric Knox—a software genius played by Sam Rockwell—under the guise of guarding him from his kidnappers. The two have sex and Dylan emerges from his bedroom swaddled in a sheet. Eric confronts Dylan and reveals that his kidnapping was a ruse designed to hoodwink her and the other two angels before he shoots her. The bullet narrowly misses Dylan. She tumbles backward, saved by the bedsheet snagging on a shard of broken glass, which allows her to fall, roll down the hillside, and land roughly in a stranger's backyard. Dylan uses cleverly placed pool floats to hide her naked body before knocking on the back door to ask for help from two teenage boys—who offer their ill-fitting clothes and miniature scooter.

I fantasized about that scene many times, although my fantasies weren't the pornographic daydreams of a teenage boy who also wishes a naked Drew Barrymore might appear at their door in the middle of the night and beg for help. When I wrapped myself in my cotton sheets, I cast myself as Barrymore. I tried to imagine what it felt like to be flushed with pleasure after sex, giddily following after your lover without feeling the need to conceal your nakedness. I wanted to know what it felt like to be a woman who is desired, who might be the object of some teenage boy's fantasy.

My uncle mimicked the stereotypical, high-pitched vocal fry of a gay man, which didn't sound much different than my voice at the time; I was always being mistaken for my mother on the phone, even by her own sister—a fact that both excited and ashamed me. He caught my eye in the rearview mirror and grinned at me. The bullet felt enormous, as if it had expanded, swelling until the shell pressed against the insides of my rib cage. The pain was unbearable, yet I managed to ignore it. I persuaded myself that I could feel nothing if I thought of the wound as childish curiosity, a fun game that I would lose interest in as I matured. This wasn't the first time I decided to feel nothing, and it wouldn't be the last.

Why does it always feel like other people are able to recognize and name my identity before I can?

I felt nothing when my brother told me that my mother asked if I was transgender after she saw photos of me performing at my university's drag show in a limp, blond bob wig, comically overapplied eye makeup, and a red satin minidress I thrifted and occasionally wore about my apartment. Like a passive-aggressive teenager trying to be subversive, I posted the photos to my Facebook knowing my mother would see them. I laughed about it on the phone with my brother and insisted that I wasn't trans. But when I hung up, I felt uneasy, like after telling a harmless white lie that I know will unravel and embarrass me; I couldn't help but wonder, *Why does it always feel like other people are able to recognize and name my identity before I can?*

I felt nothing the frigid March night my first boyfriend, who I had been dating for three months, told me that he didn't like when I wore heels or feminine clothes after we got home from a poetry reading at Women and Children First bookstore. He suggested that identifying as nonbinary was a phase that I would grow out of. He insisted that he was gay and therefore only attracted to men. When I asked what that meant for our relationship, he said, "We'll just have to see." He kissed me goodnight in the doorway and told me that he loved me for the first time. After he left, I waited until I heard him reach the bottom of the stairs to quietly lock the door. I broke up with him the next day, knowing that, despite all the hours he spent admiring my body, he had not seen the bullet hole, could not smell it festering sickly sweet, could not feel the sweltering heat of the inflamed wound like an old radiator's steam.

I felt nothing the time a man I had been dating for a few months walked me home from dinner and, while we were standing and flirting outside my apartment, groped me and said, "Just wanted to make sure that you didn't cut it off since the last time I saw you." I drily replied, "Not yet." He continued to talk, but I had lost any ability to understand language. I deflected his suggestion that we could hang out in my apartment for a bit and told him that I had to be up early the next day. He begrudgingly ordered an Uber and asked, "Do I at least get a kiss before I go?" I gave him a quick peck on the lips and stepped inside. I swiftly locked the door behind me. Later that night, I stood in the bathroom and tucked my genitals between my legs, squeezing my thighs together to give the illusion that I had a neat, triangular vagina. I squinted, stared at my naked body with my semi-blurred vision, laid my hand over my groin, and forcefully pressed until I felt one of my testicles retract. My legs started to tremble. A notification lit up my phone. It was the groper. He wrote, "I had a nice time tonight. Wish you were here in bed with me." I separated my thighs and watched my dick hang dispiritedly between my legs before snatching my phone off the edge of the sink and blocking him on every platform.

Feeling nothing became unbearable. I instinctively followed every trans person that came up on my social media feeds. I Googled "best trans books," made a list of all the titles from an Oprah Daily article titled "12 of the Best Books by Trans Authors That You Need to Read," and bought copies of each. I started idly researching hormone replacement therapy. But then I started dating a boy and became infatuated, so I made a bargain and convinced myself that I should wait to see how the relationship developed before deciding whether to medically transition; I believed revealing my desire to transform my body would cause him to break up with me. Only when he ended things anyway did I realize how juvenile and asinine these rationalizations had been. After we said goodbye, I walked to the liquor store and bought a bottle of wine, which I quickly downed before curling up in a fetal position on my bed and watching the hour-long special episode of *Euphoria* centered around Jules Vaughn, a trans teenager played by Hunter Schafer. Jules makes a confession to her therapist: "I feel like I've framed my entire womanhood around men.... I just, like, look at myself and I'm like how the fuck did I spend my entire life building this. Like, my body and my personality and, like, my soul around what I think men desire? It's just embarrassing. I feel like a fraud."

I feel like I've framed my entire womanhood around men.

I cried deep, body-seizing cries. She was describing a feeling that I couldn't shake; I had also framed my entire personhood around what I thought men desire. Admitting that I wanted to transition was unthinkable—I had decided that being desirable to men was the most important thing in my life and that if I wasn't desirable, I would be nothing. I knew how to date cis gay men, that older men liked my pubescent, boyish body, my flat stomach, my angular jawline, my peach-fuzz-like facial hair. But none of my relationships lasted longer than a few months. I eventually began to feel like I was putting on a performance, playing a fictionalized version of myself I thought they would find attractive. Unsurprisingly, I felt like my partners didn't understand me and balked at the idea of sharing that I frequently fantasized about having breasts, wearing dresses in public somewhere other than the gay club, growing out my hair—so I sabotaged my relationships other ways to avoid potential rejection for revealing I might be trans. Despite all the years I spent obsessively observing women, I realized I didn't know how to be desirable as a woman, and that frightened me more than anything—who would I be if I wasn't desirable?

But I had to surrender to the unknown. I needed to transition. Or at least try.

I played that *Euphoria* episode two more times and then paced around my bedroom. I caught sight of myself in my mirror and scanned myself from head to toe. I let my gaze linger on my wound, its shiny mauve edges, and I looked straight down the tunnel the bullet bored through my chest and saw a world I had seen nothing of before reflected in the mirrored face of the cartridge. In my wound I saw myself taking my estradiol pills for the first time in a park while my friend filmed me. "I hope these make my ass fat," I joked and tipped my head back, dropped the two oblong, baby-blue pills into my mouth, and washed them down with a swig of prosecco.

I saw myself being apprehended by a friendly but slightly misguided airport worker, who insisted I was mistakenly going into the men's restroom and politely pointed out the women's restroom, the first time I passed as a woman. I saw myself at a gay go-go bar in New Orleans where one of the dancers offered to give me a massage. He slid his hands underneath the skirt of my minidress and pressed his thumbs against my lumbar and whispered in my ear, "Are you wearing lotion? Your skin feels like velvet." I was dangerously tipsy at this point in the night, but I managed the common sense to not tell him it was because of the estrogen.

I saw my great-aunts calling me beautiful at my brother's wedding while wearing a sage green turtleneck dress, a pair of black heeled mules, and a flower crown made of baby's breath. I saw myself in my parents' kitchen, zesting so many limes and washing dishes under scalding water for so long that my hands cracked and bled along the furrows of my finger joints the next day. Except, the wounds felt like a badge of honor—proof that I had adopted the daughter's domestic role of feeding and cleaning up after my family. I saw myself slowly walking along Lake Michigan, trying to regulate my breathing as I prepared to call my parents. I explained that I was on hormone replacement therapy, and reassured my mother that there were no scary side effects—besides blood clots, which I could easily combat by taking an aspirin every so often. My mother replied, "I'm on hormones, too, although mine are for menopause." I laughed and asked her if it was estrogen or progesterone, surprised she made the connection that we were both undergoing HRT without drawing attention to it. As they prepared to say goodbye, my mother added, "I hope you know how much we love you."

While I looked straight at my wound, I saw an afternoon from my childhood. My friend and I were playacting husband and wife in the basement—him the husband, and me the wife. I can't remember how we decided who would be the man and who would be the woman, whether he claimed the clip-on tie first and I meekly acquiesced, or if I volunteered eagerly to play wife. I pretended to cook and served him a meal of plastic spaghetti, corn, and apple juice.

I doted on him, asking if everything tasted OK while he assured me it was perfect. I wore my mother's aquamarine pumps she set aside for my siblings and I to play dress up. When I slid my tiny, eight-year-old feet into the shoes, the heel of my foot barely extended beyond the toe, but I managed to follow my friend up the carpeted stairs. He complemented the clip-on tie with a bowler hat. We peered down the hallway, trying to figure out if either of my parents were in the kitchen, and giggled, nervous at the idea of being seen in our costumes. We could hear my mother loading dishes into the dishwasher—the water turning on and off and the clink of plates accidentally grazing. We waited for her to finish, but several minutes passed and she didn't walk our way, so we prodded each other and worked up the courage to stand in the entryway of the kitchen without saying anything. My mother laughs and yells for my father to grab his camera. We posed and my father took a picture. This might be the moment I am struck by the bullet, but it's an easy memory to confuse, the camera's flash so close to the muzzle flash of gunfire.

Afterward, we returned to the basement, put one of my mom's old dresses on the slightly damp concrete floor, and lay on top of it. We didn't say anything. Our playful demeanor has faded, replaced by a stony seriousness. He leaned in close enough to feel his breath's wetness on my lips. I didn't move. He kissed me, a curt, uninspired kiss, like politely waving at someone you'd prefer to leave unacknowledged. But he kissed me again, a softer, eager kiss, this time like brushing your arm against an attractive stranger in a large crowd. He raised his hand and pretended to fondle my breasts as we had seen actors do in the R-rated movies we sneakily watched from the second-floor balcony while my parents thought we were asleep. I realized a truth about myself at that moment: I wanted real breasts, to feel the rush of his hands, any man's hands, really, brush across my nipples again, to feel like a swatch of upholstery fabric being stroked and caressed and admired—waiting to hear them exclaim, "You're so soft and velvety. I would run my hands over you forever."

My friend stared at me with his brown calflike eyes and whispered, "You're beautiful. I love you." That was the day the bullet pierced my heart.

we know the weight is human

Tate Justus

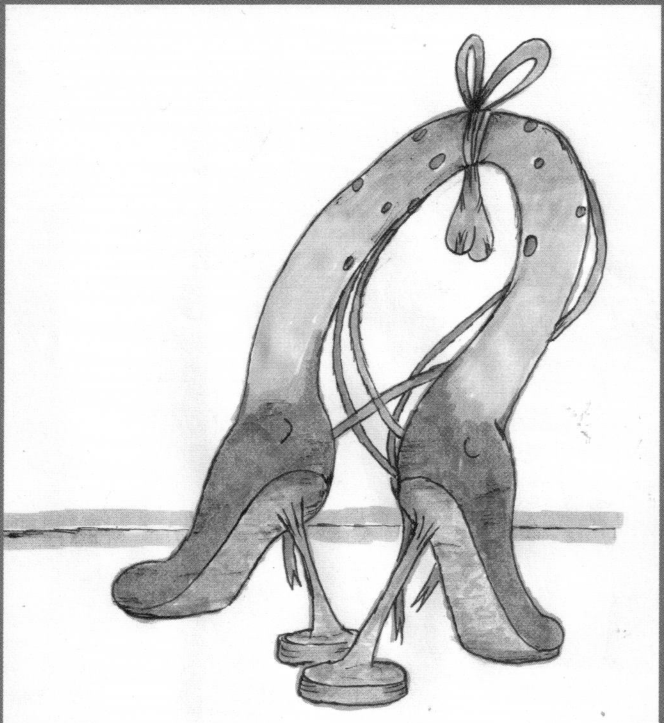

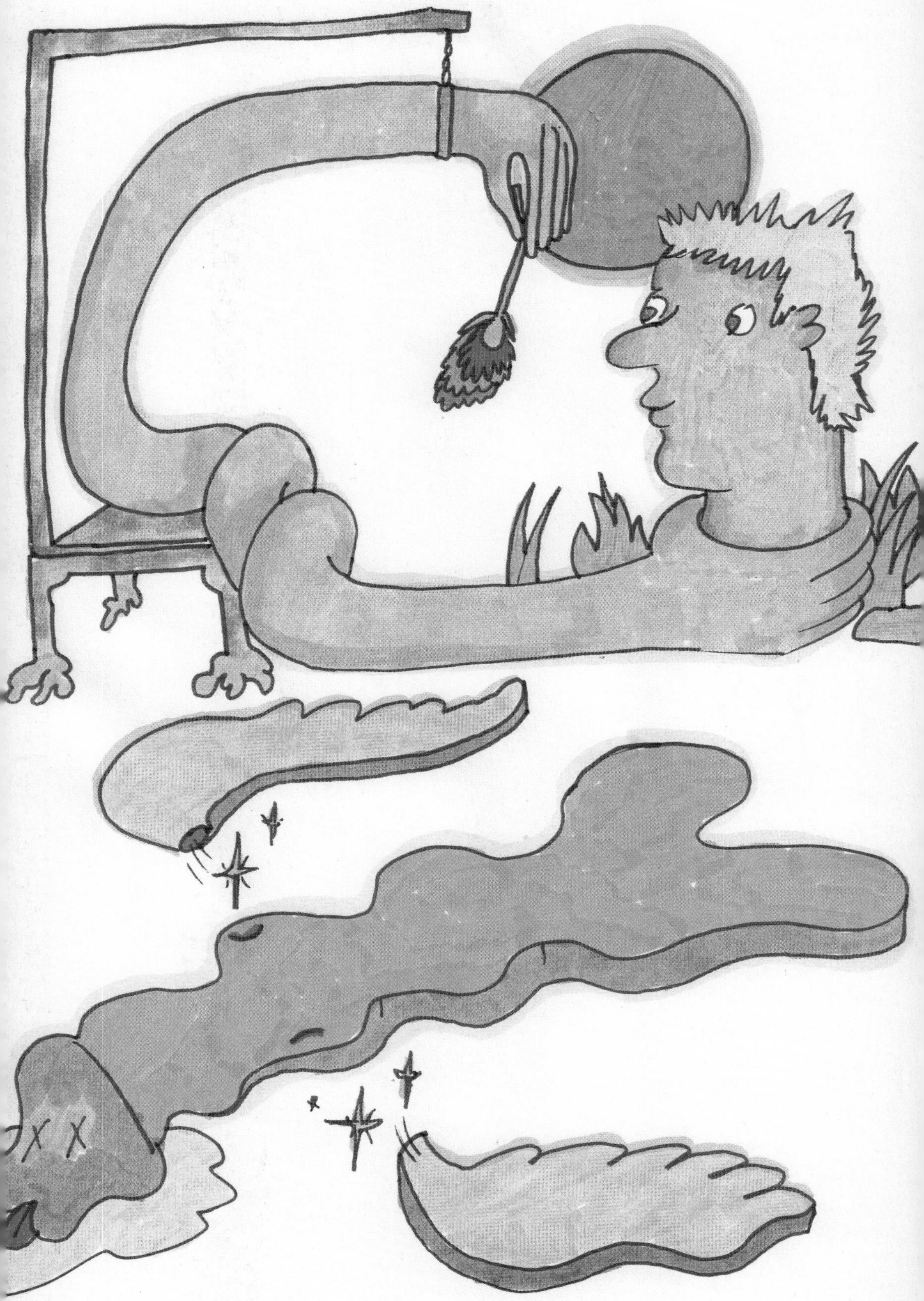

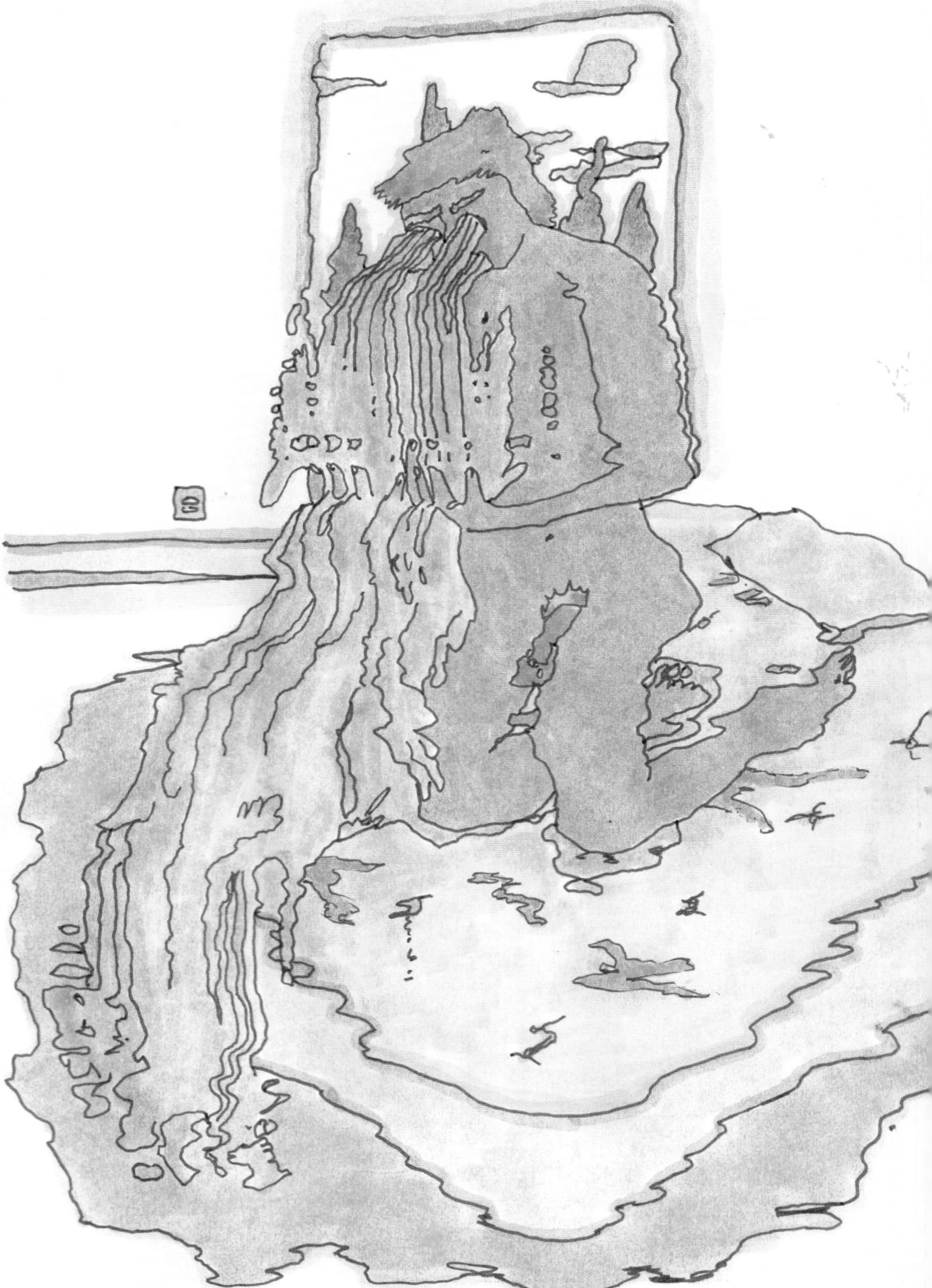

the power of animating only once the coin dropped in
the moment it chings my smile rises
all bulbs lit
show time

the crazy behavior comes out of the blue,
yet how clean and sane the quid pro quos
how heinous beetle juice interiors
and how bad the breath

it makes my face hurt in all the ways too many fake smiles do
breathing from a very guarded place
one wrong breath could give it all away
effortlessness, a secret bead of sweat down my back

i am downright Pavlovian toward the ticking of the clock
and the gleeful last minutes until I am free to go,
my body is my own again
but i have to retrieve it, where did it go

if one shape doesn't work try another
keep trying until it doesn't feel like a mask

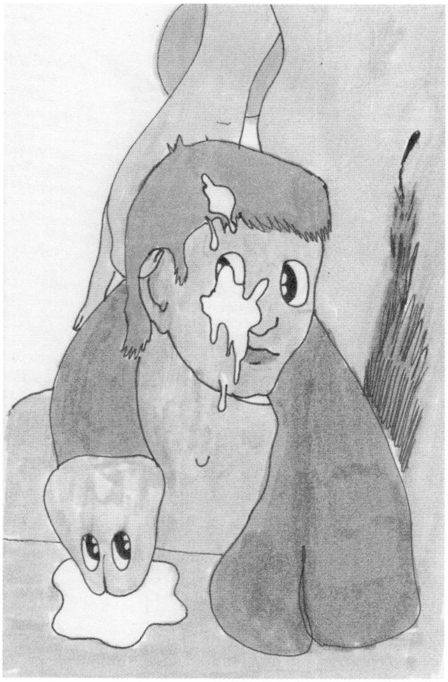

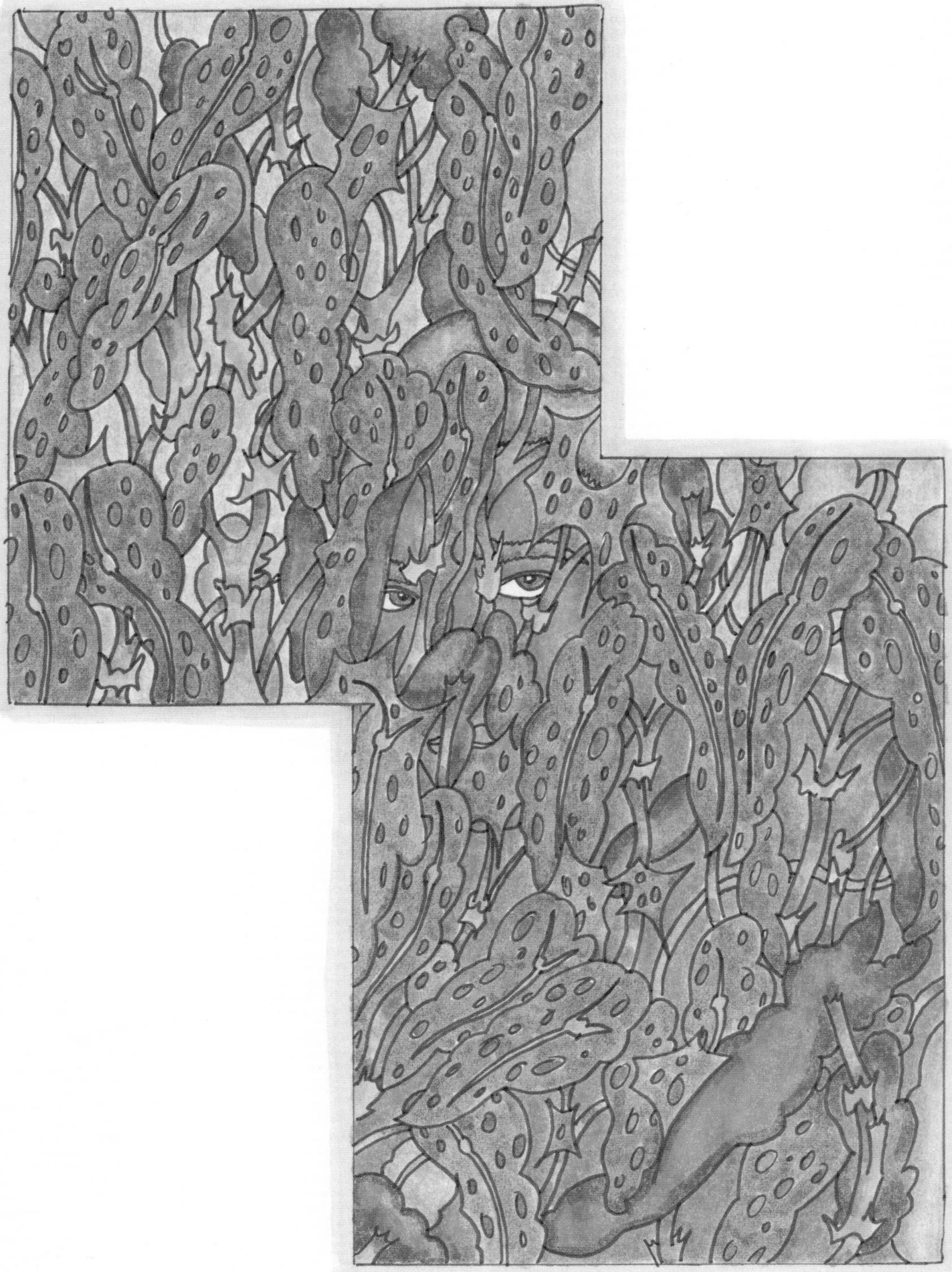

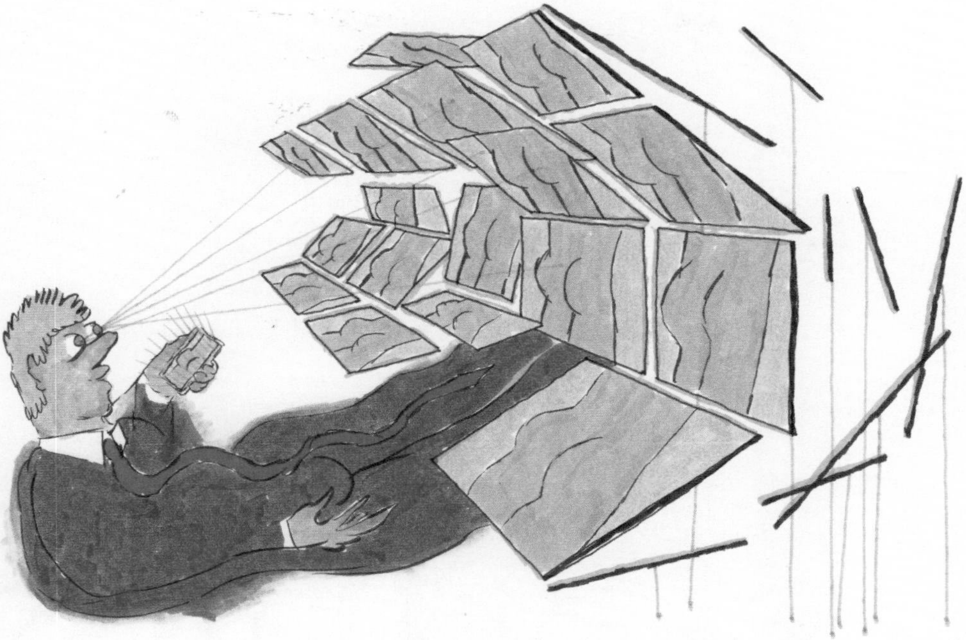

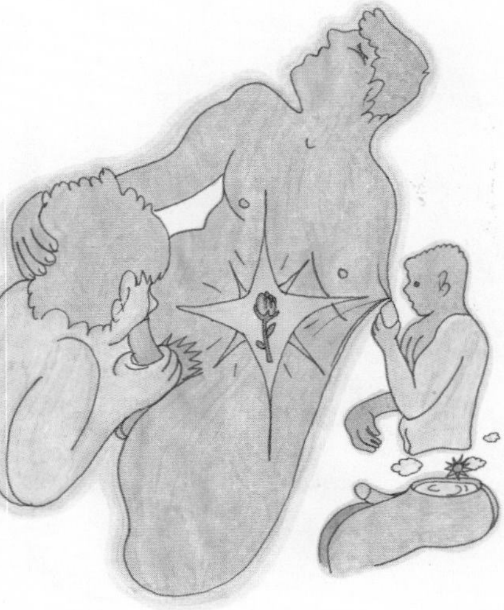

we know the weight is human
holding him down so he doesn't float away

sometimes it's a complete surprise
peeling off the layers of inevitable fruit

building the swell
the slightest grazing of skin

eyes mutually rise   are we really going there
the alphabet of sexual acts between two silent people

the last point of contact passes all the dough
where and how the money gets placed says a lot

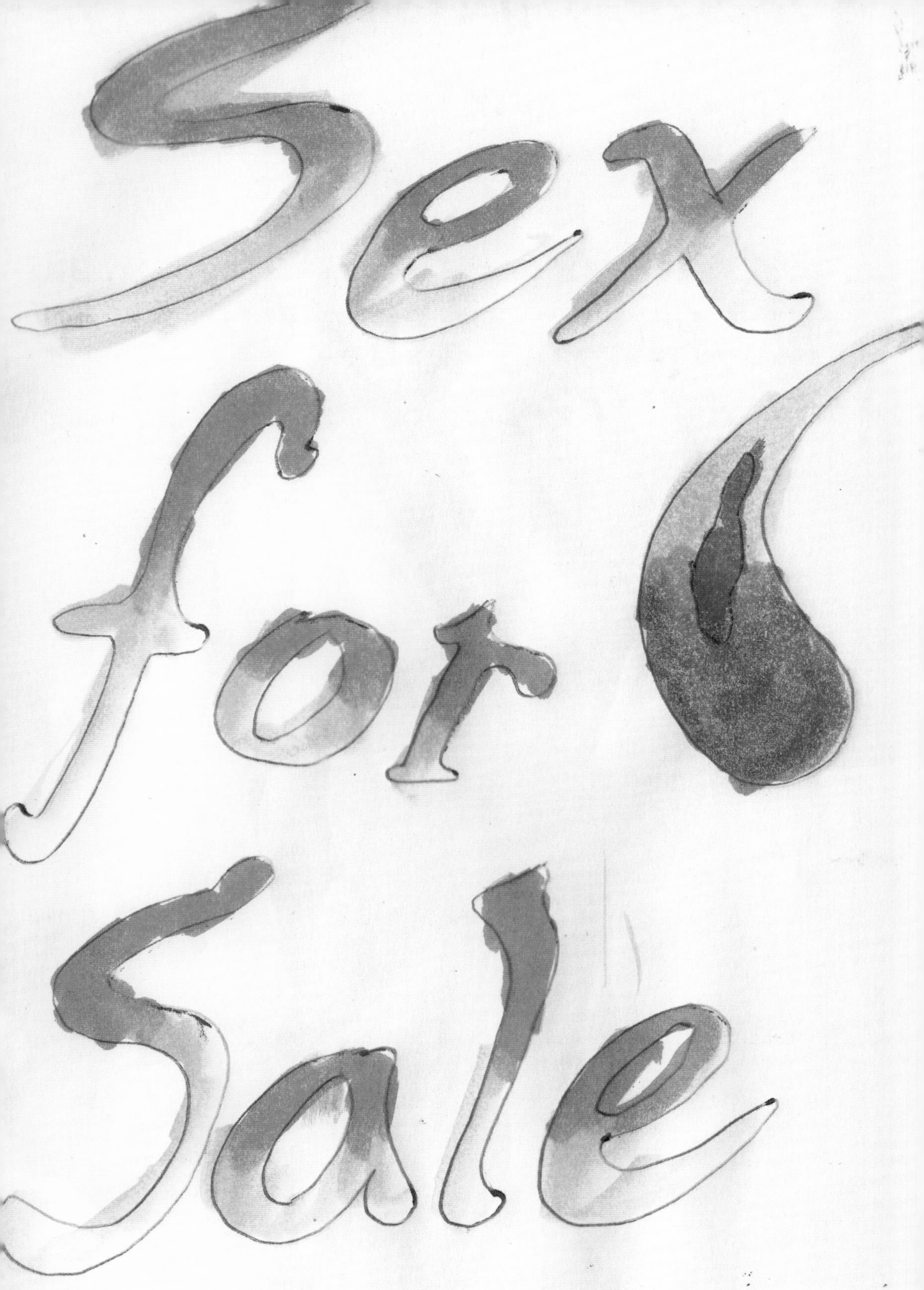
Sex
for
Sale

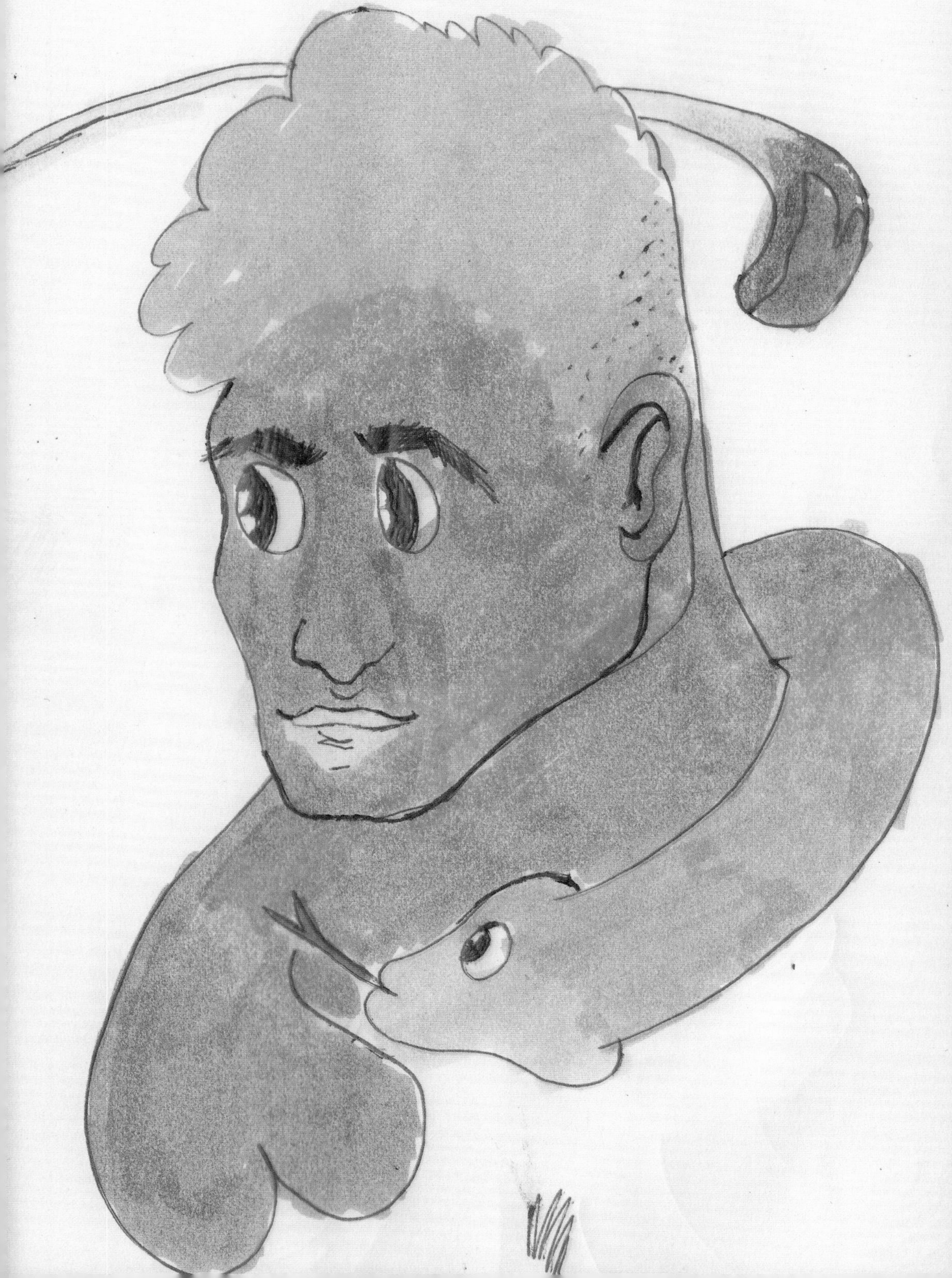

Contributors

LUKE ABBY (b. 1992) is a visual artist from Kent, England. He first picked up the camera at age fifteen. He is now based between Berlin and NYC. Abby's artistic style is described as both romantic and painterly, featuring subjects within meticulously crafted surreal environments with narrative undertones. Homoerotic motifs coupled with intimate portraits of sensuality and tenderness make up his personal oeuvre.
• lukeabby.us
• Instagram: @lukeabby

COLBY ANDERSON is the creator of *BRUNCH CLUB*, a magazine centered on uplifting and telling the stories of trans and queer people of color. He currently lives and works in Brooklyn, New York.
• brunchclubmag.com
• Instagram: @brunchclubmag
• @colbchella

JEREMY ATHERTON LIN is an essayist based in Los Angeles and East Sussex, England. His debut book, *Gay Bar*, received the National Book Critics Circle Award for Autobiography. His next, *Deep House*, is a gay love story before and after gay marriage.
• jeremyathertonlin.com
• Instagram: @jeremyathertonlin

JOHN BETTER ARMELLA is a queer Colombian novelist, poet, and journalist. His books include *China White, Locas de Felicidad: Crónicas Travestis y Otros Relatos, A la Caza del Chico Espantapájaros*, and *Limbo: Una Historia de Horror en el Caribe.*
• Twitter: @johnbetter69

MARTIN BELK is the author of *Pretty Broken Punks: lipstick, leather jeans, a death of New York.* He is a former New York City club producer and is currently completing his PhD on a prominent figure of the Edinburgh and London 1950-60s counterculture as observed through anthropologist Victor Turner's theory of liminality and communitas.
• martinbelk.com
• Instagram: @martinbelk_latesupper

SCOTT BIXBY is an award-winning political reporter at the *Daily Beast*, where he covers the White House.
• Instagram: @scotbix

STANISLAW BONIECKI was born and raised in Poland. He now lives in Brooklyn.
• @bobrowiec

SAMUEL BRADLEY is a British photographer and director known for his longform collaborations with fashion brands and musicians.
• samuelbradley.com
• Instagram: @samuelbradley

JULIAN BUCHAN is a London- and Los Angeles-based director and photographer.
• julianbuchan.com
• Instagram: @juliandbuchan

THOM JAMES CARTER is a writer based in Scotland. His nonfiction has been published by the *New Statesman, Current Affairs, WIRED, Insider, Wellcome Collection*, and more. *They Came to Slay*, his book exploring queerness and Dungeons & Dragons, was published in 2022 by 404 Ink.

DEREK CHARM is an Eisner Award-winning comic artist, illustrator, and designer. He has worked on multiple projects for Marvel, DC, and Archie Comics, and well as Pepsi, DreamWorks Animation, and Marc Jacobs.
He currently works as a character designer for WB Animation and lives in Los Angeles.
• derekcharm.co
• Instagram: @derekcharm

ALEXANDER CHEE is most recently the author of *How to Write an Autobiographical Novel*, a collection of essays. He teaches at Dartmouth College and lives in Vermont.
• alexanderchee.net
• Instagram: @cheemobile
• Twitter: @alexanderchee

ROBERT ANDY COOMBS was born in Michigan in 1987 and attended Kendall College of Art and Design (KCAD). During his third year in undergrad, Coombs sustained a spinal cord injury due to a gymnastics training accident. After a year of recovery, he returned to KCAD and received his BFA in photography in 2013. Coombs's photography explores themes of relationships, caregiving, and fetish in the intersections of disability and sexuality. Coombs graduated from the Yale School of Art amid the COVID-19 pandemic and currently resides in Miami, Florida.
• robertandycoombs.com
• Instagram: @robertandycoombs_

HAYDEN DAVIS is a multimedia artist in New York City who makes illustrations, prints, paintings, gifs, collages, quilts, zines, and more. His love of ephemera and texture inspires him to create colorful work that always has a clear human hand.
• haydenwdavis.com
• Instagram: @hayden__davis

MATHEUS DE SIMONE is a queer visual artist who lives in Brazil. His work aims to highlight tensions between spirituality, play, violence, and sexuality.
• matheusdesimone.com
• Instagram: @matheusdesimone

LIE DIRKX is a Belgian illustrator/designer working with print, textiles, and mosaics.
• liedirkx.com
• Instagram: @liedirkx

BENJAMIN EDELINE is the artistic alter ego behind MENLAYERS, an online label dedicated to and fascinated by male iconography, photography, nudity, still-life, and queer graphics from the '70s and '80s. Born in Versailles, France, Edeline lived and worked in the fashion industry in New York for the last ten years, before returning to live in Paris to focus on collage-making and photography.
• menlayers.com
• Instagram: @benjaminmenlayers

KHALID EL KHATIB is a Brooklyn-based writer and marketer who often draws inspiration from his Palestinian heritage and Iowa roots. He's contributed to dozens of magazines and websites and is (slowly) working on a book.
• khalidelkhatib.com
• Instagram: @kmelkhat

BILLY ERB aka Billy Beyond is a New York City multidisciplinary artist working mainly in photography, music, and fashion.
• billyerb.com
• billybeyond.com
• @billybeyond

based in Tulsa, Oklahoma. His work reflects how he wants to feel on a daily basis, poised with a great assertion of confidence no matter the setting. The elements of putting together characters, atmosphere, and emotion through a lens is his passion.
- rogelioesparza.com
- Instagram: @rogelio.ec

MIKE FESWICK is a creative director and producer whose work often explores concepts of desire. Mike also has a foot fetish.
- mikefeswick.com
- Instagram: @mikefeswick

SAM FINKELSTEIN is a full-time flaneur from New York City. He has walked dogs, made bubble tea, sold comedy tickets in Times Square, cooked in a four-star restaurant, tutored kids, wrapped poke burritos, and baked kosher edibles. Recently he took some mushrooms and decided to try writing.

MICHELE FOSSI has contributed as a freelance journalist to *Vogue Italia*, *L'Uomo Vogue*, and *Dust Magazine* for many years. Having earned his PhD in chemistry, he discovered that telling stories was his true passion. Berlin has been his home and workplace for more than twenty years.
- michelefossi.com
- Instagram: @michelefossi

BEN FRENCH was the recipient of the inaugural Dramatists Guild of America's Young Playwright Award, the Bill Hallberg Award, and the Sam Selden Award. His poems have appeared in *Queer Voices* and *Hello Mr*. Outside of his written work, Ben makes music under the moniker Johnny Pontiac.
- Instagram: @benjamin_french

SCOTT GALLAGHER is a Belfast-born, London-based photographer.
- scottjgallagher.com
- Instagram: @scottjgallagher

MICHAEL GEORGE is a photographer and writer based in Brooklyn, New York. His clients include *National Geographic*, the *New York Times*, *Vogue*, and dozens of other publications. Michael's storytelling has taken him from the glaciers of Antarctica to the City Palace in Jaipur, India. When you meet him, you'll probably say, "I thought you'd be taller."
- Instagram: @michaelgeorge
- Twitter: @migeophoto

CALVIN GIMPELEVICH is an NEA Literature Fellow, the recipient of a Lambda Literary Award, and the author of *Invasions* (Instar, 2018). His work has appeared in *Ploughshares*, *Kenyon Review*, and *The Best American Essays 2022*.
- calvingimplelevich.com
- Instagram: @calvin.calvin.g
- Facebook: @calvin.gimpelevich

DAN GLUIBIZZI is an artist living in Portland, Oregon.
- dangluibizzi.com
- Instagram: @dangluibizzi

GARTH GREENWELL is the author of two books of fiction, *Cleanness* and *What Belongs to You*. He lives in New York and teaches at Princeton University.
- garthgreenwell.com
- Instagram: @ggreenwell
- Twitter: @garthgreenwell

JASON HANASIK's films and photographs have been exhibited at the Smithsonian's National Portrait Gallery and featured on the BBC, in the *Guardian*, and in the *LA Times*. His monograph, *I slowly watched him disappear*, is in the research collections of the Metropolitan Museum of Art, MoMA NYC, and other institutions.
- jasonhanasik.com
- Instagram: @jasonhanasik

KITSCH HARRIS is a queer illustrator and animator in New York City.
- Instagram: @werkzine

MATTHEW HARRIS is a writer, editor, and teacher. His fiction has been published in several magazines, including *Plenitude*, the *Malahat Review*, the *Dalhousie Review*, and *Grain*. He is also the fiction editor of the *Humber Literary Review*, and he teaches English at Humber College. He is working on a novel.
- Twitter: @doublematthew

GEORGE HENSON is a translator of contemporary Latin American prose and a 2021–2023 Tulsa Artist Fellow. He shares his life and loft with Henry Pipo, a six-year-old Havanese.
- Instagram: @gberthenson

grew up in ... County, Michigan, and lives in Vienna, Austria. His work as conceptual artist and writer focuses on memory. Alongside *Camp*, he is currently preparing a biography of Count Felix Schaffgotsche, Averell Harriman's location scout for Sun Valley. He is married to Viennese art historian Christian Witt-Dörring.
- michaelhuey.com
- Instagram: @summercampheritage

TATE JUSTUS is a visual and performance artist. He grew up on the East Coast and attended the University of Chicago and Cooper Union.
- artworkarchive.com/profile/tate-justus
- Instagram: @etat_it

DELWIN KAMARA is an artist originally from Kabala, Sierra Leone. He moved to Maryland at the age of nine where he studied fine arts and graphic design before diving into the world of photography. In 2009, he relocated again to New York, where he currently lives and works. Spanning genres of portraiture, documentary, and fashion, his photographic practice is heavily influenced by the communities around him. More recently he has been exploring his own identity through his work.
- studiokamara.com
- Instagram: @kam.del

ANDREW KETCHAM writes about love. He is thirty and single.
- Instagram: @islafissure

SARAH ELIZABETH LARSON is a freelance photographer living in Chicago, focusing mainly on comedy, music, and theater. Her work has appeared in various periodicals such as the *Los Angeles Times*, *the Wall Street Journal*, the *Sun-Times*, and the *Chicago Tribune*.
- sarahelizabethlarson.com
- Instagram: @selfoto

PETER ASH LEE is a New York-based photographer and director. Born in Seoul and raised in Toronto, his work is informed by the pursuit of a contemporary standard of beauty that champions diversity and representation. Peter is also the cofounder of *Burdock*, an arts and culture publication celebrating multidimensional Asian American experiences.
- peterashlee.com
- Instagram: @peterashlee

ANIEL SEUNG LEE is a Korean merican photographer based in ew York City by way of Los Angeles, alifornia.
danielseunglee.com
Instagram: @danielseunglee

AUL LEGAULT is the author of *The ower* (Coach House Books, 2020). is previous books include *The Other oems* (Fence, 2011), a Lambda Literary ward finalist, and *The Emily Dickinson eader: An English-to-English ranslation of the Complete Poems of mily Dickinson* (McSweeney's, 2012).
theotherpaul.com
Instagram: @pmlegault
Twitter: @theotherpaul

ATHY LO is a portraiture and fashion hotographer. She was born in Taipei, aised in Vancouver, and now lives and orks in New York.
kathy-lo.com
Instagram: @kathylo15

ACK TAYLOR LOVATT is a multimedia rtist.
jacktaylorlovatt.com
Instagram: @jacktaylorlovatt

RNESTO MACIAS is a queer, Mexican merican editor who joined *Interview*'s asthead in 2018. Along with being regular contributor to *Interview*'s rint and digital editions, Macias is the ofounder of *BRUNCH CLUB*—a queer IPOC platform and print magazine— nd a contributing writer to titles such s *I-D*, *Document Journal*, *Huffpost oices*, *InStyle*, and was the managing ditor of *Hello Mr.*'s final print edition. le learned to roll joints one year ago nd lives in Brooklyn.
theinternest.wordpress.com
Instagram: @the_internest
Twitter: @internest_the

MBER BYRNE MAHONEY (Australia, 984) is a visual artist living and orking in the Hudson Valley, New York, e unceded lands of the Stockbridge- lunsee Band of Mohicans. The ncestral name Muh-he-con-ne-ok anslates to: "People of the waters at are never still." MFA, Rhode Island chool of Design, 2022.
ambermahoney.com
nstagram: @amberbmahoney

RAIG MANGUM is a writer ased in Los Angeles, California.
craigmangum.com
nstagram: @craigmangum
Twitter: @craigmangum

NOAH MICHELSON received his MFA in poetry from New York University. He is the head of *HuffPost Personal* and hosts a podcast about love and sex.
• Instagram: @noahmichelson

MARCUS MORRIS is a multidisciplinary artist whose work centers queerness and performance. Based in Brooklyn since 2012, he is currently a graduate fellow at The Ohio State University developing a project focused on his Black queer Appalachian identity called "Elegance Is Refusal."
• marcus-morris.com
• Instagram: @marcusmorris
• Twitter: @marcuslmorris

STEVE ORLANDO is a GLAAD-, Eisner-, and Ringo-nominated writer and editor, with works published by DC Comics, Image Comics, Marvel Comics, AfterShock Comics, IDW Publishing, TKO Studios, Heavy Metal, Boom! Studios, Dynamite Entertainment, and more. Outside of comics, he's written for Cartoon Network's *Ben 10* and has been featured in *National Geographic*.
• Instagram: @the.steve.orlando
• Twitter: @thesteveorlando

TOMMY "TEEBS" PICO is a poet, podcaster, TV writer, and ho.
• Instagram: @heyteebs

MASON PIPPENGER is a writer, photographer, and digital/editorial creator based in Chicago. In his work, he explores the sometimes murky waters of race, sexuality, culture, and humanity. He hopes for a pet one day and something bigger than a studio apartment. He is a dreamer.
• masonpippenger.com
• Instagram: @mason.pip
• Twitter @masonpippenger

DAVY PITTOORS is a London-based Belgian visual creative, specializing in storytelling, art direction, and curation. He works with artists, makers, and small businesses, with a focus on interiors, lifestyle, arts, and culture. Davy also has a strong interest in LGBTQ+ history and aesthetics. His projects and events often explore these subjects in a domestic setting, bringing together artists and makers whose work interrogates the multifaceted relationship between art, sexuality, and domesticity.
• davypittoors.com
• Instagram: @davypittoors

JONATHAN DANIEL PRYCE is an award-winning photographer, including the 2023 Portrait of Britain award. His work can be found in *Vogue*, *Vanity Fair*, *Esquire*, and *GQ*.

BRONTEZ PURNELL is the author of several books, including *100 Boyfriends*, which won the 2022 Lambda Literary Award in Gay Fiction, was longlisted for the 2022 Mark Twain American Voice in Literature Award and the 2021 Brooklyn Public Library Literary Prize, and was named an Editors' Choice by the *New York Times Book Review*. The recipient of a 2018 Whiting Writers' Award for Fiction and the 2022 Foundation for Contemporary Arts Robert Rauschenberg Award, he was named one of the thirty-two Black Male Writers of Our Time by *T: The New York Times Style Magazine* in 2018. Purnell is also the frontman for the band the Younger Lovers and a renowned dancer, performance artist, and zine-maker. Born in Triana, Alabama, he's lived in California for over two decades.
• Instagram: @brontezpurnell

ZHANG QINGYUN is a Chinese director and art director based in New York.
• zhangqingyun.com
• Instagram: @zhang.qingyun

ERIN RILEY is a trans social worker and sometime writer who enjoys routines that rarely change, reading, eating, and dreams of taking more risks. Erin was a Penguin Random House Australia Write It fellow in 2021. Their first book of essays, *A Real Piece of Work*, will be published by Penguin in 2023.
• Instagram: @grubkitsch

LJ ROBERTS (b.1980, Royal Oak, Michigan) is an artist and writer who creates large-scale textile installations, intricate embroideries, artist books, collages, and mixed-media sculptures. Their work illuminates oft-erased and unacknowledged queer and trans narratives, people, and places. The artist creates conceptual and geographical maps of queer life of the past, present, and future through material deviance and reimaging craft practices.
• ljroberts.net
• Instagram: @atelier.lj

MATHEW RODRIGUEZ is an award-winning writer, journalist, and editor. His work has been featured in the *Village*

INTO, the *Advocate*, *Mic*, and more. His book *Carlos Alejo Has to Lose His Chichos* is forthcoming from Farrar, Straus and Giroux.
- mathew-rodriguez.com
- Instagram: @mathewkrodriguez
- Twitter: @mathewrodriguez

JODY ROGAC is a photographer centering on fashion and portraiture. Raised in beautiful Vancouver, Canada, Rogac intuitively draws inspiration from nature. Rogac's empathy and sensitivity, coupled with her command of light, space, and depth of field, enables her to create natural compositions engrossed with refinement and intelligence. Rogac's recent clients include *Vogue*, the *Gentlewoman*, *Double*, *Time*, the *New York Times*, *Aperture*, The Row, Tory Burch, Theory, and Apple.
- jodyrogac.com
- Instagram: @jodyrogac

CHARLES ROGERS is the cocreator of *Search Party*, the critically acclaimed dark comedy series on HBO Max, which ran for five seasons. He has been named one of the Out100, *Forbes'* "30 Under 30," the *Hollywood Reporter*'s "Power Showrunners," and *Variety*'s "10 Writers to Watch."
- Instagram: @gcharlesrogers

MACK ROGERS graduated from the University of Tennessee in Knoxville with a BA in English with a concentration in creative writing. His work has appeared in *Foglifter*, *Olney* magazine, and *Susurrus*. He has a blog of dream poetry and his shower walls are covered in waterproof poems. He currently lives with his partner and their three cats in East Tennessee.
- mackrogers.com
- Instagram: @macksinamillion
- Twitter: @mackrogers_

ANDREW SA is Chicago's premier queer country crooner, an actor, and a singer/songwriter originally from California. He released an EP of covers from the popular Cosmic Country Showcase (2020), his first original single "Dark Phoenix" with B-side "Little Lamb" (2023), and he's working on his debut album with producer, songwriter, and friend H. C. McEntire (2024). *Girlfriends*, his unfinished Patsy Cline and Loretta Lynn tribute album with Patrick Haggerty, is also set to be released in 2024.
- Instagram: @lonesomeandrew

DANY SALVATIERRA is an award-winning Peruvian author of four books of fiction. He also works as an editor, translator, and DJ, and is based in Lima and Boston. You can find him at airports working on his manuscripts or watching countless hours of vintage telenovelas.
- Instagram: @d__salvatierra
- Twitter: @danysalvatierra

ANTWAUN SARGENT is a writer, curator, and a director at Gagosian. His recent books are *The New Black Vanguard: Photography Between Art and Fashion* (2019) and *Young, Gifted and Black: A New Generation of Artists* (2020). His recent exhibitions include the group show series *Social Works* and solo presentations of artists Rick Lowe, Tyler Mitchell, Awol Erizku, Amanda Williams, Virgil Abloh, and Alexandria Smith.
- Instagram: @sirsargent

DANIEL SHEA is an artist based in New York City. Recent monographs include *43-35 10th Street* (Kodoji Press, 2018) and *Ex Nihilo* (InOtherWords Press, 2019). He has two forthcoming titles with Mack Books, London. He has exhibited internationally including at the Pavilion of the United States during the Venice Biennale of Architecture; Foam Fotografiemuseum, Amsterdam; and the Museum of Contemporary Photography, Chicago. He has been a resident artist at Light Work, Syracuse. His photographs have appeared in *The New Yorker*, *Frieze*, and *Fantastic Man*.
- danielpshea.com
- Instagram: @danielpshea

JEN SILVERMAN is the author of the debut novel *We Play Ourselves*, the story collection *The Island Dwellers*, and the poetry chapbook *Bath*. Honors include fellowships from the National Endowment for the Arts (2022, Prose) and the Guggenheim (2022, Drama). Jen's plays have been produced off-Broadway, regionally, and internationally. Jen also writes for TV and film.

CHRISTOPHER SOTO's debut poetry collection, *Diaries of a Terrorist*, was published by Copper Canyon Press in 2022.
- christophersoto-poet.com
- Instagram: @loma_poetry

LANDON SPEERS's work has been described as quiet and thoughtful. With a strong curiosity to photograph both people and places, he has followed personal projects and commissions across cities, forests, deserts, and mountains. Hailing from the prairies of Western Canada, he is now based between Brooklyn and upstate New York, where he can often be found at the nearest swimming hole during the warmer months.
- landonspeers.com
- Instagram: @landonspeers

ELLIOT STOKES is an artist, illustrator, and art director based in Los Angeles. Practicing across multiple mediums, his work has been featured in numerous publications.
- elliotstokes.com
- Instagram: @elliotstokes
- Twitter: @relliotstokes

MATTHEW TAMMARO is a photographer based in Paris, France.
- matthewtammaro.com
- Instagram: @matthewtammaro

FRAN TIRADO is a writer, filmmaker, and podcaster living in Brooklyn.
- @fransquishco

ADRIAN TUAZON-McCHEYNE is a Melbourne-based photographer and has shot for various Australian print and digital magazines.
- adriantuazon.com
- Twitter: @atuazon

JASON EDWARD TUCKER is an artist, photographer, and Director of Admissions for The Oxbow School. He received his BFA in photography from the Corcoran College of Art + Design. His work explores the dissection of portraiture and etymology, which centers queer iconography as integral parts of history and himself.
- jasonedwardtucker.com
- Instagram: @jasonedwardtucker

YEZMIN VILLARREAL is a writer and editor living in Phoenix, Arizona. In 2017, they launched *Dyke Queen*, a QTPOC magazine about art, style, and literature. Villarreal was formerly an editor at the *Advocate*, *PRIDE*, and Grindr's *Into*.
- yezmin.com
- dykequeen.com
- Instagram: @yezyesyall
- @dykequeenzine

JASON VILLEMEZ writes fiction and nonfiction centering on LGBTQ people. His work has appeared in *Philadelphia Gay News*, *LGBTQ Nation*, *New Orleans*

Review, *F(r)iction*, and *Foglifter*. He lives in Philadelphia with his husband and dog.
• jasonvillemez.com
• Twitter: @JasonVillemez

OCEAN VUONG is the author of the award-winning poetry collection *Night Sky with Exit Wounds* and the *New York Times* bestselling novel *On Earth We're Briefly Gorgeous.* His most recent poetry collection *Time Is a Mother* was a *New York Times* bestseller. A recipient of the 2019 MacArthur "Genius Grant," he is also the winner of the Whiting Award and the T. S. Eliot prize. Born in Saigon, Vietnam, he is a professor in the Creative Writing MFA Program at NYU.
• oceanvuong.com
• Instagram: @ocean_vuong

BRYAN WASHINGTON is the award-winning author of *Family Meal, Memorial,* and *Lot.*
• brywashing.com

CHRIS WILLIFORD (b. 1993, Dallas, TX) is an interdisciplinary artist working in textile, print, and window display. He received his BFA in printmaking from the Maryland Institute College of Art in 2015 and his MFA in printmedia from the School of the Art Institute of Chicago in 2018. Chris is an alumnus Artist in Residence of the Massachusetts Museum of Contemporary Art (MASS MoCA). His work was published in *New American Paintings* #137 (midwest issue).
• chriswilliford.com
• Instagram: @cwilli

LIAM WOODS is a nonbinary image-maker based out of Los Angeles. Their work is characterized by the intimate storytelling of queer communities. In their six-year experience, Liam has partnered these stories with companies and publications such as Apple, Levi's, Adidas, *People* magazine, the *Los Angeles Times*, and many more.
• analoguepapi.com
• Instagram: @analoguepapi

J WORTHAM (they/them) is a sound healer, Reiki practitioner, herbalist, and community care worker oriented toward healing justice and liberation. J is also a staff writer for the *New York Times Magazine* and cohost of the podcast *Still Processing*. They occasionally publish thoughts on culture, technology, and wellness in a newsletter. J is the proud editor, along with Kimberly Drew, of the visual anthology *Black Futures* from One World, a 2020 Editors' Choice by the *New York Times Book Review*. J is also currently working on a book about the body and dissociation for Penguin Press. J mostly lives and works on stolen Munsee Lenape land, now known as Brooklyn, New York, and is committed to decolonization as a way of life.
• jennydeluxe.com
• Instagram: @jennydeluxe

HANYA YANAGIHARA lives in New York.

RILEY J. YAXLEY is a writer whose tenderhearted work evokes memories in order to contemplate the self and the ways we make sense of the world and our place in it. They earned their BA and MA in writing, rhetoric, and discourse from DePaul University.
• rileyyaxley.com
• Instagram: @gay_rage

Credits

"Forgiveness" was originally published in *Hello Mr.* Issue 10 © 2018 Christopher Soto

"The Recording" was originally published in *Hello Mr.* Issue 10 © 2018 Khalid El Khatib

"Back to Start: The 'Lady' Bunny in conversation with Martin Belk" © 2024 Martin Belk

Photo of Lady Bunny © 2020 Billy Erb
Photo of Lady Bunny © 2019 Billy Erb

Fag School #6 1/2 by Brontez Purnell © 2023 Dream Baby Press

"All These Cats Have AIDS" was previously published in *Big Fiction Magazine* © 2020 Jason Villemez

"Fire Island" © 2022 Robert Andy Coombs

"Kehinde Wiley in 3D: An Artist's Quest to Unflatten Black America" was originally published in *Hello Mr.* Issue 09 © 2017 Antwaun Sargent

Photos for "Kehinde Wiley in 3D: An Artist's Quest to Unflatten Black America" were originally published in *Hello Mr.* Issue 09 © 2017 Amber Mahoney

"The House of the Sleeping Beaus" originally appeared in Locas de Felicidad: Crónicas Travestis y Otro Relatos (La Iguana Ciega 2009) © John Better Armella. Translated by George Henson.

Red Archive © 2014 Dan Gluibizzi
The Plaid Shirt © 2015 Dan Gluibizzi

"Good Dick Is a Myth" © 2024 Mack Rogers

"We Meet Again: Familiar Faces of *Hello Mr.*" © 2024 Ernesto Macias

Photos of Nic Dorward were originally published in *Hello Mr.* Issue 01 © 2013 Adrian Tuazon-McCheyne

Photos of Ed Droste were originally published in *Hello Mr.* Issue 02 © 2013 Daniel Seung Lee

Photo of Dan Donigan was originally published in *Hello Mr.* Issue 03 © 2014 Marcus Morris

Photo of Dan Donigan was originally published in *Hello Mr.* Issue 08 © 2016 Zhang Qingyun

Photos of Saeed Jones were originally published in *Hello Mr.* Issue 04 © 2014 Michael George

Photos of Mike Hadreas were originally published in *Hello Mr.* Issue 05 © 2015 Kathy Lo

Photos of Parson James were originally published in *Hello Mr.* Issue 07 © 2016 Peter Ash Lee

Photos of Stephen Galloway were originally published in *Hello Mr.* Issue 08 © 2016 Jody Rogac

Photos of Brian Anderson were originally published in *Hello Mr.* Issue 09 © 2017 Samuel Bradley

Photos of John Early were originally published in *Hello Mr.* Issue 09 © 2017 Stanislaw Boniecki

Photos of Tunde Olaniran were originally published in *Hello Mr.* Issue 09 © 2017 Landon Speers

Photos of Olly Alexander were originally published in *Hello Mr.* Issue 10 © 2018 Scott Gallagher

"History of My Blood" © 2024 Mason Pippenger

Ocean Vuong "Notebook Fragments" from *Night Sky with Exit Wounds* (Copper Canyon Press). Copyright © 2016 by Ocean Vuong

"Camp" © 2024 Michael Huey

Photo for "Camp" by Phil Balyeat from *Straight as the Pine, Sturdy as the Oak* © 2013 Michael Huey & Christian Witt-Dörring Family Archive

"He Opened Up Somewhere Along the Eastern Shore" was originally published in *Hello Mr.* Issue 05 © 2015 Jason Hanasik

"A Compendium of Loss" was originally published in *Hello Mr.* Issue 06 © 2015 Thom James Carter

Art for "A Compendium of Loss" © 2024 Elliot Stokes

"Javi Muñoz: *Hamilton*'s new Hamilton" was originally published with the title "Javi Muñoz" in *Hello Mr.* Issue 08 © 2016 Scott Bixby

Photos of Javi Muñoz were originally published in *Hello Mr.* Issue 08 © 2016 Matthew Tammaro

"Close Encounter" was originally published in *Hello Mr.* Issue 04 © 2014 Noah Michelson

"Clear Constellations: Mapping the Cultural Pinpoints of Critic Wesley Morris" was originally published in *Hello Mr.* Issue 09 © 2017 J Wortham

"Falling Prey" was originally published on YouPorn.com © 2022 Fran Tirado

Art for "Falling Prey" © 2024 Benjamin Edeline

"Jello Boy" © 2024 Calvin Gimpelevich

"What's Left of Marcus Leatherdale" was originally published in *Hello Mr.* Issue 06 © 2015 Martin Belk

Photos of "What's Left of Marcus Leatherdale" were originally published in *Hello Mr.* Issue 06 © 2015 Jonathan Daniel Pryce

"On Watching MormonBoyz porn as a Gay Ex-Mormon" © 2024 Craig Mangum

Art for "On Watching MormonBoyz porn as a Gay Ex-Mormon" © 2024 Hayden Davis

"Queering Space" © 2024 Davy Pittoors

"1st Samuel, 1st Love" © 2024 Kitsch Harris

"How to Unerase Yourself with Garrard Conley" was originally published in *Hello Mr.* Issue 10 © 2018 Scott Bixby

"Learning I'm Susceptible to Cults" originally appeared in Andrew Ketcham's debut book of poems, *CAPTIVA* (Bullshit Lit, 2023) © Andrew Ketcham

"Maggie and Olivia, or: Flickering In and Out of Many Things" appears in Erin Riley's debut collection, *A Real Piece of Work: A Memoir in Essays*, published by Penguin Random House Australia © 2023 Erin Riley.

"Crying These Cocksuckin Tears: Remembering My Friend, Patrick Haggerty" © 2024 Andrew Sa

'hotos for "Crying These
Cocksuckin Tears: Remembering
My Friend, Patrick Haggerty" © 2022
Sarah Elizabeth Larson

Nature Poem" (Tin House) © 2017
ommy Pico

Chani Nicholas Is in Your House" was
riginally published in *Hello Mr.* Issue 10
© 2018 Alexander Chee

'hotos for "Chani Nicholas Is in Your
House" © 2024 Liam Woods

Violets" © 2024 Derek Charm and
Steve Orlando

Just Be Cool" was originally published in
Hello Mr. Issue 06 © 2015 Matthew Harris

Art for "Just Be Cool" was originally
published in *Hello Mr.* Issue 06 © 2015
.ie Dirkx

"Selected Poems from *The Walt
Whitman Reader*, an English-to-English
Translation" was originally published in
Hello Mr. Issue 07 © 2016 Paul Legault

"The Mother, The Son, and The Holy
Spirit" was originally published in *Hello
Mr.* Issue 06 © 2015 Dany Salvatierra

Maresia #4 © 2015-2022 Matheus de
Simone
Maresia #2 © 2015-2022 Matheus de
Simone
Maresia #3 © 2015-2022 Matheus de
Simone

"Screen Test" was originally published
in *Hello Mr.* Issue 07 © 2016 Daniel Shea

"Saying Hello To New Queer Voices"
© 2024 Colby Anderson and
Yezmin Villarreal

"How to Talk to Strangers" was
originally published in *Hello Mr.* Issue
06 © 2015 Bryan Washington

"The Perfect Imbalance of Raul Lopez"
was originally published in *Hello Mr.*
Issue 10 © 2018 Ernesto Macias

Photos for "The Perfect Imbalance of
Raul Lopez" were originally published
Hello Mr. Issue 10 © 2018 Delwin Kama

"The Wound" was originally published
by Sixty Inches from Center © 2022
Riley Yaxley

Art for "The Wound" was originally
published in *Hello Mr.* Issue 10 © 2018
Jack Taylor Lovatt

"we know the weight is human" © 202
Tate Justus

Photo of Ryan Fitzgibbon © 2024
Rogelio Esparza

Acknowledgments

This gay book would not be possible without the queer heroes who braved the world with their truth so that we could live proudly in ours. It is great because of the courage and sacrifice of countless souls, known and unknown, whose strength was made available to us by the stories they told.

I am infinitely grateful for the communities that have welcomed and bolstered me through this process. Thank you to my friends and family whose encouragement was always there when I needed it most. Special thanks, in no particular order, for their contributions to this monument; Fran Tirado, Zhang Qingyun, Ernesto Macias, Taahir Husain, Jennifer Hope Choi, Jackson Howard, Charles Rogers, and Nehemiah D. Frank.

A *Great Gay Book* was made during my time as an awardee of the Tulsa Artist Fellowship with studio assistance from Annie Jones and Cole Stevens. Endless appreciation for my agent, Michael Bourret, and for the generous guidance of my editor, Zack Knoll, for his dedication to this colossal project. And to the entire team at Abrams for trusting the vision and making it all happen; Diane Shaw, Denise LaCongo, Annalea Manalili, Andrew Gibeley, Danielle Kolodkin, Michael Sand, and Rebecca Kaplan.

Finally, to everyone who believed in *Hello Mr.* simply by engaging with it. Especially those who shared their talents and their time to help others realize the possibilities available to them. The list, while long, does not reflect everyone who played a role in making *Hello M*

Emily Abay
Bobby Abley
Justin Abraham Linds
TJ Acena
Austin Addison
Campbell Addy
Marcelo Agudo
Joseph Alexander
Ryker Allen
Arthur Allen
Anais & Dax
Jeremy Anderson
Jim Antonopoulos
Shayan Asadi
Luke Austin
Zac Babcock
Christopher Barnard
Geoff Barrenger
Ethan Barry Murley
David M. Bazner
Alex John Beck
Kyle Bella
Evan Benally Atwood
Trish Bendix
Sean Michael Bennett
Hilton Bertalan
Shawn Binder
Mickey Boardman
Michael Bolognino
Peter Borg
Michael Bouldin
Patrick Boyle
Ian Bradley
Marcus Branch
Joe Brennan
Luisa Brimble
Ben Brooks
Christopher Bryant
Mark Burger
Chase Burns
Tom Capelonga
Ben Capp
Micaiah Carter
Alfonso Casas
Doug Paul Case
Jun Cen
Tereza Červeňová
Cody Chandler
Phædra Charles
Juan Chavarria Jr.
Kristtian Chevere
Irene Chin
Winston Chmielinski
Tag Christof
Lily Clark
Sam Clarke
Adam W. Clifton
Zeph Colombatto
Nate Cover
Anthony Cudahy
Jon Cuevas
Marcus Cuffie
Adam Curley
Austin Dale
Paul Dalla Rosa
Alex Daly
Lacey Daniels
Ashley Denton
Kevin Derrick
Tariq Dixon
DOM&INK
Nathan Dorotiak
Paul Dotey
Ingar Dragset
Lauren Dunn
Scott Durno
Christian Dutilh
Yunus Emre Duyar
Alex Ebel
Gabriel Ebensperger
Bradley Eberts
Adam Kirk Edgerton
Andy Egelhoff
Oray Egin
Michelle Eismann
Michael Elmgreen
Jackson Epstein
Ouliana Ermolova
Patrik Ervell
James K. Evans
Sam Evans-Butler
Mina Fanous
Danny Ferrell
Sam Ferrigno
Peter Flew
Scott Ford
Tim Forster
Caleb Fox
Guy Franklin
Daniel Franzese
Louis Fratino
Evanie Frausto
Paul Frederick
Avena Gallagher
Tramaine George
Jeffrey Gerson
E. Gibbons
Adrian Gilliland
Harrison Glazier
Dylan Glynn
Adam Goldman
Sina Grace
Stephen Grace
Jonathan Randall Grant
Daniel Gray
Amit Greenberg
Josh Greene
Miles W. Griffis
Matt Grubb
Marcelo Gutierrez
Joshua Gutterman Tranen
Jason Haaf
Carlos Hache
Richard Haines
Justin Hal Pitts
Jordan Hall
Josh Hamlet
Jonathan Handel
Emmanuel Hapsis
Antoine Harinthe
Marty Harper
Spencer Harrison
Amy Harrity
Meaghan Hartland
Levi Hastings
Kort Havens
Bryce Heatherly
Andrew Heaver
Victoria Hely-Hutchinson
Gabriel Hendifar
Chad Hensley
Tess Herbert
Ryan S. Hicks
Max Hirschberger
Luke Hogan
Jacob Hoving
Seth Howard
Adam Hurly
Francisco Hurtz
Matt Huynh
Logan Jackson
Kuschan Jafarian
Mark James
Timju Jeannet
Huang Jiaqi
Ryan Tristan Jin
Myles Johnson
Abe Johnson
Gus Johnston
Mike Joosee
Kevin Junk
Tom Kalin
Ib Kamara
Akiko Kawasaki
Justin Keenan
James Keller
Michael Kelly
Robert Klebenow
Christopher Klimovski
Jesse Koehler
Ryan Kost
Adam Kremer
Johannes Kuczera
Adam J. Kurtz
Jacobo Labella
Scott LaBelle
Kenneth Lam
Matt Lambert
Brodie Lancaster
Brad Lande-Shannon
Benjamin Law
Gwendal Le Bec
Grant Legan
Samuel Leighton-Dore
Ian Lewandowski
Jonas Lindstroem
Melissa Ling
Rita Lino
Yichi Liu
Benoît Loiseau
Matthew Lowe
Ryan Lowry
Anna Lucas
Stephen Lucas
Tommy Lucas
Mabel Luna
Levi Macdonald
Brendan Maclean
Inés Maestre
Jesse Mallon
Nathan Mallon
Nick Malone
Nikolay Malyarov
Louie Mandelbaum
Carlos Mangubat
Ross Mantle
Stefano Marchionini
Lisa Marie Corso
Barry Marré
Marc Martin
Rodolfo Martinez
Mark Mason
Edouard Massih
Blair Mastbaum
Jeffery Masters
Ross McCallum
Tom McIlory
Josh McKenna
Brendan McKnight
Kevin McLellan
Joshua McLeod
Chad McPhail
Tom McQuaid
Jorge Medina
Fabrizio Mingarelli
Blair Mishleau
Evan Moffitt
Malique Morris
Max Mosher
Ben Mulcahy
Théo Münch
Mike Mutsaers
Nathan Nankervis
Jürgen Natter
Mark Neil Balson
Nick Nemechek

James Newman
Michael Newsted
Amie Norris
Denne Michele Norris
Mitchell Nugent
Gwen O'Brien
Ryan O'Connell
Sean O'Connor
Paul Octavious
Bridget Ore
Adam Osgood
Joseph Osmundson
Blake Pack
Rocco Paone Jr.
Hue Park
Tim Parker
Jim Parsons
Clément Pascal
Conor Patrick
Tsari Paxton
Orville Peck
Mark Peckmezian
Anthony Pedraza
Brent Persun
Alden Peters
Phillip Picardi
Igor Pjörrt
Nate Jun Poekert
Adam Polaski
James Powell
Benjamin Preyer
David Prior
Menelik Puryear
Michael Putnam
Taylor Putnam
Arie Rain Glorie
Daniel Rampulla
Greg Reynolds
Colin Roberson
Jott Robertson
Josiah Robinson
Sam Rodgers
Ryan Rogers
Robbie Rogers
Hernan Romero van Gompel
Chris Roney
B. Root
Rolando Rosler
Dan Rowden
Eric Rutherford
Daniel Sanchez Torres
Daniel Saniski
Scandebergs
Quinn Schoen
Chris Schoonover
Sybil Secor
Hiroyuki Seo
Khary Septh
Cameron Shepherd
Robert Sherer
Ferdi Sibbel
Pacifico Silano
Josh Silverman
Igor Smirnoff
Allie Smith
Jack Arthur Smith
Rafael Soldi
Christopher Soto
Bell Soto
Tyler Spangler
Zach Stafford
Colin Stark
Scott Stephenson
Mae Stier
Robert Storey
Michael Sun
Michael Tatalovich
Nijel Taylor
Vawdrey Taylor
Michelle Tea
Alex Testere
Rod Thomas
Teddy Tinson
Jacob Tobia
Jake Tobin Garrett
Alex Tolosa
Rosen Tomov
Fernando Torrent
Owen Torrey
Joel Tozer
Rob Truglia
Kevin Truong
Billie Turnbull
Dorian Ulises López
David Urbanke
Jordy van den Niewendijk
Esteban Vargas
Jim Verburg
Korey Vincent
Ben Wagner
Joey Wańczyk
Jacob Weinzettel
Brandon Wickenkamp
Hamish Wirgman
Jaime Woo
Michael Wooten
Megan Wray Schertler
Jimmy Wright
Royal Yates
Mitch Zachary
Victoria Zschommler

RYAN FITZGIBBON is an artist and publisher. After beginning as a communication designer at IDEO in San Francisco, California, he founded *Hello Mr.* in 2012. Fitzgibbon self-published ten issues of the magazine from Brooklyn, New York, before moving to Tulsa, Oklahoma, in January 2020. Shortly after arriving, he was diagnosed with HIV at the height of the pandemic. His work in Oklahoma to protect LGBTQ+ rights includes the expansion of HIV/AIDS care and prevention through Tulsa CARES, in addition to supporting the *Black Wall Street Times* in the production of multiple publications and the opening of a newsroom and storefront in Greenwood. Fitzgibbon is a 2021–2023 awardee of the Tulsa Artist Fellowship. ryanfitz.info • @ryanfitzgibbon

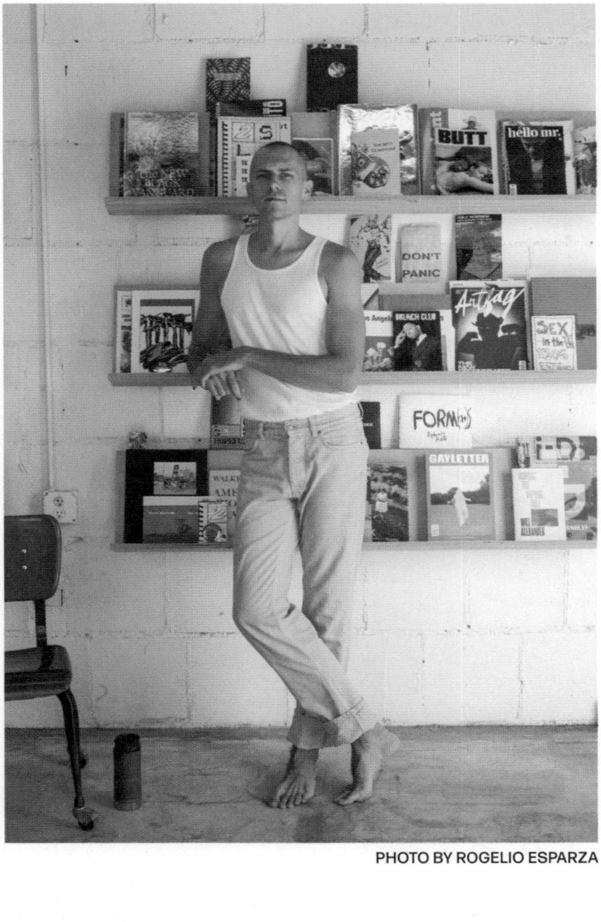

PHOTO BY ROGELIO ESPARZA